P9-DWC-155

CHART B

Tensed INTERIOR geometric Vector
Construction in Equilibrium. Minimum vol. with maximum surface.

Absolute Convergence First Orbit.
No Volume, Exterior Compression

Divergent Components of
Octave Subdivision

Convergent and Divergent Unit and
Fractional Values in High-Low
Octaves

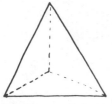

4 Equal Planes perpendicular to
[4] separate axis = 4 dimensions

Internal Tension
[5] 60° x 35° x 110° Pyramids
4 Parts

4 SMALL TETRA
1 = 1/2 or .5

[6]

4

32

[7]

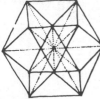

Eight equiangular equilateral
[11] surface triangles

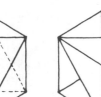

Eight components are 60° triangle
[12] base, 45° x 90° pyramids.

[13]

1/2   2

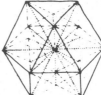

Octahedron has
[14] Dymaxion Center

16

1 2 8

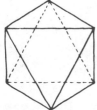

Dymaxion only solid with natural
center and radius identical from
[18] all dimensions. Monster

Dymaxion as a uniform vector field
diaphram converting or compounding
[19] 2-and-3 values.

Dymaxion is Comprehensive to
Tetra and Octahedrons and is the
[20] Decimal Octave.

1 1/2
1.25

10 with Diameter = Unity
[21] 80 with Radius or; Unity
Edge

10

80

Unit Cube has no Center of Its Own

Cube corners Borrowed From Neighboring Neuclei in Third Orbit.
[25] Cube Corners = 1/8 Octahedron

Octave of Cubes - Center - Cube
Collection has Common Center with
[26] Dymaxion - 9 Axes.

60° Triangle Base x 35° x 110°
(approx.) Pyramid equal 1/4 of tetrahedron formed on Center tetrahedron. Adopted as VOLUMETRIC UNITY.

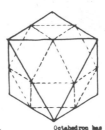

1   1 1/2
     1.5

2

60° Triangle Base x 45° x 90° has
[27] Volume of 2

[28]

12

96

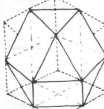

60° Triangle Base 45°x90° Pyramid
Has Tetra at Center   6 of Next
[32] Lower Octave 60x45x90 Pyramids

Individual Cube Has Tetrahedron
[33] At Its Center.

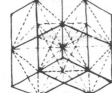

1

8

60° Triangl. Faced Square-based
Pyramid equalling 1/2 an octahedron
[34] has Volume of 8

64

(Icosahedron of unit exterior
measure has octave values of 9
(or 72,which are natural zeroes.

DIAGONAL OF SQUARE IS ITS CONTROLING DIMENSION

Unity = 2 ; Sides of Square = √1
COPYRIGHTED
[35] R.BUCKMINSTER FULLER '41,

Books by R. Buckminster Fuller

Nine Chains to the Moon

Untitled Epic Poem on the History of Industrialization

Ideas and Integrities

No More Secondhand God

Education Automation

Utopia or Oblivion

Operating Manual for Spaceship Earth

Intuition

Earth, Inc.

Synergetics

Synergetics 2

And It Came to Pass—Not to Stay

Synergetics 2

SYNERGETICS 2

Explorations in the Geometry of Thinking

R. BUCKMINSTER FULLER

in collaboration with E. J. APPLEWHITE

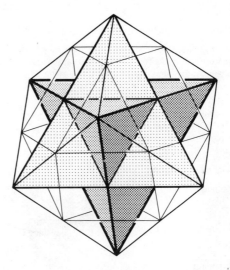

MACMILLAN PUBLISHING CO., INC.

NEW YORK

COLLIER MACMILLAN PUBLISHERS

LONDON

The Vail-Ballou Press of Binghamton, N.Y. was responsible for
the typesetting and printing of *Synergetics* and *Synergetics 2*.
Princeton Polychrome Press of Princeton, N.J. manufactured the
color plates and printed the color inserts.

Copyright © 1979 by R. Buckminster Fuller

Macmillan Publishing Co., Inc.
866 Third Avenue, New York, N.Y. 10022
Collier Macmillan Canada, Ltd.

Library of Congress Cataloging in Publication Data (Revised)

Fuller, Richard Buckminster, 1895–
  Synergetics.

  1. System theory.   2. Thought and thinking.
3. Mathematics—Philosophy.   I. Applewhite, Edgar J.
II. Title.
Q295.F84   191   74-7263   74-7264
ISBN 0-02-541870-X (v. 1)
ISBN 0-02-541880-7 (v. 2)

First Printing 1979

Printed in the United States of America

Contents

600.00 *Structure*

1000.00 *Omnitopology*

Scenarios

Each scenario is a narrative sequence of geometrical exposition written—and intended to be read—as a separate continuity.

*The author suggests that beginning readers should start their explorations at the Demass Model: it presents a broad survey of the evolution of his geometry as well as a model of Einstein's equation.

Explicit: *A note to the reader*

Synergetics 1 and *Synergetics 2* are separate volumes only because of their bulk and the chronology of their composition. They in fact comprise a single integral work. Each chapter in the first volume has been expanded in the second, and the sequence of paragraphs has been numbered to dovetail and provide a shared context.

It is the essence of synergy to produce unpredicted—indeed, unpredictable—results like the surprise geometrical discoveries of this second volume. *Synergetics 2* continues the exposition of Fuller's radical geometrical cosmos with its landscapes of unfamiliar models and metaphors; it amplifies and amends—but does not supersede—the earlier volume published in 1975; it makes more explicit the significance of certain geometrical functions that are only implicit in *Synergetics 1;* and it introduces the term *epistemography* to describe Fuller's geometry of thinking. The two books together present descriptions that are explicit as well as contextual.

Buckminster Fuller employs the discipline of a lecturer, recommencing his expositions from the beginning, reviewing the previous experiments and recalls of experiences. His written discourse, like his speech, is replete with sustained narrative sequences that recapitulate the geometrical premises, ever starting back from the beginning . . . as Fuller says, like the pole vaulter who always goes back to the end of the cinder track before repeating his sprint.

Although the apparatus of section numbers is handy as a key to context and essential for indexing and for cross-reference, it tends to obscure the logical continuity of certain passages that merit the reader's sustained attention. For this reason the Table of Contents is supplemented with a Table of Scenarios. The new reader seeking an avenue into the work should choose from the list of Scenarios as a guide; those seeking a specific topic may refer to the Table of Contents.

The index and cross-references in *Synergetics 2* refer to both volumes; references to *Synergetics 1* are in roman numbers and those in *Synergetics 2* in *italic numerals*.

—E. J. APPLEWHITE

Washington, D.C.
19 February 1979

The author's original color posters are 36 by 24 inches. They are reduced here to page size, which makes some of the captions too small to read. Therefore the captions are recapitulated in the text of *Synergetics 2* at the sections referenced.

Simplest Trigonometric Solutions

Stones may be broken into ever smaller stones but they cannot be broken into no stones. They may be broken into gravel and gravel into dust, and the dust separated into crystals which are too small to be seen except through lensed microscopes, or further broken apart into atoms which can only be seen through electromagnetic field microscopes, — but they cannot be broken into nothingnesses — only into somethings, and somethings are always systems. *

As the stones break, they have cleavage faces. They break into irregular polyhedra that are complex or single, geometrically definable systems, each of which has always an inherent insideness and outsideness. The number of faces (hedra) of polyhedra cannot be reduced to less than four (the tetrahedron). Each of the faces (hedra) are polygons. The number of sides (gons) of a polygon cannot be reduced to less than three (the triangle). The minimum polyhedron of universe is the tetrahedron, which requires a minimum of three triangles surrounding each of its four corners, whose four corners are omni-interconnected with a minimum of six edges which discretely outline the four triangular (minimum polygon) faces.

Make the V for "Victory" sign with two adjacent fingers. The V is visual. The V is a specifically visible angle. The angle is an angle independently of the length of the fingers — that is, independently of the length of the sides of the angle. Angles, triangles and tetrahedra are conceptual pattern integrities independent of size. Angles are always and only fractional parts of whole circles (of 360°). Likewise, triangles are always and only components of a priori whole physical polyhedronal systems, or of a plurality of whole polyhedronal systems, each of 720° (or whole multiples of 720°) of angles surrounding all the external vertices outliningly describing those systems. Only triangles produce structural stability. Only triangles produce pattern stability. The omni-triangulated tetrahedron is the minimum structural system of universe.

Drawing or scribing, are physical operations executed upon a physical system. Triangles can be drawn or scribed, traced, or trajectoried only upon or within an a priori physical system or defined by a constellation of three physical systems within a greater a priori system.

There are six and only six different but always orderly inter-covarying geometrical characteristics or integral parts of all triangles — three surface angle corners: A, B, C, and three sides: a, b, c, which sides in reality are always the central angles of the scribed upon system and only evidenced by their surface arcs (lines). (See drawing on "Conceptuality of Trigonometric Functions" chart).

*The energy of the blow that breaks them asunder entropically releases the energy which previously bound together the atoms of the separate somethings. Disassociative energy is radiant — entropic. Associative energy is something forming — syntropic.

Individual angular value, or the relative interrelationships, or inter-ratios, or functions of these part hold true independently of the size of the triangle, i.e., an equiangular triangle is equiangular and humanly conceptual independently of the size of any of our special case triangular experiences. The four most useful of these functions and their symbols are:

sine = sin   tangent = tan
cosine = cos   cotangent = cot

The science which measures the respective angle magnitudes of the six, ever orderly inter-covarying angles of triangles is called trigonometry. All the geometrical interrelationships of all triangles, spherical or planar, are discoveringly calculated by the same trigonometry because plane triangles are always very small spherical triangles on very large spheric systems (high frequency, symmetric systems). A circle is a spherical triangle each of whose three corner angles are 180°.

— 180°
— 120°
— 90°
— 72°
— 60°+

To find the values of all the central angles (sides) and surface (corner) angles of any spherical triangle, we can always start by dropping a perpendicular from any vertex of that triangle upon its opposite side, making it into two "right" triangles. In order to discover all six angular values of a given triangle, it is necessary that in addition to knowing the 90° corner, C, we must also know the surface or central angular values of any other two of the to-be-solved triangle's five parts: A, B, a, b, c. Many mathematicians have devised many strategic formulas for coping with trigonometric solutions, most of them involving plus or minus quadrant symbols, which invite errors of calculation.

To make the trigonometry of the sea captain's celestial navigation as simple and foolproof as possible, the mathematician, Lord Napier (1550-1617), evolved the following information, diagrams and procedures.* To avoid what is known in navigation as the "180° error" — going in exactly the opposite direction from that which will get you to where you want to go, Napier arranged the five non-90° "parts" of a triangle in a five segment "clock:"

*Lord Napier was first to use the decimal point and also invented logarithms for numbers the addition or subtraction of which gave the logarithm of the number which is the product of multiplication or the quotient of division of the two given numbers. Napier's mathematical ingenuity contributed greatly to attainment of the world oceans supremacy by the English East India Company and the British Navy which supported it as founded and directed by Queen Elizabeth the First in 1600

Napier had two equally simple ways to solve trigonometric problems without plus or minus symbols, provided any two of the five non-90° angles are known at outset. His superscript, c, means that A^c, c^c, B^c are the 180° complements of A, c, B. For instance, A^c + A = 180°, wherefore sin A^c — cos A; or tan c^c = cot c, etc.

First, we checkmark the two "known-in-advance," non-90° parts on Napier's five segment clock-like pattern. It will be evidenced that the two already knowns are always either divided from one another or are side by side.

In Napier's Case One, the two "knowns" are side by side. Napier called this the Case of "Opposites."

"OPPOSITE" CASE See Rule 1

chosen unknown for first solution

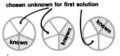

In Case Two, the two knowns are separated from one another in the clock. Napier called this the Case of "Adjacents."

"ADJACENT" CASE See Rule 2

first unknown to be solved

Napier's two easily remembered rules are:

Rule 1. The sine of any unknown part "theta," is equal to the product of the cosines of the two known opposite parts. This is written as: unknown's angle "theta's" sin = cos·cos of its two known opposite parts

Rule 2. The sine of any unknown part is equal to the product of the tangents of its two known adjacent parts. This is written as: the unknown angle "theta's" sin = tan·tan of its two known adjacent parts

Next we employ the appropriate formula with the known cosine or tangent values. Next we must remove the superscript c of the complementaries, if any, by substituting cosines for sines, sines for cosines, tangents for cotangents and cotangents for tangents.

Example: When the equation as first written is sin b = cos c^c·cos b^c the equation must be rewritten as sin b = sin c·sin b or if the equation first reads sin A^c = tan^c·tan b it must be rewritten as cos A = cot c·tan b before going on to intermultiply the functions of the two knowns whose product will be the function value of the previously unknown angle "theta". The angle values of the newly found knowns may be located in any table of trigonometric functions or may be "remembered" by computers. When the value is found for an angle's function (sin, cos, tan, cot), its specific angular value also may be read out of the tables.

R. Buckminster Fuller

Copyright 1976 R. Buckminster Fuller
Mechanicals Jack Ren Marquette

CONCEPTUALITY OF TRIGONOMETRIC FUNCTIONS

OF ANGLE 'A' AS EXPOUNDED IN SYNERGETICS

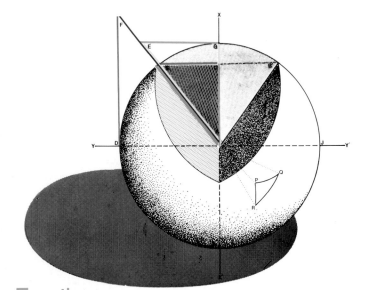

Function:

SINE is the length B——————C divided by the length A══════Radius =1══════B

COSINE is the length A——————C divided by the length A══════════════B

TANGENT is the length B——————C divided by the length A——————C

COTANGENT is the length A——————C divided by the length B——————C

SECANT is the length A════════B divided by the length A——————C

COSECANT is the length A════════B divided by the length B——————C

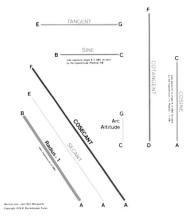

The trigonometric functions are mathematical relationships (ratios) arrived at by dividing the relative lengths of any two of a given right triangle ABC's three geometric lines by one another in unique respect to given angle A of a right triangle ABC which (though often unrealized by mathematics teachers) is always the central apex angle of a right triangle drawn on the sphere's great circle plane, with angle A occurring at the center of that sphere.

Trigonometric functions' length of line ratios are expressed as quotients of divisions of one number (R) by another (S), and may be written in several alternative ways: S/R, R is to S, R:S, R/S, $\frac{R}{S}$, R divided by S =quotient= function value. All the trigonometric function tables used by science are calculated and expressed on the basis that the radius of the sphere (ergo, of the great circle) is deliberately valued as "unity," i.e., having the numerical value of one.

In spherical trigonometry the great circle arcs bounding any surface triangle PQR are in reality external manifests of their subtended central angles. We have surface angles (surface corners) and central angles. What teachers have erroneously identified as edge lines of any triangle drawn on any surface are in fact arcs of central angles. When in primary school arithmetic we were taught about fractions, we were told that these were operations of division and that both the dividend and divisor must be of the same class — that we could not divide peanuts by elephants. This reasonable rule seemed to be contradicted when we came to trigonometry wherein we seemed to be dividing angles by edges. This dismaying confusion is so unreasonable that many drop mathematics at this juncture. It was, and as yet is, occasioned by an error of identity and not by an infraction of the rule, for what were mistakenly called edges of triangles are always central angles of the spherical system's great circle coordinates invisibly governing the geometrical inter-relationships of any substance (no matter how far distorted from its spherical norm it may be) on which substance surface any triangle can be drawn. All triangles are in effect spherical triangles. What we were taught to be plane triangles were always very small triangles on very large spheres — so large as to make the local surface seemingly flat, as with a triangle scratched by you or me upon the surface of the clear, smooth ice on a local pond on our spherical Earth's surface whose local ice surface seems — only superficially — to be flat, or "plane." All trigonometry is spherical trigonometry — and all trigonometry is operated as in the first paragraph above.

Mechanics: Jack Rex Marquette
Copyright 1976 R. Buckminster Fuller

R. Buckminster Fuller

MULTIPLICATION ONLY BY DIVISION
Three Ways of Progressive Halving
Starting from Primitive Unity or Tetrahedron

Tetrahedron with edge length 2.

Divide into 2 equal volumes.

Divide again into 2 equal volumes.

Divide into 1 regular tetrahedron and 1 irregular tetrahedron, which have equal volumes since they have equal altitudes and base areas.

Since the regular tetrahedron has a volume of 1, the irregular tetrahedron has a volume of 1.

Assemble 4 irregular tetrahedron to make 1 regular octahedron.

Octahedron has a volume of 4 (4×1).

Octahedron with a volume of 4.

Divide to make 2 – 1/2 octahedra, each with a volume of 2.

Divide to make 4 – 1/8 octahedra, each with a volume of 1/2.

Combine 4 – 1/8 octahedra with 1 regular tetrahedron . . .

to make a cube with a volume of 3.

Viewpoint altered for clarity.

Regular tetrahedron with a volume of 1.

Divide into 4 – 1/4 tetrahedra.

1/4 tetrahedron has a volume of 1/4.

Combine octahedron of volume 4 . . .

with 8 – 1/4 tetrahedra to make a rhombic dodecahedron.

Rhombic dodecahedron has a volume of 6 = [4+(8×1/4)].

---

3 regular tetrahedra each with a volume of 1.

6 regular tetrahedra.

8 regular tetrahedra.

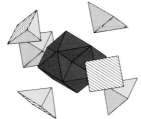

Combine 8 tetrahedra with 6 – 1/2 octahedra to make the Vector Equilibrium.

Vector Equilibrium has a volume of 20 [(8×1)+(6×2)].

1/4 tetrahedron with a volume of 1/4.

Divide into 6 equal parts each with a volume of 1/24.

This is an A Module.

1/8 octahedron with a volume of 1/2.

Divide into 6 equal parts each with a volume of 1/12.

Subtract the A Module (1/12 – 1/24) which leaves an irregular tetrahedron with a volume of 1/24.

This is a B Module.

R. Buckminster Fuller

Deceptiveness of Topology
Quanta Lost by Congruence

24 EDGES
12 VERTICES

A.

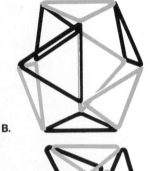

B.

C.

E.

F.

24 EDGES
CONGRUENT AS 6

12 VERTICES
CONGRUENT AS 4

G.

D.

24 EDGES
CONGRUENT AS 12

12 VERTICES
CONGRUENT AS 6

Euler's Uncored Polyhedral Formula:
$$V + F = E + 2$$

Vector Equilibrium	$12 + 14 = 24 + 2$
Octahedron	$6 + 8 = 12 + 2$
Tetrahedron	$4 + 4 = 6 + 2$

Although superficially the tetrahedron seems to have only six vector edges, it has in fact 24. The sizeless, primitive tetrahedron–conceptual independent of size–is quadrivalent, inherently having eight potential alternate ways of turning itself inside out: four passive and four active, meaning that four positive and four negative tetrahedra are congruent.

The vector equilibrium jitterbug provides the articulative model for demonstrating the always omnisymmetrical, divergently expanding or convergently contracting, intertransformability of the entire primitive polyhedral hierarchy, structuring-as-you-go, in an omnitriangularly oriented evolution.

As we explore the interbonding (valencing) of the evolving structural components, we soon discover that the universal interjoining of systems —and their foldability—permit their angularly hinged convergence into congruence of vertexes (single bond-

ing), vectors, (double bonding), faces (triple bonding), and volumetric congruence (quadri-bonding), each of whose multicongruences appear only as one aspect. The Eulerian topological accounting as presently practiced— innocent of the inherent synergetical hierarchy of intertransformability — accounts each of these multicongruent topological aspects as consisting of only one of such aspects. This misaccounting has prevented the physicists and chemists from conceptual indentification of their data with synergetics' disclosure of nature's comprehensively rational inter-coordinate mathematical system.

Only the topological analysis of synergetics can account for all the multicongruent — doubled, tripled, fourfolded — topological aspects by accounting for the initial tetravolume inventories of the comprehensive rhombic dodecahedron and vector equilibrium. The comprehensive rhombic dodecahedron has an initial tetravolume of 48 and the vector equilibrium has an inherent tetravolume of 20 and their respective initial or primitive inventories of vertexes, vectors, and faces are always present —though often imperceptibly so—at all stages in nature's comprehensive $48 - 1$ convergence transformation.

Only by recognizing the deceptiveness of Eulerian topology can synergetics account for the primitive total inventories of all aspects and thus conceptually demonstrate and prove the validity of Boltzmann's concepts as well as those of all quantum phenomena. Synergetics' mathematical accounting conceptually interlinks the operational data of physics and chemistry and their complex associabilities manifest in such disciplines as geology, biology, and others.

R. Buckminster Fuller
Copyright 1977 R. Buckminster Fuller

Synergetics' Operational   Accountability

Of All Vanishing and Elsewhere Reappearing Quanta

The Whole of synergetics' cosmic hierarchy of always symmetrically concentric, multi-staged but continually smooth, geometrical contracting from 20 to 1 tetravolumes (or quanta) and their successive whole number volumes and their topological and vectorial accounting's intertransformative convergence (or divergence) phases, and in particular this series of drawings, elucidates conceptually, and by experimentally demonstrable evidence, the elegantly exact, energetic quanta transformings by which:

(A) energy exporting structural systems precisely accomplish their entropic, seemingly annihilative quantum "losses," or "tune-outs," and

(B) new structural systems appear, or tune in, at remote elsewheres and elsewhens, thereafter to agglomerate syntropically with other seemingly "new" quanta to form geometrically into complex systems of varying magnitudes;

(C) and how such complex structural systems may accommodate concurrently both entropic exporting and syntropic importing and do so always in terms of whole, uniquely frequenced, growing or diminishing, four dimensional, structural system quantum units.

In the pre-speed-of-light's-measurement era, scientists assumed an instant, simultaneous, unitarily conceptual, normally at rest (but for the moment, and only locally, perversely restless) universe. Before the 20th century discoveries of other galaxies, and in the early days of thermodynamics and the latter's disclosure of entropy—the inexorable systemic loss of energy — scientists were prone to assume that the vast instantaneous "cosmic machine" as a thermodynamic system itself must be "running down;" that is, continually spending itself entropically and trending eventually to absolute self-annihilation.

Boltzman contradicted that assumption, saying that the a priori fact of the existence of billions of stars, radiatingly, ergo, entropically, broadcasting their energies required an as yet undiscovered but obviously operative energy redistribution system by which such stars are elsewhere and elsewhen assemblingly formed. Boltzman therefore assumed a cosmic complex of invisible energy importing centers, whose nonsimultaneous formations but sum-total, long-run, energy importing exactly balances all the long-run cosmic exportings. The entropic radiance of the exporting centers makes them visible to us while the importing centers are inherently invisible except when starlight bounces reflectively off them as does the sunlight make the Moon and the planets (Venus, Jupiter, Mars and Saturn) reflectively visible to us Earthians.

Because Boltzman could not demonstrate the astro-physical presence of such inherently invisible importing centers, his concept was not widely accepted by other scientists. Einstein, however, later supported Boltzman's concept as constituting a logical corollary of Einstein's own concept of the universe as an aggregate of nonsimultaneous, variously enduring and only partially overlapping energy events.

Though Einstein did not employ the analogy, his was in effect an endless, ropelike concept of variously enduring, finite, special case (episodes) converging in generalized principle to apparent interrelevance and overlapping one another to momentarily constitute as fat or thinly diametered a rope of meaningful concern as might preoccupy any one cosmologist at any one time.

Amongst their many sophisticated mathematical devices, the mathematician's most abstract conceptual tool is Euler's (1707-83) topology, whose three irreducible visualizable aspects of vertexes—V, planar faces or areas—F, and edges of faces or lines—E, seem to the geometrically heedless mathematical physicists and astrophysicists to have no inherent correspondence with experimentally demonstrable energetic reality.

Synergetics defines the word "structure" as meaning self-interstabilization by a complex of forces operative in six degrees of freedom which complex definition can be resolved into only one word: "triangulation." The Massachusetts Institute of Technology defines mathematics as being "the science of structure and pattern in space."

Synergetical and operational mathematics finds that: by combining topology and vectorial geometry; and by always requiring structural stability and intertransformative proofs in four dimensional electromagnetic reality for all our propositions; and by starting with minimum conceptuality of a substantive entity as having inherent insideness and outsideness—it is in evidence that the minimum polyhedron (the tetrahedron), itself consisting entirely of minimum polygons (triangles) which minimum polyhedron systematically and inherently divides all universe into (A) an excluded macrocosm, and (B) an included microcosm, and (C) the remainder of universe constituting the dividing system itself, which tune-in-able, minimum, systemic, primitive entity is apprehendible conceptually because of its contrast to the "nothingness" of presently un-tuned-in, and un-tune-in-able within the limited frequency range of the human observer's given equipment as well as in contrast to the cosmically comprehensive equilibrium of all vectors, which invisible nothingness provides the geometrically conceptual field of structuring-as-you-go reference and is known as the four dimensional isotropic vector matrix, meaning cosmically everywhere and everywhere the same energy conditions, ergo, undifferentiable, ergo untunable and unapprehendible in any special case time-size reality, but both intellectually and geometrically conceptualized in Synergetics' vectorialized, angular oriented comprehensivity. There is no "space." There is the tuned in and the at present un-tuned in. Over ten million invisible electromagnetic waves, "Radio," TV, etc. programs are surrounding you and permeating you in that which we usually call "space."

Euler shows that in respect to all uncored polyhedra the number of vertexes plus the number of faces always equals the number of edges plus the number two.

But Euler seemed equally interested in local aspects of polyhedra and found that on one plane surface V + F = E + 1 —which diversion of Euler's with nonexistent two dimensionality allowed mathematicians to detour reality. This is because academic mathematicians, themselves indifferent to physical manifestation of experimental evidence have detoured Euler's concepts into such games as that of pretended existence of a substanceless rubber sheet having no insideness but only a one-way-at-a-time facing surface with no edge thickness or obverse surface on which surface Euler's vertexes, faces and edges are distortingly redeployed.

Almost blind, Euler's compensatorily vivid imagination discovered that all visual experiences could be reduced to three prime aspects: LINES and where lines converged to VERTEXES and when lines surroundingly crossed one another, AREAS bound by those lines. Because in his topology he was concerned only with visual aspects he was able to overlook substantial textures, sounds, tastes and smells, temperatures, weights and volumes, durations, intensities, frequencies and velocities. However, Euler was so great a scientist and so mathematically competent that he evolved the fundamentals of twentieth century structural analysis employed in designing structures of land, sea, sky and extraterrestrial functioning. Willard Gibbs, the chemist, developed the Phase Rule dealing with liquid, gaseous and crystaline states of substances not realizing that his phase rule employed the same generalized mathematics as did Euler's topological vertexes, faces and edges.

● ● ●

Synergetics is concerned exclusively with physically demonstrable, ergo experimentally evidenceable phenomena and adds to Euler's topology its discovery of the mathematically generalizable constant relative interabundances of angles, volumes and all the physical characteristics of (time-space) velocity, force, wave-length and frequency, directional orientation and systems consideration by always identifying Euler's E (edges, lines) as representative only of physical energy vectors or metaphysical lines of unique interrelationships of vertexially located phenomena. It is recalled that vectors are discrete in length being the product of physical velocity times mass operating in a given, angularly describable direction in respect to a given axis of observation; and that velocity is a product of time and distance while mass is a relative density of energy events per given volume wherefore all the qualities of physical experience ergo of physical demonstrability by science are describable in a unified, four-dimensional field at which state physical universe never tarries and through which and relative to which all of nature's physical manifestations are local, differentially frequenced aberratings and pulsative omni-convergent divergent omni-interaccommodative transformings.

Since the sum of the chordally convergent angles of any triangle (right, isosceles or scalene) is always 180° the sum of the angles of any chordally defined tetrahedron (four chordally triangulated polyhedron), regular or irregular, is always 720°, ergo, all its topological and geometrical interrelationship properties are consistently "similar," ergo, universal independently of time-size considerations.

We start our vectorial, topological, structuring-as-you-go exploration with the primitive state of conceptuality (independent of size and time) of the universal tetrahedron as well as of its four triangular facets, its four corners, its twelve angles and its six most economical (chordal) linear relationships lines running between its four corners event focii.

In exploring the intertransformability of the primitive hierarchy of structuring-as-you-go, omni-triangularly oriented evolution and the inter-bonding of its evolving structural components, we soon discover that the universal interjointing of systems and their foldability permit the angularly hinged convergence into congruence of vectors, faces and vertexes, (See VE Jitterbug) each of whose multi-congruences appear only as one edge, or one vertex, or one face aspects, wherefore topological accounting as presently practiced accounts each of these multi-congruent topological aspects as consisting of only one of such aspects. Only synergetics accounts for all the congruent (doubled, tripled, fourfolded) topological aspects' presences by always accounting for the initial inventory of the comprehensive rhombic dodecahedron's tetravolumed 48-ness and the vector equilibrium's inherent tetravolume 20-ness, together with their respective initial or primitive inventories of vertexes, faces and edge lines, which are always present in all stages of the 48 — 1 convergence transformation, though often imperceptibly so.

With recognition of the foregoing topological deceptiveness and always keeping account of the primitive total inventory of such aspects, we find it possible to conceptually demonstrate and prove not only the validity of Boltzman's concepts, but of all quantum phenomena, and thereby to conceptually interlink synergetics' mathematical accounting with the operational data of physics and chemistry and their complex associabilities manifest as geology, biology, et al.

R. Buckminster Fuller

● ● ●

Now You See It. Now You Don't
Quanta Lost by Precession (Richter Transformation)

We may emphasize the faces by making "solid" polyhedra.

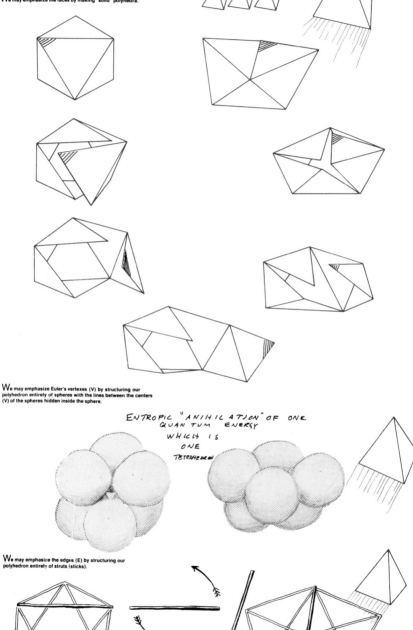

We may emphasize Euler's vertexes (V) by structuring our polyhedron entirely of spheres with the lines between the centers (V) of the spheres hidden inside the sphere.

ENTROPIC "ANIHILATION" OF ONE QUANTUM ENERGY WHICH IS ONE TETRAHEDRON

We may emphasize the edges (E) by structuring our polyhedron entirely of struts (sticks).

PRECESSION

No matter which way we do so, we find that the octahedron has 6 vertexes (spheres), 8 faces (solid surfaces), and 12 edges (struts, sticks).

R. Buckminster Fuller

But There It Is Again
Quantum Recovered in the Cube

PRIMITIVE
ELECTROMAGNETIC
WAVE - TETRAHELIX

STABLE
ASYMMETRIC

12 EDGES

=

UNSTABLE
SYMMETRIC
12 EDGES

STABILIZED
SYMMETRIC
12 EDGES

=

3 TETRAVOLUMES

3 TETRAVOLUMES

STABILIZED
ONLY BY
TWO CONCENTRIC
ALTERNATING
TETRAHEDRA

TOPOLOGICALLY

6 VERTICES, 8 FACES, 12 EDGES

12 EDGES ARE 12 VECTORS

3 VECTORS = 1 EVENT, 6 VECTORS = 1 QUANTUM

TOPOLOGICALLY

8 VERTEXES, 6 FACES, 12 EDGES

CAPTURES
12 EXTRA VECTORS
= 2 QUANTA
1 ACTIVE, 1 PASSIVE
TO MAKE
POSSIBLE STRUCTURAL
CUBE OF TETRAVOL
3

Quantum Recovered in the Vector Equilibrium

SYNTROPIC RECAPTURE (NOT BIRTH)
OF ENTROPIC "ANNIHILATION"
OF ONE ENERGY QUANTUM.

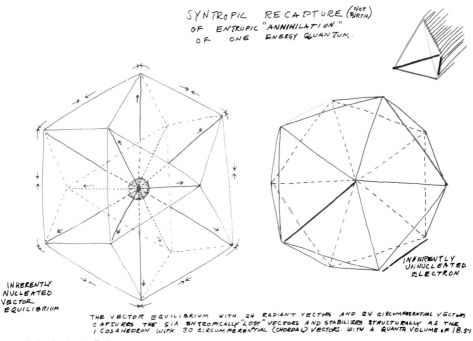

INHERENTLY
NUCLEATED
VECTOR
EQUILIBRIUM

INHERENTLY
UNNUCLEATED
ELECTRON

THE VECTOR EQUILIBRIUM WITH 24 RADIANT VECTORS AND 24 CIRCUMFERENTIAL VECTORS
CAPTURES THE SIX ENTROPICALLY "LOST" VECTORS AND STABILIZES STRUCTURALLY AS THE
1 ICOSAHEDRON WITH 30 CIRCUMFERENTIAL (CHORDAL) VECTORS. WITH A QUANTA VOLUME OF 18.51

R. Buckminster Fuller

Four Quanta Phases:
Gravity More Effective than Radiation
In Spite of Identical Vectorial Energy Potential and Because of
Single-Linked Disintegrative Patterning vs. Double-Linked Integrative Patterning

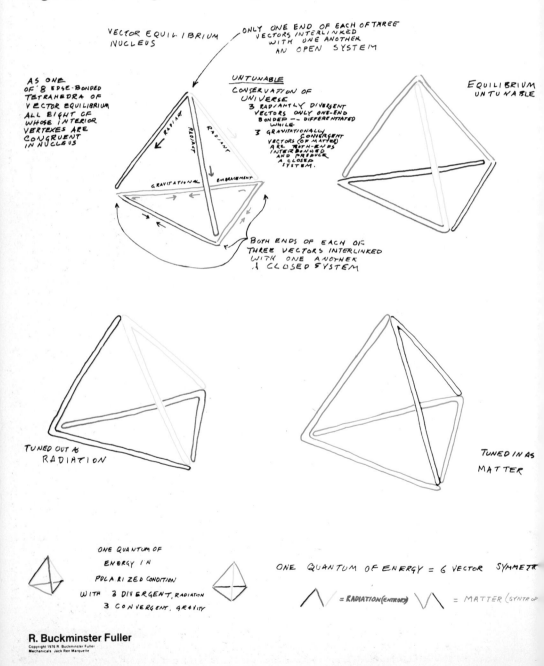

VECTOR EQUILIBRIUM
NUCLEUS

ONLY ONE END OF EACH OF THREE
VECTORS INTERLINKED
WITH ONE ANOTHER
AN OPEN SYSTEM

AS ONE
OF 8 EDGE-BONDED
TETRAHEDRA OF
VECTOR EQUILIBRIUM
ALL EIGHT OF
WHOSE INTERIOR
VERTEXES ARE
CONGRUENT
IN NUCLEUS

UNTUNABLE
CONSERVATION OF
UNIVERSE
3 RADIANTLY DIVERGENT
VECTORS ONLY ONE-END
BONDED -- DIFFERENTIATED
WHILE
3 GRAVITATIONALLY
CONVERGENT
VECTORS (OF MATTER)
ARE BOTH-ENDS
INTER-BONDED
AND PRODUCE
A CLOSED
SYSTEM.

EQUILIBRIUM
UNTUNABLE

RADIANT RADIANT RADIANT

GRAVITATIONAL EMBRACEMENT

BOTH ENDS OF EACH OF
THREE VECTORS INTERLINKED
WITH ONE ANOTHER
A CLOSED SYSTEM

TUNED OUT AS
RADIATION

TUNED IN AS
MATTER

ONE QUANTUM OF
ENERGY IN
POLARIZED CONDITION
WITH 3 DIVERGENT, RADIATION
3 CONVERGENT, GRAVITY

ONE QUANTUM OF ENERGY = 6 VECTOR SYMMETR

= RADIATION (ENTROPY)   = MATTER (SYNTROP

R. Buckminster Fuller

COSMIC HIERARCHY
of Omniinterrationally-phased, Nuclear-centered,
Convergently-divergently Intertransformable Systems

There is realized herewith a succession of concentric, 12-around-one, closest-packed spheres, each of a tetravolume of *five*; i.e., of 120 A and B Quanta Modules omniembracing our hierarchy of nuclear event patternings. This is the synergetics isometric view of the isotropic vector matrix and its omnirational, low-order whole number, equilibrious state of the micro-macro cosmic limits of the nuclearly unique, symmetrical morphological relativity and its interquantative, intertransformative, intertransactive, expansive-contractive, axially rotative, operational field. This may come to be identified as the unified field, which, as an operationally transformable complex, is conceptualizable only in its equilibrious state. (982.61)

SYMMETRICAL FORM	TETRAVOLUMES	QUANTAMODULES
F¹ Tetrahedron	1	24
F¹ Tetrahedron	1	24
F⁰ Vector Equilibrium	2.5	60
F² Double Tet (Cube)	3	72
F² Octahedron	4	96
F¹ Rhombic Triacontahedron	5	120
F² Rhombic Dodecahedron	6	144
F⁴ Vector Equilibrium	20	480
F⁴ Double Tet (Cube)	24	576

Not Shown:
SKEW-ABERATED SYMMETRICAL FORM

F⁰ Icosahedron (Disequilibrious)	5	120
F² Icosahedron (Disequilibrious)	40	960

For a full description see Synergetics: Explorations in the Geometry of Thinking Sections 982.40 through 982.73

from an original drawing by R. Buckminster Fuller

"The Spheric Spin Domain of the Rhombic Triacontahedron: 'Sphere'"

R. Buckminster Fuller

Radiant Photons

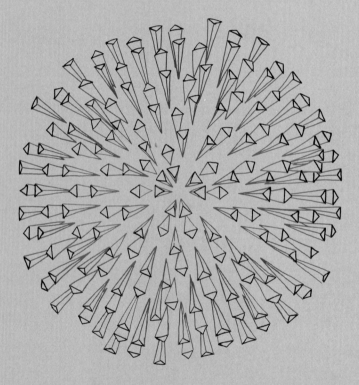

R. Buckminster Fuller

Plate 11
Dymaxion Nuclear Growth
(10 June 1948)

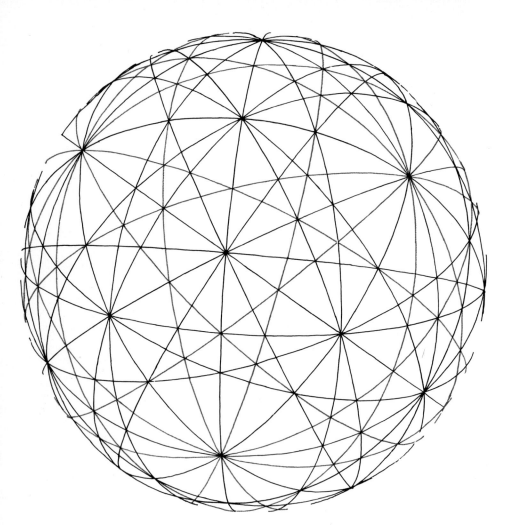

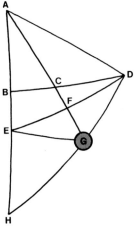

Plate 12 (See Sec. 987.133)

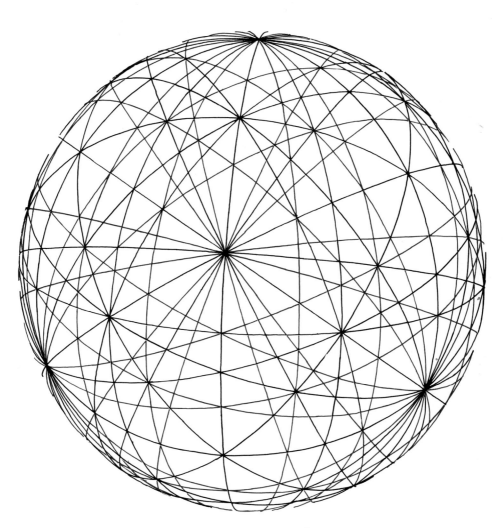

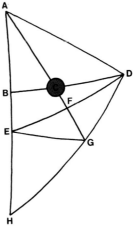

Plate 13 (See Sec. 987.134)

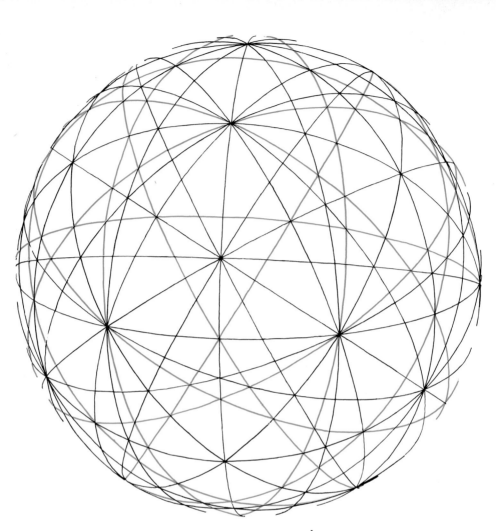

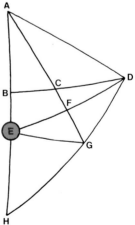

Plate 14 (See Sec. 987.135)

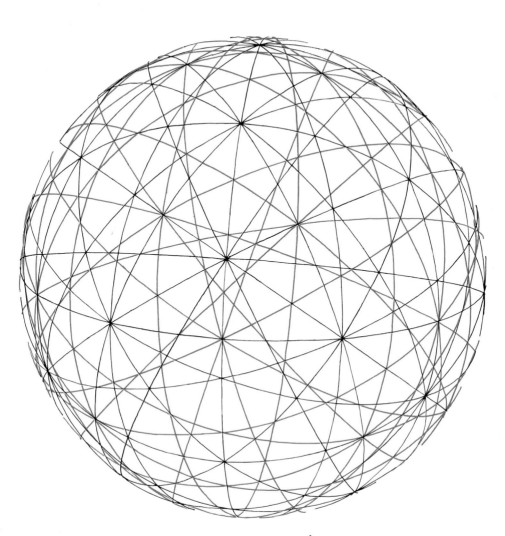

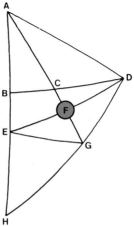

Plate 15 (See Sec. 986.136)

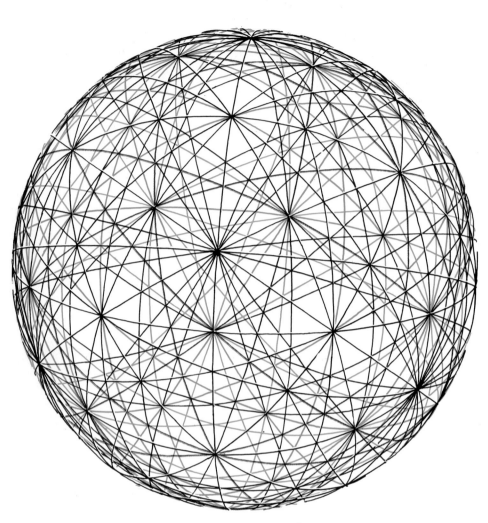

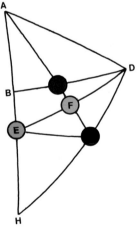

Plate 16 (See Sec. 987.137)

Humans in Universe

000.100 Introduction to 10 Color Posters

000.101 The combined land areas of Africa, Europe, and Asia embrace within their perimeters the Mediterranean, Black, Caspian, Aral, China, Arabian, Red, Baltic, and North seas: altogether their area was historically thought of only as a flat Universe sandwiched between heaven above and hell below and seemingly stretching away to infinity in all lateral directions. Yet the total land area of this flat world constitutes less than 17 percent of the subsequently-discovered-to-be-spherical Planet Earth's surface. All the great empires of written history before A.D. 1500 lay well within that "known" flat world: it was and as yet remains the spontaneous theater of popular historical conceptioning.

000.102 How did this pervading historical concept become outdated? What changed the terrestrial conceptionings adopted by the leaders of the world's power structures?

000.103 When the archaeologists' artifact-proven history of mathematics opens 4,000 years ago in Babylon and Mesopotamia, it is already a very sophisticated science. Mathematics may well have had its beginnings much earlier in India or Indochina, as it is an art and science that has traveled consistently westward. Over 3,000 years ago the Greeks made further magnificent contributions to geometry, algebra, and calculation. Then about 2,000 years ago the Roman Empire all but obliterated mathematics. A little more than 1,000 years ago Arabs and Hindus traveling through North Africa began to restore some of the ancient mathematics to the westward-evolving culture. When al-Khwarizmi's original A.D. 800 treatise on algebra was republished in Latin in Carthage in 1200, it required a further 200 years for his elucidation of the function of zero—the cipher—to be diffused into the university systems of Europe.

000.104 The cipher made possible the positioning of numbers, which in turn facilitated division and multiplication. Imagine trying to multiply or divide with Roman numerals . . . impossible! The Renaissance began with the new calculating facility introduced by the cipher. The cipher was not only an essential tool in the work of Copernicus, Kepler, Galileo, and Newton, but it also brought about Columbus' revised concepts of terrestrial navigation. It went on to instrument the mechanical and leverage calculation capabilities of Leonardo; and in the art of ship design the cipher gave birth to structural and mechanical engineering, which made possible the intertensioning and compressioning calculations of the ribbed structural strength of a sailing vessel as well as that of its vast wind-energy-driven complex of compression and tension spars, sails, and rigging—replacing the trial-and-error guesswork that had previously been used in naval and land architecture. This capability in mathematical multiplication and division opened up a whole new field of safely anticipated structural engineering and navigation.

000.105   This new anticipatory science made large engineering projects possible, but it became known to, and then was employed by, only the world's richest schemers, monarchs, nations, and pirate enterprisers. No others could afford to buy great ships.

With more powerfully engineered ships, humans emerged westward through Gibraltar to explore the Atlantic, to sail around Africa, to reach the Orient and the Pacific by water, and to circumnavigate the globe. Thus it became public knowledge that the old open-edged, infinite world system had closed back on itself in all circumferential directions to become a finite system: a closed sphere. The monarchs and merchants realized that, within that closed system, whoever commanded the line of most efficient high seas supply would become the masters of world wealth. Ships could carry cargoes that overland caravans could not.

000.106   In 1600 the East India Company was founded as a private enterprise by Queen Elizabeth and a small group of her intimates. The limited legal liability of their enterprise was granted by royal decree, and its projects were thereafter militarily sustained and protected by Great Britain's Royal Navy and colonial troops. In England the East India Company College was established to train the officers of the enterprise for their world-wide deployment; that college and its handsome campus are still in operation as of 1979. The British Empire became the first in history of which it could be said that the Sun never set.

000.107   As professor of economics at the East India Company College in 1810 Thomas Malthus became the first economic authority ever to receive in toto the vital statistics of a world-embracing spherical empire. At the very end of the 18th century Malthus published his documented thesis that humanity was multiplying its numbers at a geometric (exponential) rate of gain while increasing life-support production at only an arithmetic (linear) rate of gain. And since the Earth is a finite, closed-system sphere, it apparently became scientifically manifest that there is a fundamental inadequacy of life support on our planet. Until then all opinions on such matters had been pure guesses.

000.108 A third of a century after Malthus, Darwin attributed biological evolution to survival of only the fittest species (and individuals within species). Though he denied there was any economic significance in his theory of evolution, the economists insisted that superior physical fitness obviously governed economic survival as well. Karl Marx accepted the scientific viewpoints of both Malthus and Darwin when he declared in effect that the working class is the fittest to survive: they know how to use the tools and to cultivate the fields—the wealthy are parasites. This inaugurated the supranational concept of two world-wide political classes and two competing theories of political organization.

000.109 As a consequence of the discoveries of Malthus and Darwin all the great political ideologies have since adopted a prime philosophy that says: "You may not like our political system, but we are convinced that we have the fairest, most logical, and ingenious method of coping with the inherent inadequacy of terrestrial life support, but since there are others who disagree diametrically about the best method of coping, it can be determined only by force of arms which system is the fittest to survive." Thus survival of the physically fittest became the basis for national departments of defense with their priority of access to the most advanced science and technology. The military took command of all the highest performance materials, brains, instruments, and tools of production.

000.110 Mutually assumed survival-only-of-the-fittest is the reason why the United States and the USSR have for the past 30 years appropriated 200 billion dollars annually to buy ever more effective weapons of potential destruction. The great political and industrial power structures have all become supranational comprehensivists, while the people have been passport-chained to their respective 150 national preserves—the people have become educationally divided into "specialists" for exploitation by the supranational powers who divide to conquer and divide to keep conquered.

000.111 Up until the 20th century reality consisted of everything that humans could see, smell, touch, and hear. Then at the entry into the 20th century the electron was discovered. A century after the time of Malthus much of science became invisible with the introduction of an era of electronics, electromagnetics, and atomics. These invisible micro- and macro-exploring cosmic instruments provided for rearrangements of atomic interpositioning whose metallic alloying and chemical structuring produces ever more powerful and incisive performances per pound of physical matter employed.

000.112   Structures are complexes of visible or invisible physical events interacting to produce stable patterns. A structural system divides Universe into all Universe outside the structural system (macrocosm) and all Universe inside the structural system (microcosm). Newton's discovery of mass interattraction showed that the interattraction force of atoms, planets, stars, or galaxies increases exponentially as the interdistances decrease arithmetically, and vice versa: halve the interdistance and make fourfold the interattractive integrity of the remotely bodied structural system. That is the law of gravity. Symmetrical, noncontacting, concentric interpositioning of already-symmetrical arrays of atoms produces exponentially increased interatomic coherence of "materials."

000.113   Gravity is the inwardly cohering force acting integratively on all systems. Radiation is the outwardly disintegrating force acting divisively upon all systems.

000.114   All structural systems are comprised of tension and compression components. Stone masonry has a high compression-resisting strength of 50,000 pounds per square inch ultimate. But masonry has low tensional coherence; it can withstand only 50 pounds per square inch tensing. Stone-Age-derived masonry is a thousand times more effective in its resistance to compression than to tension.

000.115   Throughout the three million known years of the Stone Age humans relied on gravity to hold their vertical stone walls together until (as often happened) they were shaken apart by earthquakes against which they had almost no tensionally cohering resistance. Gravity pushed humanity's stone structures inward toward the Earth's center. Humans had to build their structures on bedrock "shoes" to prevent them from sinking vertically into Earth's center. Stone buildings could not float on water. But nature had invented low-weight wood of high self-cohering tensile strength (averaging approximately 10,000 p.s.i.) and of relatively low compression-resistive capability (also approximately 10,000 p.s.i.). Wood floated on water and could move useful loads horizontally; wood made good rafts for transporting humans but not for floating heavy cargoes. Thus the high tensile strength of wood, combined with the human discovery of the intertrussing principles of structuring and the low overall displacement weights involved, made possible for humans to design and fabricate air-enclosing wooden vessels whose structure and space enclosure combined to produce highly successful wooden vessels of the sea that could carry great cargoes.

000.116   In the 1850s humans arrived at the mass production of steel, an alloy of iron, carbon, and manganese having a tensile strength of 50,000 p.s.i. as well as a compression-resisting capability of 50.000 p.s.i. Steel has the same compression-resistance capability as masonry, but it also has a thousand times greater tensile capability than masonry and five times the tensile or compressive strength of wood. Steel brought mankind a structural-tension capability to match stone's previous millions of years of exclusive compressional supremacy. With far higher tensile strength per weight than wood, steel made possible even more powerful watertight, air-containing vessels than did wood, even though steel by itself does not float.

000.117   The technology of metallurgy began developing metal alloys of ever higher strength-to-weight ratios. Out of this came aluminum production by the opening of the 20th century—and aluminum alloys and stainless steel by the 1930s. These new materials made it possible to design and build engine-powered all-metal airplanes (structural vessels), which could pull themselves angularly above the horizontal and ever more steeply aloft. With the advent of successively higher strength-to-weight ratios of metal alloys and glass-reinforced plastic materials, ever more heavily laden airplanes were designed, which could climb ever more steeply and faster. Finally humans developed so much strength per weight of materials capability that they accomplished "vertol" jet plane flight and vertical space-vehicle blastoffs. Since then human scientists developing ever greater strength per weight of material have gone on to carry ever greater useful loads in vertical takeoff vehicles at ever more accelerated rates of ascent.

000.118   As of the 1970s the human mind has developed a practical tensile structuring capability of 600,000 p.s.i. The means of accomplishing this new and overwhelming structural strength has become entirely invisible. Fully 99 percent of humanity has as yet no idea that this increase in tensile capability has come about or how it came about or why it works. While humans cannot see the ever-lessening interatomic proximity of atoms and electrons of electromagnetic events, they can witness the ever more vertical takeoff-angle capabilities manifesting human comprehension of the fundamental structuring principles and their military developments and profitable commercial uses. But only vast money investments or vast governments can afford to exploit the increased technical advantages.

000.119   Before the airplane humans said, "You cannot lift yourself by your bootstraps." Today we are lifting ever lighter and stronger structural vessel "selves" by ever less effort of our scientific know-how bootstraps. No economist knows this. It is the most highly classified of military and private-enterprise secrets. Industry now converts the ever-increasing work capacity per pound of materials invested primarily to yield monetary profits for the government-subsidized private-enterprise producers of weapons.

000.120   Now in the 1970s we can state an indisputable proposition of abundance of which the world power structures do not yet have dawning awareness. We can state that as a consequence of the myriad of more-with-less, invisible, technological advances of the 20th century, and employing only well-proven technologies and already mined and ever more copiously recirculating materials, it is now technically feasible to retool and redirect world industry in such a manner that within 10 years we can have all of humanity enjoying a sustainably higher standard of living—with vastly increased degrees of freedom—than has ever been enjoyed by anyone in all history.

000.121   During this 10-year period we can also phase out all further use of fossil fuels and atomic energy, since the retooled world industry and individual energy needs will have become completely supplied by our combined harvests of electromagnetic, photosynthetic, chemical, and biological products of the daily energy income initially produced by Sun and gravity. Industry, retooled from weapons production to livingry production, will rehouse the deployed phases of world-humans by single-family, air-deliverable, energy-harvesting, only-rentable dwelling machines. When humans are convergent, they will dwell in domed-over moon-crater cities that will be energy-harvesting and -exporting centers rather than energy sinkholes.

000.122   All of the foregoing makes it possible to say that since we now know that there is a sustainable abundance of life support and accommodation for all, it follows that all politics and warring are obsolete and invalid. We no longer need to rationalize selfishness. No one need ever again "earn a living." Further living for all humanity is all cosmically prepaid.*

000.123   Why don't we exercise our epochal option? Governments are financed through taxation and would have no way of putting meters between the people and their directly received individual cosmic incomes. So too, private enterprise should no more meter the energy than it meters the air. But all of Earthians' present power structures—political, religious, or capitalist—would find their interests disastrously threatened by total human success. They are founded upon assumption of scarcity; they are organized for and sustained by the problems imposed by the assumption of fundamental inadequacies of life support.

000.124   Why does not the public itself demand realization of its option for a revolution by design science? Less than one percent of humanity now knows that the option exists; 99 percent of humanity cannot understand the

---

* Rudyard Kipling labored under the only-you-or-me philosophy, but he was inspired by thoughts that it might some day be otherwise:

> And no one will work for money and no one will
>   work for fame
> But each for the joy of working, and each in his
>   separate star,
> Shall draw the Thing as he sees It for the God of
>   Things as They are!''

—from *When Earth's Last Picture Is Painted*

mathematical language of science. The people who make up that 99 percent do not know that all that science has ever found out is that the Universe consists of the most reliable technology. They think of technology as something new; they regard it as threatening both in terms of modern weaponry and as job-eliminating competition for their life-sustaining opportunities to "earn a living." Ergo, humanity thinks it is against technology and thinks itself averse to exercising its option.

000.125   The fact that 99 percent of humanity does not understand nature is the prime reason for humanity's failure to exercise its option to attain universally sustainable physical success on this planet. The prime barrier to humanity's discovery and comprehension of nature is the obscurity of the mathematical language of science. Fortunately, however, nature is *not* using the strictly imaginary, awkward, and unrealistic coordinate system adopted by and taught by present-day academic science.

000.126   Nature's continuous self-regeneration is 100 percent efficient, neither gaining nor losing any energy. Nature is not employing the three-dimensional, omniinterperpendicular, parallel frame of the *XYZ* axial coordinates of academic science, nor is nature employing science's subsequently adopted gram/centimeter/second weight/area/time exponents. Nature does not operate in parallel. She operates in radiational divergence and gravitational convergence. She *grows* outwardly by omniintertriangulated structuring from nuclei.

000.127   Nature is inherently eight-dimensional, and the first four of these dimensions are the four planes of symmetry of the minimum structure of Universe—the omnitriangulated, equi-vector-edge tetrahedron. In respect to the conceptual pre-time-size tetrahedron's volume taken as unity 1, with its six unit-vector-edge structure, the always conceptual-independent-of-size *family* of primitive, pre-time-size, least complex polyhedra have the following exact volumes—the vector-triangulated cube 3, the octahedron 4, the rhombic triacontahedron 5, and the rhombic dodecahedron 6. When the size information is introduced, it occurs only as frequency of modular subdivision of each unit vector structuring of the primitive family's respective 1-, 2-, 3-, 4-, 5-, and 6-tetravolumes. Frequency to the third power, F^3, values then multiply the primitive, already-four-dimensional volumetric values. In physically realized time-size each has therefore $4 + 3 = 7$ dimensions, but since each system is inherently independent in Universe and therefore has *spinnability,* one more dimensional factor is required, making a total of eight dimensions in all for experientially evidencing physical reality.

000.1271   To define the everywhere-and-everywhen-transforming cosmic environment of each and every system requires several more intercovarying system dimensions—planetary, solar, galactic, intergalactic. Because of the six positive and six negative degrees of freedom governing systems-within-systems intertransforming, we have $8 + 6 = 14$ dimensional systems in cosmic relationship governance.

000.128   Nature is using this completely conceptual eight-dimensional co-ordinate system that can be comprehended by anyone. Fortunately television is spontaneously attractive and can be used to teach all the world's people nature's coordinating system—and can do so in time to make it possible for all humanity to favorably comprehend and to exercise its option to attain universal physical success, thereby eliminating forevermore all world politics and competition for the right to live. The hydrogen atom does not have to compromise its function potential by first "earning a living" before it can function directly as a hydrogen atom.

000.129   Nature's coordinate system is called Synergetics—synergy means behavior of whole systems unpredicted by any part of the system as considered only separately. The eternally regenerative Universe is synergetic. Humans have been included in this cosmic design as local Universe information-gatherers and local problem-solvers in support of the integrity of the eternal, 100-percent-efficient, self-regenerative system of Universe. In support of their cosmic functioning humans were given their minds with which to discover and employ the generalized laws governing all physical and metaphysical, omniinteraccommodative, ceaseless intertransformings of Universe.

000.130   At present 99 percent of humanity is misinformed in believing in the Malthusian concept of the fundamental inadequacy of life support, and so they have misused their minds to develop only personal and partisan advantages, intellectual cunning, and selfishness. Intellectual cunning has concentrated on how to divorce money from true life-support wealth; second, cunning has learned how to make money with money by making it scarce. As of the 1970s muscle, guns, and intellectual cunning are ruling world affairs and keeping them competitive by continuing the false premise of universal inadequacy of life support. If mind comes into supreme power within a decade, humanity will exercise its option of a design revolution and will enter a new and lasting epoch of physical success for all. If not, it will be curtains for all humanity within this century.

000.131   In complement with *Synergetics 1* and *2* the posters at color plates 1–10 may clarify for everyone the few scientific conceptions and mathematical tools necessary for universal comprehension and individual use of nature's synergetic geometrical intertransformings.

100.00 Synergy

100.00 SYNERGY

100.01 Introduction: Scenario of the Child
    100.010 Awareness of the Child
    100.020 Human Sense Awareness
    100.030 Resolvability Limits

    100.10 Subdivision of Tetrahedral Unity
      100.101 Synergetic Unity
      100.120 Icosa and Tetra
    100.20 Scenario of the Child
    100.30 Omnirational Subdividing
      100.3011 Necklace
      100.304 Cheese Tetrahedron
      100.310 Two Tetra into Cube
    100.320 Modular Subdivision of the Cosmic Hierarchy
    100.330 "Me" Ball
    100.40 Finite Event Scenario
      100.41 Foldability of Triangles into Tetrahedra
      100.415 Unfoldable Limit
    100.50 Constant Triangular Symmetry
    100.60 Finite Episoding

(101.00 Definition: Synergy)*

(120.00 Mass Interattraction)

(130.00 Precession and Entropy)

(140.00 Corollary of Synergy: Principle of the Whole System)

(150.00 Synergy-of-Synergies)

(160.00 Generalized Design Science Exploration)

180.00 Design Science and Human-Tolerance Limits

    * Titles in parentheses will be found in *Synergetics 1*

100.01 Introduction: Scenario of the Child

• [*100.01–100.63 Child as Explorer Scenario*]

100.010 **Awareness of the Child:** The simplest descriptions are those expressed by only one word. The one word alone that describes the experience "life" is "awareness." Awareness requires an otherness of which the observer can be aware. The communication of awareness is both subjective and objective, from passive to active, from otherness to self, from self to otherness.

$$\text{Awareness} = \text{self} + \text{otherness}$$

$$\text{Awareness} = \text{observer} + \text{observed}$$

100.011 Awareness is the otherness saying to the observer, "See Me." Awareness is the observer saying to self, "I see the otherness." Otherness induces awareness of self. Awareness is always otherness inductive. The total complex of otherness is the environment.

100.012 Universe to each must be
All that is, including me.
Environment in turn must be
All that is, excepting me.

(*Compare Secs. 264.10 and 1073.12.*)

100.013 Life begins only with otherness. Life begins with awareness of environment. In Percival W. Bridgman's identification of Einstein's science as *operational science,* the comprehensive inventory of environmental conditions is as essential to "experimental evidence" as is the inventory of locally-focused-upon experimental items and interoperational events.

3

100.014 The child's awareness of otherness phenomena can be apprehended only through its nerve-circuited sense systems and through instrumentally augmented, macro-micro, sense-system extensions—such as eyeglasses. Sight requires light, however, and light derives only from radiation of celestial entropy, where Sunlight is starlight and fossil fuels and fire-producing wood logs are celestial radiation accumulators; ergo, all the sensings are imposed by cosmic environment eventings.

100.015 The child apprehends only sensorially. The combined complex of different sensorial apprehendings (touch, smell, hear, see) of each special case experience are altogether coordinated in the child's brain to constitute "awareness" conceptions. The senses can apprehend only other-than-self "somethings"—for example, the child's left hand discovering its right hand, its toe, or its mother's finger. Brains differentially correlate the succession of special case informations communicated to the brain by the plurality of senses. The brain distinguishes the new, first-time-event, special case experiences only by comparing them with the set of all its recalled prior cognitions.

100.016. Although children have the most superb imaginative faculties, when they explore and arrive at new objective formulations, they rely—spontaneously and strategically—only upon their own memory of relevant experiences. With anticipatory imagination children consider the consequences of their experiments, such as a physical experiment entailing pure, unprecedented risk yet affording a reasonable possibility of success and including a preconception of the probable alternative physical consequences of their attempt. For example, they may conceivably jump over a ditch today even though it is wider than any over which they have previously leapt. They only make the attempt because they have also learned experientially that, as they grow older and bigger, they are often surprised to find that they can jump farther and higher than ever before. "How do all my muscles feel about it now?" and "Shall I or shall I not try?" become exquisitely aesthetic questions leading to synergetically integrated, physical-metaphysical, split-second self-appraisals and exclusively intuitive decisions. If it's "Everything go!" all thoughts of negative consequences are brushed aside.

100.017 Children conduct their spontaneous explorations and experiments with naive perceptivity. They have an innate urge first subjectively to *sort out, find order in, integratively comprehend,* and *synergetically memory-bank* their experience harvests as intertransformability system sets. Thereafter they eagerly seek to demonstrate and redemonstrate these sets as manifest of their comprehension and mastery of the synergetic realizability of the system's physical principles. Consequently children are the only rigorously pure physical scientists. They accept only sensorially apprehensible, experimentally redemonstrable physical evidence.

100.018 Things = events = patterns = somersaults = intertransform-ability systems . . . that's what delights a girl as she accepts her uncle's invitation to face him, take hold of his two hands, walk up his front until, falling backward—and still holding his hands—the child finds herself looping the loop, heels over head, to land with feet on the ground and head high. . . . "Wow, let's do it again!"

100.020 *Human Sense Awareness*

INFRARED THRESHOLD
(Only *micro*-instrument-apprehensible)

Tactile: Preponderantly sensing the crystalline and triple-bonded atom-and-molecule state, including all the exclusively infraoptical frequency ranges of the electromagnetic wave spectrum's human receptivity from cold "solids" through to the limit degrees of heat that are safely (nonburningly) touchable by human flesh.

Olfactoral: Preponderantly sensing the liquid and double-bonded atom-and-molecule state, including all of the humanly tunable ranges of the harmonic resonances of complex chemical liquid substances.

Aural: Preponderantly sensing the gaseous and single-bonded atom-and-molecule state, including all ranges of humanly tunable simple and complex resonance harmonics in gasses.

Visual: Preponderantly sensing the radiantly deflecting-reflecting, unbonding-rebonding, atom-and-molecule energy export states, including all ultratactile, humanly-tune-in-able, frequency ranges of electromagnetic wave phenomena.

ULTRAVIOLET THRESHOLD
(Only *macro*-instrument-apprehensible)

(See Secs. *267.02, 801.01–24,* and *1053.85.*)

100.021 The direct sensing of information may sometimes be deceptive and illusory due to such factors as coincidence, congruence, or the time-and-angle distortions of perspective. For instance, the parallel railroad tracks seem (mistakenly) to converge at the horizon, and the apparently "motionless" remote stars seem (mistakenly) fixed, while they are in fact speeding at celestial macrorates.

100.022 Children can learn from their successive observations of the rotational progression of angles that the hour and minute hands of a clock have moved; that the tree and the vine have grown; and that the pond's top has frozen into ice that surprisingly floats—getting colder usually means getting denser and heavier per given volume, which erroneously suggests that ice should sink to the pond's bottom. But the crystallization of water forms a "space frame" whose members do not fill allspace. This vacated space embraces and incorporates oxygen from the atmosphere—which makes ice lighter than water. The crystallization of water takes up more room than does the water in its liquid nonform condition. Crystallization is structurally and vectorially linear: it is not allspace-filling. Crystalline structurings are interspersed by additional atmospheric molecules occupying more volume (ergo, having less mass); the process of crystallization cracks open its closed containers. If ice did not float, if ice sank to the bottom, life would have long since disappeared from planet Earth.

100.023 Comprehensively concerned children can learn how to avoid the miscarriages of misconceptioning as induced by too-brief reviews of their progressive experiences as observed from too few viewpoints or loci. They can learn—as did Einstein—of the plurality of different, instrumentally measured, time-angle-and-size aspects of the same phenomena as viewed from different given environmental surrounding points by different observers at as close to the "same" time as possible, taken at "almost the same time" as well as at distinctly different times. The foregoing is what led Einstein to the discovery of relativity.

100.030 Resolvability Limits

100.031 The visual limits of "now-you-see-it-now-you-don't," yes-no-yes-no, something-nothing-something-nothing, dot-dash-dot-dash are relative size-scale discernibilities spoken of technically as *resolution*. These resolvability limits of the human eye may be pictured as follows:

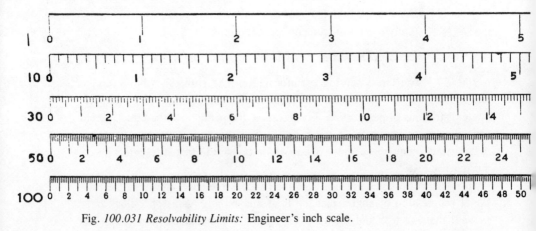

Fig. *100.031 Resolvability Limits:* Engineer's inch scale.

The finest "smooth"-surface, intercolor-crossblending, continuum photogravure printing is accomplished with a benday screen that uses 200 unique color dots per square inch of printed surface. (See Secs. *260.11* and *260.22*.)

100.032   A point-to-able something may be much too small to be optically resolved into its constituent polyhedral characteristics, yet be unitarily differentiated as a black speck against a white background. Because a speck existed yet defied their discernment of any feature, mathematicians of the premicroscope era mistakenly assumed a speck to be self-evidently unitary, indivisible, and geometrically employable as a nondimensional "point." (See Secs. *262.02–05, 264, 527.25,* and *530.11*.)

100.033   A plurality of points became the "building blocks" with which the mathematicians of the day before microscopes imaginatively constructed their lines. "Lines" became the one-dimensional, substanceless "logs" that they floored together in their two-dimensional, planar, thicklessness "rafts." Finally they stacked these planar rafts one upon another to build a "solid" three-dimensional "cube," but having none of the essential characteristics of four-dimensional reality—i.e., having neither temperature, weight, nor longevity.

100.10   Subdivision of Tetrahedral Unity

100.101   **Synergetic Unity:** Quantum mechanics commences with the totality of energy of physical Universe—energy intertransformable either as matter or as radiation. Quantum mechanics assumes conservation. Energy can be neither created nor lost. Cosmic energy is plural unity, always-and-only coexistent, complementarily complex unity, i.e., *synergetic unity,* consisting of an overlapping mix of infrequent big events and frequent little ones. Multiplication of energy events can be accomplished only by progressive subdividing of its cosmic unity.

100.102   The child-scientist's show opens with reiteration of rigorous science's one-and-only acceptable *proof:* experientially redemonstrable physical evidence. All of the scenario's proofs—and their rationally interrelated number values—derive exclusively from progressive equatorial-symmetry-halvings of Universe's minimum structural system: the tetrahedron. Multiplication occurs only through progressive fractionation of the original complex unity of the minimum structural system of Universe: the tetrahedron.

100.103   Rational numerical and geometrical values derive from (a) parallel and (b) perpendicular halving of the tetrahedron. (See Fig. *100.103*.)

    (a) The parallel method of tetrahedral bisecting has three axes of spin—ergo, three equators of halving. Parallel equatorial halving is both statically and dynamically symmetric.

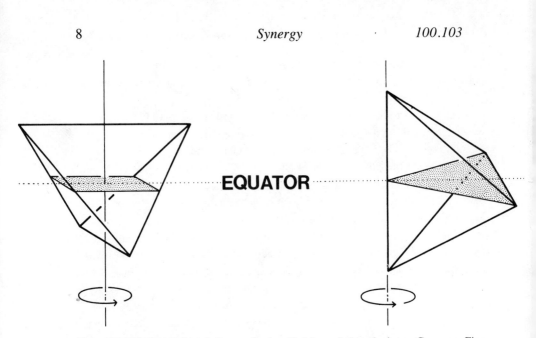

Fig. *100.103 Parallel and Perpendicular Halving of Tetrahedron:* Compare Figs.
527.08 and *987.230B*.

(b) The perpendicular method of tetrahedral bisecting has six axes of
spin—ergo, six equators of halving. Perpendicular equatorial halving
is only dynamically symmetric.

100.104 The three-way, symmetry-imposed, perpendicular bisecting of
each of the tetrahedron's four triangular faces results in an inadvertent *thirding*. This halving and inadvertent thirding physically isolate the prime number
three and its multiples and introduce the 24 A Quanta Modules. (See Sec.
911, Fig. 913.01, and Table 943.)

100.1041 The initial halvings of the triangular facets inadvertently accomplish both thirdings and quintasectings. Halving a triangle by perpendicular bisectors finds three ways of doing so. (See Fig. *100.1041*.)

100.1042 Great circles inherently halve unity. The six positive and six
negative great circles spin around the 12 positive and 12 negative poles vertexially identified by the 12-great-circle and four-great-circle intersections of
the vector equilibrium producing the pentagons from the quintasectings.

100.105 All the geometries in the cosmic hierarchy (see Table 982.62)
emerge from the successive subdividing of the tetrahedron and its combined
parts. After the initial halvings and inadvertent thirdings inherent in the bisecting of the triangles as altogether generated by all seven sets of the great-
circle equators of symmetrical-systems spin (Sec. 1040), we witness the
emergence of:

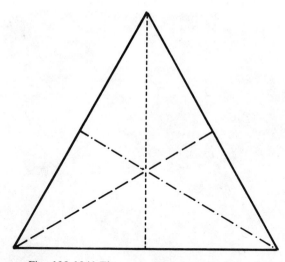

Fig. *100.1041 Three-way Bisecting of a Triangle*

—the A quanta modules
—the octa
—the "icebergs"
—the Eighth-Octa
—the cube
—the Quarter-Tetra
—the rhombic dodeca
—the B quanta modules
—the icosahedron
—the T quanta modules
—the octa-icosa, skewed-off "S" modules
—the rhombic triacontahedron
—the E quanta modules
—the Mites (quarks)
—the Sytes
—the Couplers

100.120 **Icosa and Tetra:** The icosahedron concentric within, but flushly askew, in the four-frequency truncated tetrahedron completes the whole cosmic hierarchy as subdivisioning of the primitive unity of the tetrahedron—one quantum—the minimum structural system of Universe. Looked at perpendicularly to the middle of any of the tetrahedron's four truncated faces—as a line of sight—the icosahedron appears at the center of volume of the tetrahedron as a four-dimensional symmetrical structure. (See Fig. *100.120.*)

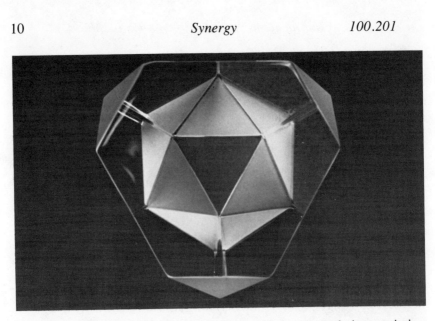

Fig. *100.120 Image of Icosa and Tetra:* Photograph of a truncated glass tetrahedron with frosted triangular facets producing an image of clustered tetrahedra that approximate an icosahedron. (See discussion at Sec. 934.)

100.20   Scenario of the Child

100.201   Our scenario, titled "Experimentally Certified Scientific Proofs," opens with a child standing outdoors, glancing all around, pausing to look more intently at an aggregate of generalized somethings, and finally focusing upon a special case something:

—a point-to-ability

—a surface of something

—a substance having "insideness and outsideness." The smallest thing we know of—the atom—has a withinness nucleus and one or more withoutness electrons.

—a big something fastened to the Earth

—picture of the Matterhorn

—minimum of three faces around a corner

—child breaks off piece of something

—separate individual "things"

—child takes hammer and breaks rock

—nature breaks big rocks

—humans blast apart rock cliff with dynamite

—picture of rocks on Earth

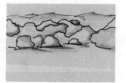

—picture of rocks on Moon

—picture of rocks on Mars

—picture of big rocks broken into smaller rocks

—picture of small rocks broken into sand

—picture of sandy beach

—picture of individual grains of sand

—minimum separable something has a minimum of four corners, each surrounded by a minimum of three faces; each face is surrounded at minimum by three edges. "Minimum somethings" consist altogether of a minimum of four corners, four faces, six edges, 12 angles, insideness, outsideness, concavity, convexity, and two poles of spinnability—a minimum total of 32 unique geometrical features (Sec. 1044)

—picture of one tetrahedron

—picture of tetrahedron turning inside out in four different ways as each of four corner vertexes plunges through their respective four opposite triangular openings to produce four different positive and four different negative tetrahedra, for a total of eight different tetrahedra

—picture of four great circle planes of tetrahedron all going through a common center to produce both the zerovolume tetrahedron and the vector equilibrium's eight tetrahedra with only nuclear-congruent vertexes

—minimum of four cosmically different tetrahedra:

—the tuned-in, at-presently-considered-complex system—a tetrahedral time-size somethingness

—the infra-tuned-in micro-tetra-nothingness

—the ultra-tuned-in macro-tetra-nothingness

—the metaphysical, only primitively conceptual, timeless-sizeless tetra.

100.30 Omnirational Subdividing

100.301 Omniquadrilaterally interconnecting the mid-edge-points of any dissimilarly-edge-lengthed quadrilateral polygon always produces four *dissimilar* quadrangles. Omnitriangularly interconnecting the mid-edge-points of any dissimilarly-edge-lengthed triangle always produces four *similar* triangles. (See Fig. 990.01.) Whereas omniinterconnecting the mid-edge-points of a cube always subdivides the cube into eight similarly equiedged cubes, interconnecting the mid-edge-points of any dissimilarly-edge-lengthed quadrangular-faced hexahedra always subdivides the hexahedron into eight always dissimilar, quadrangular-faced hexahedra. (See Fig. *100.301.*)

100.3011 **Necklace:** Here we observe the sequence of the child's necklace (Sec. 608). The child starts with an enlargement of his mother's necklace consisting of a dozen half-inch-by-12-inch aluminum tubes strung tightly together on dacron cords. The child drapes the necklace over his shoulders to assume various shapes. Then, removing one tube at a time, he finds that the necklace remains flexible . . . until all but the last three are removed and—as a triangle—it suddenly holds its shape. (Thus we arrive at the triangular definition of a structure.)

100.302 A triangle is a microaltitude tetrahedron with its apex almost congruent with one of its base triangle's vertexes. A right-angled triangle, an isosceles triangle, and a scalene triangle are all the same triangle. The seeming difference in edge lengths and angles is a consequence only of shifting the base-plane locus of the observer.

100.303 Most economically intertriangulating the midpoints of any regular equiedged or any dissimilarly edged tetrahedra will always subdivide that

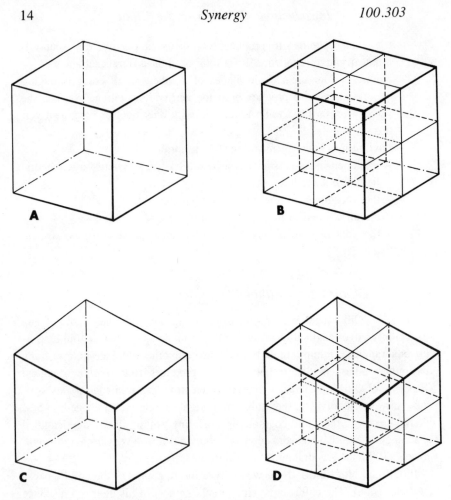

Fig. *100.301A–D Dissimilar Subdivision of Irregular Hexahedra*

tetrahedron into four similar tetrahedra and one octahedron whose volume is always four times that of any of the four similar and equivolumed tetrahedra.

100.304 **Cheese Tetrahedron:** If we make all the symmetrical Platonic solids of firm cheese, and if we slice the cube parallel to one of its faces, the remaining hexahedron is no longer equiedge-lengthed. So too with all the other Platonic solids—the dodecahedron, the octahedron, or the icosahedron—with one, and only one, exception: the tetrahedron. The cheese tetrahedron may be sliced parallel to any one, or successively all four, of its faces without losing its basic symmetry; ergo, only the tetrahedron's four-dimensional coordination can accommodate asymmetric aberrations without in any way disrupting the symmetrical integrity of the system.

100.310 **Two Tetra into Cube:** The child wants to get inside things. What is the minimum something it can get inside of? The necklace tetrahedron strung together with long-tube-beads. A child tries the necklace cube, and it collapses. The child then takes the 12 edge tubes of the collapsed cube and reassembles them as an octahedron—which holds its shape. The child also takes two sets of six tubes and makes two tetrahedra producing an omni-triangulated superficially induced cube with eight corners.

100.320 Modular Subdivision of the Cosmic Hierarchy

100.321 Any four points in Universe are always most economically interrelated by an ever-transforming tetrahedron, the whole, low-order, rational volume of whose primitive, cosmic, equiwavelengthed-and-frequenced corresponding vector equilibrium, cube, octahedron, rhombic triacontahedron, and rhombic dodecahedron—stated in tetravolumes—are always 1, $2^1/_2$, $2^1/_2$, 3, 4, 5, 6—which hierarchy of constituent geometrical structures remains eternally invariable. (See Table *1033.192.*)

100.322 The omnirational subdivision of any regular or irregular tetrahedron by the systemic triangular interconnecting of the tetrahedron's similarly frequenced, modular subdivision points of its six edges, respectively, will always subdivide the tetrahedron into the same rationally volumed geometrical constituents constituting the *cosmic hierarchy* and its A and B Quanta Modules as well as its T, E, and S Modules.

100.323 Only the tetrahedron can accommodate the asymmetric aberrations of otherness without losing the integrity of its own four-dimensional symmetry and its subdivisible volumetric rationality. The asymmetric aberrations of otherness are essential to awareness, awareness being the minimum statement of the experience life. In the accommodation of asymmetric aberration the tetrahedron permits conceptual focus upon otherness, which is primitively essential to the experience of life, for it occasions life's initial awareness. (See Fig. 411.05.)

100.330 "Me" Ball

100.331 Here we observe the child taking the *"me"* ball (Sec. 411) and running around in space. There is nothing else of which to be aware; ergo, he is as yet unborn. Suddenly one *"otherness"* ball appears. Life begins. The two balls are mass-interattracted; they roll around on each other. A third ball appears and is mass-attracted; it rolls into the valley of the first two to form a triangle in which the three balls may involve-evolute. A fourth ball appears and is also mass-attracted; it rolls into the "nest" of the triangular group . . .

and this stops all motion as the four balls become a self-stabilized system: the tetrahedron. (See Fig. 411.05. See vol. 1.)

100.40   Finite Event Scenario

100.401   Events are changes of interrelationships.

100.402   Events are changes of interrelationships between a plurality of systems or between constituents of any one system. Events are changes of interrelationships, between any one of the separate ''thing'' system's constituent characteristics—a minimum thing has separable parts. A thing is always special case. Special cases always have time-frequency relative sizing; whereas the minimum system—the tetrahedron—is generalized, prefrequency, timeless, yet conceptual—ergo, does not have separable parts, but being primitive and timeless does have primitive fractionability into structurally conceptual, timeless, omnirationally accountable, symmetrical, differential polyhedra of the cosmic hierarchy.

100.403   The cosmic hierarchy is comprised of the tetrahedron's inherent, intertransformable interrelationships—four active, four passive—all of which occur within the six primitive, potential, omnidirectional vectorial moves found in each primitive system's (timeless) event potential.

100.41   Foldability of Triangles into Tetrahedra

100.411   Every triangle is always a projected tetrahedron. Any triangle having no angle greater than 90 degrees can be folded into a tetrahedron. No squares or quadrangles may be folded into a hexahedron.

100.412   The scalene right triangle is a limit case that folds into an almost-flat tetrahedron. (See Fig. *100.412.*)

100.413   The equiangular triangle folds into a regular tetrahedron consisting of four similar, equivolume, regular tetrahedra. Their total volume equals the volume of the central octahedron (inadvertently described). (See Fig. *100.413.*)

100.414   The isosceles triangle, with all angles less than 90 degrees, folds into an irregular tetrahedron consisting of four similar irregular tetrahedra. Their total volume equals the volume of the central irregular octahedron (inadvertently described). (See Fig. *100.414.*)

100.415   **Unfoldable Limit:** The scalene triangle, having one angle greater than 90 degrees, will not fold into a tetrahedron, but it consists of 16 similar triangles. (See Fig. *100.415.*)

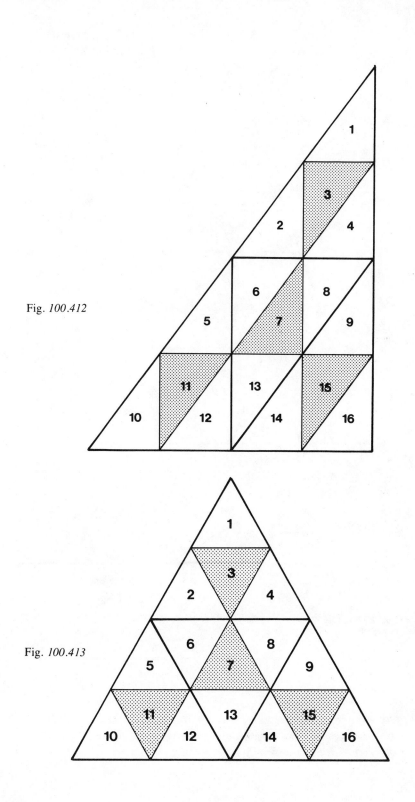

Fig. *100.412*

Fig. *100.413*

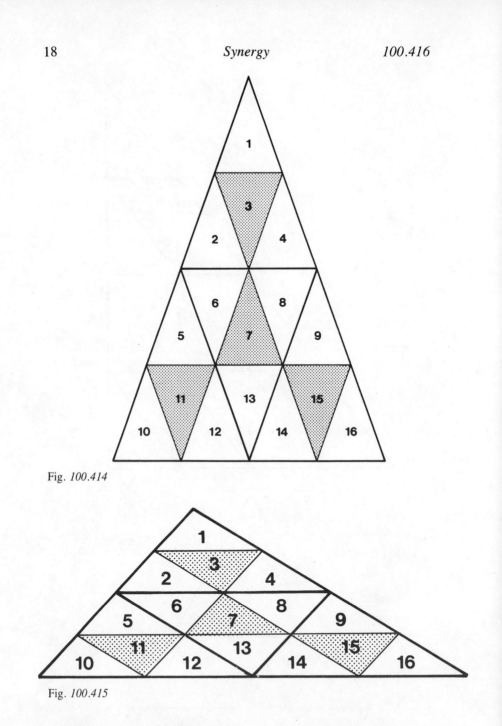

Fig. *100.414*

Fig. *100.415*

100.416 The triangle folded into a tetrahedron inadvertently describes the four exposed faces of the tetrahedron's internal octahedron. (See Figs. *100.416A–D.*)

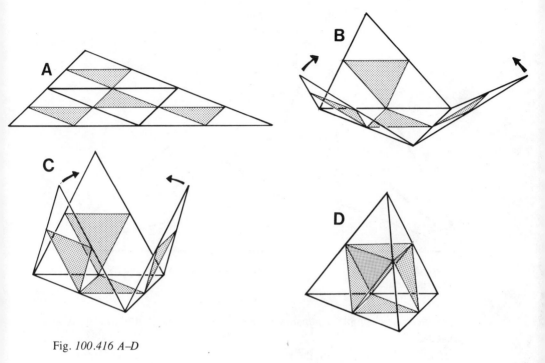

Fig. *100.416 A–D*

100.50 Constant Triangular Symmetry

100.51   Dr. Frank Morley, a professor of mathematics at Johns Hopkins University, was the author of a theorem on triangular symmetry: The three interior intersection points of the trisectors of any triangle's three angles will always describe an equiangular triangle. It may be demonstrated graphically as in Fig. *100.51.*

This theorem is akin to the tetrahedral coordinate system of synergetics (Sec. 420), which describes how the superficial dissimilarities and aberrations of the tetrahedron in no way alter any of its constant symmetries of omnirational subdivisioning.

100.60 Finite Episoding

100.61   Nonunitarily conceptual but finite Scenario Universe's only separate, differently enduring, and only overlappingly occurring, conceptual episodes, their scenery, costumes, and character parts—all being special case and temporal—are each and all demonstrably separable—ergo, finite—and only altogether coordinate, to provide the ever-aggregating *finiteness* of Scen-

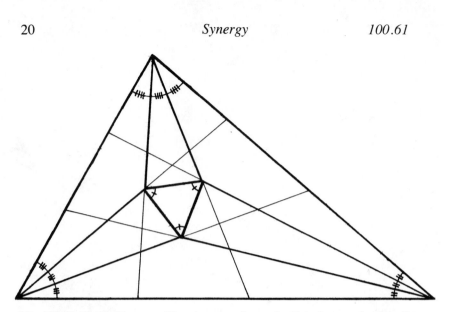

Fig. *100.51 Morley Theorem:* The trisectors of any triangle's three angles describe an equiangular triangle.

ario Universe's complex, nonsimultaneous—ergo, nonunitarily conceptual—episodes.

100.62   This moment in the evolutionary advance and psychological transformation of humanity has been held back by non-physically-demonstrable—ergo non-sensorial—conceptionless mathematical devices and by the resultant human incomprehensibility of the findings of science. There are two most prominent reasons for this incomprehensibility: The first is the non-physically-demonstrable mathematical tools. The second is our preoccupation with the sense of static, fixed "space" as so much unoccupied geometry imposed by square, cubic, perpendicular, and parallel attempts at coordination, *rather than* regarding "space" as being merely systemic angle-and-frequency information that is presently non-tuned-in within the physical, sensorial range of tunability of the electromagnetic sensing equipment with which we personally have been organically endowed.

100.63   The somethingness here and the nothingness there of statically interarrayed "space" conceptioning is vacated as we realize that the infratunable is subvisible high-frequency eventing, which we speak of as *matter,* while the ultratunable is radiation, which we speak of as *space.* The tunable is special case, sensorially apprehensible episoding.

180.00   Design Science and Human-Tolerance Limits

181.00   Humans are often spoken of as behaving like animals. Vast experimental study of animal reflexes and proclivities has disclosed reliable benign behaviors to be predictable when the creatures' vital necessities are both habitually and readily available well within critical limits of safe, healthy input periodicities of the chromosomically and DNA-RNA programmed optimum metabolic processing of the subject species creatures.

182.00   Such scientifically conducted zoological behavior studies use the words *reward* and *punishment*. By the word *reward* they do not refer to a gold medal. And their word *punishment* does not refer to whipping. The animal behavior scientist's word *reward* means that the creature is acquiring the vital life-support chemistries of air, food, and water well within the critical metabolic timing tolerance. Punishment, to these scientists, means that the creature's subconsciously generated hunger, thirst, and respiratory instincts are not met within comfortably tolerable time limits, whereafter the creature panics. Its original subconscious, spontaneous, innate trust that its environment will always provide what it wants and needs exactly when it is needed having been violated, the creature panics, and forever after its behavior pattern is unpredictable.

183.00   It is clear that with the pushing of the panic button a secondary act of subconscious behavior controls has been activated. It is one of the self-disciplined responsibilities of comprehensive, anticipatory design science always to include fail-safe, automatically switched-in, alternate circuitry for mechanical functioning whenever a prime function facility is found wanting. When a series of failures has blown out all the alternate circuits' fuses, then a sense of lethal frustration sets in that is identified as panic. Once panicked, the individuals—creatures or humans—tend to trust nothing, and their behavior then becomes utterly unpredictable. They become spontaneously suspicious of their environment in general and prone to be spontaneously hostile and aggressive.

184.00   When they are aggressive—or even worse, when they panic—both humans and animals demonstrate a subconscious drive only for self-survival. For instance, when a great theater fire disaster occurs and the flames quickly exhaust all the oxygen, people suffocate within two minutes. When the fire is over and many of the human dead are found inside unscorched, their deaths having been caused by suffocation, we discover that the otherwise loving fathers lost personal consciousness and stampeded over their own children and crushed them to death—the children for whom the conscious fathers would gladly have given their lives a hundred times over.

185.00　This frustratedly insecure or panicked animal survival drive is not a primary human behavior; it is only a secondary, subordinate, "fail-safe" behavior that occurs only when the very broad limits of physical tolerance are exceeded. When supplies are available, humans daily consume about two dry pounds of food as well as five pounds of water and seven pounds of oxygen, which their blood extracts from the 50 pounds of atmosphere that they inhale every day. Humans can go 30 days without food, seven days without water, but only two minutes without air. With 30 days' tolerance, humans have plenty of time to decide how to cope with vital food problems; with a week's waterless tolerance, they have to think and act with some expedition; with only one-and-a-half minutes' oxygenless tolerance, they rarely have time to think and cope successfully. Because the substances that humans require the least can be gone without for 30 days, nature has for millions of years used humans' hunger and the fertility potentials to force them to learn by trial and error how most competently to solve problems. But because the absence for more than a minute or so of oxygen (the substance humans use the most) could not be tolerated, nature provided the air everywhere around the world—in effect, "socialized" it.

186.00　As long as the 30-day, seven-day, two-minute tolerances, respectively, for lack of food, water, and air are not exceeded, humans' minds tend to remain in ascendance over their brain-reflexive sensing, and people are considerate of their fellow humans. When the human is stressed beyond these tolerable limits, the preconditioned-reflexing brain function takes over from the thoughtful, loving, orderly reasoning of mind. Then the secondary utterly thoughtless behavior occurs.

187.00　It is at least scientifically plausible, and possibly even scientifically validated, to say that not only all humans but all creatures are designed to behave spontaneously in a benign manner and that all creatures have toleration limits within which they continue to function with subconsciously spontaneous amiability, but that many have been stressed and distressed beyond those limits early in their lives and consequently have developed aggressive, belligerent, or outright mad proclivities. This is not to say that this switch by both creatures and humans from dominance by their primary proclivities to dominance by their secondary proclivities is an irreparable condition of life on Earth. Though Humans as yet know little about complete repair of their innate propensities, there are promising signs that such cures are not beyond attainment by the human mind.

200.00 Synergetics

*Titles in parentheses will be found in *Synergetics 1*

200.001 Definition: Synergetics

200.06 Synergetics shows how we may measure our experiences geometrically and topologically and how we may employ geometry and topology to coordinate all information regarding our experiences, both metaphysical and physical. Information can be either conceptually metaphysical or quantitatively special case physical experiencing, or it can be both. The quantized physical case is entropic, while the metaphysical generalized conceptioning induced by the generalized content of the information is syntropic. The resulting mind-appreciated syntropy evolves to anticipatorily terminate the entropically accelerated disorder.

201.10 Accommodation of Proclivities, Phases, and Disciplines

201.11 The tetrahedral and vector equilibrium models in the isotropic vector matrix provide an absolute accommodation network of energy articulation, including the *differentiated proclivities* of:

associative–disassociative
convergent–divergent–oscillating–pulsating
dynamic–kinetic
energetic–synergetic
entropic–syntropic
expansive–contractive
explosive–implosive
gravitational–radiational
hydraulic–pneumatic
importing–exporting
inside-outing–outside-inning

     involuting–evoluting
     omnidirectional–focal push–pulling
     radial–circumferential
     rotational–ovational gearing
     synchronous–dissynchronous
     torque–countertorque
     turbining–counterturbining
     vector–tensor

together with the *integrated synergetic proclivities* of:

     inward-outward and three-way aroundness;
     precessional processing of plus-minus polarization; and
     wave propagation mechanics;

together with the intertransformative behavioral
phases of:

     incandescent
     liquid
     plasmic
     thermal
     vapor;

and the mensurabilities elucidating the
disciplines of:

     biological
     chemical
     cryogenic
     crystallographic
     electrical
     genetic
     geodesic
     geodetic
     geological
     geometrical
     logical
     mathematical
     mechanical
     nonbiological structuring
     physiological
     scientific
     teleologic

thermodynamic
virological

explorations for comprehensive rational interrelationship number constants. (See Sec. 424.01.)

201.20 Synergetic Hierarchy: Grand Strategy

201.21 Although we are deeply and inescapably aware of the vast ranges of unexploited geometry, we must not permit such preoccupations to obscure our awareness of the generalized, comprehensively coordinate, arithmetical, geometrical, and factorial system employed by nature in all her energetic-synergetic transformative transactions. With the general systems' discovery of the tetrahedron as the basic structural unit of physical Universe quantation, we find that there is a fundamental hierarchy of vectorial-geometric relationships that coincides with and integrates topology, quantum mechanics, and chemistry.

201.22 All of the exact sciences of physics and chemistry have provided for the accounting of the physical behaviors of matter and energy only through separate, unique languages that require awkward translation through the function of the abstract interpreters known as the *constants*. But synergetics now embraces the comprehensive family of behavioral relationships within one language capable of reconciling all the experimentally disclosed values of the $XYZ–CG_tS$ mensuration systems adopted by science. The adoption of the tetrahedron as mensural unity, as proposed in Table 223.64, and the recognition of the isotropic vector matrix as the rational coordinate model, are all that is needed to reveal the implicit omnirationality of all chemical associating and disassociating. Thus we can provide a single language to recognize and accommodate—

> Avogadro's law of gases;
> Bohr's fundamental complementarity;
> Bridgman's operational procedure;
> Brouwer's fixed-point theorem;
> Gibbs' phase rule;
> Field equations;
> Einstein's energy equation;
> Euler's topology of points, areas, and lines;
> Kepler's third law;
> Newton's theory of gravity;
> Pauling's chemical structuring;
> Pauli's exclusion principle;

Thermodynamic laws;

L.L. Whyte's point system

202.03 **Angular Topology:** Synergetics discovers the relative abundance laws of Euler's point-area-line conceptual regularities and integrates them with geometrical angle laws, prime number progression, and a primitive geometrical hierarchy. All of this synergetic integration of topology with the angular regularities of geometrical transformabilities is conceptually generalizable independent of special case, time-space-sizing relations.

220.00   Synergetics Principles

223.00   Principle of Prime Number Inherency and Constant Relative Abundance of the Topology of Symmetrical Structural Systems

223.05 **Two Kinds of Twoness:** There are two kinds of twoness:

(1) the numerical, or morphationally unbalanced twoness; and
(2) the balanced twoness.

The vector equilibrium is the central symmetry through which both balanced and unbalanced asymmetries pulsatingly and complexedly intercompensate and synchronize. The vector equilibrium's frequency modulatability accommodates the numerically differentiated twonesses.

223.06 There are four kinds of positive and negative:

(1) the eternal, equilibrium-disturbing plurality of differentially unique, only-positively-and-negatively-balanced aberratings;
(2) the north and south poles;
(3) the concave and convex; and
(4) the inside (microcosm) and outside (macrocosm), always cosmically complementing the local system's inside-concave and outside-convex limits.

223.07 There is a fourfold twoness: one of the exterior, cosmic, finite ("nothingness") tetrahedron—i.e., the macrocosm outwardly complementing all ("something") systems—and one of the interior microcosmic tetrahedron of nothingness complementing all conceptually thinkable and cosmically isolatable "something" systems. (See Sec. *1070.*)

223.08 A pebble dropped into water precessionally produces waves that move both outwardly from the circle's center—i.e., circumferentially of the Earth sphere—and reprecessionally outwardly and inwardly from the center of the Earth—i.e., radially in respect to the Earth sphere. Altogether, this interregeneratively demonstrates (1) the twoness of local precessional system effects at 90 degrees, and (2) the Universe-cohering gravitational effects at 180 degrees. These are the two kinds of interacting forces constituting the regenerative structural integrity of both subsystem local twonesses and nonunitarily conceptual Scenario Universe. The *four* cosmically complementary twonesses and the *four* local system twonesses altogether eternally regenerate the scientific generalization known as complementarity. Complementarity is sum-totally eightfoldedly operative: four definitive local system complementations and four cosmically synergetic finitive accountabilities.

223.09   Topologically the additive twoness identifies the opposite poles of spinnability of all systems; the multiplicative twoness identifies the concave-insideness and convex-outsideness of all systems: these four are the four unique twonesses of the eternally regenerative, nonunitarily conceptual Scenario Universe whose conceptual think-aboutedness is differentially confined to local "something" systems whose insideness-and-outsideness-differentiating foci consist at minimum of four event "stars." (See Secs. 510.04 and 510.09.)

223.34   **Symmetrical Analysis of Topological Hierarchies:** Whenever we refer to an entity, it has to be structurally valid, and therefore it has to be triangulated. Being locally mixed, vectorially symmetrical but facially asymmetrical, being triangulated but not omnitriangulated, vector equilibrium may function as a system but not as a structure.

223.67   **Synergetics Hierarchy:** The Table of Synergetics Hierarchy (223.64) makes it possible for us to dispense with the areas and lines of Euler's topological accounting; the hierarchy provides a definitive description of all omnitriangulated polyhedral systems exclusively in terms of points and prime numbers.

228.00   Scenario Principle

228.12   **Scenario Principle: Considerable Set:** In considering all experiences, the mistakes of the past and the anticipations of the future are metaphysically irrelevant. We do not have to be preoccupied with hypothetical or potential experiences because we are always living in the *now*. Living in the present tense obviates impatience. (See Sec. 529.11.)

250.00　Discoveries of Synergetics

251.00　Discoveries of Synergetics: Inventory

251.021　Synergetics adds four additional topological aspects to Euler's three cosmically unique aspects of vertexes, faces, and edges. Synergetics adds (1) angles, (2) irrelevant untuned insideness and outsideness, (3) convexity and concavity, and (4) axis of spin, making a total of seven topological aspects (see Sec. 1044); synergetics has also recognized the addition of frequency as being always physically manifest in every special case.

251.15　The tetrahedral trisecting of angles: the trisection of a 180-degree angle. (See Secs. 841.16 and *841.30*)

251.16　The rational volumetric quantation or constant proportionality of the octahedron, the cube, the rhombic triacontahedron, and the rhombic dodecahedron when referenced to the tetrahedron as volumetric unity. (See Sec. 1053.21.)

251.17　The rational and symmetric surface subdivision of the icosahedron, the octahedron, the cube, and the rhombic dodecahedron by the 48 spherical triangle tiles of the vector equilibrium's 25-great-circle grid, rationally quantized in a reverse order of magnitude in whole, low-order, even numbers. (See Secs. 1053.20–21.)

251.18　The seven unique axes of great-circle spinnability that also describe the seven great circles foldable into bow ties. (See Sec. 1040.)

251.19　The definition of the omniequiangled and omnitriangulated tetrahedron, octahedron, and icosahedron, with respectively three, four, and five triangles around each of their vertexes, as altogether constituting the topological and finitely limited set of prime structural systems. (See Sec. 610.20.)

251.29　The trigonometric identification of the great-circle trajectories of the seven axes of symmetry with the 120 basic disequilibrium *LCD* triangles of the spherical icosahedron. (See Sec. *1043.*)

251.48　The disclosure of a hierarchy of rational quantation and topological interrelationships of all physically experiential phenomena that are omnirationally accounted when we assume the volume of the tetrahedron and its six vectors to constitute both metaphysical and physical quantation unity. (See Secs. 221.01 and 620.12.)

260.00   The Epistemography of Generalization and Special Case

---

•[*260.00–269.07   Nature in a Corner Scenario*]

260.10   Invisibility of Macro- and Microresolutions

260.11   The eye of a healthy human can comfortably perceive an interval of $^{1}/_{50}$th of an inch, and the human's timing sense can recognize the rhythm of identical minimum intervals lying between the black vertical lines of an engineer's white ivory measuring scale, but with optimum naked eyesight humans can only with great difficulty read on a scale that equals $^{1}/_{100}$th of an inch. Humans' eyesight cannot "resolve," i.e., differentially perceive $^{1}/_{200}$th-inch intervals between microdots of $^{1}/_{200}$th-of-an-inch diameter. For these reasons black-and-white or color printing plates for picture reproductions, which consist of subvisible benday screen dots spread $^{1}/_{200}$th of an inch apart, produce pictures whose surface information appears to humans as being realistically "continuous" and as a progressive color blending—ergo, natural.

260.12   The diameter of the spherical activity domain of a single atom, including the electrons orbiting its nucleus, is called one angstrom. And one angstrom is $^{1}/_{2,500,000}$th the diameter of the smallest humanly seeable *speck*. Moreover, the diameter of the atomic nucleus is $^{1}/_{10,000}$th of one angstrom, and the nucleus has now been found to consist of a plurality of further "particles" such as quarks, leptons, hadrons, and so forth. Humans have now developed electromagnetic sensors, have microphotographed individual atoms, and have macrophotographed a billion galaxies, each of hundreds of billions of star-population magnitudes—99.9999 percent of which information about reality is invisible to the naked human eye. (See Sec. 1238.60.) What humans have been experiencing and thinking of "realistically" as dim "somethings" or "points" in a field of omnidirectional seeming nothingness now requires experimentally provable reconsideration, epistemographic reconceptioning, and rewording.

260.20   Convergent vs Parallel Perception

260.21   All exclusively three-dimensional matrixes, consisting only of parallel lines and perpendicular rectilinear interactions—like parallel railroad tracks—inherently fail to accommodate any terminal convergence. Such matrixes fail to accommodate the inherent strategy of range-finding: the fact that the linear-distance relationship between our two human eyes—and also those of other optically equipped creatures—was designed to provide the baseline of a triangle whose opposite apex occurs at the position of a sighted object. The convergent apex angle of the object provides the human brain's computer circuitry with a limited, distance-to-object-magnitude appraising, or range-finding perceptivity, whose maximum terrestrial range is the horizon. Beyond the horizon the distances between remote objects are reduced to optically non-tunable angle-size or -frequency discernibility. Ergo, at the maximum tunability of differential-wavelength-perceptivity, our range-finding optical system produces a false image of a seemingly convergent pair of parallel railroad tracks. It is not that the tracks or the ties are coming together, but that the distance between them is subtunable.

260.211   Our two eyes form the baseline of an isosceles triangle and seek to discern the convergent angle at an opposite object apex: for instance, tracks *A* or *B,* with the distance between *A* and *B* constant. The farther away they are, they become relatively shorter and shorter chords of ever larger circles *A* and *B,* and finally they appear to be congruent. See Fig. *260.211.*

260.22   Though the diameter of Betelguese in Orion's Belt is greater than the diameter of the planet Earth's orbit around the Sun, Betelguese appears to Earthians only as a fine point of light. As in the rate of information recall by the mind from brain storage, there is also an inherent lag in the rate human optical equipment can apprehend newly perceived phenomena. The pulsative frequency of alternating current electric light is 60 cycles per second, which is designed to coincide with the frequency corresponding to humans' "second look" stroboscopic rate of apprehending. In a like manner the frequency rate of the cinema's picture-frame running is synchronized to coincide with the human rate of mental-mouthful digestibility of new information receptivity, which must check the new information with the old to permit recognition or new cognition. The static frames themselves—as in benday screen printing— are frequency-subdivided into local increments whose wavelength-spacing is infratunable by the human-brain-apprehending set. The human brain apprehends 200 info-bits per inch as omnicontinuous, despite the separate frequency islands of their different color light points, each of which is an island of different electromagnetic frequencies. All of the spots are frequency islands like events and novents (see Sec. 524.01).

260.30   Physical Experience and Closest Packing of Spheres

260.31   The *XYZ*-rectilinear coordinate system of humans fails to accommodate any finite resolution of any physically experienced challenge to comprehension. Physical experience demonstrates that individual-unit wavelength

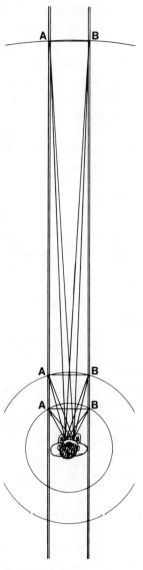

Fig. *260.211 Humans' Range-finding Optical System:* Our two eyes form the baseline of an isosceles triangle and seek to discern the convergent angle at the opposite object apex: for instance, tracks *A* or *B,* with the distance between *A* and *B* constant. Farther away they become shorter chords of ever larger circles and finally appear to be congruent.

or frequency events close-pack in spherical agglomerations of unit radius spheres. Two unit-radius spheres in tangency provide a seemingly linear pattern, but a third closest-packed sphere nests in the valley of the first two and produces triangulation. In equilateral triangular growth of closest-planar-packed unit-radius spheres the triangle's edges are never parallel. As human experience increases—event by event—the number of experience spheres along the faraway edge of the triangle of individual observations also increases. Each successive row of closest-packed spheres away from the observer always increases by one event. While the rows are parallel to one another, the outermost row can be taken perpendicularly away from the master triangle and from any one of its sides without disturbing the integrity of equiangular symmetry. This progression of symmetrical shrinkage of the triangle is a property completely different from that of the square, wherein the removal of any one outermost parallel row of closest-packed cubes from any of the four sides leaves a nonsquare, nonequiedged rectangle.

260.32   Closest-packed spheres, or spherical events, of equal frequency and wavelength produce tetrahedral agglomerations which, as events transpire, produce additional layers, each of which consists of equilateral triangles of one more edge row than the previous one. (See the event relationship law at Sec. 227.)

260.33   Because nature always operates most economically—ergo, most closest packed—and because all asymmetries are observable only relative to idealized symmetry, we find all the similar-magnitude events of experience tend to close pack triangularly in symmetrical convergent or divergent aggregations. (See Secs. *223.05, 505.62,* and 532.10.)

260.34   The *XYZ* coordinates of parallels and perpendiculars have nothing to do with the way Universe is operating. Universe is operating in radiational-divergence and gravitational-convergence. Events in parallel never get resolved; convergent events become exquisitely resolved. You cannot have a nucleus in a perpendicular or a parallel system. You can have nuclei only when you have symmetrical tetrahedral convergence.

260.40   Convergence to a Nucleus

260.41   The coordinate system of nature as manifest in synergetics is one in which nature operates in convergent-divergent, associative-disassociative agglomerating, a system in which the inherent symmetry is maintained only by the equiangular triangles. Synergetically, nature is both expansively radiant and convergently gravitational: radiant as radiation—an expansive, disintegrative, ever more disorderly coming apart—or nature as gravitationally convergent with increasing symmetry and order. Nature resolves her problems by their resolution to inherent nuclei.

260.42   The synergetic coordinate system of nature and its finite macro-micro turnaround-limited hierarchy of primitive ascending or descending timeless-sizeless, omnisymmetrically concentric, polyhedral components provides the human mind with a rational means of resolving problems by bringing nature into a corner—a convergent terminus center, a four-dimensional corner of the four-dimensional planes of the tetrahedron. Only with the four-dimensional convergence and divergence of synergetics can the human mind reduce problems to comprehension as minimum-limit systems. The minimum polygon is a triangle; the minimum polyhedron is a tetrahedron; both of their structural behaviors are unique (see Secs. 614 and 621). By their academic training humans think only in terms of parallel and rectilinear coordination, and so they tend to hold to the unresolvable parallel interpretations of their lives' experiences. They seek to maintain the status quo and—despite the organic and biologic manifests of birth and death—they fail to be able to take advantage of the cornerability of comprehension and the positional fixes provided by the four-dimensional, synergetic, convergent-divergent coordination.

260.50   Precession of Two Sets of 10 Closest-Packed Spheres

260.51   Two identical sets of 10 spheres in closest packing precess in 90-degree action to form a prime, nonnucleated, four-ball-to-the-edge tetrahedron with a total of 20 spheres. Each of the two sets of 10 balls consists of a line of four balls arranged in a tangentially cohered row nested in the long valley of a rectangle consisting of three pairs of balls tangentially cohered to one another in a parallel array, with two balls on one end and three balls on the other end. Cohering the four-ball row tangentially to the valley of the six-ball quadrangle produces a 10-ball aggregate. When brought together, these two 10-ball assemblies produce the prime, four-ball-edge tetrahedron of 20 balls, the largest single-shell tetrahedron without a nuclear ball. (This 20-ball tetrahedron is at the heart of the tetrahedral assembly of 120 balls comprised of two sets of 60 closest-packed spheres—see Sec. 417.) To bring them into tetrahedral symmetry of assembly, each four-ball edge of the two separate assemblies must be precessed (turned at right angles) to the other's four-ball edge. In these conditions the two-ball edges of the six-ball rectangle are now addressing the three-ball edges of the other quadrangle. To the trained eye and rationale of rectilinear coordination it seems illogical to address two balls to three balls or three balls to two balls. In matching such assemblies people think of doing so only in parallels or perpendiculars. (See Sec. *527.08.*)

260.52   In universally convergent-divergent coordinate growth or shrinking, each row is greater (or lesser) by one than the next. Three automatically goes to two in a convergent, planar-arrayed, structurally stable system and two automatically goes to three in a divergent, planar-arrayed, structurally stable system. Tetrahedral expansion or contraction produces a structurally stable systematic model of universal behavior. In tetrahedral growth one goes to three and three goes to six and six goes to 10 (see Sec. 415.55 and Fig. 415.55A). Tetrahedral growth from unity is special-case angularly directional. Vector equilibrium growth from unity is nuclear-divergent at a growth rate of ten times frequency to the second power plus two:

$1 \rightarrow 12$
$12 \rightarrow 42$
$42 \rightarrow 92$, etc.
(See Sec. 418.01.)

260.53   A tetrahedron has three—and only three—inherent polar symmetries; their axes run between the midpoints of the tetrahedron's three pairs of opposite edges. (See Sec. 622.) These midpoints are in edges that are oriented at 90 degrees to one another.

261.00   Getting Nature into a Corner

261.01   Getting nature into a corner is the essence of synergetics' exploratory strategy. Synergetics is the coordination of thought and physical action, the genesis of geometry, system, and structure. Physics and metaphysics are resonantly integral: the integrity of their intertransformative mathematics into all the special case, variably enduring associabilities cognized by humans as structural design. The frequency rates are the separate, static frame rates of inspection and are recognized by humans' brains as mechanics when the frequency of inspection by humans synchronizes with the cinema frames' running. The difference between structures and machinery is the same as the difference between "moving" and "static" pictures as both relate to human information comprehending. This is the grand strategy.

261.02   What Euler and all professional topologists and mathematicians called "areas" are only windows in polyhedrally conceptual systems. You look out the window at the nothingness of undimensional night—or of fog. The "faces" of presynergetics topology packaged the undimensionable nothingness into arbitrary somethingness, which thus misassumed the dimensions of the face windows and their closed-circuit edges to constitute dimensional attributes of the undimensional nothingness so framed. Academically misinformed teachers go to the blackboard, drawing a "square," and saying to the students, "A square is an area bound by a closed line of four equal-length edges and four equiangled corners," without paying any attention to the inherently existent complementations of Universe. To start off with, the phenomenon "square" is dependent on the phenomenon "blackboard," whose structural matrix alone maintained the symmetrical shape of the nonstructurally stabilized pattern of the square. (Compare Sec. 617.04.) The closed-line pattern of the square inadvertently subdivides the whole surface of the polyhedral blackboard into two areas, both bound by the closed line of four equal edges and four equal angles. The four equal edges of the large complementary square are the same length as those of the small square; the big square's corners are each 270 degrees, while the small square's corners are each 90 degrees. (Compare Sec. 810.) Moreover, the drawing of the square also inadvertently subdivides the insideness and outsideness of the blackboard into concave and convex big and little squares; it also deposits part of the Universe as "chalk" atoms onto the blackboard's agglomeration of atoms, which inadvertently rearranges the chemical element resources of Scenario Universe.

261.03   In the layer-around-layer, symmetrical closest packing of unit radius spheres around a nuclear sphere of the same radius, the number of spheres in each layer will always be 10 times the second power of the frequency of comprehensively concentric layer enclosings plus the number 2—i.e., $10F^2 + 2$. By this we discover that in the first layer, where frequency $(F) = 1$, we have $1^2 = 1$, and $10 \cdot 1 = 10$, $10 + 2 = 12$. Thus we find experimentally that 12 unit radius spheres comprehensively omni-inter-close-pack around the single nuclear sphere. Where frequency is two, in the case of the second layer, we have

$$2^2 = 4, \ 4 \cdot 10 = 40, \ 40 + 2 = 42$$

spheres symmetrically embrace the 12-ball system. Thus the number of unit radius spheres in the third layer is 92, and so forth (see Sec. 418).

261.04   Since the central or nuclear sphere has no outer layer and is only the nucleus, its frequency of layer enclosures is zero. (See Sec. 415.10.) Following our symmetrically and convergently diminishing uniform rate of contraction to its inherent minimum and terminal frequency case of zero, and applying our generalized formula $10F^2 + 2$, we have

$$0^2 = 0, \ 0 \cdot 10 = 0, \ 0 + 2 = 2$$

and we discover that unity is two. The single nuclear sphere consists of both its concave inside and its exterior convex sphere, its inbounding and outbounding co-occur at the convergent, center-of-volume turnaround point. Unity is plural and at minimum two (see Secs. 224.12 and 240.03). That the nuclear ball is inherently two has been incontrovertibly discovered by reducing nature to her omnidirectionally convergent, nuclear-center terminal case.

262.00 Conceptual Minimum

262.01   Since there was nothing more exaltedly high than heaven and nothing more degradingly low than hell, *up* and *down* were limited or terminal dimensions.

—Since humans were so tiny in respect to their laterally surrounding world, and since the tales of travelers reported greater mountains as one went inland from the sea, and since the sea ever surrounded the land, the best-informed humans assumed Earth to be an island floating on a sea that extended laterally to infinity in all horizontal directions as a plane, a plane whose surface could be made rough by god-blown winds, while the skies were filled with gods disguised as clouds blowing winds.

—Since the shortest distances between two points seemed obviously to be a straight, stretched-hair line, all the straight lines on the infinite plane of the world ran to infinity; and since humans could never reach infinity, they need not worry about where the points were located between which the straight infinite lines were stretched. All they had to do was to have two local points through which to run their "straight" line, which could thus be extended to infinity in two opposite directions. This was the genesis of "flat land," from which humans have not yet emerged. In flat land there are infinite biggest and smallest: In the vertical sense this means giants bigger than mountains and gods bigger than giants—ergo, the biggest greatest god, the biggest of visually engendered conceptioning enthroned on the highest mountain, while the invisibly smallest emerged as the elves and the evil spirits existing in things.

262.02 The human concept of a geometrical point was established eons before the inventive conceptualizing by anyone that humans might develop a microscope. The point seemed to be the terminal, smallest visual experience. The visual smallest was smaller than the smallest touchable, handleable experience. The visual smallest engendered the assumption of an infinitely smaller nondimensional point. The point is premicroscopic.

262.03 Similarly, the concept of spatial nothingness is pretelescopic, established eons before anyone knew that humans might develop a telescope. Now that humans have acquired discretely measured knowledge regarding the speed and other behavioral characteristics of all radiation, including the refraction of light, and have developed the science of optics and the chemistry of light-sensitive emulsions for phototelescopy, they have discovered a macrocosm of billions of galaxies consisting of an average of 100 billion stars each; 99.9999 percent of these progressively outwardly considered, discovered phenomena are invisible to the naked human eye. In the opposed or inwardly considered experience field the physicists have discovered and measured the unique frequency characteristics of each of the chemical elements together with frequency characteristics and other energetic characteristics of atomic components. Physicists employing the same radiation-sensitive emulsion photography—first through the human-spectrum-range microscope, subsequently through the scanning electron microscope, and after that through the field emission microscope—have photographed individual atoms. In this inwardly and diminishing magnitude progression humans have photographically harvested knowledge of physical reality that is 99.9999 percent infra- or subvisible to humans, meaning untunable within the very limited electromagnetic frequency range of the human senses' crystal-equipped radio sets. The exponential, fourth-power, historical acceleration rate of these outwardly exploding and inwardly permeating human cognitive events has become too sudden for societal digestion and recognition of the significance of what seemed to be *terminal* yesterday. The reality of the *point* and the *space* have been variously conceptualized in the purely theoretical and physically unexperienceable rationalizations of progressively misinformed humans.

262.04   Man suddenly got to thinking of the atom as the terminal, the conceptual minimum. He had the terminal case of the atom as a point, but then later found that the atoms consisted of at minimum a proton, a neutron, an electron, and an atomic nucleus, and so forth. And so for a while the atomic nucleus was the terminal limit, until humans began smashing the atom and breaking the nucleus into new component particles: Thus the quarks became the most recently apparent terminally smallest limits of considerability. But the characteristics of the quarks are very exciting because they, too, incontrovertibly manifest a complex of a plurality of interdependent and numerically consistent behaviors. So what physics is really discovering is primitive *system conceptuality* independent of time and size. And in synergetics conceptuality independent of time and size discloses a complex hierarchy of nuclear system intertransformabilities with low-order numerical and topological relationships, a complex of interrelationships consistently characterizing every one of their realizations as special case, experimentally demonstrable, sense-tuned, physical reality. (See Secs. *1052.330–340.*)

262.05   Whenever we look at something that is special case—call it a nucleus or call it a quark—we find that the special cases all break up into the complex of pure principles of conceptuality independent of size and time as elucidated by synergetics. Physically discovered, i.e., experientially, i.e., sense-tuned terminal discoveries, are always special case. Special cases have always time-incremented duration magnitudes—ergo, they are terminal.

262.06   There are no terminal generalizations. Generalizations are eternal independent of size and time. The weightless, sizeless, frequency-innocent principles are dealt with in synergetics and are exclusively mind-employable. Synergetics represents an exclusively mind-conceptual, complex system of numerically identifiable, geometrical interrelationships holding eternally true in all special case manifestations and physical discoverabilities, utterly independent of time-size. (See Sec. 445.11.)

262.07   Our Scenario Universe will continually open up more thing-and-thingness special cases and our beautiful—because eternally exquisite—generalized thingless principles will tend to become conceptually ever more lucidly clear and more evidently operative at no matter what magnitude: macro . . . medio . . . micro.

262.08　The physical is always special case; this is why we spell Universe with a capital U.

262.09　So our new understanding of reality involves an eternal extension of the tunability in pure unlimited principle. Physical energy occurs only in finite packages. Physical Universe is a discontinuity of such finite islanded events. Events and novents: so life and death—so high-frequency intermingled as to be distinguishable only by our live-event-frequency-tuning capability. Death is as-yet-untuned reality. We used to have two structurally static Universes of life and afterlife. That we seem to be accelerating toward a unified Scenario Universe field seems to be implicit.

262.10　We do not have two Universes: this world and the next world. Death is only the as-yet-unexperienced, superlow frequencies. Both death and life are complementary functions of our electromagnetic experience. (See Secs. *526.25.* and *531.10.*)

263.00　Nothingness and Tunability

263.01　Having introduced the electromagnetic concept of the infra-tunable-to-human-sense frequency range set and the ultratunable-to-human-sense frequency range set, it becomes manifest that the nothingness is simply the as-yet-not-tuned-in information. We never deal in nothingness. *Nothing* occurs only as the at-present-untuned-in information broadcasting of nature—when we tune into the next higher or lower frequency, our senses resonate again and anew and may detect significant information, as in the inadvertently discovered photographic emulsion tuning in of the theretofore-unknown unique frequencies of the inherently regenerative set of the 92 chemical elements.

263.02　Our brains are physical tuning capabilities consisting of uniquely resonant atoms and cells. Apprehension consists of resonant atoms tuning into congruently resonant atoms. There is a cosmic meshingness; an angle-and-frequency congruence similar to that of mechanical gear trains when the number of teeth per circular perimeter and the angular modulation of the valleys and peaks of the individual teeth of the larger, smaller, or unit radius gears must mesh with minimally tolerated aberrational error; wherein the aberrations of metallic gears must be compensatingly interfilled with lubricants that prevent the aberrations of one part from reaching the aberrations of the reciprocating part. In much modern machinery nylon and other plastic gears have provided interyieldability, obviating the use of lubricants. Such yielding is demonstrably employed by nature in the hydraulic-pneumatic, crystalline structuring of all biological organisms. (See Sections 522.36 and *1052.52.*)

263.03   Special cases are inherently terminal. Brain, which deals only with special case experiences, each of which is energetically terminal, demands knowledge of how everything begins and ends. But principles are eternal, a word with which the brain is not familiar. All inputs to the brain are finite. (See Sec. 504.04.)

263.04   We have what we refer to as events and novents (Sec. 524.01). Experiences are always special case event programs. The special cases of music or noise are temporarily tunably sensed frequencies, of whose message significance we become progressively aware and in between which unsensed, untunable, eternal interrelationships persist. There is no verb for eternity. Verbs are always special case.

264.00 Geometry of Self and Otherness

264.01   A point is a something, a complex entity system, but an infratunable system. A point occurs as the first moment of awareness of a looming-into-tunability of any system in Universe. A point—or a noise—appears in an angularly determinable direction within the total omnidirectional spherical sphere of reference of the individual observer's sense-informed environment. It is oriented in respect to the observer's head-to-heel axis of reference in respect to which the direction from which the somethingness of infradiscrete tunability—as well as the non-tune-outability of the static—is emanating, as distinct from the nothingness of untuned-in, omnidirectional withinness and withoutness. (See Secs. *505.65, 505.74,* and *527.25.*)

264.02   At minimum, life involves awareness, self involves otherness, and otherness involves somethingness. Awareness is of otherness: awareness of the outside superficiality of the observer's "finger" by the externality-searching optical system of the observer. Indeed, the externality-searching for the nipple of its mother's breast by the olfactorily guided external nose-mouth of the newborn constitutes initial otherness awareness. As a fertilized ovum of an integrally evolving female organism umbilically circuited with the female organism, no otherness awareness is involved except that of the mother even as she may be sensorially aware of a sore spot on her arm.

264.03   Otherness involves somethingness: This brings us to the consideration of the nature of the epistemographic evolution of experience that—at one historical moment—evolved the misconceptioning of a nothingness—ergo, dimensionless—point.

264.10 Prime Otherness: Single and Plural Otherness

264.11 While environment plus me equals Universe, Universe minus me does not equal environment.

264.12 Environment does not exist without me. I the observer am the living human experience. Life is the present experience. Experience begins with awareness. No otherness: No awareness.

264.13 I am one of the two prime othernesses: I am the single otherness; environment is the plural otherness. I am the present otherness; environment is the past otherness. By the time I have become aware, other as-yet-untuned-in events of nonunitarily conceptual Universe have transpired. Environment is inherently historical. Universe is eternally inclusive of all past, present, and future experiences plus all the at-present-untune-inable otherness of Universe. Universe is eternally general; environment is always special case.

264.14 Environment is the complex of all observed experiences of all life. Environment is the present scene, and all the remembered scenes, and all the scenes remembered by all the other scenes, which I cannot remember but memories of which are all registered in the environment to be redisclosed from time to time.

264.15 Every individual is an evolutionary pattern integrity. Each individual's environment of the moment is different from that of the next moment and from that of every other individual, though two or more individuals may think that they are mutually experiencing the same environment. The individual is the product and servant of a plurality of semisimilarities of mutual tuned-in-ness.

265.00 Unity of Triangulation

265.01 Otherness involves somethingness; This brings us to reconsideration of the nature of epistemological evolution and of the gradual transition in degrees of relative adequacy of macroscale of human comprehending and in microscale of definitive exactitude in interpreting what is being humanly experienced. Humans were included in the cosmic system's design to fulfill critical functions in respect to maintenance of the integrity of eternally regenerative Scenario Universe. To arrive full-blown and functioning in its cosmic role, humanity has been given the capability to inventory its tactical resources progressively and to reorient its functioning from an omniautomated behavior to a progressively more conscious and responsible behavioral pattern.

265.02 The epistemological evolution of individual humans has also included progressive appraisal of the relative significance of the separate scenarios of experience as periodically elucidated by the synergetically accruing concepts. Thus the sum of all human experiences seems periodically to explain how humans fit into the cosmic scheme, as that cosmic scheme itself evolves as emergingly and sum-totally appraised and disclosed by scholars—together with those cosmologists' controversial explanatory theories.

265.03 At one early historical moment in that epistemological evolution humans evolved the mathematical concept of dimensionless points, lines, and planes. Their dimensionless lines and planes were aggregates of the dimensionless points, yet these self-contradictory concepts have persisted in the children's school curricula of today, despite the fact that they were adopted long before humans had even dreamed of optical magnifying lenses, let alone electron microscopes. The philosophy that adopted such nonoperational educational devices was predicated—they said—upon "purely imaginary phenomena," and since the image-ination of the brain is entirely furnished with special case experiences of system conceptuality (see Secs. 504.04 and 1056.15), it is appropriate in this moment of instrumentally informed experience to reformulate our experience-substantiated philosophy.

265.04 Considerability (*con-sidus*—the interrelationship of a plurality of stars) is experientially furnished and is inherently systemic. The axial spinnability of all systems provides observational orientation in azimuth around the head-to-heel axis, statable in measurable fractions of circular unity. In the special case of humans as the observing system we have the head-to-heel axis of observational reference. We have therefore the human observer's system's inherent "additive twoness" provided by the system's two poles of such axial spin. In humans' organic systems we have also the multiplicative twoness of insideness-outsideness—i.e., the system's convex-concave congruity.

265.05 The observed otherness can be an organically integral part of the individual observer, for the individual human organism is—at simplest—a system comprised of a myriad of systems, which in turn are comprised of myriads of subsystems of subsystems of subsystems—to the limit of present microexploration capability. And the individual human organism will always consist of systems and never of nonsystems, for less-than-system systems are inherently nondiscoverable. (See Sec. 400.011.)

265.06 Observing individuals can be visually or tactilely aware of another (complex or subsystem) part of their own systemic organism—for example, the child's hand tactilely discovering its own foot's temperature, texture, olfactoral, taste, relative size, and conformation. This self-discovery, otherness-aroused awareness of the individual includes the child's cerebral-cortex feeling that its stomach is hungry, whereby the brain instructs the child's fourfold aural-communication-system-defining mouth, throat, tongue, and lungs to start pumping in and out of the smellable, nonorganically integral, otherness atmosphere to produce "crying" for contact with an external udder of the nonintegral otherness—the m-m-motherness from which to suck (pump) out her nonintegral otherness milk produced by her digested consumption of a plurality of nonintegral othernesses. This is an objective-subjective awareness of the complex individual's integral otherness parts.

265.07   Here is the complex integral otherness with which philosophers have for so long failed to confront themselves in their epistemological considerations. They have erroneously assumed that original, or initial, cognizable otherness exists exclusively in a separate external entity other than that of the organism of the observer. The individual is inherently complex, having four different sensing systems: the same four separate and differentially unique apprehending advantages that are always acquired to define a tetrahedron as the minimum system in Universe.

265.08   As with the "out" of in-out-and-around directions, the ultratunable is ultra to both external and internal experiences of human record. The ultratunable nothingness persists where the electromagnetic wavelengths involved are greater than the span of all humanly remembered experiences; wherefore the last time such a phenomenon occurred was prior to human experience recording, the next time its wave is to peak is unpredictable, because it always takes a minimum of two experiences to define a wavelength, but it always takes a minimum of three identical-magnitude events (waves) and their identical-magnitude wave intervals to definitively arouse humans' awareness that they are experiencing an unfamiliar wave-frequency phenomenon—ergo, to trigger humans' re-cognition capability thus to become aware of the same phenomenon being repeated for a third time (tres-pass) with the same interval of time between them occurring for the second time. (See Sec. *526.23*.)

265.09   But it takes a fourth equifrequenced and equiwavelengthed experience in the angular direction deviations of the never-occurring straightlinedness of wavilinear Scenario Universe to produce the altitude from which sensing advantage the intertriangulatability of the first three experiences may be apprehended—which triangular pattern integrity becomes realized by mind as forming the base, the three separate directions toward which three previous event corners provide altogether the six unique lines of interrelationship direction of the four experience events that constitute a system, of whose presence the observer-sensor is now initially aware. Conceptuality is tetrahedral.

265.10   The operational self-discovery of any given conceptually periodic frequency is predicated upon a minimum experience quota of four successively experienced, similar events. This is because the three original time intervals between four angularly finite events constitute the minimum number of experience intervals necessary to establish the human mind's awareness that it is experiencing an identical interval repetition between what seem to be similar events. The first interval between the first two similar experiences was entirely unanticipated and—as of the moment of first recurrence—seemed to be only an inconsequential happenstance. But the *third repeat* of a similar, angularly conformed, finite experience that is recurring at a second and similar interval of elapsed time to that intervening between the first and second experiences could—and sometimes does—arouse an intuitive sense of there being a possible time-lapse-identifying significance present in the second successively similar lapse of time between the *now-threefold* similarity of angularly conformed experiences.

265.11   On the occasion of the third similar experience intuition can—and sometimes does—educe a hypothetical assumption and prediction by the experiencing individual of the possibility or probability of the future recurrence of a fourth such similar experience, which predicative hypothesis can only be confirmed by the actual fourth-time experiencing of the similar, angularly conformed, finite event recurring on schedule after the third experiencing of the same interval of elapsed time. If this fourth finite event does occur as hypothetically predicted after the third interval of the same time lapse, it provides experimental evidence of the existence of a consistent frequency and interval system of event recurrences. This may be recorded by humans as scientifically reliable—ergo, as operationally usable data.

265.12   A frequency of four events provides the three intervals that also form the base triangle of the tetrahedron apexed by the initially unpaired, angularly finite event. The insideness and outsideness of this primitively evolved tetrahedron constitute the minimum macrocosm-microcosm-differentiating system of the Universe. This tetrahedron has six angularly directional interrelationship lines interconnecting its four finite events. (See "Observer as Tetrasystem," Sec. 267.)

265.13   The chief characteristic of *frequency* is the accommodation of special case systems. Frequency identification begins only upon the recurrence of a directionally continuous fourth similar event along any one line of vertexial interrelationships of a system—ergo, with a minimum of three similar time intervals An angle, as we learn at Sec. 515.10, is inherently a subfrequency event. Four nonsimultaneous, unique, angular event experiences occurring successively as a trajectory trending in the same direction constitute the minimum constituents for the time-size-measurable special case—i.e., temporal case—identifications.

266.00 Science and Mathematics in the Language of Electromagnetics

266.01   The ability of humans to tune in information is dependent on their being initially equipped with limited-range tuning apparatus, such as that of seeing, hearing, touching, smelling; human tunability is also dependent upon the special case data of experience stored in their recallable brain banks, the interrelatedness of which is only intuitively apprehended at first and later is experimentally reconfirmed, but comprehended only by human minds. Infra- or ultratunability at any one moment of human experience neither precludes nor promises—but can suggest to intuition—the possibility of further tunability to be developed by humans to occur beyond any time-and-event predictability of our experience-cognition projecting—quite possibly billions of years either *ago* or *hence*. The infrequency may involve wavelength intervals between the too-recent-to-be-experienced and the too-late-to-be-experienced cyclic phenomena. This brings all our synergetic, event-vector convergence-divergence into congruence with the meanings of the language of electro-magnetics.

266.02 A geodesic always is the operationally most economically accomplishable, and therefore most accommodatingly steerable, line of interrelationship existing exclusively between any two event foci. While generalizable as "straight," all geodesic realizations are superficially special-case—ergo, line events involving energy expenditures. Their lines of interrelationship accomplishment are radiationally noninstantaneous, and because of omni-in-motion Universe are wavilinear, as progressively modulated and accommodated for the differential changes of interpositioning of the interrelated events. From all that has yet been learned the gravitational or convergent forces may be assumed to be instantaneous and continually operative—ergo, always prevailing over the speed-limited radiational entropy. And being omniembracing rather than linear, gravity may also be assumed to have no directional identification.

266.03 A geodesic line is a component concept of systems' interrelationships.

266.04 So we now comprehend that humans' initial experiences of subresolvable, as-yet-discretely-non-tune .in-able, but directionally oriented awareness sensing of "twilight" *specks* or *noise* signals were reasonably defined by the human as a realistic somethingness occurring in a specific point-to-able direction, which is an as-yet-frequency-untunable system.

266.05 Self as observer is part of a system observing the integral-to-organic-system self's integral or separate otherness systems, or systemic subsystems—a system's as-yet-untuned systemic parts observing its as-yet-untuned systemic parts. The organic self has built-in, cerebrally coordinated equipment for in-tuning, as with the unique crystals of a radio set.

266.06 Humans' integral sensing and brain-operated tunability is always special-case, size-and-frequency limited. But the conceptioning and comprehending of a human's mind is concerned exclusively with relative-magnitude-and-frequency interrelationships constituting limitless synergetic systems in pure, abstract, generalized, eternal principle. All humans' minds are now and always have been capable of employing those principles as soon as they have been apprehended, experimentally verified, and mathematically quantified, to enlarge multibillionsfold both the macro- and microranges of special case, definitively exquisite harvesting of cosmic information, the significance of which is almost undetected and unrealized by humanity's common-sense, socioeconomic, and spontaneous recreational preoccupations.

266.07   The exclusive parallel-perpendicular coordination of physics—the *XYZ* Cartesian and centimeter-gram-second systems—probes blindly in fields of nonconceptuality. The exclusively convergent-divergent coordination of synergetics deals exclusively in conceptuality—conceptuality of omniinterrelatedness independent of size and time. Size depends on frequency, and frequency is cyclic. Angle, as only a fraction of a circle, is inherently subcyclic and subsize. But angle expresses a direction: This is where geometry enters into conceptuality. An angle—or a noise—has direction in respect to the head-to-heel axis or other system initiators.

267.00   Observer as Tetrasystem

267.01   The unity-at-minimum-twoness of the observed somethingness and the unity-at-minimum-twoness of the observer provide the initial four-dimensional foci of a tetrasystem. Otherness as a noise always has a direction relative to both the vertical human observer's head-to-heel axis and the horizontal axis of any pair of the human's two nostrils, ears, eyes, hands, and arms. The two polar terminals of the vertical axis derive from the initial head-to-heel axis of the observer. The diametric axis is generated subsequently and spun horizontally and cirumferentially in the observational plane of any two of its terminally sensing facilities. The two polar terminals of the head-to-heel axis and any two of the sensing terminals of the diametric observational axis are intertriangularly connectable to produce the six interrelationships of the inherent systemic tetrahedron of the observer system. The interim orbital repositioning of the observer system totality during the spin cycle inherently occasions the occurrence of the diametric axis in a plane always other than that in which the original axis of spinnability had occurred.

267.02

Tactile: touch ——————omnidirectionally outward

Olfactory——————inward

Sight: optical——————frontally oriented

Hearing ——————sidewise

Inherent tetrahedral relationship. (See Fig. *267.02A*.)

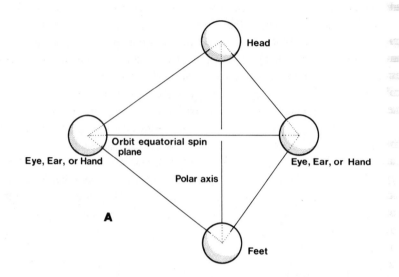

Observer is inherently a tetra-system. (See Fig. *267.02B*.)

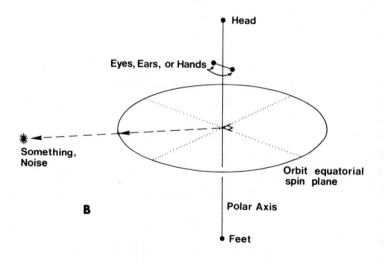

Figs. *267.02A–B Observer as Tetrasystem*

267.03   Physical self is inherently a tetrahedral observing system with four alternate, "fail-safe," distance-and-direction-sensing circuits.

267.04   Special case is angularly referenced to the inherent twoness of the polar axis of the system doing the observing, because the observer is a system and the system is four-dimensional. The fact that unity is two (Sec. 513.30) means that an observer is at minimum two, but realistically four, because the observer is a system; and the observed is at minimum two, but being a system, is realistically four. A range-finder is inherently tetrahedral.

267.05   The sensing apparatus and the action apparatus with which humans are integrally equipped are both designed to provide them with angular orientation and the triangulated observation of distance. The two ears, two eyes, two nostrils, two arms, and two legs all produce triangulated distance-to-object information. They are range-finders. Using the distance between any pair of their integral sensing instruments as the baseline of a triangle whose opposite vertex is marked by the external object they are viewing, touching, hearing, or smelling, they sense the relative magnitude of the angles at the sensing ends of the baseline—which gives them the sense of magnitude of the complementary third angle at the apex of the triangle where the sensed object is located. Range-finding is triangulation. Sensing is triangulation.

268.00   Omnioriented Tunability

268.01   We call it a triangle only because the observing system lacks the frequency tunability to see the altitude of the tetrahedron.

268.02   System insideness and outsideness means two congruent, concave-convex systems, four corner-defining *ins,* and their four opposite windows through which the omnidirectional *out* nothingness is revealed. The eight were there all the time. The fourness of self and the fourness of otherness = comprehension. Comprehension involves tuned-in octave resonance as well as omnidirectional and local angular integrity. The sum of all the angles around all of the system vertexes must add up to 720 degrees, which is not only four triangular enclosures but is also unity as two, for 360 degrees is one cycle—ergo, 720 degrees = unity two.

268.03   A system's parameters are the exact number of lucidly relevant somethings constituting the system. Parameters are the consideration. *Sidus* = star; *con-sidus*—consideration: how many interrelationships between the tunably relevant events con-sidered. There must be six or multiples of six to satisfy the generalized Eulerean topological equation.

268.04   All who have been educationally conditioned in science's formal, three-dimensional, *XYZ, CG_tS,* rectilinearly coordinate frame of omniparallel lines of conceptual reference are condemned to infinite travel in three sets of opposite directions, along and between whose infinite parallelism there are no inherent resolutions of answers to infinite questions. It is quite otherwise when they are advantaged by the inherent nucleated, omnidirectionally-concentrically enclosing, wave-frequency magnitude gradations of radiant growth or gravitational contraction of synergetics, whose convergent-divergent, systemic resonatability and tunability have the capability to run nature into terminal minimum-involvement systems of omnioriented considerability. (See Sec. *1053.171.*)

268.05　Conditioned to linear, special-case-directions thinking by the formally adopted educational systems of world-around society, humans think of life as a continuous linear experience despite all experiencing being inherently omnidirectionally informed. But they fail to consider that for every two eight-hour periods of seemingly continuous consciousness they stop conscious experiencing for eight hours—two on and two off—two on and two off. And they fail to realize that their sight is stroboscopically discontinuous and that there are inherent lags between sightings and cognitions, with the intervals between sights and cognitions too short to be cerebrally tunable. Here again we have evidence of the omnidirectional, finitely islanded, closed-system moments of *awareness,* which moments alone can be identified with what we call life. Here we have infratunable discontinuity of life occurring 60 times every second and tunably discontinuing for eight hours every 16 hours—with no human ever having the capability to prove that he is the same human who went to sleep nor that what he calls being awake is not a more vivid dream.

268.06　In view of the experimental provability—and ever reprovability—of the omnidirectionally islanded discontinuities of the packaged moments of life of which we are unaware, we must nonetheless comprehend that we have also been unconsciously "dying" 60 times a second. We must also become aware of the possibility that there is a periodicity of unconsciousness that is only as yet supratunable in terms of the as-yet-only-minuscule, cosmic duration of human experience.

268.07　This inference is also implicit in the closest-packed uniradius spheres, as photographically manifest by atomic agglomerations whose spherical domains are those of their spherical triangles' stabilized orbiting electrons' great circle patterns and their comprehensive constants of axial rotations, between whose closest packing are the spaces whose space-to-sphere ratio is one to six. Inasmuch as the rhombic triacontahedron volume is five (when the tetrahedron's volume is 1) and the allspace volume is six as manifest by the allspace-filling rhombic dodecahedron that tangentially embraces the sphere—the space-to-space ratio (or its nonexperience-to-experience, inherently spherical ratio) is clearly manifest in the co-occurring $10F^2 + 2$ and

$6F^2 + 2$ rates of concentric closest packing of uniradius spheres around a nuclear sphere in which the rate of occurrence of the concentric layers of space modules is twice that of the whole sphere layer occurring—ergo, $5F^2 + 2$ is to $6F^2 + 2$ as $5:6$. (See Secs. 983.04 and *986.860-64.*)

269.00   Topology of Ins, Outs, and Interrelationships

269.01   The self or otherness somethingnesses seem initially to be infra-tune-in-able. Thinking in terms of Euler and advantaged by all electromagnetically harvested experience, we may now employ the term *inframicrosystems* instead of "points" and *ultramacrosystems* instead of "space." The tuner and the tuned have a minimally-energy-expensive—ergo, geodesic—set of interrelationships. Tune-in-ability and tune-out-ability systems function as transceivers. Tune-out-ability is omnidirectional transmission: it does not mean shut off, as does "turning out the light." The tuner and the tuned inherently constitute an in-out transceiver system—a coordinate, concentric, convergent-divergent, frequency-differentiable system.

269.02   The silence is ultratunable; the noise is infratunable; and the music is tunability itself. Color is special case tunable.

269.03   *In* and *out* are characteristic of the tunability language of electromagnetics. *Any* or *no* direction is of equal information importance.

269.04   We can call the focals the *ins*. Focal point $= in;$ *in* vs omnidirectional. The focal *ins* are special case, while the outness is generalization. This is how conceptuality produces geometry independent of size and time. *Outness* is ultratuned conceptuality independent of time-size. *Inness* is conceptually oriented independent of size.

269.05   But there are always the outsideness and the insideness of tetrahedral system unity—the ultratunable, omnidirectionless nothingness and the infratunable, twilight-radiant-threshold-crossing, directionally oriented somethingness. Instead of Euler's vertexes, crossings, or points, we say:

—*inframicrosystems,* which are only directionally identifiable; specific directional *ins;* threshold-crossing, twilight-radiant, twilight-frequency somethingnesses tune-in-able only as noise.

—*ultramacrosystems,* which are nondirectionally identifiable; the omnidirectional *outs,* never-as-yet and maybe never-ever tunable; wherever and whenever the seeming nothingness may have color only as threshold-crossing, twilight-radiant, twilight-frequency, nondirectional, ultratunable *outness;* a number of glimpsed or window-framed views of nothingness.

—*interrelationships,* the directionally orientable, local-azimuthally-angled, cyclically-fractionated *aroundness* from this moment to that; the most economic geodesic interrelationship lines occurring as curvilinear arc segments of complex orbital accelerations. (Compare Sec. *1007.22.*)

269.06   The observer and the observed are two *ins* with one relationship. Euler said $V + A = L + 2$, but we may now say: The number of somethings + the number of nothings = the number of interrelationships + 2.

—Or we may say: The number of *ins* + the number of *outs* = the number of most economical interrelationships between the *ins* + the number 2.
—Or we may say: Observer + observed + *outness* = three elements = one interrelationship + the number 2.

The complete generalization of Euler does away with the windows. Windows were the rims of the eyeglass-framing separate views of the same nothingness.
269.07   In generalized topology we may use symbols for *ins, outs,* and *interrelationships:*

S = Somethingness *ins*
N = Nothingness *outs*
R = Minimum number of interrelationships
$\circled{S}$ = Multiplicative twoness
P = Additive twoness

$\circled{S}$ = Multiplicative twoness = Euler's + 2 unity = twoness = the inherently co-occurring, concave-convex, systemic, inward-outward dichotomy.
P = Additive twoness = Euler's + 2 unity = twoness = the two axial poles of inherent rotatability of all systems

We may say:

$$\circled{S}(S + N = R + P)$$
$$2(S + N = R + P)$$
$$2(S + N = R + 2)$$

270.00   Synergetics' Operational Accountability

270.10   Topological Accountability of All Vanishing and Elsewhere-Reappearing Quanta

270.11   The whole of synergetics' cosmic hierarchy of always symmetrically concentric, multistaged but continually smooth (click-stop subdividing), geometrical contracting from 20 to 1 tetravolumes (or quanta) and their successive whole-number volumes and their topological and vectorial accounting's intertransformative convergence-or-divergence phases, and in particular the series of posters appearing in color plates 1–10, elucidate conceptually, and by experimentally demonstrable evidence, the elegantly exact, energetic quanta transformings by which

  (a) *energy-exporting structural systems precisely accomplish their entropic, seemingly annihilative quantum "losses" or "tune-outs," and*
  (b) *new structural systems appear, or tune in at remote elsewheres and elsewhens, thereafter to agglomerate syntropically with other seemingly "new" quanta to form geometrically into complex systems of varying magnitudes, and how*
  (c) *such complex structural systems may accommodate concurrently both entropic exporting and syntropic importing, and do so always in terms of whole, uniquely frequenced, growing or diminishing, four-dimensional, structural-system quantum units.*

270.12   In the era before the measurement of the speed of light scientists assumed an instant, unitarily conceptual, normally-at-rest (but for the moment, and only locally, perversely restless) Universe. Before the 20th-century discoveries of other galaxies and in the early days of thermodynamics and its disclosure of entropy—the inexorable systemic loss of energy—the scientists were prone to assume that the vast instantaneous cosmic machine as a thermodynamic system must itself be "running down"—that is, continually spending itself entropically and trending eventually to self-annihilation.

270.13   Boltzmann contradicted that assumption by saying in effect that the a priori fact of the existence of billions of stars radiantly and entropically broadcasting their energies must require an as-yet-undiscovered but obviously operative energy redistribution system by which stars are elsewhere and elsewhen assemblingly formed. Boltzmann therefore assumed a cosmic complex of invisible energy-importing centers whose nonsimultaneous formations but sum-total, long-run energy importing exactly balances all the long-run cosmic exportings. The entropic radiance of the exporting centers makes them visible to us, while the importing centers are inherently invisible, except when starlight bounces reflectively off them as does Sunlight make the Moon—and the planets Venus, Jupiter, Mars, and Saturn—reflectively visible to us Earthians.

270.14   Because Boltzman could not demonstrate the astrophysical presence of such inherently invisible importing centers, his concept was not widely accepted by other scientists. Einstein, however, later supported Boltzmann's concept as constituting a logical corollary of Einstein's own implicit concept of the Universe as an aggregate of nonsimultaneous, variously enduring, and only partially overlapping energy events. Though Einstein did not employ the analogy, his was in effect an endless ropelike concept of variously enduring, finite, special case episodes converging in generalized principle to apparent interrelevance and overlapping one another momentarily to constitute a fat- or thin-diametered rope of meaningful concern as might preoccupy any one cosmologist at any one time.

270.15   Among their many sophisticated mathematical devices mathematicians' most advanced conceptual tool is the topology of Leonhard Euler, whose three irreducible visualizable aspects of *vertexes V, planar faces or areas F,* and *edges of faces or lines E* seem to the geometrically heedless mathematical physicists and astrophysicists to have no inherent correspondence with experimentally demonstrable energetic reality.

270.16   Synergetics defines *structure* as meaning the self-interstabilization by a complex of forces operative in six degrees of freedom. This complex definition can be resolved into only one word—*triangulation*. The faculty of the Massachusetts Institute of Technology has defined mathematics as "the science of structure and pattern in general."

270.17   Synergetics and operational mathematics find that by combining topology and vectorial geometry, and by always requiring structural stability and intertransformative proofs in four-dimensional electromagnetic reality for all propositions, and by starting with minimum conceptuality of a substantive entity as having inherent insideness and outsideness, *it is in evidence*

   —that the minimum polyhedron (the tetrahedron) consists entirely of
      minimum polygons (triangles);
   —that the minimum polyhedron systematically and inherently divides all
      Universe into (a) an excluded macrocosm, (b) an included microcosm,

and (c) the remainder of Universe constituting the dividing system itself;

—that this tune-in-able minimum, systemic, primitive entity is apprehensible conceptually because of its contrast to the "nothingness" of the
presently untuned-in and un-tune-in-able (within the limited frequency
range of the human observer's given equipment);

—that the cosmically comprehensive equilibrium of all vectors provides
the geometrically conceptual field of *structuring-as-you-go* reference
and is known as the four-dimensional isotropic vector, meaning cosmically everywhere and everywhen *the same* energy conditions—ergo
undifferentiable, ergo untunable and unapprehendible in any special
case time-size reality—but both intellectually and geometrically conceptualized in synergetics' vectorial, angular-oriented comprehensivity; and

—that there is no "space"; there is only the tuned-in and the at-present-
un-tuned-in—over ten million invisible electromagnetic waves of
radio, TV, and other broadcasts are surrounding you and permeating
you in what we usually call space.

270.18   Euler shows that in respect to all uncored polyhedra the number of
vertexes plus the number of faces always equals the number of edges plus the
number 2 ($V + F = E + 2$). But the diversion of this formula into local aspects
of polyhedra introduced a nonexistent two-dimensionality, allowing the mathematicians to detour around reality. Academic mathematicians (themselves indifferent to physical manifestation of experimental evidence) have detoured
Euler's concepts into such games as that of the pretended existence of a substanceless rubber sheet having no insideness but only a one-way-at-a-time-fac-
ing surface with no edge thickness or obverse surface. On such an imaginary
surface Euler's vertexes, faces, and edges have been distortingly redeployed.

270.19   Euler was almost blind, but with his compensatorily vivid imagination he discovered that all visual experiences could be reduced to three
prime aspects: *lines,* and where lines converge to *vertexes,* and where lines
surroundingly cross one another to describe *areas* bound by those lines. Because his topology was concerned with only visual aspects, Euler was able to
overlook substantial textures, sounds, tastes, and smells; temperatures,
weights, and volumes; durations, intensities, frequencies, and velocities. But
he was so great a scientist and so competent a mathematician that he evolved
the fundamentals of structural analysis employed in the 20th century in designing structures of land, sea, sky, and extraterrestrial functioning.

270.20   The chemist Willard Gibbs, developed the phase rule dealing with
liquid, gaseous, and crystalline states of substances, apparently not realizing

that his phase rule employed the same generalized mathematics as that of Euler's topological vertexes, faces, and edges.

270.21   Synergetics is concerned exclusively with physically demonstrable, and thus experimentally evidenceable, phenomena. Synergetics adds to Euler's topology its discovery of the mathematically generalizable constant relative interabundance of angles, volumes, and all the physical characteristics of time-space velocity, force, wavelength and frequency, directional orientation, and systems consideration—always identifying Euler's edge lines E as representative only of physical energy vectors or metaphysical lines of unique interrelationships of vertexially located phenomena. Vectors are discrete in length, being the product of physical velocity and mass operating in a given angularly describable direction in respect to a given axis of observation. Velocity is a product of time and distance, while mass is a relative density of energy events per given volume; wherefore all the qualities of physical experience are describable in a unified four-dimensional field, a state at which physical Universe never tarries, and relative to which (and through which) all of nature's physical manifestations are local, differentially frequenced aberratings and pulsative omniconvergent-divergent, omniinteraccommodative transformings.

270.22   Since the sum of the chordally convergent angles of any triangle (right, isosceles, or scalene) is always 180 degrees, the sum of the angles of any chordally defined tetrahedron, regular or irregular, is always 720 degrees; therefore, all its topological and geometrical interrelationship properties are consistently similar—ergo, universal independently of time-size considerations.

270.23   We start our vectorial, topological, structuring-as-you-go exploration with the primitive state of conceptuality (independent of size and time) of the universal tetrahedron, with its four triangular facets, its four corners, its 12 angles, and its six most economical, chordal, interrelationship lines running between its four-corner event foci.

270.24   In exploring the intertransformability of the primitive hierarchy of structuring-as-you-go, with its omnitriangularly oriented evolution and the interbonding of its evolving structural components, we soon discover that the universal interjointing of systems and their foldability permit the angularly hinged convergence into congruence of vectors, faces, and vertexes as demonstrated in the *vector equilibrium jitterbug* (Sec. 460), each of whose multicongruences appears as only one edge or one vertex or one face aspect. Topological accounting as conventionally practiced accounts each of these multicongruent aspects as consisting of only one such aspect. Only synergetics accounts for the presence of all the congruent aspects—double, triple, or fourfold—by always accounting for the initial inventory of the comprehensive tetravolume-48 rhombic dodecahedron and the 20-tetravolume vector equilibrium, together with their initial or primitive inventory of vertexes, faces, and edge lines, which are always present in all stages of the 48→1 jitterbug convergence transformation, though often imperceptibly so.

270.25   With recognition of the foregoing topological deceptiveness, and always keeping account of the primitive total inventory of such aspects, we find it possible to demonstrate conceptually and to prove the validity not only of Boltzmann's concepts but of all quantum phenomena. This makes it possible to interlink the mathematical accounting of synergetics conceptually with the operational data of physics and chemistry as well as with the complex associabilities of their related disciplines.

300.00 Universe

   * Titles in parentheses will be found in *Synergetics 1*

301.00 Definition: Universe

304.00 Our definition of Universe provides for the undiscovered and for the yet-to-be discovered. Do not worry about that farthermost star which is yet to be consciously apprehended by any human being. Do not think we have not provided for those physical or chemical phenomena as yet not observed and recorded by human or mechanical sensing devices. The existence of such phenomena may not have even been postulated, but they can all be accommodated by our definition of Universe. Because we start with whole Universe we have left out nothing: There is no multiplication by amplification of, or addition to, eternally regenerative Universe; there is only multiplication by division. The farthermost star and the most unfamiliar physical phenomena are all accommodated by further arithmetical subdividing of our aggregate of overlapping experiences. Nothing could have been *left out* when you start with whole Universe. (See Secs. 522.32, 537.31, 540.03, and 1050.13.)

310.10 Odd Ball

310.11 In synergetics we find the difference of exactly one whole integer frequently manifest in our geometrical interrelationship explorations. Beyond the one additional proton and one additional electron that progressively characterize the hierarchy of the already-discovered family of 92 regenerative chemical elements and their short-lived transuranium manifestability by high-energy physics experiments, we find time and again a single integer to be associated with the positive-negative energetic pulsations in Universe. Because the energetic-synergetic relationships are usually generalized relationships independent of size, these single rational integer differentials are frequently found to characterize the limit magnitudes of asymmetric deviations from the zerophase vector equilibrium. (See Sec. *1043*.)

310.12   The minor aberrations of otherwise elegantly matching phenomena of nature, such as the microweight aberrations of the 92 regenerative
chemical elements in respect to their atomic numbers, were not explained
until isotopes and their neutrons were discovered a few decades ago. Such
discoveries numerically elucidate the whole-integer rationalization of the
unique isotopal system's structural-proclivity agglomeratings.

310.13   There is a phenomenon that we might describe as the eternal
disquietude of the Odd Ball promulgating eternal reorderings, realignments,
and inexorable transformings to accommodate the eternal regeneration integrity of intellectually differentiable Universe. This suggests philosophically
that the individual metaphysical human viewpoint—the individual ego of the
human—is indeed an essential function of the eternally regenerative integrity
of complex law-governed Universe.

310.14   Possibly this mathematical Odd-Ball-oneness inherently regenerates the ever-reborn ego. Just when you think you are negative, you find you
are positively so. This is the eternal wellspring of positive-negative regeneration of acceleratingly heating entropy and cooling-off syntropy, which is synergetically interoperative between the inherently terminal physical differentiating and the inherently eternal metaphysical integration.

311.10   Humans as Ultimate Complexities

• [*311.10–311.18   Complex Humans Scenario*]

311.11   Synergetics presents a picture of the multioptioned operational
field of cosmic favorabilities, intertransformabilities, and complementary in-
teraccommodations within which each human individual, his life, his world,
is always one alternately elective, complex-integrity way Universe could have
evolved.

311.12   No man or woman can ever prove when they wake up in the
morning that they are the same person who they think they remember went to
sleep. They may dream that they had other dreams, but there is now no way
to prove that there are not a great many alternate "me's," and that one of
them may have awakened under one set of alternate possibilities while the
others may have awakened under other circumstances, and that each of them
thinks that it is the only "me."

311.13   Let's assume that you have the realistically imaginative capability
to invent a Universe wherein there are no substantive "things," a Universe
wherein there are only events. Life is first of all awareness. No otherness: no

awareness. Much otherness is difference-from-me-ness. Events are cognizable and re-cognizable only through awareness of the occurrence of interrelationship differences in sequentially observed conditions. Your Universe would have to be a Universe of ever-changing events, differentially adding here, subtracting there, multiplying, and dividing, reaching out or coming in, differentially including and integratingly refining, either locally gaining or losing, while continually and complexedly transforming at a plurality of rates and magnitudes. Within this Universe you also invent all the 92 regenerative chemical elements and their respectively unique, repulsive or associative behaviors compounding to form billions of unique substances while catalytically disassociating such substances to form all the chemical-element isotopal agglomeratings. You may go on to invent all the generalized principles of synergetic mass-interattractiveness and entropic radiation, as well as the latter's reflectivity and refractivity. And you will have to invent precession and all the unique frequencies of the chemical elements as well as each and all cyclic events. Then you start playing your game of Universe. You have all the stars and galaxies of stars entropically exporting energy and planets syntropically importing energies that, when they reach critical mass, become new stars as fragments of the exploded old stars become cores for the beginning of new planets. As you invent, you arrive at more and more intertransformative complexities and timing problems; the whole game gets more and more complicated. Quite clearly experiences must multiply, so the complexity of your invented Universe multiplies exponentially at a fourth-power rate in respect to the arithmetical progression of time. And since every event is always accomplished with six equieconomical, four-dimensionally directioned moves—the four dimensions being (1) inwardly, (2) outwardly, (3) circumferentially and equatorially around (axial spinning), and (4) polarized, involutionally-evolutionally, inside-outingly around—by means of the alternative, equimaximally economical optional move events you might find by the close of each event that you are six, five, four, three, or two radial zones outwardly in any direction from where you started—or right back where you started—and you soon come to the complex invention of thus-far-discovered billions of galaxies consisting of approximately 100 billion stars of the macrocosm and multibillions of invisible-to-naked-human-eye, microcosmic, associating and disassociating behavioral identities, altogether camouflaged beneath the blanket of make-believe "reality" of exclusively terrestrial politics and economic mefirstings, whose nonsensical preoccupation we call "today." It is doubtful that the million-light-year-distanced Andromeda nebula has any interest in Republicans or Democrats, communists or capitalists, or any other terrestrial partisanships.

   311.14   So it could be that human beings, wherever they occur in Universe, may be introduced as a means of coping metaphysically with the most complex kinds of local Universe problems, so that each one of us is where the problem-solving of Universe is being transacted. If we were to think of ourselves as things—as china dolls, as kinds of china dolls that would just get smashed up or would just get worn or eroded away—that wouldn't be very good thinking. It would be much closer to actual Universe to think of ourselves as an absolutely continuous complex process. We are quite possibly the most complex of the problem-solving challenges of the invention that is eternally regenerative Scenario Universe. In this way each of us might be a department of the mind of what we might call god.

311.15   It is reasonable to suppose that there must be an overall physical-metaphysical cosmic accounting system that is always omniconsiderately integrative of all the a priori set of generalized interrationship principles that we have found scientifically to be unfailingly operative in Universe. It may well be that each of us humans is an important function in sustaining the eternally regenerative integrity of Universe. The invention of the game of limited and terminal local awareness that we call "life" is in contradistinction to the concept of eternally total cosmic knowledge, intellect, and wisdom, whose totality of comprehensive comprehension would answeringly cancel out all questions and all problems, which would result in the eternally timeless, sublime $0 = 0$ equation of absolute perfection.

311.16   Local life in Universe involves the invention of time. Time involves nonsimultaneity and limited information—ergo, only partial equatability. By introducing time and the myriad differential of interevent lags consequent to the exponentially multiplying, reinterpositioning distance variables inherent in the six alternative moves for each of the myriad of differentially frequenced, never-simultaneous events, the exponentially multiplying complexity of interevent lags accounts for both the micronuclear and macroastronomical progressive range of distance differentials of experience-limited, local-Universe human observing. Since each of the only-mathematically-statable, scientifically generalized laws of physical Universe constitutes a statement of truth, and since science has discovered a plurality of observable and ever redemonstrably operative truths—all of which are always omniinteraccommodative—it may be said that truth is complex. It is mathematically hypothesizable that all of the truths are potentially integratable and that the resulting integral truth constitutes the cosmic integrity that humans intuitively sense to be in governance of Universe and speak of to one another with the inadequate sound-word god.

311.17   We can thus invent a hypothetical Universe with a limited game of individual human participation in only-locally-occuring, time-distance morphation awareness conceptualizations integratingly cognizant, as the sequential reality of human realization, of the complexedly interacting plurality of omniinteraccommodative cosmic laws that altogether enact events in pure principle, so reliably pure as to be sensorially apprehended by human brains and partially comprehended by human minds.

311.18   We may logically assume that the intellectual cosmic integrity of the timeless, sublime integral of absolute perfection must continually test its integrity of eternal regenerativity; wherefore the integral that we inadequately identify as god requires a plurality of local sensing monitors to be omnideployed in the time-distance-differentiated, nonsimultaneously conceptual, serial Universe to continually observe the local Universe events, while also being progressively advantaged with an ever larger inventory of the discovered laws governing cosmic regeneration integrity, and thus equipped, to cope metaphysically with each of the profusion of unprecedentedly unique regenerative complexities that we speak of as problems. In effect god differentiates cosmic integrity into a time-distance-differentiated plurality of limited, local, metaphysical, intellectual experiences with which to test the capability of "god" to reintegrate and restore its timeless zerophase unity.

320.00   Scenario Universe

321.03   Humans have always tried to conform their concepts of Universe to their own human prototype. Humans stop and start; sleep and wake; are born, grow, decay, and die: so humans thought the Universe must also have a beginning and an end. Now astrophycists find this to be untrue. There could never have been a primordial chaos, simply because scientists now know that the proton and neutron always and only coexist in the most exquisite interorderliness. There could never have been a time when their integrity was not an integrity.

321.04   Universe is a scenario. Scenario Universe is the finite but nonunitarily conceptual aggregate of only partially overlapping and communicated experiences of humanity. Uni-verse is a momentarily glimpsed, special-case, systemic-episode takeout. When we start synergetically with wholes, we have to deal with the scenario within which we discover episodes—like the frog the snake is swallowing.

321.05   Time is only now. Time and size are always special-case, asymmetric episodes of *now* whose systemic aberrations are referenced to the cosmic hierarchy of primitive and symmetrical geometries through which they pulsate actively and passively but at which they never stop. The rest of Scenario Universe is shapeless: untuned-in. (See Sec. 982.62 for cosmic hierarchy and compare text at Sec. *1033.103.*)

325.10   Analogy of Rope-making and Film-strips

325.11   As seen by an individual human observer or as recorded by any humanly devised instruments, Scenario Universe is progressively reaggregated within the recorded, remembered, recalled, and progressively reconsidered information inventory of ever more macro-comprehensive-outward and micro-exquisite-inward ranges of the compositely growing individual's experiencing of life-in-time.

325.12   Scenario Universe is to any and all human observers very much like a rope-making experience—a rope that grows ever greater in total complexity but not in total diameter, and is comprised of ever more exquisitely diametered and ever stronger separate and differently lengthed fibers, a rope of which each of the myriad of progressive information events are in themselves terminal.

325.13   Each fiber enters into the scenario of rope-making by being twisted with others into a small thread of successively introduced and only partially overlapping fibers. This composited thread in turn is twisted with other threads into more complex strands. The strands are twisted with strands—always consistently clockwise or counterclockwise (never both)—until the totally twisted complex is brought together with a similarly twisted but turned-around and now oppositely directioned rope of equal complexity, whereat, when side by side, their respective tendencies to untwist interwhip them together to block one another's untwisting and produce an overall stabilized rope.

325.14   Employing the concept of individual fibers in this rope-making analogy and substituting for the word *fibers* the word *photons,* we can comprehend Einstein's curved-space assumption of the manner in which the omniremotely, entropically dispersed, individual energy increments, radiationally disassociated from former star sources at maximum remoteness from other entities, now progressively enter the gravitational neighborhood of radiationally disassociated energy increments—emanated from many sources—and become thereafter progressively reassociated with one another in forming new celestial aggregates, thereafter—as substantive matter—converging to a terminal complexity and density, thereafter once more to become radiantly dispersed.

325.15   The balancing of the gravitational and radiational exchanges is again analogous to the patterns of rope-making. We simply splice together the ends of the stabilized overall ropes to produce a plurality of looped-back, cosmic rope-making in a Scenario Universe of nonsimultaneous, local, episode twistings and untwistings. While some loops are unraveling, their strayed-away strands got caught elsewhere in new intertwinings.

325.16   The whole analogy of the rope-making and unmaking can be re-transformed into the cinema concept, and the words *fibers* or *photons* being replaced by the word *atoms*. We can conceive now of all the separate atoms in the chemical compounds comprising the photo-negative celluloid ribbon of long-ago-exposed, financially exploited, stored-and-forgotten footage, the significance of whose once novel special case information has long since been incorporated in popularly accepted generalized viewpoints. The old film-strip has been chemically dissolved and its atoms disassociatively dispersed, migrated, and subsequently reassociated in a new inventory of on-the-shelf, unexposed, film-strip footage upon which may be recorded the ever-changing but progressively increasing inventory of comprehensive human experiences of tomorrow's today. In this analogy there is a plurality of fresh individual film-strips being nonsimultaneously and only overlappingly-in-time exposed for each individual observer in the Universe, as each is overlappingly intertwined into more complex information strands.

325.20   Epistemography of Scenario Universe

325.21   Synergetics always commences its considerations and explorations with finite but nonunitarily conceptual Scenario Universe, which is inherently nonsimultaneous. Scenario Universe is the totality of all humanity's consciously apprehended and communicated experiences. It is inherently prohibited for the totality of physical Universe to be quantitatively increased—ergo, in synergetics we have differentiation in the family of primitive generalized conceptual systems. Multiplication is always and only a special case, relative time-size phenomenon—ergo, multiplication is accomplished always and only as special case frequency of subdivision of the primitive epistemographic family of interassociations of primitive concepts.

325.22   All special case multiplicity is considered and expressed in unique frequency, angle, vector, and topological quantation terms. The epistemography of synergetics discovers operationally, experientially, and experimentally that the most primitive of the conceptual systems to be divided or isolated from nonunitarily and nonsimultaneously conceptual Scenario Universe must inherently consist of the simplest minimum considerability none of whose components can exist independently of one another. The system components of minimum considerability are inherently recollectable only because they are experientially components of observable otherness. The words to describe inherencies of systems were invented by humans in spontaneous recognition of co-occurring observabilities. The word *part* could have been invented by humans only after having discovered a holistically considerable system.

325.23   Within the time frame of any one given observer *simultaneous* means the unitary consideration of a plurality of experientially observable, concurrently focal episodes with differently occurring births, deaths, and longevities—but they are overlappingly co-occurring with their omnidirectionally comprehensive environment. Omnicircumstance conditions are often forgotten in the recall of only the focal episodes of the considered systems' most prominent central memorabilities. Con-sideration—or the simultaneous co-reviewing of a plurality of stars—is always simultaneous. But simultaneous is not instantaneous. Apprehending and comprehending require a time lapse. Simultaneous is episodal in Scenario Universe. Because our sight is only a light-wave frequency phenomenon, *instantaneous* cannot accommodate apprehension because instantaneity inherently lacks time span or wavelength.

326.00   Universe as Metaphysical and Physical

• [*326.00–326.50   Metaphysics Scenario*]

326.01   The support of life on our planet consists of two kinds—metaphysical and physical. Both cosmic and terrestrial energetic regeneration, organic and inorganic, are physical; while the know-what of pure science and the know-how of applied science are both metaphysical. The know-what of science's experimental evidence informs technology's know-how to employ efficiently the substantive resources and synergetic metaphysical patterns progressively found to be operative in Universe. These are essential to the maintenance of life on board our planet as well as in mounting local-Universe exploring excursions from our mother-spaceship Earth.

326.02   All that is physical is energetic. All that is metaphysical is synergetic.

326.03   All the energetic physical consists of two phases—(1) energy associative as matter, and (2) energy disassociative as radiation—with each being reconvertible into the other. All the synergetic metaphysical consists of two phases—(1) subjective information acquisition by pure science exploration, and (2) objectively employed information by applied science invention.

326.04   We can refine all the tools and energy capability of single and commonwealth into two main constituents—the physical and the metaphysical. The physical consists of specific, measurable energy quantities; the metaphysical consists of specifically demonstrable know-how capabilities. Only the metaphysical can designedly organize the physical, landscape-forming events to human advantage, and do so while also maintaining

(a) the regenerative integrity of the complex ecological-physiological support of human life aboard our planet, and

(b) the integrity of the chemical-element inventory of which our planet, its biosphere and co-orbiting hydraulic, atmospheric, ozonic radiation-shielding spheres, ionosphere, Van Allen belts, and other layerings all consist.

326.05 Only the physical is alterable; the metaphysical is unalterable. All the physical is continually intertransforming in orderly ways discoverable only by the weightless metaphysical mind. The local physical systems are everywhere energy exportive, which is humanly misinterpreted to be entropic and dissynchronously expansive only because the exported energies are electromagnetically (i.e., nonsubstantially) dispatched *only as information*— which is purely metaphysical—to be always eventually imported as information by electromagnetic reception in elsewhere-newborn, regenerative assemblages of cosmic systems. The local exportings appear to be dissynchronous only when viewed from too short a time span to permit the tuned-in occurrence of the next synchronous moment of the eons-apart frequencies often involved in celestial electromagnetics.*

326.06 We look at the stars, and they look very randomly scattered throughout the sky. But we can say that the number of direct and unique interrelationships between all the stars is always $\frac{N^2 - N}{2}$. This equation demonstrates the principle of order underlying all superficially appearing disorderliness or randomness (see Sec. 227) and tells us quite clearly and simply that we are mathematically justified in assuming order to be always present despite the superficially appearing disorder. This gives us a personal sense of the order-discovering and -employing power of the weightless mind and at the same time a sense of our human anatomy's negligible magnitude in Universe when juxtaposed to the vast array of stars visible to the naked human eye. The stars observable on clear nights—the naked-eye-visible stars—constitute but a meager fraction of all the stars of our own "Milky Way" galaxy. Beyond this there is the 99.99 times greater array of the only-telescopically-visible, 200 billion other already photographically identified galaxies, each consisting of an average of 100 billion stars, all coordinately operative within a 22-billion-

---

* Whether communication is by telephone hook-up or by wireless radio, what you and I transmit is only weightless metaphysical information. Metaphysical, information appreciative, you and I are not the telephones nor the wired or wireless means of the metaphysical information transmitting.

light-year-diameter sphere of Earth-planet-mounted instrumental observation and Earthians' photographic recording. This spherical-sweepout sphere of astronomical observation by minuscule humans on Earth describes a sphere of 123-plus-21-zeros-miles in diameter, all of which adds up at the present moment to each of the four billion humans on Earth having an exclusive personal quota of 25 billion stars or suns operatively available to their energetic regeneration, just awaiting his metaphysical know-how development, with the metaphysical assurance already established that the Universe is eternally regenerative. Energy crises are crises of ignorance induced by lethal self-interest.

326.07 This cosmic-accounting analysis discloses the omniuniversal orderliness that the scientist finds always to be underlying all of the only-ignorantly-apprehended illusions of randomness. This tells us that the seeming disorder of physical entropy is only superficial and explains why metaphysical thought can always find the syntropic orderliness that cancels out all disorderliness. Disorderliness is nonthinking. Exclusively energetic brain, which stores the sensorial input data of all the special-case experiences, cannot find the synergetic interrelationships existing only *between* and never *in* any of the special-case systems considered only separately, any more than a library building in itself can find the unique interrelationships existing between the separate data that it houses. Only mind—the magnificent, weightless, metaphysical, pattern-seeking-and-apprehending function—has demonstrated the capability to intuitively apprehend and mathematically contrive the experimental means for identifying the significant, only-between-and-not-of, only mathematically expressible, eternal relationships, which altogether permit a seemingly inexhaustible variety of cosmic interrelationship patterning, and thereby human mind's capability to participate in the ceaseless complex of orderly intertransformings in such a manner as continually to abet the human mind's unique local-Universe functioning in maintenance of the cosmic integrity of eternal regeneration.

326.08 So long as humans progressively employ and develop their syntropic, energetic, metaphysical mind's capability to locally abet cosmic integrity, just so long will that metaphysical capability continue to operate in this particular local Universe's ecologically regenerative, planetary team aboard spaceship Earth. If, however, the entropic, energetically exploiting, antisynergetic, exclusively partisan profit motive—political or financial—continues to dominate and rule humans by force of arms, then the Earthian ecology team will become self-disqualifying for further continuance as a potentially effective local sustainer of cosmic-regeneration integrity. This is the net of what has now become metaphysically evidenced regarding the potential significance of humans aboard planet Earth. It is the nature of the contest between brain and mind. Brain is selfishly exclusive; mind is cosmically inclusive. Brain now commands the physical power to overwhelm humanity. But it is also the nature of mind's design science capability to render all humanity physically successful, thus eliminating human preoccupation with the struggle and thereby freeing all humanity to become metaphysically preoccupied with fulfilling its cosmic-regeneration functioning.

326.09   The physical Universe is an aggregate of frequencies. The human brain's senses are able to tune in directly only about one-millionth of the exclusively-mind-discovered and now experimentally proven and usable electromagnetic ranges of energetic reality. To this magnificent extent has the metaphysical brought humans into potential mastery of the physical. But thus far their physically most powerful political masters, misassuming ignorantly that there is fundamental inadequacy of life support, continue to exploit the fear that this induces in individuals, not for the individuals' sake but for concern and love for their dependents. Thus individuals concerned for the welfare of their dependents fearfully yield their economic-strategy mandates to the power-wielding brains of exclusively partisan ideologists.

326.10 Precession of Side Effects and Primary Effects

326.11   In recognizing the residual ignorance of variously dominant Earthian power-structure partisans of this particular cosmic-history moment, we do not impute malevolence or wrongdoing; we are only recognizing the checks-and-balances mechanisms of nonsimultaneously occurring and only partially overlapping Scenario Universe's vast variety of local conception-to-birth gestation rates. These gestations are the product of the associative energies' frequency synchronizations as well as of the concomitant rate of local disassociative energies, the dyings-off.

326.12   In the regenerative integrity of the cosmic design the locally supportive, human mind's understanding operative on planet Earth has to be midwife at the birth and experiential development of critical information inventorying; it must also sustain the total—Garden of Eden—ecological regenerativity as naturally accomplished by intense high-frequency information transmitted by the electromagnetics of chemical elements of the star Sun and receivingly translated by the Earth's land-borne vegetation and water-borne algae into photosynthetic sorting, reorganizing, and combining of the planet Earth's inventory of carbon, hydrogen, and other chemical elements. Some of these energies are redistributed to the biosphere, and some reenter directly into the integral metabolic multiplication and proliferation by all biological organisms of the hydrocarbon molecules and their concomitant environmentally supportive, chemical exchanging events. To function successfully in gales and

storms while exposing adequate leafage to the Sun, the dry Earthborne vegetation must send into the soil and rocks roots that draw water from the soil to
cool themselves against dehydration by the heat of radiation exposure as well
as to provide the vegetation with noncompressible, hydraulic structuring as
well as with hydraulic distribution of the many eccentric, locally concentrated
energy stressings of the vegetation's structure. Because the vegetation is
rooted, it cannot reach the other vegetation to procreate. To solve this regenerative problem Universe inventively designed a vast variety of mobile creatures—such as birds, butterflies, worms and ants—to intertraffic and cross-
pollinate the vast variety of vegetation involved in the biochemical refertiliza-
tion complexities of ecology, as for instance does the honeybee buzz-enter the
flowers to reach its honey while inadvertently cross-fertilizing the plants.
Each biological specimen is structurally designed by the programmed codings
of DNA-RNA and is chromosomically programmed to go directly to immediately rewarding targets while inadvertently, or unknowingly, producing (what
are to it) "side effects" that inadvertently sustain the main objective of Universe, which is the sustenance of the synergetic circuitry of terrestrial ecology
and thereby as well to sustain the cosmic regeneration.

326.13   Humans, like the honeybee, are born ignorant, preprogrammed
with hunger, thirst, and respiratory drives to take in chemical elements in
crystalline, liquid, and gaseous increments, as well as with procreativeness
and parental-protectiveness drives. With their directly programmed drives
humans inadvertently produce (what are to them) side effects, which results in
their doing the right cosmic regenerative tasks for all the wrong reasons—or
without any reason at all. This preliminary phase of preconditioned human
reflexing, while lasting millions of years, is a gestative-phase behavior that
becomes obsolete as humans' metaphysical mind discovers the principles of
precession and discovers—only through vast, cumulative trial and error—the
pattern experience of both terrestrial and cosmic ecology; whereafter humans
will progressively recommit their endeavors in support of the recycling and
orbitally regenerative effects, precessionally interproduced by all independently orbiting cosmic systems. This abrupt 90-degree reorientation constitutes the evolutionary stage through which humanity is now passing, wherein
humanity will progressively exchange its exclusive preoccupation with self-
preservation for that of supporting omniinclusive, cosmic integrity.

326.20   Pyramid of Generalizations

326.21   The physical Universe is characterized by local-system entropy,
an ever-increasing, locally expansive randomness, and an ever-increasing diffusion, as all the different and nonsimultaneous transformations and reorienta-

tions occur. While the entropy and disorderliness of physically exportive Universe increase and expand, we have the metaphysical Universe countering syntropically with energy importing, orderly sorting, and comprehensive contraction and storage of energy. In the metaphysically organized, syntropic-importing phase of cosmic-energy events we have the human mind digesting and sorting out all the special case experiences and generalizing therefrom the persistent relationships existing *between* and not *in* the special characteristics of all the special cases. All the eternal, weightless principles apparently governing both the physical and metaphysical Universe are experimentally detected and digested into mathematical generalizations, of which only a very few are as yet known.

326.22   The whole process of generalizing generalizations forms a pyramid whose base consists of all the special cases of direct physical experiences. We can say, "We take a piece of rope and tense it," when we do not in fact have a rope in our hands. We have all had so many rope experiences that we can generalize our communication of the concept. This is a first-degree generalization. The discovery of always and only coexisting tension and compression is a second-degree generalization. Finding a whole family of always and only coexisting phenomena is a third-degree generalization; and conceiving therefrom "relativity" is a fourth-degree generalization.

326.23   In this pyramid of generalizations the human mind goes way beyond the biologicals in its development of the diminishing conceptual Universe—diminishing because, being progressively reduced and refined from a plurality of first-degree to a plurality of second-degree generalizations, and finally to as concise a form as $E = Mc^2$, which may some day be even more economically expressed as it is synergetically digested into ever more comprehensive and exquisite cosmic comprehension by metaphysically evolving human minds. So we find the metaphysical not only comprehending the physical—which should have been expected—but also encompassing and omni-accounting all the physical with the tetrahedron and thereafter reducing Universe's structural system myriadness to unity. The metaphysical, as with the circumferentially united, great-circle chord vectors of the vector equilibrium, masteringly coheres the physical by more effective use of the same quanta of energy. (See Sec. 440.08.)

326.24   Discovery of an acceptable hypothesis for explaining the role of humans as an essential metaphysical function of Universe, along with discovery of the mathematical proof of the tetrahedron as the true minimum limit structural system of Universe and its subdivision of Universe into macro- and microcosms as the sizeless conceptual system basis for generalizing general system theory, all develop as a consequence of our asking ourselves the question: How may we organize our self-disciplining on behalf of all humanity and in support of the integrity of eternal cosmic regeneration to deal comprehensively and capably with the maximum and minimum of limiting factors of the combined and complementary metaphysical and physical prime subdivisions of Universe?

326.25   The *theory of functions* holds for Universe itself. Universe consists at minimum of both the metaphysical and the physical. The inherent, uniquely differentiable, but constantly interproportional twoness of physical Universe was embraced in Einstein's one-word metaphysical concept, "relativity," and in a more specific and experimentally demonstrable way in the physicists' concept of complementarity.

326.30 Comprehensive Universe

326.31   Comprehensive Universe combines both the metaphysical Universe and the physical Universe. The local physical system is the one we experience sensorially: the conceptual metaphysical system is one we never experience physically but only consider in thought. As we discover in our grand synergetic strategy, we commence all problem-solving most advantageously at the supreme, terminally comprehensive level of Universe—that is, at the generalized-principle level. Thereafter we separate out from nonunitarily conceptual Scenario Universe one single, thinkable, experientially definable, holistic concept, which definition function inadvertently discloses the inherent polyhedral geometry of all conceptually sizeless thought referencing. We go on to find out through topological mathematics how to demonstrate that the difference between the cosmically total metaphysical and physical Universe and any one experiential physical system, or any one conceptually thinkable system, is just one (positive and negative) tetrahedron, or one unity-of-twoness. This is to say that the difference between the finite (because an aggregate of finites) but nonunitarily conceptual total Scenario Universe (which we used to call infinity) and the physical Scenario Universe of energy with which physics deals, is just one finitely positive and one complementary, finitely negative tetrahedron. The exclusively conceptual metaphysical Universe is also proven to be a finite scenario because it too is an aggregate of locally terminal—ergo, finite—intellectual conceptioning experiences. The total Universe is just one (plus and minus) tetrahedron more than either the exclusively physical or exclusively metaphysical conceptualized Universe. (See Sec. 620.12.)

326.32   What man used to call infinite, I call finite, but nonunitarily conceptual—ergo, nonsimultaneously thinkable. What man used to call finite, I call definite, i.e., definable, conceptually—ergo, thinkably definable. The plus and minus, sizelessly conceivable, tetrahedral differences are all finitely and rationally calculable.

326.40   Metaphysical and Physical: Summary

Metaphysical cogitates reliably in respect to equilibrium.

Physical abhors equilibrium.

That which is communicated, i.e., understood, is *metaphysical*.

The means of communication is *physical*.

Metaphysical is unlimited and generalizable independent of time-space-sizing.

Physical is limited, experienceable, and is always special case time-space-sized.

Metaphysical is unweighable, imponderable, and cannot move an electromagnetically or mass-attracted, levered needle.

Physical is always apprehensible by an instrument's needle leverage actuated by weight, pressure, heat, or electromagnetics.

Metaphysical discoveries clarify ever more comprehensively, inclusively, and are more economically communicable in their progressive description of the eternally changeless, and the rate of the more economic restatability continually accelerates.

Physical events are ever transforming and ever more acceleratingly entropic.

Humans are *metaphysical*. You and I are awareness, which is the identity of the weightless life.

The *physical,* automatedly rebuilding, information-gathering device we sensorially apprehend as our anatomy, employed by metaphysical mind, consists entirely of inanimate atoms and is therefore entirely physical.

Conceptioning is *metaphysical*.

Sensing is *physical,* and the sensed is physical and always inherently special case.

Waves are *metaphysical* pattern integrities.

Metaphysical pattern integrity waves articulate as *physical* phenomena such as water, air, or electromagnetic fields, and thus communicate their nonsensorially apprehensible presence through the displacement of the sensibly detectable *physical* phenomena.

Symmetry is *metaphysical*.

Asymmetry is *physical*.

Equilibrium is metaphysical.

Disequilibrium is physical.

Conceptuality is *metaphysical* and weightless. Reality is metaphysically conceptualized information transmitted only through physical senses.

Realizations are special case *physical*, brain-sensed phenomena.

The *metaphysical* evolution of human awareness slows as it approaches the omniintegrated verity— physically unattainable by the only-physically-sensing, anatomical machine designed specifically only for limited operation with the highly specialized local Universe conditions of the Earthian biosphere.

Physical systems alone accelerate as they unravel entropically, ever approaching the speed of a noninterfered-with electromagnetic, spherically expansive wave (186,000 mps.)^2

The generalized conceptions of *metaphysical* evolution tend ever to decelerate, simplify, consolidate and ultimately unify.

The special case transformings of physical evolution tend ever to accelerate, differentiate, and multiply.

Generalization is *metaphysical:* mind function. Design is generalized metaphysical conceptioning.

Tools, artifacts, and all humanly contrived extracorporeal facilities designed by mind are always special-case, brain-processed, physically sensible phenomena.

Theoretical and applied science is conceptually *metaphysical*.

Applied science always results in special-case, brain-sensible, limited-longevity phenomena.

Metaphysically operative mind cannot design a generalized tool of unlimited and eternal capability, which unlimited and eternal capability is manifest only in purely metaphysical, weightless principles. Principles have no beginning-ending or other temporal limitations. Principles are truths.

We can invent only *physical*. The human mind, translating the generalized principles only through special-case, individual, brain-operated anatomical tools, can realize only phenomena of special case, limited-capacity capability and durability.

326.50 Metaphysical and Physical: Cross-references

400.00   System

 *Titles in parentheses will be found in *Synergetics 1.*

400.01 Definition: System

400.55 Polyhedra: Polyhedra consist only of polyhedra. Polyhedra are always pro tem constellations of polyhedra. Polyhedra are defined only by polyhedra—and only by a minimum of four polyhedra.

400.56 All systems are polyhedra: All polyhedra are systems.

400.57 The observed or tuned-in polyhedra whose plurality of corners, faces, and edges and frequency of subdividing are tunably discernible to the tuning-in station (the observer) consist of corners that are infra-threshold-tunable polyhedra and whose faces or openings are ultra-threshold tunables.

400.65 Summary: Six Positive and Negative Motions

400.651 Energetic Functions: Twoness is synergetic. The twoness of inherent otherness of awareness is synergetic. Twoness inherently induces the dynamic quality of oscillatory propagation unpredicted by one-integer-plus-one-integer as empty set. Synergetic twoness and the primitive topological complexity of minimum systems themselves and the presently-non-tuned-in but always inherently coexisting macro-micro otherness inherently produces the ever-interaccommodative, intertransforming, ceaseless *restlessness,* an intercomplementary characteristic inherent in energetic functions.

400.652 Resultants of pluralities of copotentials of initial freedoms of unique, reciprocally displacing event patterning, of necessity, occasion fundamental conversion of Euler's empty integer *plus twoness* into the synergetic—or unpredicted—inherent nuclear cohesion.

400.653 Structural Functions: Structural functions are summarized at Sec. 610.10. (Compare also Sec. *502.05.*)

400.654 **Summary:** There are six basic motions in Universe. All of them are positive and negative: active and passive. The first five are individually experienceable and popularly familiar; the last—precession—is less popularly familiar:

— *Spin:* Spinning is horizontal or vertical axial rotation. Spinnability has to be totally independent of the system's local surface transformations.

— *Orbit:* No path of travel may be 180-degree linear in a multibodied, gravity-cohered, omnimotional Universe. The initial reality of all travel is orbital as a composite resultant of all tensive restraints. As the Sun's pull on the Earth produces orbiting, orbiting electrons produce directional field pulls. As 99.99 percent of the bodies in motion in physical Universe are operating orbitally, orbiting must be thought of as normal. (Spinning and orbiting together is dancing.) Orbits are regenerative feedback circuits.

— *Inside-out:* Anything with a hole in it turns inside-out. The tetrahedron turns inside-out through any of its four space-window faces. Kissing humans turn partially inside-out as they "pucker" their lips.

— *Expansion-contraction:* Expansion is radiant divergence, and contraction is gravitational convergence.

— *Torque:* Torque and countertorque are local twists in which one pole spins right and the other pole spins left.

— *Precession:* Precession is the effect of bodies in motion on other bodies in motion in interrelationship patterns of other than 180 degrees. Reactions and resultants are precessional, bringing about orbits and not straight lines. For instance, the effect of the Sun traveling around our galaxy center at 700,000 miles per hour upon the Earth cotraveling with the Sun; the precessional effect of gravity between the two is an effect at 90 degrees to the Sun pull, which makes the Earth both spin and orbit around the Sun.

400.66 Basic Motions and Degrees of Freedom

400.661 There are six positive and six negative exercises of the motion freedoms (see Sec. *400.654*), but the freedoms themselves come from the fact that the minimum structural system in Universe consists of six vectors: the tetrahedron. The tetrahedron has a minimum of six edges.

400.662 The tetrahedron is a fourfold symmetry: As the minimum something it has four faces of symmetry and four vertexes of symmetry and six edge vectors providing the minimum degrees of freedom. Any one face has three edges, and the total of six edge vectors in the structure defines the set of events. With every turn to play in Universe we always get six moves: So the minimum something is the minimum play. (Compare Sec. 537.10, Fig. 608.01, and Sec. 825.27.)

400.663   The minimum six vectors can be interarrayed at all kinds of angles provided they all add to 720 degrees—the variable interangling provides the degrees of freedom. We find in topology that all minimum systems have vertexes, faces, and edges and that the number of edges in Universe is always evenly divisible by six. These are the six active and passive degrees of freedom, and they are always there. They do not operate in a plane; they are omnidirectionally interarranged.

400.664   The six basic motions are complex consequences of the six degrees of freedom. If you want to have an instrument held in position in respect to any cosmic body such as Earth, it will take exactly six restraints: no more, no less. If we have only five restraints, then the tetrahedron will change its shape. Shape requires six restraints. Exactly six systemic interrestraints produce structure. Six restraints are essential to structure and to pattern stability.

400.665   Anything that holds its shape has a minimum of six positive and negative integral restraints so that the system itself can spin or the system itself can orbit. The system itself can inside-out. These are system behaviors, and the six degrees of restraint are integral.

400.666   The six basic integral system cosmic motions have six internal structure-producing restraints and six external unique motion-producing restraints. (If a system is frozen as part of a larger system, it will have to lose one of its restraints.) Internally and externally there are 12 alternate optimally equieconomical degrees of cosmic freedom, all of which must be coped with to produce cosmic order.

400.70   Visibility and Invisibility of Systems

400.71   There are six uniquely differentiable components of all systems and of all thoughts: (1) insideness; (2) outsideness; and (3) (4) (5) (6) the four star events (see Sec. 510) that do the systemic defining of the insideness and the outsideness, which inadvertently display:

—six interrelationships, which in turn inadvertently define:
—four triangle windows, which, again inadvertently, reveal the untuned-in programs potentially occurring between the six most economical omniinterrelationships whose triangular edge-defining lines inadvertently exclude the macro-outsideness and definingly include the micro-insideness.

400.72   Therefore there are six parts of Universe: four of them are always humanly conceptualizable and always define the successively considerable domains of human thought, while the other two of the six cosmic parts are always untuned-in, ergo, invisible; i.e., the ultramacrotunable otherness and the inframicrotunable otherness.

400.73   The visibility of conceptuality is always so preoccupying of human senses and minds as to render spontaneously forgettable our only-progressively-acquired knowledge of the vast ranges of the known-to-exist but nonsimultaneously tunable—ergo, *invisible*—otherness of Scenario Universe.

401.08   **Tetherball:** In the "me" ball in Universe 12 structural restraints are necessary to eliminate all the degrees of freedom because all the initial four restraints are connected to the surface of the "me" sphere and not to its center. The four points of tangency describe a square, and they permit local twist and torque because a square is unstable. So each tension has to be replaced by three tension restraints to produce a tensegrity structure within which the "me" ball may be omninonredundantly immobilized.

410.00   Closest Packing of Spheres

415.17   **Nucleated Cube: The "External" Octahedron:** The minimum allspace-filling nuclear cube is formed by adding eight Eighth-Octahedra to the eight triangular facets of the nucleated vector equilibrium of tetravolume-20, with a total tetravolume involvement of 4 + 20 = 24 quanta modules. This produces a cubical nuclear involvement domain (see Sec. *1006.30*) of tetravolume-24: 24 × 24 = 576 quanta modules. (See Sec. 463.05 and Figs. *415.17A–F.*)

415.171   The nuclear cube and its six neighboring counterparts are the volumetrically maximum members of the primitive hierarchy of concentric, symmetric, pre-time-size, subfrequency-generalized, polyhedral nuclear domains of synergetic-energetic geometry.

415.172   The construction of the first nuclear cube in effect restores the vector-equilibrium truncations. The minimum to be composited from closest-packed unit radius squares has 55 balls in the vector equilibrium. The first nucleated cube has 63 balls in the total aggregation.

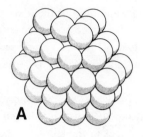

A

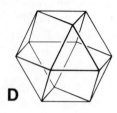

D

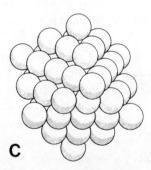

B

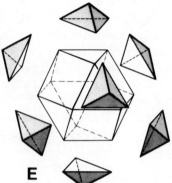

E

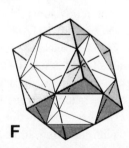

C

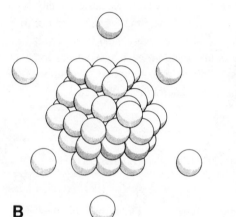

F

Fig. *415.17 Nucleated Cube: The "External" Octahedron: ABC* show that eight additional closest-packed spheres are required to form the minimum allspace-filling nuclear cube to augment the nuclear vector equilibrium. *DEF* show the eight Eighth-Octa required to complete the polyhedral transformation. (Compare Fig. *1006.32.*)

419.10 Nuclear Domain and Elementality

419.11   Where the primitive polyhedron considered is the vector equilibrium, the closest-packed-sphere-shell growth rate is governed by the formula $10F^2 + 2$ (Sec. 222). Where the most primitive polyhedron is the tetrahedron, the growth rate is governed by the formula $2F^2 + 2$; in the cases of the octahedron and the cube see Sec. 223.21. The formula is reliably predictable in the identification of the chemical elements and their respective neutron inventories for each shell. The identifications are related exclusively to the unique nuclear domain pattern involvements.

419.12   When a new nucleus becomes completely surrounded by two layers, then the exclusively unique pattern surroundment of the first nucleus is terminated. Thereafter, at three enclosure levels or more, the initial nucleus is no longer the unique nucleus. The word *elemental* relates to the original unique patterning around any one nucleus of closest-packed spheres. When we get beyond the original unique patterning, we find the patternings repeating themselves, and we enter into the more complex structurings of the molecular world.

419.13   Uranium-92 is the limit case of what we call *inherently self-regenerative chemical elements*. Beyond these we get into demonstrations of non-self-regenerative elements with the split-second life of Negative Universe. These demonstrations are similar to having a rubber ball with a hole in its skin and stretching that hole's rubber outwardly around the hole until we can see the markings on the inner skin that correspond to markings on the outer skin—but when we release the ball, the momentarily outwardly displayed markings on the inside will quickly resume their internal positions.

419.14   As we see in Sec. 624, the inside-outing of Universe occurs only at the tetrahedral level. In the nucleated, tetrahedral, closest-packed-sphere-shell growth rates the outward layer sphere count increases as frequency to the second power *times two plus two*—with the outer layer also always doubled in value.

419.20 Elemental Identification of First and Second Shell Layers

419.21   The outer layer of the vector equilibrium aggregates always equals the shell wave frequencies to the second power times 10 plus two. The sum of all the layers equals the number of neutrons of the elements, and the outer layer is always complemented by an equal number of active nucleons, which, if added to the sum of the previously encompassed neutron layer, equals the isotope number.

419.22 The omnidirectional closest packing of spheres in all six symmetrical conformations of the primitive hierarchy of polyhedra probably provides models for all the chemical elements in a hierarchy independent of size in which the sum of the spheres in all the layers and the nuclear sphere equals the most prominent number of neutrons, and the number in the outer layer alone equals the number of protons of each atom. In the VE symmetry of layer growth the sum of the spheres is one and the outer layer is one: the initial sphere represents the element hydrogen, with the atomic number 1, having one neutron and one proton. The second VE assembly layer, magnesium, with the atomic number 12, has 12 protons and 24 neutrons. The third layer, molybdenum, with the atomic number 42, has 42 protons and a majority of 54 neutrons. The fourth layer, uranium, with the atomic number 92, has 92 protons and an isotopal majority of 146 neutrons. (Compare Secs. *986.770* and *1052.32*.)

419.23 Table: Number of Protons and Neutrons in Magnesium, Molybdenum, and Uranium

Element	Protons		Neutrons		Abundance
Hydrogen	1	+	1	= 2	
Magnesium	12	+	12	= 24	78.6 %
	12	+	13	= 25	10.11
	12	+	14	= 26	11.29
Molybdenum	42	+	52	= 94	9.12
	42	+	53	= 95	15.7
	42	+	54	= 96	16.5
	42	+	55	= 97	9.45
	42	+	56	= 98	23.75
Uranium	92	+	142	= 234	0.0051
	92	+	143	= 235	0.71
	92	+	146	= 238	99.28

Vector Equilibrium Shell Growth Rate: $10 F^2 + 2$

Zero Frequency	$1 + 1 = 2$
Initial Frequency	$12 \times 2 = 24$
Frequency^2	$42 + 42 + 12 = 96$
Frequency^3	$92 + 92 + 42 + 12 = 238$

419.30 **Closest-sphere-packing Analogy to Atomic Structure:** In 1978 Philip Blackmarr, a student of synergetics from Pasadena, proposed a novel analogy of closest-sphere-packing geometry to electron-proton-neutron interrelationships and atomic structure. He took note of the following four facts;

(1) In the closest packing of unit radius spheres each spheric and interspheric space domain is equally and symmetrically embraced by allspace-filling rhombic dodecahedra. (Sec. 426.20.)

(2) The concentrically embracing shells of the vector equilibrium have a successive population growth rate of $10F^2 + 2$, resulting in 12 spheres in the first layer, 42 in the second, 92 in the third, and 162 in the fourth. (See Chart 415.03.)

(3) In the concentric successive shells of closest-packed spheres a new nucleus does not appear until the fifth frequency—the fifth shell layer. (Secs. 414 and 415.30.)

(4) The ratio of the electron mass to the proton mass is 1 : 1836. (Sec. 433.02.)

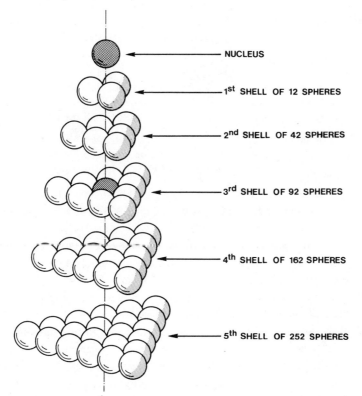

NUCLEUS

1st SHELL OF 12 SPHERES

2nd SHELL OF 42 SPHERES

3rd SHELL OF 92 SPHERES

4th SHELL OF 162 SPHERES

5th SHELL OF 252 SPHERES

Fig. *419.30 Realized Nucleus Appears at Fifth Shell Layer:* In concentric closest packing of successive shell layers potential nuclei appear at the third shell layer, but they are not realized until surrounded by two shells at the fifth layer.

Bearing those four facts in mind Blackmarr employed a symmetrical four-shell aggregate of 308 rhombic dodecahedra to represent the total allspace-filling domains of the 308 spheres of the maximum limit nuclear domain. He then intuitively divided the number 1836 by 6, the latter being the volume of the rhombic dodecahedron in respect to the volume of the tetrahedron as one. The number $1836/6 = 306$ becomes significant as it represents the total number of neutron spheric domains in the vector equilibrium concentric shell packing—*less* the number *two* of their integral number to serve as poles of the axis of spin of the symmetrical system. The spheres in the successive shell layers—12, 42, 92, 162—add up to 308; $308 - 2 = 306$. (Compare Sec. 418.)

419.31   Blackmarr then hypothetically identified the electron as the volume of the unit-vector-edge tetrahedron as ratioed to the volume of the four-frequency vector equilibrium, representing a symmetrical and "solid" agglomeration of 308 rhombic dodecahedra (with two of the outer-layer rhombic dodecahedra assigned to serve as the symmetrically opposite poles of the system's axis of spin), or of 308 unit-radius spheres and their interspaces. This evidences that the space filled by the 308 rhombic dodecahedra is the maximum, cosmic-limit, unit-vector, symmetrical polyhedral space occupiable by a single nucleus.

419.32

| The volume of the ELECTRON (which is that of one regular vector-edged negative tetrahedron) | The volume of the rhombic-dodecahedron-composed four-frequency VECTOR EQUILIBRIUM | = | $\dfrac{1}{1836}$ |
| The volume of the POSITRON (which is that of one regular vector-edged positive tetrahedron) | The volume of the rhombic-dodecahedron-composed four-frequency VECTOR EQUILIBRIUM | = | $\dfrac{1}{1836}$ |

419.33   Here is an elegant realization that two spheres of the outer-layer spheres (or rhombic dodecahedra) of the symmetrical system have to serve as the polar axis of the system spin. (See Secs. 223 and *1044*.)

419.34   Thus by experimental evidence we may identify the electron with the volume of the regular, unit-vector-radius-edge tetrahedron, the simplest symmetrical structural system in Universe. We may further identify the *electron tetrahedra* with the maximum possible symmetrical aggregate of concentrically-packed, unit-radius spheres symmetrically surrounding a single nucleus—there being 12 new potential nuclei appearing in the three-frequency shell of 92 spheres, which three-frequency shell, when surroundingly embraced by the four-frequency shell of 162 spheres, buries the 12 candidate new nuclei only one shell deep, whereas qualifying as full-fledged nuclei in their own right requires two shells all around each, which 12, newborn nuclei event calls for the fifth-frequency shell of 252 spheres.

419.35   Together with the closest-packed spheres of the outer layer of the icosahedron of frequencies 1 and 4 (and of the outer layers of the closest-packed spheres of the one—and only one—nucleus-embracing, symmetrically and closest-packed, unit-radius sphere aggregates in the form of the octahedron, rhombic dodecahedron, rhombic triacontahedron, and enenicontahedron) as well as the already identified four-frequency vector equilibrium, the rhombic dodecahedron is the maximum nuclear domain within which the pre-time-size set of chemical-element-forming atoms' proton-neutron-and-electron interrelationship events can and may occur.

419.36 All of the foregoing is to say that the size of one spinnable proton consisting of 308 rhombic dodeca closest packed in the symmetrical form of the four-frequency vector equilibrium is 1836 times the size of one prime, pre-time-size, prefrequency, unit-vector-edge tetrahedron or of one electron. Multiplication only by division means that the time-size frequencies of the elements (other than hydrogen) occur as various concentric-shell symmetry phases of the single-nucleus-embracing, symmetrically closest-packed, single-nucleus aggregates in the multiconcentric-layered forms of the vector equilibrium, tetrahedron, octahedron, rhombic dodecahedron, rhombic triacontahedron, and cube.

419.37 Synergetics has long associated the electron with the icosahedron. Icosahedra cannot accommodate concentric shells; they occur as single-layer shells of closest-packed, unit-radius spheres. Since the *proton* has only the outer shell count, it may be identified with the icosa phase by having the total volume of the rhombic-dodecahedron-composed four-frequency vector equilibrium transformed from the 306 (non-axial) *nucleon* rhombic dodecahedron into each of the closest-packed, single-layer icosahedra shells as an emitted wave entity. The rhombic dodecahedron *neutrons* are packed into concentric layers of the vector equilibria to produce the various isotopes. For example:

$$\text{VE } f^1 = 12 \text{ neutrons}$$
$$\text{VE } f^2 = 42 \quad ''$$
$$\text{VE } f^3 = \underline{92 \quad ''}$$
$$146 \text{ neutrons in Uranium}$$
$$\text{Icosa } f^3 = 92 \text{ protons}$$
$$(238 \text{ nucleons in Uranium})$$
$$92 \text{ Tetra} = 92 \text{ electrons in Uranium}$$

420.00 Isotropic Vector Matrix

421.031 Function of Nucleus in Isotropic Vector Matrix: Every vector has two ends both of which join with other vectors to produce both structural systems and total cosmic integrity of regeneration. Every vector unites two ends.

421.20 Ideal Vectorial Geometry of Nucleated Systems

421.21 It is experientially suggested that the structural interpatterning principles apparently governing all atomic associability behaviors are characterized by triangular and tetrahedral accommodation, wherein the tetrahedron's six positive and six· negative vectorial edge forces match a total of 12 universal degrees of freedom. The tetrahedron's exclusively edge-congruent-agglomeratability around any one nuclear point produces the vector equilibrium. These structural, pattern-governing, conceptualizable principles in turn govern all eternally regenerative design evolution, including the complex patterning of potential, symmetrically and asymmetrically limited, pulsative regenerations, only in respect to all of which are ideas conceivable. These patternings are experientially manifest in synergetics' closed-system topological hierarchy through which we can explore the ramifications of the idealistic vectorial geometry characteristics of inherently nucleated systems and their experientially demonstrable properties. (For possible relevance to the periodic table of the elements see Sec. 955.30.)

426.04 Spherics: Employing the rhombic dodecahedron as the hub at the vector crossings of the octet truss (the isotropic vector matrix) provides unique economic, technical, and geometric advantages: its 12 facets represent the six pairs of planes perpendicular to the six degrees of freedom. (See Sec. 537.10.) Its 12 diamond faces also provide the even-numbered means of allowing the vectors to skew-weave around the nucleus at critical-proximity distances without touching the nucleus or one another. Because two or more lines cannot go through the same point at the same time, this function of the rhombic dodecahedron's hub makes all the difference between regenerative success or failure of Universe. (See Figs. 955.52 and *426.04*.)

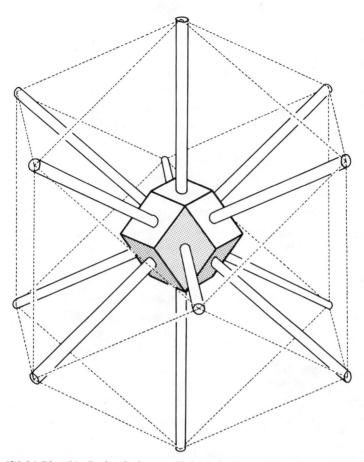

Fig. *426.04 Rhombic Dodecahedron as Hub at the Vector Crossings within the Isotropic Vector Matrix*

440.00   Vector Equilibrium as Zero Model

440.09   **Zerophase:** Being the zerophase of energy the vector equilibrium is inherently invisible and non-empirically-discoverable, which accounts for its having been for so long unrecognized as the spontaneous equilibrious model. As specialists, scientists seek only the somethings. The vector equilibrium is the only model of nonbeing zero-inflection at the nonmoment of omniintertransformabilities, where anything can happen and must happen single-atomically within and multiatomically without. Specializing science, seeking only somethings, inherently overlooked the nonthing vector equilibrium. Vector equilibria in isotropic vector matrixes produce the discontinuity of particles, while the vector-weaving around the VE nuclei produce the continuity of wave phenomena.

440.10   The vector equilibrium is the most abstract of all the always-and-only abstract scientific generalizations, for it is the heart of all interrelationships existing between—and not in or of—any of all the empirically apprehended intertransforms of the ever-and-everywhere intertransforming Scenario Universe. The vector equilibrium is the zerophase—ergo, inexpressible—interrelationship of all Universe events.

440.11   The word *vacuum* relates specifically to gaseous phenomena. Nature's abhorrence of a vacuum induces physical relationships only in respect to the gaseous states. The vector equilibrium is the nothingness phase of all states of physical Universe: it is the generalization of nothingness, within which generalization the absolute vacuum is a special case event in the gaseous state. The vector equilibrium is such a physically abhorred nonstate as to be the eternal self-starter—ergo, the eternal re-self-starter, ever regenerating the off-zero perturbations, oscillations, and all the wave propagation of all humanly experienceable physical and metaphysical phenomena.

440.12   The sense-coordinating brain of each and every human, like sound or light, has a limit speed of apprehending. There is no instant cerebral cognition. These apprehension lags automatically impose off-center human cognition, which occasions the sense of time in a timeless eternity. The sense of time occasions the conception of life and serial experience. The inherently invisible vector equilibrium self-starters life and ever regenerates life.

441.021   **Zerovolume Tetrahedron:** The zerovolume phenomenon altogether avoids the operationally prohibited concept of a plurality of lines going through the same point at the same time. In the zerovolume tetrahedron each of the four great circles is folded into a "bow tie" pair of double-bonded tetra, each of which is double-bonded to the three others. The eight vertexes of the eight tetrahedra at each of their four open corners only seemingly pass through each other, whereas each converges to the other and turns around divergently outward at 60 degrees, thus producing a nucleus with an energy potential of eight but presenting the topologically visual aspect and enumeration of only one. (See Secs. 623.20, *1033.020* and *1053.810.*)

460.00   Jitterbug: Symmetrical Contraction of Vector Equilibrium

461.00   Recapitulation: Polyhedral Progression in Jitterbug

461.10 **Deceptiveness of Topology:** *Quanta Loss By Congruence:* (See poster, color plate 4.) The vector equilibrium jitterbug provides the articulative model for demonstrating the always omnisymmetrical, divergently expanding or convergently contracting intertransformability of the entire primitive polyhedral hierarchy, *structuring-as-you-go,* in an omnitriangularly oriented evolution.

461.11 As we explore the interbonding (valencing) of the evolving structural components, we soon discover that the universal interjoining of systems—and their foldability—permit their angularly hinged convergence into congruence of vertexes (single-bonding), or congruence of vectors (double-bonding), or congruence of faces (triple-bonding), or volumetric congruence (quadrivalent), but each of the multicongruences appears as only one vertex or one edge or one face aspect. The Eulerean topological accounting as presently practiced—innocent of the inherent synergetical hierarchy of intertransformability—accounts each of these multicongruent topological aspects as consisting of only one such aspect. This misaccounting has prevented the physicists and chemists from conceptual identification of their data with synergetics' disclosure of nature's comprehensively rational intercoordinate mathematical system.

461.12 Only the topological analysis of synergetics can account for all the multicongruent—two-, three-, fourfold—topological aspects by accounting for the initial tetravolume inventories of the comprehensive rhombic dodecahedron and the vector equilibrium. The rhombic dodecahedron has an initial tetravolume of 48, and the vector equilibrium has an inherent tetravolume of 20. Their respective initial or primitive inventories of vertexes, vectors, and faces are always present (though often imperceptibly so) at all stages in nature's comprehensive 48→1 convergence transformation.

461.13 Although superficially the tetrahedron seems to have only six vectors, we witness in the jitterbug transformation that it has in fact 24. (See poster 4 and Fig. 461.08.) The sizeless, primitive tetrahedron—conceptual independent of size—is quadrivalent, inherently having eight potential alternate

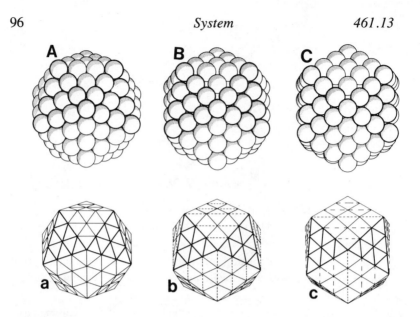

Fig. *466.00 Energy-valve Functions of Closest Sphere Packing:* This series illustrates the skew-transformation of the 92-ball icosahedral aggregate to a vector equilibrium conformation and its return to the icosahedral state.

Figs. 466A–G illustrate closest-sphere-packing transformations.

Figs. 466a–g illustrate polyhedral resultants.

ways of turning itself inside out: four passive and four active, meaning that four positive and four negative tetrahedra are congruent.

461.14   Only by recognizing the deceptiveness of Eulerean topology can synergetics account for the primitive total inventories of all aspects and thus conceptually demonstrate and prove the validity of Boltzmann's concepts as well as those of all quantum phenomena. Synergetics mathematical accounting conceptually interlinks the operational data of physics and chemistry and their complex associabilities manifest in such disciplines as geology, biology, and others.

465.40   Triangular-cammed, In-out-and-around Jitterbug Model (Short Title)

465.41   The four axes of the vector equilibrium provide the four-dimensionally articulatable model of motion freedoms unimpeded by other motions of either contiguous or remote systems of Universe while copermitting the concurrently articulating both omnidirectional wave propagation and gravita-

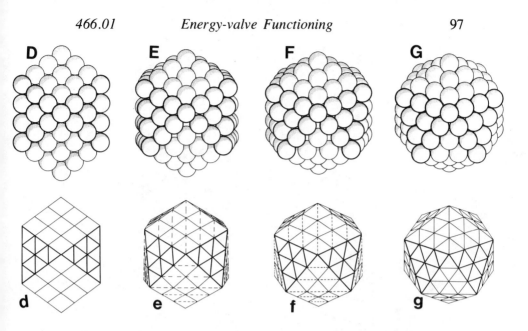

tionally convergent embracement. We can also call it by the short title: triangular-cammed, in-out-and-around jitterbug model. (See Fig. 465.01.)

465.42 The "opposite" of the engineers' equal-and-opposite action and reaction is a strictly 180-degree linear conceptioning, conceived on a planar drawing. Macro is not opposite to micro: these are opposed, inward-and-outward, explosive-contractive, intertransformative accommodations such as those displayed by the eight-triangular-cammed, perimeter-tangent, contact-driven, involuting-evoluting, rubber doughnut jitterbug. In such a model macro and micro are not planarly opposed: they are the poles of inward-outward, omnidirectional, locally vertexing considerations of experience. (See Fig. 465.10.)

466.00   Energy-valve Functioning of Outer Shell of Nuclear Domains

466.01. An earlier version of Fig. *466.01* was first published by the author in 1944: it illustrates the energy-valving aspects of the closest-packed spheres interfunctionings as they occur within the three-frequency, 92-ball outer layer of the vector equilibrium as it "jitterbuggingly" skew-transforms into the icosahedral state, then returns to the vector equilibrium state, passes

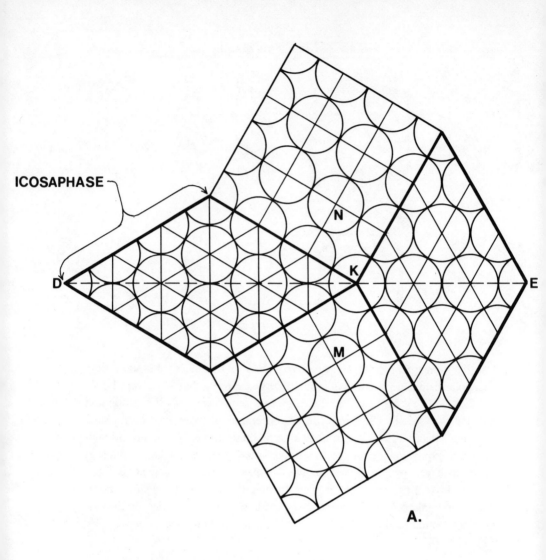

ICOSAPHASE

D ◀— — — — — — — — — — — — — — — — — — — ▶ E

N

K

M

A.

Fig. *466.01 Reciprocal Motion of Nine Internal Spheres Propagates Wave by Diago-*
nal Elongation: (The original version of this drawing was copyrighted by R. Buckminster Fuller in 1944.) This is a planar representation of the closest-packed spheres in
the outer layer as they skew-transform between the icosahedral and vector equilibrium
phases.

A. Apex sphere *K* surrounded by two 16-ball grids *M* and *N*, and by short-axis
   diamond *E* and long-axis diamond *D*.

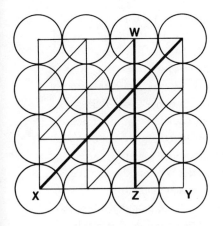

B.

C.

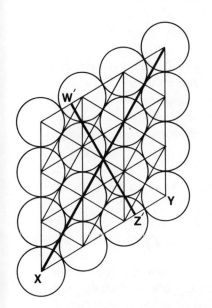

D.

E.

B. The 90-degree alignment of the 16 balls of any one of the six square faces of the vector equilibrium.

C. Plan view of the closest-sphere-packing aspects of any one of the vector equilibrium's four pairs of nuclear tetrahedra as they begin to torque in the jitterbug process.

D. Short-axis diamond.

E. Long-axis diamond.

through, and again transforms to the alternately skewed icosahedral state—repeat and repeat.

466.02   The 90-degree interalignment of the 16 balls of any one of the six square faces of the vector equilibrium (Fig. B) is inherently unstable. The 16 balls resolve their instability by forming any one of two alternate types of most closely packed diamonds (Figs. D and E) with either a short cross axis or a long diagonal axis. Both types are equiedged, equiarea, and most densely packed, and they occupy less area than their equiedged square counterparts. This is quickly evidenced geometrically because both the square (Fig. B) and the diamond (Fig. D) have the same-length base edge *XY,* but the altitude *WZ* of the square is greater than the altitude *WZ* of the diamond.

466.03   As displayed in a planar array, Fig. A, there is an apex sphere *K* surroundingly shared by the innermost corners (vertexes) of two square-faced, 16-ball grids, *M* and *N,* as well as by the two diamonds—the short-axis diamond E and the long-axis diamond D.

466.04   The apex sphere *K*'s neighboring spheres are uncomfortable because *K* is surrounded by seven spheres and not six. Only six can closest pack around one in any given plane. One of the two adjacent spheres *M* or *N* from the two square-faced grids will get pushed in, and the other one will be pushed out, depending upon which way the vector-equilibrium-to-icosahedron jitterbug transformation is rotating around apex sphere *K.* The "in-and-out" pumping of spheres *M* and *N* acts as an energy-propagating valve.

466.05   Fig. C is a plan view of the closest-sphere-packing manifestation of any one of the vector equilibrium's four pairs of nuclear tetrahedra as they commence to torque in the jitterbug process. An isometric sketch of this net 39-ball aggregation is given at Fig. 466.31. Note that this torqued pair of nuclear tetrahedra employs three of the vector equilibrium's six axes. The two unengaged axes of the equator are starved and inoperative.

466.10   High-frequency Sphericity Approaches Flatness

466.11   Where we have six balls in a planar array closest packed around one nucleus, we produce six top and six bottom concave tetrahedral valleys surrounding the nucleus ball. We will call the top set of valleys the northern set and the bottom set the southern set. Despite there being six northern valleys we find that we can nest only three close-packed (triangulated) balls in the valleys. This is because we find that the balls nesting on top of the valleys occupy twice as much planar area as that afforded by the six tetrahedral valleys. Three balls can rest together on the top in omni-close-packed tangency with one another and with the seven balls below them; and three balls can similarly rest omniintertangentially in the bottom valleys as their top and bottom points of tangency bridge exactly across the unoccupied valleys, allowing room for no other spheres. This produces the symmetrical nuclear vector equilibrium of 12 closest-packed spheres around one. (See Fig. *466.13A*.)

466.12   The three balls on the top can be lifted as a triangular group and rotated 60 degrees in a plane parallel to the seven balls of the hexagonal equatorial set below them; this triangular group can be then set into the three previously vacant and bridged-over valleys. As this occurs, we have the same 12 spheres closest packed around one with an overall arrangement with the two triangular sets of three on the top, three on the bottom, and six around the equator. The top and the bottom triangular sets act as poles of the system, which—as with all systems—has inherent free spinnability. In both of the two alternate valley occupations the northern polar triangle is surrounded alternately by three squares and three triangles, reading alternately—triangle, square, triangle, square, triangle, square. (See Fig. *466.13B*.)

466.13   In one polar triangular valley occupation the squares of the northern hemisphere will be adjacent to the triangles of the southern hemisphere. This is the vector-equilibrium condition. In the alternate valley nesting position at the equator the equatorial edges of the squares of the northern hemisphere will abut the squares of the southern hemisphere, and the triangles of the northern hemisphere will abut those of the southern, producing a polarized symmetry condition. In the vector-equilibrium condition we have always and everywhere the triangle-and-square abutments, which produces a four-dimensional symmetry system. (See Sec. 442 and Fig. *466.13C*.)

466.14   There is then a duality of conditions of the same 12 nucleus-surrounding first omni-inter-closest-packed layer: we have both a polarized symmetry phase and an equilibrious symmetry phase. Under these alternate conditions we have one of those opportunities of physical Universe to develop a pulsative alternation of interpatterning realizations, whereby the alternations in its equilibrium phase do not activate energy, while its polarized phase does activate energetic proclivities. The equilibrious phase has no associative proclivities, while the polarized phase has associative proclivities. In the polarized phase we have repulsion at one end and attraction at the other: potential switchings on and off of energetic physical Universe. (See Figure *466.13D*.)

466.15   When modular frequency enters into the alternately vector equilibrium⟷polarized conformations, the vertexes of the multifrequenced nuclear system are occupied by uniradius spheres, whereat it is evidenced that the equatorial continuity set of spheres can be claimed either by the northern or southern set of triangles and squares, but they cannot serve both simultaneously. Here again we have alternating conditions—starving or fulfilling—of

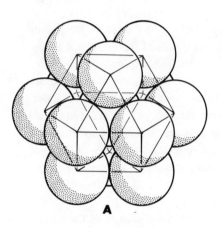
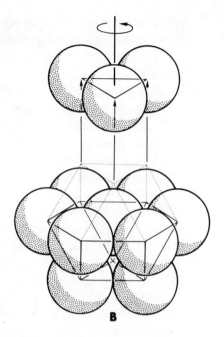

A

B

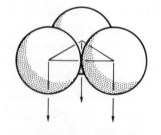
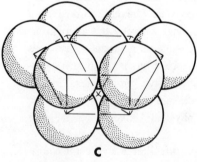
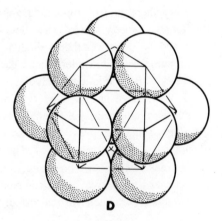

C

D

Fig. 466.13

A. *Twelve Closest-packed Spheres around One:* Symmetrical nuclear vector equilibrium.

B. *Twelve Closest-packed Spheres around One:* Rotation of top triangular group.

northern and southern himispheres matching or nonmatching triangles and squares, with the central equilibrium condition having a large plurality of alternately realizable behaviors under variously modified conditions affected further as frequency increases the numbers of edge-vertex-occupying spheres.

466.16   As the frequencies of vector equilibria or icosahedra increase, the relative size of the occupied arcs of the great circles involved become of ever lesser magnitude. At a high frequency of larger spheres—for example, planet Earth—the conditions of patterning around the 12 external vertexes of the vector equilibria or icosahedra appear to be approximately flat, in contrast to the sharp concavity/convexity of the nonfrequenced convergence of the four planes around the corners of the vector equilibrium and the convergence of the five planes around the corners of the icosahedron.

466.17   In very-high-frequency nuclear systems the approach to flatness from the four planes to five planes tends to induce a 360-degreeness of the sums of the angles around the critical 12 vertexes—in contrast to the 300-degree condition existing in both the unfrequenced vector equilibrium and icosahedron. That is what Fig. *466.01* is all about.

466.18   In Figs. *466.01* and *466.41* there is introduced an additional 60-degree equilateral triangle, in surroundment of every directly-nuclear-emanating vertex K. The 12 vector-equilibrium K vertexes are always in direct linear relationship with the system nucleus (see Sec. 414). The additional degrees of angle produced by the high-frequency local flattening around K vertexes introduces a disturbance-full exterior shell condition that occasions energetic consequences of a centrifugal character.

466.20 Centrifugal Forces

466.21   As we get into ultra-ultra-high-frequency, and as we get to greater and greater sphericity, by virtue of the inherent spin, we can account for the vector equilibrium becoming the sphere of lesser radius, becoming the sphere of approximately tetravolume 5, while the relative flatness around the critical K vertexes relates to the centrifugal forces involved.

466.22   People think of centrifugal force as picturable by arrows expelled radially (perpendicularly) outward. But in fact centrifugal force operates as a

---

C. *Twelve Closest-packed Spheres around One:* Alternate nestability in polar triangular valley.

D. *Twelve Closest-packed Spheres around One:* Alternate polarized symmetry of vector equilibrium.

hammer-thrower's hammer does: it departs from the system tangentially, not radially. Since the outward tangent ends reach ever farther away, there is a net only-indirectly-radial force realized. This common misapprehension of the assumed 180-degreeness of centrifugal forces has greatly misled human thinking and has obscured comprehensions of precession.

466.23   At certain high frequencies the energy displacements tend to occur that do not tend to occur at low- or no-frequency conditions, which brings us into the realm of possibly comprehending the photon-emitting radiation limits of operation within the 92 regenerative chemical elements and the split-second articulatability of transuranium nuclear systems when bombarded with ultra-ultra-high-frequency energy missiles. The lower the frequency, the higher the required bombardment energies.

466.30   Nuclear Tetrahedra Pairs: Closest-sphere-packing Functions

466.31   In Fig. 466.01-C is a plan view of the closest-sphere-packing manifestation of any one of the vector equilibrium's four pairs of nuclear tetrahedra as they commence to torque in the jitterbug process. An isometric sketch of this net 39-ball aggregation is given in Fig. 466.31. Note that this torqued, north-south-pole, axial pair of tetrahedra employs three of the vector equilibrium's six axes. The other three unengaged axes lying in the equator are starved and inoperative—angularly acceleratable independently of the north-south axial motion.

466.32   In Fig. 466.01-C we see the internal picture from the nucleus to the vertexes displaying the hexagonal pattern emerging at F^3.

466.33   There can be only one pair of tetrahedra operative at any one time. The other three pairs of tetrahedra function as standby auxiliaries, as in the triangular-cammed, in-out-and-around, rubber cam model described in Secs. 465.01 and 465.50.

466.34   The active triangular face has to share its vertexes with those of the adjacent square-face grids. This transformation relates to the transformation of the octahedron and the rhombic dodecahedron.

466.35   In the outer layer of 92 balls—two of which are extracted for the axis of spin—there are eight triangular faces. There are four balls in the center of each of the six square faces.

$$6 \times 4 = 24. \quad 92 - 24 = 68. \quad 68/8 = 8^1/_2.$$

We need 20 balls for a pair of complete polar triangles.

$$68 - 20 = 48. \quad 48/8 = 6; \text{ a pair of 6s} = 12.$$

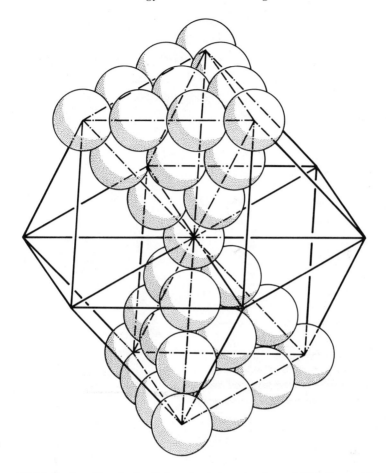

Fig. *466.31 Nuclear Tetrahedra Pairs:* An isometric view of 39-ball aggregate of torqued, north-south pole, axial pair of tetrahedra at nucleus of vector equilibrium.

Thus there are only 12 available where 20 are required for a polar pair. In any one hemisphere the vertex balls *A, B, C* used by a polar triangle make it impossible to form any additional polar units.

466.40 Universal Section of Compound Molecular Matrix

466.41   The illustration at the back-end paper was first published by the author in 1944. It displays the surface shell matrix of an ultra-high-frequency sphere in which a local planar flatness is approached. The vertexes are energy centers, just as in the isotropic vector matrix where 12 exterior corner vertexes of the vector equilibria are always connected in 180-degree tangential direct radial alignment with the nuclear sphere.

466.42   This compound molecular matrix grid provides a model for molecular compounding because it accommodates more than one tetrahedron.

466.43   This matrix is not isotropic. It is anisotropic. It accommodates the domain of a nucleus.

500.00 Conceptuality

500.00   CONCEPTUALITY

501.00   Definition: Conceptuality
  501.131   Omnidirectional Halo
  501.20   Cosmic Timetable of Cyclic Events

502.00   Experience
  502.03   Complexity

503.00   Happenings
  503.031   Starting Point

504.00   Special Case
  504.011   Events
  504.10   Truth as Special Case Realizations

505.00   Pattern
  505.50   Abstract vs Energetic
  505.60   Minimum-Limit Case
  505.70   Topology of Minimum Awareness
  505.80   Background Nothingness

506.00   Knot
  506.40   Yin-Yang

(507.00   Parity)*

(508.00   Number)

(509.00   Considerable Set)

(510.00   Star Events)

(511.00   Energy Event)

(512.00   Locality)

513.00   Vectorial Orientation and Observation
  513.08   Articulation

(514.00   Axis of Reference)

515.00   Frequency
  515.15   Complementary Angles

(516.00   Frequency Modulation)

(517.00   Interference)

(518.00   Critical Proximity)

(519.00   Point)

(520.00   Wavilinearity: Fixes)

---

*Titles in parentheses will be found in *Synergetics 1*.

501.00   Definition: Conceptuality

501.131   Omnidirectional Halo: Every time we have annihilation into eternity, it is not lost in principle; it is only locally lost in the relative inaccuracy that we must have to differentiate and to have awareness.

501.20   Cosmic Timetable of Cyclic Events

501.21   An angle is a convergent-divergent pattern: in terms of human experience it is a directionally focused happening—an event—an eVe-nt—a conVening—interference eVent whose V-angle of conVergence is a linear crossing fiX and, as such, is mentally conceptual and finitely think-about-able independent of the outwardly extendable length of the two lines. Even though the lines diverge outwardly—inferentially toward infinity—the angle formed by their inwardly converging lines is finite.

501.22   By the same logic a triangle or three-angled polygon is not only thinkably conceptual independent of size, but all its lines also terminate in angular convergences. Ergo, the triangle has no loose ends; the triangle is integrally and comprehensively finite. The triangle demonstrates finite conceptuality independent of time-sizing.

501.23   Conceptuality is always referenced to previous experience. The triangle is conceptually independent of time-sizing because it is a generalization of many triangular experiences. All of Euler's generalized topological trio of *vertexes, faces,* and *edges*—his irreducible family of three unique geometrical aspects and their respectively unique constancies of always-and-only-co-occurring relative abundance $V + F = E + 2$—are all conceptually finite and considerable independent of special-case geometric shaping and sizing.

501.24   The relative size of any phenomenon is measurable only in time, for it takes time to measure. The relative magnitudes or microtudes of phenomena are measurable in equal, elapsed-time-per-whole-cycle increments relative to a specified cyclic system. (See Secs. *265.08* through *265.13, 526.23,* and *1033.601.*) The prime time increments and their respective frequency of recurrence within specific cyclic periods as employed by science are those of the only-gravitationally-intercohered galactic and nuclear systems. The celestial galaxies and the atomic nuclei alike are axially and orbitally unrestrained angular momentums of independently operative energy substances. The relative frequencies of the macrocelestial and microatomic systems and their local, individual, integral, inwardly-outwardly-pulsative, intertransforming characteristics have been reliably and informedly measured and interreferenced to constitute the cosmic timetable of cyclic events.

502.00 Experience

502.03 **Complexity:** Experiences are never elementary; ergo, they are always complex. The concept *one* as unity is only available in respect to one-half of twoness. There is no experience without the finite furniture of twoness.

502.04 Thinking is inherently exclusive. Experience, which comes before thinking, is inherently inclusive.

502.05 Experience is always special case but always governed by generalized laws. Among the generalized laws governing experience is the law that there are three directional aspects of all experience: in, out, and around. These directions manifest an inward-outward pulsing and a surface-articulated patterning. The pulsing patterning has six consequences:

(1) the change in size wave frequency;

(2) the plurality of precessionally induced surface vertex-vortex rotations of the expansive-contractive pulsations acting as omninonpolar vertex, alternately winding and unwinding, alternately and symmetrically to take in the slack of the contracting system or unwinding locally to permit symmetrical expansion;

(3) the inherent axial rotation of the whole system;

(4) the inherent orbitally occasioned surface changings occasioned by external forces operating precessionally upon the conceptual system considered;

(5) the precessionally induced inside-outing transformations; and

(6) the local-surface spiral wrinklings caused by axial torque; i.e., when opposite poles rotate in opposite directions (as with the Earth's

clockwise rotation of high-pressure, clear-weather atmospheric motions and the counterclockwise, spirally wrinkled, cloud-cover pattern of the low-pressure stormy weather in the Northern Hemisphere and the oppositely spiraling behaviors in the Southern Hemisphere in respect to the same fair and stormy weather conditions).

503.00   Happenings

503.031   Starting Point: The vector equilibrium nucleus of the isotropic vector matrix is the zero starting point for happenings or nonhappenings: it is the empty theater and empty Universe intercoordinatingly ready to accommodate any act and any audience.

504.00   Special Case

504.011   *Events:* Energy events and structures are always special case (see Sec. 1075).

504.10   Truth as Special Case Realizations

504.11   We may say that thinking about the truth alters truth, but only to the extent of defining it. We may always clarify and redefine the truth by making it more comprehensively considerate and more incisively exquisite. Truth alters truth only by refining the definition. The substance of the sensing and instrumental control of the physical means of communication is always refinable and tends toward the ephemeralization of doing ever more with ever less, but you can never get to the exact, most economical statement of the truth, for the very communication will have ephemeralized to pure metaphysics. Truths are like generalized principles: interaccommodative and non-intercontradictory. Truths are special case realizations of the generalized principles; by these very aspects are they discovered to be truths.

504.12   The experience of life inevitably brings inspirational glimpsing of the cosmic orderly vectors, all of which point convergingly to the absolute. The synergetic integral of all truths—being absolute—is incomprehensible to temporality.

504.13   Truth is special case. Truths tend to articulate generalized principles. All the cosmic generalized principles are omniembracing. Truth, like gravity, is nonlinear; it is omniembracing. Of all the creatures on our planet only humans have demonstrated the ability to discover progressive truths.

504.14   As humans are physically situate halfway between the largest and smallest known bio-organisms, they are also halfway between the astro-largest and nuclear-smallest physical phenomena; humans thus find themselves between an absolute, omnidirectional, equilibrious, dimensionless, metaphysical core contained within a spheric twilight zone of macro-almost-true and themselves containing a spheric twilight zone of micro-almost-true. As humans are in the middle of the cosmic scheme metaphysically, truth itself is an unreachable, omnidirectional, cosmic center. The truth is zero eternal. Temporality = tempo-reality = time-reality. In temporality you cannot reach the truth. You cannot be exact because truth is zero. Absolute truth is an omnizerophase condition. The metaphysical comprehension passes through, expandingly and contractively, but fails ever to remain at the zero core of equilibrious truth.

504.15   As we reduce the tolerance for error, we begin to get near the eternal, which is what we call the truth. But we will never quite get there. The inexhaustibly attractive and truthfully inspired thoughts of human minds ever approach an evolutionary refinement while constantly intertransforming as a precessional consequence of progressively experienced complexes of omniinteraccommodative, intercomplementary transactional events; the process results in ever-closer proximity to perfect equilibrium of all intertransformative forces, but it never attains such equilibrium.

504.16   Truth may be dealt with only as relative relationships of interactions of dynamic principles. Degrees of accuracy are refinements that in no way affect the fundamental reliability of the directional or angular sense toward centralized truths. Truth is a relationship; it is a direction rather than an attainment. The search for truth is a yielding to the integrity of the intellect, revealing information and nuances that are ever more impressive, more delicate, and more exciting.

504.17   Truth is the progressive diminution of residual error. The generalizations are eternal. The more accurately we state the truth, the less frequently it becomes necessary to modify our statement of it. We have to change what we say less and less. Eventually it works back to the eternality of No Change.

505.50   Abstract vs Energetic

•[*505.50–505.83   Pattern Scenario*]

505.51   The science of pattern is mathematical. As the fundamental communications system of all the sciences mathematics is both the most comprehensive and the most abstract of the sciences. Experimentally discovered mathematical relationships permit generalized statements of such laws as are found to be governing all science, and all sciences must use mathematics. Nonexperimentally disclosed mathematical relationships can be imaginatively evolved, however, but they may or may not have identity with physical Universe behavior. It is for instance mathematically feasible to explore a hypothetical Universe theoretically devoid of any one of the family of mathematical operations, such as, for instance, a Universe in which there is only multiplication and no division, or an exclusively two-dimensional Universe.

505.52   Employing only mathematics in the analysis of physically verifiable data (which always includes all the known physically relevant variables) can provide information to humans within minutes regarding cosmic events that in themselves take years to transpire, even though they occur at the speed of light.

505.53   Synergetics conceptualizes in generalized principles, in contradistinction to special-case empirics. We may logically hypothesize either (a) that mathematics is entirely physical, or (b) that the physical is in reality pure abstract principle. You can play the game either way: both are valid, but not simulaneously. There are certainly not two absolutely separate and independently operating Universes: the abstract Universe of the mathematician and the energetic Universe of the physiochemist.

505.60   Minimum-Limit Case

505.61   You cannot have a line that is less than a line, or a fix that is less than a fix, or a virgin that is less than a virgin. Nature comes to minimum-limit case with all her points in order to feel very comfortable. But the resolution is not linear or planar: it is omnidirectional; it is hierarchical in ascending or descending hierarchies.

505.62   You grow or decrease. You get better or worse. In parallelism things do not converge. Science is not getting the right answers because scientists do not think divergently and convergently. If you are in parallel, you can never get to any conclusion whatsoever. Waves require hierarchies. (See Sec. 260.20.)

505.63   Only *means* are parallel: *means* are the averages of the limits. Dealing in probability calculus scientists can deal only with averages of limits; wherefore they explore and speculate only in terms of parallels. Min-max limits are inherently omnidirectional—inherently divergently expansive toward max-limits and convergently contractive toward min-limits. There are no experimentally demonstrable, absolute-maximum limits. Only the minimum limit is demonstrably absolute—even when it looks like a point.

505.64   All the characteristics of a system are absolute because each of its components is the minimum-limit case of its conceptual category, for all conceptuality—as Euler discovered and proved—consists at minimum of points, areas, and lines.

505.65   An area is a nothingness. A plurality of areas are views of nothingness through separate frames. A point is a somethingness. A line is a relationship between two somethingnesses. An enlarged, apparently single somethingness may prove to be resolvable into a plurality of somethingnesses between which the lines of interrelationship fence off the nothingness into a plurality of separately viewable nothingnesses. Points are unresolvable, untunable somethingnesses occurring in the twilight zone between visible and supravisible experience. (See Secs. *262.02* and *264.01*.)

505.70   Topology of Minimum Awareness

505.71   *Awareness* seems to be the one minimal word best expressing the experience of life. Awareness is inherently plural, for it consists of the individual system that becomes aware and the first minimum otherness of which it is aware: such otherness may be integrally internal or externally separate of the observing system. We say, "No otherness: no awareness" (Sec. 905.02). A philosopher may question that statement, saying, "No, you are wrong because awareness can be exclusively of self." But we reply by recapitulating the inherent minimum topology of awareness:

—minimum self and minimum otherness are both systems, each having both insideness and outsideness;
—one part of a system cannot exist without the other;
—an experienceable point is substantial;
—all substance has insideness and outsideness;
—all substances are divisible into minimum substances;
—each minimum substance is always a whole system; and

—each system always has insideness and outsideness and four minimum-system-defining events, all of which events are inherently nonsimultaneous and only overlappingly co-occurring.

505.72   Ergo, the minimum cognition employs the information-sensing, remembering, and recognizing circuitry of the organic substance's minimum self-sensing awareness, which could only be at a minimum *one* as a system of four minimum-event components, being aware of its own integral system's otherness-defining components. Ergo, experientially, no otherness: no awareness. Q.E.D.

505.73   All minimum otherness or all minimum-observer *self* are both plural unity with mutual interawareness. Interawareness means one system aware of another system or the outsideness of a system aware of its system's insideness.

505.74   The observer and the observed constitute two points differentiated against an area of nothingness with an inherent interrelationship line of awareness running between the two points. (See Sec. 264.01.) Thus there is a minimum set of four awareness aspects of life:

(1) the observer;
(2) the observed;
(3) the line of interrelationship; and
(4) the background nothingness against which the somethingness is observed.

505.80   Background Nothingness

505.81   When we draw a spherical triangle on the Earth's surface (Fig. 812.03), it demonstrates an aspect of geometry apparently not recognized by Euler. The spherical triangle also demonstrates self and otherness. The spherical triangle is the first awareness: there is an inherent twoness in the triangle's insideness and outsideness; and the axis of the two poles constitutes the two points of self and otherness. The *background nothingness* of these two points represents an area not contained by a line. Euler apparently did not realize that there could be an area not contained by a line.

505.82   From Euler we know that the number of locally identified minimum entities called *points* plus the number of separate *areas* equals the number of *lines* plus the number two. In minimum awareness we have two identified entities which, being local points, must have directional fixedness against a background of nothingness. Ergo, in minimum awareness two points plus one area of nothingness have one inherent line of most economical interrelationship between the two points. These two points plus one area equal the number of lines—in this case "one" plus Euler's abstractly accommodative two. (The line of interrelationship is another aspect of the prime vector. See Sec. *540.10.*)

505.83   The Euler "plus one" abstractly accommodates two in the minimum awareness model:

$$\text{points} + \text{area} = \text{lines} + 2$$
$$2 + 1 = 1 + 2$$
$$3 = 3$$

Three of two kinds = three of two other kinds = six of four kinds = the six vector-edge relationships existing between the four different event-point fixes. *Points* are subdifferentiable systems—i.e., microsystems of events too close to be resolved from one another. *Areas* are supradifferentiable systems—i.e., macrosystems of event points too far apart to resolve. The *nothingness* area is unbounded by any visible closed line. Nothingness is the part of the system unencompassed by the observer. (See Sec. *1052.350.*)

506.00   Knot

506.40   Yin-Yang

506.41   Each lobe of a baseball is simply a precessed triangle of a tetrahedron. The baseball is yin-yang, not in a plane but in Universe: it is telling us that complementarities interprecess omnidirectionally and not just in a plane, as the planar yin-yang suggests.

506.42   The spherical tetrahedron can be demonstrated by placing a light inside a translucent plastic sphere. The light at the system center casts the shadow lines of the tetrahedron's four vertexes and their six interconnecting edges outwardly and symmetrically onto the plastic sphere to produce the outlines of a spherical tetrahedron. We may then inscribe four circles around each of the four vertexes of the spherical tetrahedron of such a unit radius so that each of the four circles is tangent to each of the three others. We can take a sharp-edged cutting tool and severingly trace around the perimeter of one circle to its point of tangency with the next adjacent circle, and there we can inflect the cutting tool to cut around the next tangent circle to its next point of tangency, where once more we can inflect the cutting tool's severance trace to follow around the next circle to reach the next tangent point, repeating the procedure until we finally return to the point of original cutting. Upon completion of the severance tracing we find we have cut apart the surface of the spherical tetrahedron into two similar, equiarea sections, each of which corresponds to the two similar, dumbbell-profiled, skin sections of a baseball. With these two similar half-sphere surface sections precessingly aimed toward one another in such a manner that the bulge of one section registers symmetrically with the half-circle opening on the other, we find that we can sew the edges of the sections together around a core to produce a baseball.

506.43   When you look at the baseball with the inflection point of its S-pattern stitching, located at the center of the visible hemisphere's circular profile, aimed directly at you, you will see that the baseball's surface pattern is the same inflection pattern as that of the most profound symbol of the orient: yin-yang. Long ago human minds of the orient must have discovered precession, tetrahedra, and symmetry. (See Sec. 1056.12.)

513.00   Vectorial Orientation and Observation

513.08   Articulation: The articulations are ever reenacted, each time hoping to reduce the tolerance magnitude of residual inaccuracy of either observation or articulation.

515.00   Frequency

515.15   Complementary Angles

515.151   The initial angle and its cyclically complementary angle are defined by the relative proportions of one whole circle into which the whole circle is divided by any two different radii of the circle.

515.152   The greater the even number of equal intervals into which the circumference of the circle is divided, the more accurately may the proportioning of the circle's central-angle-divisioning be described. If the circle is divided into 360 degrees and if the initial angle considered is 60 degrees, then its complementary angle is 300 degrees. If the initial angle is 90 degrees, its complementary is 270 degrees. If the initial angle is 180 degrees, its complementary is also 180 degrees. This ambiguity, if not thoughtfully considered, can bring about fatal "wrong-way" errors of direction-taking in navigational calculations. What looks like a local fragment of a "straight" line constitutes a complementary pair of 180-degree angles generated around the center-point of the line.

515.153   An assumedly straight line both of whose ends are hypothetically considered to be leading in opposite directions to infinity also may have an arbitrarily selected dividing point located (locally conceptually) upon it from which the oppositely extending lines emanate—or upon which point the opposite lines converge to form a 180-degree angle. Both of the oppositely-and-outwardly-bound lines of extension from the 180-degree angular convergence point are inferentially interminable. Ergo, as hypothetically assumed to be "straight" lines, they are paradoxically half-finite and half-infinite. This is a paradox consequent to humanity's misassumption of the existence of the phenomenon of "straight" lines, an error that occurred in turn only as a consequence of the inadequate experience of people at the time they adopted the fallacious assumption. Such misconceptions are the logical consequence of humans having always been born naked, helpless, and ignorant, though superbly equipped cerebrally, utterly dependent upon only trial-and-error-based exploration and survival stratagems.

525.00   Solids: Matter

525.10   Frequency and Interval

525.11   Mass is a statement of relative event frequency per volume. For example, there may be something too massive for me to put my finger through because it has too high an event frequency.

526.10   Systematic Inclusion and Exclusion of Space

•[*526.10–526.35   Space Scenario*]

526.101   Space is the antithesis of solid. Both are misnomers. *Solid* (or *mass*) refers to locals of too high an event frequency for our physical members to penetrate or conceivably tune in. *Space* refers to locals of an event frequency per volume too low for our apprehending equipment to tune in.

526.11   Space is systemic inadvertency. Space is all the observer's untuned-in information.

526.12   Space is the inescapable awareness of unaccounted otherness: the otherness is unconsidered but always and only co-occurrent with system considerations.

526.13   Space is finite as a complementary of finite Scenario Universe. As a co-occurrent, complementary function of finite but non-unitarily-conceptual and non-unitarily-tune-in-able Scenario Universe, space is finite. Space does not have *de*finable properties. Only systems have definable characteristics.

526.14   The cognitive awareness of space derives from definition of system characteristics whose topological interrelationships inherently and oherently divide Universe into insideness microcosmic space and outsideness macrocosmic space. Systems have 32 topological characteristics (enumerated at Sec. 1044).

526.15   Systems capture. Systems exclude. Systems capture all the special case, twilight-zone, only-grossly-tuned-in but as-yet-differentially-undefinable, outwardly neighboring "otherness" systems as well as all the inward, untunable, nonsystem space. Systems exclude the twilight zone of only-partially-tuned-out, no-longer-differentially-definable, outwardly neighboring otherness systems as well as all the outward, untunable, nonsystem space. Systems capture all the infratunable, concentric tween-waves that are too-high-frequency for experience-intuited-expectancy space nothingness and exclude all the ultratunable, concentric tween-waves that are two-low-frequency for experience-intuited-expectancy space nothingness.

526.16   "Solids" are the frequencies that are too high for differential tune-in-ability. Space is the integral of all the frequencies that are too low for tune-in-ability.

526.17   Included spaces and excluded spaces are both concentric. Tuning = dismissal of irrelevancies. Those too large and of too low frequency are dismissed omnidirectionally. Those too small and of too high frequency are dismissed inwardly. The tuning phenomenon is either inward or omnidirectional.

526.18   Insideness is the captured nothingness. Insideness becomes the conceptually embraced, system-defined space. Outsideness is the conceptual-system-defined, outwardly uncaptured nothingness. Without systems there can be no space awareness. (Compare Sec. *1053.824*.) Systems are awareness concepts. Space is nonconceptual awareness.

526.19   Space is a finite but nondefinable complementary relationship function of the definability of singular or plural system characteristics and their interrelationships. System is all the relevant thought, all the think-about-ableness. Space is all the unthink-about-able irrelevancy.

526.191   Space is the aggregate of all the vector equilibrium nulls of all magnitudes and frequencies of all isotropic vector matrixes always potentially articulatable in all directions from any point of origin.

526.20   Visual Aspects of Space

526.21   Where there is no radiation, there is no light. If it had always been "night," I doubt that people would have invented the word *space*. At night you have no sense of otherness—no sense of space complementation of system-defining limits. Space is a "visual" word, touch being an ultra-high-frequency "visualization."

526.22   Space is concentric and multisystem partitionable. Space is never linear. It takes four events to define three intervals. The special case events only appear to be linear because they are always successively experienced. Potential periodicity—special case, time-size—is initially cognizable when recurring after the same interval as that recalled as existing between the first and second similar systemic events experienced, but only upon the third recurrence of the similar systemic experience event do we have four similar systemic events to define three similar intervals—ergo, to confirm the periodicity that could only be intuitively anticipated after the third similar event experience had marked a second similar between-events interval.

526.23   It takes a minimum of four similar-system-experiencing event recurrences to produce three similar between-event intervals and differentially excite a recollected pattern cognition that confirms the periodicity—a periodicity that was only intuitively and speculatively anticipated at the time of the third similar-system experiencing. The confirmatory fourth event and its third similarly intervalled recurrence cognition in turn introduce the inherently minimum sixness of convergent interrelationships of any four subdifferentiable points of tunably identifiable system experiences—which four, together, always define the four corners of a larger system. (Compare Secs. *265.08–13, 501.24, 987.073,* and *1033.601.*)

526.24   Our eyesight is stroboscopic at 60 cycles per second. Because of the lags in apprehension we are not aware of the "between-takes" intervals. We do not sensingly realize that the nothingness is concentrically permeating the concentrically waved recurrent somethingnesses.

526.25   The phenomenon death is as yet ultratunable system experience. We have no way of knowing whether any single, dual, or triple recurring experience events are to be followed by a fourth, as-yet-unexperienced, similar event which, if and when it occurs, may constitute a system-tuning-in, live realization of the omnioccurring, infratunable, tunable, and ultratunable systems' concentric intervalling. Death is intervalling. Life and death are always and only co-occurrent, life being concentrically successive tuning-ins and death being the as yet nontuned-in. (See Secs. *262.10* and *531.10.*)

526.26 *Out* is any-directional. You go in to go out because *out* is not only any direction but is all directions—electromagnetically speaking it is "tuned-out." (See Sec. 905.21.) *In* is what we are thinking about now. *In* is the momentary reality into which we are *tuned.* All the rest is for the moment *tuned-out* but equally real as the information or experience is progressively *tuned-in.*

526.27 Physics finds that Universe has no solid things surrounded by, and interspersed with, space. Life is an inventory of tuning-ins and tuning-outs of experience. Birth is the first tuning in; death may not be the last.

526.30 Systematic Communication of Space

526.31 Space is the invisible complementation of the cognitive system. Like the rubber glove, cognition is left hand; space is inside-out right hand, and vice versa.

526.32 Space is the unconsidered complement of the conceptually considered episode and its only neighboringly overlapped episodes of Scenario Universe. Space is the untuned-in complement of considerability and conceptuality.

tuned & untuned

in & out

526.33 Special case is always tune-in-able. Special case is imaginable by brain. Conceptuality is a function of mind. Conceptuality is a priori independent of special case frequency tunability. Conceptuality is generalized, and the space complementation of generalized conceptuality is generalized. Space is generalization. Death is the omnidirectional otherness of as-yet physically realized Scenario Universe. Death is the as-yet unborn set of all the unconsidered special cases of all the as-yet undiscovered—ergo, as-yet-unconsidered—generalized principles.

526.34 Conceptuality and its complementary space generalizations do not account or embrace the a priori mystery, the integrity of eternally regenerative Scenario Universe. All the inherent, concentric, systemic conceptuality, its internal spatial intervals, and its external spatial embracement are altogether both subordinate and supraordinate to the nonconsiderability of such a priori mystery as . . . How come Universe?

526.35 Systems divide all of Universe. Thought divides all of Universe. Thought is inherently systemic—whose inherency always has its oherency of space. Only systems can communicate space. Space is systems-defined-and-deferred awareness of potentially tunable otherness.

527.00 Dimension

527.08 **Convergence and Divergence:** We do not arrive at dimensionality by virtue of perpendicular or parallel assembly. Dimensionality in synergetics provides for assembly only by convergence and divergence. This accounts for the spontaneous and continued frustration of conventional mathematical accounting when confronted with the problem of assembling a nonpolarized, omnisymmetrical object by joining two identical halves of the multifrequenced, closest-sphere-packed tetrahedra, each of which has five similar facets—two of which are equiangled triangles, two of which are trapezoids, and the fifth is a nonequiedged parallelogram. Matching of any of these facets produces asymmetrical, polarized objects. One of the nonequiedged parallelograms must be precessionally rotated to cross the other at 90 degrees, where it will be seen that the converging-diverging patterns of the two halves are symmetrically realized. (See Secs. *260.50* and 417 and Fig. *527.08*.)

527.09 **Series vs Parallel Circuitry:** The difference between gravitation and radiation is analogous to the difference between parallel wiring and

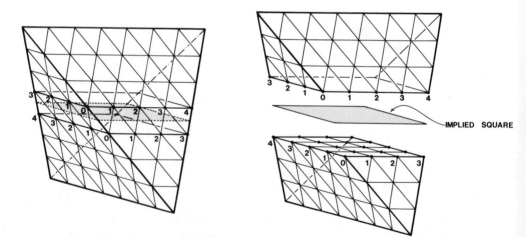

Fig. *527.08 Assembly by Convergence and Divergence:* A regular tetrahedron may be divided into two identical halves by an *implied square* section. The two halves may be separated and reassembled by precessional rotation. This is an illustration of rotational symmetry. (See Fig. 417.01 and Loeb Contribution L.) For other examples of the evolution of ''Chef's Cap'' polyhedra, see Figs. *100.103* and *987.230B*.

series wiring in electricity. Series wiring is like the wire-strung lights on an old-fashioned Christmas tree: If one light goes out, the whole string goes out. In parallel wiring, when one light goes out, the other lights remain operative. This is a demonstration of integration and disintegration. *Series* wiring is a disintegrative system, an open system. *Parallel* wiring is an integrative system, a closed system. It is not the "parallelism" that matters but the fact that the circuit is closed. The word *parallel* came into use only because of the diagram first used to demonstrate the principle as well as the fact that the closed-circuit wire is conveniently doubled back upon itself and bound into one "lead" for house-wiring purposes. The fact that the vectors are drawn in parallel is only a convenience for the construction industry. The same-length vectors—ergo, the same energy magnitude involvement—used correctly, can provide either function. Here we have the convergent integration and divergent disintegration language of synergetics identified in the language of electricity. (See Secs. *260.20,* 541.05, 647, Fig *527.09,* and Loeb Contribution, N.)

527.25 **Nonpolar Points:** All systems have poles—ergo, spin axes—ergo, they are polarizably identifiable. Nonpolarized simply means that the spin axis is unrecognized under the conditions considered. There is no such thing as a nonpolarized point, because if you tuned in the subvisible system—

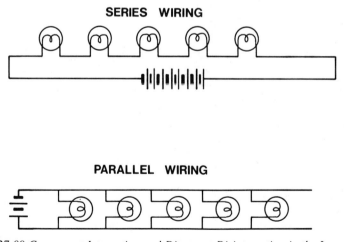

Fig. *527.09 Convergent Integration and Divergent Disintegration in the Language of Electricity:* "Series" wiring is disintegrative, an open system. "Parallel" wiring is integrative, a closed system.

appearing only as a directionally positioned microsomething—to visible comprehension, you would find that as a system it has poles and that it has a potential of seven alternately employable poles (see Sec. 1040). So we may call a "point" a focal center—i.e., a "noise" with a direction—but it is inherently an as-yet undistinguished system, with all of the latter's characteristics (see Sec. *264.01*).

527.26   There is inherent polarity in all observation, which always introduces the additive twoness:

Nonpolarized = unrecognized
    Focal event = infratunable system

527.70   Primitive Dimensionality

527.701   In synergetics *primitive* means systemic conceptuality independent of size. (Compare Sec. *1033.60*.)

527.702   Geometers and "schooled" people speak of length, breadth, and height as constituting a hierarchy of three independent dimensional states—"one-dimensional," "two-dimensional," and "three-dimensional"—which can be conjoined like building blocks. But length, breadth, and height simply do not exist independently of one another nor independently of all the inherent characteristics of all systems and of all systems' inherent complex of interrelationships with Scenario Universe.

527.703   The educational authorities in the art and science of "plane" and "solid" geometry disregard the *environmental otherness:* They assume an infinitely extendible imaginary plane upon which they mark apart two infradimensional imaginary points A and B between which they can draw an imaginary shortest straight line whose "length" AB constitutes their academic mathematicians' first-dimensional state. They then mark apart on the same infinite imaginary plane third and fourth points C and D, which are then linearly interconnected by another "straight" line CD in the same imaginary plane with, parallel to, and at an AB distance from, line AB, with a third line CA drawn in the same plane perpendicular to line AB at A, and a fourth line DB in the same imaginary plane drawn perpendicular to line AB at B, whereby either of the lines CA or DB constitutes the "breadth," which is the educators' second-dimensional state. They then erect four AB-long lines perpendicular to the first imaginary plane at points A', B', C' and D', respectively. They then draw the imaginary straight lines $A'B'$, $B'C'$, $C'D'$, and $D'A'$. With all this so-called construction—which would collapse in the presence of gravitational reality—they have now attained their third-dimensional state of "height" above their two-dimensional square plane base. This assumedly produces three-dimensional reality, which by virtue of their constructional strategy

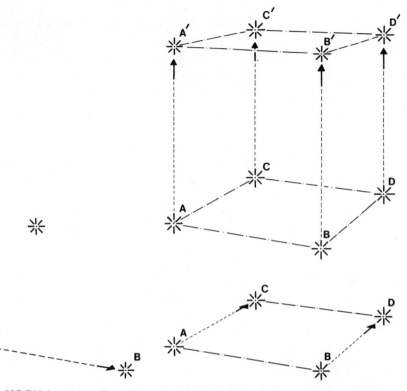

Fig. 527.703 *Imaginary Three Dimensionality:* Parallel and perpendicular construction strategies of "plane" and "solid" geometry assume that reality can be measured only in cubes.

suggests to them that reality is only cubically measurable or comprehensible.

527.704　　　There is also trouble with the word *fundamental*. It means foundational when there are no foundations . . . no two-dimensional planar base. The Earth and other objects are co-orbiting the Sun at 60,000 miles per hour and are gravitationally tethered to one another. The word *foundation* implies an impossible standing-still-somewhere in Universe . . . on a solid and square or planar base.

527.705　　　We may use the word *primitive* only to describe the initial self-starting conditions of awareness and think-about-ability of the minimum essential components of any evolutionary system's divergent or convergent considerability. Thus the primitive conceptual angle as one myopically viewed corner of the 12 corners of the minimum system has greater meaning than the expression *fundamental particle* employed by the high-frequency research physicists. The statements of this paragraph are strictly within the concerns of epistemography.

527.706   Infinity is only a consequence of subdividing finity. Because synergetics has conceptuality independent of size, it permits—indeed, requires—systemic conceptuality before the subdividing commences. There is no a priori size. There is no experimentally demonstrable systemic one-dimensional line extending to infinity. Size commences only with subdivision, with frequency. Subdivision may be considered as potentially limitless, provided infinite time. But time is always a special case limited characteristic of special case time-size systems. Time is not generalizable. Generalized principles are all eternal. Eternal is not a whole lot of time. Eternal is independent of and devoid of time. Infinity is micro rather than macro—hence the difficulty of research physicists in their search for the one last "building block" or fundamental particle.

527.707   The minimum family of inherent systemic omnicosmic interrelationships is inherently primitive and eternal. Primitive dimensionality is expressible only in terms of the interproportionality of the components of whole minimum systems—ergo, in prefrequency primitive tetravolume proportionality and the latter's primitive topological characteristics. There can be no partial systems. Systems can be divided multiplyingly only into whole systems.

527.708   There is a cosmic hierarchy of primitively symmetric systemic states of intertransformability or interassociabilities of prime polyhedra. (See Sec. 982.62.)

527.71   Substance Is Systemic

527.711   People think of a point as the most primitive thing with which to initiate geometrical conceptioning. A point is a microevent of minutiae too meager, they say, to be dignified with dimensionality: Ergo, they assume a point to be only an "imaginary fix." But speaking in the experiential language of science, whatever is optically point-to-able is a substance, and every substance has insideness and outsideness—ergo, is systemic: Ergo, all point-to-ables can never be less than the minimum system: the tetrahedron. Points always amplify optically to be identifiable as systemic polyhedra.

527.712   All conceptual consideration is inherently four-dimensional. Thus the *primitive* is a priori four-dimensional, being always comprised of the four planes of reference of the tetrahedron. There can never be any less than four primitive dimensions. Any one of the stars or point-to-able "points" is a system—ultratunable, tunable, or infratunable but inherently four-dimensional.

529.00 Time

529.40 Now Hourglass

The macro-microcosm of minimum frequency of omnidirectional self-
interference restraints, whose greatest degrees of outward expansion occur when the last of the least-frequent, self-interfering
cycles is completed (and cycles, being geodesic great circles,
must always interfere with one another twice in each wave-
and-frequency cycle, which *twiceness* imposes eternally
regenerative cosmic resonance with inherent quanta-,
wave-, frequency-, time, interference-, mass-, and
effort-aspects), in exquisite speed-of-light, 700-
million-miles-per-hour, self-interfering radiation patterns energetically self-tying into
concentric knots of relative mass in a
mathematically idealized variety of
symmetrical-asymmetrical atomic
assemblages, whose local sub-
visibly resolvable micro-
orbiting induces the su-
perficially deceptive,
motionless thingness
of mini-micro-
microcosm of
NOW
which progres-
sive, experience-
won, knowledge mul-
tiplies by progressive, intellectually contrived, instrumentally implemented, exploratory subdividing into microscopically ever-greater
speeds of transformation through insect-phase
magnitudes dividing into the micro-organisms
phase, and then dividing progressively into molecular
and atomic phases; then phasing into radioactivity at 700-
million-miles-per-hour, expanding once more into the micro-
eternity of no-time into the macrocosm and repeat, ad infinitum. . . .

530.00   Nonsimultaneity

530.10   Nonsimultaneity of Scenario Universe

530.11   Any point can tune in any other point in Universe (Sec. 960.08). Between any two points in Universe there is a tetrahedral connection (see Sec. 961.30). Thus systematic connection of two points results in the interconnecting of four points. But none of the four event points of the tetrahedron are simultaneous. They are all overlappingly co-occurrent, each with different beginnings and endings. All of the atoms are independently introduced and terminaled; many are in gear—that is, synchronously tuned—but many are also way out of gear, untuned, or "noisy."

530.12   Nouns can co-occur at the same time, but verbs cannot. Events can never be omnicongruently simultaneous, which would mean having all the component four events' beginnings and endings always simultaneous. Events occur. Occur is a time word. The overlappingness of Scenario Universe (see Sec. 320) makes events appear simultaneous when they are not. Events are only overlappingly co-occurrent but never omnisimultaneous.

530.13   All the four unique electromagnetic frequencies of the 92 chemical elements are uniquely different, yet many are intersynchronizable in overlapping occurring alloys, whose unique sets of interattractive interrelationships produce the synergetically unique behaviors of those specific alloys.

531.00   Life

531.04   **Organisms:** Atoms are inanimate systems. Physically we consist entirely of atoms. When we die, all the atoms are there. Whatever life was, it was not the inanimate atom systems that persist after death. At the virus level of professional concern the scientists say you can identify all the physical substances present as inanimate crystals. Biological science initiated the investigations that successively discovered cells, genes, chromosomes, and other biological design controls. Needing to check their design control theories, they employed the swift succession of generations of the fruit fly and then discovered the even swifter succession of the generations of the tobacco mosaic virus. This brought the scientists into a very new realm of virology where they found nuclear physicists, biologists, and chemists all involved. Though the virologists have discovered DNA-RNA bioprogramming controls, they have found only inanimate atomic constituents. Because their whole series of events started with biology, they have as yet—unthinkingly and mistakenly—retained the "animate" relationship. Biology began with the whole seemingly living organisms consisting of protoplasm and viruses, but they misidentified the viral substances as physically "animate," when life is not physical. The error lies in the fact that humanity long ago misassumed that the organism employed by life is the life itself instead of merely the vehicle—as if the telephone was the communication itself instead of merely the instrument.

531.05 The now overspecialized scientists seem to have forsaken epistemological *significances;* they seem to have lost their gift for philosophical thinking. So the focus on the animate aspect of physical things has been continued by the church. Many religious organizations establish their power by maintaining that life is the physical apparatus it employs and by basing their ideals on "living" physical images. If life were the physical, we really could make synthetic men, laboratory animals, and artificial intelligence; we never will. We can make brainy robots, but we cannot make thinking, loving life.

531.06 Science is arriving at a phase of required new comprehension in which we will be discovering that all of the physical cases experimentally discovered are only special cases of the generalized principles of generalized systems—i.e., the vector equilibrium.

531.10 Life and Death

531.11 Life's employed apparatus is microconstituted by the unique frequency identifications of the chemical elements and their compounded atoms, as well as the humanly tune-in-able "color" frequencies of the comprehensive electromagnetic spectrum's concentrically interpositioned occurrences—usually published in a chart of positions along any one radius of the comprehensive concentric system. Death's reality is constituted by all the vector equilibrium null intervals between and beyond—inwardly and outwardly—the comprehensive electromagnetic frequencies. (See Secs. *262.10* and *526.25.*)

532.00 Symmetry

532.17 **Oscillation of Symmetry and Asymmetry:** Symmetry is only generalized. In cosmic-event averaging symmetry is ever implicit in the preponderantly-almost-symmetrical, spontaneous symmetry-referenceability of all asymmetry. Symmetry is systemic. Symmetry has nothing to do with the scenario series; it has nothing to do with local, special case realizations. You can find balances in series—positive and negative energies—but absolute symmetry is characteristic only of generalized systems. (See Secs. 223.05 and *260.33*.)

532.18   Crystallography is always special-case and is always confronted with near-symmetric asymmetry; ergo, crystallography must recognize and reference its special case aspects to generalized symmetry. Generalized symmetric conceptuality is only manifest as the vector equilibrium and its involvement domain. The regular—regular means absolutely uniangular— tetrahedron is absolute and generalized, thus never physically realized. All physical reality is special case. This is why Universe has a capital U.

533.00   Precession

533.07   **Intereffects:** All bodies of Universe interaffect all other bodies in varying degrees; and all the intergravitational effects are precessionally angular modulation, and all the interradiation effects are frequency modulations.

533.08   Precession is the intereffect of individually operating cosmic systems upon one another. Since Universe is an aggregate of individually operative systems, all of the intersystem effects of Universe are precessional, and the 180-degree imposed forces usually result in redirectional resultants of 90 degrees. Gravity's 180-degree circumferential, omniembracement effect results in a 90-degree inwardly effected pressure that gains rapidly in intensity as the initially sixfold leverage advantage of the circumferentially tensed embracement gains exponentially in locally induced pressure as the radial distance outwardly from the sphere's center is decreased.

533.09   The Sun's direct 180-degreeness interattraction pull upon Earth begets precessionally the latter's 90-degreeness orbiting around the Sun. And Earth's circumferential orbiting direction begets Earth's own 90-degreeness of axial rotation.

533.10   Precessional 180-degree efforts beget 90-degree effects such as the Sun's radiation impoundment on Earth by the photosynthesis of agriculture (around the land) and photosynthesis of algae (around the waters of Earth), which regeneration occurs as precessionally impounded life-sustaining foods. The 180-degree Sun radiation effect precesses Earth's atmosphere in 90-degree circumferential direction as wind power, which wind power in turn precesses the windmills into 90-degree rotating.

533.11   All the metaphysical generalizations of physical principles produce indirect physical acceleration effects that are precessional.

533.12   Leverage, Sun power, wind power, tidal power, paddles, oars, windlasses, fire, metallurgy, cooking, slings, gears, electromagnetic generators, and metabolics are all 180-degree efforts that result in 90-degree precessional intereffects.

533.20   Precession and Degrees of Freedom

533.21   Despite the angularly modified resultant complexities of omnidirectionally operative precessional forces upon ever-varyingly interpositioned cosmic bodies, Universe may be manifesting to us that there is always and only operative an omniintegrated cosmic coordination of cosmic independents' actions and reactions, wherein with radial broadcasting of energy there is an exponentially increasing diffusion as well as disturbance-diminishing resultant energy effectiveness, producing widely varying angular aberrations of the precession, wherein nonetheless there is always an initial individual-to-individual operative attractiveness whereby

180-degreeness begets 90-degreeness

and

90-degreeness begets 180-degreeness,

all of whose angularly aberrated complexity of resultant directional effects always pulsate in respect to a neutral or static 60-degreeness, which (only statically) imposes an everywhere-else 60-degreeness of resultants, which in turn induces the coexistence of the isotropic vector matrix.

533.22   The 56 axes of cosmic symmetry (see Sec. 1042.05) interprecess successively to regenerate the centripetal-centrifugal inwardness, outwardness, and aroundnesses of other inwardnesses, outwardnesses, and aroundnesses as the omnipulsative cycling and omniinterresonated eternally regenerative Universe, always accommodated by the six positive and six negative alternately and maximally equieconomical degrees of freedom characterizing each and every event cycle of each and every unique frequency-quantum magnitude of the electromagnetic spectrum range.

535.00   Halo Concept

535.20   Building

535.21   A building can be thought of as a clock, i.e., as a feedback circuitry wherein local pushings and pullings are structurally regenerative and ever-self-restabilizing. The spirally overlapping critical path of progressive accomplishments that led to humans reaching the Moon and returning safely to Earth involved not a linear months-and-years progression but an around-the-Sun-by-Earth orbiting and an around-the-Earth-by-Moon orbiting progression of accomplished events wherein humans progressively established one feedback circuitry system overlapping another, and another, more than a million times, as the year of Earth-Moon orbiting of 365 axially-rotated-in-orbit days drew to orbital close at a galactic merry-go-round repositioning in the cosmic theater that finds the planet Earth and its 92-million-miles-away Sun six billion miles away from where their Earth-Sun year began. And all of these celestially complex "goings-on" had to be competently comprehended and attended in order for humans to ferry both outward and returning between the complexedly moving Earth and the ever-more-complexedly orbiting, spinning, and galaxying Sun-Earth-Moon team.

535.22   Thus with each year the spiraled critical-path "rope" of omniinterrelated, locally overlapping, circuitry-feedback closures integrated synergetically to produce the finally realized Earth-Moon inter-round-tripping of humans as the whole show co-orbited the Sun. The entire complex operation resulted in an ever-expanding spontaneous involvement of Earthians in an ever-increasing range of local Universe affairs. (See Sec. *1130.20*.)

537.00   Twelve Universal Degrees of Freedom

537.06   **Four Sets of Actions, Reactions, and Resultants**: Nature always employs only the most economical intertransformative and omnicosmic interrelatedness behavioral stratagems. With each and every event in Universe—no matter how frequently recurrent—there are always 12 unique, equieconomical, omnidirectionally operative, alternate-action options, which 12 occur as four sets of three always interdependent and concurrent actions, reactions, and resultants. This is to say that with each high frequency of recurring turns to play of each and all systems there are six moves that can be made in 12 optional directions. (See Secs. 251.46, 421.20, 521.06 and Fig. *537.10*.)

537.08   **Universe Divisible by Two**: Everything in Universe is divisible by two. There will always be two poles to any system. Unity is two.

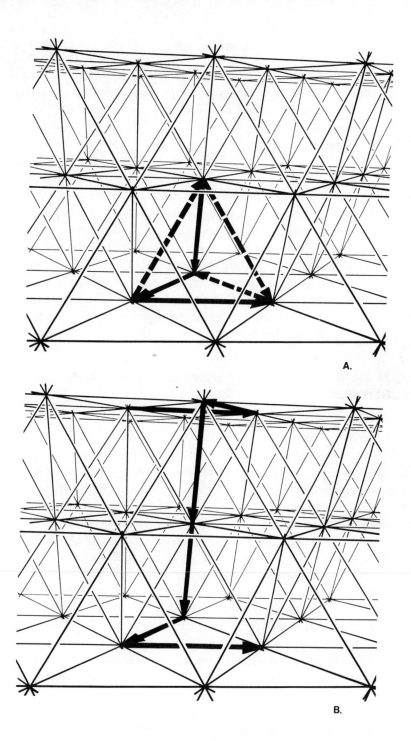

Fig. *537.10 Six Vectors for Every Point:* With each high frequency of recurrent turns to play, there are six moves that can be made in 12 optimal directions.

537.09 All the aspects of the constant relative abundances of points, areas, and lines are divisible by two: four faces, four points, and six edge lines. Thus there are six vectorial moves for every event; each of the vectorial moves is reversible, hence 12. Positional differentials in Universe derive only from the sixness of the 12 degrees of freedom.

537.131 **Six Vectors for Every Point:** The behavioral interpatterning frame of reference of the six degrees of freedom in respect to omnidirectionality is of course the vector equilibrium, which embraces the three-dimensionality of the cube and the six-dimensionality of the vector equilibrium. Experience is inherently omnidirectional; ergo, there is always a minimum of 12 "others" in respect to the nuclear observing self. The 24-positive- and 24-negative-vectored vector equilibrium demonstrates an initially frequenced, tetrahedrally quantized unity of 20; ergo, the Universe, as an aggregate of all humanity's apprehended and comprehended experiences, is at minimum a plurality of 24 vectors. (See Secs. 981.12 and *1224.21*.)

537.40 Game of Universe: Individuality and Degrees of Freedom

537.41 We may define the individual as one way the game of Universe could have eventuated to date. Universe is the omnidirectional, omnifrequency game of chess in which with each turn of the play there are 12 vectorial degrees of freedom: six positive and six negative moves to be made. This is a phenomenon of frequencies and periodicities. Each individual is a complete game of Universe from beginning to end. This is why each of us individuals is so much alike and yet completely different, a unique and individual way of playing the game with each of the omnidirectional degrees of freedom. With the six positive and the six negative omnidirectional degrees-of-freedom moves to be made at each turn of the play, the individual can move to any cosmic point that is not occupied and can move back over the same points or move on to new ones. (See Fig. 537.10.) Intellect as "god" can play all these incredibly different games in all these different ways and at all the differential rates at the same time. (See Sec. 1002.12.)

537.42 The individual differentiates position in Universe. The six degrees of freedom operate at *every* turn of the play. Just think of the frequencies per second of each of the chemical elements that make up the individual human body and then think of the periodicities of those frequencies.

537.43 That each individual is a complete integrity is one of the reasons I don't have to make any effort in loving my fellow human. (In the first-person plural of *we-even* the *I* even classes itself with the *other*. Each individual integrity has a steering effect, and like all steering effects it goes from one aberration to another. Certain individuals may be very wide aberrations from all the corruption that's going on in Universe, acting as just one of those infrequent and very wide aberrations so that Universe can hold its center. At that center sphere is the *two,* and you turn inside-out—and only the tetrahedron turns inside out. The other side of the Universe is not like the other side of the river; it is an inside-outing.)

537.44   We regard each individual as the special case, but consciousness as the generalization. Like the bumper sticker, "The Real World is Special Case." Reality is special case. You and I are sitting here, and no one else can be sitting right where we are. This is the kind of reality that the newspapers miss: they write about reality as if we were all the same realities, as if we were all the same things. If you and I are sitting here, we couldn't possibly be anywhere else.

537.45   There are many different realities. This is the difference between reality and generalization. There is only one generalization. The only reason the radio works is that it has no interference. The game of Universe can be played on any one of the fantastically large number of the quadrillions of quadrillions of frequencies: the game can be played any way just so long as there is no interference on the frequency you are using, so long as there are not two pieces in the same vector equilibrium at the same time.

537.46   What is important about the individual and important about the Universe is that neither is exempt from any of the rules. Universe is the sumtotal, and the individual is the special case. Universe is the aggregate of all the generalized principles. Each individual is one of the illions of ways the game of Universe could be played.

537.50   Freedom and Will

537.51   I think I tend to avoid using the word *will* because I spontaneously associate it with the term "free will" and all the controversies regarding the history of such human beliefs. I have felt that all such controversies lack adequate knowledge of science's generalized laws. To me it is obvious that no amount of individual will can nullify any cosmic law. It is also obvious to me that few know of and comprehend the significance of nature's having six positive and six negative equieconomical alternative moves to make with each turn to play in cosmic events.

537.52   It is clear to me that most humans tend to think in a linear, Go-or-

No-go, greenlight-redlight manner. To me, *will* is an optionally exercisable control by mind over brain—by wisdom over conditioned reflex—that becomes realizable when mind is adequately convinced regarding which of the 12 alternatives will produce the most comprehensively considerate vital advantage for all.

537.53   In a lesser way *will* becomes operative when the individual finds himself in terminal peril and has only seconds to "pull out" of a tailspin, when he becomes "cool," that is, when he discovers swiftly which of the alternative moves can save him, and exercises his will to execute the survival procedures.

537.54   Will determines what we should do in all the special case circumstances. Will is not a muscle thing—not the clenched fist—at all. People say I have a strong will, but what I have is a fairly clear view of the options of humanity and the commitments to their realization. It is thus that I determine what course to take in the special cases confronting us.

540.00   Frame of Reference

540.10   Prime Vector

540.11   All structural accounting of nature is accomplished with rational quantities of tetrahedra. The *XYZ* coordinates may be employed to describe the arrangements, but only in awkward irrationality, because the edge of the cube is inherently irrational in respect to the cube's facial diagonal. The hypotenuses actually function only as the edges of the positive and negative tetrahedra, which alone permit the cube to exist as a structure. The hypotenuses connect the sphere centers at the cube corners; they function concurrently and simultaneously as the natural structuring of tetrahedra edges in the omnidirectional isotropic vector matrix; as either hypotenuse or tetra edge they are *prime vectors*.

540.12   Of the eight corners of the cube only four coincide with the sphere centers of closest-packed, unit-radius spheres; therefore only the cube's facial diagonals can interconnect closest-packed spheres. One closed set of six cube-face diagonals can interconnect only four sphere-center corners of the prime tetrahedron, which alone provides the structural stability of the cube, whose eight-cornered, structural-stability completeness requires the saturation of the alternate set of six diagonals in each of the cube's six faces. This alternate set of six diagonals intertriangulates the other four sphere centers of the cube's eight corners. The cube diagonals and the edges of the tetrahedra structuring the cube are two aspects of the same phenomenon. The tetra-edge, cube-face diagonals connecting the two sets, of four corners each, of the cube's total of eight corners are the *prime vectors* of the vector equilibrium and of the isotropic vector matrix.

540.13   The second power of the length of the prime vector that constitutes the diagonal of the cube's face equals the sum of the second powers of any two edges of the cube. Because these two edges converge at the cube's corner to form one standing wave that may be multifrequenced to apparently coincide with the cube's facial diagonal, we discover that this relationship is what we are talking about in the deliberately nonstraight line. It is the same mathematical relationship demonstrated in the ancients' proof of the Pythagorean theorem, wherein the square of the hypotenuse is proven to be equal to the sum of the squares of the triangle's two legs. Thus the deliberately nonstraight line displays an evolutionary transformation from coincidence with the two sides of the parallelogram to coincidence with the seemingly straight, wavilinear diagonal of the parallelogram.

540.14   Prime vector may be considered variously as:

   —the axis of intertangency (Secs. 521.21 and 537.22);
   —the control line of nature (Sec. 982.21);
   —the deliberately nonstraight line (Sec. 522);
   —the diagonal of the cube (Sec. 463);
   —diametric unity (Sec. *986.160* and Fig. *986.161*);
   —half-vectors (Sec. 537.21);
   —the hypotenuse (Sec. 825.26);
   —the internuclear vector modulus (Sec. 240.40);
   —the line of interrelationship (Secs. *505.74* and *505.82*);
   —the line between two sphere centers (Sec. 537.21);
   —linear mensuration unity (Sec. 982.51);
   —the radial line (Sec. 537.21);
   —the T Quanta Module edge (Sec. *1033.130*);
   —the tetra edge (Sec. 982.53);
   —unit radius (Sec. 1106.23).

540.30   Four-frequency Hyperbolic Paraboloid

540.31   A flat, four-sided frame (*A*) can be folded to define a nonplanar hyperbolic paraboloid (*B, C, D*).

540.32   The edges of the four-sided frame are joined with lines parallel to its edges. This forms the basic grid of the hyperbolic paraboloid. When the frame is in planar position (*A*), all the grid lines are of equal length. As opposite vertexes of the frame are lifted, the grid lines change lengths at unequal rates. Figure *540.30* is a four-frequency system that in closed position (*E*) reveals there are two different cross-lengths in addition to the length of the frame edge. Although the lengths shorten as the altitude increases, there are always only two different cross-lengths for a four-frequency hyperbolic paraboloid. The moment the four-sided frame is no longer planar, the fact of two different axis lengths is revealed.

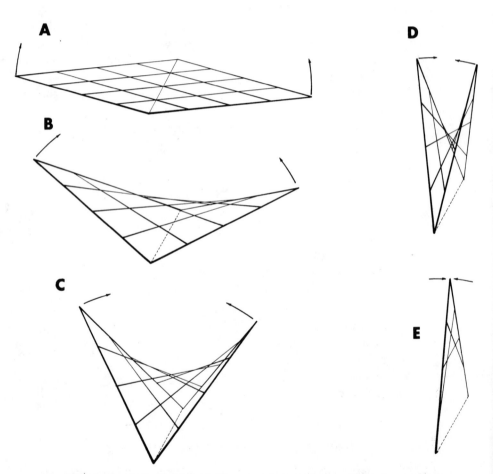

Fig. *540.30 Hyperbolic Paraboloid:* There are always only two different cross-lengths for a four-frequency hyperbolic paraboloid. As opposite vertexes of the frame are lifted, the grid lines change length at unequal rates. The moment the four-sided frame is no longer planar, the fact of two different axis lengths is revealed.

540.40 Multidimensional Accommodation

540.41   Vectors, like all real experiences, are inherently terminal. The relative lengths of the vectors are the products of the mass and velocity of the energy events, as expressed in unified scale in relation to other co-occurring energy events. All co-occurring vectors have unique angles of direction as angularly referenced multidimensionally to a given observer's system axis, spin orientation, and system-orbit direction at the time of observation. All angularly referenced relationships inherently involve fourth-dimensional accommodation (and fifth-power accommodation, when referenced to the cosmic scenario). These relationships can be conceptually comprehended in synergetics but can be expressed only in complex formula terms in the XYZ-CG_tS system.

541.00 Radiation and Gravity

541.01A   Radiation distributes energy systems outwardly in omnidiametric directions. Radiation fractionates whole systems into multidiametrically dispatched separate packages of the whole. The packaging of spherical unity is accomplished by radii-defined, central-angle partitioning of the spherical whole into a plurality of frequency-determined, simplest central divisioning, thus producing a plurality of three-sided cornucopias formed inherently at minimum limit of volumetric accommodation by any three immediate adjacent central angles of any sphere or of any omnitriangulated polyhedron. The threefold central-angle vertex surroundment constitutes the inner vertex definition of a radially amplified tetrahedral packet of energy, while the three inner faces of the energy package are defined by the interior radial planes of the sphere of omnidiametric distribution. (There is a great-circle plane common to any two radii.) The fourth, or outermost face of the energy package is the spherical surface triangle of the tetrahedron which always occurs at the radial distance outwardly traveled from the original source at the speed of radiation, symbolized as lower-case c. (See color plate 10.)

541.15 Local Conservation and Cosmic Regeneration

541.16   The excess effectiveness of gravity over radiation equals the excess of cosmic integrative forces over cosmic disintegrative forces. This gain of syntropy over entropy is invested in the constant intertransformations and transpositionings of eternally regenerative Scenario Universe. (See Secs. 231 and 320.)

541.17 The vector equilibrium provides a vector model of these functions: the 24 circumferential vectors of the vector equilibrium close back upon themselves and are united in the interconnection of their ends, providing integrative effectiveness of the circumferential vectors vs the individually acting, disintegrative abandonment of the total associative effectiveness of the 24 radial vectors of the vector equilibrium. These represent, respectively, the total gravitational forces of Universe and the total radiational forces of Universe, rendering the total integrative forces of Universe to be inherently more efficient than the total disintegrative forces of Universe. The excess efficiency of the integrative over the disintegrative provides an energy bonus that is cosmically reinvested in local intertransformings of nonsimultaneous, nonunitarily conceptual, almost-totally-invisible-to-humans Scenario Universe.

541.18 Thus gravity uses energy more efficiently than radiation, which accounts for the eternal dominance of syntropy over entropy. The energy conserved is invested in the constant transformative transpositioning of the eternal regeneration of Universe. The dominance of syntropy over entropy is the dominance of the metaphysical over the physical and guarantees an eternal resolution of all conflicts between the physical and the metaphysical in favor of the metaphysical. Mind will always win over energy. Omniconsiderate love will always win out over ruthless selfishness, but the score is only cosmically accounted and the meager, momentarily-visible-and-tunable considerations cannot so inform the inherently limited comprehension of the local players. The players may easily be deluded into misassuming that momentary victories won by treachery or physical force are of lasting importance. The invisible design provides for the only-slowly-gestating self-education of humanity from naked, helpless ignorance at birth, through individual trial-and-error coping with necessities, to omnigraduation into functioning with omnireliable., omniloving, intellectual-integrity-governing individuals of an omnifaithfully operative and truthful society. The cosmic design often employs precession to guide the ignorant players into inadvertently producing the evolutionarily necessary regenerative integrity functions, while the ignorant are consciously preoccupied only in vain and selfishly expedient ends.

541.19 The cosmic excess of integrative effectiveness and constancy is manifest in the successively repeatable, self-intertransformative "jitterbug" articulation of the vector equilibrium as it contracts rotationally, symmetrically, and precessionally, thereby successively to transform from the 20-quanta-volume vector equilibrium to the 4-volume octahedron to the volume-of-1 positive tetrahedron to the volume-of-1 negative tetrahedron. (See Illus. 460.08 and 461.08.) The jitterbug articulation turns around at the negtive tetrahedron to reexpand therefrom, returning through all of those volumetric stages to its original 20-volume integrity, to be alternately recontracted through all the 20-to-1 and 1-tetravolume-to-20 without any break ever occurring in the circuitry integrity of the vector-chord closures and intertriangulation in the four planes of the four-dimensional symmetry. The syntropic integrity capability of the vector-equilibrium jitterbug articulation also discloses the means by which nature can effect as much as a 20-to-1 symmetrical and locally volumetric disappearance from visibility.

541.40   Islanded Radiation and Tensional Constancy

541.41   Radiation is special case, systematically centered, and discontinuously islanded. Gravity is continuous tension omni-inter-between all systems. Because gravitational, intertensional intensivity varies as the second power of the arithmetical interdistancing variations, whose unique variations are locally periodic, it manifests periodic intensities of tidal pulls, but the overal tensional integrity is constant independent of local variabilities in intensity.

541.42   Electromagnetic radiation is distributive and entropic; its frequency magnitudes represent multiplication by division. Gravity is nondivisive and syntropic; its conservation is accomplished by holistic embracement of variable intensities. Gravity is integral. Holistic gravity has no frequency.

541.43   Earth's biospheric inventory of water is radially dispersed outwardly by vaporization and omnilocally condensed as inwardly "falling" drops of rain, which are gravitationally and convergently collected as ocean.

512.00   Quality

>   . . . then, if we are not able to hunt the Good with one idea
>   only, with three we may catch our prey: Beauty, Symmetry,
>   Truth are the three. . . .
>
>   —Plato, *Philebus*

542.01   This triadic concept is exclusively planar—ergo, nonexistent. What is inadvertently omitted is the observer of the planar triad, whose observer position marks the fourth corner of the tetrahedron, the minimum system.

542.02   The observer-plus-the-observed, Beauty, Symmetry, and Truth

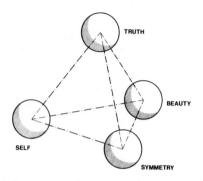

Fig. *542.02 Tetrahedral Analysis of Plato's Triad:* The triadic concept of Beauty, Symmetry, and Truth inadvertently omitted the function of the observer. The tetrahedron is the unique symmetrical set of minimum interrelationships.

are the four unique system-defining characteristics. It is possible that Plato might have approved a systematic reordering of his statement to read: The observer (as a truth) observing three other truths constitutes a system whose macro-micro-Universe-differentiating capability displays inherent symmetry and beauty—symmetry of four vertexes subtending four faces and symmetry of any two opposite pairs of its six edges precessionally subtending one another, together with the beauty of accomplishing such symmetry and Universe-differentiating with the minimum of structural system interrelationships. (See Fig. *542.02.*)

542.03 The qualitative interrelationships of this beautiful and symmetrical system are expressed in the generalized formula $N = \dfrac{N^2 - N}{2}$, in which $N = 4$, the number of vertexes of the minimum system constituting the tetrahedron; wherefore

$$4^2 = 16, \quad 16 - 4 = 12, \quad \frac{12}{2} = 6.$$

Six is the set of the uniquely symmetrical interrelationships of the minimum system.

542.04 Beauty and symmetry are inherent and make superficially "good" the three additional interrelationships: thankfulness, maximum economy, and wisdom. They also make "good" all the remaining cases on balance—the 32 cases (Sec. 1044) of all the simplest cosmically conceptual and structurally realizable systems of Universe.

542.05 Is there a *qualitative* systems attribute? Can special case system events and characteristics be appraised *qualitatively?* My answer is that you and I are always off-center. All special case realizations of generalized principles are always aberrated realizations. Since there is no simultaneity, there is always realization lag. Consciousness is aberration. But the lags are always accompanied by experientially evolved inventions of more efficient operational means of decreasing the magnitude of tolerated errors—i.e., off-center aberrations.

542.06 Evolutingly we always acquire the means to come closer to the truth, but in all special-case temporality and its asymmetric resonance we can never reach statically concentric congruence with truth.

542.07 Quality describes the relative proximity—concentrically attained—of absolute congruence with convergently directioned, dimensionless truth.

543.00 Reality and Inexactitude

543.01 Reality is the special case, episodic, high-frequency recall of like experiences within our individual scenario lives. Reality is nothing but high-frequency recurrence of the awareness of a dominant generalized principle remanifesting itself in our special case awareness sequences.

543.02 The cognitive is self-startered by mind's outer-rampart-guardian intuition and by mind's aesthetic delicacy of tolerance of pro tem imperfection. The intellect differentiates the reactions and discernments of our sense apprehending. The intellect-invented differentiations become operative when the high frequency of unrecognized events accelerates in pure principle to thicken up as do storm clouds: "Something's about to happen. . . . Now it's happening."

543.03 What you and I call matter are the high-frequency recurrences of interprinciple, interangular-action accommodations . . . the deflectings . . . the thickenings . . . sometimes intensifying to *hurt* or *bang!*

543.04 The cyclic timing of our only-apparently continuous sight—as photoframes—differs greatly from the cyclic timing of our other senses, each of which has its separate harmonic ranges and velocities (Sec. 801.09).

543.05 The apprehending of reality is a mind function. Reality = inexactitude.

543.10 Local and Cosmic Exactitude

543.11 Metaphysical principles are absolutely exact, absolutely inelastic, and absolutely intolerant of error: these are the generalized principles. Despite elegant mathematical expression, they may never be exactly defined by their human mind discoverers. (At Sec. 986.702 we see Einstein's once seemingly perfect equation $E = Mc^2$ having to be improved to read $E = 2V^2$, as vectorial expression of the T Module and E Module relationships—the vectors being a more economical expression of the product of mass and velocity.)

543.12   But there exists a plurality of such non-positionally-realized but eternally coexistent generalized principles whose integrated relative degree of relevance to any one episode or event of the individual's experience scenario is inherently inexact. These inexact events are always special case effects of the momentary integration of a plurality of generalized principles.

543.13   The wave-frequency characteristics of energy (either seemingly disassociative as radiation or seemingly associative as matter) are propagated by the elasticity of the mind's tolerance of the inexactitude-shrouded but nonetheless-recognized generalized principle. In complex social phenomena, we speak of this tolerance as love, which spontaneously forgives, allows, or tolerates outright macro-error or micro-deviation from exquisite exactitude.

543.14   The realities of you and I are typical special cases of the infinity of inexactitudes of the individual cognition lags and re-cognitions of the generalized integral of all generalized principles—love.

543.15   It was only the recall of the total of all the love that I had known in my childhood that turned around my determination in 1927 to throw myself away and instead to employ the throwaway-self toward repaying all lives for my unforgettable experiencings of the infinite tolerance of love as it had embraced and permeated (both) my infant, childhood, and juvenile years. My commitment to this repayment in turn led to the discovery of the cumulative total of loving understanding of all humanity in all time as ever regenerated in parents and grandparents for all its children and by the ever regenerative tolerance of children for parents.

543.20   Gravity and Love

543.21   The scientific word for the integral of all the special case realizations of gravity is love.

543.22   Love is the integral of gravity and radiation. Energy as either radiation or matter is the summa frequency, local-in-Universe, aberrational palpitation of comprehensive gravity embracement. Energy manifests itself as the palpitating, gravity-tolerated, aberrational pulsings-through of the plurality of exact centers of pure principles. This plurality of principles, being inherently different one from the other, have ever-varying interdomain proximities that produce varying push-pulls of the plurality of generalized principles influencing the locally-tuned-in event, which proximity variations depend on which set of principles are most informationally relevant in comprehending both the local and cosmic significance of any given local experience event.

543.23   All the foregoing abets our comprehension of the truth toward which all experience leads—to the truth that the physical is only a misapprehension of the metaphysical and that the reality is absolutely truthful love.

543.24   There is only the metaphysical. The physical can never be *only*— because it is only partially experienceable and think-aboutable.

543.25   It is the love-gravity toleration of high-frequency-recurrent aberrations from any one absolute principle's exact center, along with the varying yielding toward other centers, that permits those from-time-to-time, love-intellect-mind-intuited discoveries of the mathematical variation rates of interrelationship changes evolutionarily existing between the nondimensional plurality of pure principles. This infinitely regenerated and loving comprehension breeds realizations of the infinitude of intercombining the plurality of principles, which infinitude of realizations and complex interrelationships of variable-relevance tolerance effects altogether constitute both the over-all theme and the separate, unique, individual experience episodes of any one life at any one time. (Compare Secs. *541.18* and 1005.20.)

600.00 Structure

* Titles in parentheses may be found in *Synergetics 1*.

600.01   Definition: Structure

608.20   Even- and Odd-Number Reduction of Necklace Polygons

608.21   We undertake experimental and progressive reduction of the tubularly beaded necklace's multipolygonal flexibility. The reduction is accomplished by progressive one-by-one elimination of tubes from the assembly. The progressive elimination alters the remaining necklace assemblage from a condition of extreme accommodation of contouring intimacies and drapability over complexedly irregular, multidimensional forms until the assembly gradually approaches a number of remaining tubes whose magnitude can be swiftly assessed without much conscious counting. As the multipolygonal assembly approaches a low-number magnitude of components of the polygons, it becomes recognizable that an *even* number of remaining tubes can be arranged in a symmetrical totality of inward-outward, inward-outward points, producing a corona or radiant starlike patterning, or the patterning of the extreme crests and troughs of a circular wave. When the number of tubular beads is *odd*, however, then the extra tube can only be accommodated by either a crest-to-crest or a trough-to-trough chord of the circle. This is the pattern of a gear with one odd double-space tooth in each circle. If the extra length is used to join two adjacent crests chordally, this tooth could mesh cyclically as a gear only with an equal number of similarly toothed gears of slightly larger diameter, where the extra length is used to interconnect the two adjacent troughs chordally. (See Fig. *608.21*)

608.22   Even-numbered, equilength, tubular-bead necklaces can be folded into parallel bundles by slightly stretching the interconnection tension cable on which they are strung. Odd numbers cannot be so bundled.

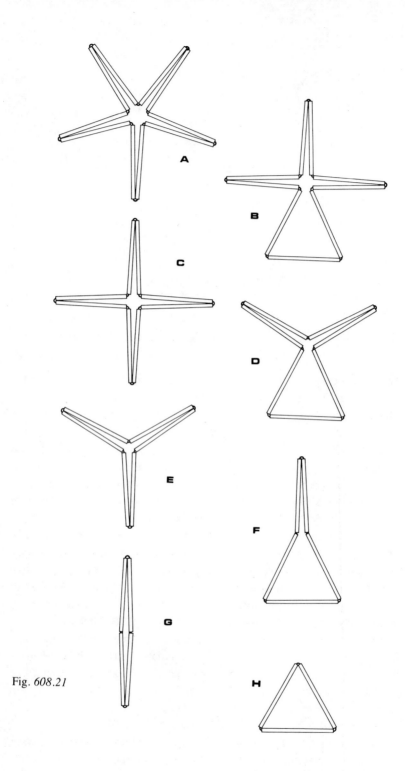

A

B

C

D

E

F

G

H

Fig. *608.21*

608.23   Congruence with Mariner's Compass Rose: As the number of remaining tubes per circle become less than 40, certain patterns seem mildly familiar—as, for instance, that of the conventional draftsman's 360-degree, transparent-azimuth circle with its 36 main increments, each subdivided into 10 degrees. At the 32-tube level we have congruence with the mariner's compass rose, with its four cardinal points, each further subdivided by eight points (see Fig. *608.23*).

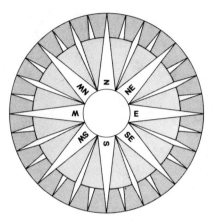

Fig. *608.23 Mariner's Compass Rose:* This pattern accommodates 32 necklace tubes per circle.

608.24   Next in familiarity of the reduced numbers of circular division increments comes the 12 hours of the clock. Then the decimal system's azimuthal circle of 10 with 10 secondary divisions. Circles of nine are unfamiliar. But the octagon's division is highly familiar and quickly recognized. Septagons are not. Powerfully familiar and instantly recognized are the remaining hexagon, pentagon, square, and triangle. There is no twogon. Triangle is the minimum polygon. Triangle is the minimum-limit case.

608.25   All the necklace polygons prior to the triangle are flexibly drapable and omnidirectionally flexible with the sometimes-square-sometimes-diamond, four-tube necklace as the minimum-limit case of parallel bundling of the tubes. The triangle, being odd in number, cannot be bundled and thus remains not only the minimum polygon but the only inflexible, nonfoldable polygon.

608.30   *Triangle as Minimum-altitude Tetrahedron*

608.31   In Euclidean geometry triangles and other polygons were misinformedly thought of as occurring in two-dimensional planes. The substanceless, no-altitude, planar polygons were thought to hold their shape—as did any polygonal shape traced on the Earth's surface—ignoring the fact that the shape of any polygon of more than three edges is maintained only by the four-dimensional understructuring. Only the triangle has an inherent and integral structural integrity.

608.32   The triangular necklace is not two-dimensional, however; like all experienceable structural entities it is four-dimensional, as must be all experienceably realized polygonal models even though the beads are of chalk held together by the tensile coherence of the blackboard. Triangles at their simplest consist experientially of one minimum-altitude tetrahedron.

610.00   Triangulation

610.24   Limit Cases: Macro, Medio, and Micro: Considered geometrically, triangles are the only self-stabilizing polygonal patterns—ergo, only triangles are structurally stable. Since we cannot construct a polyhedral system of only two triangles around each corner (because a polyhedral system must by definition have an insideness and an outsideness in order definitively and closingly to separate the Universe into macrocosm and microcosm), and since we cannot have six equilateral triangles around each vertex of a polyhedral system (for each of the six would themselves separate out from the others to form flat planes and could not close back to join one another to separate Universe definitively into macrocosm and microcosm)—ergo, the tetrahedron, octahedron, and icosahedron constitute the minimum, middle, and maximum cases of omnitriangulated—ergo, stabilized—structural subdividings of Universe into macro, medio, and micro Universe divisions.

610.30   Structural Harmonics

610.31   The conceptual sequence in the left column of Fig. 610.20 illustrates the basic octave behavior of structural transformations. The first three figures—tetra, octa, icosa—represent the positive outside-out set of primitive structural systems. Three equiangular triangles around each corner add to tetra; four around each corner add to octa; five around each corner add to icosa; but six 60-degree angles around each corner add to 360 degrees; ergo, produce an infinitely extendible plane; ergo, fail to return upon themselves embracingly to produce a system's insideness and outsideness; ergo, thus act as the zerophase of maximum evolution changing to the involution phase of maximum nothingness. As the transformation sequence changes from divergent evolution to convergent involution, from five, then four, then three equiangular triangles around each corner, it thereby produces successively the inside-out icosa, octa, and tetra, until the convergent involutional contraction attains the phase of maximum nothingness. At the minimum zero bottom of the sequence the inside-out tetra revolves outside-out to minimum somethingness of tetravolume 1 as the transformation diverges expansively to the maximum vector-equilibrium somethingness of tetravolume 20, thereafter attaining maximum nothingness and evolution-to-involution conversion. (See Sec. *1033*.)

610.32   At six-vector hexagonality we have the vector equilibrium at maximum zero evolution-to-involution conversion.

610.33   The minimum zero tetrahedron with which the series commences repeats itself beneath the bottom figure to permit the accomplishment of octave harmony at minimum zero conversion whose terminal nothingnesses accommodate the overlapping interlinkages of the octave terminals: thus do–re–mi–fa–sol–la–ti–do.

620.00   Tetrahedron

621.30   Camera Tripod

621.31   A simple model of the effective conservation of regenerative Universe is to be had in a camera tripod which, when its legs are folded and parallel, finds the centers of gravity and mass of its three individual legs in close proximity to one another. As the legs are progressively hinged outward from one another, the respective centers of mass and gravity recede from one another. From Newton's second law we know that as bodies increase their distance apart at an arithmetical rate, their interattractiveness decreases at a rate of the second power of the distance change—i.e., at double the distance the interattraction decreases to one-quarter intensity. Since the legs are fastened to one another at only one end (the top end), if the floor is slippery, the three bottom ends tend to slide apart at an accelerated rate.

621.32   We may think of the individual legs of the tripod as being energy vectors. The "length" of a vector equals the mass times the velocity of the force operative in given directions. We now open the equilengthed tripod legs until their bottom terminals are equidistant from one another, that distance being the same length as the uniform length of any one of the legs. Next we take three steel rods, each equal in length, mass, and structural strength to any one of the tripod legs, which renders them of equal force vector value to that of the tripod set. Next we weld the three rods together at three corner angles to form a triangle, against whose corners we will set the three bottom ends of the three downwardly and outwardly thrusting legs of the tripod. As gravity pulls the tripod Earthward, the tendency of these legs to disassociate further is powerfully arrested by the tensile integrity of the rod triangle on the ground, in which both ends of all three are joined together.

621.33   Assuming the three disassociative vectorial forces of the tripod legs to be equal to the associative vectorial force of the three-welded-together rods, we find the three-jointed closed system to be more effective than the one-jointed system. In this model the associative group in the closed triangle represents the gravity of Universe and the disassociative group—the tripod legs—represents the radiation of Universe. The whole model is the tetrahedron: the simplest structural system.

621.34   Think of the head of the camera tripod as an energy nucleus. We find that when nuclear energy becomes disassociated as radiation, it does so in a focused and limited direction unless it is intercepted and reflectively focused in a concave mirror. Radiation is inherently omnidirectional in its distribution from the nucleus outward, but it can be directionally focused. Gravity is totally embracing and convergently contractive toward all its system centers of Scenario Universe, and it cannot be focused. Like the circular waves made by an object dropped in the water, both gravitational and radiational growth-in-time patterns are concentrically arrayed; gravity convergently and contractively concentric, radiation divergently and expansively concentric. Frequency of concentricity occurrence is relative to the cyclic system considered.

625.10   Macro-Micro Invisible Tetrahedra

625.11   In finite but nonunitarily conceptual Scenario Universe a minimum-system tetrahedron can be physically realized in local time-and-space Universe—i.e., as tune-in-able only within human-sense-frequency-range capabilities and only as an inherently two-in-one tetrahedron (one convex, one concave, in congruence) and only by concurrently producing two separate invisible tetrahedra, one externalized macro and one internalized micro—ergo, four tetrahedra.

625.12   The micro-tetra are congruent only in our Universe; in metaphysical Universe they are separate.

640.00   Tension and Compression

642.10   Tetrahedral Models of Functions

642.11   Covarying functions are tetrahedrally modelable. A series of co-varying tetrahedral models is presented in Secs. 961.10–48.

646.10   Spherical Behavior of Gravity and Bonding

•[*646.10–646.22   Spherical Gravity Scenario*]

646.11   Gravitational behavior is an operational concept embracing the following discoveries:

(1) Spheres contain the most volume with the least surface.

(2) Nature always employs only the most economical intertransformative and omniscosmically interrelated behavioral stratagems.

(3) With each event in Universe there are always 12 unique degrees of freedom (see Sec. *537.06*).

(4) Falling bodies manifest a mathematically uniform, second-power, ex-ponential rate of acceleration (discovered by Galileo).

(5) Hidden within the superficial disorder of individual omnidifferences differences of size; differences in distance from the Sun; and differences in Sun-orbiting rates—there nonetheless exists an elegantly exact, one-to-one mathematical correspondence in the Sun's planets' intercoordinate behaviors manifest by the equiareas of the radii- and arc-bounded, piece-of-apple-pie-shaped, areal sweepouts, within an identical time span, of all the Sun's planets as they orbit elliptically around the Sun at vast distances from one another, all accomplished without any visible mechanical interlinkage such as gears, yet whose orbiting around the Sun (rather than flying off tangentially from those orbits by centrifugal force, as do the round iron balls released by hammer-throwing athletes) altogether suggests that some incredibly powerful

interattractiveness is operative. (All of the foregoing planetary behavior was discovered by Kepler. Compare Sec. *791.01*.)

(6) The above discoveries (1–5) were correlated by Newton to reveal:

First, that the prime interattractiveness magnitude existing between two mutually remote bodies, as compared to the prime interattractiveness existing between any other two mutually remote bodies, is arrived at by multiplying each of the respective couples' separate masses by one another; and

Second, as a cosmic generalization of the second-power, time-distance acceleration rate of Galileo's Earthward-falling bodies, Newton discovered the second-power mathematical rate of interattractiveness gain occurring with each halving of the intervening distance of any two given celestial bodies; whereby it was thereafter shown by other astronomers that there are interrelationship behaviors manifest in physical Universe that are in no wise indicated to be interoperative between those bodies by any or all of the unique and integral geometrical, chemical, or physical characteristics of any one of the mass-interattracted bodies when either one is only separately considered.

(7) Synergy means behavior of whole systems unpredicted by the integral characteristics of any of the systems' separate parts; thus it has come to pass that it has been synergetically *proven* that Copernicus was right, for the exponentially ever-increasing interattractiveness of bodies freed of other external restraints must induce their ultimate huddling together in the most economical volume-to-enclosing-surface manner, which, as the number of converging bodies increases, is that of the *spherical* conformation.

646.12 The spherical behavior of gravity is illustrated in the trending series of intertransforming events that would take place as two large, independent spherical masses, such as two asteroids, fell into one another and their multitudinous individual atoms began to sort themselves into most economical interarray. Interestingly enough, this is the opposite of what transpires with biological cell dichotomy.

646.13 Electromagnetic radiant energy is entropic; gravitational energy is syntropic (see Sec. *1052.80*).

646.14 Speaking mathematically, the surface area growth is always at a second-power rate of increase in respect to the linear dimension's rate of increase. As Newton's linear distance apart was measured arithmetically, we can understand systematically why the relative interattraction of the bodies varies as the second power, which represents their relative surface rates of change, but this does not explain why there is any interattraction. Interattraction is eternally mysterious.

646.15 **Circumferential Behavior of Gravity: Hammer Men and Closest Packing:** Sheet-metal workers never seem to think of what they are doing in terms of what their work does to the atoms, of the ways the atoms accommodate to their work. The hammer men have learned that they can gather the metal together in a way that hammers it thicker. It is easy to conceive of hammering metals thinner, but few of us would think spontaneously of hammering metals thicker. But the hammer men are quite able to do this, to hammer the metal in such a way as to increase its bulk. They can start with a flat sheet of metal and hammer it thicker, as you would knead dough together after it has been rolled out thin with a rolling pin. But you push the dough together horizontally with your hands; you do not pummel it vertically from above. The skilled sheet-metal workers can do just that with the metal, though amateurs might assume it to be illogical, if not impossible. (See Secs. 1024.13–15 and 1024.21).

646.16 We can conceive of heating metal until it becomes liquid and flows together. Thus the blacksmith's heating of his horseshoes to a bright red, to a condition just short of melting; this makes it easy for us to think of the cherry-red metal as being in a plastic or semimolten condition that permits the smith to smite it into any preferred shapes—thicker or thinner. But the sheet-metal men hammer cold, hard sheet metal into any shape without preheating.

646.17 What the hammer men do intuitively without sensing it consciously is to hit the indestructible atoms tangentially, as a billiards player might "kiss" the object ball with his cue ball. Thus does the hammer inadvertently impel atoms sidewise, often to roll atop the next-nearest "spherical" aggregate of atoms. The aggregate of atoms is spherical because of the electrons' orbiting combined with the atoms' spinning at so high a rate as usually to present a dynamically spherical surface. Hammer men do not think about their work as bounce-impelling the spherical atoms around as if they were a bunch of indestructible ball bearings stuck together magnetically, as a conse quence of which the accelerated ball bearings would cleave-roll to relodge themselves progressively in certain most-economically-traveled-to, closest-packed, internested rearrangements.

646.18 Atoms dislodged from the outer layer of the omniintermagnetized ball bearings would always roll around on one another to relocate themselves in some closest-packing array, with any two mass-interattracted atoms being at least in tangency. When another dynamic-spherical-domain atom comes into closest-packing tangency with the first two, the mutual interattractiveness interrolls the three to form a triangle. Three in a triangle produce a "planar" pattern of closest packing. When a fourth ball bearing lodges in the nest formed between and atop the first three, each of the four balls then touches three others simultaneously and produces a tetrahedron having a concave-faceted void within it. In this tetrahedral position, with four-dimensional symmetry of association, they are in circumferential closest packing. Having no mutual sphere, they are only intercircumferentially mass-interattracted and cohered: i.e., *gravity* alone coheres them, but gravity is hereby seen experimentally to be exclusively circumferential in interbonding.

646.19   With further spherical atom additions to the initial tetrahedral aggregate, the outermost balls tend to roll coherently around into asymmetrical closest-packing collections, until they are once more symmetrically stabilized with 12 closest packing around one and as yet exercising their exclusively intercircumferential interattractiveness, bound circumferentially together by four symmetrically interacting circular bands, whereby each of the 12 surrounding spheres has four immediately adjacent circumferential shell spheres interattracting them circumferentially, while there is only one central nuclear ball inwardly—i.e., radially attracting each of them. In this configuration they form the vector equilibrium.

646.20   In the vector-equilibrium configuration of closest-packed, ''spherical'' atoms we have clarification of the *Copernican nostalgia,* or synergetic proclivity, of the circumferentially arrayed spheres to associate symmetrically around the nucleus sphere or the nucleus void, which, as either configuration—the vector equilibrium or the icosahedron—rotates dynamically, producing a spherical surface. But the modus operandi of *four* symmetrically intertriangulated gravitational hoops (in the case of the vector equilibrium) and the *six* hoops (in the case of the icosahedron) is lucidly manifest. If we take out the central ball, or if it shrinks in diameter, we will discover synergetics' jitterbug model (see Sec. 460), showing that the 12 circumferential spheres will closest pack circumferentially until each of the 12 circumferentially arrayed balls is tangent to five surrounding balls, and thus they altogether form the icosahedron.

646.21   Gravity has been described by Arthur Koestler as the nostalgia of things to become spheres. The nostalgia is poetic, but the phenomenon is really more of a necessity than it is a nostalgia. Spheres contain the most volume with the least surface: Gravity is circumferential: Nature is always most economical. Gravity is the most effective embracement. Gravity behaves spherically *of necessity,* because nature is always most economical.

646.22   The hammer man probably does not think about these properties of atoms. The fact is that the spheres do not actually touch each other. They are held together only mass-interattractively, and their electron paths are of course at distances from their atomic nuclei equivalent relatively to that of the distance of the Earth from the Sun, as proportioned to the respective radii of these vastly different-sized spheres. Thus the hammer man can push the atoms only as the physical laws allow them to be moved. Nature accommodates his only-superficially contrived hammering strategies, while all the time all those atoms are intercohered by gravity—which the hammer associates only with falling objects. Almost nothing of the reality of our present life meets the human eye; wherefore our most important problems are invisible.

700.00 Tensegrity

700.00   TENSEGRITY

(700.01   Definition: Tensegrity)*

(710.00   Vertexial Connections)

(720.00   Basic Tensegrity Structures)

(730.00   Stabilization of Tension in Tensegrity Columns)

(740.00   Tensegrity Masts: Miniaturization)

(750.00   Unlimited Frequency of Geodesic Tensegrities)

(760.00   Balloons)

(770.00   System Turbining in Tensegrity Structures)

(780.00   Allspace Filling)

*Titles in parentheses will be found in *Synergetics 1*

790.00 Tensegrity Structures

•[*790.10–795.11 Tensegrity Scenario*]

790.10 Definition

790.11 Everyone thinks he knows the meaning of the word *structure*. We point to a stone wall or a bridge or a barn and say, "That's a structure." What is common to a steel bridge, a wooden barn, a jumbo jet, an iceberg, a starfish, a star, a fern, a diamond jewel, an elephant, a cloud, and a human baby? They are all structures. Some are more versatile than others; some last longer than others. Why? Why do the stone or wood or steel cohere at all? If we understood a little more about structure, it could lead to a better understanding of the political and economic dilemmas of our time. Political and economic systems are structures—often so ill-conceived as to require constant local patching and mending. Even structural engineering has as yet failed to comprehend adequately or to define and cope with structure.

790.12 We all have experiences of *pushing* and *pulling*, and we think of them as 180-degree experiences directly away from us or toward us. But (as we shall soon discover) pushing and pulling both produce 90-degree resultants, which we mistakenly call "side effects." Our side effects are nature's primary effects, and vice versa. Pushing is outwardly explosive from a center of effort: that is why a ping pong ball can ride on the parting outward and downward of the waters of an only-vertically-aimed fountain nozzle. Gravity and magnetism are embracingly contractive around—and radially inward toward—a center of gravity. With gases, *pull* is a partial vacuum whereas *push* is an explosion: attraction vs propulsion, tension vs compression.

790.13 Tension and compression always and only coexist and covary inversely. We experience tension and compression continuously as they interaccommodate the eternally intertransforming and eternally regenerative interplay of the gravitational and radiational forces of Universe.

790.14   The gravitational or omnidirectional tension totality in Universe is quantitatively equal to the totality of the radiational or explosive compression of Universe, but the sum total of tensional coherence is more effectively arranged than the sum total of explosively disintegrative forces. This is why Universe is finite. (See Sec. 231.)

790.15   Barrel: A barrel as the sum total of its staves and its encircling hoop bands illustrates the cosmic gravity-vs-radiation balance. (See Figs. 705.01–.02.) The staves are wedges—each stave is wedged between two other truncated-triangle wooden staves. When seen in cross-section, each stave is the outer-arc-chord-truncation segment of a long, thin, isosceles triangle whose inner, sharply pointed section—truncated and dispensed with— would have had its apex at the central axis of the barrel. Each stave's outer chord is always a little wider than its inner chord, wherefore the staves cannot fall inward of one another but could very readily move outwardly and apart, were it not for the tension bands that go completely around the barrel and close back on themselves as a finite integrated system.

790.16   The staves are separate, disassociative, inherently disintegrative, and self-differentiating, while the barrel's external ring-bands are self-integrating: though separate, the two groups of members are operating complementarily to produce union. It is the embracing tension that successfully maintains the integrity of the barrel despite the disintegrative tendencies of the individual staves. The push-pull components are more effective associatively than they are separately. The disintegrative explosive force is embracingly cohered by the gravitational. So it is with Universe.

790.17   Push and pull, disassociative and associative in omnidirectional balance, characterize the essence of structure.

790.18   Column: If you load the top center of a thin column, it tends to bend like a banana—its radius of curvature in the bending area gets smaller and smaller. (See Fig. 640.20.) A tensed line tends to get straighter and straighter, though never absolutely straight. Physics has not found any straight lines. Physics has found only waves—the superficially straighter waves being of ever higher frequency and ever shorter wavelength, and always locally and discontinuously particled.

790.19   Compression tends to break a slender one-wavelength column into two columns of two wavelengths, thus tending to focus the ever smaller radius between them into one point, which increases the leverage of either half to consummate the breakage. (See Fig. 640.20G.)

790.20   By contracting their girth, tensed lines of tension tend to pull their fibers together ever more tightly so that the atoms get nearer to one another—their mass interattractiveness increases as the second power of the decrease in the distance between the atoms. (See Fig. 641.01B.) Tensional strength increases initially, and therewith lies its capability to cope with loading; when the girth contraction rate is exceeded by the elongation of the tension member, the atoms recede from one another and coherence decreases rapidly.

790.21   Ropes can be pulled around corners. Neither stiff poles nor flexible ropes can be pushed around corners. Tension has a greater distance range of capability than has compression: witness the compression masts and the only-tensionally-suspended long center spans of the great suspension bridges. Tensional capabilities are always more versatile and energetically effective than are compressional capabilities. The variable live loads of suspension bridges are applied directly only to its cables, which distribute the loads evenly. In the same way the tensed tubes of automobile tires receive the shock loads locally and distribute them evenly.

790.22   The taller a column is in proportion to its mid-girth cross-section dimension, the less the load it will bear before it tends to buckle, which means to bend twistingly outward in one direction, and—if further loaded—ultimately to break into two columns. In principle, tension members of structures have no limit ratio of cross-section-to-length. With materials of higher and higher tensile strength it is possible to make longer and longer and thinner and thinner tension cables—approaching a condition of very great length and no cross-section at all. (See Figs. 641.01C-D.) With better and better alloys it is possible to make longer and longer, thinner and thinner, clear-span suspension bridges. People tend erroneously to think of those cables as "solid"—and of the steel as solid—but they are not solid: the atoms are not touching one another. The distances between the nuclei of the atoms and their orbiting electrons—as measured in diameters of their nuclei—are approximately the same proportionally as the distance between our star Sun and its planets. The individual atoms are in sufficiently critical proximity to be sustainingly attracted to one another as are the Earth and Moon, which obviously are not touching each other. In aeronautical terms they are all in dynamic "flying formation." As the Earth and the Moon co-orbit the Sun, and as the Sun and its planets together are in flight formation in our galactic system's merry-go-round, and as the billions of galaxies omnirecede from one another, they are all intersecured by comprehensive mass attraction. The mutual interpull force between Sun, Earth, and Moon is manifest rotationally around opposite sides of the Earth by the twice-a-day tides as quadrillions of tons of water are progressively pulled outward from Earth's surface jointly by the Moon and the Sun—and then are allowed to subside. In the Milky Way periphery of our galaxy the stars do not touch one another: they are in critical proximity. The Universe itself is held together by tension—invisible, substanceless tension that allows for local motions and transformations.

790.23   The same structural laws of Universe operate at both macro- and microlevels: they are the structural laws of our planet Earth.

790.24   Architecture on our planet Earth is the design process of building macrostructures out of microstructures, the building of visible structures out of invisible structures.

791.00   Cosmic Structuring

791.01   With the advent of mathematical calculating capability into the public domain only 500 years ago, we had the beginnings of mathematically derived knowledge of cosmic structuring principles. To understand the significance of these principles we begin with Isaac Newton. Newton was inspired by the prior discoveries of Kepler, Galileo, and Copernicus, and he derived his laws of motion from consideration of their basic concepts, as follows:

(1) Kepler discovered that all of the Sun's then known six planets orbit the Sun in elliptical paths.

(2) The planets are of different sizes, each going around the Sun at different rates and at vastly different distances from the Sun.

(3) In a given amount of time all of the planets "sweep out" equal areas. For instance, in a period of 21 days each planet describes a relatively short elliptical arc of travel around the Sun. If we connect the two ends of those arcs by the shortest radial lines to the Sun, and if we make proportionally accurate diagrams of each of the six pie-shaped pieces of sky enclosed by the respective arc-and-radii-bound areas, and if we use Kepler's carefully measured dimensions of those arcs and radii, we will find that the several triangular pieces of pie are very different in shape—ranging from very thin and long to very short and wide—but when calculated for area, they are all found to be of exactly identical areas. (Compare Sec. *646.11.*)

(4) The coordination of these planetary motions was found to be exquisitely accurate but hidden invisibly in disparate observational data. Considered separately, each planet had unique behavioral characteristics that could not be explained by any mechanics of physical contact such as that of a train of teeth-meshed gears. The planets and the Sun are vast distances apart. Kepler must have noted that a weight on the end of a string hand-swung by a human around the head will—when released into orbit—travel tangentially and horizontally

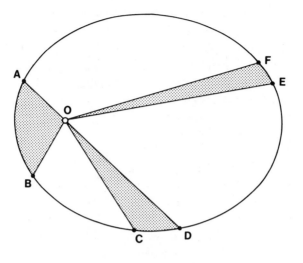

Area AOB = Area COD = Area EOF

Fig. *791.01(3) Diagram of Equal Area Planetary Sweepouts:* Each of the irregular pie-shaped pieces of sky enclose identical areas.

away from the human, while being progressively diverted toward Earth by the gravitational pull. Thus Kepler concluded that invisible tensile forces were intercohering the orbiting planets with the Sun and, to a lesser extent, with each other.

(5) Galileo's measurement of the accelerating acceleration in the rate of bodies falling freely toward Earth indicated that each time the distance between the falling body and the Earth was halved, the speed of falling increased fourfold.

(6) Newton was also impressed by the enormous magnitude of the tidal pulling of the Earth's waters by the Moon and the Sun.

(7) The astronomers and navigators had established information governing the seemingly "fixed" interpositions of certain celestial star patterns at any given moment of the year as viewed from any given position on Earth. Of course, much of the celestial sphere patterning is obscured from any human observer on Earth's surface by the vast bulk of our planet. But Newton knew from personal experience that the position (as calculated by spherical geometry) of any one of the viewable stars as measured in angular height above the observer's horizon in any given compass direction at any chronometer-recorded moment of time on any given annual calendar day will permit the observer to make accurate calculation of his position on Earth.

791.02   In consideration of all the foregoing seven concepts—and much other information—Isaac Newton concluded that the relative magnitude of interpull forces of planetary coordination was proportional to the masses of the bodies involved. He concluded that the interpull between two apples would be so insignificant in proportion to the pull of massive Earth upon both apples that the two apples near one another on the table would be so powerfully pulled against the table as to manifest no measurable pull toward each other. Apparently the extraordinary interpulling of Universe could only be manifested in free space; thus it had never been noticed by humans in their preoccupation with Earthian affairs.

791.03   Newton reasoned from Kepler's work that if he swung a weight around his head and then let go of it, it would start off in a horizontal line but become overpowered by gravity and swiftly veer away 90 degrees vertically toward Earth. Thus Newton formulated his first law of motion, that all bodies will persist in a state of rest or in a line of motion *except* as affected by other bodies.

791.04   Newton reasoned that if Earth were to be annihilated, it would relinquish its pull on the Moon, and then the Moon would be free to fly off tangentially on an approximately linear course. He chose a night of full Moon at a given moment of clock time to observe the Moon—well above the horizon—predictably positioned against the celestial pattern of the "fixed" stars. He then calculated the line of tangential direction along which a released Moon would travel as traced against the sky pattern. Newton then observed and calculated the rate at which the Moon would travel away from the theoretical trajectory of release and "fall" toward the Earth as they both orbited the Sun at 60,000 miles per hour.

791.05   As a result of this observation and calculation Newton found that the path of the Moon's "fall" agreed exactly with the falling body data of Galileo. Wherefore Newton concluded it was celestially manifest that

(1) relative to all known bodies, the magnitude of mutual interattraction between any two bodies is proportional to the product of their paired and intermultiplied masses; and

(2) whenever the distance between two bodies is halved, the force of their interattraction increases fourfold, which is to say that the interattraction varies exponentially at a second-power rate as the distance between the considered bodies varies at only an arithmetical rate.

791.06   For millennia humans had endeavored to explain the apparently random independence, the seemingly uncoordinated individual motions, of the five planetary bodies visible from Earth, orderly interpositioned against the background of the vast myriads of "fixed" stars of the celestial sphere. What Newton had discovered is relevant to our comprehension of the universal nature of structures. He had discovered a pair of integral characteristics of two bodies, with one interrelationship varying at an exponential rate and the other interrelationship covarying arithemtically. Kepler and Newton had found synergetic behaviors of whole systems that were unpredicted by the behaviors or the integral characteristics of any parts of the system considered separately. Kepler and Newton had found synergy.

791.07   If you were a contemporary of Kepler or Newton and were to have asked them what the mass interattraction called "gravity" *is*, they would have told you that they had no way of knowing. And there is as yet no way to explain the interrelationship behaviors found experimentally to exist "between" and not "of" any two objects in Universe. The relationships they discovered are elegantly reliable, but they are also an absolute a priori mystery.

791.08   Humanity has inherited an inventory of generalized laws of Universe from the Copernicus-Kepler-Galileo-Newton discoveries, which they in turn inherited from their Greek, Mesopotamian, Egyptian, Indian, and Chinese predecessors. There is no information to suggest that the inventory has been completed. All of the generalized laws can be expressed in mathematical terms. They are all eternally operative and interaccommodative. Together, the thus-far-discovered generalized laws guarantee the integrity of nonsimultaneous, only partially overlapping, Scenario Universe.

792.00 Design

792.01   The word *design* is used in contradistinction to random happenstance. *Design* is intellectually deliberate. Design means that all the components of the composition are interconsiderately arranged. In a design the component behaviors, proclivities, and mathematical behaviors are interaccommodative. The family of generalized principles constitutes an eternal cosmic design whose interrelationships are expressible only in abstract mathematical terms.

792.02   Speaking in terms of generalized law, *structure* is always and only the consequence of a complex of six energy events—three dominantly tensive and three dominantly compressive—with each set interacting in complement to produce a self-regeneratively stabilized pattern.

792.03   Contrary to common opinion (even that of engineers), structures are always dynamic and never static. All structural realizations are special case. Structural realizations have specific longevities; they are entropic; they give off energy. The energies are often syntropically replaceable in the consequence of structural transformations.

792.04 Any and all of what humans identify as substances are structural systems. Any and all structure consists entirely of atoms. Atoms are not things: they are energy events occurring in pure principle. Each and every experimentally evidenced atom is a complex of unique structural-system interrelationships—both internal and external—that manifest generalized pattern integrities in special case scenario continuities.

792.10 **Universe:** Universe is synergetic. Universe is synergetically consequent to all the generalized principles, known or unknown. Universe is not a structure. Universe embraces all structures and more. While a plurality of generalizations governs all structures, *realized* structuring is always special case. Structures are synergetic consequences of the intimate interaction of a complex of special case factors. Superficially, the overall limits of the manifold omniintertransformability of structures are unitarily conceptual.

792.20 **Scenario Universe:** Scenario Universe embraces all the non-simultaneous, only-local-in-time-and-place structurings, destructurings, unstructurings, and restructurings. All the somethingnesses are structures. All the nothingness is unstructure. All the somethingnesses are special case. All the nothingness is generalized.

792.30 **Tension and Compression:** Everything we call structure is synergetic and exists only as a consequence of interactions between divergent compressional forces and convergent tension forces.

792.31 I take a piece of rope and tense it. As I purposely tense it, I inadvertently make it more taut. But I was not tensing the rope for the purpose of making it taut; my brain was only trying to elongate the rope. As I do so, however, the girth is inadvertently contracting and the rope is inadvertently getting harder. In getting harder the cross-section of the rope is contracting radially in a plane at 90 degrees to the axis of my purposeful tensing, thus inadvertently producing the always and only coexisting action-reaction-and-resultant complementations of myopic preoccupation.

792.32 Next I purposely produce compression. I take tempered steel rods, each three feet long and one-eighth of an inch in diameter. The rods bend flexively. We find that two rods cannot get closer to one another than in parallel tangency of their circular cross-sections. A third rod cannot get closer to the other two than by nestling in the parallel valley between them. With each of the three rods in parallel tangency, the centers of their three circular cross-sections form an equilateral triangle.

792.33 Hexagons consist of six equiangular triangles. Hexagons have six circumferential points and a center point—seven in all—all equidistant from their neighbors. Six rods now huddle in closest-packed tangency around the original rod. (See Fig. 412.01.) And 12 more rods may be huddled around the first seven to complete an additional hexagonal perimeter. Successive perimeters aggregate, each time with six more rods than those of the previous ring. The outermost rods will be tangentially closest packed in triangular stabilization with their neighbors; the rod at the center is at the symmetrical nucleus of the aggregate. We note in nature that the rodlike Earthward trajectories of closely falling, inter-mass-attracted raindrops passing through freezing temperatures nucleate in hexagonal snowflake arrays under just such hexagonal close-packing laws.

792.34   The Greek architects found experientially that when the height of a stone column exceeded its girth by 18 diameters, it tended to fail by buckling out of the central stone cylinder section. The length-to-diameter ratio of a compressional column is called its *slenderness ratio.* Continuous steel columns are more stable than stone columns and may be used structurally with slenderness ratios as high as 30 to 1—these are long columns. Short columns—with a slenderness ratio of 12 to 1—tend to fail by crushing rather than by buckling.

792.35   For our further experiment in *purposeful compression* we assemble a column 36 inches high with a minimum girth diameter of three inches. It requires 547 of our 36-inch-long, one-eighth-inch-diameter rods to produce this 12-to-1 short column. Each individual rod is slender and highly buckleable, but bound circumferentially together for its full length by tightly wound steel wire. The rods will close-pack symmetrically in a hexagonal set of 13 concentric rings around a nuclear rod: the maximum diameter will be three and three-eighths inches. We can then add forged steel caps over the hexagonal ends of this integrated short column.

792.36   We may next insert the column perpendicularly between the upper and lower jaws of a hydraulic press and load the composite column in vertical compression. We know from our earlier trial that each rod taken by itself can bend when end-loaded. Being close-packed together, they cannot bend further inwardly toward the center rod: they can only bend outwardly, straining the binding wire wrapped around the rods and causing them ultimately to yield to the severe outward force at the column's mid-girth. The bunched ends are held together by the hexagonal steel caps as the force of the hydraulic press increases. This results in the whole column twisting mildly and bulging out to become cigar-shaped as seen in vertical profile. If loaded sufficiently, the bundle approaches sphericity.

792.37   This experiment indicates that our purposeful loading of the column in compression inadvertently results in its girth increasing in diameter, which brings about *tension* in the horizontally bound wires. An inadvertent tension occurs in a plane at 90 degrees to the axis of compression.

792.40 **Tidal Complementarities:** By two visibly different experiments—one with rope and the other with steel rods—we have demonstrated experimentally that tension and compression always and only coexist. One can be at *high tide* of visibility and the other coincidentally at *low tide,* or vice versa. These tidal covariables are typical complementarities: they are not mirror images of one another, but must always balance one another complexedly in physical equations. Both demonstrate 90-degree inadvertent resultants. In engineering this behavior is known as the *Poisson effect,* and in physics it is known as *precession.*

792.50 **Spherical Islands:** Short columns loaded on their neutral axes tend to bulge toward sphericity of conformation. In the spherical form—and only in the spherical—we find that the system has no unique axis. Any diametric loading in the sphere is in effect a neutral axis. In coping with compressive loads, spheres act most effectively regardless of which is the loaded axis. Since spheres have the greatest volume with the least surface, loads are evenly distributed radially from the center to all of the enclosing mass. Thus ball bearings constitute the most effective of universal load-bearing designs for compressional functioning.

792.51 We find nature preferentially investing her compressionally assigned energy tasks in sphericals—whether stars, planets, asteroids, oranges, or atoms. Universe isolates all her major compression functions in spherical islands that are vastly remote from one another and that are intercohered only by Kepler's and Newton's invisible tension: *gravity.* The star Sun gravitationally precesses its compressionally islanded planets to orbit around it; the atomic nucleus gravitationally precesses its islanded electrons to orbit around it. Nature's cosmic structuring strategy employs only discontinuous islanded compression and only omni-everywhere continuous tension, *gravity.* Paradoxically, Earthian engineers as yet design their structures only as compressional continuities, sometimes tied together by tension rods and reinforcements. Humans still use a primarily direct-compressional Stone Age logic, using tension only as a secondary reinforcement. Nature—both macrocosmically and microcosmically—uses a primary tensional logic, with compression as a secondary islanded back-up.

792.52 The Stone Age logic said that the wider and heavier the walls, the more happily secure would be the inhabitants. The advent of metal alloys in the 20th century has brought an abrupt change from the advantage of structural ponderousness to the advantage of structural lightness. This is at the heart of all ephemeralization: that is the dymaxion principle of doing ever more with ever less weight, time, and ergs per each given level of functional performance. With an average recycling rate for all metals of 22 years, and with comparable design improvements in performance per pound, ephemeralization means that ever more people are being served at ever higher standards with the same old materials.

793.00 Tree Structures

793.01   Among nature's most efficient—and therefore most beautiful—designs are the structuring of the great trees. To examine the structural effectiveness of trees we can make an experiment. Take two suitcases, each weighing 50 pounds, one in each hand. Try to hold them out horizontally at arm's length. It is easy for our arms to hang them vertically from our shoulders, but the more horizontally they are held, the more difficult. It is almost impossible to hold out 50 pounds horizontally. Yet look at a tree's shoulders where the branches are attached. Look at the branch of a tree with the same girth as that of your shoulder when your arm is extended and flexed. Such a tree branch may weigh 500 pounds—ten times what you can hold out horizontally. Many larger-shouldered tree branches weighing five tons and more are held out horizontally. "Wing root" is an aeronautical engineering term for shoulder—that is, where the plane's airframe fuselage joins the jet-pod-carrying aluminum wing. These air transport wing roots accomplish great load-bearing tasks with very low weight ratios. The way trees hold out five-ton branches while yielding in streamline and flexing gracefully without breaking in great winds is a design accomplishment unparalleled in aeronautical engineering—even in the wing roots of jumbo jets and supersonic fighters. How can a tree do that? Biological structures cope hydraulically with all compressional loadings.

793.02   The paramount function of trees is to expose as much leafage as possible under varying wind conditions in order to impound Sun radiation. By a complex of relationships with other biologicals, this impoundment supports life on our planet, since few mammals can directly convert Sun energy into life support. Since the function of trees requires maximum leafage exposure, their progeny will prosper best when planted outside the shadow of the parent. Each tree seed is a beautiful flying machine designed to ride the wind until reaching propitious soil. Because few seeds will find propitious sites in this random distribution, the tree launches many thousands of seeds. The seeds contain the geometric design instructions for associating the locally available resources of air and water and the atomic chemistries of the locally available soil and rock in the environs of seed-landing.

793.03   Seeds contain coded programs for associating local atoms in triple-bonded crystal structures. Triple-bonded structures have high tensile capabilities, and when further interbonded they produce long, overlapping, fibrous sacs to be filled with local water and air derivatives. These close-packed, liquid-filled fibrous sacs compound first to produce the "wood" of the tree's roots and trunk. What nature ships in the seeds are the DNA-RNA coded instructions on how to utilize the resources of the locally occurring water, gases, and chemical elements at the planting site. The high-tensile fiber sacs are filled with liquid sap developed from water brought in from the roots by osmosis. By one-way capillary valving the hydrogen and oxygen of the water combine with the carbon- and oxygen-laden gases of the atmosphere to produce the hydrocarbon crystal cells of the tree while at the same time giving off to the atmosphere oxygen atoms with which the growth of mammals will be respiratorially sustained.

793.04   Enormous amounts of water are continuously being elevated through the one-way, antigravity valving system. The tree feeds the rain-forming atmosphere by leaking atomized water out through its leaves while at the same time sucking in fresh water through its roots. The tree's high-tensile fiber cell sacs are everywhere full of liquid. Liquids are noncompressible; they distribute their local stress loadings evenly in all directions to all the fiber cell sacs. The hydraulic compression function firmly fills out the predesigned overall high-tensile fiber shaping of the tree. In between the liquid molecules nature inserts tiny gaseous molecules that are highly compressible and absorb the tree's high-shock loadings, such as from the gusts of hurricanes. The branches can wave wildly, but they rarely break off unless they are dehydratively dying—which means they are losing the integrity of their hydraulic, noncompressible load-distribution system. Sometimes in an ice storm the tree freezes so that the liquids cannot distribute their loads; then the branches break off and fall to the ground.

793.05   In trees the liquids distribute the loads and the gases absorb the shocks in an overall high-tension crystalline fiber network predesigned by the DNA-RNA programming. The system transmits its hydraulic load-distribution impulses through each liquid-filled cell's contacts with adjacent liquid-loaded sacs. Starting with one tetrahedral bud "shoot," the tree grows as a series of concentric tetrahedral cones. Revolved tetrahedra generate cones. The constant reorienting of the direction from which the Sun radiation is coming, the frequent shift in the wind direction, and the consequent drag forces on the tetra-tree produce a conic revolution effect on the tree growth. Each year a new cambium layer cone grows over the entire outside of the previous year's tetra-cone. Each branch of the tree also starts as a tetrahedral shoulder cone sprouting out of the main tree cone.

793.06   This high-tension sac's web design with its hydraulic compression coping and pneumatic shock absorbing is much the same structural system nature employs in the design of human beings. To be sure, with humans the liquid does not freeze under normal environmental conditions; nature creates a good-health temperature control of 98.6 degrees F. for all its humans. Instead of the larger tetra cone form, over which the tree builds from the roots outward into its successive live layers, nature introduced in the mobile mammals the skeleton around which all their hydraulically actuated muscles and cushioning cells are grown in crystalline patterns as scheduled by the DNA-RNA program and as thereafter automated by genetic coding.

793.07   When humans tried to make solid crystalline machinery and ship it from here to there over the ground, the objects could move only very slowly without being shattered. So pneumatic tires were put on the wheels so as to distribute the working loads throughout all the freely moving compressional molecules, which in turn distribute the workload energies over the whole uniformly tensioned surface of the high-tensile tire casing. The aeronautical engineers finally adopted nature's biological structuring strategies to cope with 150 tons of fully loaded jumbo jets coming out of the sky to land at 150 miles per hour—with the music going and the people putting on their coats, paying no attention to the extraordinary engineering accomplishment. The plane's tires are pneumatic. Rubber makes the first contact. Pneumatics take the shock load. Next the hydraulic struts distribute the shock loading evenly through metered orifices, and all the shock load energy is thereafter distributed as heat through the high conductivity aluminum walls of the hydraulic system. The heat is completely dispersed by the metal surfaces. Only in the landing gear of great airplanes have humans employed nature's really beautiful structuring of crystalline tension in complement with hydraulic compression and pneumatic elasticity for shock absorption.

794.00 Geodesic Domes

794.01   The great structural systems of Universe are accomplished by islanded compression and omnicontinuous tension. *Tensegrity* is a contraction of *tensional integrity* structuring. All geodesic domes are tensegrity structures, whether the tension-islanded compression differentiations are visible to the observer or not. Tensegrity geodesic spheres do what they do because they have the properties of hydraulically or pneumatically inflated structures.

794.02   Pneumatic structures—such as footballs—provide a firm shape when inflated because the kinetically accelerated atmospheric molecules are trying to escape and are impinging outwardly against the skin, stretching outwardly into whatever accommodating roundness has been designed into the omniembracing tension system. (Compare Sec. 760.) When more molecules are introduced into the enclosure by an air pump, their overcrowding increases the pressure. A fleet of ships maneuvering under power needs more sea room than does another fleet of ships moored side by side. The higher the speed of the individual ship, the greater the minimum turning radius and the more sea room required. This means that the enclosed and pressurized molecules in pneumatic structural systems are accelerated in outward-bound paths by the addition of more molecules by the pump; without additional room each must move faster to get out of the way of the others.

794.03　Pressurized liquid or gaseous molecules try to escape from their confining enclosure. When a football is kicked on one outside spot the outward-bound molecules impact evenly on the entire inside surface of the football's flexible skin. The many outward-bound impactings force the skin outwardly and firmly in all directions; the faster the molecules move, the more powerful their impact, and the harder and more resilient the football. The effect is dynamic; there is no firm or static condition. The outward forces are met by the compressive embracement of the tensile envelope enclosure.

794.04　Geodesic domes are designed as enclosing tensile structures to meet discretely—ergo, nonredundantly—the patterns of outwardly impinging forces. A fishing net's mesh need be no finer than that through which the smallest fish worth catching cannot pass. If we know exactly the size of the fish we wish to catch, and how many of them are going to hit the net, exactly where, at what force, at what angle, and when, we then have a model for the realistic engineering analysis of geodesic domes.

794.05　The conventional engineering profession has been analyzing geodesics strictly in terms of compression, on a crystalline, non-load-distributing, "post and lintel" basis. For this reason the big geodesic domes erected so far have been many times overbuilt, way beyond the appropriate safety factor of 2:1 as adopted by aeronautical science. The building business uses safety factors of 5 or 6:1. The greater the ignorance of the art, the greater the safety factor demanded by probability mathematics. The greater the safety factor, the greater the redundance and the less the freedom of load distribution.

794.06　We have a mathematical phenomenon known as a geodesic. A geodesic is the most economical relationship between any two events. A special case geodesic finds that a seemingly straight line is the shortest distance between two points in a plane. Geodesic lines are the shortest surface distances between two points on the outside of a sphere. Spherical great circles are geodesics.

794.07 A great circle is a line formed on the surface of a sphere by a plane passing through the sphere's center. The Earth's equator is a great-circle geodesic; so too are the Earth's meridians of longitude. Any two great circles of the same system must cross each other twice in a symmetrical manner, with their crossings always 180 degrees apart.

794.08 Each of any three great circles of a sphere not having common polar crossings must cross each of the others twice. This makes for a total of four crossings for each of the three great circles and a total of six crossings for the whole set of three great circles; the whole set of three great circles entirely divides the entire sphere into four hemispherically opposed pairs of similar spherical triangles, and—in one special case—into the eight similar spherical triangles of the regular spherical octahedron. All cases are thus omnitriangular spherical octahedra, regular or irregular.

794.09 Because both ends of spherical chords always impinge on their sphere at identical angles, molecules of gas reactively accelerate chordally away from one another in a spherical enclosure, trying to proceed in straight-line trajectories. The molecules must follow the *shortest-distance,* geodesic great-circle law, and the angular reflectance law; they will carom around the inside of the sphere or football or balloon only in circular paths describing the greatest diameter possible, therefore always in the planes of great circles except as deflected by other forces.

794.10 When two force vectors operating in great-circle paths inside a sphere impinge on each other at any happenstance angle, that angle has no amplitude stability. But when a third force vector operating in a third great-circle path crosses the other two spherical great circles, eight great-circle-edged triangles are formed with their four sets of two inherent, opposite-hemisphered, mirror-image triangles.

794.11 With successive inside-surface caromings and angular intervector impingements, the dynamic symmetry imposed by a sphere tends averagingly to equalize the angular interrelationships of all the millions of triangle-forming sets of those three great circles. The intershunting triangulation in great-circle paths automatically tends averagingly to produce a spherically closed system of omnisimilar triangles. This means that if there were only three great circles, they would tend swiftly to interstabilize comprehensively as the spherical octahedron, all of whose surface angles and arcs average as 90 degrees.

794.12 If we successively shoot at the same high velocity three steel ball bearings of the same size and weight into a smoothly walled, spherical steel container, and if we do that shooting through a carefully timed pop-open-and-pop-closed hole, and if we aim the ball bearing gun as far away from the sphere center as the pop-open hole permitted, each of the three balls would start describing a great-circle path of bouncings off the sphere. Each would have to cross the other four times and would carom off each other as well, swiftly to work toward the spherical octahedron.

794.13   Because each of the three gas molecules must have its reactor molecule, we will always have six initial great circles operative in the pressurized pneumatic containers; all the additional molecules will be six-teamed, and each team of six will increase the system frequency by one, and all the teams will averagingly parallel one another.

794.14   The great-circle chords of all polyhedra are always found to be systematically developed out of sets of exactly six great-circle chords—never more or less. These six vectors are the six vectors of the energy quantum. The 12 vector-edged chords of the octahedron equal the two sets of six chord vectors: two quanta. The 30 vector-edged chords of the icosahedron equal the five sets of six chord vectors: five quanta. In the tetrahedron one quantum of structurally invested energy encloses one unit of volume. In the octahedron one quantum of structurally invested energy encloses two units of volume. In the icosahedron one quantum of energy invested in structure encloses almost four units of volume. Of the three prime structural systems of Universe, the tetrahedron is the strongest per unit of volume enclosed; the octahedron is "middling"; and the icosahedron is least strong, but encloses the greatest volume per unit of invested energy. Whenever nature uses the icosahedron, the maximum volume enclosure per units of invested energy is the principal function served. For this reason all pneumatic and hydraulic structuring of nature employs icosahedral spherical geometry. When maximum structural strength per unit of invested energy is the principal function served, nature uses the tetrahedron. When the principal function to be served is a balance of strength and volume, nature uses the octahedron as her preferred structural system.

794.15   A vast number of molecules of gas interacting in great circles inside of a sphere will produce a number of great-circle triangles. The triangles, being dynamically resilient, mutually intertransform one another to evolve an "averaging" of the random-force vectors, resulting in angular self-interstabilizing as a pattern of omnispherical symmetry. The aggregate of all the inter-great-circlings resolves typically into a regular pattern of 12 pentagons and 20 triangles, or sometimes more complexly into 12 pentagons, 30 hexagons, and 80 triangles described by 240 great-circle chords.

794.16   This is the pattern of the geodesic tensegrity sphere. The numbers of hexagons and triangles and chords may be multiplied in regular arithmetical or geometrical series, but the 12—and only 12—pentagons will persist as constants, as will the number of triangles occur in multiples of 20, and the number of edges in multiples of 6.

794.17   In the geodesic tensegrity sphere each of the entirely independent, compressional-chord struts represents two oppositely directed and force-

paired molecules. The paired-outward caroming of the two chord ends produces a single radially outward force of each chord strut. The tensegrity
compressional chords do not touch one another: they operate independently,
each trying to escape outwardly from the sphere, but they are restrained by
the spherical tensional integrity's closed-network system of great-circle con-
nectors, which alone can complete the great-circle paths between the ends of
the entirely separate, non-directly-interconnecting, compressional chords.
Were the chordal struts to be pushing circumferentially from the sphere, their
ends would touch one another or slide by one another, but the tension lines
show clearly that the struts each pull away from their nearest neighbor and
strain to escape radially outward of the system.

794.18   Central angles of great circles are defined by two radii, the outer
ends of which are connected by both an arc and a chord—which arc and chord
are directly proportional to each unique such central angle. The chord and two
radii form an isosceles triangle. The distance between the mid-arc and the
mid-chord is called the *arc altitude*. Every point on a great-circle arc is at
full-radius distance from the sphere's center. In developing the triangular
subgridding of the icosahedral geodesic prime structural system, the great-
circle arc edges of the icosahedron (each of which has a central angle of 63
degrees, 26 minutes, and several seconds) are equally subdivided into two,
three, or four equal-arc increments—or as many more equal-arc increments as
the engineering calculation finds desirable in consideration of all the optional
variables, such as the diameter of the structure, the structural properties of the
materials with which it is to be produced, and the logistics of delivery, installation, and assembly.

794.19 **Frequency**: Whatever the number of the equal subdivisions of
the icosa arc—whose subdivision points are to be interconnected with a three-
way omnitriangulated grid of great-circle arcs—that icosa arc edge subdivision number is spoken of as the *frequency* of the system. The higher the
frequency of the system, the lesser in dimension will each of the arc, chord,
and arc-altitude increments become. All these dimensions covary at identical
rates and are therefore uniformly proportional for any given frequency. Uniform dimensions, chord factors, and ratios may be listed for any size dome;
the only numerical variable in geodesic spheroidal structures is that of the system's radius.

794.20   Because each islanded compression strut in a tensegrity sphere
addresses its adjacent (but untouched) struts at an angle of approximately 60
degrees, that strut is aimed at but does not reach the midpoints of the adjacent
struts. Each of the struts is a chord of the sphere, with its ends at greater distance from the center of the sphere than the radial distance of the midpoint of

the chordal strut—that difference in distance being exactly that of the arc altitude. The arc altitude decreases as the system frequency is increased, which occurs logically as the system radius increases.

794.21   The mid-girth of each chordal compression strut is proportional to its length and is always substantial. The strut is most efficient when cigar-shaped and pin-ended. As the frequency increases and the arc altitude decreases, there develops a special size geodesic sphere, wherein—employing the most economical material for the struts—the mid-girth of the chordal strut is exactly the same as the arc altitude, at which point the pin-ends of the struts approaching at 60 degrees may exactly touch the mid-girths of the impinged-upon struts. But this kind of touching does not mean pushing against, because the struts (as their tension slings show) are trying to escape radially outward from the dome center. What this touching does is to dampen the vibratory resonance of the tensegrity sphere.

794.22   One of the impressive behavioral characteristics of tensegrity spheres, witnessed at low frequencies, is that when any two islanded struts 180 degrees apart around the sphere are pulled outwardly from one another, the whole sphere expands symmetrically. When the same two 180-degrees-apart struts are pushed toward one another, the whole sphere contracts symmetrically. When the polar pulling apart or pushing together ceases, the tensegrity sphere assumes a radius halfway between the radii of the most pullingly expandable and pushingly contractable conditions; that is, it will rest in dynamic equilibrium.

794.23   When the tension-member lengths between the islanded struts are everywhere the same, the twanging of any of them sounds the same vibration note as any and all the others. Tightening any one tension member or increasing the length of any one strut tightens the whole system uniformly, as is tunably demonstrable. The equilibrium state, which tensegrity spheres spontaneously assume, is the state wherein all the parts are most comfortable but are always subject to spherical oscillatability. Thus the coming into contact of the pin-end cigar struts with the neighboring struts' mid-girth points provides a condition at which—if the pin-point is locked to the mid-strut—it will be prevented from leaving its most energetically efficient state of repose, and the locking together will prevent either the expansion or contraction of the sphere and will mute its resonance and deaden its springiness.

794.24   At the low-frequency, push-pull, contraction-expansion susceptible state, tensegrity spheres act like basketballs. Bouncing them against the floor makes them contract locally, after which they spring back powerfully to their original shape, which impels them back against gravity. Geodesic spheres are in strict physical fact true pneumatic structures with a discrete number of oppositely paired molecules—and their respective atomic colonies—all averagingly aggregated together in the form of the islanded struts instead of being in their invisible gaseous state.

795.00 Reduction to Practice

795.01   We can take advantage of the fact that lumber cut at the "two-by-four" size represents the lumber industry's most frequently used and lowest-cost structural lumber. The average length of the two-by-fours is 12 feet. We can take the approximately two-inch dimension as the mid-girth size of a strut, and we can use an average of 10-foot lengths of the tensilely strongest two-by-four wood worked by the trade (and pay the premium to have it selected and free of knotholes). We can then calculate what size of the spherical dome—and what frequency—will produce the condition of "just-kissing" contact of the two-by-four ends of the islanded two-by-four chordal struts with the mid-girth contact points of one another. This calculates out to a 12-frequency, 72-foot-diameter sphere that, if truncated as a three-quarter sphere, has 20 hexagonal openings around its base, each high enough and wide enough to allow the passage of a closed body truck.

795.02   We calculated and produced such a 72-foot, three-quarter-sphere geodesic dome at the Edwardsville campus of Southern Illinois University in 1962. The static load testing of all the parts as well as the final assembly found it performing exactly as described in the above paragraphs. The static load testing demonstrated performance on the basis of the load-distributing capabilities of pneumatics and hydraulics and exceeded those that would have been predicted solely on the basis of continuous compression.

795.03   As the world's high-performance metallic technologies are freed from concentration on armaments, their structural and mechanical and chemical performances (together with the electrodynamic remote control of systems in general) will permit dimensional exquisiteness of mass-production-forming tolerances to be reduced to an accuracy of one-hundredth-thousandths of an inch. This fine tolerance will permit the use of hydraulically pressure-filled glands of high-tensile metallic tubing using liquids that are nonfreezable at space-program temperature ranges, to act when pressurized as the discontinuously isolated compressional struts of large geodesic tensegrity spheres. Since the fitting tolerances will be less than the size of the liquid molecules, there will be no leakage. This will obviate the collapsibility of the air-lock-and-pressure-maintained pneumatic domes that require continuous pump-pressurizing to avoid being drag-rotated to flatten like a candle flame in a hurricane. Hydro-compressed tensegrities are less vulnerable as liquids are noncompressible.

795.04   Geodesic tensegrity spheres may be produced at enormous *city-*

enclosing diameters. They may be assembled by helicopters with great economy. This will reduce the investment of metals in large tensegrity structures to a small fraction of the metals invested in geodesic structures of the past. It will be possible to produce geodesic domes of enormous diameters to cover whole communities with a relatively minor investment of structural materials. With the combined capabilities of mass production and aerospace technology it becomes feasible to turn out whole rolls of noncorrosive, flexible-cable networks with high-tensile, interswaged fittings to be manufactured in one gossamer piece, like a great fishing net whose whole unitary tension system can be air-delivered anywhere to be compression-strutted by swift local insertions of remote-controlled, expandable hydro-struts, which, as the spheric structure takes shape, may be hydro-pumped to firm completion by radio control.

795.05   In the advanced-space-structures research program it has been discovered that—in the absence of unidirectional gravity and atmosphere—it is highly feasible to centrifugally spin-open spherical or cylindrical structures in such a manner that if one-half of the spherical net is prepacked by folding below the equator and being tucked back into the other and outer half to form a dome within a dome when spun open, it is possible to produce domes that are miles in diameter. When such structures consist at the outset of only gossamer, high-tensile, low-weight, spider-web-diameter filaments, and when the spheres spun open can hold their shape unchallenged by gravity, then all the filaments' local molecules could be chemically activated to produce local monomer tubes interconnecting the network joints, which could be hydraulically expanded to form an omniintertrussed double dome. Such a dome could then be retrorocketed to subside deceleratingly into the Earth's atmosphere, within which it will lower only slowly, due to its extremely low comprehensive specific gravity and its vast webbing surface, permitting it to be aimingly-landed slowly, very much like an air-floatable dandelion seed ball: the multi-mile-diametered tensegrity dome would seem to be a giant cousin. Such a space-spun, Earth-landed structure could then be further fortified locally by the insertion of larger hydro-struttings from helicopters or rigid lighter-than-air-ships—or even by remote-control electroplating, employing the atmosphere as an electrolyte. It would also be feasible to expand large dome networks progressively from the assembly of smaller pneumatic and surface-skinning components.

795.06   The fact that the dome volume increases exponentially at a third-power rate, while the structural component lengths increase at only a fraction more than an arithmetical rate, means that their air volume is so great in comparison to the enclosing skin that its inside atmosphere temperature would remain approximately tropically constant independent of outside weather variations. A dome in this vast scale would also be structurally fail-safe in that the amount of air inside would take months to be evacuated should any air vehicle smash through its upper structure or break any of its trussing.

795.07   In air-floatable dome systems metals will be used exclusively in tension, and all compression will be furnished by the tensionally contained, antifreeze-treated liquids. Metals with tensile strengths of a million p.s.i. will be balance-opposed structurally by liquids that will remain noncompressible even at a million p.s.i. Complete shock-load absorption will be provided by the highly compressible gas molecules—interpermeating the hydraulic molecules—to provide symmetrical distribution of all forces. The hydraulic compressive forces will be evenly distributed outwardly to the tension skins of the individual struts and thence even further to the comprehensive metal- or glass-skinned hydro-glands of the spheroidally enclosed, concentrically-trussed-together, dome-within-dome foldback, omnitriangulated, nonredundant, tensegrity network structural system.

795.08   **Design Strategies:** All the calculations required for the design of geodesic domes may be derived from the three basic triangles of the three basic structural systems:

    —the 120 right spherical triangles of the icosahedron,
    —the 48 right spherical triangles of the octahedron, and
    —the 24 right spherical triangles of the tetrahedron.

All the great-circle behaviors occurring around the whole sphere take place within just one of those three basic right triangles and repeat themselves in all others.

795.09   The data mathematically developed within the three basic triangles become constants for spheres of any size. What we need to know structurally is the length of the chordal lines between any two adjacent points in the three-way great-circle grid and the angles at which they intersect. The spherical surface angles of the sphere and the central angles may all be expressed in the same decimal fractions, which remain constant for any size sphere since they are fractions of a unit finite whole system. We assign the name *chord factors* to all the constant lengths of a sphere's connecting lines, whether between any two spherical surface points or between two concentric spheres that are intertriangularly trussed. We assign the word *frequency* to the number of uniform-edge subdivisions of the spherical arc edges of the basic spherical triangles.

795.10   There is a set of unique chord factors for each frequency. There are six alternate ways of organizing the triangular subgridding, some of which permit planar base cutoffs of the sphere at other than its equator. Various fractions of the sphere are permitted, as some produce more overall structural economy for differing applications than others. The most economical total lengths for a given frequency are also the most equilibriously comfortable—that is, where it requires the least energy to maintain its integrity under any and all environmental conditions.

795.11   Competent designing of geodesic tensegrity domes also requires monitoring the evolving increases in performance of the various chemical materials and metal alloys available. The full design science responsibility includes developing, prototyping, testing, production, engineering, tooling, manufacturing, transporting from factory to use point, assembly, and removing and recycling of the materials: only from consideration of each such successive cycle can we learn how to do it again more efficiently and satisfactorily to society.

800.00 Operational Mathematics

810.00 One Spherical Triangle Considered as Four

812.05 **Background Nothingness**: One spherical triangle *ABC* drawn on the Earth's surface inadvertently produces four triangles as the corners of the surface triangle are inherently related to the center of the Earth *D,* and their lines of interrelatedness together with the three edge lines of the surface triangle describe a tetrahedron. (See Fig. 812.03.) Drawing a triangle on the surface of the Earth (as described at Sec. 810) also divides the surface of the Earth into two areas—one large, one small—both of which are bound by a closed line with three edges and three angles. The large triangle and the small triangle have both concave and convex aspects—ergo, four triangles in all. Euler did not recognize the background nothingness of the outside triangles. (See Sec. *505.81.*)

812.06 Under the most primitive pre-time-size conditions the surface of a sphere may be exactly subdivided into the four spherical triangles of the spherical tetrahedron, each of whose surface corners are 120-degree angles, and whose "edges" have central angles of 109° 28′. The area of a surface of a sphere is also exactly equal to the area of four great circles of the sphere. Ergo, the area of a sphere's great circle equals the area of a spherical triangle of that sphere's spherical tetrahedron: wherefore we have a circular area exactly equaling a triangular area, and we have avoided use of *pi* (*π*).

820.00 Tools of Geometry

826.00 Unity of Peripheral and Radial Modularity

826.02A **Hammer Throw**: The picture of the hammer throw and gyro-

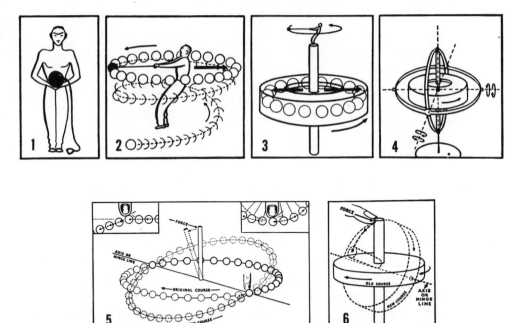

Fig. *826.02A Hammer Throw:* The weight on the cord accumulates energy as the man swings it around his head in a circular pattern that illustrates angular acceleration. When the weight is released it goes into linear acceleration as modified by any secondary restraints.

scope appearing in *Synergetics 1* was incomplete. The complete sequence of six line drawings appears here in revised Fig. *826.02A*.

826.10 Otherness Restraints and Elliptical Orbits

826.11 Angular acceleration is radically restrained accumulation of circular momentum; angular deceleration is the local depletion of angular momentum.

826.12 Release from angular acceleration appears to be linear acceleration, but the linearity is only theoretical. Linear acceleration is the release from the restraint of the nearest accelerator to the angularly accelerative or decelerative restraint of the integrated vectorial resultant of all the neighboringly dominant, forever-otherness restraints in Universe. Linear acceleration never occurs, because there is no cosmic exemption of otherness.

826.13 The hammer thrower releases his "hammer's" ball-and-rod assembly from his extended arm's-end grasp, seemingly allowing the hammer to take a tangentially linear trajectory, but Earth's gravitational pull immediately takes over and converts the quasistraight trajectory into an elliptical arc of greater orbiting radius than before. But the arc is one of ever-decreasing radius as the Earth's gravity takes over and the hammer thrower's steel ball seemingly comes to *rest* on the Earth's surface, which is, however, in reality traveling around the Earth's axis in synchronized consonance with the other huddled together atoms of the Earth's surface. Near the Earth's equator this would be at a circular velocity of approximately 1000 miles an hour, but near the Earth's poles the velocity would be only inches per hour around the Earth's axis. Both Earth, hammer thrower, and thrown hammer are traveling at 60,000 miles an hour around the Sun at a radial restraint distance of approximately 92 million miles, with the galaxies of Universe's other nonsimultaneously generated restraints of all the othernesses' overlappingly effective dominance variations, as produced by degrees of neighboring energy concentrations and dispersions. It is the pulsation of such concentrations and dispersions that brings about the elliptical orbiting.

826.14   This is fundamental complementarity as intuited in Einstein's curved space prior to the scientific establishment of *generalized complementarity,* which we may now also speak of as the "generalized otherness" of Universe. This is why *there can be only curved space.* (See Sec. 1009.52.)

826.15   Isaac Newton's first law of motion, "A body persists in a state of rest or in a straight line except as affected by other forces," should now be restated to say, "Any one considered body persists in any one elliptical orbit

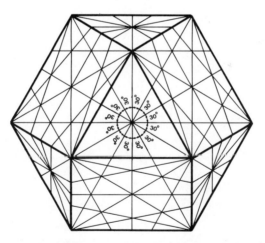

Fig. *841.30 Trisection by Inherent Axial Spin:* The 12 great circles of the vector equilibrium inherently *trisect* each of its eight equiangular faces, centrally subdividing each of them into twelve 30-degree angles.

until that orbit is altered to another elliptical orbit by the ceaselessly varying interpositionings and integrated restraint effects imposed upon the considered body by the ever-transforming generalized cosmic otherness." A body is always responding orbitally to a varying plurality of otherness forces.

840.00   Foldability of Four Great Circles of Vector Equilibrium

841.30   Trisection by Inherent Axial Spin of Systems

841.31   The 12 great circles of the vector equilibrium's hemispherical self-halvings inherently—and inadvertently—centrally *trisect* each of the vector equilibrium's eight equiangle spherical triangles, centrally subdividing those triangles into twelve 30-degree angles.

900.00   Modelability

*Titles in parentheses may be found in *Synergetics 1*

900.01 Definition: Modelability

900.10 Modelability

900.11 Modelability is topologically conceptual in generalized principle independent of size and time: ergo, conceptual modelability is metaphysical.

900.12 Conceptual formulation is inherently empirical and as such is always special case sizing and always discloses all the physical characteristics of existence in time.

900.20 Synergetics

900.21 Synergetics is a book about models: humanly conceptual models; lucidly conceptual models; primitively simple models; rationally intertransforming models; and the primitively simple numbers uniquely and holistically identifying those models and their intertransformative, generalized and special case, number-value accountings.

900.30 Model vs Form

900.31 Model is generalization; form is special case.

900.32 The brain in its coordination of the sensing of each special case experience apprehends forms. Forms are special case. Models are generalizations of interrelationships. Models are inherently systemic. Forms are special case systems. Mind can conceptualize models. Brains can apprehend forms.

900.33 Forms have size. Models are sizeless, representing conceptuality independent of size.

901.00 Basic Disequilibrium LCD Triangle

901.19 **Omnirational Control Matrix:** *Commensurability of Vector Equilibrium and Icosahedron* The great-circle subdivisioning of the 48 basic equilibrious *LCD* triangles of the vector equilibrium may be representationally drawn within the 120 basic disequilibrious *LCD* triangles of the icosahedron, thus defining all the aberrations—and their magnitudes—existing between the equilibrious and disequilibrious states, and providing an omnirational control matrix for all topological, trigonometric, physical, and chemical accounting.

920.00 Functions of A and B Modules

923.00 Constant Volume

923.15 **One Tetra Edge Constant:** Using a constant-volume, vectorially edged tetrahedron *ABCD* with six edges *AB, AC, AD, BC, BD,* and *CD,* and with only one of those six edge lengths holding a constant length *AB,* all five of the tetrahedron's other edge lengths may covary as the tetrahedron rotates around the fixed edge length *AB,* which acts as an axis of rotation. While the axis *AB* is precessionally tilted within its celestial theater, it is experientially demonstrable that—without changing the tetrahedron's volume or its constant-length vector *AB*—its two other corners *C* and *D* may interconnect the *AB*-fixed-length-axis points with any other two points in Universe no matter how remote from one another. This is the reason why electromagnetic waves can interlink any points in Universe in response to a given constant wavelength *AB.* (Compare Secs. 426.40, *530.11,* 960.08, and 961.10–40.)

930.00 Tetrahelix Unzipping Angle

933.08 **Closest Packing of Different-sized Balls:** It could be that the *GCTA* tetrahelix derives from the closest packing of different-sized balls. The Mites and Sytes (see Sec. 953) could be the tetrahedra of the *GCTA* because they are both positive-negative and allspace filling.

935.00   Octahedron as Conservation and Annihilation Model

• [*935.00–938.16   Annihilation Scenario*]

935.10   Energy Flow and Discontinuity

935.11   Though classic science at the opening of the 18th century had achieved many remarkably accurate observations and calculations regarding the behaviors of light, individual scientists and their formal societies—with one notable exception—remained unaware that light (and radiation in general) has a speed. Ole Roemer (1644–1710), both Royal Astronomer and Royal Mathematician of Denmark, was that exception. Roemer's observations of the reflected light of the revolving moons of the planet Jupiter made him surmise that light has a speed. His calculations from the observed data very closely approximated the figure for that speed as meticulously measured in vacuo two centuries later, in the Michelson-Morley experiment of 1887. Though Roemer was well accredited by the scientists and scientific societies of Europe, this hypothesis of his seemed to escape their cosmological considerations. Being overlooked, the concept did not enter into any of the cosmological formulations (either academic or general) of humanity until the 20th century.

935.12   Until the 20th century scientists in general assumed the light of all the stars to be instantaneously and simultaneously extant. Universe was an instantaneous and simultaneous system. The mid-19th-century development of thermodynamics, and in particular its second law, introduced the concept that all systems always lose energy and do so in ever-increasingly disorderly and expansive ways. The academicians spontaneously interpreted the instantaneity and simultaneity of Universe as requiring that the Universe too must be categorized as a system; the academicians assumed that as a system Universe itself must be losing energy in increasingly expansive and disorderly ways. Any expenditure of energy by humans on Earth—to whom the stars in the heavens were just so much romantic scenery; no more, no less—would hasten the end of the Universe. This concept was the foundation of classical conservatism—economic, political, and philosophical. Those who "spent" energy were abhorred.

935.13   This viewpoint was fortified by the hundred-years-earlier concept of classical science's giant, Isaac Newton, who in his first law of motion stated that all bodies persist in a state of rest, or in a line of motion, except as affected by other bodies. This law posits a cosmic norm of *at rest:* change is abnormal. This viewpoint as yet persists in all the graphic-chart coordinates used by society today for plotting performance magnitudes against a time background wherein the baseline of "no change" is the norm. Change is taken spontaneously as being inherently abnormal and is as yet interpreted by many as being cause for fundamental social concern.

935.14 With the accurate measurement, in 1887, of the speed of light in vacuo, science had comprehensively new, experimentally redemonstrable challenges to its cosmogony and cosmology. Inspired by the combined discoveries of the Brownian movement, black body radiation, and the photon of light, Einstein, Planck, and others recognized that energy-as-radiation has a top speed—ergo, is finitely terminaled—but among them, Einstein seems to have convinced himself that his own cosmological deliberations should assume Boltzmann's concept to be valid—ergo, always to be included in his own exploratory thoughts. There being no experimental evidence of energy ever being created or lost, universal energy is apparently conserved. Wherefore Boltzmann had hypothesized that energy progressively and broadcastingly exported from various localities in Universe must be progressively imported and reassembled at other localities in Universe.

935.15 Boltzmann's concept was analogous to that upon which was developed the theory and practice of the 20th-century meteorological weather forecasting, which recognizes that our terrestrial atmosphere's plurality of high-pressure areas are being progressively exhausted at different rates by a plurality of neighboring low-pressure areas, which accumulate atmospheric molecules and energy until they in turn become new high-pressure areas, which are next to be progressively exhausted by other newly initiated low-pressure areas. The interpatterning of the various importing-exporting centers always changes kaleidoscopically because of varying speeds of moisture formation or precipitation, speeds and directions of travel, and local thermal conditions.

935.16 Though they did not say it that way, the 20th-century leaders of scientific thinking inferred that physical Universe is apparently eternally regenerative.

935.17 Einstein assumed hypothetically that energies given off omnidirectionally with the ever-increasing disorder of entropy by all the stars were being antientropically imported, sorted, and accumulated in various other elsewheres. He showed that when radiant energy interferes with itself, it can, and probably does, tie itself precessionally into local and orderly knots. Einstein must have noted that on Earth children do not disintegrate entropically but multiply their hydrocarbon molecules in an orderly fashion; little saplings grow in an orderly way to become big trees. Einstein assumed

Earthian biology to be reverse entropy. (This account does not presume to re-capitulate the actual thought processes of Einstein at any given point in the development of his philosophy; rather it attempts to illustrate some of the in-evitable conclusions that derive from his premises.)

935.18   What made it difficult for scientists, cosmologists, and cos-mogonists to comprehend about Boltzmann's concept—or Einstein's implicit espousal of it—was the inherent *discontinuity* of energy events implicit in the photon as a closed-system package of energy. What happened to the energy when it disappeared? For disappear it did. How could it reappear elsewhere in a discontinuous system?

935.20 Precessional Transformation in Quantum Model

935.21   One quantum of energy always consists of six energy vectors, each being a combined push-pull, positive-negative force. (See Secs. 600.02 through 612.01 and Fig. 620.06.) Twelve unique forces: six plus and six minus. Six vectors break into two sets of three each. Classical engineers as-sumed that each action had its equal and opposite reaction at 180 degrees; but since the discovery of the speed of light and the understanding of nonsimul-taneity, we find that every action has not only a reaction but also a *resultant*. Neither the reaction nor the resultant are angularly "opposite" in 180-degree azimuth from the direction of action. The "equal and opposite" of classical engineering meant that both action and reaction occurred in opposite direc-tions in the same straight line in the same geometrical plane. But since the recognition of nonsimultaneity and the speed of light, it has been seen that ac-tion, reaction, and resultant vectors react omnidirectionally and precessionally at angles other than 180 degrees. (See Fig. 511.20.)

935.22   As we enter the last quarter of the 20th century, it is recognized in quantum mechanics and astrophysics that there could never have existed the traditionally assumed, a priori universal chaos, a chaos from which it was also assumed that Universe had escaped only by the workings of chance and the long-odds-against mathematical probability of a sequence of myriad-illions of coincidences, which altogether produced a universal complex of orderly evo-lutionary events. This nonsense was forsaken by the astrophysicists only a score of years ago, and only because science has learned in the last few de-cades that both the proton and the neutron always and only coexist in a most orderly interrelationship. They do not have the same mass, and yet the one can be transformed into the other by employing both of their respective two energy side effects; i.e., those of both the proton and the neutron. Both the proton and the neutron have their respective and unique two-angle-forming patterns of three interlinked lines, each representing their action, reaction, and resultant vectors.

935.221 **Coming-Apart Phase: Coming-Apart Limit:** The astrophysicists say that no matter how far things come apart, fundamentally they never come farther apart than proton and neutron, which always and only coexist.

935.23 The names of the players, the positions they play, and the identifying letters they wear on the three-vector teams of proton and neutron, respectively, are identified as follows. The proton's three-vector team consists of

(1) the *action* vector, played by its captain, the *proton,* wearing the letters *BD;*

(2) the *reaction* vector, played by the *electron,* wearing the letters *AD;* and

(3) the *resultant* vector, played by the *antineutrino,* wearing the letters *BC.*

The neutron's three-vector team consists of

(1) the *action* vector, played by its captain, the *neutron,* wearing the letters *AC;*

(2) the *reaction* vector, played by the *positron,* wearing the letters *CD;* and

(3) the *resultant* vector, played by the *neutrino,* wearing the letters *AB.*

Either one of these two teams of three-vector events is identified in quantum mechanics as being a half-quantum (or one-half spin or one-half Planck's constant). When two half-quanta associate, they produce one unit of quantum. (See Sec. 240.65.) These two sets of three vectors each combine to produce the six vector edges of the tetrahedron, which is the minimum structural system of Universe: one quantum of energy thus becomes structurally and systematically conceptual. (See Fig. *935.23.*) One quantum of energy equals one tetrahedron. Humanist writers and broadcasters take notice that science has regained conceptuality. Science's intertransformabilities and intercomplementarities are modelably demonstrable. The century-long chasm that has separated science and the humanities has vanished.

935.24 The tetrahedral model of the quantum as the minimum structural system of Universe is a prime component in producing the conceptual bridge to span the vast chasm identified by C. P. Snow as having for so long existed between the one percent of the world people who are scientists and the 99 percent of humanity comprehendingly communicated with by the writers in literature and the humanities. This chasm has been inadvertently sustained by the use of an exclusively mathematical language of abstract equations on the part of scientists, thus utterly frustrating the comprehension of the scientists' work by the 99 percent of humanity that does not communicate mathematically.

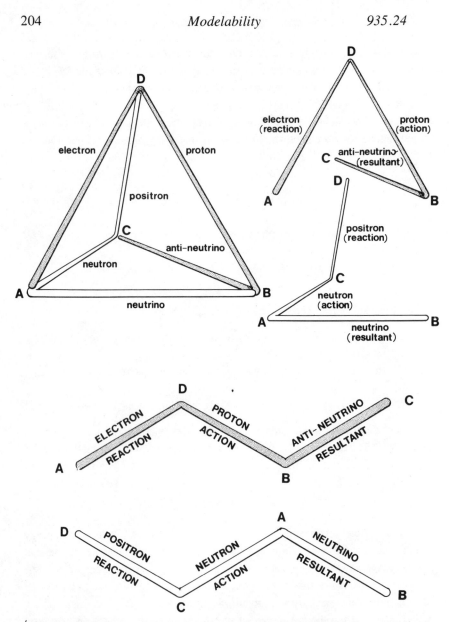

Fig. 935.23 *Proton and Neutron Three-vector Teams:* The proton and neutron always and only coexist as action vectors of half-quanta associable as quantum.

This book, *Synergetics*, contains the conceptualizing adequate to the chasm-bridging task, and it does so in vectorially structured geometry and in exclusively low-order prime numbers in rational whole-number accounting.

935.25   As an instance of chasm-spanning between science and the humanities by conceptually transformative energy-quanta accounting, synergetics conceptually elucidates the Boltzmann import-export, entropy-syntropy transaction and the elegant manner in which nature accommodates the "hidden ball" play of now-you-see-it-now-you-don't energy transference.

936.00 Volumetric Variability with Topological Constancy

936.10 Symmetrical and Asymmetrical Contraction

936.11 An octahedron consists of 12 vector edges and two units of quantum and has a volume of four when the tetrahedron is taken as unity. (See Table 223.64.) Pulling two ends of a rope in opposite directions makes the rope's girth contract precessionally in a plane at 90 degrees to the axis of purposeful tensing. (Sec. 1054.61.) Or if we push together the opposite sides of a gelatinous mass or a pneumatic pillow, the gelatinous mass or the pneumatic pillow swells tensively outward in a plane at 90 degrees to the line of our purposeful compressing. This 90-degree reaction—or resultant—is characteristic of precession. Precession is the effect of bodies in motion upon other bodies in motion. The gravitational pull of the Sun on the Earth makes the Earth go around the Sun in an orbit at 90 degrees to the line of the Earth–Sun gravitational interattraction. The effect of the Earth on the Moon or of the nucleus of the atom upon its electron is to make these interattractively dependent bodies travel in orbits at 90 degrees to their mass-interattraction force lines.

936.12 The octahedron represents the most commonly occurring crystallographic conformation in nature. (See Figs. 931.10 and 1054.40.) It is the most typical association of energy-as-matter; it is at the heart of such association. Any focused emphasis in the gravitational pull of the rest of the Universe upon the octahedron's symmetry precesses it into asymmetrical deformation in a plane at 90 degrees to the axis of exaggerated pulling. This forces one of the 12 edge vectors of the octahedron to rotate at 90 degrees. If we think of the octahedron's three *XYZ* axes and its six vertexes, oriented in such a manner that *X* is the north pole and *X'* is the south pole, the other four vertexes—*Y, Z, Y', Z'*—all occur in the plane of, and define, the octahedron's equator. The effect of gravitational pull upon the octahedron will make one of the four equatorial vectors disengage from its two adjacent equatorial vertexes, thereafter to rotate 90 degrees and then rejoin its two ends with the north pole and south pole vertexes. (See Fig. *936.12* and color plate 6.)

936.13 When this precessional transformation is complete, we have the same topological inventories of six vertexes, eight exterior triangular faces, and 12 vector edges as we had before in the symmetrical octahedron; but in the process the symmetrical, four-tetrahedra-quanta-volume octahedron has been transformed into three tetrahedra (three-quanta volume) arranged in an

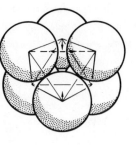
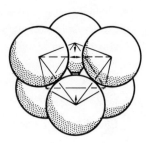

A.   B.   C.

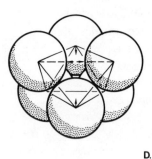
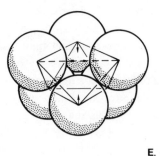
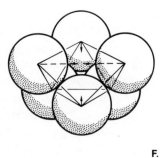

D.   E.   F.

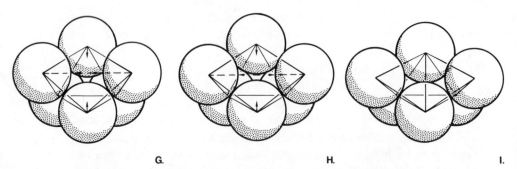

G.   H.   I.

Fig. *936.12 Octahedron as Conservation and Annihilation Model:* If we think of the octahedron as defined by the interconnections of six closest-packed spheres, gravitational pull can make one of the four equatorial vectors disengage from its two adjacent equatorial vertexes to rotate 90 degrees and rejoin the north and south vertexes in the transformation completed as at I. (See also color plate 6.)

arc section of an electromagnetic wave conformation with each of the two end tetrahedra being face bonded to the center tetrahedron. (See Sec. 982.73.)

936.14   The precessional effect has been to rearrange the energy vectors themselves in such a way that we have gone from the volume-four quanta of the symmetrical octahedron to the volume-three quanta of the asymmetric tetra-arc-array segment of an electromagnetic wave pattern. Symmetric matter has been entropically transformed into asymmetrical and directionally focused radiation: one quantum of energy has seemingly disappeared. When the radiation impinges interferingly with any other energy event in Universe, precession recurs and the three-quantum electromagnetic wave retransforms syntropically into the four-quantum octahedron of energy-as-matter. And vice versa. Q.E.D. (See Fig. *936.14.*)

936.15   The octahedron goes from a volume of four to a volume of three as one tensor is precessed at 90 degrees. This is a demonstration in terms of tension and compression of how energy can disappear and reappear. The process is reversible, like Boltzmann's law and like the operation of syntropy and entropy. The lost tetrahedron can reappear and become symmetrical in its optimum form as a ball-bearing-sphere octahedron. There are six great circles doubled up in the octahedron. Compression is radiational: it reappears. Out of the fundamental fourness of all systems we have a model of how four can become three in the octahedron conservation and annihilation model.

936.16   See the Iceland spar crystals for the octahedron's double vector-edge image.

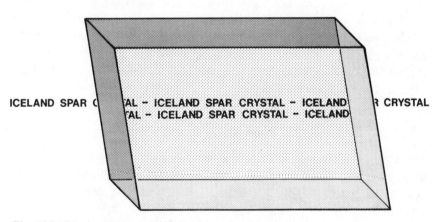

Fig. *936.16 Iceland Spar Crystal:* Double vector image.

936.17   The interior volume of the concave-vector-equilibrium-shaped space occurring interiorly between the six uniradius octahedral collection of closest-packed spheres is greater than is the concave-octahedrally-shaped space occurring interiorly between the four uniradius tetrahedral collection of closest-packed spheres, which tetrahedral collection constitutes the minimum structural system in Universe, and its interior space is the minimum interior space producible within the interstices of closest-packed uniradius spheres.

936.18　Thus the larger interior space within the omnitriangularly stable, six-vertex-ball, 12-vector-edge octahedron is subject to volumetric compressibility. Because its interior space is not minimal, as the octahedron is omniembracingly tensed gravitationally between any two or more bodies, its six balls will tend precessionally to yield transformingly to produce three closest-packed, uniradius, sphere-vertex-defined, face-bonded tetrahedra.

936.19　As we tense the octahedron, it strains until one vector (actually a double, or unity-as-two, vector) yields its end bondings and precesses at 90 degrees to transform the system into three double-bonded (face-bonded) tetrahedra in linear arc form. This tetra-arc, embryonic, electromagnetic wave is in neutral phase. The seemingly annihilated—but in fact only separated-out—quantum is now invisible because vectorless. It now becomes invisibly face-bonded as one invisible tetrahedron. The separated-out quantum is face-bonded to one of the furthermost outward triangular faces occurring at either end of the tetra-arc array of three (consisting of one tetra at the middle with each of the two adjacent tetra face-bonded to it); the fourth invisible tetrahedron is face-bonded to one or the other of the two alternatively vacant, alternatively available furthermost end faces of the tetra-arc group. With this fourth, invisible tetrahedral addition the overall triple-bonded tetrahedral array becomes either rightwardly or leftwardly spiraled to produce a four-tetrahedron tetrahelix, which is a potential, event embryo, electromagnetic-circuitry gap closer. Transmission may thereafter be activated as a connected chain of the inherently four-membered, individual-link continuity. This may explain the dilemma of the wave vs the particle. (See Sec. 973.30, Fig. *936.19,* and color plates 6 and 7.)

936.20　Conceptual Conservation and Annihilation

936.21　The octahedron as the conservation and annihilation model provides an experiential and conceptual accounting for the question: What happens to entropically vanishing quanta of energy that have never been identified as discretely lost when new quanta appeared elsewhere and elsewhen? Were these appearing and disappearing quanta being encountered for the first time as we became capable of penetrating exploration of ever vaster ranges of Universe?

936.22　Boltzmann hypothesized and Einstein supported his working assumption—stated in the conceptual language of synergetics—that there can be no a priori stars to radiate entropically and visibly to the information-importing, naked eyes of Earthian humans (or to telescopes or phototelescopy or electromagnetic antennae) if there were not also invisible cosmic importing centers. The importing centers are invisible because they are not radiantly ex-

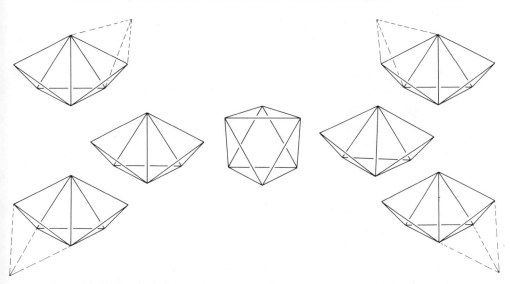

Fig. *936.19 Tetrahedral Quantum is Lost and Reappears in Transformation between Octahedron and Three-tetra-arc Tetrahelix:* This transformation has the precessional effect of rearranging the energy vectors from 4-tetravolumes to 3-tetravolumes and reverse. The neutral symmetric octahedron rearranges itself into an asymmetric embryonic wave pattern. The four-membered individual-link continuity is a potential electromagnetic-circuitry gap closer. The furthermost ends of the tetra-arc group are alternatively vacant. (See also color plate 6.)

porting; they are in varying stages of progressive retrieving, accumulating, sorting, storing, and compressing energies. The cosmic abundance of the myriads of such importing centers and their cosmic disposition in Scenario Universe exactly balances and conserves the integrity of eternally regenerative Universe.

936.23   In Scenario Universe (in contrast to a spherically-structured, normally-at-rest, celestially-concentric, single-frame-picture Universe) the episodes consist only of such frequencies as are tune-in-able by the limited-frequency-range set of the viewer.

936.24   There is no such phenomenon as space: there is only the at-present-tuned-in set of relationships and the untuned intervalling. *Points* are twilight-border-line, only amplitude-tuned-in (AM), directionally oriented, static squeaks or pips that, when frequency-tuned (FM), become differentially discrete and conceptually resolvable as topological systems having withinness and withoutness—ergo, at minimum having four corner-defining yet subtunable system pips or point-to-able corner loci. In systemic cosmic topology Euler's vertexes (*points*) are then always only twilight energy-event loci whose discrete frequencies are untunable at the frequency range of the reception set of the observer.

937.00 Geometry and Number Share the Same Model

937.10 Midway Between Limits

937.11   The grand strategy of quantum mechanics may be described as progressive, numerically rational fractionating of the limit of total energy involved in eternally regenerative Universe.

937.12   When seeking a model for energy quanta conservation and annihilation, we are not surprised to find it in the middle ranges of the geometrical hierarchy of prime structural systems—tetrahedron, octahedron, and icosahedron (see Sec. 610.20). The tetrahedron and icosahedron are the two extreme and opposite limit cases of symmetrical structural systems: they are the minimum-maximum cosmic limits of such prime structures of Universe. The octahedron ranks in the neutral area, midway between the extremes.

937.13   The prime number characteristic of the tetrahedron is 1; the prime number characteristic of the icosahedron is 5. Both of these prime numbers—1 and 5—are odd numbers, in contradistinction to the prime number characteristic of the middle-case structural-system octahedron, which is 2, an even number and the *only even numbered prime* number. Again, we are not surprised to find that the octahedron is the most common crystal conformation in nature.

937.14   The tetrahedron has three triangles around each vertex; the octahedron has four; and the icosahedron has five. The extreme-limit cases of structural systems are vertexially locked by odd numbers of triangular gears, while the vertexes of the octahedron at the middle range have an even number of reciprocating triangular gears. This shows that the octahedron's three great circles are congruent pairs—i.e., six circles that may seem to appear as only three, which quadrivalent doubling with itself is clearly shown in the jitterbug model, where the 24 vector edges double up at the octahedron phase to produce 12 double-congruent vector edges and thus two congruent octahedra. (See Fig. 460.08D.)

937.15   The octahedron is doubled-up in the middle range of the vector equilibrium's jitterbug model; thus it demonstrates conceptually the exact middle between the macro-micro limits of the sequence of intertransformative events. The octahedron in the middle of the structural-system hierarchy provides us with a clear demonstration of how a unit quantum of energy seemingly disappears—i.e., becomes annihilated—and vice versa.

937.20 Doubleness of Octahedron

937.21   The octahedron always exhibits the quality of doubleness. When the octahedron first appears in the symmetrical contraction of the vector equi-

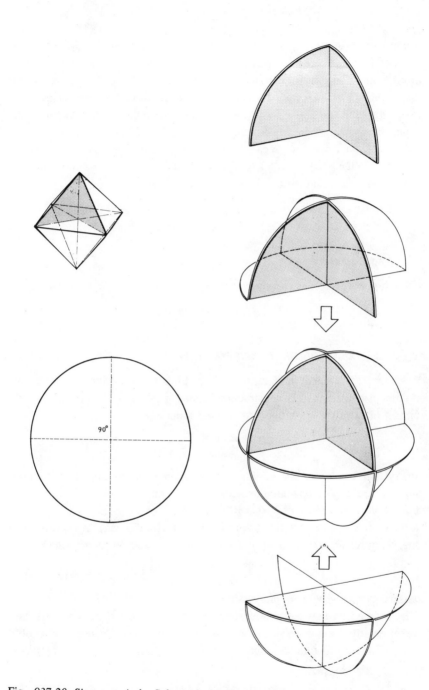

Fig. 937.20 *Six-great-circle Spherical Octahedron:* The doubleness of the octahedron is illustrated by the need for two sets of three great circles to produce its spherical foldable form.

librium jitterbug system, it appears with all of its vectors doubled (see Fig. 460.08D). It also takes *two* sets of three great circles each to fold the octahedron. You might think you could do it with one set of three great circles, but the foldability of the octahedron requires two sets of three great circles each. (See Secs. 835 and 836.) There are always six great circles doubled up in the octahedron to reappear only as three. (See Fig. *937.20*.)

937.22   And we also recall that the octahedron appears as the prime number 2 in the geometrical hierarchy, while its volume is 4 when the tetrahedron is taken as volumetric units (see Table 223.64).

The tetrahedron's prime number identity is 1
The octahedron's prime number identity is 2
Both cubes and rhombic dodecahedra are   3
And icosahedra and vector equilibria are   5

They first occur volumetrically, respectively, as

1, 4, 3, 6, 18.51, and 20.

937.30   Octahedron as Sphere of Compression

937.31   The slenderness ratio in gravitationally tensed functioning has no minimum overall limit of its structural-system length, as compared to the diameter of the system's midlength cross section; ergo,

$$\frac{\text{tensile length}}{\text{diameter}} = \frac{\alpha}{0}$$

In crystalline compression structures the column length minimum limit ratio is 40/1. There may be a length/diameter compression-system-limit in hydraulics, but we do not as yet know what it is. The far more slender column/diameter ratio attainable with hydraulics permits the growth of a palm tree to approach the column/diameter ratio of steel columns. We recognize the sphere—the ball bearing, the spherical island— $\frac{\text{column}}{\text{diameter}} = \frac{1}{1}$ constituting the optimal, crystalline, compressive-continuity, structural-system model. (See Fig. 641.01.) The octahedron may be considered to be the optimum crystalline structural representation of the spherical islands of compression because it is double-bonded and its vectors are doubled.

938.00   Jitterbug Transformation and Annihilation

938.10   Positive and Negative Tetrahedra

938.11   The tetrahedron is the minimum-limit-case structural system of Universe (see Secs. 402 and 620). The tetrahedron consists of two congruent tetrahedra: one concave, one convex. The tetrahedron divides all of Universe into all the tetrahedral nothingness of all the cosmic outsideness and all the tetrahedral nothingness of all the cosmic insideness of any structurally conceived or sensorially experienced, special case, uniquely considered, four-starry-vertex-constellared, tetrahedral system somethingness of human experience, cognition, or thinkability.

938.12   The tetrahedron always consists of four concave-inward hedra triangles and of four convex-outward hedra triangles: that is eight hedra triangles in all. (Compare Fig. 453.02.) These are the same eight—maximally deployed from one another—equiangular triangular hedra or facets of the vector equilibrium that converge to differential inscrutability or conceptual zero, while the eight original triangular planes coalesce as the four pairs of congruent planes of the zero-volume vector equilibrium, wherein the eight exterior planes of the original eight edge-bonded tetrahedra reach zero-volume, eightfold congruence at the center point of the four-great-circle system. (Compare Fig. 453.02.)

938.13   The original—only vertexially single-bonded, vectorially structured—triangles of the vector-equilibrium jitterbug transform by symmetrical contraction from its openmost vector-equilibrium state, through the (unstable-without-six-additional-vector inserts; i.e., one vectorial quantum unit) icosahedral stage only as accommodated by the nuclear sphere's annihilation, which vanished central sphere reappears transformedly in the 30-vector-edged icosahedron as the six additional external vectors added to the vector equilibrium to structurally stabilize its six "square" faces, which six vectors constitute one quantum package. (See Fig. *938.13*.)

938.14   Next the icosahedron contracts symmetrically to the congruently vectored octahedron stage, where symmetrical contraction ceases and precessional torque reduces the system to the quadrivalent tetrahedron's congruent four positive and four negative tetrahedra. These congruent eight tetrahedra further precess into eight congruent zero-altitude tetrahedral triangles in planar congruence as one, having accomplished this contraction from volume 20 of the vector equilibrium to volume 0 while progressively reversing the vector edges by congruence, reducing the original 30 vector edges (five quanta) to zero quanta volume with only three vector edges, each consisting of eight congruent vectors in visible evidence in the zero-altitude tetrahedron. And all

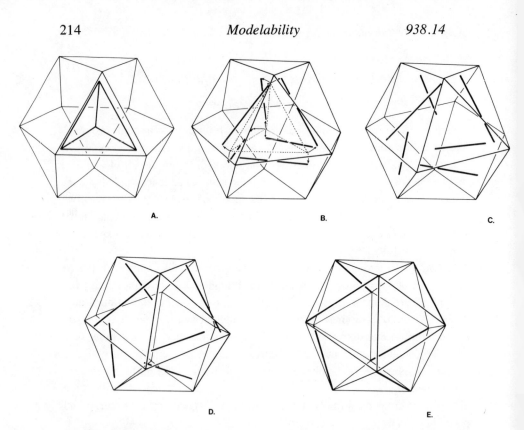

A.   B.   C.

D.   E.

Fig. *938.13 Six Vectors of Additional Quantum Vanish and Reappear in Jitterbug Transformation Between Vector Equilibrium and Icosahedron:* The icosahedral stage in accommodated by the annihilation of the nuclear sphere, which in effect reappears in transformation as six additional external vectors that structurally stabilize the six "square" faces of the vector equilibrium and constitute an additional quantum package. (See also color plate 7.)

this is accomplished without ever severing the exterior, gravitational-embracing bond integrity of the system. (See Figs. 461.08 and 1013.42.)

938.15   The octahedron is produced by one positive and one negative tetrahedron. This is done by opening one vertex of each of the tetrahedra, as the petals of a flower are opened around its bud's vertex, and taking the two open-flowered tetrahedra, each with three triangular petals surrounding a triangular base, precessing in a positive-negative way so that the open triangular petals of each tetrahedron approach the open spaces between the petals of the other tetrahedron, converging them to produce the eight edge-bonded triangular faces of the octahedron. (See Fig. *938.15.*)

938.16   Because the octahedron can be produced by one positive and one negative tetrahedron, it can also be produced by one positive tetrahedron alone. It can be produced by the four edge-bonded triangular faces of one pos-

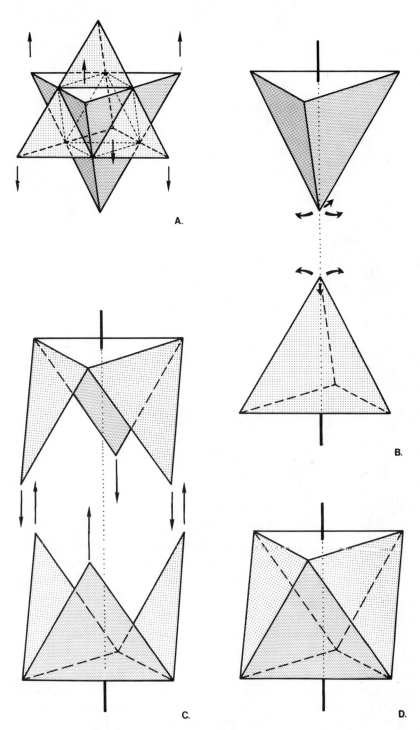

A.

B.

C.

D.

Fig. 938.15 *Two Tetrahedra Open Three Petal Faces and Precess to Rejoin as Octahedron*

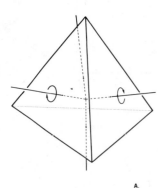
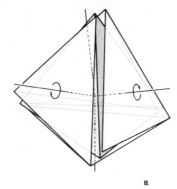
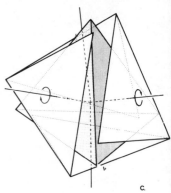

A.　　　　　　　　B.　　　　　　　　C.

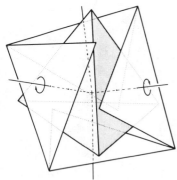
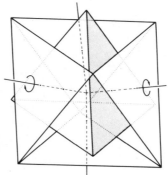
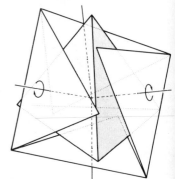

D.　　　　　　　　E.　　　　　　　　F.

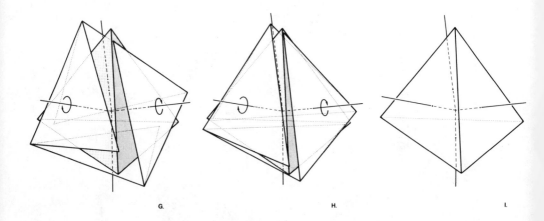

G.　　　　　　　　H.　　　　　　　　I.

Fig. *938.16 Octahedron Produced from Precessed Edges of Tetrahedron:* An octahedron may be produced from a single tetrahedron by detaching the tetra edges and precessing each of the faces 60 degrees. The sequence begins at *A* and proceeds through *BCD* to arrive at *E* with an octahedron of four positive triangular facets interspersed symmetrically with four empty triangular windows. From *F* through *I* the sequence returns to the original tetrahedron.

itive tetrahedron, each being unbonded and precessed 60 degrees to become only vertex-interbonded, one with the other. This produces an octahedron of four positive triangular facets interspersed symmetrically with four empty triangular windows. (See Fig. *938.16.*)

950.00   Allspace Filling

954.10A   Allspace-filling Hierarchy as Rationally Quantifiable in Whole Volume Units of *A* or *B* Modules (*Revised*)

Synergetics' Name	*Quanta Module Volume*	*Type Polyhedron*	*Symmetrical or Asymmetrical*
Mite	3	Tetrahedron	Asymmetrical
Syte (3 types)			
Bite	6	Tetrahedron	Asymmetrical
Rite	6	Tetrahedron	Asymmetrical
Lite	6	Hexahedron	Asymmetrical
Coupler	24	Octahedron	Asymmetrical
Cube	72	Hexahedron	Simple Symmetrical
Rhombic dodecahedron	144	Dodecahedron	Simple Symmetrical
Tetrakaidecahedron	18,432	Tetradecahedron	Complex Symmetrical

980.00   Pi *and Synergetics Constant*

982.61A   Cosmic Hierarchy of Omnidirectionally-phased Nuclear-centered, Convergently-divergently Intertransformable Systems: There is realized herewith a succession of concentric, 12-around-one, closest-packed spheres omniembracing our hierarchy of nuclear event patternings. The synergetics poster in color plate 9 depicts the synergetics isometric of the isotropic vector matrix and its omnirational, low-order-whole-number, equilibrious state of the macro-micro cosmic limits of nuclearly unique, symmetrical morphological relativity in their interquantation, intertransformative, intertransactive, expansive-contractive, axially rotative, operational field. This may come to be identified as the unified field, which, as an operationally transformable complex, is conceptualized only in its equilibrious state.

982.62A *Table of Concentric, 12-around-one, Closest-packed Spheres Omniembracing Our Hierarchy of Nuclear Event Patternings (Revised):*

Symmetrical Form	Tetravolumes	A and B Quanta Modules
F^0 Tetrahedron	1	24
F^0 Vector equilibrium	2.5	60
F^0 Double-Tet cube	3	72
F^0 Octahedron	4	96
F^0 Rhombic triacontahedron*	5 +	120 +
F^0 Rhombic dodecahedron	6	144
F^2 Vector equilibrium	20	480
F^2 Double-Tet cube	24	576

*The spheric spin domain of the rhombic triacontahedron "sphere."

986.00 T and E Quanta Modules: Structural Model of $E = mc^2$: *The Discovery that the E Quanta Module Is the True, Experimentally Evidenceable Model of* $E = mc^2$

•[*986.00–986.874 Demass Model Scenario*]

986.010 *Narrative Recapitulation*

986.011 The exposition herein recounts and recapitulates the original surprise and excitement of the progressive, empirically verified conceptionings; the family of relevant experimental-evidence recalls; the modus operandi; the successive, only-evolutionarily-discovered inputs; and the synergetic comprehension of the omniinterresultant cosmic significance of these strategically employable, synergetically critical additions to human knowledge and their technologically realizable insights.

986.020 *Elementary School Definitions*

986.021 My first mathematics and geometry teachers taught me games that I learned to play well enough to obtain swiftly the answers for which their (only-axiomatically-argued) assumptions called. Webster's dictionary states tersely the definitions of the games they taught me. Webster's definitions are carefully formulated by leading academic authorities and represent the up-to-the-minute concensus of what the educational system assumes *geometry, mathematics,* and *science* to consist.

986.022   Webster defines *geometry* as "the mathematics of the properties, measurements, and relationships of points, lines, angles, surfaces, and solids"—none of which we ourselves observe can exist experientially (ergo, science-verifiably), independently of the others; ergo, they cannot be isolatable "properties" or separate characteristics.

986.023   Physics has found no surfaces and no solids: only localized regions of high-frequency, self-interfering, deflecting, and consequently self-knotting energy events. These self-interference patterns occur in pure principle of ultra-high-frequency intervals and on so minuscule a scale as to prohibit intrusion by anything so dimensionally gross and slow as our fingers. We cannot put our fingers between any two of all the numbers occurring serially between the integer 1 and the integer 2,000,000,000,000—two trillion—as aggregated linearly in one inch. This is the approximate number of atomic domains (the x-illion-per-second, electron-orbited atoms' individual spinout domains) tangentially arrayable in a row within an experience inch.

986.024   Within each of the electron-orbited spheric domains the respective atomic nuclei are centered as remotely distant from their orbiting electrons as is our Sun from its orbiting planets. Within each of these nuclei complex, high-frequency events are occurring in pure principle of interrelationship.

986.025   How do you see through a solid-glass window? Light passes through glass. Light is high-frequency radiation passing unobstructedly at 700 million miles per hour with lots of time and room "to spare" between the set of energy events that constitute the atomic-event constellation known as "glass." (In lenses the light caroms off atoms to have its course deliberately and angularly altered.)

986.026   Webster's definition of *mathematics* is "the science of dealing with quanitites, forms, etc., and their relationships by the use of numbers and symbols."

986.027   Webster defines *science* as "systematized knowledge derived from observation and study."

986.028   In respect to those definitions I was taught, between 1905 and 1913 at the private preparatory school then most highly regarded by Harvard, that "the properties of a point" are nonexistent—that a point is nondimensional or infradimensional, weightless, and timeless. The teacher had opened the day's lesson by making a white chalk mark on the cleanly washed-off blackboard and saying, "This is a point." I was next taught that a line is one-dimensional and consists of a "straight" row of nondimensional points—and I am informed that today, in 1978, all schoolchildren around the world are as yet being so taught. Since such a line lacks three-dimensionality, it too is nonexistent to the second power or to "the square root of nonexistence." We were told by our mathematics teacher that the plane is a raft of tangentially parallel rows of nonexistent lines—ergo, either a third power or a "cube root of nonexistence"—while the supposedly "real" cube of three dimensions is a rectilinear stack of those nonexistent planes and therefore must be either a fourth power or a fourth root of nonexistence. Since the cube lacked weight, temperature, or duration in time, and since its empty 12-edged frame of nonexistent lines would not hold its shape, it was preposterously nondemonstrable—ergo, a treacherous device for students and useful only in playing the game of deliberate self-deception. Since it was arbitrarily compounded of avowedly nonexistent points, the socially accepted three-dimensional reality of the academic system was not "derived from observation and study"—ergo, was to me utterly unscientific.

986.030 Abstraction

986.031   The scientific generalized eternal principle of *leverage* can be experientially demonstrated, and its rate of lifting-advantage-gain per each additional modular increment of lifting-arm length can be mathematically expressed to cover any and all special case temporal realizations of the leverage principle. Biological species can be likewise generalizingly defined. So in many ways humanity has been able to sort out its experiences and identify various prominent sets and subsets of interrelationship principles. The special-case "oriole on the branch of that tree over there," the set of all the orioles, the class of all birds, the class of all somethings, the class of all anythings—any one of which anythings is known as X . . . that life's experiences lead to the common discovery of readily recognized, differentiated, and remembered generalizable sets of constantly manifest residual interrelationship principles—swiftly persuaded mathematical thinkers to adopt the symbolism of algebra, whose known and unknown components and their relationships could be identified by conveniently chosen empty-set symbols. The intellectuals call this *abstraction*.

986.032   Abstraction led to the discovery of a generalized family of plus-and-minus interrelationship phenomena, and these generalized interrelationships came to be expressed as ratios and equations whose intermultiplicative, divisible, additive, or subtractive results could—or might—be experimentally (objectively) or experientially (subjectively) verified in substantive special case interquantation relationships.

986.040 Greek Geometry

986.041 It was a very different matter, however, when in supposed scientific integrity mathematicians undertook to abstract the geometry of structural phenomena. They began their geometrical science by employing only three independent systems: one supposedly "straight"-edged ruler, one scribing tool, and one pair of adjustable-angle dividers.

986.042 Realistically unaware that they were on a spherical planet, the Greek geometers were first preoccupied with only plane geometry. These Greek plane geometers failed to recognize and identify the equally important individual integrity of the system upon whose invisibly structured surface they were scribing. The Euclidean mathematicians had a geocentric fixation and were oblivious to any concept of our planet as an includable item in their tool inventory. They were also either ignorant of—or deliberately overlooked—the systematically associative minimal complex of inter-self-stabilizing forces (vectors) operative in structuring any system (let alone our planet) and of the corresponding cosmic forces (vectors) acting locally upon a structural system. These forces must be locally coped with to insure the local system's structural integrity, which experientially demonstrable force-interaction requirements are accomplishable only by scientific intertriangulations of the force vectors. Their assumption that a square or a cube could hold its own structural shape proves their obliviousness to the force (vector) interpatternings of all structurally stable systems in Universe. To them, structures were made only of stone walls—and stone held its own shape.

986.043 The Ionian Greeks seem to have been self-deceived into accepting as an absolute continuum the surface of what also seemed to them to be absolutely solid items of their experience—whether as randomly fractured, eroded, or ground-apart solids or as humanly carved or molded symmetrical shapes. The Ionian Greeks did not challenge the self-evident *axiomatic* solid integrity of their superficial continuum, surface-face-area assumptions by such thoughts as those of the somewhat later, brilliantly intuitive, scientific speculation of Democritus, which held that matter might consist of a vast number of invisible minimum somethings—to which he gave the name "atoms." All of the Euclidean geometry was based upon *axioms* rather than upon experimentally redemonstrable principles of physical behavior.

986.044 Webster's dictionary defines *axiom* (etymologically from the Greek "to think worthy") as (1) a maxim widely accepted on its intrinsic merit, and (2) a proposition regarded as self-evident truth. The dictionary defines *maxim* as (1) a general truth, fundamental principle, or rule of conduct, and (2) a saying of a proverbial nature. *Maxim* and *maximum* possibly integratingly evolved as "the most important *axiom*." Max + axiom = maxim.

The assumption of commonly honored, customarily accredited axioms as the fundamental "building-blocks" of Greek geometry circumvented the ever-experimentally-redemonstrable qualifying requirement of all serious scientific considerations.

986.045   The Ionian Greeks assumed as fundamental geometric components their line-surrounded areas. These areas' surfaces could be rough, smooth, or polished—just as the smooth surface of the water of the sea could be roughened without losing its identity to them as "the surface." Looking upon plane geometry as the progenitor of subsequently-to-be-developed solid geometry, it seemed never to have occurred to the Euclideans that the surface on which they scribed had shape integrity only as a consequence of its being a component of a complex polyhedral system, the system itself consisting of myriads of subvisible structural systems, whose a priori structural integrity complex held constant the shape of the geometrical figures they scribed upon—the polyhedral system, for instance, the system planet Earth upon whose ground they scratched their figures, or the stone block, or the piece of bark on which they drew. Even Democritus's brilliant speculative thought of a minimum thing smaller than our subdimensional but point-to-able speck was speculative exploration a priori to any experimentally induced thinking of complex dynamic interactions of a plurality of forces that constituted *structuring* in its most primitive sense. Democritus did not think of the atom as a kinetic complex of structural shaping interactions of energy events operating at ultra-high-frequency in pure principle.

986.046   Cubical forms of wood and stone with approximately flat faces and corner angles seemed to the Euclidean-led Ionians to correspond satisfactorily with what was apparently a flat plane world to which trees and humanly erected solid wooden posts and stone columns were obviously perpendicular—ergo, logically parallel to one another. From these only-axiomatically-based conclusions the Ionians developed their arbitrarily shaped, nonstructural, geometrical abstractions and their therefrom-assumed generalizations.

986.047   The Greeks' generalized geometry commenced with the planar relationships and developed therefrom a "solid" geometry by in effect standing their planes on edge on each of the four sides of a square base and capping this vertical assembly with a square plane. This structure was then subdivided by three interperpendicularly coordinate lines—X, Y, and Z—each with its corresponding sets of modularly interspaced and interparalleled planes. Each of these three sets of interparallel and interperpendicular planes was further subdivisible into modularly interspaced and interparallel lines. Their sets of interparallel and interperpendicular planar and linear modulations also inherently produced areal squares and volumetric cubes as the fundamental, seemingly simplest possible area-and-volume standards of uniform mensuration whose dimensioning increments were based exclusively on the uniform linear module of the coordinate system—whose comprehensive interrelationship values remained constant—ergo, were seemingly generalizable mathematically quite independently of any special case experiential selection of special case lengths to be identified with the linear modules.

986.048   The Euclidean Greeks assumed not only that the millions of points and instant planes existed independently of one another, but that the complex was always the product of endlessly multipliable simplexes—to be furnished by an infinite resource of additional components. The persistence of the Greeks' original misconceptioning of geometry has also so distorted the conditioning of the human brain-reflexing as to render it a complete 20th-century surprise that we have a finite Universe: a finite but nonunitarily-and-non-simultaneously accomplished, eternally regenerative Scenario Universe. In respect to such a scenario Universe multiplication is always accomplished only by progressively complex, but always rational, subdivisioning of the initially simplest structural system of Universe: the sizeless, timeless, generalized tetrahedron. Universe, being finite, with energy being neither created nor lost but only being nonsimultaneously intertransformed, cannot itself be multiplied. Multiplication is cosmically accommodated only by further subdivisioning.

986.049   If the Greeks had tried to do so, they would soon have discovered that they could not join tetrahedra face-to-face to fill allspace; whereas they could join cubes face-to-face to fill allspace. Like all humans they were innately intent upon finding *the* "Building-Block" of Universe. The cube seemed to the Greeks, the Mesopotamians, and the Egyptians to be just what they needed to account their experiences volumetrically. But if they had tried to do so, they would have found that unit-dimensioned tetrahedra could be joined corner-to-corner only within the most compact omnidirectional confine permitted by the corner-to-corner rule, which would have disclosed the constant interspace form of the octahedron, which complements the tetrahedron to fill allspace; had they done so, the Ionians would have anticipated the physicists' 1922 discovery of "fundamental complementarity" as well as the 1956 Nobel-winning physics discovery that the complementarity does not consist of the mirror image of that which it complements. But the Greeks did not do so, and they tied up humanity's accounting with the cube which now, two thousand years later, has humanity in a lethal bind of 99 percent scientific illiteracy.

986.050   Unfamiliarity with Tetrahedra

986.051   The distorted conditioning of human reflexing and reasoning persisted in overwhelming the academic point of view—and still does so up to this moment in history. This is nowhere more apparent than in the official re-action to the data and photographs taken on planet Mars by the planet Earth's scientists from their multistage-rocket-despatched *Mariner 9* and *Viking* or-biters:

> But even at the present limits of resolution, some surprising formations have been seen, the most inexplicable of which are *the three-sided pyra-mids* found on the plateau of Elysium. Scientists have tried to find a nat-ural geological process that would account for the formation of these pyr-amids, some of which are *two miles across at the base,* but as yet their origin is far from being explained. Such tantalizing mysteries may not be fully solved until astronauts are able to make direct observations on the Martian surface.*

986.052   In 1977 the NASA scientists scrutinized the robot-photographed pictures of the close-in Martian scene and reported the—to them—surprise presence on Mars of two (two-mile-base-edged) three-sided pyramids the size of Mount Fuji. The NASA scientists were unfamiliar with the tetrahedron. They remarked that these forms, with whose simplest, primitive character they were unacquainted, must have been produced by wind-blown sand ero-sion, whereas we have discovered that tetrahedra are always and only a priori to nature's processes of alteration of her simplest and most primitive polyhe-dral systems.

986.053   Also suggestive of the same blindness to nature's reality suffered by the academic world and the scientists who lead it, was van't Hoff's late-19th-century identification of the primitive significance of the tetrahedron in the structuring of organic chemistry. (See Sec. 931.60.) His hypothesis was at first scoffed at by scientists. Fortunately, through the use of optical in-struments he was able to present visual proof of the tetrahedral configuration of carbon bonds—which experimentally reproduced evidence won him the first Nobel prize awarded a chemist. The Greeks of three millennia ago and today's "educated" society are prone to assume that nature is primitively dis-orderly and that symmetrical shapes are accomplished only by human contriv-ing.

986.060   Characteristics of Tetrahedra

986.061   The tetrahedron is at once both the simplest system and the simplest structural system in Universe (see Secs. 402 and 620). All systems have a minimum set of topological characteristics of vertexes, faces, and

---

* David L. Chandler, "Life on Mars," *Atlantic,* June 1977.

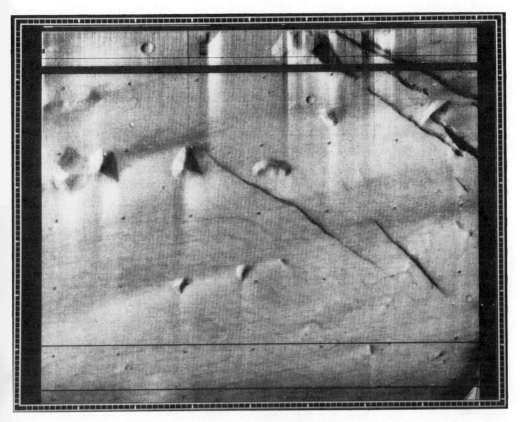

Fig. *986.052 Robot Camera Photograph of Tetrahedra on Mars:* On their correct but awkward description of these gigantic polyhedra as "three-sided pyramids" the NASA scientists revealed their unfamiliarity with tetrahedra.

edges (see Secs. *1007.22* and *1041.10*). Alteration of the minimum structural system, the tetrahedron, or any of its structural-system companions in the primitive hierarchy (Sec. 982.61), may be accomplished by either external or internal contact with other systems—which other systems may cleave, smash, break, or erode the simplest primitive systems. Other such polyhedral systems may be transformingly developed by wind-driven sandstorms or wave-driven pebble beach actions. Those other contacting systems can alter the simplest primitive systems in only two topological-system ways:

(1) by truncating a vertex or a plurality of vertexes, and
(2) by truncating an edge or a plurality of edges.

Faces cannot be truncated. (See Fig. *986.061*.)

986.062   As we have learned regarding the "Platonic solids" carvable from cheese (Sec. 623.10), slicing a polyhedron parallel to one of its faces

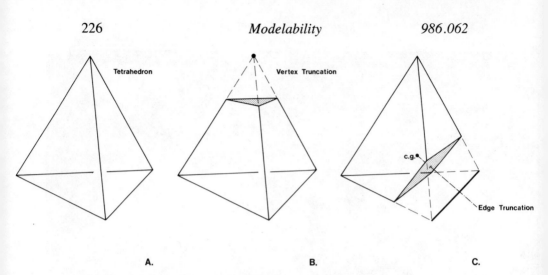

Fig. *986.061 Truncation of Tetrahedra:* Only vertexes and edges may be truncated. (Compare Figs. *987.241* and *1041.11.*)

only replaces the original face with a new face parallel to the replaced face. Whereas truncating a vertex or an edge eliminates those vertexes and edges and replaces them with faces—which become additional faces effecting a different topological abundance inventory of the numbers of vertexes and edges as well. For every edge eliminated by truncation we gain two new edges and one new face. For every corner vertex eliminated by truncation our truncated polyhedron gains three new vertexes, three new edges, and one new face.

986.063   The cheese tetrahedron (Sec. 623.13) is the only one of the primitive hierarchy of symmetrical polyhedral systems that, when sliced parallel to only one of its four faces, maintains its symmetrical integrity. It also maintains both its primitive topological and structural component inventories when asymmetrically sliced off parallel to only one of its four disparately oriented faces. When the tetrahedron has one of its vertexes truncated or one of its edges truncated, however, then it loses its overall system symmetry as well as both its topological and structural identification as the structurally and topologically simplest of cosmic systems.

986.064   We may now make a generalized statement that the simplest system in Universe, the tetrahedron, can be design-altered and lose its symmetry only by truncation of one or more of its corners or edges. If all the tetrahedron's four vertexes and six edges were to be similarly truncated (as in Fig. 1041.11) there would result a symmetrical polyhedron consisting of the original four faces with an addition of 10 more, producing a 14-faceted symmetrical polyhedron known as the tetrakaidecahedron, or Kelvin's "solid," which (as shown in Sec. 950.12 and Table 954.10) is an allspace filler—as are also the cube, the rhombic dodecahedron, and the tetrahedral Mites, Sytes, and

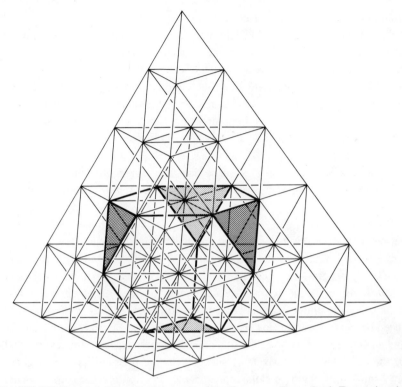

Fig. *986.062 Truncated Tetrahedron within Five-frequency Tetra Grid:* Truncating the vertexes of the tetrahedron results in a polyhedron with four triangular faces and four hexagonal faces. (Compare Figs. *1041.11* and *1074.13.*)

Couplers. All that further external alteration can do is produce more vertex and edge truncations which make the individual system consist of a greater number of smaller-dimension topological aspects of the system. With enough truncations—or knocking off of corners or edges—the system tends to become less angular and smoother (smoother in that its facets are multiplying in number and becoming progressively smaller and thus approaching subvisible identification). Further erosion can only "polish off" more of the only-microscopically-visible edges and vertexes. A polished beach pebble, like a shiny glass marble or like a high-frequency geodesic polyhedral "spheric" structure, is just an enormously high-frequency topological inventory-event system.

986.065   **Joints, Windows, and Struts:** As we have partially noted elsewhere (Secs. 536 and 604), Euler's three primitive topological characteristics—*vertexes, faces,* and *lines*—are structurally identifiable as *joints, windows,* and push-pull *struts,* respectively. When you cannot see through the windows (faces), it is because the window consists of vast numbers of sub-visible windows, each subvisible-magnitude window being strut-mullion-framed by a complex of substructural systems, each with its own primitive topological and structural components.

986.066   Further clarifying those structural and topological primitive com-ponentation characteristics, we identify the structural congruences of two or more joined-together-systems' components as two congruent single vertexes (or joints) producing one single, univalent, universal-joint intersystem bond-ing. (See Secs. 704, 931.20, and Fig. 640.41B.) Between two congruent pairs of interconnected vertexes (or joints) there apparently runs only one ap-parent (because congruent) line, or interrelationship, or push-pull strut, or hinge.

986.067   Returning to our early-Greek geometry initiative and to the as-yet-persistent academic misconditioning by the Greeks' oversights and misin-terpretations of their visual experiences, we recall how another non-Ionian Greek, Pythagoras, demonstrated and "proved" that the number of square areas of the unit-module-edged squares and the number of cubical module volumes of the unit-module-edged cubes correspond exactly with arithmetic's second-powerings and third-powerings. The Greeks, and all mathematicians and all scientists, have ever since misassumed these square and cube results to be the only possible products of such successive intermultiplying of geome-try's unit-edge-length modular components. One of my early mathematical discoveries was the fact that all triangles—regular, isosceles, or scalene—may be modularly subdivided to express second-powering. Any triangle whose three edges are each evenly divided into the same number of intervals, and whose edge-interval marks are cross-connected with lines that are inherently parallel to the triangle's respective three outer edges—any triangle so treated will be subdivided by little triangles all exactly similar to the big triangle thus subdivided, and the number of small similar triangles subdividing the large master triangle will always be the second power of the number of edge mod-ules of the big triangle. In other words, we can say "triangling" instead of "squaring," and since all squares are subdivisible into two triangles, and since each of those triangles can demonstrate areal second-powering, and since nature is always most economical, and since nature requires structural integrity of her forms of reference, she must be using "triangling" instead of "squaring" when any integer is multiplied by itself. (See Sec. 990.)

986.068   This seemed to be doubly confirmed when I discovered that any nonequiedged quadrangle, with each of its four edges uniformly subdivided into the same number of intervals and with those interval marks intercon-nected, produced a pattern of dissimilar quadrangles. (See Fig. 990.01.) In the same manner I soon discovered experimentally that all tetrahedra, octahedra, cubes, and rhombic dodecahedra—regular or skew—could be unitarily subdivided into tetrahedra with the cube consisting of three tetra, the octahedron of four tetra, and the rhombic dodecahedron of six similar tetra; and that when any of these regular or skew polyhedras' similar or dissimilar edges and faces were uniformly subdivided and interconnected, their volumes would always be uniformly subdivided into regular or skew tetrahedra, and that N^3 could and should be written and spoken of as $N^{\text{tetrahedroned}}$ and not as N^{cubed}.

986.069   Nature would use the tetrahedron as the module of subdivision because nature has proven to the physicists and the other physical scientists that she always chooses the most economic realization. Cubes require three times as much Universe as do tetrahedra to demonstrate volumetric content of systems because cubic identification with third-powering used up three times as much volume as is available in Universe. As a result of cubic mensuration science has had to invent such devices as "probability" and "imaginary numbers." Thus "squaring" and "cubing," instead of nature's "triangling" and "tetrahedroning," account for science's using mathematical tools that have no physical-model demonstrability—ergo, are inherently "unscientific."

986.070   Buildings on Earth's Surface

986.071   In the practical fortress and temple building of the earliest known Mesopotamians, Egyptians, and Greeks their cubes and omnirectilinear blocks seemed readily to fill allspace as they were assembled into fortress or temple walls with plumb bobs, water-and-bubble levels, straightedges, and right-triangle tools. No other form they knew—other than the cube—seemed to fill allspace as demonstrated in practical masonry; wherefore they assumed this to be scientifically demonstrated proof of the generalizability of their mathematically abstracted plane- and solid-geometry system and its *XYZ* coordination.

986.072   Because of the relatively diminutive size of humans in respect to the size of our planet, world-around society as yet spontaneously cerebrates only in terms of our immediate world's seeming to demonstrate itself to be a flat plane base, all of the perpendiculars of which—such as trees and humans and human-built local structures—appear to be rising from the Earth parallel to one another—ergo, their ends point in only two possible directions, "up" or "down." . . . It's "a wide, wide world," and "the four corners of the Earth."

986.073   It was easy and probably unavoidable for humanity to make the self-deceptive blunders of assuming that a cube held its shape naturally, and not because the stone-cutters or wood-cutters had chosen quite arbitrarily to make it in this relatively simple form. Human's thought readily accepted— and as yet does—the contradictory abstract state "solid." The human eye gave no hint of the energetic structuring of the atomic microcosm nor of the omnidynamic, celestial-interpositioning transformations of both macro- and micro-Universe.

986.074   Prior to steel-framed or steel-reinforced-concrete construction methods, humans' buildings that were constructed only of masonry could not be safely built to a height of over 20 stories—approximately 200 feet high. Such a masonry building was Chicago's turn-of-the-20th-century world-record Monadnock Building, whose base covered a small but whole city block. It is not until we reach a height of 100 stories—approximately 1000 feet high— that two exactly vertical square columns, each with base edges of 250 feet, built with exactly vertical walls, and touching one another only along one of each of their base edges, will show a one-inch space between them. The rate their vertical walls part from one another is only $1/1000$th of an inch for each foot of height.

986.075   Masons' and carpenters' linear measuring devices are usually graduated only to $1/16$th of an inch, and never finer than $1/32$nd of an inch. Thus differentials of a thousandth of an inch are undetectable and are al-together inadvertently overlooked; ergo, they get inadvertently filled-in, or cross-joined, never to have been known to exist even on the part of the most skilled and conscientious of building craftsmen, whose human eyes cannot see intervals of less than $1/100$th of an inch.

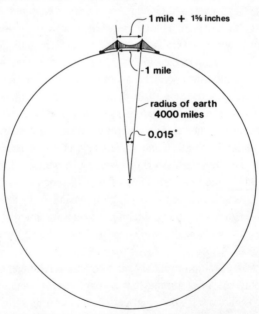

Fig. *986.076* *Diagram of Verrazano Bridge:* The two towers are not parallel to each other.

986.076   If two exactly-vertical-walled city skyscrapers are built side by side, not until they are two and one-half miles high (the height of Mount Fuji) will there be a space of one foot between the tops of their two adjacent walls. (See Fig. 986.076.) Of course, the farther apart the centers of their adjacent bases, the more rapidly will the tops of such high towers veer away from one another:

> The twin towers of New York's Verrazano Bridge are 693 feet high . . . soaring as high as a 70-story skyscraper . . . set almost a mile from each other, the two towers, though seemingly parallel, are an inch and five-eighths farther apart at their summits than at their bases because of the Earth's curvature.*

986.077   It is easy to understand how humans happened to think it "illogical" to have to consider that all the perpendiculars to a sphere are radii of that sphere—ergo, never parallel to one another. Our humans-in-Universe scale is inherently self-deceptive—ergo, difficult to cope with rigorously.

986.080   Naive Perception of Childhood

986.081   The inventory of experimentally demonstrated discoveries of science which had accrued by the time of my childhood gave me reason to question many of the "abstractions" of geometry as I was being instructed in that subject. Axioms were based on what only seemed "self-evident," such as the stone block or the "cubical" wooden play blocks of my nursery. To society they "obviously held their shape." I do not think that I was precocious or in any way a unique genius. I had one brother; he was three years younger than I. His eyesight was excellent; mine was atrocious. I did not get my first eyeglasses until my younger brother was running around and talking volubly. He could see things clearly; I could not. Our older sister could also see things clearly. I literally had to feel my way along—tactilely—in order to recognize the "things" of my encountered environment—ergo, my deductions were slow in materializing. My father called my younger brother "stickly-prickly" and he called me "slow-and-solid"—terms he adopted from "The Jaguar and the Armadillo" in Kipling's Just So Stories.

986.082   I was born cross-eyed on 12 July 1895. Not until I was four-and-a-half years old was it discovered that I was also abnormally farsighted. My vision was thereafter fully corrected with lenses. Until four-and-a-half I could see only large patterns—houses, trees, outlines of people—with blurred color-

*The Engineer (New York: Time-Life Books, 1967.) If the towers are 12,000 miles apart— that is, halfway around the world from one another—their tops will be built in exactly opposite directions—ergo, at a rate of two feet farther apart for each foot of their respective heights.

ing. While I saw two dark areas on human faces, I did not see a human eye or a teardrop or a human hair until I was four. Despite my newly gained ability—in 1899—to apprehend details with glasses, my childhood's spontaneous dependence upon only big-pattern clues has persisted. All that I have to do today to reexperience what I saw when I was a child is to take off my glasses, which, with some added magnification for age, have exactly the same lens corrections as those of my first five-year-old pair of spectacles. This helps me to recall vividly my earliest sensations, impressions, and tactical assumptions.

986.083   I was sent to kindergarten before I received my first eyeglasses. The teacher, Miss Parker, had a large supply of wooden toothpicks and semidried peas into which you could easily stick the sharp ends of the toothpicks. The peas served as joints between the toothpicks. She told our kindergarten class to make structures. Because all of the other children had good eyesight, their vision and imagination had been interconditioned to make the children think immediately of copying the rectilinearly framed structures of the houses they saw built or building along the road. To the other children, horizontally or perpendicularly parallel rectilinear forms were structure. So they used their toothpicks and peas to make cubic and other rectilinear models. The semidried peas were strong enough to hold the angles between the stuck-in toothpicks and therefore to make the rectilinear forms hold their shapes—despite the fact that a rectangle has no inherent self-structuring capability.

986.084   In my poor-sighted, feeling-my-way-along manner I found that the triangle—I did not know its name—was the only polygon—I did not know that word either—that would hold its shape strongly and rigidly. So I naturally made structural systems having interiors and exteriors that consisted entirely of triangles. Feeling my way along I made a continuous assembly of octahedra and tetrahedra, a structured complex to which I was much later to give the contracted name "octet truss." (See Sec. 410.06). The teacher was startled and called the other teachers to look at my strange contriving. I did not see Miss Parker again after leaving kindergarten, but three-quarters of a century later, just before she died, she sent word to me by one of her granddaughters that she as yet remembered this event quite vividly.

986.085   Three-quarters of a century later, in 1977, the National Aeronautics and Space Administration (NASA), which eight years earlier had put the first humans on the Moon and returned them safely to our planet Earth, put out bids for a major space-island platform, a controlled-environment structure. NASA's structural specifications called for an "octet truss"—my invented and patented structural name had become common language, although sometimes engineers refer to it as "space framing." NASA's scientific search for the structure that had to provide the most structural advantages with the least pounds of material—ergo, least energy and seconds of invested time—in order to be compatible and light enough to be economically rocket-lifted and self-erected in space—had resolved itself into selection of my 1899 octet truss. (See Sec. 422.)

986.086 It was probable also that my only-insectlike, always-slow, cross-referencing strategy of touching, tasting, smelling, listening, and structurally testing by twisting and pounding and so forth—to which I spontaneously resorted—made me think a great deal about the fact that when I broke a piece of glass or a stone or a wooden cube apart, it did not separate naturally into little cubes but usually into sharp pointed shapes. In the earliest of my memories I was always suspicious of the integrity of cubes, which only humans seemed to be introducing into the world. There were no cubical roses, eggs, trees, clouds, fruits, nuts, stones, or anything else. Cubes to me were unnatural: I observed humans deliberately sawing ice into large rectilinear cakes, but window glass always broke itself into predominantly triangular pieces; and snowflakes formed themselves naturally into a myriad of differently detailed, six-triangled, hexagonal patterns.

986.087 I was reacting normally in combining those spontaneous feelings of my childhood with the newly discovered knowledge of the time: that light has speed (it is not instantaneous, and comes in smallest packages called photons); that there is something invisible called electricity (consisting of "invisible behaviors" called electrons, which do real work); and that communication can be wireless, which Marconi had discovered the year I was born—and it is evident that I was reacting normally and was logically unable to accept the customarily honored axioms that were no longer "self-evident."

986.088 My contemporaries and I were taught that in order to design a complete and exact sphere and have no materials left over, we must employ the constant known as *pi* (π), which I was also taught was a "transcendentally irrational number," meaning it could *never be resolved*. I was also informed that a singly existent bubble was a sphere; and I asked, To how many places does nature carry out *pi* when she makes each successive bubble in the white-cresting surf of each successive wave before nature finds out that *pi* can never be resolved? . . . And at what moment in the making of each separate bubble in Universe does nature decide to terminate her eternally frustrated calculating and instead turn out a fake sphere? I answered myself that I don't think nature is using *pi* or any of the other irrational fraction constants of physics. Chemistry demonstrates that nature always associates or disassociates in whole rational increments. . . . Those broken window shards not only tended to be triangular in shape, but also tended to sprinkle some very fine polyhedral pieces. There were wide ranges of sizes of pieces, but there were no pieces that could not "make up their minds" or resolve which share of the original whole was theirs. Quite the contrary, they exploded simultaneously and unequivocally apart.

986.089 At first vaguely, then ever more excitedly, precisely, and inclusively, I began to think and dream about the optimum grand strategy to be employed in discovering nature's own obviously elegant and exquisitely exact mathematical coordinate system for conducting the energetic transactions of eternally regenerative Universe. How does nature formulate and mass-produce all the botanical and zoological phenomena and all the crystals with such elegant ease and expedition?

986.090 The Search for Nature's Coordinate System

986.091 Several things were certain: nature is capable of both omnidirectional disorderly, dispersive, and destructive expansion and omnidirectional collective, selective sorting and constructive contraction; and rays of candlelight are not parallel to one another. I decided to initiate my search for nature's coordinate system by assuming that the coordinate system must be convergently and divergently interaccommodative. That the seasons of my New England childhood brought forth spectacular transformations in nature's total interpatterning; that the transformations were not simultaneous nor everywhere the same; that there were shaded and Sun-shined-upon area variables; and that they were all embraced by a comprehensive coordination—altogether made me dream of comprehending the comprehensively accommodating coordinate system that had no separate departments of chemistry, physics, biology, mathematics, art, history, or languages. I said nature has only one department and only one language.

986.092 These thoughts kept stimulating my explorations for the totally accommodative coordinate system. Einstein's conclusion—that the definitive, maximum possible speed of light rendered astronomical phenomena an aggregate of nonsimultaneous and only partially overlapping, differently enduring energy events—greatly affected the increasing inventory of my tentative formulations of the interaccommodative requirements of the cosmic coordination system which I sought. I was driven by both consciously and subconsciously sustained intuition and excitement. This was very private, however. I talked to no one about it. It was all very remote from that which seemed to characterize popular interest.

986.093 The youthful accruals of these long-sustained private observations, cogitations, and speculations were enormously helpful when I decided at the age of 32, in my crisis year of 1927, to abandon the game of competitive survival (a game I had been taught to believe in as thought-out, managed, and evolved entirely by others) and instead to rely completely upon my own thinking and experience-suggested inclinations . . . to find out how Universe is organized and what it is doing unbeknownst to humans. Why are humans here in Universe? What should we be doing to fulfill our designed functioning in Universe? Surely all those stars and galaxies were not designed only to be romantic scenery for human moods. What am I designed to be able to comprehend about Universe? What are we humans designed to be able to do for one another and for our Universe?

986.094 **Expanding Universe:** My determination to commit myself completely to the search for nature's raison d'être and for its comprehensive coordinate system's mathematics was greatly reinforced by the major discovery of the astronomer E. P. Hubble in 1924. He discovered an expanding macrocosmic system with all the myriads of galaxies and their respective stellar components at all times maintaining the same interangular orientations and relative interdistancings from one another while sum-totally and omnisymmetrically expanding and moving individually away from one another, and doing so at astronomical speeds. This discovery of Hubble's became known as Expanding Universe.

986.095 The only way humans can expand their houses is by constructing lopsided additions to their rectilinearly calculated contriving. People found that they could "blow up" rubber-balloon spheres to increase their radii, but they couldn't blow up their buildings except by dynamite. They called their wooden "2 x 4," and "2 x 6," and "2 x 8-inch" cross-section, wooden-timber nail-ups "balloon framing," but why they selected that name was difficult to explain.

986.096 My insights regarding nature's coordinate system were greatly enhanced by two of Milton Academy's greatest teachers: Homer LeSourd in physics and William Lusk Webster Field ("Biology Bill") in biology. During the summer vacation of 1906, at 11 years of age I designed and built my first small but exciting experimental dwelling on our family's small mid-Penobscot Bay island. Living all my youthful summers on that island, with its essential boat-building, boat-modifying, boat-upkeep, and boat-sailing, followed by five years as a line officer in the regular U.S. Navy with some of my own smaller-craft commands, some deck-officering on large craft of the new era's advanced technology ships, together with service involving airplanes, submarines, celestial navigation, ballistics, radio, and radiotelephone; then resignation from the Navy followed by five more private-enterprise years developing a new building system, inventing and installing its production tools, managing the production of the materials, and erecting therewith 240 residences and small commercial buildings—altogether finally transformed my sustained activity into full preoccupation with my early-boyhood determination some day to comprehend and codify nature's omniintertransformative, omnidirectional, cosmic coordination system and its holistic, only-experientially-proven mathematics. In 1928, inspired and fortified by Hubble's Expanding Universe discovery, I gave the name and its symbol 4-D to my mathematical preoccupations and their progressively discovered system codifying. In 1936 I renamed my discipline "Energetic Vectorial Geometry." In 1938 I again renamed it "Energetic-synergetic Geometry," and in 1970 for verbal economy contracted that title to "Synergetics." (See Fig. *986.096.*)

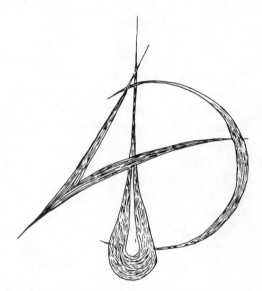

Fig. *986.096 4-D Symbol:* Adopted by the author in 1928 to characterize his fourth-dimensional mathematical explorings.

986.100   Sequence of Considerations

986.101   At the outset of my lifelong search for nature's omnirational coordination system of mathematical interaccounting and intertransformability I proceeded through a sequence of considerations which may be enumerated as follows:

986.110   Consideration 1: Energetic Vectors

986.111   I first determined to employ only vectors for lines. I realized that operationally all lines are always trajectories of energy events, either as the energy invested by humans in the work of carving or depositing linearly— which we call "drawing" a line—or as the inanimately articulated energy of force lines.

986.112   Vectors always represent energy forces of given magnitude operating at given angles upon given entities at given loci, and vectors may always be demonstrated by lines representing given mass moving at given velocity in unique angular direction in respect to a given axis of observation. Vectors do not occur singly: They occur only as the total family of forces interacting in any given physical circumstance.

986.113   Vectors always have unique length, that length being the product of the mass and the velocity as expressed in a given modular system of measurement. Vectors do not have inherent extendibility to infinity—as did the lines of my boyhood's schoolteachers. Vectors are inherently terminal. Vectors bring into geometry all the qualities of energetic reality lacking in Euclidean geometry: time and energy—energy differentially divergent as radiation (velocity) and energy integratively convergent as matter (mass). Velocity and mass could be resolved into numerically described time and temperature components.

986.120   Consideration 2: Avogadro's Constant Energy Accounting

986.121   Avogadro discovered that under identical conditions of pressure and heat all elements in their gaseous state always consist of the same number of molecules per given volume. Since the chemical elements are fundamentally different in electron-proton componentation, this concept seemed to me to be *the* "Grand Central Station" of nature's numerical coordinate system's geometric volume—that numerically exact volumes contain constant, exact numbers of fundamental energy entities. This was the numerical and geometrical constancy for which I was looking. I determined to generalize Avogadro's experimentally proven hypothesis that "under identical conditions of heat and pressure all gases disclose the same number of molecules per given volume." (See Secs. 410.03–04.)

986.122   Here were Physical Universe's natural number quantations being constantly related to given volumes. Volumes are geometrical entities. Geometrically defined and calculated volumes are polyhedral systems. Polyhedra are defined by edge lines, each of which must be a vector.

986.123   Within any given volumetrically contained gaseous state the energy kinetics of molecules are everywhere the same. The outward pressure of air against the enclosing tube wall and casing of any one automobile tire is everywhere the same. Pressure and heat differentials involve isolated conditions—isolated by containers; ergo, special cases. To me this meant that we could further generalize Avogadro by saying that "'under identical, uncontained, freely self-interarranging conditions of energy all chemical elements will disclose the same number of fundamental somethings per given volume.'' This constant-volume-population-and-omniequilibrious-energy relationship would require physically demonstrable, substantive, geometrical combining of a given number of unique energetic-event entities per unit volume with constant-angularly-defined positional orientation integrities. This meant that the vectorially structured shapes of the volumes accommodating given numbers of most primitive energy events must be experientially demonstrable.

986.130   Consideration 3: Angular Constancy

986.131   I said that since vectors are physically modelable structural components, they produce conceptual structural models of energy events, and since my hypothetical generalization of Avogadro's law requires that ''all the conditions of energy be everywhere the same,'' what does this condition look like as structured in vectorial geometry? Obviously all the vectors must be the same length and all of them must interact at the same angles. I said: It will make no difference what length is employed so long as they are all the same length. Linear size is special case. Special case occurs only in time. Angles are cosmically constant independently of time-size considerations.

986.140   Consideration 4: Isotropic Vector Model

986.141   I said, Can you make a vector model of this generalization of Avogadro? And I found that I had already done so in that kindergarten event in 1899 when I was almost inoperative visually and was exploring tactilely for a structural form that would hold its shape. This I could clearly feel was the triangle—with which I could make systems having insides and outsides. This was when I first made the octet truss out of toothpicks and semidried peas, which interstructuring pattern scientists decades later called the ''isotropic vector matrix,'' meaning that the vectorial lengths and interanglings are everywhere the same. (See Sec. 410.06.)

986.142   This matrix was vectorially modelable since its lines, being vectors, did not lead to infinity. This isotropic vector matrix consists of six-edged tetrahedra plus 12-edged octahedra—multiples of six. Here is an uncontained omniequilibrious condition that not only could be, but spontaneously would be, reverted to anywhen and anywhere as a six-dimensional frame of transformative-evolution reference, and its vector lengths could be discretely tuned by uniform modular subdivisioning to accommodate any desired special case wavelength time-size, most economically interrelated, transmission or reception of physically describable information. (Compare Secs. 639.02 and *1075.10*.)

986.143   Since the vectors are all identical in length, their intersection vertexes become the nuclear centers of unit-radius spheres in closest-packed aggregation—which closest packing is manifest by atoms in their crystal growth. All the foregoing brought the adoption of my vectorial geometry's everywhere-the-same (isotropic) vector matrix as the unified field capable of accommodating all of Physical Universe's intertransformative requirements.

986.150   Consideration 5: Closest Packing of Spheres

986.151   I had thus identified the isotropic vector matrix with the uniform linear distances between the centers of unit radius spheres, which aggregates became known later—in 1922—as ''closest-packed'' unit-radius spheres (Sec. 410.07), a condition within which we always have the same optimum number of the same ''somethings''—spheres or maybe atoms—per given volume, and an optimally most stable and efficient aggregating arrangement known for past centuries by stackers of unit-radius coconuts or cannonballs and used by nature for all time in the closest packing of unit-radius atoms in crystals.

986.160   Consideration 6: Diametric Unity

986.161   The installation of the closest-packed unit-radius spheres into their geometrical congruence with the isotropic vector matrix showed that each of the vectors always reaches between the spheric centers of any two

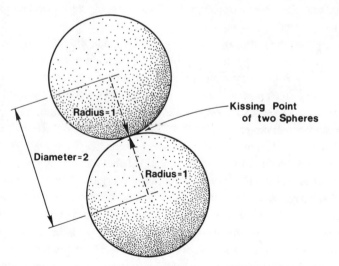

Fig. *986.161 Diametric Unity:* The vectors of the isotropic vector matrix interconnect the spheric centers of any two tangentially adjacent spheres. The radii of the two spheres meet at the *kissing point* and are each one-half of the system vector. Unity is plural and at minimum two.

tangentially adjacent spheres. This meant that the radius of each of the *kissing* spheres consists of one-half of the interconnecting vectors. Wherefore, the radius of our closest-packed spheres being half of the system vector, it became obvious that if we wished to consider the radius of the unit sphere as unity, we must assume that the value of the vector inherently interconnecting two unit spheres is *two*. Unity is plural and at minimum two. Diameter means dia-*meter*—unit of system measurement is two.

986.162   Fig. 986.161 shows one vector D whose primitive value is two. Vectors are energy relationships. The phenomenon relationship exists at minimum between two entities, and the word *unity* means union, which is inherently at minimum two. "Unity is plural and at minimum two" also at the outset became a prime concept of synergetics vectorial geometry. (See Sec. 540.10.)

986.163 $1R + 1R = 2R$

$2R = $ Diameter

Diameter is the relative-conceptual-size determinant of a system. A diameter is the prime characteristic of the symmetrical system. The separate single system = unity. Diameter describes unity. Unity = 2. (See Secs. 905.10 and *1013.10.*)

986.164   One by itself is nonexistent. Existence begins with awareness. Awareness begins with observable otherness. (See Secs. 264 and 981.)

986.165   Understanding means comprehending the interrelationship of the observer and the observed. Definitive understanding of interrelationships is expressed by ratios.

986.166   At the outset of my explorations I made the working assumption that unity is two, as combined with the experimentally demonstrable fact that every system and every systemic special case sphere is at once both a concave and a convex sphere—ergo, always inherently two spheres. Reflective concave surfaces convergently concentrate all impinging radiation, and reflective convex surfaces divergently diffuse all impinging radiation. Though concave and convex are inherently congruent as they are always-and-only *co*existing, they are also diametrically opposed physical behavior phenomena—ergo, absolutely different because the one diffuses the energies of Universe, producing macrocosmic dispersion, and the other concentrates the energies of Universe, producing microcosmic convergence. Concave and convex are explicitly two opposites cosituate (congruent) geometrically as one. This led me to the working assumption at the outset of my—thus far—60-year exploration for nature's own coordinate system, that unity is inherently plural and at minimum is to be dealt with as the value two, which twoness might well coexist with other numbers of inherent properties of primary-existence systems.

986.170   Consideration 7: Vector Equilibrium

986.171   I then identified this closest-packed-spheres isotropic vector matrix as a generalized field condition of the everywhere-and-everywhen most economically interaccommodating of any plurality of nuclearly convergent-divergent, importively organizing, and exportingly info-dispensing energy events—while also providing for any number of individually discrete, overlappingly co-occurrent, frequency differentiated info-interexchangings—ergo, to be always accommodative of any number of co-occurrent, individual-pattern-integrity evolutionary scenarios.

986.172   Thus the eternally regenerative Universe, embracing the minimum complex of intercomplementary transformations necessary to effect total regeneration, becomes comprehensively accommodated by the only generalizably definable Scenario Universe as the condition of the *vector equilibrium*, an everywhere-everywhen condition at which nature refuses to pause, but through which most economically accommodating field of operational reference she pulsates her complex myriads of overlapping, concurrent, local inter-transformings and aberrative structurings. I then invented the symbol to identify vector equilibrium.

986.180   Consideration 8: Concentric Polyhedral Hierarchy

986.181   Thereafter I set about sorting out the relative numbers and volumes of the most primitive hierarchy of symmetrically structured polyhedral-event ''somethings''—all of which are always concentrically congruent and each and all of which are to be discovered as vertexially defined and structurally coexistent within the pre-time-size, pre-frequency-modulated isotropic vector matrix. (See Sec. and Fig. 982.61.)

986.190   Consideration 9: Synergetics

986.191   This book *Synergetics* (volumes 1 and 2) embraces the record of the lifetime search, research, sorting-outs, and structural-intertransforming experiments based upon the foregoing eight considerations, all of which I had adopted by 1927. This 1927 inventory has been progressively amplified by subsequent experience-induced considerations.

986.200　Narrative Exposition of Spherical Accommodation

986.201　Consideration 10: The Spheric Experience: Energetic-reality Accounting vs Abstract-cubic Accounting

986.202　In *Synergetics 1*, Secs. 962 through 966, I developed the first-, second-, and third-power values of my numerical factors for converting the *XYZ* coordinate system's edge lengths, square areas, and cubical volumes to my 1927-discovered synergetic system's unit VE vectorial edge lengths, triangular areas, and tetrahedral volumes.* (See Table 963.10.)

986.203　The synergetics coordinate system—in contradistinction to the *XYZ* coordinate system—is linearly referenced to the unit-vector-length edges of the regular tetrahedron, each of whose six unit vector edges occur in the isotropic vector matrix as the diagonals of the cube's six faces. We also recall that the eight corners of the cube are defined and structured omnitriangularly by the symmetrically interarrayed and concentric pairs of positive and negative tetrahedra (Figs. 110A and 110B).

986.204　Since the cube-face diagonal is the edge of the six-vector-edged, four-planes-of-symmetry tetrahedron, and since synergetics finds the unit-vector-edged tetrahedron to be the simplest structural system in Universe, the tetrahedron's vector edge logically becomes the most economically primitive simplex module of relative length in synergetics' coordinate system of exploratory reference. Thus the tetrahedron's unit vector edge of unity 2 is manifest as nature's coordinate primitive-length module for assessing:

second-power triangular area, $2^2 = 4$

as well as for assessing that vector's

third-power tetrahedral volume, $2^3 = 8$,

These areas and volumes become the logical unit of areal and volumetric reference in accounting the relative geometrical area and volume values of the entire hierarchy of primitive, concentrically congruent, symmetrical polyhedra as these naturally occur around any vertex of the isotropic vector matrix, and that matrix's experimentally demonstrable, maximum-limit set of seven axes of polyhedral symmetries, which seven symmetries (Sec. 1040) accommodate and characterize the energetic special case formulations of all great-circle gridding.

986.205　The synergetics hierarchy of topological characteristics as presented in Table 223.64 of *Synergetics 1* (which was contracted for with Mac-

---

* My chart of these conversion factors, which I at first called the Dymaxion constants, was privately published in 1950 at North Carolina State University, and again in 1959 in *The Dymaxion World of Buckminster Fuller*, written with Robert W. Marks.

millan in 1961 and published by them in 1975), discloses the rational values of the comprehensive coordinate system of nature, which my 60-year exploration discovered. In 1944 I published a paper disclosing this rational system. At that time I was counseled by some of my scientist friends, who were aware that I was continuing to make additional refinements and discoveries, that premature publication of a treatise of disclosure might result in the omission of one or more items of critical information which might be later discovered and which might make the difference between scientific acceptance or rejection of the disclosures. Reminded by those scientist-artist friends that we have only one opportunity in a lifetime out of many lifetimes to publish a prime-science-reorienting discovery, I postponed publishing a comprehensive treatise until in 1970, at the age of 75, I felt it could no longer be delayed.

986.206   The eleventh-hour publishing of *Synergetics 1* coincided with my busiest years of serving other obligations over a period calling for a vast number of tactical decisions regarding the methodology of producing what proved to be a 780-page book. Typical of the problems to be swiftly resolved are those shortly to be herewith recounted. The accounting also discloses the always surprisingly productive events that ensue upon mistake-making that are not only discovered and acknowledged, but are reexplored in search of the significance of the mistakes' having occurred.

986.207   Because the *XYZ*-coordinate, three-dimensional system values are arrived at by successive multiplying of the dimensions, volume in that system is an inherently three-dimensional phenomenon. But in synergetics the primitive values start holistically with timeless-sizeless tetrahedral volume unity in respect to which the cube's primitive value is 3, the octahedron's relative timeless-sizeless value is 4, the rhombic triacontrahedron's is 5, and the rhombic dodecahedron's is 6. In synergetics, when time-size special-case realizations enter into the consideration, then the (only-interrelated-to-one-another) primitive volumes of the synergetic hierarchy are multiplied by frequency of the edge modulation to the third power. Since innate primitive volume is a base-times-altitude three-dimensional phenomenon, and since all the synergetics hierarchy's time-size realization volumes are inherently six-dimensional, I was confronted with an exploratory tactical quandary.

986.208   The problem was to arrive at the numerical volume value for the sphere in the synergetics hierarchy, and the dilemma was whether I should apply my synergetics' volumetric constant to the first power or to the third power of the *XYZ*-coordinate system's volumetric values as arrived at by the conventional *XYZ*-coordinate system's method of calculating the volume of a sphere of radius vector = 1. This operation is recorded in Sec. 982.55 of *Synergetics 1,* where I misconceptualized the operation, and (without reviewing how I had calculated the constant for converting *XYZ* to synergetics) redundantly took the number 1.192324, which I assumed (again in mistaken carelessness) to be the third-power value of the synergetics-conversion constant, and I applied it to the volumetric value of a sphere of unit vector diameter as already arrived at by conventional *XYZ*-referenced mathematics, the conventional *XYZ*-coordinate volumetric value for the volume of a sphere of radius 1 being 4.188, which multiplied by 1.192324 gave the product 4.99—a value so close to 5 that I thought it might possibly have been occasioned by the unresolvability of tail-end trigonometric interpolations, wherefore I tentatively accepted 4.99 as probably being exactly 5, which, if correct, was an excitingly significant number as it would have neatly fitted the sphere into the hierarchy of primitive polyhedra (Sec. 982.61). My hindsight wisdom tells me that my subconscious demon latched tightly onto this 5 and fended off all subconsciously challenging intuitions.

986.209 But what I had mistakenly assumed to be the third-power synergetics constant was in fact the ninth power of that constant, as will be seen in the following list of the synergetics constant raised to varying powers:

Table 986.209

Synergetics Power Constants
$S^1 = 1.019824451$
$S^2 = 1.040041912$
$S^3 = 1.060660172$
$S^4 = 1.081687178$
$S^5 = 1.103131033$
$S^6 = 1.125$
$S^9 = 1.193242693$
$S^{12} = 1.265625$

986.210 In our always-experimental-evidenced science of geometry we need only show ratio of proportion of parts, for parts of primitive polyhedra have no independent existence. Ergo, no experimental proof is required for $\sqrt[2]{}$ roots and $\sqrt{}$ roots. Though those numbers are irrational, their irrationality could not frustrate the falling apart of the polyhedral parts, because the parts are nonexistent except as parts of wholes, and exact proportionality is not required in the structuring.

986.211 Whatever the workings of my subconscious may have been, the facts remain that I had erroneously concluded that the 5 was the tetravolume of the sphere whose diameter was our unit vector whose value was 2. In due course I received a letter from a mathematician, Ramsey Campbell, whose conventional calculations seemed to show that I was wrong. But I was not convinced that his conventional results were not also erroneous, inasmuch as they had been "cubically" arrived at rather than tetrahedrally referenced.

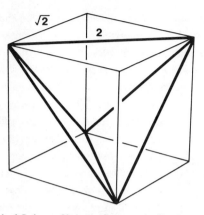

Fig. *986.210 Diagonal of Cube as Unity in Synergetic Geometry:* In synergetic geometry mensural unity commences with the tetra edge as prime vector. Unity is taken not from the cube edge but from the edge of one of the two tetra that structure it. (Compare Fig. 463.01.) Proportionality exactly known to us is not required in nature's structuring. Parts have no existence independent of the polyhedra they constitute.

986.212   At this point a young associate of mine, Robert Grip—who was convinced that I was misconvinced—and who knew that I would alter my position only as confronted by physically demonstrable evidence, made a gallon-sized, water-holding tetrahedron and a sphere whose diameter was identical with the prime vector length of the tetrahedron's edge. The water content—the volume—of the sphere was indeed 4.43 units—.57 less than 5.

986.213   The cubically-arrived-at spherical volume (A) of a sphere of diameter equal to the unit edge of the *XYZ* coordinate system's cube is 4.188. To convert that spherical volume value (A) to that of sphere (B) whose diameter is equal to the diagonal of the face of the *XYZ* system's cube, we multiply the volume of sphere (A) by the synergetics hierarchy's volumetric constant, which is obtained by taking synergetics' unit VE vector linear constant 1.0198 and raising it to its third-power—or volumetric—dimension, which is $1.0198 \times 1.0198 \times 1.0198$, which equals 1.0606. Multiplying the *XYZ* system's cube-edge-diametered (A) sphere's volume of 4.1888 by the synergetics' volumetric constant of 1.0606 gives us 4.4429, which is the sought-for volume of the sphere (B). I thanked Mr. Campbell and acknowledged my error.

986.214   I then said to my mathematical associates, Robert Grip and Chris Kitrick, that there is no single item that more effectively advances research than the unblocking of our thought processes—through experiential evidence—of a previously held erroneous assumption. Wherefore my intuition told me that my error may have been stubbornly clung to because there might be something very important to be discovered in this region of investigation. There is possibly some enlightening significance in the fact that I had intuitively applied (and again forsaking the first correction, had doubly reapplied) my third-power synergetics' conversion factor to an already-three-dimensional cubic-volume quantation, which on the occasion of these retreatments had erroneously seemed to me to be as yet three powers short of the minimum primitive realizable somethingness.

986.215   Why did I think as I did? Why was I puzzled? I was not confused about arithmetical operations per se. We conventionally arrive at the area of a square by multiplying the square's edge length by itself, and we arrive at the volume of a cube by multiplying its edge length times itself twice—that is, we identify the square's area by the second power of its edge length, and we identify a cube's volume by the third power of its edge length. All that seems simple and clear . . . until we discover that the cube does not exist and cannot exist until it has at least three other observable attributes: weight, duration, and temperature. Given the quantitative inputs for those coordinate factors, the cube as yet fails to "exist," because as calculated it is now "solid," and physics has discovered and proven that no such solid phenomenon exists; wherefore the cubical domain has to be substantively populated by atoms which have a variety of interspacing and interpositioning behavioral patterns.

986.216   Also, in order to exist the cube must have both tension and compression forces so arranged and quantated as to produce a self-stabilizing, independent behavior in the presence of the cosmic complex of coexisting force events. For it to exist there also must be introduced coordinate factors that account for the fact that this special case cube is keeping locatable company with the planet Earth with which it is traveling around the Sun at approximately 60,000 miles per hour.

986.217   As the Earth and the Sun whirl circumferentially in company with the other hundred billion stars of the galactic system, and as all the while the galactic system keeps company with all the now-known billion such galaxies whose uniformly angled retreat from one another at an astronomical speed altogether constitutes what is called the Expanding Universe . . . if we wrote out the formula for integrating all those quantities and for realistically diagramming its geometry and its dimensions, we would have to admit that the dimensions of the cube did not as yet produce existence. There would as yet be required the set of coordinate factors stating when and where the cube was born, how old it was at the moment of its dimensioning, and what its exact remaining longevity would be—and with all that, we have not disclosed its smell, its resonance factor, its electromagnetic-wave propagation length and frequencies. My quandary was one of adequately identifying and calculating the magnitude of relevant dimensions for the "considered set" (Section 509).

986.218   My quandary also included, "Which exactly are the attributes that are being disclosed by the successive powerings?" With all the foregoing considerations I resolved upon the following set as that which I would employ in publishing *Synergetics*.

986.219   Since our dimensional control is the prime vector, and since a vector's relative size represents mass times velocity, and since mass has a priori both volume and weight, it inherently introduces one more dimension to velocity's a priori two-dimensional product of time and distance. Ergo, vectors are in themselves primitive, pre-time-size, potentially energizable, three-dimensional phenomena. Any special case time-size phenomena must also be multiplied by frequency of subdivision of the primitive system taken volumetrically to the third power. We seem thus to have arrived at nine dimensions—i.e., ninth powering—and we have altogether identified geometrical realization as being at least nine-dimensional.

986.220   This is how I came to adopt my ninth-power factor for conversion from *XYZ* coordination to synergetics coordination. Employing the *XYZ*-coordinated volume of 4.188790205, I multiplied it by the appropriate factor (see table 986.209, where we find that $S^9 = 1.193242693$), which produced the inherently imperfect (only chord-describable rather than arc-describable) sphere of 4.998243305. This I knew was not a primitive three-dimensional or six-dimensional *volume*, and I assumed it to be the value of potential *energy* embraceable by a sphere of vector radius = 1. Ergo, both my conscious and subconscious searchings and accountings were operating faultlessly, but I was confusing the end product, identifying it as *volume* instead of as potential *energy*.

986.221   I was astonished by my error but deeply excited by the prospect of reviewing the exponentially powered values. Looking over the remaining valid trail blazings, I ruminated that the proximity to 5 that provoked the 4.998243305 figure might have other significance—for instance, as a real ninth-dimensional phenomenon. There was some question about that constant 1.193242693 being a sixth-dimension figure: $N^3 \cdot N^3 = N^6$, which operation I had—in my forgetfulness and carelessness—inadvertently performed. Or the figure I had arrived at could be taken as nine-dimensional if you assume primitive demonstrability of minimum something always to have a combined a priori volumetric-and-energetic existence value, which is indeed what synergetics vectorial structuring does recognize to be naturally and demonstrably true. (See Sec. 100.20.)

986.222   Synergetics demonstrates that the hierarchy of vectorially defined, primitive, triangularly self-stabilized, structural-system polyhedra is initially sixth-dimensional, being both a vectorially six-way coordinate system (mass × velocity) as well as being tetrahedrally—ergo, four-dimensionally-coordinate*—ergo, $N^6 \cdot N^4 = N^{10}$ somethings; and that they grow expansively in time-size—ergo, in volume at the rate of F^3—ergo, in time-size $D^{10} \cdot D^3 = D^{13}$, a 13-dimensional special-case-somethingness of reality.

986.223 We have learned in synergetics by physical experiment that in agglomerating unit-radius, closest-packed spheres around a nuclear sphere of the same unit radius, successively concentric symmetrical layers of the nuclear surroundment occur in a pattern in which the number of spheres in the outer shell is always the second power of the frequency of modular-system subdivision of the vector-defined edges of the system, and that when the primitive interhierarchy's relative volumetric values are multiplied by frequency to the third power—and an additional factor of six—it always gives the symmetrical system's total cumulative volume growth, not only of all its progressively concentric, closest-packed, unit-radius spheres' combined shells, but also including the volume of the unit-radius, closest-packed sphere shells' *interstitial spaces,* as altogether embraced by the exterior planes of the primitive polyhedra of reference. (See Sec. 971 and, in the drawings section, Fig. 970.20, "Dymax Nuclear Growth" (10 June 1948), and "Light Quanta Particle Growth" (7 May 1948); also drawings published in 1944 appearing as end papers to *Synergetics 2.*)

986.230 System Spinnability

986.231 Synergetics assumes an a priori to time-size, conceptually primitive, relative volumetric value of all the hierarchy of primitive polyhedra; and it also assumes that when we introduce frequency, we are also introducing *time* and *size* (see Secs. 782.50 and 1054.70), and we are therefore also introducing all the degrees of freedom inherent in time-size realizations of energetic-system behavior—as for instance the phenomenon of inherent *system spinnability*.

986.232 With the introduction of the phenomenon of system spinnability around any one or several or all of the hierarchy of concentric symmetric systems' seven axes of symmetry (Sec. 1040), we observe experientially that such inherent system spinnability produces a superficially spherical appearance, whose time-size realizations might be thought of as being only the dynamic development in time-size aspects of the primitive static polyhedral

---

*It was a mathematical requirement of *XYZ* rectilinear coordination that in order to demonstrate four-dimensionality, a fourth perpendicular to a fourth planar facet of the symmetric system must be found—which fourth symmetrical plane of the system is not parallel to one of the already-established three planes of symmetry of the system. The tetrahedron, as synergetics' minimum structural system, has four symmetrically interarrayed planes of symmetry—ergo, has four unique perpendiculars—ergo, has four dimensions.

states. We recall the scientific nondemonstrability of the Greek sphere as defined by them (Secs. 981.19 and 1022.11). We also recall having discovered that the higher the frequency of the unit-radius-vertexed, symmetrical polyhedra of our primitive cosmic hierarchy, the more spherical do such geodesic-structured polyhedra appear (compare Sec. *986.064*). I realized that under these recalled circumstances it could be safely assumed that *a sphere does not exist in the primitive hierarchy of pre-time-size polyhedral conceptioning,* whose timeless-sizeless—ergo, eternal—perfection alone permitted consideration of the vector equilibrium's isotropic vector matrix as the four-dimensional frame of reference of any time-size intertransforming aberrations of realizable physical experience. Such perfection can be only eternal and timeless.

986.233   Timeless but conceptually primitive polyhedra of differently-lengthed-and-radiused external vertexes can be dynamically spinnable only in time, thereby to produce circular profiles some of whose longer radii dominantly describe the superficial, illusory continuity whose spherical appearance seems to be radially greater than half the length of the prime vector. (See Fig. *986.314.*)

986.234   Thus the only-superficially-defined spherical appearance is either the consequence of the multiplicity of revolving vertexes of the polyhedron occurring at a distance outwardly of the unit vector radius of the prime polyhedral hierarchy, or it could be inherent in the centrifugal deformation of the polyhedral structure. Wherefore I realized that my having unwittingly and redundantly applied the synergetics constant of the sixth power—rather than only of the third power—and my having applied that sixth-power factor to the theretofore nonexistent static sphere of the Greeks' energy-and-time deprived three-dimensionality, was instinctively sound. Thus the erroneous result I had obtained must not discourage my intuitive urge to pursue the question further. I had inadvertently produced the slightly-greater-than-vector-radiused, high-frequency "spheric" polyhedron.

986.235   It seemed ever more evident that it could be that *there is no true sphere in Universe.* This seemed to be confirmed by the discovery that the sum of the angles around all the vertexes of any system will always be 720 degrees—one tetra—less than the number of the system's external vertexes times 360 degrees (Sec. 224). It could be that the concept conjured up by the mouthed-word *sphere* itself is scientifically invalid; ergo, it could be that the word *sphere* is not only obsolete but to be shunned because it is meaningless and possibly disastrously misleading to human thought.

986.240 The Sphere Experimentally Defined

986.241   The best physically demonstrable definition of the ''spheric'' experience is: an aggregate of energy events approximately equidistant, multidirectionally outwardly from approximately the same central event of an only approximately simultaneous set of external events—the more the quantity of external points measuringly identified and the more nearly simultaneous the radius-measuring events, the more satisfactorily ''spherical.'' With each of all the outward unit-radius events most economically and most fully triangularly interchorded with their most immediate neighbors—chords being shorter than their corresponding arcs—we find that the ''spheric'' experience inherently describes only high-frequency, omnitriangularly faceted polyhedra. By geometrical definition these are geodesic structures whose volumes will always be something less than a theoretically perfect omni-arc-embraced sphere of the same radius as an omni-chord-embraced geodesic sphere's uniformly radiused outer vertexes.

986.242   As is demonstrated in Sec. 224, the sum of the angles around all the vertexes of any system will always be 720 degrees less than the number of vertexes multiplied by 360 degrees. By the mathematicians' definition a perfect arc-embraced sphere would have to have 360 degrees around every point on its surface, for the mathematicians assume that for an infinitesimal moment a sphere's surface is congruent with the tangent plane. Trigonometry errs in that it assumes 360 degrees around every spherical surface point.

986.300 Minimum-Maximum System Limits

986.301 Consideration 11: Maximum-limit Case

986.302   The explorer gains assurance by discovering the relevant minimum-maximum limit cases—the min-max limits of the variables—of the system under consideration.

986.303   For instance, we have learned through experimental evidence, the cosmic hierarchy of primitive polyhedra has a limit set of seven axes of great-circle symmetries and spinnabilities. They are the 3, 4, 6 (VE), 12, 10, 15, 6 (icosa) great-circle-spinnable systems. (See Table 986.304 and Sec. 1040.) Within that inherently limited hierarchy of seven symmetries, the triacontahedron, with its 15 different great circles' self-hemispherings and 120 triangular interconfigurings, produces the maximum-limit number of identical polyhedral surface self-facetings of all great-circle systems in Universe (Sec. 400).

Table 986.304:   Limit Set of Seven Axes of Spinnability

Generalized Set of All Symmetrical Systems:	Spinnable System Great Circles:
#1	3
#2	4
#3	6 (VE)
#4	12
#5	10
#6	15
#7	6 (icosa)

(Compare Secs. 1041.01 and 1042.05.)

986.310   Strategic Use of Min-max Cosmic System Limits

986.311   The maximum limit set of identical facets into which any system can be divided consists of 120 similar spherical right triangles *ACB* whose three corners are 60 degrees at *A,* 90 degrees at *C,* and 36 degrees at *B.* Sixty of these right spherical triangles are positive (active), and 60 are negative (passive). (See Sec. 901.)

986.312   These 120 right spherical surface triangles are described by three different central angles of 37.37736814 degrees for arc *AB,* 31.71747441 degrees for arc *BC,* and 20.90515745 degrees for arc *AC*—which three central-angle arcs total exactly 90 degrees. These 120 spherical right triangles are self-patterned into producing 30 identical spherical diamond groups bounded by the same central angles and having corresponding flat-faceted diamond groups consisting of four of the 120 angularly identical (60 positive, 60 negative) triangles. Their three surface corners are 90 degrees at *C,* 31.71747441 degrees at *B,* and 58.2825256 degrees at *A.* (See Fig. *986.502.*)

986.313   These diamonds, like all diamonds, are rhombic forms. The 30-symmetrical-diamond system is called the rhombic triacontahedron: its 30 mid-diamond faces (right-angle cross points) are approximately tangent to the unit-vector-radius sphere when the volume of the rhombic triacontahedron is exactly tetravolume-5. (See Fig. *986.314.*)

986.314   I therefore asked Robert Grip and Chris Kitrick to prepare a graphic comparison of the various radii and their respective polyhedral profiles of all the symmetric polyhedra of tetravolume 5 (or close to 5) existing

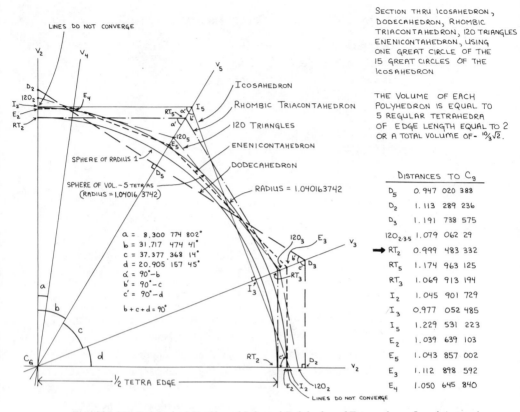

SECTION THRU ICOSAHEDRON, DODECAHEDRON, RHOMBIC TRIACONTAHEDRON, 120 TRIANGLES ENENICONTAHEDRON, USING ONE GREAT CIRCLE OF THE 15 GREAT CIRCLES OF THE ICOSAHEDRON

THE VOLUME OF EACH POLYHEDRON IS EQUAL TO 5 REGULAR TETRAHEDRA OF EDGE LENGTH EQUAL TO 2 OR A TOTAL VOLUME OF- $^{10}/_3\sqrt{2}$.

DISTANCES TO C_9	
D_5	0.947 020 388
D_2	1.113 289 236
D_3	1.191 738 575
$120_{2\cdot3\cdot5}$	1.079 062 29
➡ RT_2	0.999 483 332
RT_5	1.174 963 125
RT_3	1.069 913 194
I_2	1.045 901 729
I_3	0.977 052 485
I_5	1.229 531 223
E_2	1.039 639 103
E_5	1.043 857 002
E_3	1.112 898 592
E_4	1.050 645 840

Fig. *986.314 Polyhedral Profiles of Selected Polyhedra of Tetravolume-5 and Approximately Tetravolume-5:* A graphic display of the radial proximity to one another of exact and neighboring tetravolume-5 polyhedra, showing central angles and ratios to prime vector.

within the primitive cosmic hierarchy (Sec. 982.62)—i.e. other than those of tetravolumes 1, 2, 3, 4, and 6—which carefully drafted drawing of the tetravolume-5 polyhedra (and those polyhedra "approximately" tetravolume 5) my colleagues did prepare (see Fig. *986.314*). These exactly tetravolume-5 polyhedra are, for example—

    (a) the icosahedron with outer edges of unit vector length;
    (b) the icosahedron of outer vertex radius of unit vector length;
    (c) the regular dodecahedron of unit vector edge; and
    (d) the regular dodecahedron of unit vector radius

—all of which show that they have only a slightly greater radius length than that of the prime vector.

    986.315 The chart of the polyhedral profiles (Fig. *986.314*) shows the triacontahedron of tetravolume 5 having its mid-diamond-face point C at a distance outward radially from the volumetric center that approximately equals the relative length of the prime vector. I say "approximately" because the trigonometrically calculated value is .999483332 instead of 1, a 0.0005166676 radial difference, which—though possibly caused in some very meager degree by the lack of absolute resolvability of trigonometric calculations themselves—is on careful mathematical review so close to correct as to be unalterable by any known conventional trigonometric error allowance. It is also so correct as to hold historical significance, as we shall soon discover. Such a discrepancy is so meager in relation, for instance, to planet Earth's spheric diameter of approximately 8,000 miles that the spherical surface aberration would be approximately the same as that existing between sea level and the height of Mount Fuji, which is only half the altitude of Mount Everest. And even Mount Everest is invisible on the Earth's profile when the Earth is photographed from outer space. The mathematical detection of such meager relative proportioning differences has time and again proven to be of inestimable value to science in first detecting and then discovering cosmically profound phenomena. In such a context my "spherical energy content" of 4.99, instead of exactly 5, became a thought-provoking difference to be importantly remembered.

986.316   By careful study of the Grip-Kitrick drawings of tetravolume-5 polyhedra it is discovered that the graphically displayed zones of radial proximity to one another of all the tetravolume-5 symmetric polyhedra (Fig. *986.314*) describe such meager radial differences at their respective systems' outermost points as to suggest that their circumferential zone enclosed between the most extremely varied and the most inwardly radiused of all their axially spun vertexes of the exact tetravolume-5 polyhedra may altogether be assumed to constitute the zone of limit cases of radiantly swept-out and pulsating tetravolume-5 kinetic systems.

986.317   Recognizing that polyhedra are closed systems and that there are only seven cases of symmetrical subdivisioning of systems by the most economical great-circle spinnings (and most economically by the chords of the great-circle arcs), we discover and prove structurally that the maximum-limit abundance of a unit-symmetrical-polyhedral-system's identical facetings is the rhombic triacontahedron, each of whose 30 symmetrical diamond planar faces may be symmetrically subdivided into four identical right triangles $(30 \times 4 = 120)$, and we find that the triacontahedron's 120-spherical-right-triangled frame of system reference is the maximum-limit case of identical faceting of any and all symmetrical polyhedral systems in Universe. This maximum-limit-system structuring proof is accomplished by the physically permitted, great-circle-spun, hemispherical self-halvings, as permitted by any

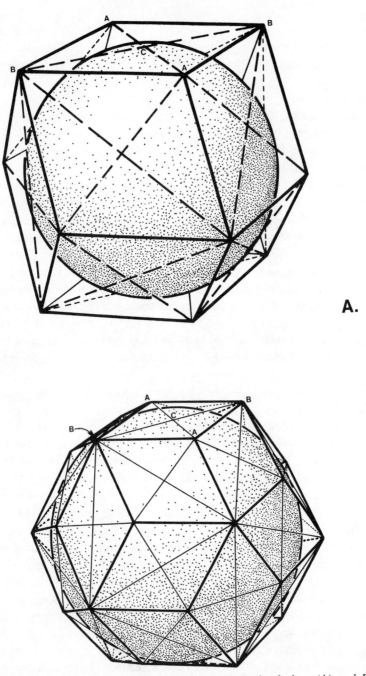

A.

B.

Fig. 986.405 *Respective Subdivision of Rhombic Dodecahedron* (A) *and Rhombic Triacontahedron* (B) *into Diamond-faced Pentahedra: O* is at the respective volumetric centers of the two polyhedra, with the short axes *A-A* and the long axes *B-B* (diagrams on the right). The central and surface angles of the two pentahedra differ as shown.

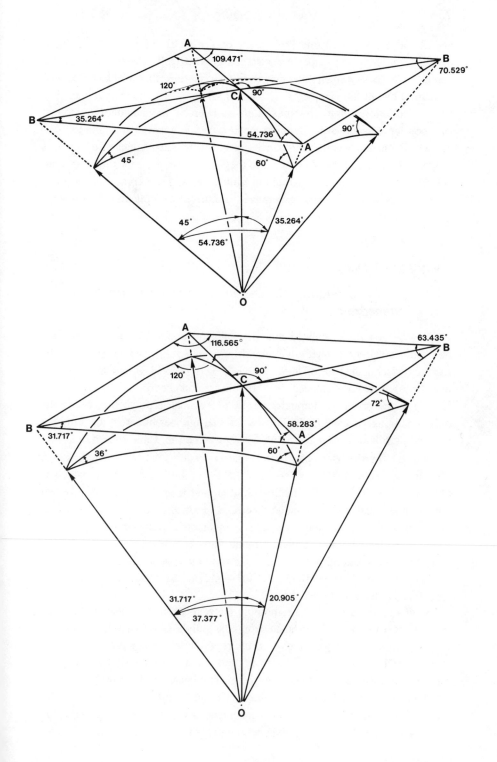

and all of the seven cosmic limit cases of symmetric systems' being spun-defined around all the respective system's geometrically definitive (ergo, inherent) axes of symmetrical spinnability. It is thus that we learn experimentally how all the symmetric systems of Universe self-fractionate their initial system unities into the maximum number of omniangularly identical surface triangles outwardly defining their respective internal-structure tetrahedra whose angles—central or surface—are always independent of a system's time-size considerations. And because they are independent of time-size considerations, such minimum-maximum limit-case ranges embrace all the symmetrical polyhedral systems' generalized-primitive-conceptuality phenomena.

986.400   T Quanta Module

986.401   Consideration 12: Dynamic Spinning of Rhombic Triacontahedron

986.402   I then speculated that the only-by-spinning-produced, only superficially apparent "sphericity" could be *roundly* aspected by spinning the rhombic triacontahedron of tetravolume 5. This rational volumetric value of exactly 5 tetravolumes placed the rhombic triacontahedron neatly into membership in the primitive hierarchy family of symmetric polyhedra, filling the only remaining vacancy in the holistic rational-number hierarchy of primitive polyhedral volumes from 1 through 6, as presented in Table *1053.51A*.

986.403   In the isotropic vector matrix system, where R = radius and PV = prime vector, $PV = 1 = R$—ergo, PVR = prime vector radius, which is always the unity of VE. In the 30-diamond-faceted triacontahedron of tetravolume 5 and the 12-diamond-faceted dodecahedron of tetravolume 6, the radius distances from their respective symmetric polyhedra's volumetric centers 0 to their respective mid-diamond faces C (i.e., their short-and-long-diamond-axes' crossing points) are in the rhombic triacontahedral case almost exactly PVR—i.e., 0.9994833324 PVR—and in the rhombic dodecahedral case exactly PVR, 1.0000 αPVR.

986.404   In the case of the rhombic dodecahedron the mid-diamond-face point C is exactly PVR distance from the polyhedral system's volumetric (nucleic) center, while in the case of the rhombic triacontahedron the point C is at approximately PVR distance from the system's volumetric (nucleic) center. The distance outward to C from the nucleic center of the rhombic dodecahedron is that same PVR length as the prime unit vector of the isotropic vector matrix. This aspect of the rhombic triacontahedron is shown at Fig. *986.314*.

986.405   The symmetric polyhedral centers of both the rhombic dodecahedron and the rhombic triacontahedron may be identified as 0, and both of their respective external diamond faces' short axes may be identified as *A–A* and their respective long axes as *B–B*. Both the rhombic dodecahedron's and the triacontahedron's external diamond faces *ABAB* and their respective volumetric centers 0 describe semiasymmetric pentahedra conventionally labeled as *OABAB*. The diamond surface faces *ABA* of both *OABAB* pentahedra are external to their respective rhombic-hedra symmetrical systems, while their triangular sides *OAB* (four each) are internal to their respective rhombic-hedra systems. The angles describing the short *A–A* axis and the long *B–B* axis, as well as the surface and central angles of the rhombic dodecahedron's *OABAB* pentahedron, all differ from those of the triacontahedron's *OABAB* pentahedron.

986.410   T Quanta Module

986.411   The respective 12 and 30 pentahedra *OABAB* of the rhombic dodecahedron and the triacontahedron may be symmetrically subdivided into four right-angled tetrahedra *ABCO,* the point *C* being surrounded by three right angles *ABC, BCO,* and *ACO.* Right-angle *ACB* is on the surface of the rhombic-hedra system and forms the face of the tetrahedron *ABCO,* while right angles *BCO* and *ACO* are internal to the rhombic-hedra system and from two of the three internal sides of the tetrahedron *ABCO.* The rhombic dodecahe-

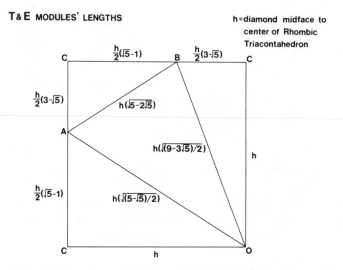

· Fig. *986.411A   T and E Quanta Modules: Edge Lengths:* This plane net for the T Quanta Module and the E Quanta Module shows their edge lengths as ratioed to the octa edge. Octa edge = tetra edge = unity. ·

T & E MODULES' ANGLES

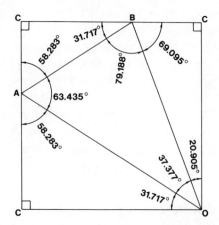

Fig. *986.411B T and E Quanta Module Angles:* This plane net shows the angles and the foldability of the T Quanta Module and the E Quanta Module.

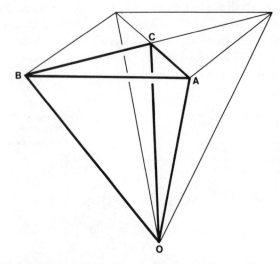

Fig. *986.411C T and E Quanta Modules in Context of Rhombic Triacontahedron*

dron consists of 48 identical tetrahedral modules designated $ABCO^d$. The triacontahedron consists of 120 (60 positive and 60 negative) identical tetrahedral modules designated $ABCO^t$, for which tetrahedron $ABCO^t$ we also introduce the name *T Quanta Module*.

986.412   The primitive tetrahedron of volume 1 is subdivisible into 24 A Quanta Modules. The triacontahedron of exactly tetravolume 5, has the maximum-limit case of identical tetrahedral subdivisibility—i.e., 120 subtetra.

Thus we may divide the 120 subtetra population of the symmetric triacontahedron by the number 24, which is the identical subtetra population of the primitive omnisymmetrical tetrahedron: $120/24 = 5$. Ergo, volume of the A Quanta Module = volume of the T Quanta Module.

986.413   The rhombic dodecahedron has a tetravolume of 6, wherefore each of its 48 identical, internal, asymmetric, component tetrahedra $ABCO^d$ has a regular tetravolume of $6/48 = 1/8$. The regular tetrahedron consists of 24 quanta modules (be they A, B, C, D,* or T Quanta Modules; therefore $ABCO^d$, having $1/8$-tetravolume, also equals three quanta modules. (See Fig. 986.413.)

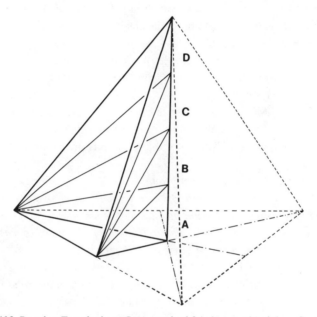

Fig. 986.413 *Regular Tetrahedron Composed of 24 Quanta Modules:* Compare Fig. 923.10B.

986.414   The vertical central-altitude line of the regular, primitive, symmetrical tetrahedron may be uniformly subdivided into four vertical sections, each of which we may speak of as quarter-prime-tetra altitude units—each of which altitude division points represent the convergence of the upper apexes of the A, B, C, D, A', B', C', D', A", B", C", D" . . . equivolume modules (as illustrated in Fig. 923.10B where—prior to the discovery of the E "Einstein" Module—additional modules were designated E through H, and will henceforth be designated as successive $ABCD$, $A'B'C'D'$, $A"B"C"D"$ . . . groups).

* C Quanta Modules and D Quanta Modules are added to the A and B Quanta Modules to compose the regular tetrahedron as shown in drawing B of Fig. 923.10.

The vertical continuance of these unit-altitude differentials produces an infinite series of equivolume modules, which we identify in vertical series continuance by groups of four repetitive *ABCD* groups, as noted parenthetically above. Their combined group-of-four, externally protracted, altitude increase is always equal to the total internal altitude of the prime tetrahedron.

986.415   The rhombic triacontahedron has a tetravolume of 5, wherefore each of its 120 identical, internal, asymmetric, component tetrahedra $ABCO^t$, the T Quanta Module, has a tetravolume of $^5/_{120} = ^1/_{24}$ tetravolume—ergo, the volume of the T Quanta Module is identical to that of the A and B Quanta Modules. The rhombic dodecahedron's 48 $ABCO^d$ asymmetric tetrahedra equal three of the rhombic triacontahedron's 120 $ABCO^t$ T Quanta Module asymmetric tetrahedra. The rhombic triacontahedron's $ABCO^t$ T Quanta Module tetrahedra are each $^1/_{24}$ of the volume of the primitive "regular" tetrahedron—ergo, of identical volume to the A Quanta Module. The A Mod, like the T Mod, is structurally modeled with one of its four corners omnisurrounded by three right angles.

986.416   1 A Module = 1 B Module = 1 C Module = 1 D Module = 1 T Module = any one of the unit quanta modules of which all the hierarchy of concentric, symmetrical polyhedra of the VE family are rationally comprised. (See Sec. 910).

986.417   *I find that it is important in exploratory effectiveness to remember—as we find an increasingly larger family of equivolume but angularly differently conformed quanta modules—that our initial exploration strategy was predicated upon our generalization of Avogadro's special-case (gaseous) discovery of identical numbers of molecules per unit volume for all the different chemical-element gases when individually considered or physically isolated, but only under identical conditions of pressure and heat. The fact that we have found a set of unit-volume, all-tetrahedral modules—the minimum-limit structural systems—from which may be aggregated the whole hierarchy of omnisymmetric, primitive, concentric polyhedra totally occupying the spherically spun and interspheric accommodation limits of closest-packable nuclear domains, means that we have not only incorporated all the min-max limit-case conditions, but we have found within them one unique volumetric unit common to all their primitive conformational uniqueness, and that the volumetric module was developed by vectorial—i.e., energetic—polyhedral-system definitions.*

986.418   None of the tetrahedral quanta modules are by themselves all-space-filling, but they are all groupable in units of three (two A's and one B—which is called the Mite) to fill allspace progressively and to combine these units of three in *nine* different ways—all of which account for the structurings of all but one of the hierarchy of primitive, omniconcentric, omnisymmetrical

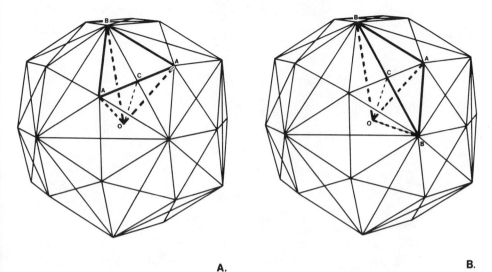

A.   **B.**

Fig. *986.419 T Quanta Modules within Rhombic Triacontahedron:* The 120 T Quanta Modules can be grouped two different ways within the rhombic triacontahedron to produce two different sets of 60 tetrahedra each: 60 *BAAO* and 60 *BBAO*.

polyhedra. There is one exception, the rhombic triacontahedron of tetravolume 5—i.e., of 120 quanta modules of the T class, which T Quanta Modules as we have learned are of equivolume to the A and B Modules.

986.419   The 120 T Quanta Modules of the rhombic triacontahedron can be grouped in two different ways to produce two different sets of 60 tetrahedra each: the 60 *BAAO* tetrahedra and the 60 *BBAO* tetrahedra. But rhombic triacontahedra are not allspace-filling polyhedra. (See Fig. *986.419.*)

986.420   Min-max Limit Hierarchy of Pre-time-size Allspace-fillers

986.421   Of all the allspace-filling module components, the simplest are the three-quanta-module Mites, consisting of two A Quanta Modules (one A positive and one A negative) and of one B Quanta Module (which may be either positive or negative). Thus a Mite can be positive or negative, depending on the sign of its B Quanta Module. The Mites are not only themselves tetrahedra (the minimum-sided polyhedra), but they are also the simplest minimum-limit case of allspace-filling polyhedra of Universe, since they consist of two energy-conserving A Quanta Modules and one equivolume energy-dispersing B Quanta Module. The energy conservation of the A Quanta Module is provided geometrically by its tetrahedral form: four different right-triangled facets being all foldable from one unique flat-out whole triangle

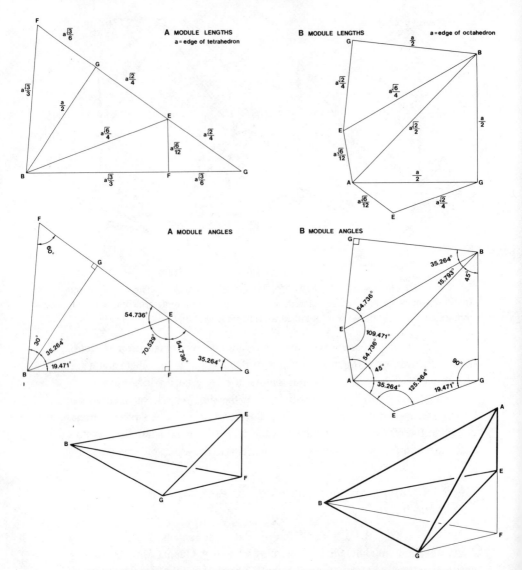

Fig. *986.421 A and B Quanta Modules:* The top drawings present plane nets for the modules with edge lengths of the A Modules ratioed to the tetra edge and edge lengths of the B Modules ratioed to the octa edge. The middle drawings illustrate the angles and foldability. The bottom drawings show the folded assembly and their relation to each other. Tetra edge = octa edge. (Compare Figs. 913.01 and 916.01.)

(Fig. 913.01), which triangle's boundary edges have reflective properties that bounce around internally to those triangles to produce similar smaller triangles: Ergo, the A Quanta Module acts as a local energy holder. The B Quanta

Module is not foldable out of one whole triangle, and energies bouncing around within it tend to escape. The B Quanta Module acts as a local energy dispenser. (See Fig. *986.421.*)

986.422   **Mite:** The simplest allspace-filler is the Mite (see Secs. 953 and *986.418*). The positive Mite consists of 1 *A* + mod, 1 *A* − mod, and 1 *B* + mod; the negative Mite consists of 1 *A* + mod, 1 *A* − mod, and 1 *B* − mod. Sum-total number of modules . . . . 3. MITE((See color plate 17.)

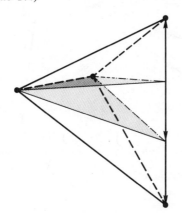

986.423   Around the four corners of the tetrahedral Mites are three right triangles. Two of them are similar right triangles with differently angled acute corners, and the third right triangle around that omni-right-angled corner is an isosceles.

986.424   The tetrahedral Mites may be inter-edge-bonded to fill allspace, but only because the spaces between them are inadvertent capturings of Mite-shaped vacancies. Positive Mite inter-edge assemblies produce negative Mite vacancies, and vice versa. The minimum-limit case always provides inadvertent entry into the Negative Universe. Sum-total number of modules is . . . . $1\frac{1}{2}$

986.425   Mites can also fill allspace by inter-face-bonding one positive and one negative Mite to produce the Syte. This trivalent inter-face-bonding requires twice as many Mites as are needed for bivalent inter-edge-bonding. Total number of modules is 3

986.426   **Syte:** The next simplest allspace-filler is the Syte. (See Sec. 953.40.) Each Syte consists of one of only three alternate ways of face-bonding two Mites to form an allspace-filling polyhedron, consisting of 2 *A* + mods, 2 *A* − mods, 1 *B* + mod, and 1 *B* − mod. Sum-total number of modules 6

986.427   Two of the three alternate ways of combining two Mites produce tetrahedral Sytes of one kind:

BITE (See color plate 17)   RITE (See color plate 19)

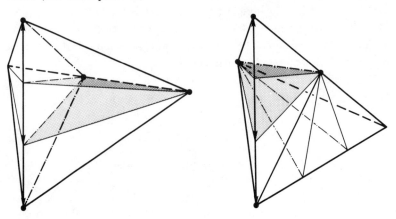

while the third alternate method of combining will produce a hexahedral Syte.

LITE (See color plate 18)

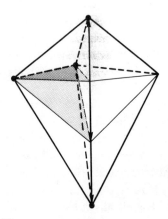

Fig. *986.427 Bite, Rite, Lite:*

986.428   **Kite:** The next simplest allspace-filler is the Kite. Kites are pentahedra or half-octahedra or half-Couplers, each consisting of one of the only two alternate ways of combining two Sytes to produce two differently shaped pentahedra, the Kate and the Kat, each of 4 *A* + mods, 4 *A* − mods, 2 *B* + mods, and 2 *B* − mods. Sum-total number of modules   12

986.429   Two Sytes combine to produce two Kites as

KATE (See color plate 20)   KAT (See color plate 21)

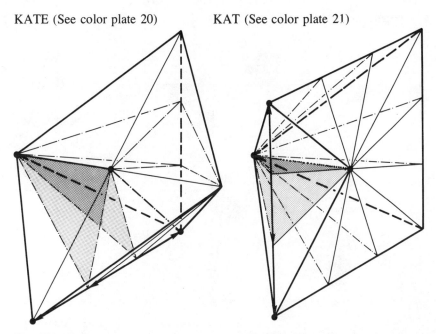

Fig. 986.429 *Kate, Kat.*

986.430   **Octet:** The next simplest allspace-filler is the Octet, a hexahedron consisting of three Sytes—ergo, 6 A + mods, 6 A − mods, 3 B + mods,
and 3 B − mods. Sum-total number of modules 18

OCTET (See color plate 22)

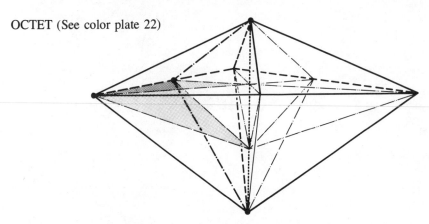

986.431   **Coupler:** The next simplest allspace-filler is the Coupler, the
asymmetric octahedron. (See Secs. 954.20–.70.) The Coupler consists of two
Kites—ergo, 8 A + mods, 8 A − mods, 4 B + mods, and 4 B − mods. Sum-total number of modules 24

COUPLER (See color plate 23)

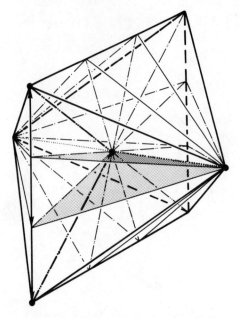

986.432 Cube: The next simplest allspace-filler is the Cube, consisting of four Octets—ergo, 24 A + mods, 24 A − mods, 12 B + mods, and 12 B − mods. Sum-total number of modules 72

CUBE (See color plate 24)

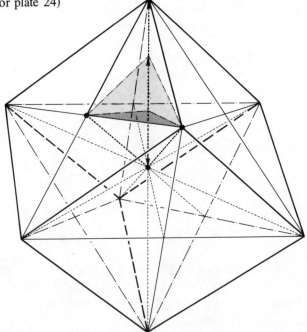

986.433 **Rhombic Dodecahedron:** The next and last of the hierarchy of primitive allspace-fillers is the rhombic dodecahedron. The rhombic dodecahedron is the domain of a sphere (see Sec. 981.13). The rhombic dodecahedron consists of 12 Kites—ergo, 48 A + mods, 48 A − mods, 24 B + mods, and 24 B − mods. Sum-total number of modules 144

RHOMBIC DODECAHEDRON (See color plate 25)

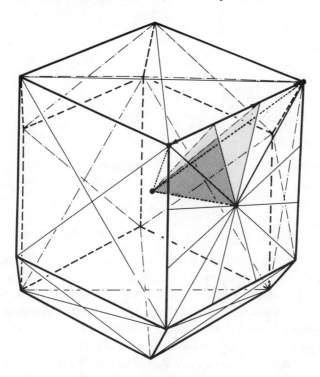

986.434 · This is the limit set of simplest allspace-fillers associable within one nuclear domain of closest-packed spheres and their respective interstitial spaces. There are other allspace-fillers that occur in time-size multiplications of nuclear domains, as for instance the tetrakaidecahedron. (Compare Sec. 950.12.)

986.440 *Table: Set of Simple Allspace-fillers*

This completes one spheric *domain* (i.e., sphere plus interstitial space) of one unit-radius sphere in closest packing, each sphere being centered at every other vertex of the isotropic vector matrix.

Name:	Face Triangles	Type Hedra	A Quanta Modules	B Quanta Modules	Sum-Total Modules
MITE	4	tetrahedron	2	1	3
SYTE					
BITE⎤	4	tetrahedron	4	2	6
RITE⎦	4	tetrahedron	4	2	6
LITE	6	hexahedron	4	2	6
KITE					
KATE	5	pentahedron	8	4	12
KAT	5	pentahedron	8	4	12
OCTET	6	hexahedron	12	6	18
COUPLER	8	octahedron	16	18	24
CUBE	6	hexahedron	48	24	72
RHOMBIC DODECAHEDRON	12	dodecahedron	96	48	144

(For the minimum time-size special case realizations of the two-frequency systems, multiply each of the above *Quanta Module* numbers by eight.)

986.450   Energy Aspects of Spherical Modular Arrays

986.451   The rhombic dodecahedron has an allspace-filling function as the domain of any one sphere in an aggregate of unit-radius, closest-packed spheres; its 12 mid-diamond-face points C are the points of intertangency of all unit-radius, closest-packed sphere aggregates; wherefore that point C is the midpoint of every vector of the isotropic vector matrix, whose every vertex is the center of one of the unit-radius, closest-packed spheres.

986.452   These 12 inter-closest-packed-sphere-tangency points—the C points—are the 12 exclusive contacts of the "Grand Central Station" through which must pass all the great-circle railway tracks of most economically inter-distanced travel of energy around any one nuclear center, and there-from—through the C points—to other spheres in Universe. These C points of the rhombic dodecahedron's mid-diamond faces are also the energetic centers-of-volume of the Couplers, within which there are 56 possible unique in-terarrangements of the A and B Quanta Modules.

986.453   We next discover that two *ABABO* pentahedra of any two tangentially adjacent, closest-packed rhombic dodecahedra will produce an asymmetric octahedron *OABABO'* with O and O' being the volumetric centers (nuclear centers) of any two tangentially adjacent, closest-packed, unit-radius spheres. We call this nucleus-to-nucleus, asymmetric octahedron the Coupler, and we found that the volume of the Coupler is exactly equal to the volume of one regular tetrahedron—i.e., 24 A Quanta Modules. We also note that the Coupler always consists of eight asymmetric and identical tetrahedral Mites, the minimum simplex allspace-filling of Universe, which Mites are also identifiable with the quarks (Sec. *1052.360*).

986.454   We then discover that the Mite, with its two energy-conserving A Quanta Modules and its one energy-dispersing B Quanta Module (for a total combined volume of three quanta modules), serves as the cosmic minimum allspace-filler, corresponding elegantly (in all ways) with the minimum-limit case behaviors of the nuclear physics' quarks. The quarks are the smallest discovered "particles"; they always occur in groups of three, two of which hold their energy and one of which disperses energy. This quite clearly identifies the quarks with the quanta module of which all the synergetics hierarchy of nuclear concentric symmetric polyhedra are co-occurrent.

986.455   In both the rhombic triacontahedron of tetravolume 5 and the rhombic dodecahedron of tetravolume 6 the distance from system center *O* at *AO* is always greater than *CO,* and *BO* is always greater than *AO.*

986.456   With this information we could reasonably hypothesize that the triacontahedron of tetravolume 5 is that static polyhedral progenitor of the only-dynamically-realizable sphere of tetravolume 5, the radius of which (see Fig. *986.314*) is only .04 of unity greater in length than is the prime vector radius *OC,* which governs the dimensioning of the triacontahedron's 30 midface cases of 12 right-angled corner junctions around mid-diamond-vertex *C,* which provides the 12 right angles around *C*—the four right-angled corners of the T Quanta Module's *ABC* faces of their 120 radially arrayed tetrahedra, each of which T Quanta Module has a volume identical to that of the A and B Quanta Modules.

986.457   We also note that the radius *OC* is the same unitary prime vector with which the isotropic vector matrix is constructed, and it is also the VE unit-vector-radius distance outwardly from *O,* which *O* is always the common system center of all the members of the entire cosmic hierarchy of omniconcentric, symmetric, primitive polyhedra. In the case of the rhombic triacontahedron the 20 *OA* lines' distances outwardly from *O* are greater than *OC,* and the 12 *OB* lines' distances are even greater in length outwardly from *O* than *OA.* Wherefore I realized that, when dynamically spun, the great-circle chord lines *AB* and *CB* are centrifugally transformed into arcs and thus sprung apart at *B,* which is the outermost vertex—ergo, most swiftly and forcefully outwardly impelled. This centrifugal spinning introduces the spherical excess of 6 degrees at the spherical system vertex *B.* (See Fig. *986.405.*) Such yielding increases the spheric appearance of the spun triacontahedron, as seen in contradistinction to the diamond-faceted, static, planar-bound, polyhedral state aspect.

986.458   The corners of the spherical triacontahedron's 120 spherical arc-cornered triangles are 36 degrees, 60 degrees and 90 degrees, having been sprung apart from their planar-phase, chorded corners of 31.71747441 degrees, 58.28252559 degrees, and 90 degrees, respectively. Both the triacontahedron's chorded and arced triangles are in notable proximity to the well-known 30-, 60-, and 90-degree-cornered draftsman's flat, planar triangle. I realized that it could be that the three sets of three differently-distanced-outwardly vertexes might average their outward-distance appearances at a radius of only four percent greater distance from *O*—thus producing a moving-picture-illusioned "dynamic" sphere of tetravolume 5, having very mildly greater radius than its static, timeless, equilibrious, rhombic triacontahedron state of tetravolume 5 with unit-vector-radius integrity terminaled at vertex *C*.

986.459   In the case of the spherical triacontahedron the total spherical excess of exactly 6 degrees, which is one-sixtieth of unity $= 360$ degrees, is all lodged in one corner. In the planar case 1.71747441 degrees have been added to 30 degrees at corner *B* and subtracted from 60 degrees at corner *A*. In both the spherical and planar triangles—as well as in the draftsman's triangle—the 90-degree corners remain unchanged.

986.460   The 120 T Quanta Modules radiantly arrayed around the center of volume of the rhombic triacontahedron manifest the most spherical appearance of all the hierarchy of symmetric polyhedra as defined by any one of the seven axially rotated, great circle system polyhedra of the seven primitive types of great-circle symmetries.

986.461   What is the significance of the spherical excess of exactly 6 degrees? In the transformation from the spherical rhombic triacontahedron to the planar triacontahedron each of the 120 triangles releases 6 degrees. $6 \times 120 = 720$. 720 degrees $=$ the sum of the structural angles of one tetrahedron $= 1$ quantum of energy. The difference between a high-frequency polyhedron and its spherical counterpart is always 720 degrees, which is one unit of quantum—ergo, it is evidenced that spinning a polyhedron into its spherical state captures one quantum of energy—and releases it when subsiding into its pre-time-size primitive polyhedral state.

986.470   Geodesic Modular Subdivisioning

986.471   A series of considerations leads to the definition of the most spherical-appearing limit of triangular subdivisioning:

   (1) recalling that the experimentally demonstrable "most spherically-appearing" structure is always in primitive reality a polyhedron;

   (2) recalling that the higher the modular frequency of a system the more

spheric it appears, though it is always polyhedral and approaching
not a "true sphere" limit but an unlimited multiplication of its polyhedral facetings;

(3) recalling that the 120 outer surface triangles of the icosahedron's 15
great circles constitute the cosmic maximum limit of system-surface
omni-triangular-self-subdivisioning into centrally collected tetrahedron components; and

(4) recalling that the icosahedron's 10- and 6-great-circle equators of
spin further subdivide the 15 great circles' outer 120 *LCD* triangles
into four different right triangles, *ADC, CDE, CFE,* and *EFB* (see
Fig. 901.03),

then it becomes evident that the icosahedron's three sets of symmetrical great-
circle spinnabilities—i.e., $6 + 10 + 15$ (which totals 31 great circle self-halvings)—generate a total of 242 unit-radius, external vertexes, 480 external triangles, and 720 internal triangles (which may be considered as two congruent
internal triangles, each being one of the internal triangular faces of the 480
tetrahedra whose 480 external triangular faces are showing—in which case
there are 1440 internal triangles). The 480 tetrahedra consist of 120 *OCAD*,
120 *OCDE*, 120 *OCEF*, and 120 *OFEB* tetrahedra. (See Fig. *986.471*.) The
480 internal face-congruent tetrahedra therefore constitute the "most spheric-
appearing" of all the hemispheric equators' self-spun, surface-subdividing entirely into triangles of all the great circles of all the primitive hierarchy of
symmetric polyhedra.

986.472 In case one thinks that the four symmetrical sets of the great
circles of the spherical VE (which total 25 great circles in all) might omnisub-
divide the system surface exclusively into a greater number of triangles, we
note that some of the subdivision areas of the 25 great circles are not triangles
(see quadrant *BCEF* in Fig. 453.01—third printing of *Synergetics 1*—of
which quadrangles there are a total of 48 in the system); and note that the total
number of triangles in the 25-great-circle system is 288—ergo, far less than
the 31 great circles' 480 spherical right triangles; ergo, we become satisfied
that the icosahedron's set of 480 is indeed the cosmic maximum-limit case of
system-self-spun subdivisioning of its self into tetrahedra, which 480 consist
of four sets of 120 similar tetrahedra each.

986.473 It then became evident (as structurally demonstrated in reality by
my mathematically close-toleranced geodesic domes) that the spherical trigonometry calculations' multifrequenced modular subdividing of only one of
the icosahedron's 120 spherical right triangles would suffice to provide all the
basic trigonometric data for any one and all of the unit-radius vertex locations
and their uniform interspacings and interangulations for any and all frequen-

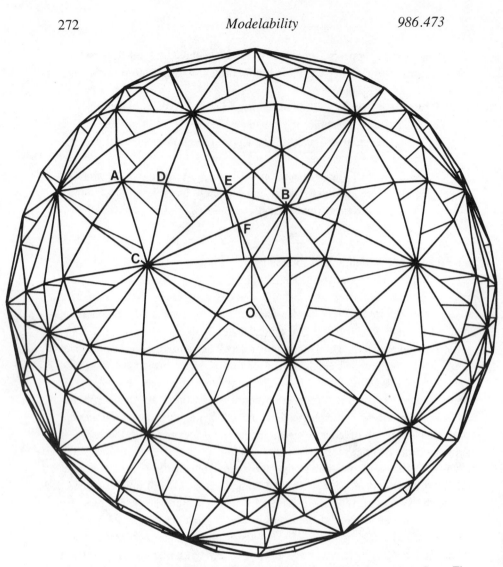

Fig. 986.471 *Modular Subdivisioning of Icosahedron as Maximum Limit Case:* The 120 outer surface right spherical triangles of the icosahedron's 6, 10, and 15 great circles generate a total of 242 external vertexes, 480 external triangles, and 480 internal face-congruent tetrahedra, constituting the maximum limit of regular spherical system surface omnitriangular self-subdivisioning into centrally collected tetrahedral components.

cies of modular subdividings of the most symmetrical and most economically chorded systems' structuring of Universe, the only variable of which is the special case, time-sized radius of the special-case system being considered.

986.474   This surmise regarding nature's most-economical, least-effort design strategy has been further verified by nature's own use of the same geodesics mathematics as that which I discovered and employed in my domes. Nature has been using these mathematical principles for eternity. Humans were unaware of that fact. I discovered these design strategies only as heretofore related, as an inadvertent by-product of my deliberately undertaking to find nature's coordination system. That nature was manifesting icosahedral and VE coordinate patterning was only discovered by other scientists after I had found and demonstrated geodesic structuring, which employed the synergetics' coordinate-system strategies. This discovery by others that my discovery of geodesic mathematics was also the coordinate system being manifest by nature occurred after I had built hundreds of geodesic structures around the world and their pictures were widely published. Scientists studying X-ray diffraction patterns of protein shells of viruses in 1959 found that those shells disclosed the same patterns as those of my widely publicized geodesic domes. When Dr. Aaron Klug of the University of London—who was the one who made this discovery—communicated with me, I was able to send him the mathematical formulae for describing them. Klug explained to me that my geodesic structures are being used by nature in providing the "spherical" enclosures of her own most critical design-controlling programming devices for realizing all the unique biochemical structurings of all biology—which device is the DNA helix.

986.475   The structuring of biochemistry is epitomized in the structuring of the protein shells of all the viruses. They are indeed all icosahedral geodesic structures. They embracingly guard all the DNA-RNA codified programming of all the angle-and-frequency designing of all the biological, life-accommodating, life-articulating structures. We find nature employing synergetics geometry, and in particular the high-frequency geodesic "spheres," in many marine organisms such as the radiolaria and diatoms, and in structuring such vital organs as the male testes, the human brain, and the eyeball. All of these are among many manifests of nature's employment on her most critically strategic occasions of the most cosmically economical, structurally effective and efficient enclosures, which we find are always mathematically based on multifrequency and three-way-triangular gridding of the "spherical"—because high-frequenced—icosahedron, octahedron, or tetrahedron.

986.476   Comparing the icosahedron, octahedron, and tetrahedron—the isosahedron gives the most volume per unit weight of material investment in its structuring; the high-frequency tetrahedron gives the greatest strength per unit weight of material invested; and the octahedron affords a happy—but not as stable—mix of the two extremes, for the octahedron consists of the prime number 2, $2^2 = 4$; whereas the tetrahedron is the odd prime number 1 and the icosahedron is the odd prime number 5. Gear trains of even number reciprocate, whereas gear trains of an odd number of gears always lock; ergo, the tetrahedral and icosahedral geodesic systems lock-fasten all their structural systems, and the octahedron's compromise, middle-position structuring tends to yield transformingly toward either the tetra or the icosa locked-limit capabilities—either of which tendencies is pulsatively propagative.

986.480 Consideration 13: Correspondence of Surface Angles and Central Angles

986.481 It was next to be noted that spherical trigonometry shows that nature's smallest common denominator of system-surface subdivisioning by any one type of the seven great-circle-symmetry systems is optimally accomplished by the previously described 120 spherical-surface triangles formed by the 15 great circles, whose central angles are approximately

$$20.9°$$
$$37.4°$$
$$\underline{31.7°}$$
$$90°$$

whereas their surface angles are 36 degrees at A, 60 degrees at B, and 90 degrees at C.

986.482 We recall that the further self-subdividing of the 120 triangles, as already defined by the 15 great circles and as subdividingly accomplished by the icosahedron's additional 6- and 10-great-circle spinnabilities, partitions the 120 *LCD* triangles into 480 right triangles of four types: *ADC, CDE, CFE,* and *EFB*—with 60 positive and 60 negative pairs of each. (See Figs. 901.03 and *986.314.*) We also recall that the 6- and 10-great-circle-spun hemispherical gridding further subdivided the 120 right triangles—*ACB*—formed by the 15 great circles, which produced a total of 12 types of surface angles, four of them of 90 degrees, and three whose most acute angles subdivided the 90-degree angle at C into three surface angles: *ACD*—31.7 degrees; *DCE*—37.4 degrees; and *ECB*—20.9 degrees, which three *surface angles,* we remember, correspond exactly to the three *central angles COB, BOA,* and *COA,* respectively, of the triacontahedron's tetrahedral T Quanta Module *ABCO^t*.

986.500 E Quanta Module

986.501 Consideration 14: Great-circle Foldable Discs

986.502 With all the foregoing events, data, and speculative hypotheses in mind, I said I think it would be worthwhile to take 30 cardboard great

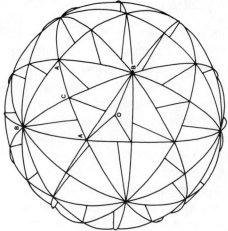

D.

B.

C.

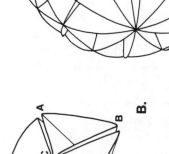

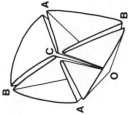
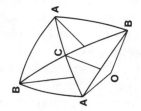

$$\angle COA = 20.90515745° = \text{arc sin} \left(\frac{\sin 18°}{\sin 60°} \right)$$

$$\angle AOB = 37.37736814° = \text{arc sin} \left(\frac{\sin 18°}{\sin 60° \sin 36°} \right)$$

$$\angle BOC = 31.71747441° = \text{arc sin} \left(\frac{\sin 18°}{\sin 36°} \right)$$

A.

Fig. 986.502 Thirty Great-circle Discs Foldable into Rhombic Triacontahedron System: Each of the four 90-degree quadrants, when folded as indicated at A and B, form separate T Quanta Module tetrahedra. Orientations are indicated by letter on the great-circle assembly at *D.*

circles, to divide them into four 90-degree quadrants, then to divide each of the quadrants into three angles—*COA,* 20.9 degrees; *AOB,* 37.4 degrees; and *BOC,* 31.7 degrees—and then to score the cardboard discs
with fold lines in such a manner that the four lines *CO* will be negatively out-folded, while the lines *AO* and *BO* will be positively infolded, so that when they are altogether folded they will form four similar-arc-edged tetrahedra *ABCO* with all of their four *CO* radii edges centrally congruent. And when 30 of these folded great-circle sets of four T Quanta Module tetrahedra are each triple-bonded together, they will altogether constitute a sphere. This spherical assemblage involves pairings of the three intercongruent interface triangles *AOC, COB,* and *BOA;* that is, each folded great-circle set of four tetra has each of its four internal triangular faces congruent with their adjacent neighbor's corresponding *AOC, COB,* and *BOC* interior triangular faces. (See Fig. *986.502.*)

986.503 I proceeded to make 30 of these 360-degree-folding assemblies and used bobby pins to lock the four *CO* edges together at the *C* centers of the diamond-shaped outer faces. Then I used bobby pins again to lock the 30 assemblies together at the 20 convergent *A* vertexes and the 12 convergent *B* sphere-surface vertexes. Altogether they made a bigger sphere than the calculated radius, because of the accumulated thickness of the foldings of the construction paper's double-walled (trivalent) interfacing of the 30 internal tetrahedral components. (See Fig. *986.502D.*)

986.504 Instead of the just previously described 30 assemblies of four identical spherically central tetrahedra, each with all of their 62 vertexes in the unit-radius spheres, I next decided to make separately the 120 correspondingly convergent (non-arc-edged but chorded) tetrahedra of the tetravolume-5 rhombic triacontahedron, with its 30 flat *ABAB* diamond faces, the center *C* of which outer diamond faces is criss-crossed at right angles at *C* by the short axis *A–A* of the diamond and by its long axis *B–B,* all of which diamond bounding and criss-crossing is accomplished by the same 15 great-circle planes that also described the 30 diamonds' outer boundaries. As noted, the criss-crossed centers of the diamond faces occur at *C,* and all the *C* points are at the prime-vector-radius distance outwardly from the volumetric center *O* of the rhombic triacontahedron, while *OA* is 1.07 of vector unity and *OB* is 1.17 of vector unity outward, respectively, from the rhombic triacontahedron's symmetrical system's center of volume *O.* (See Figs. *986.504A* and *986.504B.*)

986.505 To make my 120 *OABC* tetrahedra I happened to be using the same construction paperboard I had used before in making the 30 arc-edged great-circle components. The construction paperboard happened to come in sheets 24 by 36 inches, i.e., two feet by three feet. In making the previously

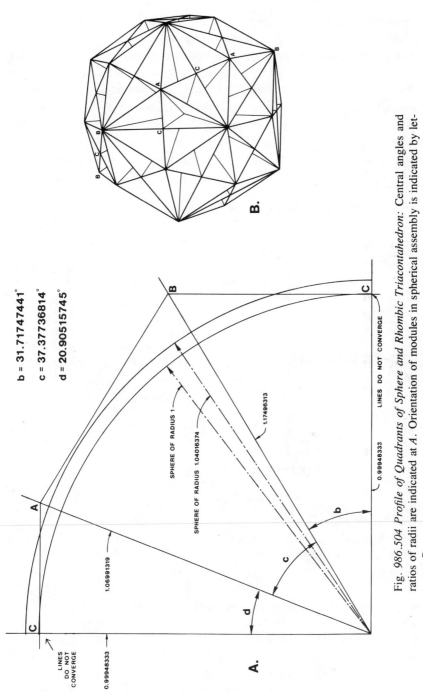

b = 31.71747441°

c = 37.37736814°

d = 20.90515745°

Fig. 986.504 *Profile of Quadrants of Sphere and Rhombic Triacontahedron:* Central angles and ratios of radii are indicated at *A.* Orientation of modules in spherical assembly is indicated by letters at *B.*

described spherical triacontahedron out of these 24-by-36-inch sheets, I had decided to get the most out of my material by using a 12-inch-diameter circle, so that I could lay out six of them tangentially within the six 12-inch-square modules of the paperboard to produce the 30 foldable great circles. This allowed me to cut out six intertangent great circles from each 24-by-36-inch construction paper sheet. Thirty great circles required only five sheets, each sheet producing six circles. To make the 12 separate T Quanta Module tetrahedra, I again spontaneously divided each of the same-size sheets into six squares with each of the six circles tangent to four edges of each square (Fig. *986.505*).

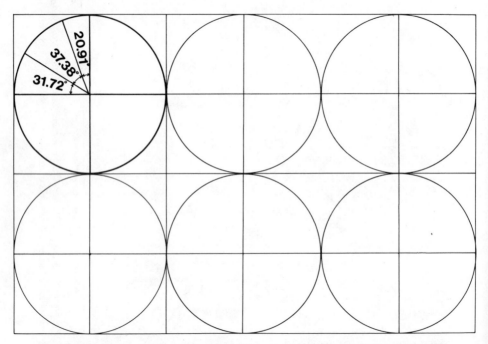

Fig. *986.505 Six Intertangent Great-circle Discs in 12-inch Module Grid:* The four 90-degree quadrants are folded at the central angles indicated for the T Quanta Module.

986.506 In starting to make the 120 separate tetrahedra (60 positive, 60 negative—known as T Quanta Modules) with which to assemble the triacontahedron—which is a chord-edged polyhedron vs the previous "spherical" form produced by the folded 15-great-circle patterning—I drew the same 12-inch-edge squares and, tangentially within the latter, drew the same six 12-inch-diameter circles on the five 24-by-36-inch sheets, dividing each circle into four quadrants and each quadrant into three subsections of 20.9 degrees, 37.4 degrees, and 31.7 degrees, as in the T Quanta Modules.

986.507   I planned that each of the quadrants would subsequently be cut from the others to be folded into one each of the 120 T Quanta Module tetrahedra of the triacontahedron. This time, however, I reminded myself not only to produce the rhombic triacontahedron with the same central angles as in the previous spheric experiment's model, but also to provide this time for surfacing their clusters of four tetrahedra $ABCO$ around their surface point C at the mid-crossing point of their 30 flat diamond faces. Flat diamond faces meant that where the sets of four tetra came together at C, there would not only have to be four 90-degree angles on the flat surface, but there would be eight internal right angles at each of the internal flange angles. This meant that around each vertex C corner of each of the four T Quanta Modules $OABC$ coming together at the diamond face center C there would have to be three 90-degree angles.

986.508   Looking at my "one-circle-per-each-of-six-squares" drawing, I saw that each sheet was divided into 24 quadrant blanks, as in Fig. 986.508A. Next I marked the centers of each of the six circles as point O, O being the volumetric center of the triacontahedral system. Then I realized that, as trigonometrically calculated, the flat, diamond-centered, right-angled, centrally criss-crossed point C of the triacontahedron's outer faces had to be at our primitive unit-vector-length distance outwardly from the system center O, whereas in the previous arc-edged 30-great-circle-folded model the outer vertex C had been at full-spherical-system-radius distance outwardly from O. In the spherical 15-great-circle-model, therefore, the triacontahedron's mid-flat-diamond-face C would be at .07 lesser radial distance outwardly from O than would the diamond corner vertexes A and vertex A itself at a lesser radial distance outwardly from O than diamond corner vertex B. (See Fig. 986.504A.)

986.509   Thinking about the C corner of the described tetrahedron consisting entirely of 90-degree angles as noted above, I realized that the line C to A must produce a 90-degree-angle as projected upon the line OC'', which latter ran vertically outward from O to C'', with O being the volumetric center of the symmetrical system (in this case the rhombic triacontahedron) and with C'' positioned on the perimeter exactly where vertex C had occurred on each of the previous arc-described models of the great circles as I had laid them out for my previous 15 great-circle spherical models. I saw that angle ACO must be 90 degrees. I also knew by spherical trigonometry that the angle AOC would have to be 20.9 degrees, so I projected line OA outwardly from O at 20.9 degrees from the vertical square edge OC.

986.510   At the time of calculating the initial layout I made two mistaken assumptions: first, that the 0.9995 figure was critically approximate to 1 and could be read as 1; and second (despite Chris Kitrick's skepticism born of his confidence in the reliability of his calculations), that the .0005 difference must

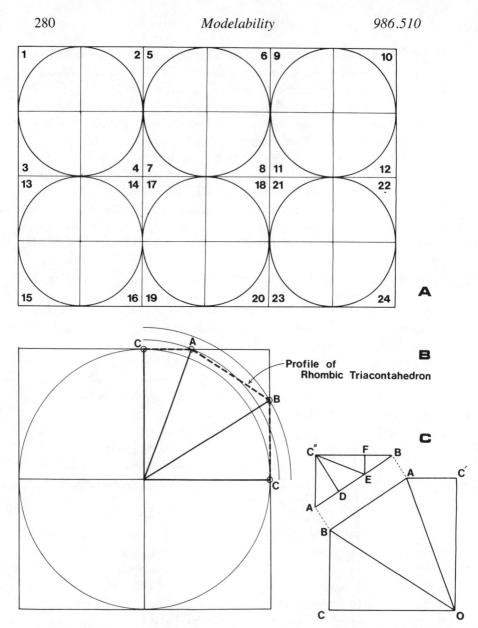

Fig. *986.508 Six Intertangent Great-circle Discs:* Twelve-inch module grids divided into 24 quadrant blanks at *A*. Profile of rhombic triacontahedron superimposed on quadrant at *B*.

be due to the residual incommensurability error of the inherent irrationality of the mathematicians' method of calculating trigonometric functions. (See the Scheherazade Numbers discussed at Sec. 1230.) At any rate I could not lay out with drafting tools a difference of 0.0005 of six inches, which is 0.0030 of an inch. No draftsman can prick off a distance even ten times that size. (I continue to belabor these mistaken assumptions and the subsequent acknowledgments of the errors because it is always upon the occasion of my enlightened admission of error that I make my greatest discoveries, and I am thus eager to convey this truth to those seeking the truth by following closely each step of this development, which leads to one of the most exciting of known discoveries.)

986.511 In order to produce the biggest model possible out of the same 24-by-36-inch construction paper blanks, I saw that vertex *A* of this new T Quanta Module model would have to lie on the same 12-inch circle, projecting horizontally from *A* perpendicularly (i.e., at right angles), upon *OX* at *C*. I found that the point of 90-degree impingement of *AC* on *OX* occurred slightly inward (.041, as we learned later by trigonometry), vertically inward, from *X*. The symbol *X* now occurs on my layout at the point where the previous spherical model's central diamond vertex *C* had been positioned—on the great-circle perimeter. Trigonometric calculation showed this distance between *C* and *X* to be 0.041 of the length of our unit vector radius. Because (1) the distance *CO* is established by the right-angled projection of *A* upon *OX;* and because (2) the length *CO* is also the prime vector of synergetics' isotropic vector matrix itself, we found by trigonometric calculation that when the distance from *O* to *C* is 0.9995 of the prime vector's length, that the tetravolume of the rhombic triacontahedron is exactly 5.

986.512 When the distance from *O* to *C* is 0.9995, then the tetravolume of the rhombic triacontahedron is exactly 5. *OC* in our model layout is now exactly the same as the vector radius of the isotropic vector matrix of our "generalized energy field." *OC* rises vertically (as the right-hand edge of our cut-out model of our eventually-to-be-folded T Quanta Module's model designing layout) from the eventual triacontahedron's center *O* to what will be the mid-diamond face point *C*. Because by spherical trigonometry we know that the central angles of our model must read successively from the right-hand edge of the layout at 20.9 degrees, 37.4 degrees, and 31.7 degrees and that they add up to 90 degrees, therefore line *OC'* runs horizontally leftward, outward from *O* to make angle *COC'* 90 degrees. This is because all the angles around the mid-diamond criss-cross point *C* are (both externally and internally) 90 degrees. We also know that horizontal *OC'* is the same prime vector length as vertical *OC*. We also know that in subsequent folding into the T Quanta Module tetrahedron, it is a mathematical requirement that vertical *OC* be congruent with horizontal *OC'* in order to be able to have these edges fold together to be closed in the interior tetrahedral form of the T Quanta Module. We also know that in order to produce the required three 90-degree angles (one surface and two interior) around congruent *C* and *C'* of the finished T Quanta Module, the line $C'B$ of our layout must rise at 90 degrees vertically from C' at the leftward end of the horizontal unit vector radius OC'. (See Fig. *986.508C.*)

986.513   This layout now demonstrates three 90-degree corners with lines OC vertical and OC' horizontal and of the same exact length, which means that the rectangle $COC'C''$ must be a square with unit-vector-radius edge length OC. The vertical line $C'C''$ rises from C' of horizontal OC' until it encounters line OB, which—to conform with the triacontahedron's interior angles as already trigonometrically established—must by angular construction layout run outwardly from O at an angle of 31.7 degrees above the horizontal from OC' until it engages vertical $C'C''$ at B. Because by deliberate construction requirement the angle between vertical OC and OA has been laid out as 20.9 degrees, the angle AOB must be 37.4 degrees—being the remainder after deducting both 20.9 degrees and 31.7 degrees from the 90-degree angle lying between vertical OC and horizontal OC'. All of this construction layout with OC' horizontally equaling OC vertically, and with the thus-far-constructed layout's corner angles each being 90 degrees, makes it evident that the extensions of lines CA and $C'B$ will intersect at 90 degrees at point C'', thus completing the square $OC'C''C$ of edge length OC, which length is exactly 0.999483332 of the prime vector of the isotropic vector matrix's primitive cosmic-hierarchy system.

986.514   Since ACO, COC', and $OC'B$ are all 90-degree angles, and since vertical CO = horizontal $C'O$ in length, the area $COC'C''$ must be a square. This means that two edges of each of three of the four triangular faces of the T Quanta Module tetrahedron, and six of its nine prefolded edges (it has only six edges after folding), are congruent with an exactly square paperboard blank. The three triangles OCA, OAB, and OBC' will be folded inwardly along AO and BO to bring the two CO and CO' edges together to produce the three systemically interior faces of the T Quanta Module.

986.515   This construction method leaves a fourth right-triangular corner piece $AC''B$, which the dividers indicated—and subsequent trigonometry confirmed—to be the triangle exactly fitting the outer ABC-triangular-shaped open end of the folded-together T Quanta Module $OABC$. O'' marks the fourth corner of the square blank, and trigonometry showed that $C''A = C'B$ and $C''B = AC$, while AB of triangle OBA by construction is congruent with AB of triangle $AC''B$ of the original layout. So it is proven that the vector-edged square $COC'C''$ exactly equals the surface of the T Quanta Module tetrahedron $CABO$. (See Fig. *986.515.*)

986.516   The triangle $AC''B$ is hinged to the T Quanta Module along the mutual edge AB, which is the hypotenuse of the small $AC''B$ right triangle. But as constructed the small right triangle $AC''B$ cannot be hinged (folded) to

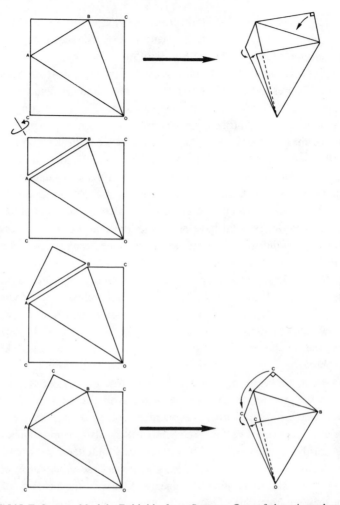

Fig. 986.515 T Quanta Module Foldable from Square: One of the triangular corners may be hinged and reoriented to close the open end of the folded tetrahedron.

close the T Quanta Module tetrahedron's open-end triangular area ABC— despite the fact that the hinged-on triangle $AC''B$ and the open triangle ABC are dimensionally identical. $AC''B$ is exactly the right shape and size and area and can be used to exactly close the outer face of the T Quanta Module tetrahedron, *if*—but only if—it is cut off along line BA and is then turned over so that its faces are reversed and its B corner is now where its A corner had been. This is to say that if the square $COC'C''$ is made of a cardboard sheet with a red top side and a gray underside, when we complete the tetrahedron folding as previously described, cut off the small corner triangle $AC''B$ along line BA, reverse its face and its acute ends, and then address it to the small triangular *ABC* open end of the tetrahedron *CABO,* it will fit exactly into place, but with the completed tetrahedron having three gray faces around vertex *O* and one red outer face *CAB.* (See Fig. 986.508C.)

986.517   Following this closure procedure, when the *AC"B* triangles of each of the squares are cut off from *COC'C"* along line *AB,* and right triangle *AC"B* is reversed in face and its right-angle corner *C"* is made congruent with the right-angle corner *C* of the T Quanta Module's open-end triangle, then the *B* corner of the small triangle goes into congruence with the *A* corner of the open-end triangle, and the *A* corner of the small triangle goes into congruence with the *B* corner of the open-end triangle—with the 90-degree corner *C* becoming congruent with the small triangle's right-angle corner *C".* When all 120 of these T Quanta Module tetrahedra are closed and assembled to produce the triacontahedron, we will have all of the 360 gray faces inside and all of the 120 red faces outside, altogether producing an externally red and an internally gray rhombic triacontahedron.

986.518   In developing the paper-folding pattern with which to construct any one of these 120 identical T Quanta Module tetrahedra, we inadvertently discovered it to be foldable out of an exact square of construction paper, the edge of which square is almost (0.9995 of the prime vector 1) identical in length to that of the prime vector radius of synergetics' closest-packed unit-radius spheres, and of the isotropic vector matrix, and therefore of the radii and chords of the vector equilibrium—which synergetics' vector (as with all vectors) is the product of mass and velocity. While the unit-vector length of our everywhere-the-same energy condition conceptually idealizes cosmic equilibrium, as prime vector (Sec. 540.10) it also inherently represents everywhere-the-same maximum cosmic velocity unfettered in vacuo—ergo, its linear velocity (symbolized in physics as lower-case *c*) is that of all radiation—whether beamed or piped or linearly focused—the velocity of whose unbeamed, omnidirectionally outward, surface growth rate always amounts to the second-powering of the linear speed. Ergo, omniradiance's wave surface growth rate is c^2.

986.519   Since the edge length of the exactly 5.0000 α volumed T Quanta Module surface square is .9995 of the prime vector 1.0000 α, the surface-field energy of the T Quanta Module of minimum energy containment is .9995 V^2, where 1.0000 αV is the prime vector of our isotropic vector matrix. The difference—.0005—is minimal but not insignificant; for instance, the mass of the electron happens also to be .0005 of the mass of the proton.

986.520   Einstein's Equation

986.521   Remembering that in any given dimensional system of reference the vector's length represents a given mass multiplied by a given velocity, we have in the present instance the physical evidence that the surface area of the T Quanta Module tetrahedron exactly equals the area of the edge length—.9995—"squared." In this case of the T Quanta Module the edge length of .9995 of the foldable square (the visibly undetectable) is .0005 less than the length of the prime vector of 1.000.

986.522   The generalized isotropic vector matrix's prime vector to the second power—"squared"—becomes physically visible in the folded-square T tetra modules. (Try making one of them yourself.) This visible "squaring" of the surface area of the exactly one-energy-quantum module tetrahedron corresponds geometrically to what is symbolically called for in Einstein's equation, which language physics uses as a nonengineering-language symbolism (as with conventional mathematics), and which does not preintermultiply mass and velocity to produce a vector of given length and angular direction—ergo, does not employ the integrated vectorial component VE—ergo, must express V^2 in separate components as M (mass) times the velocity of energy unfettered in vacuo to the second power, c^2. However, we can say $Mc^2 = V^2$, the engineering expression V^2 being more economical. When $T =$ the T Quanta Module, and when the T Quanta Module = one energy quantum module, we can say:

$$\text{one module} = 0.9995^2$$

986.523   In the Einstein equation the velocity—lower-case c—of all radiation taken to the second power is omnidirectional—ergo, its quasispheric surface-growth rate is at the second power of its radial-linear-arithmetic growth rate—ergo, c^2. (Compare Secs. 1052.21 and 1052.30.) Thus Einstein's equation reads $E = Mc^2$, where E is the basic one quantum or one photon energy component of Universe.

986.524   With all the foregoing holding true and being physically demonstrable, we find the vector minus .0005 of its full length producing an exactly square area that folds into a tetrahedron of exactly one quantum module, *but*, we must remember, with a unit-integral-square-surface area whose edge length is .0005 less than the true V^2 vector, i.e., less than Mc^2. But don't get discouraged; as with the French *Vive la Différence*, we find that difference of .0005 to be of the greatest possible significance . . . as we shall immediately learn.

986.540   Volume-surface Ratios of E Quanta Module and Other Modules

986.541   Now, reviewing and consolidating our physically exploratory gains, we note that in addition to the .9995 V^2-edged "square"-surfaced T

Quanta Module tetrahedron of exactly the same volume as the A, B, C, or D Quanta Modules, we also have the E Quanta Module—or the "Einstein Module"—whose square edge is exactly vector $V = 1.0000 \alpha$, but whose volume is 1.001551606 when the A Quanta Module's volume is exactly 1.0000 α, which volume we have also learned is uncontainable by chemical structuring, bonding, and the mass-attraction law.

986.542　When the prime-unit vector constitutes the radial distance outward from the triacontahedron's volumetric center O to the mid-points C of each of its mid-diamond faces, the volume of the rhombic triancontahedron is then slightly greater than tetravolume 5, being actually tetravolume 5.007758031. Each of the rhombic triacontahedron's 120 internally structured tetrahedra is called an E Quanta Module, the "E" for Einstein, being the transformation threshold between energy convergently self-interfering as matter $= M$, and energy divergently dispersed as radiation $= c^2$. Let us consider two rhombic triacontahedra: (1) one of radius .9995 V of exact tetravolume 5; and (2) one of radius 1.0000 α of tetravolume 5.007758031. The exact prime-vector radius 1.0000 α rhombic triacontahedron volume is .007758031 (1/129th) greater than the tetravolume 5—i.e., tetravolume 5.007758031. This means that each E Quanta Module is 1.001551606 when the A Quanta Module is 1.0000.

986.543　The 0.000517 radius difference between the .999483-radiused rhombic triacontahedron of exactly tetravolume 5 and its exquisitely minute greater radius-1.0000 α prime vector, is the exquisite difference between a local-in-Universe energy-containing module and that same energy being released to become energy radiant. Each of the 120 right-angle-cornered T Quanta Modules embraced by the tetravolume-5 rhombic triacontahedron is volumetrically identical to the A and B Quanta Modules, of which the A Modules hold their energy and the B Modules release their energy (Sec. 920). Each quanta module volume is .04166—i.e., $^1/_{24}$ of one regular primitive tetrahedron, the latter we recall being the minimum symmetric structural system of Universe. To avoid decimal fractions that are not conceptually simple, we multiply all the primitive hierarchy of symmetric, concentric, polyhedral volumes by 24—after which we can discuss and consider energetic-synergetic geometry in always-whole-rational-integer terms.

986.544　We have not forgotten that radius 1 is only half of the prime-unit vector of the isotropic vector matrix, which equals unity 2 (Sec. *986.160*). Nor have we forgotten that every square is two triangles (Sec. 420.08); nor that the second-powering of integers is most economically readable as "triangling"; nor that nature always employs the most economical alternatives—but we know that it is momentarily too distracting to bring in these adjustments of the Einstein formula at this point.

986.545   To discover the significance of the "difference" all we have to do is make another square with edge length of exactly 1.000 α (a difference completely invisible at our one-foot-to-the-edge modeling scale), and now our tetrahedron folded out of the model is an exact geometrical model of Einstein's $E = Mc^2$, which, expressed in vectorial engineering terms, reads $E = V^2$; however, its volume is now 0.000060953 greater than that of one exact energy quanta module. We call this tetrahedron model folded from one square whose four edge lengths are each exactly one vector long the E Module, naming it for Einstein. It is an exact vector model of his equation.

986.546   The volumetric difference between the T Module and the E Module is the difference between energy-as-matter and energy-as-radiation. The linear growth of 0.0005 transforms the basic energy-conserving quanta module (the physicists' *particle*) from matter into one minimum-limit "photon" of radiant energy as light or any other radiation (the physicists' *wave*).

986.547   Einstein's equation was conceived and calculated by him to identify the energy characteristics derived from physical experiment, which defined the minimum radiation unit—the photon—$E = Mc^2$. The relative linear difference of .000518 multiplied by the atoms' electrons' nucleus-orbiting diameter of one angstrom (a unit on only $1/40$-millionth of an inch) is the difference between *it is matter* or *it is radiation*. . . . Vastly enlarged, it is the same kind of difference existing between a soap bubble existing and no longer existing—"bursting," we call it—because it reached the critical limit of spontaneously coexistent, cohesive energy as-atoms-arrayed-in-liquid molecules and of atoms rearranged in dispersive behavior as gases. This is the generalized critical threshold between *it is* and *it isn't*. . . . It is the same volume-to-tensional-surface-enclosing-capability condition displayed by the soap bubble, with its volume increasing at a velocity of the third power while its surface increases only as velocity to the second power. Its tension-embracement of molecules and their atoms gets thinned out to a one-molecule layer, after which the atoms, behaving according to Newton's mass interattraction law, become circumferentially parted, with their interattractiveness decreasing acceleratingly at a second-power rate of the progressive arithmetical distance apart attained—an increase that suddenly attains critical demass point, and there is no longer a bubble. The same principle obtains in respect to the T Quanta Module→E Quanta Module—i.e., matter transforming into radiation.

986.548   The difference between the edge length of the square from which we fold the E Quanta Module and the edge length of the square from which we fold the T Quanta Module is exquisitely minute: it is the difference between the inside surface and the outside surface of the material employed to fabricate the model. In a 20-inch-square model employing aluminum foil

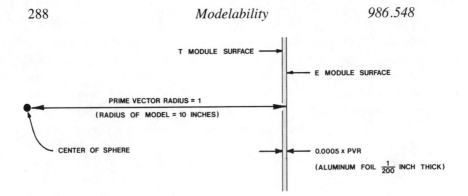

$^1/_{200}$th of an inch thick, the E Module would be congruent with the outside surface and the T Module would be congruent with the inside surface, and the ratio of the edge lengths of the two squares is as 1 is to .0005, or .0005 of prime vector radius of our spherical transformation. This minuscule modelable difference is the difference between *it is* and *it isn't*—which is to say that the dimensional difference between matter and radiation is probably the most minute of all nature's dimensioning: it is the difference between inside-out and outside-out of positive and negative Universe.

986.549 Because we have obtained an intimate glimpse of matter becoming radiation, or vice versa, as caused by a minimum-structural-system tetrahedron's edge-length growth of only 129$^1/_2$ quadrillionths of an inch, and because we have been paying faithful attention to the most minute fractions of difference, we have been introduced to a whole new frontier of synergetics exploration. We have discovered the conceptual means by which the 99 percent of humanity who do not understand science may become much more intimate with nature's energetic behaviors, transformations, capabilities, and structural and de-structural strategies.

986.550   *Table: Relative Surface Areas Embracing the Hierarchy of Energetic Quanta Modules: Volumes are unit. All Module Volumes are 1, except the radiant E Module, whose Surface Area is experimentally evidenced Unity:*

ENERGY PACKAGE   /   SURFACE AREA

V = Vector (linear)

V = Mass × velocity = Energy Package

V^2 = Energy package's surface

1 Unit vector of isotropic vector matrix

Vector × Vector = Surface (Energy as local energy system-containment capability) = Outer array of energy packages.*

Mass = F = Relative frequency of primitive-system-subdivision energy-event occupation.

	"SURFACE" AREA	VOLUME	
A Quanta Module	.9957819158	1 ⎫	HOLD
T Quanta Module	.9989669317	1 ⎭	ENERGY
"Einstein" E Module	1.0000000000	1.00155 ⎫	
B Quanta Module	1.207106781	1	
C Quanta Module	1.530556591	1	
D Quanta Module	1.896581995	1	
A′ Module	2.280238966	1	
B′ Module	2.672519302	1	RELEASE
C′ Module	3.069597104	1	ENERGY
D′ Module	3.469603759	1	
A″ Module	3.871525253	1	
B″ Module	4.27476567	1	
C″ Module	4.678952488	1	
D″ Module	5.083841106	1 ⎭	

(For a discussion of C and D Modules see Sec. *986.413*.)

986.560   *Surprise Nestability of Minimod T into Maximod T*

986.561   The $6 + 10 + 15 = 31$ great circles of icosahedral symmetries (Fig. 901.03) produce the spherical-surface right triangle $AC''B$; CAB is sub-

---

*The VE surface displays the number of closest-packed spheres of the outer layer. That surface = F^2; ergo, the number of energy-package spheres in outer layer shell = surface, there being no continuum or solids.

divisible into four spherical right triangles *CDA, CDE, DFE,* and *EFB.* Since there are 120 *CAB* triangles, there are 480 subdivision-right-surface triangles. Among these subdivision-right triangles there are two back-to-back 90-degree surface angles at *D—CDA* and *CDE*—and two back-to-back 90-degree surface angles at *F—CFE* and *EFB.* The surface chord *DE* of the central angle *DOE* is identical in magnitude to the surface chord *EB* of the central angle *EOB,* both being 13.28 degrees of circular azimuth. Surface chord *FB* of central angle *FOB* and surface chord *AD* of central angle *AOD* are identical in magnitude, both being 10.8 degrees azimuth. In the same manner we find that surface chord *EF* of central angle *EOF* constitutes the mutual edge of the two surface right triangles *CFE* and *BFE,* the central-angle magnitude of *EOF* being 7.77 degrees azimuth. Likewise, the central angles *COA* and *COF* of the surface chords *CA* and *CF* are of the same magnitude, 20.9 degrees. All the above data suggest a surprising possibility: that the small corner triangle *AC″B* itself can be folded on its three internal chord lines *CD, CE,* and *EF,* while joining its two edges *AC* and *CF,* which are of equal magnitude, having central angles of 20.9 degrees. This folding and joining of *F* to *A* and of *B* to *D* cancels out the congruent-letter identities *F* and *D* to produce the tetrahedron *ABEC.* (See Fig. *986.561.*)

986.562　We find to our surprise that this little flange-foldable tetrahedron is an identically angled miniature of the T Quanta Module *OABC^t* and that it can fit elegantly into the identically angled space terminating at *O* within the inner reaches of vacant *OABC,* with the miniature tetrahedron's corner *C* becoming congruent with the system's center *O.* The volume of the Minimod T is approximately $1/18$ that of the Maximod T Quanta Module or of the A or B Modules.

986.570　Range of Modular Orientations

986.571　Now we return to Consideration 13 of this discussion and its discovery of the surface-to-central-angle interexchanging wave succession manifest in the cosmic hierarchy of ever-more-complex, primary structured polyhedra—an interchanging of inside-out characteristics that inherently produces positive-negative world conditions; ergo, it propagates—inside-to-outside-to-in—pulsed frequencies. With this kind of self-propagative regenerative function in view, we now consider exploring some of the implications of the fact that the triangle *C'AB* is foldable into the E Quanta Module and is also nestable into the T Quanta Module, which produces many possibilities:

1. The triangle *AC'B* will disconnect and reverse its faces and complete the enclosure of the T Quanta Module tetrahedron.

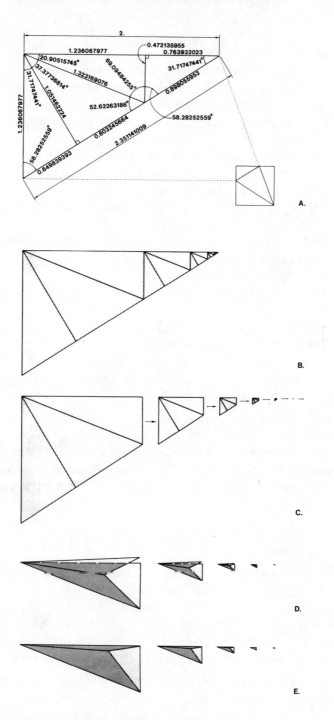

Fig. 986.561 T and E Modules: Minimod Nestabilities: Ratios of Angles and Edges: The top face remains open: the triangular lid will not close, but may be broken off and folded into smaller successive minimod tetra without limit.

2. The 120 T Quanta Modules, by additional tension-induced twist, take the *AC"B* triangles *AB* ends end-for-end to produce the additional radius outwardly from *O* to convert the T Quanta Modules into "Einstein" E Quanta Modules, thus radiantly exporting all 120 modules as photons of light or other radiation.

3. The triangle *AC"B* might disconnect altogether, fold itself into the miniature T Quanta Module, and plunge inwardly to fill its angularly matching central tetrahedral vacancy.

4. The outer triangle may just stay mishinged and flapping, to leave the tetrahedron's outer end open.

5. The outer triangle might come loose, fold itself into a miniature T Quanta Module, and leave the system.

6. The 120 miniature T Quanta Modules might fly away independently—as, for instance, cosmic rays, i.e., as minimum modular fractions of primitive systems.

7. All 120 of these escaping miniature T Quanta Modules could reassemble themselves into a miniature $^1/_{120}$ triacontahedron, each of whose miniature T Module's outer faces could fold into mini-mini T Modules and plunge inwardly in ever-more-concentrating demonstration of implosion, ad infinitum.

There are 229,920 other possibilities that any one of any other number of the 120 individual T Module tetrahedra could behave in any of the foregoing seven alternate ways in that vast variety of combinations and frequencies. At this borderline of ultrahigh frequency of intertransformability between matter and electromagnetic radiation we gain comprehension of how stars and fleas may be designed and be born.

968.580 Consideration 15: Surface Constancy and Mass Discrepancy

986.581   Those *AC"B* triangles appear in the upper left-hand corner of either the T Module's or the E Module's square areas *COC'C"*, one of which has the edge length .994 *V* and the other the edge length of 1.0000 α *V*. Regardless of what those *AC"B* triangles may or may not do, their *AC"B* areas, together with the areas of the triangles *ACO, ABO,* and *BCO,* exactly constitute the total surface area of either the T Module or the E Module.

Surface of T Module = $.994V^2$
Surface of E Module = $1.00000\ \alpha\ V^2$

986.582   The outer triangle *AC"B* of the T Quanta Module is an inherent energy conserver because of its foldability into one (minimum-something) tetrahedron. When it folds itself into a miniature T Module with the other 119

T Modules as a surface-closed rhombic triacontahedron, the latter will be a powerful energy conserver—perhaps reminiscent of the giant-to-dwarf-Star behavior. The miniature T Module behavior is also similar to behaviors of the electron's self-conservation. This self-conserving and self-contracting property of the T Quanta Modules, whose volume energy (ergo, energy quantum) is identical to that of the A and B Modules, provides speculative consideration as to why and how electron mass happens to be only $1/1836$ the mass of the proton.

986.583   Certain it is that the T Quanta Module→E Quanta Module threshold transformation makes it clear how energy goes from matter to radiation, and it may be that our little corner triangle $AC''B$ is telling us how radiation retransforms into matter.

986.584   The volume of the T Quanta Module is identical with the volumes of the A and B Quanta Modules, which latter we have been able to identify with the quarks because of their clustering in the cosmically minimum, allspace-filling three-module Mites as A +, A −, and B, with both A's holding their energy charges and B discharging its energy in exact correspondence with the quark grouping and energy-holding-and-releasing properties, with the A Modules' energy-holding capabilities being based on their foldability from only one triangle, within which triangle the reflection patterning guarantees the energy conserving. (See Secs. 921 and *986.414*)

986.585   As we study the hierarchy of the surface areas of constant volume 1 and their respective shapes, we start with the least-surface A Quanta Module which is folded out of one whole triangle, and we find that no other triangle is enclosed by one triangle *except* at the top of the hierarchy, where in the upper left-hand corner we find our Minimod T or Minimod E tetrahedron foldable out of our little triangle $AC''B$, whose fold-line patterning is similar to that of the triangle from which the A Quanta Module is folded. In between the whole foldable triangular blank of the A Quanta Module and the whole foldable triangular blank of the Minimod T or Minimod E, we have a series of only asymmetrical folding blanks—until we come to the beautiful squares of the T and E Quanta Modules, which occur just before we come to the triangles of the minimod tetrahedra, which suggests that we go from radiation to matter with the foldable triangle and from matter to radiation when we get to the squares (which are, of course, two triangles).

986.600   Surface-Volume Ratios in the Atomic Theater

986.610   Considerations, Recalls, and Discoveries

986.611   Our inventory of considerations, recalls, and discoveries is now burgeoning but remains *omniinterrelevant*. Wherefore we continue recalling and reconsidering with a high probability factor that we will make further discovery based on our past experience.

986.620 Demass Breakpoint Model of Macrotude-microtude Difference Between Matter and Radiation

986.621 Let me here introduce a physical experiment that will give us a personal feeling of appreciation of the importance to all humanity of all humanity's being able to *see with its own eyes* what Einstein's equation represents—the breakpoint between matter and radiation (critical mass and atomic-energy release)—and above all to give all humanity experienceable, knowable access to all that science has ever discovered regarding Universe, plus much more than science has ever discovered. With all this experienceability of most advanced scientific discovery all humanity will come to appreciate the otherwise utterly incredible exquisiteness of mathematical exactitude with which Universe (which is nature) functions.

986.622 What we employ for such self-instruction at a human-sense-detectable level to appreciate the meager difference between the "T" square's .9995 edge length and the "E" square's 1.00000 α edge length is to perform the physical task of producing two squares, which the human eyes can see and fingers can feel are of different sizes. Unaided by a lens, only the most skilled human eyes can see something that is one one-hundredth of an inch (expressed as .01 inch). A carpenter works at no finer than $1/32$nd of an inch. To make a difference of .0005 undeniably visible to any average human we would have to use the popularly adopted $1/16$th of an inch, which is that of the common school ruler. This $1/16$th of an inch is expressed decimally as 0.0625. To make .005 of an inch visible we multiply it by 100, which makes it .05. One hundred inches is eight and a half feet—the average room-ceiling height. If we make two squares with 100-inch edges ($8^1/2$ feet "square") out of wooden planks and timber, we cannot hold their dimensions to such a close tolerance of error because the humidity and temperature variations will be greater than .05 inch. Even if we make the $8^1/2$-foot squares of steel and aluminum plate, the expansion and contraction under common weather temperature changes will be greater than .05 inch.

986.623 Using machine tools machinists can "dress" their products to tolerances as fine as .0001 inch.

986.624 Fiberglass-and-epoxy resin is the substance that has the minimum presently known temperature-and-humidity-caused expansion and contraction rates of all practically producible materials. Wherefore: two square plates two inches thick with edge lengths of $8^1/2$ feet could be machine-tool "dressed" and placed vertically face to face in a temperature-controlled slot with one of each of both of their bottom innermost 90-degree corners jammed tightly into a "machined" corner slot, which would then make it possible to "see" with human eyes the difference in square size between the "T" and the "E" squares.

986.625   Even if we "machined" two steel cubes with an edge-length difference of .0005 inch, they would stack one on top of the other with their two vertical surfaces appearing as a polished continuum—the space between them being also subvisible.

986.626   But nature's energy-as-matter transformed into energy-as-radiation are operations conducted at a size scale far different from our experientially imagined experiments. Nature operates her matter-to-radiation energy exchanging at the atomic level. The nucleus of the atom is where energy-as-matter is self-interferingly knotted together in most primitive polyhedral-patterning event systems. The atomic nucleus diameter is $1/100,000$ the diameter of its electron-orbited domain—which domain is spoken of by scientists as "the atom." One atomic diameter is called the angstrom and is the prime measurement unit of the physicists—macrophysicists or microphysicists, astro or nuclear, as they might well be designated.

986.627   Referring to those two $8^1/_2$-foot (the size of Barnum's circus human giant) in height and 2-inches-thick square plates of machine-dressed fiberglass-epoxy resin and their minimum-human-sense-detectability difference of dimension, we find that the angstrom-atomic theater of energy-exchanging performance is only $1/126,500,000,000$ the size of the minimum average human sense detectability. This figure, put into human-experience-sensing terms, is the distance that a photon of light expanding radially at 186,000 miles per second will travel-reach between the time humans are born and the time they reach their nineteenth birthday.

986.628   What is important for us to realize here is that synergetics mathematics, beginning with the most primitive hierarchy of min-max geometrical relationships, expresses relationships that exist independently of time-size. So we humans can think intimately about structural principles of any size. These primitive structural principles disclose inherent geometrical nuclei in respect to which all of Universe's convergent-divergent, gravitational and radiational, contracting into matter and expanding into electromagnetics, and vice versa, together with their terminal angular and frequency knotting and unknotting events comprehensively and comprehendingly occur. And since the sum-total of both macro- and micro-physical science evidences 100-percent conservation of the energy of eternally regenerative Scenario Universe, each smallest differential fraction is of infinite importance to the integrity of Universe.

986.629   And since Physical Universe demonstrates the principle of least effort, i.e., maximum efficiency to be infallibly operative, Universe does the most important tasks in the most exquisite manner; ergo, it is in the most exquisitely minute fractions that she hides her most important secrets. For all the foregoing synergetics' disclosure of a means of comprehending and operating independently of size provides human mind with not only a cosmic advantage but with all the responsibility such a cosmic decision to invest such an advantage in us implies. With these thoughts we address ourselves now to considering not only the critical cosmic surface-volume relationships but also their unique behavior differentials.

986.630 Interkinetic Limits

986.631 In a structural system's interbalancing of compression and tension forces the tensed components will always embrace the compression components—as does gravity always comprehensively embrace all radiation—ergo, tension is always outermost of all systems, macrocosmic or microcosmic.

986.632 Take any bendable substance and bend it. As you do so, the outer part of the bend stretches and the inner part compresses. Tension always has the greater radius—ergo, leverage advantage—ergo, gravity is always comprehensive of radiation (Compare Sec. 1051.50)

986.633 In experiential structural reality the so-called sphere is always and only an ultra-high-frequency geodesic polyhedron; ergo, it is always chord-circumferenced and chord-convergent-vertexed rather than arc-circum-ferenced and arc-vertexed; ergo, it is always and only quasispherical, which quasispherical structural form is experimentally demonstrable as enclosing the most volume with the least surface of any and all symmetrical, equiangular, structural systems. Because of the foregoing we find it desirable to rename the spheric experience, using from now on the word *spheric* in lieu of the nonex-istent, experimentally nondemonstrable "sphere."

986.634 As an asymmetrical or polarized structural system, the hemis-pheric-ended cylinder has the same surface-to-volume ratio as that of a sphere with an identical diameter—the latter cylinders as well as their hemi-spherical terminals consist structurally only of high-frequency, triangularly chorded stuructures. The spheric and the hemispheric-terminalled cylinders alike contain the most volume with the least surface of all symmetrical poly-hedra. At the other extreme of the surface-to-volume ratio, the equiangular tetrahedron encloses the least volume with the most surface of any and all om-nisymmetrical structural systems. The more asymmetrical the tetrahedron, the more surface is required to envelop a given volume. It may be assumed, therefore, that with a given quantity of the same energy invested as molecu-larly structured, system-containing capability, it is less tensionally stressful to enclose a regular equiangular tetrahedron than it is to enclose any asymmetrical tetrahedron.

986.635   In respect to total surface areas of asymmetrical tetrahedra of unit (i.e., identical volume) enclosure, it is experimentally demonstrable that the greater the difference between the most acute angle and the most obtuse of its 12 surface angles, the greater the surface-to-volume ratio will be, and therefore the greater the tensional stressing of its outermost cohering components—ergo, the greater the challenge to the containment of its structural-system integrity. (See Sec. 923 and Fig. 923.10.) According to Newton's law the mass interattraction of two separate bodies deteriorates exponentially as the distance apart decreases arithmetically; ergo, the relative interproximity of the atoms within any molecule, and the relative interproximity of the molecules as structurally interarrayed within any and all volume-containment systems—and the resultant structural-integrity coherences of those systems—trend acceleratingly toward their theoretical atom-and-molecule-interattractive-proximity limits. These chemical-structure-integrity limits are visibly demonstrated to the human eyes by the bursting of bubbles or of children's overfilled balloons or of any other internally overpressured fluid-pneumatic, molecular-membraned containers when the membrane impinging and ricocheting interkinetic acceleration of an increasingly introduced population of contained gas molecules separates the molecules of the container membrane beyond their critical-proximity limits. These critical-atomic-and-molecular-proximity limits are mathematically and gravitationally similar to the proximity limits governing the velocity and distance outward from planet Earth's surface at which a rocket-launched vehicle can maintain its orbit and not fall back into the Earth.

986.700   Spheric Nature of Electromagnetic Waves

986.701   Consideration 16: and Realization of Synergetic Significance

986.702   Since we have learned that nature's second-powering is triangling and not squaring (Sec. 990), and since each square is always two similar triangles, we must express Einstein's equation, where E is the product of M and c^2, as:

$$E = 2V^2$$

986.710 Recapitulation of Geometry-and-energy Recalls

986.711 I must add to the inventory of only-synergetically-interrevealing significant discoveries of this chronicle a recapitulation of additional ''recalls'':

 (1) The absolute constancy of cheese polyhedra;
 (2) that the tetrahedron is the quantum of energy;
 (3) that the nonpolar vertexes of the polar-edge-''tuned'' tetrehedron can connect any other two points in Universe;
 (4) that the unit-volume progression of quanta modules accounts for electromagnetic intertuning;
 (5) that the tetrahedron in turning itself inside-out accounts for electromagnetic-wave propagation;
 (6) that polyhedra should be reidentified as *polyvertexia,* the simplest of which is the *tetravertex;*
 (7) that the tetravertex is the simplest spheric system;
 (8) that the vector equilibrium provides a field for universal energy accommodation; and
 (9) that the vector equilibrium shell growth rate predicts the proton and neutron population of the elements.

986.720 Absolute Constancy: Cheese Polyhedra

986.721 My first observation of the polyhedral hierarchy was introduced in Sec. 223.64, Table 224.20, and Fig. 400.30. That hierarchy may be considered as cheese polyhedra in which there is an experimental redemonstrability of absolute constancy of areal, volumetric, topological, and symmetry characteristics, which constancy is exclusively unique to triangles and tetrahedra and is maintained despite any and all asymmetrical aberrations of those triangles and tetrahedra, as caused

 —by perspective distortion;
 —by interproportional variations of relative lengths and angles as manifest in isosceles, scalene, acute, or obtuse system aspects (see quadrangular versus triangular accounting in Figs. 990.01 and *100.301.*);
 —by truncatings parallel to triangle edges or parallel to tetrahedron faces; or
 —by frequency modulations,

in contradistinction to complete loss of symmetry and topological constancy of all polygons other than the triangle and of all polyhedra other than the tetrahedron as caused by any special-case, time-size alterations or changes of the perspective point from which the observations of those systems are taken.

986.722   In connection with this same cheese tetrahedron recall we remember (1) that we could push in on the face A of the tetrahedron at a given rate of radial contraction of the system, while pulling out face B at a matching rate of radial expansion of the system, which "couple" of local alterations of the system left the tetrahedron unaltered in shape or size throughout the transformation (Sec. 623) and just as it was both before and after the "coupled" transformings took place, the only altered consequence of which was that the tetrahedron's center of volume had migrated; and we remember (2) that we could also push in on the same tetrahedron's face C and pull out on face D at a coupled rate other than the coupled rate of radial expansion and contraction of the A-B face-coupling's intercomplementary transformings; by all of which we learn that the tetrahedron can accommodate two disparate rates of change without in any way altering its own size and only altering its center-of-volume positioning in respect to any other system components of the local Universe consideration. (See color plate 26.)

986.723   It must be noted, however, that because of the generalized non-simultaneity of cosmic events, there exists an inherent lag between the pushing in of face A and the pulling out of face B, which induces an inherent interim wave-depression or a wave-breaking pulsating of the coupling functionings of the tetrahedron's accommodation of transmission of two disparately frequenced energetic communications.

986.724   Second, I recall—as in Secs. 920.01 and 921.10 and Fig. 923.10—that the tetrahedron is the quantum of energy.

986.725   Third, I recall that the single-tuned-length axis of the edge-axis-rotatable tetrahedron's two nonaxis polar vertexes may be deployed to connect up with any two other points in Universe without altering the tetrahedron's unit volume or its tuned-axis length. (See Sec. 961.30.)

986.726   Fourth, I recall that the tetrahedron's 24 A Modules and the latter's B, C, D; A', B', C', D'; A'', B'', C'', D'' . . . α (see Fig. 986.726, which is a detail and relabeling of Fig. 923.10B) together with the T and E Modules provide transformative significance of being the constant-unit-volume progression of ever-more-asymmetrically-transforming stages of the constant-unit-volume tetrahedra, with the uniform-stage transforming being provided by five of the six edges of each of the constant-volume tetrahedra being covaryingly and ever-progressively-disparately altered—with the sixth edge alone of each and all stages of the transformation remaining unaltered in frequency and wavelength magnitude. The concurrent

—constant-volume-and-wavelength transformings, and
—system rotating around and angular tilting of the constant, unaltered-

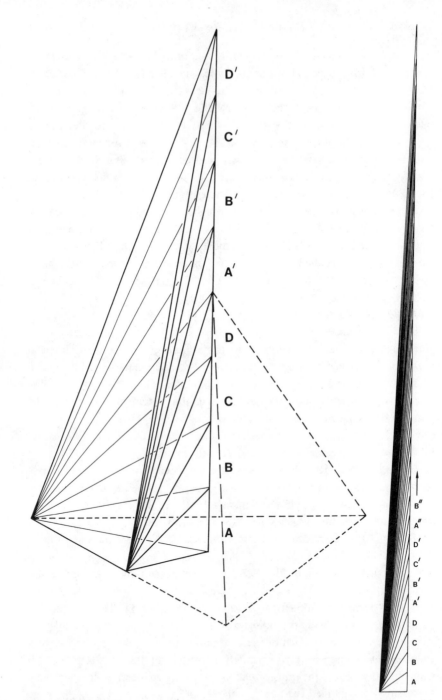

Fig. 986.726 Constant-unit-volume Progressions of Asymmetric Tetrahedra: In this progression of ever-more-asymmetric tetrahedra, only the sixth edge remains constant. Tetrahedral wavelength and tuning permits any two points in Universe to connect with any other two points in Universe.

in-length, sixth edge's axial altitude in respect to the all-other-in-Universe experiences' omniinterangular orientations,

altogether both permit and accommodate any two other points *X* and *Y* in Universe being interconnected not only with one another, but also with the two points *A* and *B* that define the unaltered sixth edge *AB* of the constant-volume and constant-*AB*-edge-length, omni-Universe-interconnecting tetrahedron *ABXY;* all of which permits the constant sixth edge *AB* length to serve as the anywhere and anywhen in Universe to be established transceiver's wavelength-defining and frequency-selecting and tuning interconnecting any given two points in Universe with any two other points in Universe; ergo, with all other points in Universe, granted only sufficient elapsed time for rotational realization of the frequency of repetition of the wavelength vector's velocity factor to reach any given loci in Universe with a given volumetric-unit quantum of energy. (This is the significance of Fig. 923.10.)

986.727   Fifth, I recall as recounted in Sec. 961.40 that the more elongated the unit-volume tetrahedron of only one-edge-length-constancy (the sixth edge), the less becomes the unit-volume tetrahedron's least-altitude aspect as related to its other interdimensional aspects, wherefore there is attained a condition wherein the controlling sixth edge's wavelength is greater than half the tetrahedron's least-altitude aspect—at which condition the tetrahedron spontaneously turns itself inside-out, ergo, turns itself out—not out of Universe, but out of tune-in-able range. Prior to this spontaneous tuning-out range we have a vast range of now-partially-tuned-in-and-now-tuned-out, which altogether propagates finitely packaged, tuned-in energy information occurring in packages yet recurring in constant, contained wavelength intervals that introduce what has hitherto been considered to be the paradoxical aspect of electromagnetic phenomena, of which it has been misassumed that as of any one moment we can consider our electromagnetic phenomena as being continuous-wave phenomena or as discontinuous-particle phenomena—both simultaneous. We thus learn that no such paradox exists. (Compare Secs. 541.30, 961.46–48, 973.30, and *1072.32*.)

986.728   Sixth, we recall that there are no solids or absolute continuums; ergo, there are no physically demonstrable faces or sides of *hedra;* ergo, we reidentify the system-conceptioning experiences heretofore spoken of as polyhedra, by the name *polyvertexia,* the simplest of which is the *tetravertex,* or "four-fix" system.

986.729   Seventh, we recall that the tetravertex is not only the simplest limit case—i.e., the topologically most economically definable polyvertex system case—but also the simplest spheric-system experience case. (See Secs. 1024.10–25, 1053.40–62, 1054. 1054.30, and Fig. 1054.40.)

986.730 **The Spheric Experience:** *We now scientifically redefine the spheric experience as an aggregate of vertex-direction-pointed-to (fixed) sub-tune-in-able microevent centers surrounding a system center at equal-radius distances from the system center. Four such surrounding, vertex-convergence-indicated, microevent fixes are redemonstrably proven to be the minimum number of such a microcenter-surrounding aggregate geometrically adequate to constitute systemic subdivision of Universe into macrocosm and microcosm by convergent envelopment, which inherently excludes the thus-constituted system's macrocosm and inherently includes the thus-constituted system's microcosm, in which spheric experiencing the greater the population of equi-radiused-from-system-center microevent fixes, the more spheric the experience, and the earliest and simplest beyond the tetrahedron being the hierarchy of concentric, symmetric, primitive polyhedra.*

986.740 Microenergy Transformations of Octet Truss

986.741 These last nine major recalls (Sec. *986.711*) are directly related to the matter-to-radiation transitional events that occur as we transit between the T and the E Quanta Modules. First, we note that bubbles are spherics, that bubble envelopes are liquid membranes, and that liquids are bivalent. Bivalent tetrahedral aggregates produce at minimum the octet truss. (See Sec. *986.835* et seq.) The octet truss's double-bonded vertexes also require two layers of closest-packed, unit-radius spheres, whose two layers of closest-packed spheres produce an octet truss whose interior intermembranes are planar while both the exterior and interior membranes are domical.

986.742 Sufficient interior pressure will stretch out the bivalent two-sphere layer into univalent one-sphere layering, which means transforming from the liquid into the gaseous state, which also means transforming from interattractive proximity to inadequate interattractive proximity—ergo, to self-diffusing, atoms-dispersing gaseous molecules. This is to say that the surface-to-volume relationship as we transform from T Quanta Module to E Quanta Module is a transformative, double-to-single-bond, liquid-to-gas transition. Nothing "bursts." . . . Bursting is a neat structural-to-destructural atomic rearrangement, not an undefinable random mess.

986.743 Small-moleculed, gaseous-state, atomic-element, monovalent integrities, wherein the atoms are within mass-interattractive critical-proximity range of one another, interconstitute a cloud that may entrap individual molecules too large for escape through the small-molecule interstices of the cloud. A cloud is a monovalent atomic crowd. Water is a bivalent crowd of atoms. Clouds of gasses, having no external membrane, tend to dissipate their molecule and atom populations expansively, except, for instance, within critical proximity of planet Earth, whose Van Allen belts and ionosphere are overwhelmingly capable of retaining the atmospheric aggregates—whose mini-energy events such as electrons otherwise become so cosmically dispersed as to be encountered only as seemingly "random" rays and particles.

986.744   This cosmic dispersion of individual microenergy event components—alpha particles, beta particles, and so on—leads us to what is seemingly the most entropic disorderly state, which is, however, only the interpenetration of the outer ramparts of a plurality of differently tuned or vectored isotropic-vector-matrix VE systems.

986.750   Universal Accommodation of Vector Equilibrium Field: Expanding Universe

986.751   Recalling (a) that we gave the vector equilibrium its name because nature avoids the indeterminate (the condition of equilibrium) by always transforming or pulsating four-dimensionally in 12 different ways through the omnicentral VE state, as in one plane of which VE a pendulum swings *through* the vertical;

> —and recalling (b) that each of the vertexes of the isotropic vector matrix could serve as the nuclear center of a VE;
>
> —and recalling (c) also that the limits of swing, pulse, or transform through aberrations of all the VE nucleus-concentric hierarchy of polyhedra have shown themselves to be of modest aberrational magnitude (see the unzipping angle, etc.);
>
> —and recalling (d) also that post-Hubble astronomical discoveries have found more than a million galaxies, all of which are omniuniformly interpositioned angularly and are omniuniformly interdistanced from one another, while all those distances are seemingly increasing uniformly;
>
> —all of which recalls together relate to, explain, and engender the name Expanding Universe.

986.752   We realize that these last four recalls clearly identify the isotropic vector matrix as being the operative geometrical field, not only when atoms are closest packed with one another but also when they are scattered entropically into the cosmically greatest time-size galaxies consisting of all the thus-far-discovered-to-exist stars, which consist of the thus-far-discovered evidence of existent atoms within each star's cosmic region—with those atoms interarrayed in a multitude of all-alternately, equi-degrees-of-freedom-and-frequency-permitted, evolutionary patterning displays ranging from interstellar gasses and dusts to planets and stars, from asteroids to planetary turtles . . . to coral . . . to fungi . . . et al. . . . . Wherefore the Expanding Universe of uniformly interpositioned galaxies informs us that we are witnessing the isotropic vector matrix and its local vector equilibria demonstrating integrity of accommodation at the uttermost time-size macrolimits thus far generalizable within this local 20-billion-year-episode sequence of eternally regenerative Universe, with each galaxy's unique multibillions of stars, and each of these stars' multibillions of atoms all intertransforming locally to demonstrate the adequacy of the isotropic vector matrix and its local vector equilibria to accommodate the totality of all local time aberrations possible within the galaxies' total system limits, which is to say within each of their vector equilibrium's intertransformability limits.

986.753   Each of the galaxies is centered within a major VE domain within the greater isotropic vector matrix geometrical field—which major VE's respective fields are subdividingly multiplied by isotropic matrix field VE centerings to the extent of the cumulative number of tendencies of the highest frequency components of the systems permitted by the total time-size enduring magnitude of the local systems' individual endurance time limits.

986.754   In the seemingly Expanding Universe the equidistant galaxies are apparently receding from each other at a uniform rate, as accounted for by the pre-time-size VE matrix which holds for the largest scale of the total time. This is what we mean by multiplication only by division within each VE domain and its total degrees of freedom in which the number of frequencies available can accommodate the full history of the cosmogony.

986.755   The higher the frequency, the lower the aberration. With multiplication only by division we can accommodate the randomness and the entropy within an entirely regenerative Universe. The high frequency is simply diminishing our point of view.

986.756   The Expanding Universe is a misnomer. What we have is a progressively diminishing point of view as ever more time permits ever greater frequency of subdivisioning of the totally tunable Universe.

986.757   What we observe sum-totally is not a uniformly Expanding Universe, but a uniformly-contracting-magnitude viewpoint of multiplication only by division of the finite but non-unitarily-conceptual, eternally regenerative Scenario Universe. (See Secs. *987.066* and *1052.62*.)

986.758   Because the higher-frequency events have the shortest wavelengths in aberration limits, their field of articulation is more local than the low-frequency, longer-wavelengths aberration limit events—ergo, the galaxies usually have the most intense activities closer into and around the central VE regions: all their entropy tendency is accommodated by the total syntropy of the astrophysical greatest-as-yet-identified duration limit.

986.759   We may now direct our attention to the microscosmic, no-time-size, closest-packed unity (versus the Galactic Universe macro-interdistanced unity). This brings us to the prefrequency, timeless-sizeless VE's hierarchy and to the latter's contractability into the geometrical tetrahedron and to that quadrivalent tetrahedron's ability to turn itself inside-out in pure principle to become the novent tetrahedron—the "Black Hole"—the presently-non-tuned-in phenomena. And now we witness the full regenerative range of generalized accommodatability of the VE's isotropic matrix and its gamut of "special case" realizations occurring as local Universe episodes ranging from photons to molecules, from red giants to white dwarfs, to the black-hole, self-inside-outing, and self-reversing phase of intertransformability of eternally regenerative Universe.

986.760   Next we reexplore and recall our discovery of the initial time-size frequency—multiplication by division only—which produces the frequency F, F^2, F^3 layers of 12, 42, 92 closest-packed spheres around a nuclear sphere. . . . And here we have evidencible proof of the persistent adequacy of the VE's local field to accommodate the elegantly simple structural regenerating of the prime chemical elements, with the successive shell populations demonstrating physically the exact proton-neutron population accounting of the first minimum-limit case of most symmetrical shell enclosings, which corresponds exactly with the ever-experimentally-redemonstrable structural model assemblies shown in Sec. *986.770.*

986.770   Shell Growth Rate Predicts Proton and Neutron Population of the Elements

986.771   Thus far we have discovered the physical modelability of Einstein's equation and the scientific discovery of the modelability of the transformation from matter to radiation, as well as the modelability of the difference between waves and particles. In our excitement over these discoveries we forget that others may think synergetics to be manifesting only pure coincidence of events in a pure-scientists' assumed-to-be model-less world of abstract mathematical expressions, a world of meaningless but alluring, simple geometrical relationships. Hoping to cope with such skepticism we introduce here three very realistic models whose complex but orderly accounting refutes any suggestion of their being three successive coincidences, all occurring in the most elegantly elementary field of human exploration—that of the periodic table of unique number behaviors of the proton and neutron populations in successive stages of the complexity of the chemical elements themselves.

986.772   If we look at Fig. 222.01 (*Synergetics* 1), which shows the three successive layers of closest-packed spheres around the prime nuclear sphere, we find the successive layer counts to be 12, 42, 92 . . . that is, they are "frequency to the second power times 10 plus 2." While we have been aware for 40 years that the outermost layer of these concentric layers is 92, and that its first three layers add to

$$
\begin{array}{r}
12 \\
42 \\
\underline{92} \\
146
\end{array}
$$

which 146 is the number of neutrons in uranium, and uranium is the 92nd element—as with all elements, it combines its total of inner-layer neutrons with its outer-layer protons. In this instance of uranium we have combined the 149 with 92, which gives us Uranium-238, from which count we can knock out four neutrons from eight of the triangular faces without disturbing symmetry to give us Uranium-234.

986.773   Recently, however, a scientist who had been studying synergetics and attending my lectures called my attention to the fact that the first closest-packed layer 12 around the nuclear sphere and the second embracing closest-packed layer of 42 follow the same neutron count, combining with the outer layer number of protons—as in the 92 uranium-layer case—to provide a physically conceptual model of magnesium and molybdenum. (See Table 419.21.)

986.774   We can report that a number of scientists or scientific-minded laymen are communicating to us their discovery of other physics-evolved phenomena as being elegantly illustrated by synergetics in a conceptually lucid manner.

986.775   Sum-totally we can say that the curve of such events suggests that in the coming decades science in general will have discovered that synergetics is indeed the omnirational, omniconceptual, multialternatived, omnioptimally-efficient, and always experimentally reevidenceable, comprehensive coordinate system employed by nature.

986.776   With popular conception of synergetics being the omniconceptual coordinate system of nature will come popular comprehension of total cosmic technology, and therefore popular comprehension that a competent design revolution—structurally and mechanically—employing the generalized principles governing cosmic technology can indeed render all humanity comprehensively—i.e., physically and metaphysically—successful, i.e., becoming like "hydrogen" or "leverage"—regular member functions of an omnisuccessful Universe.

986.800 Behavioral Proclivities of Spheric Experience

986.810 Discard of Abstract Dimensions

986.811   Inspired by the $E = Mc^2$ modelability, I did more retrospective reconsideration of what I have been concerned with mathematically throughout my life. This reviewing led me to (1) more discoveries, clarifications, and definitions regarding spheres; (2) the discard of the concept of axioms; and (3) the dismissal of three-dimensional reality as being inherently illusory—and the discard of many of mathematics' abstract devices as being inherently "roundabout," "obscurational," and "inefficient."

986.812   Reversion to axioms and three-dimensional "reality" usually occurs on the basis of "Let's be practical . . . let's yield to our ill-informed reflex-conditioning . . . the schoolbooks can't be wrong . . . no use in getting out of step with the system . . . we'll lose our jobs . . . we'll be called nuts."

986.813   Because they cannot qualify as laws if any exceptions to them are found, the generalizable laws of Universe are inherently eternal-timeless-sizeless. Sizing requires time. Time is a cosmically designed consequence of humanity's having been endowed with innate *slowness* of apprehension and comprehension, which lags induce time-lapse-altered concepts. (Compare Sec. 529.09.)

986.814   Time-lapsed apprehension of any and all energy-generated, human-sense-reported, human-brain-image-coordinated, angular-directional realization of any physical experiences, produces (swing-through-zero) momentums of misapprehending, which pulsatingly unbalances the otherwise equilibrious, dimensionless, timeless, zero-error, cosmic intellect perfection thereby only inferentially identified to human apprehending differentiates the conceptioning of all the special case manifests of the generalized laws experienced by each and every human individual.

986.815   Academic thought, overwhelmed by the admitted observational inexactitude of special case human-brain-sense experiences, in developing the particular logic of academic geometry (Euclidean or non-Euclidean), finds the term "identical" to be logically prohibited and adopts the word "similar" to identify *like* geometrical entities. In synergetics, because of its clearly defined differences between generalized primitive conceptuality and special-case time-size realizations, the word "identical" becomes logically permitted. This is brought about by the difference between the *operational* procedures of synergetics and the *abstract* procedures of all branches of conventional geometry, where the word "abstract" deliberately means "nonoperational," because only axiomatic and non-physically-demonstrable.

986.816   In conventional geometry the linear characteristics and the relative sizes of lines dominate the conceptioning and its nomenclature—as, for instance, using the term "equiangular" triangle because only lengths or sizes of lines vary in time. Lines are unlimited in size and can be infinitely extended, whereas angles are discrete fractions of a discrete whole circle. Angles are angles independently of the lengths of their edges. (See Sec. 515.10.) Lengths are always special time-size cases: angles are eternally generalized. . . . We can say with scientific accuracy: "identical equiangular triangles." (See Fig. 986.816.)

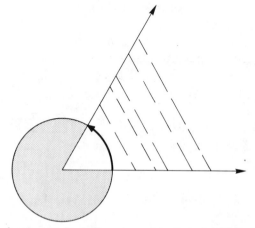

Fig. 986.816 *Angles Are Angles Independent of the Length of their Edges:* Lines are "size" phenomena and unlimited in length. Angle is only a fraction of one cycle.

986.817   In summary, lines are "size" phenomena and are unlimited in length. Size measuring requires "time." Primitive synergetics deals only in angles, which are inherently whole fractions of whole circular azimuths.

986.818   Angles are angles independent of the length of their edges. Triangles are triangles independent of their size. Time is cyclic. Lacking one cycle there is no time sense. Angle is only a fraction of one cycle.

986.819   Synergetics procedure is always from a given whole to the particular fractional angles of the whole system considered. Synergetics employs multiplication only by division. . . . only by division of finite but non-unitarily-conceptual Scenario Universe, subdivided into initially whole primitive systems that divide whole Universe into all the Universe outside the system, all the Universe inside the system, and the little bit of Universe that provides the relevant set of special case stars of experience that illuminatingly define the vertexes of the considered primitive generalized system of consideration. (See Sec. 509.) Conventional geometry "abstracts" by employment of nonexistent—ergo, nondemonstrable—parts, and it compounds a plurality of those nonexistents to arrive at supposedly real objects.

986.820   Because the proofs in conventional geometry depend on a plurality of divider-stepped-off lengths between scribed, punched, or pricked indefinably sized point-speck holes, and because the lengths of the straightedge-drawn lines are extendible without limit, conventional geometry has to assume that any two entities will never be exactly the same. Primitive synergetics has only one length: that of the prime unit vector of the VE and of the isotropic vector matrix.

986.821   Synergetics identifies all of its primitive hierarchy and their holistic subdivisions only by their timeless-sizeless relative angular fractional subdivisions of six equiangular triangles surrounding a point, which hexagonal array equals 360 degrees, if we assume that the three angles of the equiangular triangle always add up to 180 degrees. Synergetics conducts all of its calculations by spherical trigonometry and deals always with the central and surface angles of the primitive hierarchy of pre-time-size relationships of the symmetrically concentric systems around any nucleus of Universe—and their seven great-circle symmetries of the 25 and 31 great-circle systems (Sec. 1040). The foldability of the four great-circle planes demonstrates the four sets of hexagons omnisurrounding the cosmic nucleus in omni-60-degree angular symmetry. This we call the VE. (See Sec. 840.) Angular identities may be operationally assumed to be identical: There is only one equiangular triangle, all of its angles being 60 degrees. The 60-ness comes from the 60 positive and 60 negative, maximum number of surface triangles or T Quanta Modules per cosmic system into which convergent-divergent nuclear unity may be subdivided. The triangle, as physically demonstrated by the tube necklace polygons (Sec. 608), is the only self-stabilizing structure, and the equiangular triangle is the most stable of all triangular structures. Equiangular triangles may be calculatingly employed on an "identical" basis.

986.830   Unrealizability of Primitive Sphere

986.831   As is shown elsewhere (Sec. 1022.11), synergetics finds that the abstract Greek "sphere" does not exist; nor does the quasisphere—the sense-reported "spheric" experiencings of humans—exist at the primitive stage in company with the initial cosmic hierarchy of timeless-sizeless symmetric polyhedra as defined by the six positive and six negative cosmic degrees of freedom and their potential force vectors for adequately coping with all the conditions essential to maintain the individual integrity of min-max primitive, structural, presubdivision systems of Universe.

986.832   The sphere is only dynamically developed either by profiles of spin or by multiplication of uniformly radiused exterior vertexes of ever-higher frequency of modular subdivisioning of the primitive system's initial symmetry of exterior topology. Such exclusively time-size events of sufficiently high frequency of modular subdivisioning, or high frequency of revolution, can transform any one of the primitive (eternal, sizeless, timeless) hierarchy of successive $= 2^1/_2$, 1, $2^1/_2$, 3, 4, 5, 6-tetravolumed concentrically symmetric polyhedra into quasispherical appearances. In respect to each such ever-higher frequency of subdividing or revolving in time, each one of the primitive hierarchy polyhedra's behavioral appearance becomes more spherical.

986.833 The volume of a static quasisphere of unit vector length (radius = 1) is 4.188. Each quasisphere is subexistent because it is not as yet spun and there is as yet no time in which to spin it. Seeking to determine anticipatorily the volumetric value of the as-yet-only-potential sphere's as-yet-to-be-spun domain (as recounted in Secs. *986.206–214*), I converted my synergetics constant 1.0198255 to its ninth power, as already recounted and as intuitively motivated to accommodate the energetic factors involved, which gave me the number 1.192 (see Sec. *982.55*), and with this ninth-powered constant multiplied the incipient sphere's already-third-powered volume of 4.188, which produced the twelfth-powered value 4.99206, which seems to tell us that synergetics' experimentally evidenceable only-by-high-frequency-spinning polyhedral sphere has an unattainable but ever-more-closely-approached limit tetravolume-5.000 α with however a physically imperceptible .007904 volumetric shortfall of tetravolume-5, the limit 4.99206 being the maximum attainable twelfth-powered dynamism—being a sphericity far more perfect than that of any of the planets or fruits or any other of nature's myriads of quasispheres, which shortfallers are the rule and not the exceptions. The primitively nonconceptual, only-incipient sphere's only-potentially-to-be-demonstrated domain, like the square root of minus one, is therefore a useful, approximate-magnitude, estimating tool, but it is not structurally demonstrable. The difference in magnitude is close to that of the T and E Quanta Modules.

986.834 Since structure means an interself-stabilized complex-of-events patterning (Sec. *600.01*), the "spheric" phenomenon is conceptually—sensorially—experienceable only as a time-size high-frequency recurrence of events, an only-by-dynamic sweepout domain, whose complex of involved factors is describable only at the twelfth-power stage. Being nonstructural and involving a greater volumetric sweepout domain than that of their unrevolved structural polyhedral domains, all quasispheres are compressible.

986.835 Independently occurring single bubbles are dynamic and only superficially spherical. In closest packing all interior bubbles of the bubble aggregate become individual, 14-faceted, tension-membrane polyhedra, which are structured only by the interaction with their liquid monomer, closed-system membranes of all the trying-to-escape, kinetically accelerated, interior gas molecules—which interaction can also be described as an omniembracing restraint of the trying-to-escape gaseous molecules by the sumtotal of interatomic, critical-proximity-interattracted structural cohesion of the tensile strength of the bubble's double-molecule-layered (double-bonded) membranes, which comprehensive closed-system embracement is similar to the cosmically total, eternally integral, nonperiodic, omnicomprehensive embracement by gravitation of the always-and-only periodically occurring, differentiated, separate, and uniquely frequenced nonsimultaneous attempts to disintegratingly escape Universe enacted by the individually differentiated sum-total entities (photons) of radiation. Gravity is always generalized, comprehensive, and untunable. Radiation is always special case and tunable.

986.836   Bubbles in either their independent spherical shape or their aggregated polyhedral shapes are structural consequences of the omnidirectionally outward pressing (compression) of the kinetic complex of molecules in their gaseous, single-bonded, uncohered state as comprehensively embraced by molecules in their liquid, double-bonded, coherent state. In the gaseous state the molecules operate independently and disassociatively, like radiation quanta—ergo, less effective locally than in their double-bonded, integrated, gravity-like, liquid-state embracement.

986.840 Primitive Hierarchy as Physical and Metaphysical

986.841   A special case is time-size. Generalization is eternal and is independent of time-size "Spheres," whether as independent bubbles, as highfrequency geodesic polyhedral structures, or as dynamically spun primitive polyhedra, are always and only special case time-size (frequency) physical phenomena.   The omnirational primitive-numbered-tetravolume-interrelationships hierarchy of concentric symmetric polyhedra is the only generalized conceptuality that is both physical and metaphysical. This is to say that the prime number and relative abundance characteristics of the topology, angulation, and the relative tetravolume involvements of the primitive hierarchy are generalized, conceptual metaphysics. Physically evidenced phenomena are always special case, but in special cases are manifests of generalized principles, which generalized principles themselves are also always metaphysical.

986.850 Powerings as Systemic-integrity Factors

986.851   Synergetics is everywhere informed by and dependent on experimental evidence which is inherently witnessable—which means conceptual—and synergetics' primitive structural polyhedra constitute an entire, infralimit-to-ultra-limit, systemic, conceptual, metaphysical hierarchy whose entire interrelationship values are the generalizations of the integral and the "internal affairs" of *all systems* in Universe—both nucleated and nonnucleated. Bubbles and subatomic A, B, T, and E Quanta Modules are nonnucleated containment systems. Atoms are nucleated systems.

986.852   The systemically internal interrelationship values of the primitive cosmic hierarchy are all independent of time-size factorings, all of which generalized primitive polyhedra's structurings are accommodated by and are governed by six positive and six negative degrees of freedom. There are 12 integrity factors that definitively cope with those 12 degrees of freedom to produce integral structural systems—both physical and metaphysical—which integrity factors we will henceforth identify as *powerings*.

986.853   That is, we are abandoning altogether the further employment of the word *dimension,* which suggests (a) special case time-size lengths, and (b) that some of the describable characteristics of systems can exist alone and not as part of a minimum system, which is always a part of a priori eternally regenerative Universe. In lieu of the no longer scientifically tenable concept of "dimension" we are adopting words to describe time-size realizations of generalized, timeless, primitive systems as event complexes, as structural self-stabilizations, and structural intertransformings as first, second, third, etc., local powering states and minimum local systemic involvement with conditons of the cosmic totality environment with its planetary, solar, galactic, complex-galactic, and supergalactic systems and their respective macro-micro isotropicities.

986.854   In addition to the 12-powered primitive structurings of the positive and negative primitive tetrahedron, the latter has its primitive hierarchy of six intertransformable, tetravolumed, symmetrical integrities which require six additional powerings to produce the six rational-valued, relative-volumetric domains. In addition to this 18-powered state of the primitive hierarchy we discover the integrally potential six-way intertransformabilities of the primitive hierarchy, any one of which requires an additional powering factor, which brings us thus far to 24 powering states. Realization of the intertransformings requires time-size, special case, physical transformation of the metaphysical, generalized, timeless-sizeless, primitive hierarchy potentials.

986.855   It is demonstrably evidenceable that the physically realized superimposed intertransformability potentials of the primitive hierarchy of systems are realizable only as observed from other systems. The transformability cannot be internally observed. All primitive systems have potential external observability by other systems. "Otherness" systems have their own inherent 24-powered constitutionings which are not additional powerings—just more of the same.

986.856   All systems have external relationships, any one of which constitutes an additional systemic complexity-comprehending-and-defining-and-replicating power factor. The number of additional powering factors involved in systemic self-systems and otherness systems is determined in the same manner as that of the fundamental interrelationships of self- and otherness systems, where the number of system interrelationships is $\dfrac{n^2 - n}{2}$.

986.857 Not including the $\dfrac{n^2 - n}{2}$ additional intersystems-relationship powerings, beyond the 24 systemically integral powers, there are six additional, only-otherness-viewable (and in some cases only multi-otherness viewable and realizable), unique behavior potentials of all primitive hierarchy systems, each of which behaviors can be comprehensively accounted for only by additional powerings. They are:

25th-power = axial rotation of the system
26th-power = orbital travel of the system
27th-power = expansion-contraction of the system
28th-power = torque (axial twist) of the system
29th-power = inside-outing (involuting-evoluting) of the system
30th-power = intersystem precession (axial tilting) of the system
31st-power = external interprecessionings amongst a plurality of systems
32nd-power = self-steering of a system within the galaxy of systems (precessionally accomplished)
33rd-power = universal synergistic totality comprehensive of all intersystem effects and ultimate micro- and macroisotropicity of VE-ness

986.860   Rhombic Dodecahedron 6 Minus Polyhedron 5 Equals Unity

986.861 High-frequency, triangulated unit-radius-vertexed, geodesically interchorded, spherical polyhedral apparencies are also structural developments in time-size. There are therefore two kinds of spherics: the high-frequency-event-stabilized, geodesic, structural polyhedron and the dynamically spun, only superficially "apparent" spheres. The static, structural, multifaceted, polyhedral, geodesic sphere's vertexes are uniformly radiused only by the generalized vector, whereas the only superficially spun and only apparently profiled spheres have a plurality of vertexial distances outward from their systemic center, some of which distances are greater than unit vector radius while some of the vertexes are at less than unit vector radius distance. (See Fig. *986.314.*)

986.862 Among the symmetrical polyhedra having a tetravolume of 5 and also having radii a little more or a little less than that of unit vector radius, are the icosahedron and the enenicontahedron whose mean radii of spherical profiling are less than four percent vector-aberrant. There is, however, one symmetrical primitive polyhedron with two sets of its vertexes at greater than unit radius distance outwardly from their system's nucleic center; that is the rhombic dodecahedron, having, however, a tetravolume of 6. The rhombic dodecahedron's tetravolume of 6 may account for the minimum intersystemness in pure principle, being the space between omni-closest-packed unit-radius spheres and the spheres themselves. And then there is one symmetric primitive polyhedron having a volume of exactly tetravolume 5 and an inter-pattern radius of .9995 of one unit vector; this is the T Quanta Module phase rhombic triacontahedron. There is also an additional rhombic triacontahedron of exact vector radius and a tetravolume of 5.007758031, which is just too much encroachment upon the rhombic dodecahedron 6 minus the triacontahedron $5 \rightarrow 6 - 5 = 1$, or one volumetric unit of unassigned cosmic "fail-safe space": BANG—radiation-entropy and eventual turnaround precessional fall-in to syntropic photosynthetic transformation into one of matter's four states: plasmic, gaseous, liquid, crystalline.

986.863 All the hierarchy of primitive polyhedra were developed by progressive great-circle-spun hemispherical halvings of halvings and trisectings of halvings and quintasectings (see Sec. *100.1041*) of halvings of the initial primitive tetrahedron itself. That the rhombic triacontahedron of contact-facet radius of unit vector length had a trigonometrically calculated volume of 4.998 proved in due course not to be a residual error but the "critical difference" between matter and radiation. This gives us delight in the truth whatever it may be, recalling that all the discoveries of this chronicle chapter were consequent only to just such faith in the truth, no matter how initially disturbing to misinformed and misconditioned reflexes it may be.

986.870 Nuclear and Nonnuclear Module Orientations

986.871 The rhombic triacontahedron may be fashioned of 120 trivalently bonded T Quanta Module tetrahedra, or of either 60 bivalently interbonded positive T Modules or of 60 bivalently interbonded negative T Modules. In the rhombic triacontahedron we have only radiantly arrayed basic energy modules, arrayed around a single spheric nuclear-inadequate volumetric domain with their acute "corners" pointed inwardly toward the system's volumetric center, and their centers of mass arrayed outwardly of the system— ergo, prone to escape from the system.

986.872 In the tetrahedron constructed exclusively of 24 A Modules, and in the octahedron constructed of 48 A and 48 B Modules, the asymmetric tetrahedral modules are in radical groups, with their acute points arrayed outwardly of the system and their centers of mass arrayed inwardly of the system—ergo, prone to maintain their critical mass interattractive integrity. The outer sharp points of the A and B Modules are located at the centers of the four or six corner spheres defining the tetrahedron and octahedron, respectively. The fact that the tetrahedron's and octahedron's A and B Modules have their massive centers of volume pointing inwardly of the system all jointly interarrayed in the concentric layers of the VE, whereas in the rhombic triacontahedron (and even more so in the half-Couplers of the rhombic dodecahedron) we have the opposite condition—which facts powerfully suggest that the triacontahedron, like its congruent icosahedron's nonnuclear closest-possible-packed omniarray, presents the exclusively radiational aspect of a "one" or of a "no" nuclear-sphere-centered and isolated most "spheric" polyhedral system to be uniquely identified with the nonnuclear bubble, the one-molecule-deep, kinetically-escape-prone, gas-molecules-containing bubble.

986.8721 In the case of the rhombic dodecahedra we find that the centers of volume of their half-Couplers' A and B Modules occur almost congruently with their respective closest-packed, unit-radius sphere's outward ends and thereby concentrate their energies at several spherical-radius levels in respect to a common nuclear-volume-adequate center—all of which suggests some significant relationship of this condition with the various spherical-radius levels of the electron "shells."

986.873 The tetrahedron and octahedron present the "gravitational" model of self-and-otherness interattractive systems which inherently provide witnessable evidence of the systems' combined massive considerations or constellations of their interbindings.

986.874 The highly varied alternate A and B Module groupings permitted within the same primitive rhombic dodecahedron, vector equilibrium, and in the Couplers, permit us to consider a wide spectrum of complexedly reorientable potentials and realizations of intermodular behavioral proclivities lying in proximity to one another between the extreme radiational or gravitational proclivities, and all the reorientabilities operative within the same superficially observed space (Sec. 954). All these large numbers of potential alternatives of behavioral proclivities may be circumferentially, embracingly arrayed entirely within the same superficially observed isotropic field.

987.00   Multiplication Only by Division

•[*987.00–987.416 Multiplication by Division Scenario*]

987.010   Operational Scenario in Proof of Multiplication Only by Progressive Divisioning of Simplest Vectorially Structured Polyhedra

987.011   Six equi-zero-magnitude, mass-times-velocity-produced vectors representing the six equi-energetic, differently angled (i.e., differently directioned) cosmic forces that always cointeract to freshly reinitiate minimum local structuring in Universe, constitute the minimum-maximum cosmic set of coordinates necessary to formulate a definitive system. A system is the first finite unitarily conceptual subdivision of finite but nonunitarily conceptual Scenario Universe. (See Sec. 400.011 and especially Fig. 401.)

987.012   A system is a polyhedral pattern—regular or irregular—that definitively closes back upon itself topologically to subdivide Universe locally into four parts: (1) all the Universe outside the system, the macrocosm; (2) all the Universe within the system, the microcosm; (3) the convex-outside little bit of the Universe of which the system itself is constituted; and (4) the concave-inside little bit of the Universe of which the system is constituted.

987.013   The tetrahedron, with its six equi-lengthed vector edges and four vertexes and with its four triangular windows, is experimentally demonstrable to be the topologically simplest structural system of Universe.

987.020   Topological Uniqueness

987.021   Recognizing that angles are conceptual independent of the lengths of the lines converging to form them, it follows that a triangle or a tetrahedron or any polygons or polyhedra are conceptual—and conceptually *different*—quite independent of the time-size lengths of the lines defining the polyhedra. All primitive non-space-time differences are exclusively angular and topological.

987.022   The topological variables of systems are identified exclusively as the unique number of vertexes (points), faces (areas), and edges (lines) of the system considered.

987.030   Finite Synergetics

987.031   Starting with mass = zero and velocity = zero (i.e., $MV = 0$), as the energy-quantum product of the six vectors of the minimum structural system in Universe (that is, each of the tetrahedron's six equi-lengthed edges individually = 0), the mathematical art and science known as *Synergetics* provides a cosmically comprehensive mathematical strategy of employing always and only physically demonstrable, omnidimensional, quantum-compatible *multiplication only by division* of a no-gain-no-loss, no-beginning-no-ending, omnicomplexedly and nonsimultaneously overlapping, ceaselessly and differently intertransforming, eternally self-regenerative, 100-percent-efficient, energetic Universe.

987.032   The omnidirectionally multiplying amplification of information in Universe is arrived at only by discretely progressive subdivision of the structural system that has been already experimentally and operationally demonstrated to be the simplest—the regular tetrahedron.

987.033   Synergetics progressively divides and progressively discovers the omnirational tetrahedral-related volumes (see Table *1033.192* for table of tetravolume values) and the other topological and angular characteristics of the great-circle-spun, hemisystem cleavages and their respective fractionation resultants. This progressive synergetic division and discovery describes the entire primitive hierarchy of timeless-sizeless, omnisymmetrical, omniconcentric, omniintertransformative, intercommensurable,* systemic polyhedral structures. (See cosmic hierarchy at Table 982.62.)

987.040   Macro-medio-micro Mensuration Limits

987.041   Primitive unity is at minimum a union of two uniquely individual quantum vectorizations of each member of the primitive minimum polyhedral system hierarchy, each of whose polyhedra described by the quantum vectorizations are complementarily intravolumed and intra-energetic. The quantum-vectored polyhedra of the primitive hierarchy are always *relative* volumetrically, topologically, and vectorially—

   —*micro* to the tetrahedron as the minimum structural system of Universe, and

   —*macro* to the icosahedron as the maximum volume for the least energy investment structural system of Universe.

Intercommensurable means the uniform proportional interequatability of two or more separate, volumetrically interrational, geometrical sets. These sets have different divisors, which are noninterrational but interproportionally constant and successively intertransformative.

987.042 *Micro tetra* and *macro icosa* always and only coact as cosmic unity equaling at least two. This incommensurable pair serves as the two only separately rational—but proportionately constant and interequatable—mensuration reference limits in all geometrical, topological, chemical, and quantum-coordinate scientific interconsiderability.

987.043 The *medio octahedron* serves as the average, between-limits, most structurally expedient, and most frequently employed of the three prime structural systems of Universe. It is significant that the limit case pair *micro tetra* and *macro icosa* are both prime numbers—1 and 5—whereas the *medio octa* is a second power of 2, the only prime even number in Universe: $2^2 = 4$.

987.044 The self-regeneration of the nonsimultaneously and only-partially-overlappingly-episoded, beginningless and endless Scenario Universe inherently requires in pure principle an eternal incommensurability of—at minimum two—overall symmetrical and concentric system intertransformative behaviors and characteristic phases.

987.050 Intercommensurable Functions of Jitterbug

987.051 The vector equilibrium of tetravolume-20 = prime 5 × prime 2^2, is rationally coordinate with the tetrahedron representing the prime number 1 and with the octahedron representing the prime number 2. But the 20-tetravolume (5×2^2) VE is inherently incommensurable with the icosahedron, which represents the prime number 5 compounded with $\sqrt{2}$, even though the VE and icosa are concentrically and omnisymmetrically intertransformable (see Secs. 461.02–06).

987.052 The mathematical span between the second power of 2, $(2^2 = 4)$ and the second root of 2, $(\sqrt{2})$—which is the same proportional relationship as that existing between $\sqrt{2}$ and 1—is the constant proportional accommodating median between tetra 1 and octa 2 and between the first two prime numbers: between the most primitive odd and even, between the most primitive yes and no of the primitive binary system—ergo, of all computer mathematics.

987.053 The 2 as constant proportional equity median is clearly evidenced as each of the VE's six square unit-length-vector-edged faces jitterbuggingly transform into the two unit-vector-edged equilateral triangles. We recall that the diagonal of each square was the hypotenuse of a right-angle-apexed, unit-vector-edged isosceles triangle whose hypotenuse jitterbuggingly contracted in length to the length of each of the unit-vector edges. We have the well-known formula for the second power of the hypotenuse equaling the sum of the second powers of the right triangle's right-angle sides, and since the right-angle-apexed isosceles triangle's sides were of unit-vector length = 1, the second powers of both equal 1. The sum of their second powers was 2, and the length of the square's hypotenuse diagonal $= \sqrt{2}$. Ergo, the total linear alteration of the VE $\rightarrow$ icosa was the contraction of $\sqrt{2} \rightarrow 1$. This introduces one of nature's most profound incommensurability equations, wherein

$$2 : \sqrt{2} = \sqrt{2} : 1$$

987.054   Proportionately expressed this equation reads:

$$\text{VE} : \text{icosa} = 2 : \sqrt{2} = \sqrt{2} : 1$$

Fractionally expressed the equation reads:

$$\frac{\text{VE}}{\text{icosa}} = \frac{2}{\sqrt{2}} = \frac{\sqrt{2}}{1}$$

Thus we have a sublime equation of constant proportionality of otherwise inherently incommensurate value sets.

987.055   In the jitterbug, as the 20-tetravolume VE contracts symmetrically through the icosahedral phase with a tetravolume of 18.51229587, and then ever symmetrically contracts to the bivalent octahedral phase of tetravolume-4, the six-membered axis of the concentric system does not rotate while the other 18 nonaxis "equatorial" members rotate around the axis. (Fig. 460.08.)

987.056   As the system contraction continues beyond the octahedron stage of tetravolume-4, the axis also torques and contracts as the octahedron either (1) contracts symmetrically and rotationally into the regular tetrahedron of tetravolume-1 (or counterrotates into the alternate regular tetrahedron of tetravolume-1), or (2) flattens by contraction of its axis to form zerovolume, edge-congruent pair of triangular patterns; thereafter the triangle's three corners are foldable alternately into the quadrivalent positive or the quadrivalent negative regular tetrahedron of tetravolume-1.

987.057   Since all 24 internal radiation vectors had been removed before the jitterbugging, leaving only the 24 external gravitation vectors, the transformation is systematically comprehensive and embraces all the complex unities of the VE and icosa and their only-proportionally-equatable, separately rational, geometrical membership sets. Though the tetra and icosa are incommensurable with each other, the octahedron is transformatively commensurable with either.

987.058   The inherent volumetric incommensurability of VE and icosa (and their respective four- and three-unique-symmetrical-great-circle-system sets), compounded with the ability of the octahedron to intertransformably interconnect these two otherwise incommensurables, produces the energetic oscillations, resonances, and intertransformings of the eternally regenerative Universe. This eternal disquietude regeneration of Universe is also accommodated by the fact that the tetra and VE are a priori incommensurable with the icosa. Despite this the rhombic triacontahedron of tetravolume-5 (as a product of the icosa's 15-great-circle cleavaging), while under the oscillatory pressuring, is volumetrically and rationally coordinate with the tetrahedron and the state we speak of as matter—and when it is under the negative tensive pressure of the oscillatory Universe, it transforms from matter to radiation. (See scenario of T and E Modules at Sec. *986*.)

987.060 Isotropic Limits

987.061 Cosmic regeneration, metaphysical and physical, involves phases of maximum asymmetry or of random pattern uniqueness. The self-regeneration propagated by the eternal war of incommensurability occurs at the medio phase of Universe; the propagation commences at the middle and proceeds syntropically outward or recedes syntropically inward from the maxi-entropic center in both macro and micro directions with the ultrasyntropic isotropic macrophase being manifest in the interspacing of the galaxies and with the infra syntropic, isotropic microphase being manifest kinetically in time-size as "cosmic background radiation" and statically (timelessly, sizelessly) in the closest packing of unit radius spheres, like the aggregates of atoms of any one element.

987.062 The median turbulence and kaleidoscopically nonrepetitive, random, individually unique, local patterning events occur between the four successive, symmetrically orderly, "click-stop" phases of the hierarchy of primitive polyhedra: VE, icosa, octa, and tetra. Between the four maximum symmetrical phases the (overall symmetrical, internally asymmetrical) evolutionary events of Universe are empirically and operationally manifest by the VE jitterbugging: they are infinitely different as multiplication only by division is infinitely employed. Time-size infinity is embraced by primitive finity.

987.063 In the VE jitterbug the local patterning events of Universe rotate outwardly to the macro isotropicity of VE, which can rotate beyond macro to converge symmetrically again through the central phase of the icosa → octa transformation. The maximum incommensurability occurs between the latter two, whereafter octa transforms to tetra. The tetra occurs at the microphase of radiation isotropicity and itself transforms and rotates via the negative tetra, expanding again through the negative phases of the octa's duo-twoness → octa → icosa → alternate VE.

987.064 VE is potentially pattern-divisible both positively and negatively and both internally and surfacewise. Icosahedron is potentially pattern-divisible both positively and negatively and both internally and surfacewise. The octahedron has internal comprehensive (duo-tet) twoness of 2^2, 2, $\sqrt{2}$. Tetrahedron is likewise both positively and negatively integrally intertransformable.

987.065   The incommensurability of the icosa derives from its lack of a nucleus. The VE is inherently nucleated. The primitive tetra is nonnuclear but acquires a nucleus with frequency. The icosa cannot acquire a nucleus whatever the frequency. (See Sec. *466* and Fig. *466.01* for jitterbug transformation pumping out of nuclear sphere.)

987.066   Since multiplication is accomplished only by division, we observe that the macroisotropicity of seemingly Expanding Universe is equally explicable as the shrinking relative magnitude of the system viewpoint of the observer. (See Secs. *986.756–57* and *1052.62*.)

987.067   Octaphase: The eternally inherent incommensurability of the regenerative turmoil of eternally self-regenerative Universe occurs always at its mediophase of intertransforming between VE and icosa and between icosa and tetra: at these mediophases the never-repeating maxi-asymmetry patterns are generated.

987.070   Topological Minima

987.071   In synergetics all topological characteristics are interconformationally conceptual independent of size; for instance, a vertex is one of the convergence loci of a system's inherent plurality of conceptual interrelationships.

987.072   Since vertexes are omnidimensional, system topology deals with the loci of interrelationship convergences at any one of the system's set of defining loci—with a closest-packing-of-spheres-imposed maximum of 12 unit-radius convergences around any one unit-radius locus sphere. In the latter case vertexes may be predominantly identified as spheres of unit radius and may identify a prime nucleated system.

987.073   The minimum conceptual system in Universe is the regular tetrahedron, which consists of a minimum of four vertexes that can be represented as four approximately intertangent, equiradius spheres. Vertex-representing spheres do not occur in Universe or become conceptually considerable in sets of less than four. (This process is described at Secs. *100.331* and 411. A minimum of four successive events and three intervals is required to define a frequency cycle; see Sec. *526.23*.) In the same way lines—or *edges*, as they are spoken of in topology—occur only in sets of six, as the most economical interrelationships of vertexes of polyhedral systems.

987.074   The minimum system in Universe is the tetrahedron; its unit-radius spheres at each of the four vertexes have a minimum of six intersystem vertexial relationships. We have learned that topological system vertex interrelationships always occur in sets of six. The formula for the number of system interrelationships is $\dfrac{n^2 - n}{2}$, wherein n is the number of system vertexes (or unit radius spheres). A tetrahedron has four vertexes: $4^2 = 16$, minus $n4 = 12$, divided by $2 = 6$—i.e., the number of unique vertex interrelationship lines of the minimum structural system—the tetrahedron—is six.

987.075　Although Alfred North Whitehead and Bertrand Russell did not recognize the full conceptual implications, their "new mathematics" of set theory and empty sets were tour de force attempts by the leading abstract non-conceptual mathematicians of their day to anticipate the inevitable historical convergence of their mathematics with the inherently conceptual topology of Euler, as well as with the phase rule of Gibbs in chemistry, the simplified quantum mechanics of Dirac in physics, and the homogenizing biochemistry and physics of virology's DNA-RNA design programming—all remotely but inexorably rendezvousing with Boltzmann's, Einstein's, and Hubble's astrophysics and cosmology to constitute unitary science's unitary self-regenerative, untenably equilibrious, cosmic-coordinate system to be embraced and accommodated by the epistemography of synergetics.

987.076　What are known in the terminology of topology as *faces*—the polyhedron's *hedra* sides or facets—are known in synergetics as *windows*, being the consequences of system-vertex interrelationship lines framing or viewing "windows of nothingness"—windows opening to a nonconvergence, to nonrelatedness, to the untuned-in. Nothingness is the *at-present-untuned-in* information of each special case individual's special local-in-Universe, momentary, tuned-in, preoccupying consideration. Vertexes are tuned-in; *hedra* are untuned-in, ergo *out*. *Hedra* faces are system *outs*.

987.077　Unit radius spheres are unit-wavelength, tuned-in, event loci; topological faces (Greek *hedra*) are all the windows looking out upon all the rest of the Universe's presently-untuned-in information in respect to the considered or tuned-in system.

987.078　Since two system-interrelationship lines (vectorially energetic in pure principle) cannot pass through the same point at the same time, the windows' "corners" are always superimposed time-crossing aspects—one crossing behind or in front of, but not touching, the other. The topological windows of synergetics are polygonal aspects of the system's interrelationships and not of physical lines.

987.079　Synergetics' experimentally produced, minimum-structural-system subdivisions of Universe have four tuned-in vertexial loci, four windows looking toward all the untuned-in complementary balance of Universe, and six vertexial interrelationship vector lines, with all the latter occurring as outermost system features. The minimum nonnucleated structural system does not require internal vertexes.

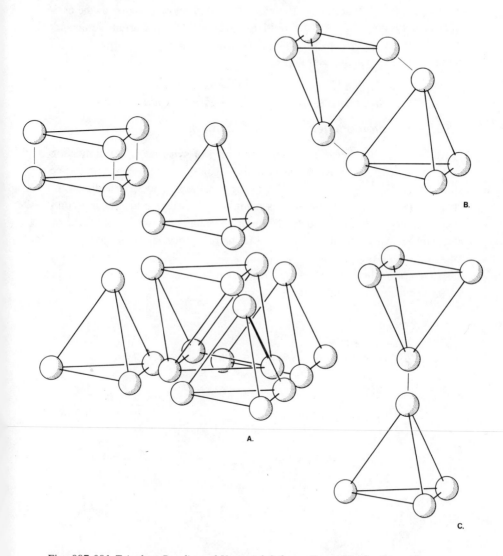

Fig. *987.081 Trivalent Bonding of Vertexial Spheres Form Rigids:* At c: *Gases* are monovalent, single-bonded, omniflexible, inadequate-interattraction, separatist, compressible. At b: *Liquids* are bivalent, double-bonded, hinged, flexible, viscous integrity. At a: *Rigids* are trivalent, triple-bonded, rigid, highest tension coherence.

987.080 Vertexial Spheres Form Rigids

987.081 In addition to the four vertexial spheres of the precleavage primitive tetrahedron, we find after the cleavage all six vertexial unit-radius-vertex spheres of the octahedron also occurring in the outermost structure of the nonnucleated system. Neither the primitive tetrahedron nor the primitive octahedron have internal or nuclear unit-radius-vertex spheres. For an illustration of these structural "rigids" see Fig. *987.081*.

987.100 Great-circle-spun Symmetries and Cleavagings

987.110 Intercommensurability Functions

987.111 In the great-circle-spun cleavaging of synergetics' multiplication only by division there are seven primitive symmetries of spinnability. (See Sec. 1040.) Four symmetries belong directly to the separate tetrahedral commensurability, and three symmetries belong to the separate icosahedral commensurability, with the integrity of eternal interrelationship being provided by the symmetrically contractive, concentric intertransformability of the two sets of symmetry at the jitterbug VE→icosa stage. This symmetrically embraced intertransformable stage corresponds to the constant interproportionality stage of the VE and icosa manifest as

$$2 : \sqrt{2} = \sqrt{2} : 1.$$

987.120 Sequence of Symmetries and Cleavagings

987.121 Table

	Symmetry Sequence	*Cleavage Sequence*
	Symmetry #1: —three great circles	Cleavage #1
	Symmetry #2: —four great circles	Cleavage #4
TETRA	Symmetry #3: —six great circles (VE)	Cleavages #2 & 3
	Symmetry #4: —12 great circles	

Thereafter we have the jitterbug transformation of the VE → icosa and the further progressive halvings of:

	Symmetry #5	
	—six great circles (icosa)	Cleavage #6
ICOSA	Symmetry #6 —15 great circles	Cleavage #5
	Symmetry #7 —10 great circles (producing the S Modules and T & E Modules)	Cleavage #7

(See also Secs. 1025.14, 1040, *1041.10*.)

987.122   Starting with the regular tetrahedron the progressive primitive subdividing of synergetics is initially accomplished only by the successive equatorial halvings of the progressively halved-out parts of the first four of the only seven cosmic symmetries of axial spin of the primitive structural systems.

987.130 Primary and Secondary Great-circle Symmetries

987.131   There are seven other *secondary* symmetries based on the pairing into spin poles of vertexes produced by the complex secondary crossings of one another of the seven original great circle symmetries.

987.132   The primary and secondary icosa symmetries altogether comprise $121 = 11^2$ great circles. (See Fig. *987.132E*.)

987.133   The crossing of the primary 12 great circles of the VE at G (see Fig. 453.01, as revised in third printing) results in 12 new axes to generate 12 new great circles. (See color plate 12.)

987.134   The crossing of the primary 12 great circles of the VE and the four great circles of the VE at C (Fig. 453.01) results in 24 new axes to generate 24 new great circles. (See color plate 13.)

987.135   The crossing of the primary 12 great circles of the VE and the six great circles of the VE at E (Fig. 453.01) results in 12 new axes to generate 12 new great circles. (See color plate 14.)

987.136   The remaining crossing of the primary 12 great circles of the VE at F (Fig. 453.01) results in 24 more axes to generate 24 new great circles. (See color plate 15.)

987.137   The total of the above-mentioned *secondary* great circles of the VE is 96 new great circles (See Fig *987.137B*.)

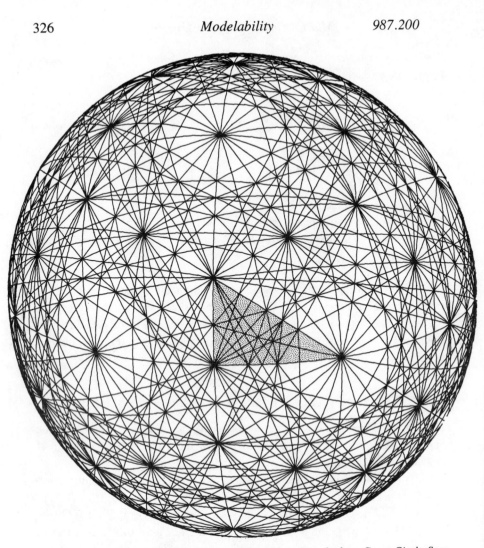

Fig. *987.132E Composite of Primary and Secondary Icosahedron Great Circle Sets:*
This is a black-and-white version of color plate 30. The Basic Disequilibrium 120
LCD triangle as presented at Fig. 901.03 appears here shaded in the spherical grid. In
this composite icosahedron spherical matrix all of the 31 primary great circles appear
together with the three sets of secondary great circles. (The three sets of secondary
icosahedron great circles are shown successively at color plates 27–29.)

987.200   Cleavagings Generate Polyhedral Resultants

987.210   Symmetry #1 and Cleavage #1

987.211   In Symmetry #1 and Cleavage #1 three great circles—the lines
in Figs. 987.210 A through F— are successively and cleavingly spun by using

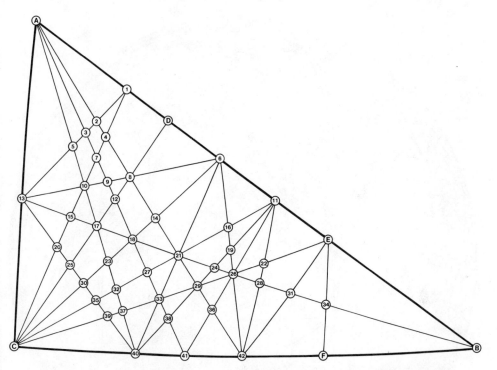

Fig. *987.132F Net Diagram of Angles and Edges for Basic Disequilibrium 120 LCD Triangle:* This is a detail of the basic spherical triangle shown shaded in Fig. *987.132E* and at Fig. *901.03.* It is the key to the trigonometric tables for the spherical central angles, the spherical face angles, the planar edge lengths, and the planar face angles presented at Table *987.132G.*

the midpoints of each of the tetrahedron's six edges as the six poles of three intersymmetrical axes of spinning to fractionate the primitive tetrahedron, first into the 12 equi-vector-edged octa, eight Eighth-octa (each of ½-tetravolume), and four regular tetra (each of 1-tetravolume).

987.212   A simple example of Symmetry #1 appears at Fig. 835.11. Cleavage #1 is illustrated at Fig. *987.210E.*

987.213   Figs. *987.210A-E* demonstrate Cleavage #1 in the following sequences: (1) The red great circling cleaves the tetrahedron into two asymmetric but identically formed and identically volumed "chef's hat" halves of the initial primitive tetrahedron (Fig. *987.210A*). (2) The blue great circling cleavage of each of the two "chef's hat" halves divides them into four identically formed and identically volumed "iceberg" asymmetrical quarterings of the initial primitive tetrahedron (Fig. *987.210B*). (3) The yellow great circling cleavage of the four "icebergs" into two conformal types of equivolumed one-Eighthings of the initial primitive tetrahedron—four of these

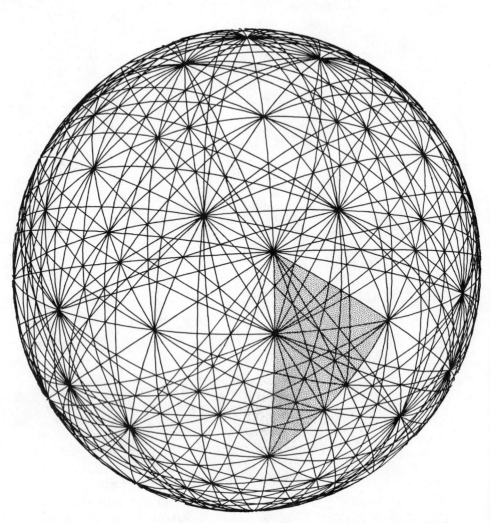

Fig. *987.137B Composite of Primary and Secondary Vector Equilibrium Great Circle Sets:* This is a black-and-white version of color plate 16. The Basic Equilibrium 48 LCD triangle as presented at Fig. 453.01 appears here shaded in the spherical grid. In this composite vector equilibrium spherical matrix all the 25 primary great circles appear together with the four sets of secondary great circles. (The four sets of secondary vector equilibrium great circles are shown successively at color plates 12–15.)

Fig. *987.137C Net Diagram of Angles and Edges for Basic Equilibrium 48 LCD Triangle in Vector Equilibrium Grid:* This is a coded detail of the basic spherical triangle shown shaded in Fig. *987.137B* and at Fig. 453.01. It is the key to the trigonometry tables for the spherical central angles, the spherical face angles, the planar edge lengths, and the planar face angles presented at Table *987.137D*. (The drawing shows the spherical phase: angle and edge ratios are given for both spherical and planar phases.)

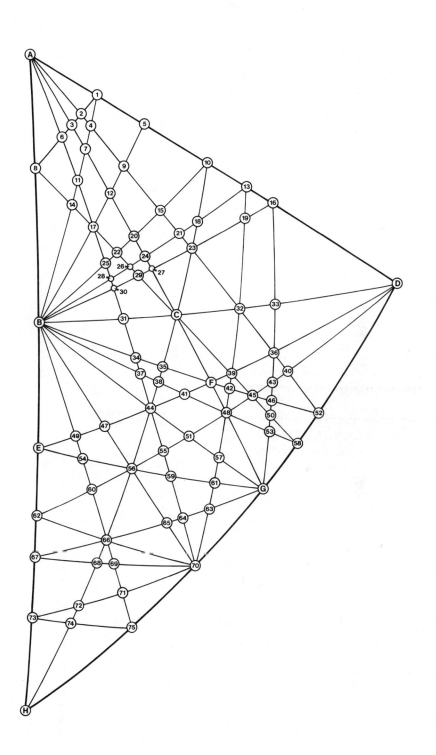

one-Eighthings being regular tetra of half the vector-edge-length of the original tetra and four of these one-Eighthings being asymmetrical tetrahedra
quarter octa with five of their six edges having a length of the unit vector = 1
and the sixth edge having a length of $\sqrt{2} = 1.414214$. (Fig. *987.210C*.)

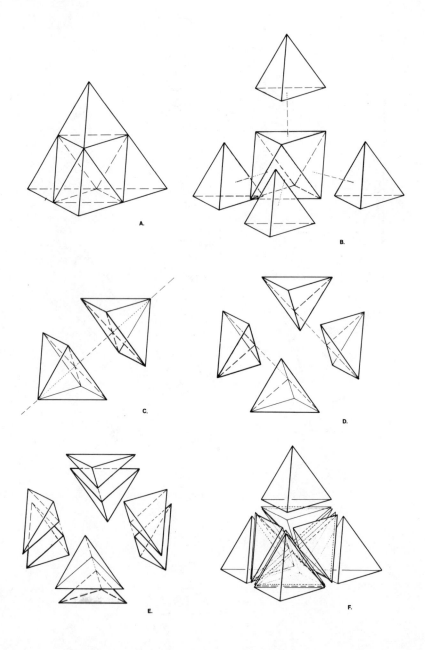

987.220 Symmetry #2 and Cleavage #4:

987.221   In Symmetry #2 and Cleavage #4 the four-great-circle cleavage of the octahedron is accomplished through spinning the four axes between the octahedron's eight midface polar points, which were produced by Cleavage #2. This symmetrical four-great-circle spinning introduces the nucleated 12 unit-radius spheres closest packed around one unit-radius sphere with the 24 equi-vector outer-edge-chorded and the 24 equi-vector-lengthed, congruently paired radii—a system called the vector equilibrium. The VE has 12 external vertexes around one center-of-volume vertex, and altogether they locate the centers of volume of the 12 unit-radius spheres closest packed around one central or one nuclear event's locus-identifying, omnidirectionally tangent, unit-radius nuclear sphere.

987.222   The vectorial and gravitational proclivities of nuclear convergence of all synergetics' system interrelationships intercoordinatingly and intertransformingly permit and realistically account all *radiant* entropic growth of systems as well as all *gravitational* coherence, symmetrical contraction, and shrinkage of systems. Entropic radiation and dissipation growth and syntropic gravitational-integrity convergency uniquely differentiate synergetics' natural coordinates from the *XYZ*–centimeter-gram-second abstract coordinates of conventional formalized science with its omniinterperpendicular and omniinterparallel nucleus-void frame of coordinate event referencing.

987.223   Symmetry #2 is illustrated at Fig. 841.15A.

987.230 Symmetries #1 & 3; Cleavages #1 & 2

987.231   Of the seven equatorial symmetries first employed in the progression of self-fractionations or cleavages, we use the tetrahedron's six mid-

---

Fig. *987.210 Subdivision of Tetrahedral Unity: Symmetry #1:*

A. Initial tetrahedron at two-frequency stage.
B. Tetrahedron is truncated: four regular corner tetra surround a central octa. The truncations are not produced by great-circle cleavages. C, D, and E show great-circle cleavages of the central octahedron. (For clarity, the four corner tetra are not shown.) Three successive great-circle cleavages of the tetrahedron are spun by the three axes connecting the midpoints of opposite pairs of the tetra's six edges.
C. First great-circle cleavage produces two Half-Octa.
D. Second great-circle cleavage produces a further subdivision into four irregular tetra called "Icebergs."
E. Third great-circle cleavage produces the eight Eighth-Octahedra of the original octa.
F. Eight Eighth-Octa and four corner tetras reassembled as initial tetrahedron.

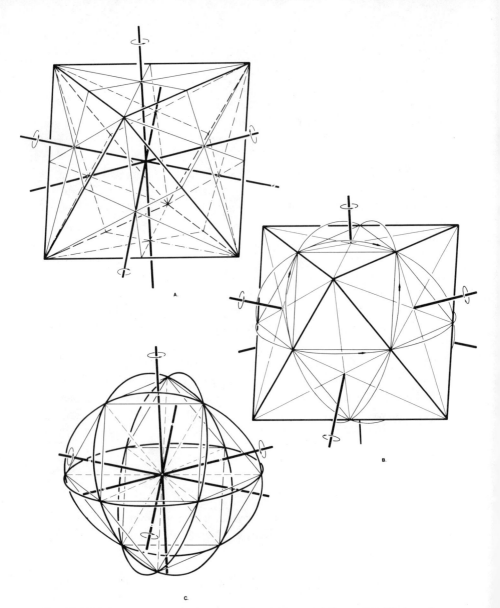

Fig. *987.221 Four-great-circle Systems of Octahedron and Vector Equilibrium: Symmetry #2:*

A. Six-great-circle fractionation of octahedron (as shown in Figs. *987.240B* and *C*) defines centers of octa faces; interconnecting the pairs of opposite octa faces provides the octahedron's four axes of symmetry—here shown extended.

B. Four mid-face-connected spin axes of octahedron generate four great circle trajectories.

C. Octahedron removed to reveal inadvertent definition of vector equilibrium by octahedron's four great circles. The four great circles of the octahedron and the four great circles of the vector equilibrium are in coincidental congruence. (The vector equilibrium is a truncated octahedron; their triangular faces are in parallel planes.)

edge poles to serve as the three axes of spinnability. These three great-circle spinnings delineate the succession of cleavages of the 12 edges of the tetra-contained octahedron whose six vertexes are congruent with the regular tetrahedron's six midedge polar spin points. The octahedron resulting from the first cleavage has 12 edges; they produce the additional external surface lines necessary to describe the two-frequency, non-time-size subdividing of the primitive one-frequency tetrahedron. (See Sec. *526.23,* which describes how four happenings' loci are required to produce and confirm a system discovery.)

987.232   The midpoints of the 12 edges of the octahedron formed by the first cleavage provide the 12 poles for the further great-circle spinning and Cleavage #2 of both the tetra and its contained octa by the six great circles of Symmetry #3. Cleavage #2 also locates the center-of-volume nucleus of the tetra and separates out the center-of-volume-surrounding 24 A Quanta Modules of the tetra and the 48 B Quanta Modules of the two-frequency, tetra-contained octa. (See Sec. 942 for orientations of the A and B Quanta Modules.)

987.240 Symmetry #3 and Cleavage #3

987.241   Symmetry #3 and Cleavage #3 mutually employ the six-polar-paired, 12 midedge points of the tetra-contained octa to produce the six sets of great-circle spinnabilities that in turn combine to define the two (one positive, one negative) tetrahedra that are intersymmetrically arrayed with the common-nuclear-vertexed location of their eight equi-interdistanced, outwardly and symmetrically interarrayed vertexes of the "cube"—the otherwise nonexistent, symmetric, square-windowed hexahedron whose overall most economical intervertexial relationship lines are by themselves unstructurally (non-triangularly) stabilized. The positive and negative tetrahedra are internally trussed to form a stable eight-cornered structure superficially delineating a "cube" by the most economical and intersymmetrical interrelationships of the eight vertexes involved. (See Figs. *987.240* and *241.*)

987.242   In this positive-negative superficial cube of tetravolume-3 there is combined an eight-faceted, asymmetric *hourglass* polyhedron of tetravolume-$1\frac{1}{2}$, which occurs interiorly of the interacting tetrahedra's edge lines, and a complex asymmetric *doughnut* cored hexahedron of tetravolume-$1\frac{1}{2}$, which surrounds the interior tetra's edge lines but occurs entirely inside and completely fills the space between the superficially described "cube" defined by the most economical interconnecting of the eight vertexes and the interior $1\frac{1}{2}$-tetravolume *hourglass* core. (See Fig. *987.242E.*)

987.243   An illustration of Symmetry #3 appears at Fig. 455.11A.

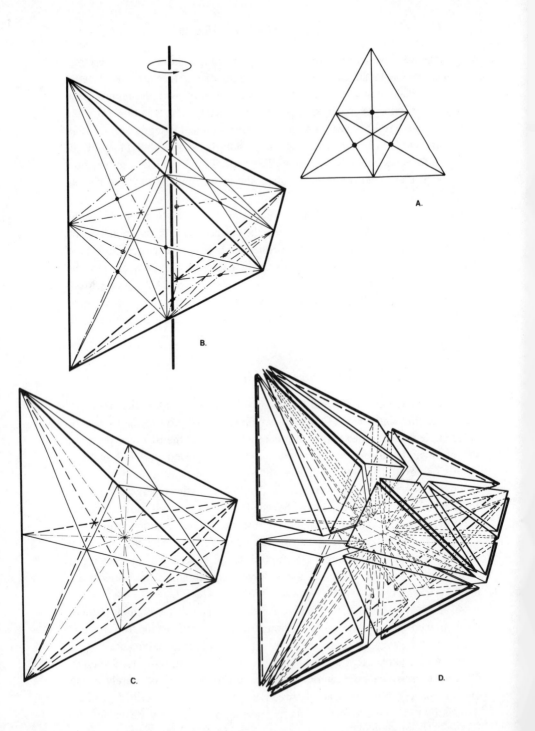

A.

B.

C.

D.

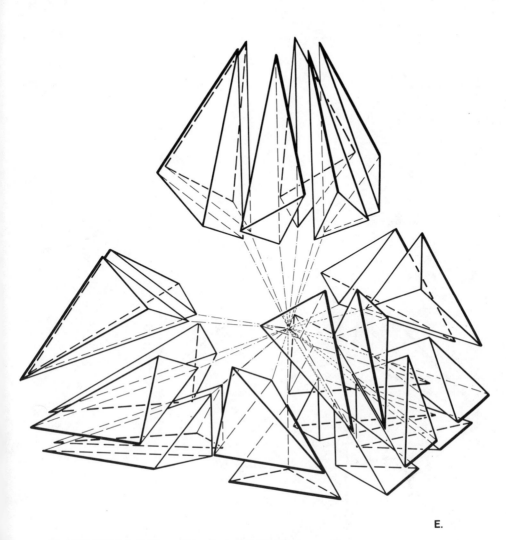

E.

Fig. 987.230 Subdivision of Tetrahedral Unity: Symmetry #3:

A. The large triangle is the tetrahedron face. The smaller inscribed triangle is formed by connecting the mid-points of the tetra edges and represents the octa face congruent with the plane of the tetra face.

B. Connecting the midpoints of the opposite pairs of the internal octahedron's 12 edges provides the six axes of spin for the six great circle system of Symmetry #3. The perpendicular bisectors at A and B are projections resulting from the great circle spinning. B also shows an oblique view of the half-Tetra or "Chef's Caps" separated by the *implied square*. (For other views of Chef's Caps compare Figs. *100.103B* and *527.08A&B*.)

C. The six great circle fractionations subdivide the tetrahedron into 24 A Quanta Modules.

D. Exploded view of the tetrahedron's 24 A Quanta Modules.

E. Further explosion of tetrahedron's A Quanta Modules.

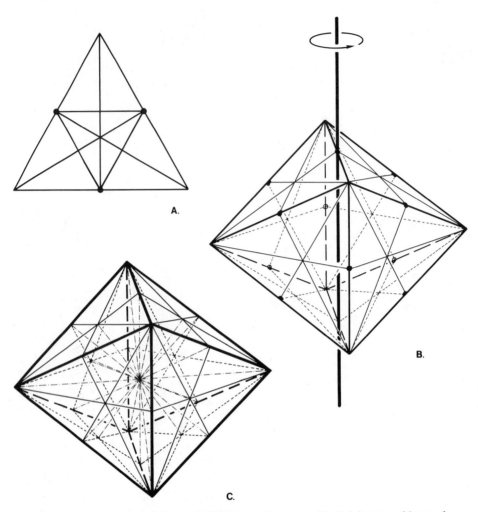

A.

B.

C.

Fig. 987.240 Subdivision of Tetrahedral Unity: Symmetry #3: Subdivision of Internal Octahedron:

A. Bisection of tetrahedron face edges describes a congruent octahedron face.
B. The spinning of the internal octahedron on axes through the opposite mid-edges generates the six great circle system of Symmetry #3.
C. The six great circle fractionations subdivide the octahedron into 48 Asymmetric Tetrahedra; each such Asymmetric Tetrahedron is comprised of one A Quanta Module and one B quanta Module.
D. Exploded view of octahedron's 48 Asymmetric Tetrahedra.

D.

987.250   Other Symmetries

987.251   An example of Symmetry #4 appears at Fig. 450.10. An example of Symmetry #5 appears at Fig. 458.12B. An example of Symmetry #6 appears at Fig. 458.12A. An example of Symmetry #7 appears at Fig. 455.20.

987.300   Interactions of Symmetries: Spheric Domains

987.310   Irrationality of Nucleated and Nonnucleated Systems

987.311   The six great circles of Symmetry #3 interact with the three great circles of Symmetry #1 to produce the 48 similar-surface triangles *ADH*

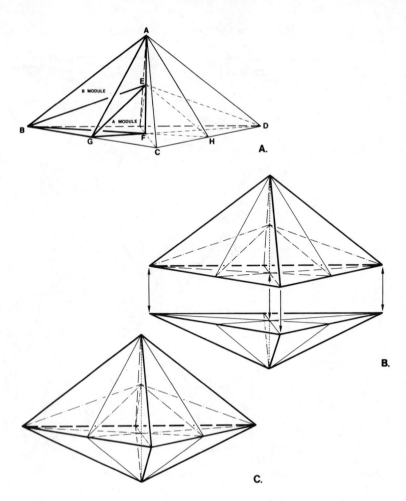

Fig. *987.241 Subdivision of Tetrahedral Unity: Octet: Duo-Tet Cube: Rhombic Dode-cahedron:*

A. Eighth-Octa composed of six asymmetric tetrahedra. Each asymmetric tetrahedron is composed of one A Quanta Module and one B Quanta Module. The drawing is labeled to show the relationship of the A Modules and the B Modules. Vertex A is at the center of volume of the octahedron and F is at the midface of any of the octahedron's eight triangular faces.

B. Proximate assembly of Eighth-Octa and Quarter-Tetra to be face bonded together as Octet.

C. *Octet:* (Oc-Tet = octahedron + tetrahedron.) An Eighth-Octa is face bonded with a Quarter-Tetra to produce the Octet. (See Sec. *986.430.*) The Octet is composed of 12 A Quanta Modules and 6 B Quanta Modules. (Compare color plate 22.)

D, E. *Duo-Tet Cube:* Alternate assemblies of eight Octets form Duo-Tet Cube. Each Duo-Tet Cube = 3-tetravolumes.

F. *Rhombic Dodecahedron:* Two Duo-Tet Cubes disassociate their Octet components to be reassembled into the Rhombic Dodecahedron. Rhombic Dodecahedron = 6-tetravolumes.

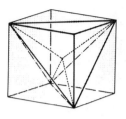

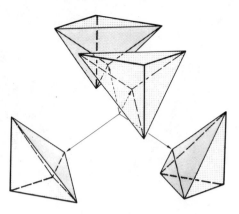

D.

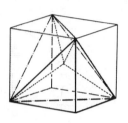

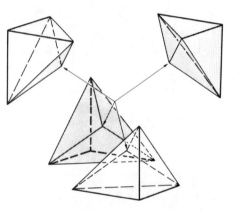

E.

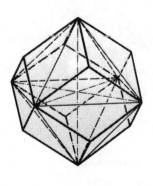

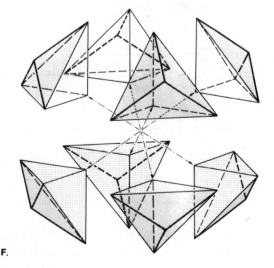

F.

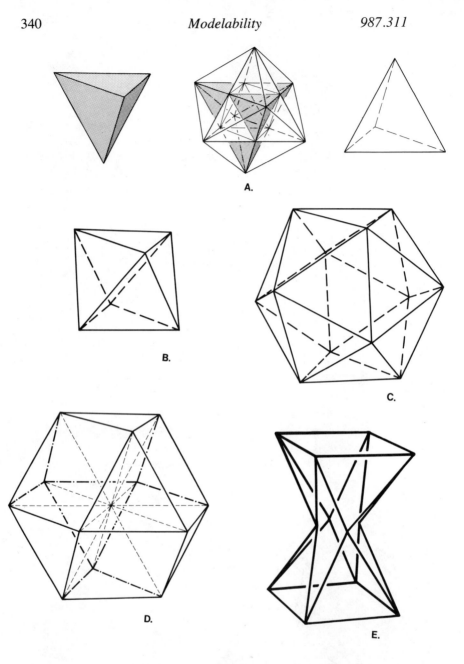

Fig. 987.242 *Evolution of Duo-Tet Cube and Hourglass Polyhedron:*

A. One positive regular tetrahedron and one negative regular tetrahedron are intersymmetrically arrayed within the common nuclear-vertexed location. Their internal
   trussing permits their equi-inter-distanced vertexes to define a stable eight-cornered
   structure, a ''cube.'' The cube is tetravolume-3; as shown here we observe

and *AIH* at Fig. *987.210N*. The 48 similar triangles (24 plus, 24 minus) are the surface-system set of the 48 similar asymmetric tetrahedra whose 48 central vertexes are congruent in the one—VE's—nuclear vertex's center of volume.

987.312   These 48 asymmetric tetrahedra combine themselves into 12 sets of four asymmetric tetra each. These 12 sets of four similar (two positive, two negative) asymmetric tetrahedra combine to define the 12 diamond facets of the rhombic dodecahedron of tetravolume-6. This rhombic dodecahedron's hierarchical significance is elsewhere identified as the allspace-filling domain of each closest-packed, unit-radius sphere in all isotropic, closest-packed, unit-radius sphere aggregates, as the rhombic dodecahedron's domain embraces both the unit-radius sphere and that sphere's rationally and exactly equal share of the intervening intersphere space.

987.313   The four great circles of Symmetry #2 produce a minimum nucleated system of 12 unit-radius spheres closest packed tangentially around each nuclear unit-radius sphere; they also produce a polyhedral system of six square windows and eight triangular windows; they also produce four hexagonal planes of symmetry that all pass through the same nuclear vertex sphere's exact center.

987.314   These four interhexagonalling planes may also be seen as the tetrahedron of zero-time-size-volume because all of the latter's equi-edge *lengths*, its face *areas*, and system *volumes* are concurrently at zero.

987.315   This four-great-circle interaction in turn defines the 24 equilengthed vectorial radii and 24 equi-lengthed vector chords of the VE. The 24 radii are grouped, by construction, in two congruent sets, thereby to appear as only 12 radii. Because the 24 radial vectors exactly equal energetically the circumferentially closed system of 24 vectorial chords, we give this system the name vector equilibrium. Its most unstable, only transitional, equilibrious state serves nature's cosmic, ceaseless, 100-percent-energy-efficient, self-regenerative integrity by providing the most expansive state of intertransformation accommodation of the original hierarchy of primitive, pre-time-size, "click-stop" *rational* states of energy-involvement accountabilities. Here we

1½-tetravolumes of "substance" within the eight vertexes and 1½-tetravolumes of complementation domain within the eight vertexes. The overall cubic domain consists of three tetravolumes: one outside-out (1½) and one inside-out (1½). The same star polyhedron appears within a vector equilibrium net at Fig. *1006.32*.

B. Octahedron: tetravolume-4
C. Icosahedron; tetravolume-18.51229586
D. Vector equilibrium: tetravolume-20
E. Eight-faceted asymmetric Hourglass Polyhedron: tetravolume-1½. These complex asymmetric doughnut-cored hexahedra appear within the star polyhedron at A.

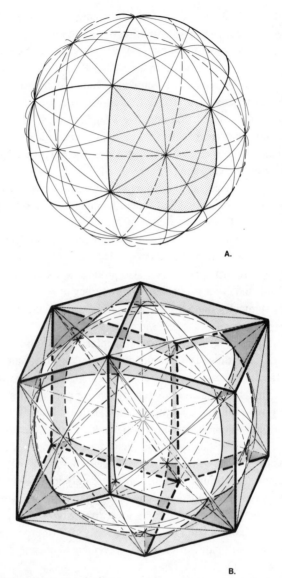

A.

B.

Fig. 987.312 Rhombic Dodecahedron:

A. The 25 great circle system of the vector equilibrium with the four great circles
   shown in dotted lines. (Compare Fig. 454.06D, third printing.)
B. Spherical rhombic dodecahedron great circle system generated from six-great-circle
   system of vector equilibrium, in which the two systems are partially congruent.
   The 12 rhombuses of the spherical rhombic dodecahedron are shown in heavy
   outline. In the interrelationship between the spherical and planar rhombic
   dodecahedron it is seen that the planar rhombus comes into contact with the sphere
   at the mid-face point.

have in the VE the eight possible phases of the initial positive-negative tetrahedron occurring as an inter-double-bonded (edge-bonded), vertex-paired, self-inter-coupling nuclear system.

987.316   With the nucleated set of 12 equi-radius vertexial spheres all closest packed around one nuclear unit-radius sphere, we found we had eight tetrahedra and six Half-octahedra defined by this VE assembly, the total volume of which is 20. But all of the six Half-octahedra are completely unstable as the 12 spheres cornering their six square windows try to contract to produce six diamonds or 12 equiangular triangles to ensure their interpatterning stability. (See Fig. *987.240*.)

987.317   If we eliminate the nuclear sphere, the mass interattraction of the 12 surrounding spheres immediately transforms their superficial interpatterning into 20 equiangular triangles, and this altogether produces the self-structuring pattern stability of the 12 symmetrically interarrayed, but non-spherically-nucleated icosahedron.

987.318   When this denucleation happens, the long diagonals of the six squares contract to unit-vector-radius length. The squares that were enclosed on all four sides by unit vectors were squares whose edges—being exactly unity—had a diagonal hypotenuse whose length was the second root of two—ergo, when VE is transformed to the icosahedron by the removal of the nuclear sphere, six of its $\sqrt{2}$-lengthed, interattractive-relationship lines transform into a length of 1, while the other 24 lines of circumferential interattraction remain constant at unit-vector-radius length. The difference between the second root of two (which is $1.414214 - 1$, i.e., the difference is .414214) occurs six times, which amounts to a total system contraction of 2.485284. This in turn means that the original

$$24 + 8.485284 = 32.485284$$

overall unit-vector-lengths of containing bonds of the VE are each reduced by a length of 2.485284 to an overall of exactly 30 unit-vector-radius lengths.

987.319   This 2.485284 α excess of gravitational tensional-embracement capability constitutes the excess of intertransformative stretchability between the VE's two alternatively unstable, omnisystem's stable states and its first two similarly stable, omnitriangulated states.

987.320   Because the increment of instability tolerance of most comprehensive intertransformative events of the primitive hierarchy is an irrational increment, the nucleus-void icosahedron as a structural system is inherently incommensurable with the nucleated VE and its family of interrational values of the octahedral, tetrahedral, and rhombic dodecahedral states.

987.321   The irrational differences existing between nucleated and non-nucleated systems are probably the difference between proton-nucleated and proton-neutron systems and nonnucleated-nonneutroned electron systems, both having identical numbers of external closest-packed spheres, but having also different overall, system-domain, volumetric, and system-population involvements.

987.322 There is another important systemic difference between VE's proton-neutron system and the nonnucleated icosahedron's electron system: the icosahedron is arrived at by removing the nucleus, wherefore its contraction will not permit the multilayering of spheres as is permitted in the multi-layerability of the VE—ergo, it cannot have neutron populating as in the VE; ergo, it permits only single-layer, circumferential closest packings; ergo, it permits only single spherical orbiting domains of equal number to the outer layers of VE-nucleated, closest-packed systems; ergo, it permits only the behavioral patterns of the electrons.

987.323 When all the foregoing is comprehended, it is realized that the whole concept of multiplication of information by division also embraces the concept of removing or separating out the nucleus sphere (vertex) from the VE's structurally unstable state and, as the jitterbug model shows, arriving omnisymmetrically throughout the transition at the structural stability of the icosahedron. The icosahedron experimentally evidences its further self-fractionation by its three different polar great-circle hemispherical cleavages that consistently follow the process of progressive self-fractionations as spin-halved successively around respective #5, #6, and #7 axes of symmetry. These successive halvings develop various fractions corresponding in arithmetical differentiation degrees, as is shown in this exploratory accounting of the hierarchy of unit-vector delineating multiplication of information only by progressive subdividing of parts.

987.324 When the tetrahedron is unity of tetravolume-1 (see Table 223.64), then (in contradistinction to the vector-radiused VE of tetravolume-20)

—the vector-diametered $VE = +2^{1/2}$

$$\text{or} = -2^{1/2}$$

—a rational, relative primitive prime number 5 tetravolume is also only realizable with half of its behavioral potentials in the presently-tune-in-able macrocosm and the other half of its total 5 behavioral potential existent in the presently-tune-out-able microcosm; thus,

—an overall $+5$ tetravolume potential $-2^{1/2}$—ergo, $+5-2^{1/2} = +2^{1/2}$

or

—an overall -5 tetravolume potential $+2^{1/2}$—ergo, $-5+2^{1/2} = -2^{1/2}$

987.325 The positive and negative tetrahedra, when composited as symmetrically concentric and structurally stable, have eight symmetrically interarranged vertexes defining the corners of what in the past has been mistakenly identified as a primitive polyhedron, popularly and academically called the "cube" or hexahedron. Cubes do not exist primitively because they are structurally unstable, having no triangularly-self-stabilizing system pattern. They occur frequently in nature's crystals but only as the superficial aspect of a conglomerate complex of omnitriangulated polyhedra.

987.326 This positive-negative tetrahedron complex defines a hexahedron of overall volume-3—$1^1/_2$ inside and $1^1/_2$ outside its intertrussed system's inside-and-outside-vertex-defined domain.

> —The three-great-circle symmetrical cleavaging (#1) of the primitive tetrahedron produces the vector-edged octahedron of tetravolume-4.
> —The vector-radiused rhombic triacontahedron, with its .9994833324 unit-vector-radius perpendicular to its midface center produces a symmetrical polyhedron of tetravolume-5.
> —With its 12 diamond-face-centers occurring at unit-vector-radius, the rhombic dodecahedron has a tetravolume-6.

The rhombic dodecahedron exactly occupies the geometric domain of each unit-vector-radius sphere and that sphere's external share of the symmetrically identical spaces intervening between closest-packed unit-radius spheres of any and all aggregates of unit-radius, closest-interpacked spheres. In this closest-packed condition each sphere within the aggregate always has 12 spheres symmetrically closest packed tangentially around it. The midpoints of the 12 diamond faces of the rhombic dodecahedron's 12 faces are congruent with the points of tangency of the 12 surrounding spheres. All the foregoing explains why unit-radius rhombic dodecahedra fill allspace when joined together.

987.327 Repeating the foregoing more economically we may say that in this hierarchy of omnisymmetric primitive polyhedra ranging from 1 through 2, $2^1/_2$, 3, 4, 5, and 6 tetravolumes, the rhombic dodecahedron's 12 diamond-face-midpoints occur at the points of intertangency of the 12 surrounding spheres. It is thus disclosed that the rhombic dodecahedron is not only the symmetric domain of both the sphere itself and the sphere's symmetric share of the space intervening between all closest-packed spheres and therefore also of the nuclear domains of all isotropic vector matrixes (Sec. 420), but the rhombic dodecahedron is also the maximum-limit-volumed primitive polyhedron of frequency-1.

987.400 Interactions of Symmetries: Secondary Great-circle Sets

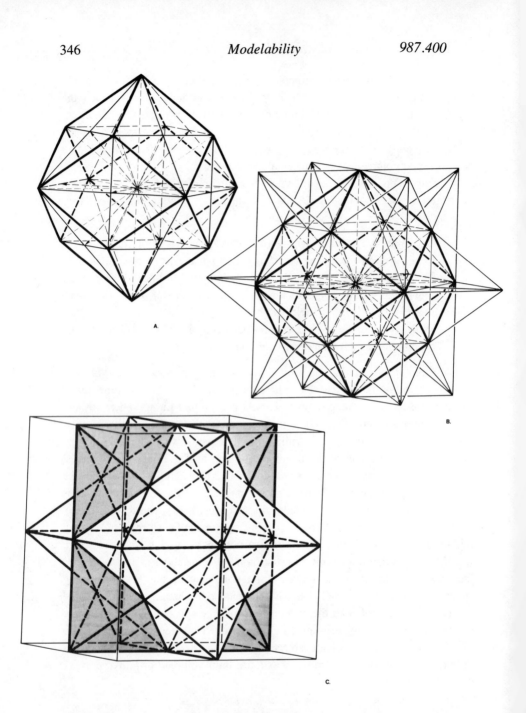

Fig. *987.326 Stellated Rhombic Dodecahedron:*

A. Rhombic dodecahedron with diamond faces subdivided into quadrants to describe mid-face centers. Interior lines with arrows show unit radii from system center to mid-face centers. This is the initial rhombic dodeca of tetravolume-6.

B. The rhombic dodecahedron system is ''pumped out'' with radii doubled from unit

987.410   Icosa Phase of Rationality

987.411   The 96 secondary great circles of the VE divide the chorded edge of the VE (which is the unit vector radius of synergetics) into rational linear fractions of the edge length—i.e., $^1/_2$, $^3/_{10}$, $^1/_4$, $^1/_6$, $^1/_{10}$—and these fractions embrace all the intercombinings of the first four prime numbers 1, 2, 3, and 5.

987.412   For an illustration of how the four VE great circles of 60-degree central angles subdivide the central-angle chord increments, see Fig. *987.412*.

987.413   Next recalling the jitterbug transformation of the VE into the icosa with its inherent incommensurability brought about by the

$$2 : \sqrt{2} = \sqrt{2} : 1$$

transformation ratio, and recognizing that the transformation was experimentally demonstrable by the constantly symmetrical contracting jitterbugging, we proceed to fractionate the icosahedron by the successive 15 great circles, six great circles (icosa type), and 10 great circles whose self-fractionation produces the S Modules* as well as the T and E Modules.

987.414   But it must be recalled that the experimentally demonstrable jitterbug model of transformation from VE to icosa can be accomplished through either a clockwise or counterclockwise twisting, which brings about 30 similar but positive and 30 negative omniintertriangulated vector edge results.

987.415   The midpoints of each of these two sets of 30 vertexes in turn provide the two alternate sets of 30 poles for the spin-halving of the 15 great circles of Symmetry #6, whose spinning in turn generates the 120 right spherical triangles (60 positive, 60 negative) of the icosahedral system.

987.416   The 120 right triangles, evenly grouped into 30 spherical diamonds, are transformed into 30 planar diamonds of central angles identical to those of the 30 spherical diamonds of the 15 great circles of the icosa. When the radius to the center of the face of the rhombic triacontahedron equals .9994833324. . . . of the unit vector radius of Synergetics (1.000), the rhombic triacontahedron has a tetravolume of 5 and each of its 120 T Quanta Mod-

---

    radius to radius = 2, or twice prime vector radius. This produces the stellated rhombic dodecahedron of tetravolume-12.

C. The stellated rhombic dodecahedron vertexes are congruent with the mid-edge points of the cube of tetravolume-24. A composite of three two-frequency Couplers (each individually of tetravolume-8) altogether comprises a star complex of tetravolume-12, sharing a common central rhombic dodeca domain of tetravolume-6. The stellated rhombic dodeca of tetravolume-12 is half the volume of the 24-tetravolume cube that inscribes it. (Compare the Duo-Tet Cube at Fig. *987.242A*.)

* See Sec. *988*.

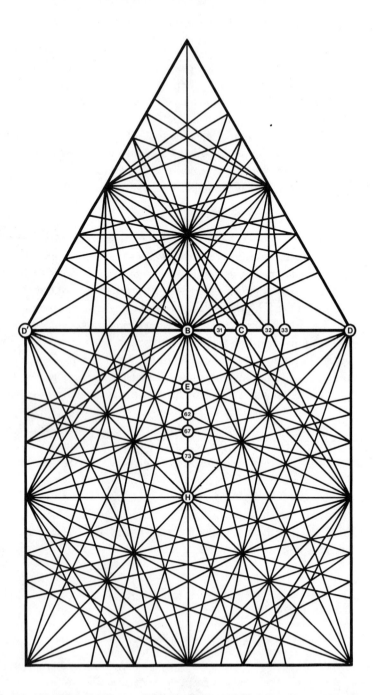

Fig. 987.412 *Rational Fraction Edge Increments of 60-degree Great-circle Subdividings of Vector Equilibrium:* When these secondary VE great-circle sets are projected

ules has a volume of one A Module. When the radius equals 1, the volume of the rhombic triacontahedron is slightly larger (5.007758029), and the corresponding E Module has a volume of 1.001551606 of the A Module. (See Sec. *986.540.*)

988.00   Icosahedron and Octahedron: S Quanta Module

988.100   Octa-icosa Matrix

988.110   The icosahedron positioned in the octahedron describes the S Quanta Modules. (See Fig. *988.100.*) Other references to the S Quanta Modules may be found at Secs. *100.105, 100.322,* Table *987.121,* and *987.413.*

988.111   As skewed off the octa-icosa matrix, they are the volumetric counterpart of the A and B Quanta Modules as manifest in the nonnucleated icosahedron. They also correspond to the $^1/_{120}$th tetrahedron of which the triacontahedron is composed. For their foldable angles and edge-length ratios see Figs. *988.111A-B.*

988.12   The icosahedron inscribed within the octahedron is shown at Fig. *988.12.*

988.13   The edge lengths of the S Quanta Module are shown at Fig. *988.13A.*

988.14   The angles and foldability of the S Quanta Module are shown at Fig. *988.13B.*

---

upon the planar VE they reveal the following rational fraction edge increments:

D′ − D = 1 VE edge

$$\frac{B\text{-}31}{D'\text{-}D} = \frac{1}{10} \qquad \frac{B\text{-}C}{D'\text{-}D} = \frac{1}{6}$$

$$\frac{B\text{-}D}{D'\text{-}D} = \frac{1}{2} \qquad \frac{B\text{-}E}{D'\text{-}D} = \frac{1}{6}$$

$$\frac{B\text{-}73}{D'\text{-}D} = \frac{3}{8} \qquad \frac{B\text{-}H}{D'\text{-}D} = \frac{1}{2}$$

D′ − D = 1 VE radius

$$\frac{B\text{-}32}{D'\text{-}D} = \frac{1}{4} \qquad \frac{B\text{-}33}{D'\text{-}D} = \frac{3}{10}$$

$$\frac{B\text{-}62}{D'\text{-}D} = \frac{1}{4} \qquad \frac{B\text{-}67}{D'\text{-}D} = \frac{3}{10}$$

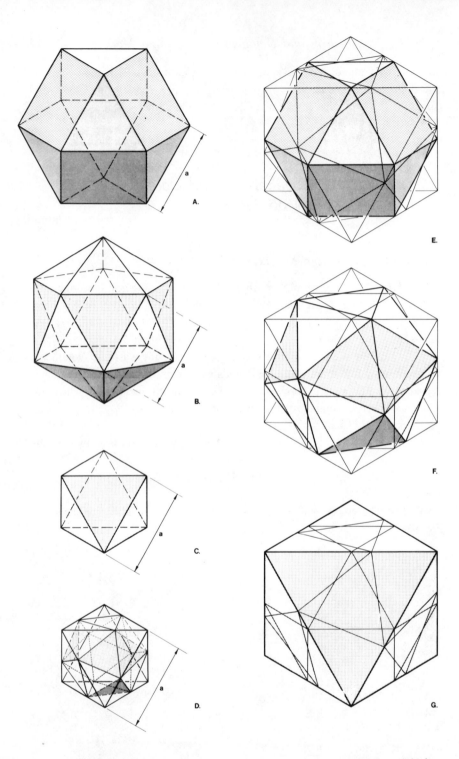

Fig. *988.00 Polyhedral Evolution: S Quanta Module:* Comparisons of skew polyhedra.

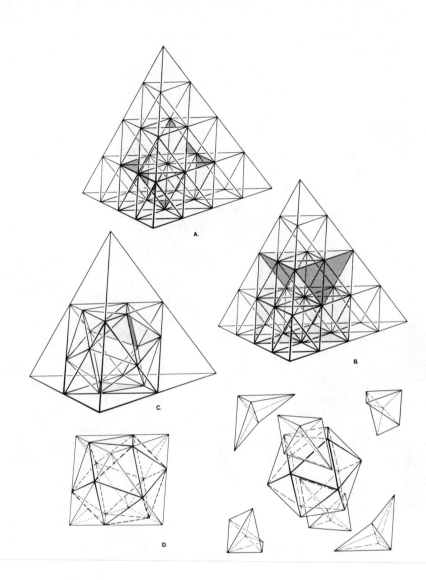

Fig. *988.100 Octa-Icosa Matrix: Emergence of S Quanta Module:*

A. Vector equilibrium inscribed in four-frequency tetrahedral grid.
B. Octahedron inscribed in four-frequency tetrahedral grid.
C. Partial removal of grid reveals icosahedron inscribed within octahedron.
D. Further subdivision defines modular spaces between octahedron and icosahedron.
E. Exploded view of six pairs of asymmetric tetrahedra that make up the space inter-
   vening between octa and icosa. Each pair is further subdivided into 24 S Quanta
   Modules. Twenty-four S Quanta Modules are added to the icosahedron to produce the
   octahedron.

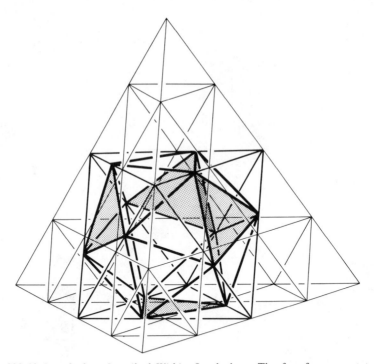

Fig. 988.12 *Icosahedron Inscribed Within Octahedron:* The four-frequency tetrahedron inscribes an internal octahedron within which may be inscribed a skew icosahedron. Of the icosahedron's 20 equiangular triangle faces, four are congruent with the plane of the tetra's faces (and with four external faces of the inscribed octahedron). Four of the icosahedron's other faces are congruent with the remaining four internal faces of the icosahedron. Two-fifths of the icosa faces are congruent with the octa faces. It requires 24 S Quanta Modules to fill in the void between the octa and the icosa.

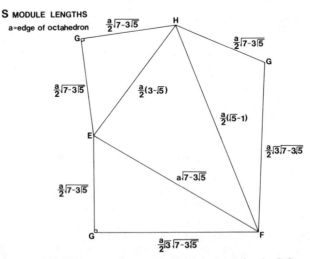

Fig. 988.13A *S Quanta Module Edge Lengths:* This plane net for the S Quanta Module shows the edge lengths ratioed to the unit octa edge (octa edge = tetra edge.)

S MODULE ANGLES

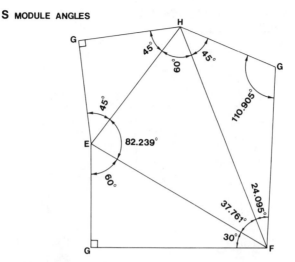

Fig. *988.13B S Quanta Module Angles:* This plane net shows the angles and fold-ability of the S Quanta Module.

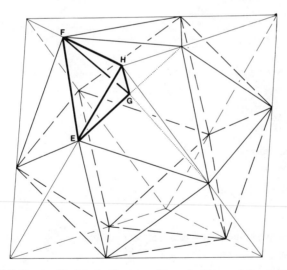

Fig. *988.13C S Quanta Module in Context of Icosahedron and Octahedron*

988.20 Table: Volume-area Ratios of Modules and Polyhedra of the Primitive Hierarchy:

	Volume	Area	Volume/Area	Area/Volume
A Module	1*	1*	1	1
T "	1	1.0032	0.9968	1.0032
E "	1.0016	1.0042	0.9974	1.0026
S "	1.0820	1.0480	1.0325	0.9685
B "	1	1.2122	0.8249	1.2122
Tetrahedron	24	6.9576	3.4495	0.2899
Icosahedron**	70.0311	10.5129	6.6615	0.1501
Cube	72	12.0508	5.9747	0.1674
Octahedron	96	13.9151	6.8990	0.1449
Rhombic dodecahedron	144	17.6501	8.1586	0.1226
Icosahedron	444.2951	36.0281	12.3319	0.0811

* Volume and area of A Module considered as unity.
** Icosahedron inside octahedron.

995.00   Vector Models of Magic Numbers

995.11A   The sequence is as follows:

(*Magic Numbers*)

One-frequency tetrahedron:
6 vectors times $^1/_3$ = 2

Two-frequency tetrahedron:
24 vectors times $^1/_3$ = 8

Three-frequency tetrahedron:
60 vectors times $^1/_3$ = 20

Three frequency tetrahedron + two-frequency
  tetrahedron:
60 vectors + 24 vectors times $^1/_3$ = 28

Four-frequency tetrahedron + one-frequency
  icosahedron:
120 vectors + 30 vectors times $^1/_3$ = 50

Five-frequency tetrahedron + one-frequency
  tetrahedron + one-frequency icosahedron:
210 + 6 + 30 vectors times $^1/_3$ = 82

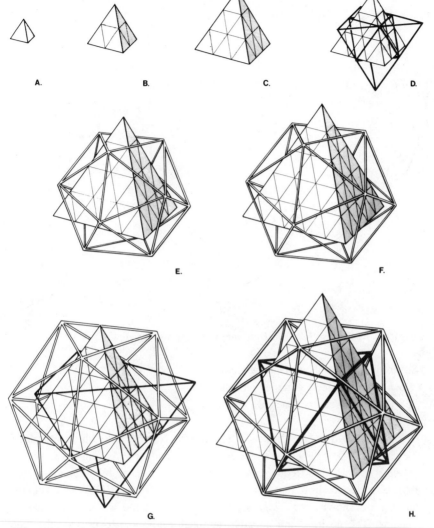

A.   B.   C.   D.

E.   F.

G.   H.

Fig. *995.03A Vector Models of Atomic Nuclei: Magic Numbers:* In the structure of
atomic nuclei there are certain numbers of neutrons and protons which correspond to
states of increased stability. These numbers are known as the magic numbers and have
the following values: 2, 8, 20, 28, 50, 82, and 126. A vector model is proposed to account for these numbers based on combinations of the three fundamental omnitriangulated structures: the tetrahedron, octahedron, and icosahedron. In this system all
vectors have a value of one-third. The magic numbers are accounted for by summing
the total number of vectors in each set and multiplying the total by ⅓. Note that although the tetrahedra are shown as opaque, nevertheless all the internal vectors defined
by the isotropic vector matrix are counted in addition to the vectors visible on all the
faces of the tetrahedra.

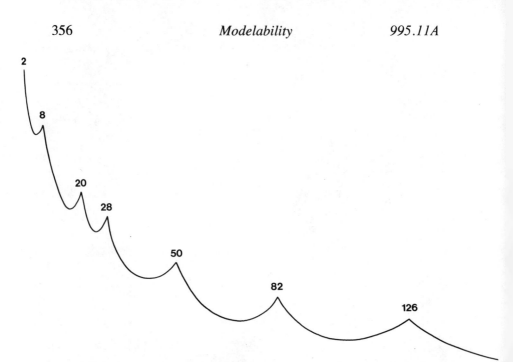

Fig. *995.31A Reverse Peaks in Descending Isotope Curve: Magic Numbers*

Six-frequency tetrahedron + one-frequency
  octahedron + one-frequency icosahedron:
336 + 12 + 30 vectors times $^1/_3$ = 126

995.12 **Magic Number 28**: The Magic Number 28, which introduces
the cube and the octahedron to the series, was inadvertently omitted from *Synergetics 1*. The three-frequency tetrahedron is surrounded by an enlarged two-frequency tetrahedron that shows as an outside frame. This is a negative tetrahedron shown in its *halo aspect* because it is the last case to have no nucleus. The positive and negative tetrahedra combine to provide the eight corner points for the triangulated cube. The outside frame also provides for an octahedron in the middle. (See revised Figs. *995.03A* and *995.31A*.)

1000.00 Omnitopology

1000.00   OMNITOPOLOGY

1001.00   Inherent Rationality of Omnidirectional Epistemology
   *(1001.10 Spherical Reference)**
   1001.20   Field of Geodesic Event Relationships
   1005.10   Inventory of Omnidirectional Intersystem Precessional Effects
   1005.15   Volume and Area Progressions
      1005.60   Generalization and Polarization
      1005.611   Metabolic Generalizations
   (1006.10   Omnitopology Defined)
   1006.30   Vector Equilibrium Involvement Domain
   1006.40   Cosmic System Eight-dimensionality
   1007.10   Omnitopology Compared with Euler's Topology
   1007.20   Invalidity of Plane Geometry
   1009.00   Critical Proximity
      1009.50   Acceleration
      (1009.60   Hammer-thrower)
      1009.69   Comet

(1010.00   Prime Volumes)
   (1011.00   Omnitopology of Prime Volumes)
   (1012.00   Nucleus as Nine = None = Nothing)
   1013.00   Geometrical Function of Nine
   1013.10   Unity as Two: Triangle as One White Triangle and One Black Triangle
   1013.20   Complementarity and Parity
   1013.30   Eight Three-petaled Tetrahedral Flower Buds
   1013.40   Nine Schematic Aspects of the Tetrahedron
   1013.50   Visible and Invisible Tetrahedral Arrays
      1013.51   Visibly Demonstrable: Physical
      1013.52   Invisible But Thinkable: Metaphysical
      1013.60   Quantum Jump Model

(1020.00   Compound Curvature: Chords and Arcs)

(1030.00   Omniequilibrium)
   (1031.10   Dynamic Symmetry)
   (1032.00   Convex and Concave Sphere-packing Intertransformings)

1033.00   Intertransformability Models and Limits
   1033.010   Involvement Field Integrates Topology, Electromagnetics, Chemistry, and Cosmology
      1033.020   Four-triangular-circuits Tensegrity
      1033.030   Untenable Equilibrium Compulsion
   1033.10   Octave System of Polyhedral Transformations
   1033.120   Click-stop Subdivisioning
   1033.180   Vector Equilibrium: Potential and Primitive Tetravolumes

*Titles in parentheses may be found in *Synergetics 1*

1001.00 Inherent Rationality of Omnidirectional Epistemology

1001.20 Field of Geodesic Event Relationships

1001.21 Since the myriads of eccentricities of cyclic periodicities of omni-everywhere-and-everywhen complex intermotions of intertransforming Universe inherently defy any "fixed" overall frame of cosmic motion referencing; and *since* the omnicosmic presence of mass-attractive and tensionally operative gravity means that no so-called straight line can be generated by any one body, as all bodies are affected by other bodies in varying degrees; and *since* all bodies are in motion either independently or in company with other bodies and are axially rotating on precessionally skewed axes as they elliptically orbit their dominant bodies (or dominant collection of bodies); *wherefore,* any point on any body progressively describes only an overall pattern in Universe of a cyclic, curlicue, wavilinear, elliptically-orbiting-within-elliptically-orbiting of larger systems.

1001.22 Within the total cosmic complexity the directions taken by each and all of the moving bodies are always the paths of least resistance. Because the paths are those of least resistance, all events of all transforming and traveling entities require the least energy to accomplish their complex action programmed passages—ergo, their accomplished curvilinear courses are always the most economical lines of travel. These most economical routes of travel are known as geodesic lines. Geodesics are not only nature's most economical lines of interrelationship travel, but ipso facto they are also nature's shortest-time-of-travel lines.

1001.23 When using string to secure the cover on a cubical box whose edges are two feet long, people spontaneously surround the box in a direction perpendicular to the cube's edges and, having run the string completely around the cubical box in one direction, they do so again in a plane at right angle to the first wind-around. This takes 16 feet of string and a pair of mid-top and mid-bottoms knots to securely bind-in all six faces of the cube. However, all six faces can be surrounded and the cover held secure almost twice as economically by using only one string eight-and-one-half-feet long and following the geodesic line that winds around the corners of the cube from mid-edge to adjacent mid-edge to produce an equiedged hexagon whose length of line-of-string-reach-around is the shortest distance around all six faces of a cube, wherefore the string cannot slide off the cube. To make this most economical path dynamically evident, hold a cube between the index fingers of your left and right hands with the left index finger pressed against one top corner of the cube and your right index finger pressed against the corner of the bottom of the cube most diagonally opposite the first corner pressed. Now, holding the box firmly between the two index fingers and stretching your arms in front of you with your fingers at the same level above the floor, ask someone to spin the box around the axis between your two fingers; as they do so, you will see the top and bottom profile of the spinning box and its six free corners rotating in two pairs of three each to produce two hills in the top and bottom profiles of the revolving box with a valley between them running around the box's equator of spinning. Along the bottom-most valley runs the hexagonally wound eight-and-one-half-feet-long string in its geodesic valley of least distance around all six faces.

1001.24 When a man shoots a bird in flight, he aims at a point where he thinks the bird will be by the time the bullet can travel that far; he must also allow for gravitational pull Earthward and cross-wind deflection of the bullet's always-consequently-corkscrew line of travel. The corkscrew line of successful travel between gun and bird is the most energy-economical trajectory. It is a geodesic line. If the man chooses the seemingly straight, "shortest" line between himself and the bird at the time he is aiming—which is the way he was taught by geometry in school—he will miss the bird.

1001.25 The misconception of a "straight" line and its popular adoption into humanity's education system as constituting the "shortest distance between two points" takes no consideration of what the invisible, dynamic, atomically structured system may be which provides the only superficially flat paper-and-lead-pencil-pattern of interrelationship graphing of the line running between the two points considered. Nor does the straight-line shortest-distance assumption consider what a "point" is and where it begins and ends—ergo, it cannot determine where and when its dimensionless points have been reached, and it cannot determine what the exact length of that shortest distance between "points" may be.

1001.26 Such self-deceiving misinterpretations of experiences have been introduced by education into human sensing and traditional reasoning only because of humanity's microstature and microlongevity in respect to the terrestrial environment and geological time. Individual humans have also been overwhelmed by the momentum of tradition, the persuasions of "common sense," and a general fear of questioning long-established and ultimately power-backed authority and tradition. Thus has innocent humanity been misinformed or underinformed by the spoken-word-relayed inventory of only popularly explained, naked-eye impressions of local environment experiences as they have occurred throughout millions of years prior to humanity's discovery and development of instrumentally accommodated, macroscoped and microscoped exploration of our comprehensive environment. The experientially obtained, macro-micro, instrumentally measured data found no evidence of the existence of dimensionless "points," "lines," and "planes," nor of dimensioned "solids," nor of any "thing," nor of any noun-designatable, thing-substantiated, static entities. The experiments of human scientists have disclosed only verb-describable events—four-dimensionally coordinate behaviors of complexedly and ceaselessly intertransforming events, wavilinear event trajectories, interferences, and resonant event fields.

1005.10   Inventory of Omnidirectional Intersystem Precessional Effects

1005.15   **Volume and Area Progressions:** Omnidirectional precession involves both volumetric progressions and areal progressions that are interaccommodative as radial (volumetric) precessions and circumferential (surface) precessions resulting per given unit of energy input into the system. The ratios of these concentric progressions are illustrated at Figs. *1005.15A-D*.

1005.60   Generalization and Polarization

1005.611   **Metabolic Generalizations:** Within economics we may be able to demonstrate the existence of a metabolic process generalization which is akin to, if not indeed implicitly inherent in, a composite of Boltzman's, Einstein's, and others' concept of a cosmically regenerative omniintercomplementation of a diversity of energetic export-import centers whose local cosmic episodes nonsimultaneously ebb and flow to accommodate the entropically and syntropically, omniversally, omniregenerative intertransformings of the nonsimultaneous intercomplementations of nonunitarily conceptual but finite Scenario Universe. How can economics demonstrate a generalization from the utterly uninhibited viewpoint of the individual human? It is said that stones do not have hunger. But stones are hygroscopic and do successively import and export both water and energy as heat or radiation. New stones progressively aggregate and disintegrate. We may say stones have both

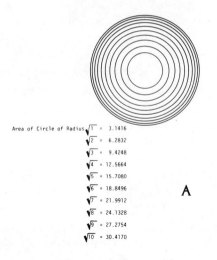

Area of Circle of Radius $\sqrt{1}$ = 3.1416

$\sqrt{2}$ = 6.2832

$\sqrt{3}$ = 9.4248

$\sqrt{4}$ = 12.5664

$\sqrt{5}$ = 15.7080

$\sqrt{6}$ = 18.8496

$\sqrt{7}$ = 21.9912

$\sqrt{8}$ = 24.1328

$\sqrt{9}$ = 27.2754

$\sqrt{10}$ = 30.4170

A

PROGRESSION OF CONCENTRIC SPHERES WITH VOLUME DIFFERENCE EQUAL
TO VOLUME OF CENTRAL SPHERE

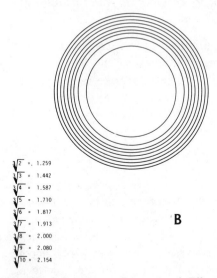

$\sqrt[3]{2}$ =. 1.259

$\sqrt[3]{3}$ = 1.442

$\sqrt[3]{4}$ = 1.587

$\sqrt[3]{5}$ = 1.710

$\sqrt[3]{6}$ = 1.817

$\sqrt[3]{7}$ = 1.913

$\sqrt[3]{8}$ = 2.000

$\sqrt[3]{9}$ = 2.080

$\sqrt[3]{10}$ = 2.154

B

Fig. *1005.15 Omnidirectional Intersystem Precessional Effects: Volume and Area Progressions:*

A. Progression of concentric circles with area difference equal to area of central circle.
B. Progression of concentric spheres with volume difference equal to volume of central sphere.
C. Doubling areas of progressive concentric circles
D. Doubling volumes of progressive concentric spheres

DOUBLING AREAL OF PROGRESSIVE CONCENTRIC CIRCLES

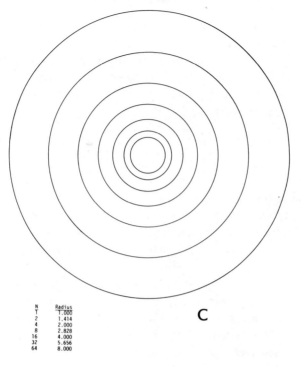

N	Radius
1	1.000
2	1.414
4	2.000
8	2.828
16	4.000
32	5.656
64	8.000

C

DOUBLING VOLUMES OF PROGRESSIVE CONCENTRIC SPHERES

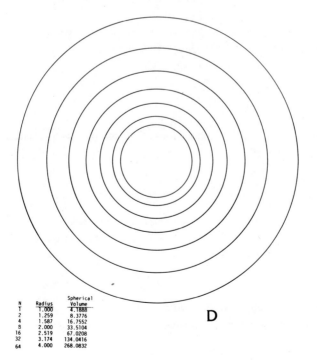

N	Radius	Spherical Volume
1	1.000	4.1888
2	1.259	8.3776
4	1.587	16.7552
8	2.000	33.5104
16	2.519	67.0208
32	3.174	134.0416
64	4.000	268.0832

D

syntropically importing "appetites" and self-scavenging or self-purging entropic export proclivities.

1005.612 When a person dies, all the chemistry remains, and we see that the human organism's same aggregate quantity of the same chemistries persists from the "live" to the "dead" state. This aggregate of chemistries has no metaphysical interpreter to communicate to self or to others the aggregate of chemical rates of interacting associative or disassociative proclivities, the integrated effects of which humans speak of as "hunger" or as the need to "go to the toilet." Though the associative intake "hunger" is unspoken metaphysically after death, the disassociative discard proclivities speak for themselves as these chemical-proclivity discard behaviors continue and reach self-balancing rates of progressive disassociation. What happens physically at death is that the importing ceases while exporting persists, which produces a locally unbalanced—thereafter exclusively exporting—system. (See Sec. *1052.59.*)

1005.613 It follows that between conception and birth—physically speaking—"life" is a progression of *predominantly importive* energy-importing-and-exporting transactions, gradually switching to an *exportive* predominance—ergo, life is a synthesis of the absolutely exportive entropy of radiation and the absolutely importive syntropy of gravity.

1005.614 The political, religious, and judicial controversies prevailing in the late 1970s with regard to abortion and "the right to life" will all ultimately be resolved by the multiplying elucidation for popular comprehension of science's discovery at the virological level that the physical and chemical organism of humans consists entirely of inanimate atoms. From this virological discovery it follows that the *individual life* does not exist until the umbilical cord is cut and the child starts its own metabolic regeneration; prior to that the life in the womb is merely composed of the mother organism, as is the case with any one individual egg in her ovary. Life begins with individually self-startered and sustained energy importing and dies when that independent importing ceases.

1006.30 Vector Equilibrium Involvement Domain

1006.31 The unfrequenced vector equilibrium has 12 external vertexes and one internal vertex of the nuclear sphere embraced by the 12 uniradius closest-packed spheres around it; the omniinterconnecting vectors between the 12-around-one spheric centers define the vector equilibrium *involvement domain.*

1006.32 We learn from the complex jitterbugging of the VE and octahedra that as each sphere of closest-packed spheres becomes a space and each

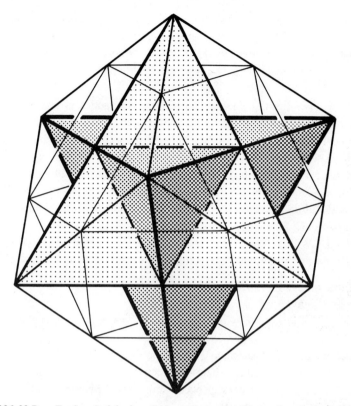

Fig. *1006.32 Duo-Tet Star Polyhedron Defines Vector Equilibrium Involvement Domain:*
The Duo-Tet star polyhedron that first appears in Fig. *987.242A* is shown here within a
vector equilibrium net. The complex also illustrates the eight Eighth-Octa that must be
added to the eight triangular faces of the vector equilibrium to form th nucleated cube—the
total complex of which functions as the vector equilibrium nuclear involvement domain.
A closest-sphere-packing evolution of this same transformation (adding eight Eighth-Octa
to the VE's six triangular faces) appears at Fig. *415.17.*

space becomes a sphere, each intertransformative component requires a te-
travolume-12 "cubical" space, while both require 24 tetravolumes. The total
internal-external closest-packed-spheres-and-their-interstitial-spaces involvement domains of the unfrequenced 20-tetravolume VE is tetravolume-24.
This equals either eight of the nuclear cube's (unstable) tetravolume-3 or two
of the rhombic dodecahedron's (stable) tetravolume-6. The two tetravolume-
12 cubes or four tetravolume-6 dodecahedra are intertransformable aspects of
the nuclear VE's local-involvement domain. (See Fig. *1006.32.*)

1006.33   The vector equilibrium at initial frequency, which is frequency^2,
manifests the fifth-powering of nature's energy behaviors. Frequency begins
at two. The vector equilibrium of frequency^2 has a prefrequency inherent tet-

ravolume of 160 ($5 \times 2^5 = 160$) and a quanta-module volume of $120 \times 24 = 1 \times 3 \times 5 \times 2^8$ nuclear-centered system as the integrated product of the first four prime numbers: 1, 2, 3, 5. Whereas a cube at the same frequency accommodates only eight cubes around a nonnucleated center. (Compare Sec. *1033.632*.)

1006.34 For the first moment in history synergetics is providing operational comprehensibility of the fourth-and-fifth-dimensional-coordinated, most economical behaviors of physical Universe as well as of their intellectual, metaphysical conceptuality. We have arrived at a new phase of comprehension in discovering that all of the physical cases experimentally demonstrable are only special cases of the generalized principles of the subfrequency, subtime, and subsize patterning integrity of the nucleus-containing, closest-packed isotropic vector matrix system.

1006.35 With reference to our operational definition of a sphere (Sec. 224.07), we find that in an aggregation of closest-packed uniradius spheres:

Tetravolume 1 = minimum F^0 F^0 tetrasphere

Tetravolume 5 = maximum F^h F^h sphere

                (h = high frequency geodesic icosasphere, Sec. 985.01)

Tetravolume 6 = maximum F^h F^h sphere (high-frequency icosa plus the intersphere volumetric involvement domain of each closest-packed uniradius sphere = rhombic dodecahedron)

1006.36 In respect to each uniradius, omni-closest-packed spherical domain of 6:

Maximum   = 5 plus tetra quanta inside   ⎫
icosa sphere F^h 1 minus tetra quantum   ⎬ integrating as +4
                  outside   ⎭

Tetra   = 1 plus tetra quantum inside ⎫
Sphere F^0 5 minus tetra quanta outside ⎬ integrating as −4

1006.37 For other manifestations of the vector equilibrium involvement domain, review Sections *415.17* (Nucleated Cube) and *1033* (Intertransformability Models and Limits), *passim*.

1006.40 Cosmic System Eight-dimensionality

1006.41 We have a cosmically closed system of eight-dimensionality: four dimensions of convergent, syntropic conservation → +4, and four dimensions of divergent, entropic radiation → − 4 intertransformabilities, with

the non-inside-outable, symmetric octahedron of tetravolume 4 and the polarized semiasymmetric Coupler of tetravolume 4 always conserved between
the interpulsative 1 and the rhombic dodecahedron's maximum-involvement
6, (i.e., $1 + 4 + 1$); ergo, the always double-valued—2^2—symmetrically perfect octahedron of tetravolume 4 and the polarized asymmetric Coupler of tetravolume 4 reside between the convergently and divergently pulsative extremes of both maximally aberrated and symmetrically perfect (equilibrious)
phases of the generalized cosmic system's always partially-tuned-in-and-
tuned-out eight-dimensionality.

1007.10 Omnitopology Compared with Euler's Topology

1007.16   While the counting logic of topology has provided mathematicians with great historical expansion, it has altogether failed to elucidate
the findings of physics in a conceptual manner. Many mathematicians were
content to let topology descend to the level of a fascinating game—dealing
with such Moebius-strip nonsense as pretending that strips of paper have no
edges. The constancy of topological interrelationships—the formula of relative interabundance of vertexes, edges, and faces—was reliable and had a
great potential for a conceptual mathematical strategy, but it was not identified operationally with the intertransformabilities and gaseous, liquid, and
solid interbondings of chemistry and physics as described in Gibbs' phase
rule. Now, with the advent of vectorial geometry, the congruence of synergetic accounting and vectorial accounting may be brought into elegant
agreement.

1007.20 Invalidity of Plane Geometry

1007.21   We are dealing with the Universe and the difference between
conceptual thought (see Sec. 501.101) and nonunitarily conceptual Universe
(see *Scenario Universe,* Sec. 320). We cannot make a model of the latter, but
we can show it as a scenario of meaningfully overlapping conceptual frames.

1007.22   About 150 years ago Leonhard Euler opened up the great new
field of mathematics that is topology. He discovered that all visual experiences could be treated as conceptual. (But he did not explain it in these
words.) In topology, Euler says in effect, all visual experiences can be resolved into three unique and irreducible aspects:

—vertexes, faces, and edges (Secs. 223.04 and 1006.20)
   or, as unique dimensional abundances:
—points, areas, and lines (Sec. 527.11)
   or, as structural identifications:

—joints, windows, and struts (Sec. *986.053*)

  or, as we say in synergetics topology:

—crossings, openings, and trajectories (Sec. 524.30)

  or the more generalized:

—events, nonevents, and traceries

  or more refined as:

—fixes, discontinuities, and continuities

  or in most refined synergetics:

—events, novents, and even interrelatabilities (Sec. *269.05*).

1007.23 In topology, then, we have a unique aspect that we call a line, not a straight line but an event tracery. When two traceries cross one another, we get a fix, which is not to be confused in any way with a noncrossing. Fixes give geographical locations in respect to the system upon which the topological aspects appear. When we have a tracery or a plurality of traceries crossing back upon one another to close a circuit, we surroundingly frame a limited view of the omnidirectional novents. Traceries coming back upon themselves produce windowed views or areas of novents. The areas, the traces, and the fixes of crossings are never to be confused with one another: all visual experiences are resolved into these three conceptual aspects.

1007.24 Look at any picture, point your finger at any part of the picture, and ask yourself: Which aspect is that, and that, and that? That's an area; or it's a line; or it's a crossing (a fix, a point). Crossings are loci. You may say, "That is too big to be a point"; if so, you make it into an area by truncating the corner that the point had represented. You will now have two more vertexes but one more area and three more lines than before. Euler's equation will remain unviolated.

1007.25 A circle is a loop in the same line with no crossing and no additional vertexes, areas, or lines.

1007.26 Operationally speaking, a plane exists only as a facet of a polyhedral system. Because I am experiential I must say that a line is a consequence of energy: an event, a tracery upon what system? A polyhedron is an event system separated out of Universe. Systems have an inside and an outside. A picture in a frame has also the sides and the back of the frame, which is in the form of an asymmetrical polyhedron.

1007.27 In polyhedra the number of V's (crossings) plus the number of F's, areas (novents-faces) is always equal to the number of L's lines (continuities) plus the number 2. If you put a hole through the system—as one cores an apple making a doughnut-shaped polyhedron—you find that $V + F = L$. Euler apparently did not realize that in putting the hole through it, he had removed the axis and its two poles. Having removed two axial terminal (or polar) points from the inventory of "fixes" (loci-vertexes) of the system, the $V + F = L + 2$ equation now reads $V + F = L$, because two V's have been deducted from the inventory on the left side of the equation.

1007.28 Another very powerful mathematician was Brouwer. His theorem demonstrates that if a number of points on a plane are stirred around, it will be found after all the stirring that one of the points did not move relative to all the others. One point is always the center of the total movement of all the points. But the mathematicians oversimplified the planar concept. In synergetics the plane has to be the surface of a system that not only has insideness and outsideness but also has an obverse and re-exterior. Therefore, in view of Brouwer, there must also always be another point on the opposite side of the system stirring that also does not move. Every fluidly bestirred system has *two* opposed polar points that do not move. These two polar points identify the system's neutral axis. (See Sec. 703.12.)

1007.29 Every system has a neutral axis with two polar points (vertexes–fixes). In synergetics topology these two polar points of every system become constants of topological inventorying. Every system has two polar vertexes that function as the spin axis of the system. In synergetics the two polar vertexes terminating the axis identify conceptually the abstract—supposedly nonconceptual—function of nuclear physics' "spin" in quantum theory. The neutral axis of the equatorially rotating jitterbug VE proves Brouwer's theorem polyhedrally.

1007.30 When you look at a tetrahedron from above, one of its vertexes looks like this:

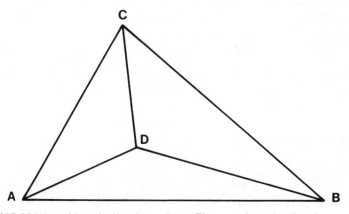

Fig. *1007.30 View of Tetrahedron from Above:* There are four triangles: three surround the top vertex; the fourth is implicit in the base.

You see only three triangles, but there is a fourth underneath that is implicit as the base of the tetrahedron, with the Central vertex D being the apex of the tetrahedron. The crossing point (vertex-fix) in the middle only superficially appears to be in the same plane as *ABC*. The outer edges of the three triangles you see, *ACD, CDB, ADB,* are congruent with the hidden base triangle, *ABC.* Euler assumed the three triangles *ACD, CDB, ADB* to be absolutely congruent with triangle *ABC.* Looking at it from the bird's-eye view, unoperationally, Euler misassumed that there could be a nonexperienceable, no-thickness plane, though no such phenomenon can be experientially demonstrated. Putting three points on a piece of paper, interconnecting them, and saying that this "proves" that a no-thickness, nonexperiential planar triangle exists is operationally false. The paper has thickness; the points have thickness; the lines are atoms of lead strewn in linear piles upon the paper.

1007.31   You cannot have a something-nothingness, or a plane with no thickness. Any experimental event must have an insideness and an outsideness. Euler did not count on the fourth triangle: he thought he was dealing with a plane, and this is why he said that on a plane we have $V + F = L + 1$. When Euler deals with polyhedra, he says "plus 2." In dealing with the false plane he says "plus 1." He left out "1" from the right-hand side of the polyhedral equation because he could only see three faces. Three points define a minimum polyhedral facet. The point where the triangles meet in the center is a polyhedral vertex; no matter how minimal the altitude of its apex may be, it can never be in the base plane. Planes as nondemonstrably defined by academic mathematicians have no insideness in which to get: *ABCD* is inherently a tetrahedron. Operationally the fourth point, *D,* is identified or fixed subsequent to the fixing of *A, B,* and *C.* The "laterness" of *D* involves a time lag within which the constant motion of all Universe will have so disturbed the atoms of paper on which *A, B,* and *C* had been fixed that no exquisite degree of measuring technique could demonstrate that *A, B, C,* and *D* are all in an exact, so-called flat-plane alignment demonstrating *ABCD* to be a zero-altitude, no-thickness-edged tetrahedron.

1009.00   Critical Proximity

1009.50   Acceleration

1009.57   An apparent straight line is not only locally wavilinear but a short-section arc of a greater system passing through a lesser system. (See Figs. *1009.57A–B.*) Universe lines return upon themselves.

1009.60   Hammer-Thrower

1009.69   Comet: A comet is a celestial itinerant, a cosmic skyways vacuum cleaner trying to accommodate an aggregation of stardust as it travels

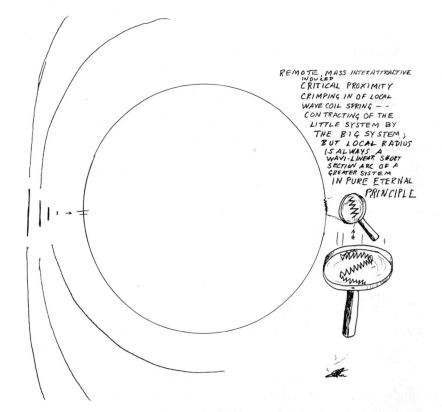

REMOTE MASS INTERATTRACTIVE
INDUCED
CRITICAL PROXIMITY
CRIMPING IN OF LOCAL
WAVE COIL SPRING – –
CONTRACTING OF THE
LITTLE SYSTEM BY
THE BIG SYSTEM;
BUT LOCAL RADIUS
IS ALWAYS A
WAVI-LINEAR SHORT
SECTION ARC OF A
GREATER SYSTEM
IN PURE ETERNAL
PRINCIPLE

Fig. *1009.57A Critical Proximity Crimping-in of Local Wave Coil-spring:* Consideration of the little system by the big system. Local radius is always a wavilinear short section arc of a great system in pure principle.

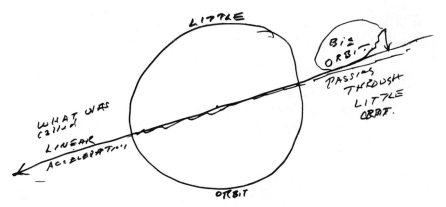

LITTLE

BIG ORBIT

PASSING THROUGH LITTLE ORBIT.

WHAT WAS called LINEAR ACCELERATION

ORBIT

Fig. *1009.57B Big Orbit Passing through Little Orbit:* What was called linear acceleration is an unrecognized arc of a bigger system.

successively through the orbital neighborhoods of planets, stars, and other comets. The radiation pressures from the nearest stars, however, tend to blow the vacuum cleaner's stardust gleanings out into a bagless "dustbag," causing what we erroneously speak of as the comet's tail. These "tail" displays should be spoken of as Sun-radiation blowout trajectories. As comets come into critical proximity of syntropically importing planets, the stardust aggregates of their inverted "tails" are gravitationally depleted by the planets they pass, as much of that stardust is attracted into the planets or moons to become part of those import centers' syntropic buildup in a multibillions-of-years syntropic preparation of their stored-energy aggregates to be converted into the state of an entropically exporting star.

1013.00   Geometrical Function of Nine

•[1013.00–1013.64   *Geometry of Nine Scenario*]

1013.10   Unity as Two: Triangle as One White Triangle and One Black Triangle

1013.11   Fish fan their tails sideways to produce forward motion. Snakes wriggle sideways to travel ahead. Iceboats attain speeds of 60 miles per hour in a direction at right angles to wind blowing at half that speed. These results are all precessional.

1013.12   The minialtitude tetrahedron seen as a flattened triangle has a synergetic surprise behavior akin to precession. We can flip one simple white triangle over and find that the other side is black. One triangle must thus be considered as two triangles: the obverse and reverse, always and only coexisting almost congruent polar end triangles of the almost zerolong prism.

1013.13   Polarity is inherent in congruence.

1013.14   Every sphere has a concave inside and a convex outside. Convex and concave are not the same: concave reflectors concentrate energy; radiation and convex mirrors diffuse the radiant energy.

1013.15   Unity is plural and at minimum two. Unity does not mean the number one. One does not and cannot exist by itself.

1013.16   In Universe life's existence begins with awareness. No otherness: no awareness. The observed requires an observer. The subjective and objective always and only coexist and therewith demonstrate the inherent plurality of unity: inseparable union.

1013.20 Complementarity and Parity

1013.21   Physics tends to think of complementarity and parity as being the interrelationship characteristics of two separate phenomena. Complementarity was discovered half a century ago, while parity was first recognized only 20 years ago. In fact the non-mirror-imaged complementations are two aspects of the same phenomenon. The always-and-only-coexisting non-mirror-image complementations also coexist as inseparable plural unity.

1013.30 Eight Three-petaled Tetrahedral Flower Buds

1013.31   We can interconnect the three mid-edged points of an almost-zero-altitude tetrahedron, a thin-material triangle, thus subdividing a big triangle into four smaller similar triangles. We recall that the big triangle must be considered as two triangles; the obverse may be white and the reverse may be black. We can fold the three corner triangles around the three lines separating them from the central triangle, thereby producing two different tetrahedra. Folding the corner triangles under or over produces either a white tetrahedron with a black inside or a black tetrahedron with a white inside. Since the outside of the tetrahedron is convex and the inside is concave, there are two very real and separate tetrahedra in evidence. Eight faces (four black, four white) have been evolved from only four externally viewable triangles, and these four were in turn evolved from one (unity-is-plural) triangle—an almost-zero-altitude tetrahedral system or an almost-zero-altitude prismatic system.

1013.32   Both the positive and negative concave tetrahedra have four different black faces and four different white faces. We can differentiate these eight faces by placing a red, a green, a yellow, and a blue dot in the center of each of their respective four white inside faces, and an orange, a purple, a brown, and a gray dot in the center of each of their outside black triangles successively.

1013.33   Each of the two tetrahedra can turn themselves inside out as their three respective triangular corners rotate around the central (base) triangle's three edge hinges—thus to open up like a three-petaled flower bud. Each tetrahedron can be opened in four such different flower-bud ways, with three triangular petals around each of their four respective triangular flower-receptacle base faces.

1013.34   The four separate cases of inside-outing transformability permit the production of four separate and unique positive and four separate and unique negative tetrahedra, all generated from the same unity and each of which can rank equally as nature's simplest structural system.

1013.40   Nine Schematic Aspects of the Tetrahedron

1013.41   Every tetrahedron, every prime structural system in Universe, has nine separate and unique states of existence: four positive, four negative, plus one schematic unfolded nothingness, unfolded to an infinite, planar, neither-one-nor-the-other, equilibrious state. These manifest the same schematic "game" setups as that of physics' quantum mechanics. Quantum mechanics provides for four positive and four negative quanta as we go from a central nothingness equilibrium to first one, then two, then three, then four high-frequency, regenerated, alternate, equiintegrity, tetrahedral quanta. Each of the eight tetrahedral quanta also has eight invisible counterparts. (See Figs. 1012.14A, .14B, and .15.)

1013.42   When the four planes of each of the eight tetrahedra move toward their four opposite vertexes, the momentum carries them through zero-volume nothingness of the vector equilibrium phase. All their volumes decrease at a third-power rate of their linear rate of approach. As the four tetrahedral planes coincide, the four great-circle planes of the vector equilibrium all go through the same nothingness local at the same time. Thus we find the vector equilibrium to be the inherent zero-nineness of fundamental number behavior. (See color plate 31.)

1013.50   Visible and Invisible Tetrahedral Arrays

1013.51   Visibly Demonstrable: Physical

Four white, three-petaled flowers
1 red   base
1 green base
1 yellow base
1 blue   base
Four black, three-petaled flowers
1 orange base
1 purple base
1 brown base
1 gray   base

1013.52   *Invisible But Thinkable: Metaphysical*

Four white, three-petaled flowers
1 orange base
1 purple base
1 brown base
1 gray   base

Four black, three-petaled flowers
1 red   base
1 green base
1 yellow base
1 blue   base

1013.60 Quantum Jump Model

1013.61   All of the triangularly petaled tetrahedra may have their 60-degree corners partially open and pointing out from their bases like an opening tulip bud. We may take any two of the 60-degree petaled tetrahedra and hold them opposite one another while rotating one of them in a 60-degree turn, which precesses it axially at 60 degrees, thus pointing its triangular petals toward the other's 60-degree openings. If we bring them together edge to edge, we will produce an octahedron. (Compare Sec. *1033.73.*)

1013.62   The octahedron thus produced has a volume of four tetrahedra. Each of the separate tetrahedra had one energy quantum unit. We now see how one quantum and one quantum may be geometrically joined to produce four quanta. Another quantum jump is demonstrated.

1013.63   Each of the two tetrahedra combining to make the octahedron can consist of the eight unique combinations of the black and the white triangular faces and their four red, green, yellow, and blue center dots. This means that we have an octahedron of eight black triangles, one of eight white, and one of four white plus four black, and that the alternation of the four different color dots into all the possible combinations of eight produces four times 26—which is the 104 possible combinations.

1013.64   Where $N = 8$ and there are four sets of 8, the formula for the number of combinations is:

$$\frac{4\,(N^2 - N)}{2} \therefore \frac{4\,(64 - 8)}{2} = \frac{4 \times 56}{2} = 112$$

This result has a startling proximity to the 92 unique regenerative chemical elements plus their additional non-self-regenerative posturanium atoms.

1033.00   Intertransformability Models and Limits

•[*1033.00–1033.92   Involvement Field Scenario*]

1033.010   Generation of the Involvement Field in Which Synergetics Integrates Topology, Electromagnetics, Chemistry and Cosmology

1033.011   Commencing with the experimentally demonstrated proof that the tetrahedron is the minimum structural system of Universe (i.e., the vectorially and angularly self-stabilizing minimum polyhedron consisting of four minimum polygons in omnisymmetrical array), we then discover that each of the four vertices of the tetrahedron is subtended by four "faces," or empty triangular windows. The four vertices have proven to be only whole-range tunable and point-to-able noise or "darkness" centers—which are primitive (i.e., as yet frequency-blurred), systemic somethings (see Secs. *505.65, 527.711*, and *1012.33*) having six unique angularly intersightable lines of interrelationship whose both-ends-interconnected six lines produce four triangular windows, out through which each of the four system-defining somethings gains four separate views of the same omninothingness of as-yet-untuned-in Universe. As subtunable systems, points are substances, somethings—ergo, we have in the tetrahedron four somethings symmetrically arrayed against four nothingnesses. (Four INS versus four OUTS.)

1033.012   The four somethingnesses are mass-interattractively interrelated by six interrelationship tensors—each tensor having two other interconnected tensor restraints preventing one another and their four respective vertexial somethings from leaving the system. Like a three-rubber-banded slingshot, each of the four sets of three restraining, but in fact vertexially convergent, tensors not only restrains but also constrains their respective four *somethings* to plunge aimedly into-through-and-out their respectively subtended triangular windows, into the unresisting nothingess, and penetrating that nothingness until the stretchable limit of the three tensors is reached, whereat they will be strained into reversing the direction of impelment of their vertexial somethings. Thus we discovered the tetrahedron's inherent proclivity to repeatedly turn itself inside out, and then outside-out, and reverse. Thus the tetrahedron has the means to convert its tuned-in-ness to its turned-out-and-tuned-outness, which inherently produces the frequencies of the particular discontinuities of electromagnetic Universe.

1033.013 Because there are four symmetrically arrayed sets of nothingnesses subtending four somethings, there are four ways in which every minimum structural system in Universe may be turned inside out. Ergo, every tetrahedron is inherently eight tetrahedra, four outside-out and four inside-out: the octave system.

1033.014 We deliberately avoid the terms positive and negative and—consistent with experience—may use the words *active* and *passive* respectively for outside-out and inside-out. Active means "now in use"; passive means "not in use now."

1033.015 Since the somethings are the INS and the nothingness is OUT, outside-out and inside-out are experientially meaningful. There are inherently a plurality of different nothingness OUTS consisting of all the potential macro- and microranges of "presently untuned-in" systemic frequencies.

1033.016 Experientiality, which is always in time, begins with an observer and an observed—i.e., two somethings, two INdividuals—with the observed other individual only differentially perceivable against the omninothingness, the presently untuned-IN, ergo OUT. (The observer and the otherness may be integral, as in the complex individual—the child's hand discovering the otherness of its own foot, or the tongue-sense discovering the taste of the tactile-sensing thumb, or the outside thumb discovering the insideness of the mouth.)

1033.017 We have elsewhere reviewed the progressive tangential agglomeration of other "spherical" somethings with the otherness observer's spherical something (Secs. 411.01–08) and their four-dimensional symmetry's systemic intermotion blocking and resultant system's interlockage, which locking and blocking imposes total system integrity and permits whole-system-integrated rotation, orbiting, and interlinkage with other system integrities.

1033.018 Since we learned by experimental proof that our four-dimensional symmetry accommodates three axial freedoms of rotation motion (see the Triangular-cammed, In-out-and-around, Jitterbug Model, Sec. 465), while also permitting us to restrain* one of the four axes of perpendicularity to the four planes, i.e., of the INS most economically—or perpendicularly—approaching the tensor relationship's angularly planed and framed views through to the nothingness, we find that we may make a realistic model of the omniinvolvement field of all eight phases of the tetrahedron's self-intertransformability.

1033.019 The involvement field also manifests the exclusively unique and inviolable fourfold symmetry of the tetrahedron (see Cheese Tetrahedron,

---

* "Restrain" does not mean motionless or "cosmically at rest." Restrain does mean "with the axis locked into congruent motion of another system." Compare a system holding in relative restraint one axis of a four-axis wheel model.

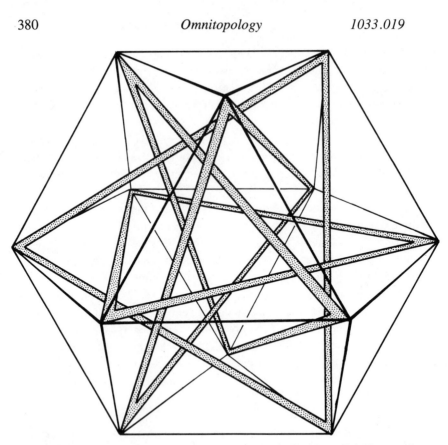

Fig. *1033.019 Circuit Pattern Tensegrity:* In Anthony Pugh's model 12 struts form four interlocking but nontouching triangular circuits. The plane of each triangle of struts bisects the vector equilibrium which its vertexes define. Each triangle of struts is inscribed within a hexagonal circuit of tensors.

Sec. 623), which permits us always to move symmetrically and convergently each—and inadvertently any or all—of the four triangular window frames perpendicularly toward their four subtending somethingness-converging-point-to-able IN foci, until all four planes pass through the same threshold between INness and OUTness, producing one congruent, zerovolume tetrahedron. The four inherent planes of the four tensegrity triangles of Anthony Pugh's model* demonstrate the nothingness of their four planes, permitting their timeless—i.e., untuned—nothingness congruence. (See Fig. *1033.019.*) The tuned-in, somethingness lines of the mathematician, with their inherent self-interferences, would never permit a plurality of such lines to pass through the same somethingness points at the same time (see Sec. 517).

---

*This is what Pugh calls his "circuit pattern tensegrity," described on pages 19–22 of his *An Introduction to Tensegrity* (Berkeley: University of California Press, 1976.)

1033.020 **Four-triangular-circuits Tensegrity:** The four-triangular-circuits tensegrity relates to the four great circles of the vector equilibrium. The four great circles of the vector equilibrium are generated by the four axes of vector equilibrium's eight triangular faces. Each of the four interlocking triangles is inscribed within a hexagonal circuit of vectors—of four intersecting hexagonal planes of the vector equilibrium. These tensegrity circuits relate to the empty tetrahedron at its center. (See Secs. *441.021, 938.12,* and *1053.804.*)

1033.021 Our omniinvolvement tetrahedral-intertransformability, isotropic-vector-matrix-field of any given relative frequency can accommodate both the tetrahedron's most complexedly expansive-divergent domain and its most convergence-to-untuned-nothingness identification, while also maintaining the integrity of its inherent isolatability from both all otherness and all nothingness.

1033.022 The involvement field also identifies the unique cosmically inviolate environment domain of convergent-divergent symmetrical nuclear systems, i.e., the vector equilibrium's unique domain provided by one "external" octahedron (see Sec. 415.17), which may be modeled most symmetrically by the 4-tetravolume octahedron's symmetrical subdivision into its eight similar asymmetric tetrahedra consisting of three 90-degree angles, three 60-degree angles, and six 45-degree angles, whose 60-degree triangular faces have been addressed to each of the vector equilibrium's eight outermost triangular windows of each of the eight tetrahedra of the 20-tetravolume vector equilibrium.

1033.023 Any one triangular plane formed by any three of the vertexial somethings' interrelationship lines, of any one omnitriangulated tetrahedral system, of any isotropic vector matrix grid, can move in only four-degrees-of-freedom directions always to reach to-or-fro limits of vertexial convergences, which convergences are always zerovolume.

1033.030 Untenable Equilibrium Compulsion

1033.031 In the 20-tetravolume vector equilibrium we have four passive and four active tetrahedra vertexially interconnected. The eight tetrahedra have a total of 32 vertexes. In the 20-tetravolume vector equilibrium each tetrahedron has three of its vertexial somethings outwardly arrayed and one vertexial something inwardly arrayed. Their 24 externally arrayed vertexes are *congruently paired* to form the 12 vertexes of the vector equilibrium, and their eight interior vertexial somethings are *nuclear congruent;* ergo, four-forcedly-more-vector-interconstrained than any of their externally paired vertexial something sets: an untenable equilibrium compulsion (UEC). (Compare Secs. 1012.11 and *1224.13*.)

1033.032   The untenable equilibrium compulsion (UEC) inherently impels the nucleus toward and through any of the nucleus's eight externally subtended triangular windows, the three corners of each of which are two-tensor-restrained (six tensors per triangular window) by the gravitationally embracing, circumferentially closed tensors. This empowers the nuclear eightfold-congruent somethings to exit pulsatingly through the windows to a distance one-half that of the altitude of the regular tetrahedron, which is describable to the eight divergent points by mounting outwardly of the eight Eighth-Octahedra on each of the eight triangular window frames of the vector equilibrium, which thereby describe the cube of 24 tetravolumes (i.e., eight of the primitive, Duo-Tet-described cubes of three tetravolumes). These eight external pulsative points are inherently center-of-volume terminalled when nuclear systems are closest packed with one another. Thus we find the total nuclear domain of Universe to have a tetravolume of 24. When the vector equilibrium nucleus has no closest-packed-around-it, nucleated vector equilibrium systems, then the eightfold nuclear impelment works successively to expel its energies pulsatingly and radiantly through all eight of its windows.

1033.10   Octave System of Polyhedral Transformations

1033.101   The systematic outsideness is the macrountuned: the ultra-tunable. The systemic insideness is the micrountuned: the infratunable. The system is the discretely tuned-in conceptuality.

1033.102   The closest-packed spheres are simply the frequencies that are activated, that get into closest proximity as a continuum of the outsideness:

> —the critical proximity spherical zone, which is fall-in-here or fall-in-there or independently in orbit for shorter or longer time spans;
> —the boundary layer;
> —the mass-interattractively tensioned (trampoline) field, which is as deeply near as any proximate systems can come to "tangency";
> —the threshold zone of tuned-in but non-frequency-differentialed; when a system is at the threshold, it is non-frequency-modulated, hence only a point-to-able noise or gray, nondescript color.

1033.103   If there were a geometric outsideness and insideness, we would have a static geometrical Universe. But since the insideness and outsideness are the as-yet-untuned-in or no-longer-tuned-in wavelengths and their frequencies, they require only Scenario Universe, its past and future. Only the NOW conceptualizing constitutes a geometry—the immediate conceptual, special-case, systemic episode in a scenario of nonunitarily conceptual, nonsimul-taneous, and only partially overlapping, differently enduring, differently mag-nituded, special-case, systemic episodes, each in itself a constellation of con-stellations within constellations of infra- or ultratunably frequenced, special case frequenced systems (Compare Sec. 321.05.)

1033.104 The isotropic-vector-matrix-field has an infinite range of elec-tromagnetic tunings that are always multiplying frequency by division of the a priori vector equilibrium and its contained cosmic hierarchy of timeless-sizeless primitive systems' unfrequenced state. At maximum their primitive comprehensive domain is that of the six-tetravolume, 24-A-and-B-quanta-moduled, unfrequenced rhombic dodecahedron, the long axis of whose 12 diamond faces is also the *prime vector* length of the isotropic vector matrix. At primitive minimum the unfrequenced state is that of the six-A-and-B-quanta-moduled Syte. Both the maximum and minimum, primitive, greatest and least primitive common divisors of Universe may be replicatively em-ployed or convergently composited to produce the isotropic vector matrix field of selectable frequency tunability, whose key wavelength is that of the relative length of the uniform vector of the isotropic vector matrix as initially selected in respect to the diameter of the nucleus of the atom.

1033.11 Every electromagnetic wave propagation generates its own cos-mic field. This field is a four-dimensional isotropic vector matrix that can be readily conceptualized as an aggregation of multilayered, closest-packed, unit-radius spheres. (See Fig. *1033.111A.*) Unit-radius spheres pack tangen-tially together most closely in 60-degree intertriangulations. Atoms close-pack in this manner. The continuum of inherent outsideness of all systems enters every external opening of all closest-packed, unit-radius sphere aggregates, permeating and omnisurrounding every closest-packed sphere within the total aggregate. Between the closest-packed, unit-radius spheres the intervening voids constitute a uniform series of unique, symmetrical, curvilinear, geomet-rical shapes, and the successive centers of volumes of those uniform phase voids are uniformly interspaced—the distance between them being always the same as the uniform distances between adjacent closest-packed spheres.

1033.111 Each of the closest-packed, unit-radius spheres is itself a geode-sic sphere, a spherical sieve with triangular openings: a tetra-, octa-, or ico-sasphere of some frequency of modular subdivision. (Compare the fallacy of the Greek sphere as described at Secs. 981.19, 1022.11–13, 1106.22, and 1107.21.) Wherefore, each of the closest-packed spheres is permeable by higher-frequency, shorter-wavelength, electromagnetic propagations; ergo, appropriately frequenced fields may pass through the isotropic vector matrix's electromagnetic field of any given wavelengths without interference. Not only does each closest-packed sphere consist of a plurality of varifrequenced ver-

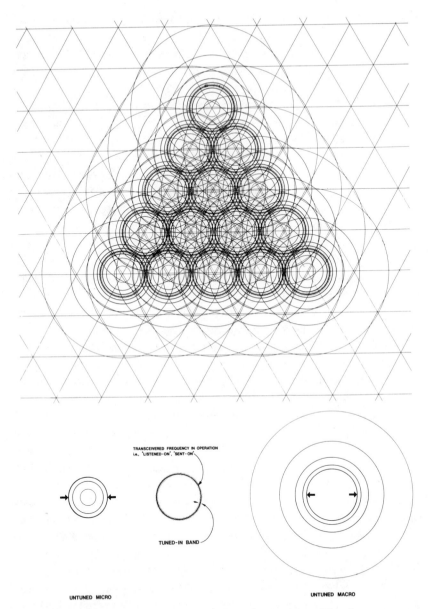

Fig. *1033.11 Electromagnetic Field of Closest-packed spheres:* This figure represents one of the four planes of symmetry of the closest-packed unit-radius spheres, of the isotropic vector matrix. Between the untuned macro and the untuned micro is the transceivered frequency operation of the tuned-in and transmitted information.

Fig. *1033.111A Photograph of Southeast Asian Reed Sphere Woven on Three-way Grid.*

tices interconnected by chords that define the triangular sieve, but also these vertexial somethings are mass-interattractively positioned and have their own boundary layer (trampoline) cushions; ergo, they are never in absolute tangency.

1033.112 The isotropic vector matrix grid illustrates that frequency multiplication may be accomplished only by division. The unit-radius spheres of the isotropic vector matrix electromagnetic fields close-pack in four planes of symmetry, permitting four-dimensional electromagnetic wavebands. The three-way, spherical, electromagnetic, basketry interweaving is illustrated at Fig. *1033.111B*. There are six great-circle equators of the six axes formed by the 12 vertices of the spherical icosahedron. The centers of area of the spherical triangles thus formed describe the terminals of the electromagnetic waveband widths. The widths of the bands of frequency tunability are determined by the truncatability of the spherical icosahedron's six bands as they run between the centers of area of the adjacent triangles.

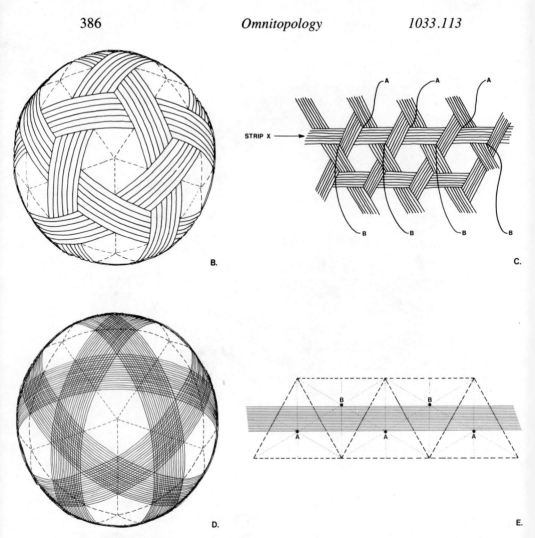

Fig. *1033.111 B–D:*

B. Diagram of three-way grid sphere.
C. Band widths of frequency tunability.
D. Six great circle band widths of spherical icosahedron
E. Centers of volumes of tetrahedra are control matrix for electromagnetic band widths.

1033.113   Note that the centers of area of the adjacent spherical triangles are alternately staggered so as to define a broad path within which the electromagnetic waveband is generated.

1033.120   Click-stop Subdivisioning

1033.121   In synergetic geometry we witness the transformation of all spheres into their local complementary intervoid domains as the local intervoid domains transform into closest-packed, unit-radius spheres. (See Fig. 1032.31.) The multifrequenced tetrahedral, octahedral, and icosahedral geodesic subdivisioning of spherical projections of the primitive polyhedral systems describes how the complex interbonding of substances occurs; it is further described by the varying radii of the closest-packed spheres and the complex of isotropic vector matrixes required to accommodate the varying radii as well as their ultra- and infrapermeating: this elucidates the resonance of substances as well as the unique electromagnetic frequencies of chemical elements. Here is the grand synergetic nexus integrating electromagnetics, chemistry, and topology.

1033.122   Synergetics arouses human awareness of the always-and-only-co-occurring, non-tuned-in cosmic complementations of our only-from-moment-to-moment systematically tuned-in conceptionings. Synergetics' always symmetrical, complementarily expanding and contracting intertransformings disclose a succession of "local way stations." Progressive arrival at these convergent-divergent "way station" states discloses a succession of immediately neighboring, larger-to-smaller, symmetrical polyhedra of diminishingly numbered topological characteristics, which all together constitute a cosmic hierarchy of symmetrical, rationally volumed, most primitive, pattern-stabilization states. Superficially the states are recognizable as the family of Platonic polyhedra.

1033.123   Throughout the convergent phase of the transformation continuum, all the vertices of these successive Platonic forms and their intertransformative phases are always diminishingly equidistant from the same volumetric center. The omnisymmetrical contraction is accommodated by the angular closing—scissor-hinge-wise—of immediately adjacent edges of the polyhedra. The vertices of each of these intertransforming symmetric states, as well as their intermediate transforms, are always positioned in a sphere that is progressively expanding or contracting—depending on whether we are reading the cosmic hierarchy as energetic volumes from 1 to 24 or from 24 to 1.

1033.124   As the originally omnisymmetrical, 20-tetravolume vector equilibrium of 12 vertices, 14 faces, and 24 vector edges shrinks its vertex-described spherical domain, it may receive one quantum of energy released entropically by some elsewhere-in-Universe entropic radiation, as most frequently occurring when octahedra of matter are precessed and the octahedron's tetravolume 4 is reduced to tetravolume 3 (see Octahedron as Conservation and Annihilation Model, Sec. 935), the tetrahedron thus annihilated being one quantum lost entropically without any alteration of the Eulerean topological characteristics as an octahedron. Since each quantum consists of six vector edges that can now be entropically dispersed, they may be syntropically harvested by the 20-tetravolume vector equilibrium, and, constituting one quantum of energy, they will structurally stabilize the shrinking 20-tetravolume vector equilibrium → 4-tetravolume octahedron system in the intermediate symmetrical form of the icosahedron. As the icosahedron of 12 vertices, 20 faces, and 30 edges $(24 + 6)$ shrinks its spherical domain, it can do so only by compressing the one energy quantum of six syntropically captured vector edges into the six vertical somethings of the octahedron, thereby allowing 12 faces to unite as six—all the while the icosahedron's ever-shrinking spherical surface pattern alters uniformly, despite which its topological inventory of 12 vertices, 14 faces, and 24 edges remains constant until the simultaneous moment of vertex, face, and edge congruence occurs. Simultaneously each of the paired vertices and edges—as well as the six compressed vector edges—now appears as one; and each of the congruent pairs is now topologically countable only as one—in this instance as the six vertices, eight faces, and 12 edges of the suddenly realized octahedron of tetra-volume 4.

1033.125   The simultaneous vanishing of the previously shuttling and lingering topological characteristics from the previously stable icosahedral state, and the instant appearance of the next neighboring state—the octahedron, in its simplest and completely symmetrical condition—is what we mean by a "click-stop" or "way station" state.

1033.126   Assessing accurately the "click-stop" volumes of the intertransformative hierarchy in terms of the volume of the tetrahedron equaling one, we find that the relative tetravolumes of these primitive polyhedra—when divergent—are successively, 1, $2^{1}/_{2}$, 3, 2^{2}, 5, 6, 20, 24, and then—converging—from 24, 20, 6, 5, 2^{2}, 3, $2^{1}/_{2}$, 1. These omnirational, whole-number, "click-stop" volumes and their successive topological characteristic numbers elegantly introduce—and give unique volumetric shape to—each of all of the first four prime numbers of Universe: 1, 2, 3, 5. (Compare Sec. *100.321.*)

1033.127   These click-stop, whole-tetravolumed, symmetrical geometries have common centers of volume, and all are concentrically and intersymmetrically arrayed within the rhombic dodecahedron. In this concentric symmetric array they constitute what we call the *cosmic hierarchy* of primitive conceptuality of thought and comprehension. Intuitively hypersensitive and seeking to explain the solar system's interplanetary behaviors, Johannes Kepler evolved a concentric model of some of the Platonic geometries but, apparently frustrated by the identification of volumetric unity exclusively with the cube, failed to discover the rational cosmic hierarchy—it became the extraordinary experience of synergetics to reveal this in its first written disclosure of 1944.

1033.128 It is visually manifest both between and at the "click-stop" states that the smooth intertransforming is four-dimensional, accommodated by local transformations around four axes of system symmetry. The systems' vertices always remain spherically arrayed and describe a smooth, overall-spheric-continuum-contraction from the largest to the smallest tune-in-able-by-the-numbers system states occurring successively between the beyond-tune-in-able system ranges of the macronothingness and the beyond-tune-in-able micronothingness.

1033.180 Vector Equilibrium: Potential and Primitive Tetravolumes

1033.181 The potential activation of tetravolume quantation in the geometric hierarchy is still subfrequency but accounts for the doubling of volumetric space. The potential activation of tetravolume accounting is plural; it provides for nucleation. Primitive tetravolume accounting is singular and subnuclear.

1033.182 When the isolated single sphere's vector equilibrium of tetravolume $2^1/_2$ is surrounded by 12 spheres to become a nuclear sphere, the vector equilibrium described by the innermost-economically-interconnecting of the centers of volume of the 12 spheres comprehensively and tangentially surrounding the nuclear sphere—as well as interconnecting their 12 centers with the center of the nuclear sphere—has a tetravolume of 20, and the nuclear group's rhombic dodecahedron has a tetravolume of 48.

1033.183 The tetravolume-6 rhombic dodecahedron is the domain of each closest-packed, unit-radius sphere, for it tangentially embraces not only each sphere, but that sphere's proportional share of the intervening space produced by such unit-radius-sphere closest packing.

1033.184 When the time-sizing is initiated with frequency², the rhombic dodecahedron's volume of 6 is eightfolded to become 48. In the plurality of closest-packed-sphere domains, the sphere-into-space, space-into-sphere *dual* rhombic dodecahedron domain has a tetravolume of 48. The total space is 24—with the vector equilibrium's Eighth-Octahedra extroverted to form the rhombic dodecahedron. For every space there is always an alternate space: This is where we get the 48-ness of the rhombic dodecahedron as the macrodomain of a sphere:

$$2^1/_2 \times 8 = 20$$
$$6 \times 8 = 48$$

1033.185 The 12 spheric domains around one nuclear sphere domain equal 13 rhombic dodecahedra—nuclear $6 + (12 \times 6) = $ tetravolume 78.

Table: Prime Number Consequences of Spin-halving of Tetrahedron's Volumetric Domain Unity

	Tetravolumes:	*Great Circles:*
Vector Equilibrium As Zerovolume Tetrahedron: eternally congruent intro-extrovert domain	$0 = +2^1/_2, -2^1/_2,$ $-2^1/_2, +2^1/_2,$ (with plus-minus limits differential of 5) ever-inter-self-canceling to produce zerovolume tetrahedron	4 complete great circles, each fully active
Tetra: eternally incongruent	$+1 (+1$ or $-1)$	6 complete great circles, each being $^1/_3$ active, vector components
Octa: eternally congruent yet nonredundant, complementary positive-negative duality	$2 (2 \times 2 = 4)$	2 congruent (1 positive, 1 negative) sets of 3 great circles each; i.e., a total of 6 great circles but visible only as 3 sets
Duo-Tet Cube: intro-extrovert tetra, its vertexially defined cubical domain, edge-outlined by 6 axes spun most-economically-interconnected edges of cube	3 "cube"	6 great circles $^2/_3$ active
Rhombic Triacontahedron: $1 \times 2 \times 3 \times 5 = 30$	5 "sphere" both statically and dynamically the most spheric primitive system	15-great-circle-defined, 120 T Modules
Rhombic Dodecahedron:	6 closest-packed spheric domain	12 great circles appearing as 9 and consisting of 2 congruent sets of 3 great circles of octa plus 6 great circles of cube
Vector Equilibrium: nuclear-potentialed	20 (potential)	4 great circles describing 8 tetrahedra and 6 half-octahedra

The constant octave system interrelationship is tunable to an infinity of different frequency keys:

Active Tetravolumes

Always and only co-occur-ring	Convergent Tetrahedron (Active: now you see it)	1
	Divergent Tetrahedron (Passive: now you don't)	1

Infratunable microcosmic zero (Four great-circle planes as zerovolume tetrahedron)	0

	Convergent-divergent tetrahedron, always and only dynamically coexisting, unity is plural and at minimum two: active or passive	1
	Vector-diameter vector equilibrium: congruently $2^1/_2$ convergent and $2^1/_2$ divergent	$2^1/_2$
The Eight Tunable Octave "Notes"	Duo-tet Cube, star-tetra geodesic cubic domain: $1^1/_2$ passive and $1^1/_2$ active	3
	Octahedron as two passive tetra and two active tetra	4
	Vector-radius rhombic triacontahedron	5 +
	Rhombic dodecahedron	6
	Vector-radius vector equilibrium	20
	Vector equilibrium plus its external octahedron	24

Sphere-into-space-space-into-sphere dual rhombic dodecahedron domain	48

Ultratunable macrocosmic zero (Four great-circle planes as zerovolume vector equilibrium)	0

1033.30 Symmetrical Contraction of Vector Equilibrium: Quantum Loss

1033.31 The six square faces of the vector equilibrium are dynamically balanced; three are oppositely arrayed in the northern hemisphere and three in the southern hemisphere. They may be considered as three—alternately polarizable—pairs of half-octahedra radiantly arrayed around the nucleus, which altogether constitute three whole "internal" octahedra, each of which when halved is structurally unstable—ergo, collapsible—and which, with the vector equilibrium jitterbug contraction, have each of their six sets of half-octahedra's four internal, equiangular, triangular faces progressively paired into congruence, at which point each of the six half-octahedra—ergo, three quanta—has been annihilated.

1033.32 In the always-omnisymmetrical progressive jitterbug contraction the vector equilibrium—disembarrassed of its disintegrative radial vectors—does not escape its infinite instability until it is symmetrically contracted and thereby structurally transformed into the icosahedron, whereat the six square faces of the half-octahedra become mildly folded diamonds ridge-poled along the diamond's shorter axis and thereby bent into six ridge-pole diamond facets, thus producing 12 primitively equilateral triangles. Not until the six squares are diagonally vectored is the vector equilibrium stabilized into an omnitriangulated, 20-triangled, 20-tetrahedral structural system, the icosahedron: the structural system having the greatest system volume with the least energy quanta of structural investment—ergo, the least dense of all matter.

1033.33 See Sec. 611.02 for the tetravolumes per vector quanta structurally invested in the tetra, octa, and icosa, in which we accomplish—

Tetra = 1 volume per each quanta of structure
Octa = 2 volume per each quanta of structure
Icosa = 4 (approximate) volume per each quanta of structure

1033.34 This annihilation of the three octahedra accommodates both axial rotation and its linear contraction of the eight regular tetrahedra radiantly arrayed around the nucleus of the vector equilibrium. These eight tetrahedra may be considered as four—also alternately polarizable—pairs. As the axis rotates and shortens, the eight tetra pair into four congruent (or quadrivalent) tetrahedral sets. This omnisymmetrically accomplished contraction from the VE's 20-ness to the quadrivalent octahedron of tetravolume-4 represents a topologically unaccounted for—but synergetically conceptualized—annihilation of 16 tetravolumes, i.e., 16 energy quanta, 12 of which are synergetically accounted for by the collapse of the three internal octahedra (each of four quanta); the other four-quanta loss is accounted for by the radial contraction of each of the VE's eight tetrahedra (eight quanta) into the form of Eighth-Octahedra (each of a tetravolume of $^1/_2$—ergo, $8 \times ^1/_2 = 4 =$ a total of four quanta.

1033.35   The six new vector diagonals of the three pairs of opposing half-octahedra become available to provide for the precession of any one of the equatorial quadrangular vectors of the half-octahedra to demonstrate the inter-transformability of the octahedron as a conservation and annihilation model. (See Sec. 935.) In this transformation the octahedron retains its apparent topological integrity of $6V + 8F = 12E + 2$, while transforming from four tetravolumes to three tetravolumes. This tetrahelical evolution requires the precession of only one of the quadrangular equatorial vector edges, that edge nearest to the mass-interattractively precessing neighboring mass passing the octahedron (as matter) so closely as to bring about the precession and its consequent entropic discard of one quantum of energy—which unbalanced its symmetry and resulted in the three remaining quanta of matter being transformed into three quanta of energy as radiation.

1033.36   This transformation from four tetravolumes to three tetravolumes—i.e., from four to three energy quanta—cannot be topologically detected, as the Eulerean inventory remains $6V + 8F = 12E + 2$. The entropic loss of one quantum can only be experimentally disclosed to human cognition by the conceptuality of synergetics' omnioperational conceptuality of inter-transformabilities. (Compare color plates 6 and 7.)

1033.40   Asymmetrical Contraction of Vector Equilibrium: Quantum Loss

1033.41   The vector equilibrium contraction from tetravolume 20 to the tetravolume 4 of the octahedron may be accomplished symmetrically (as just described in Sec. *1033.30*) by altogether collapsing the unstable six half-octahedra and by symmetrical contraction of the 12 radii. The angular collapsing of the 12 radii is required by virtue of the collapsings of the six half-octahedra, which altogether results in the eight regular tetrahedra being concurrently reduced in their internal radial dimension, while retaining their eight external equiangular triangles unaltered in their prime-vector-edge lengths; wherefore, the eight internal edges of the original tetrahedra are contractively reduced to eight asymmetric tetrahedra, each with one equiangular, triangular, external face and with three right-angle-apexed and prime-vector-base-edged internal isosceles-triangle faces, each of whose interior apexes occurs congruently at the center of volume of the symmetrical octahedron—ergo, each of which eight regular-to-asymmetric-transformed tetrahedra are now seen to be our familiar Eighth-Octahedra, each of which has a volume of $^1/_2$-

tetravolume; and since there are eight of them $(8 \times \frac{1}{2} = 4)$, the resulting octahedron equals tetravolume-4.

1033.42　　This transformation may also have been accomplished in an alternate manner. We recall how the jitterbug vector equilibrium demonstrated the four-dimensional freedom by means of which its axis never rotates while its equator is revolving (see Sec. 460.02). Despite this axis and equator differentiation the whole jitterbug is simultaneously and omnisymmetrically contracting in volume as its 12 vertexes all approach their common center at the same radial contraction rate, moving within the symmetrically contracting surface to pair into the six vertices of the octahedron—after having passed symmetrically through that as-yet-12-vectored icosahedral stage of symmetry. With that complex concept in mind we realize that the nonrotating axis was of necessity contracting in its overall length; ergo, the two-vertex-to-two-vertex-bonded "pair" of regular tetrahedra whose most-remotely-opposite, equiangular triangular faces' respective centers of area represented the two poles of the nonrotated axis around which the six vertices at the equator angularly rotated—three rotating slantwise "northeastward" and three rotating "southeastward," as the northeastward three spiraled finally northward to congruence with the three corner vertices of the nonrotating north pole triangle, while concurrently the three southeastward-slantwise rotating vertices originally situated at the VE jitterbug equator spiral into congruence with the three corner vertices of the nonrotating south pole triangle.

1033.43　　As part of the comprehensively symmetrical contraction of the whole primitive VE system, we may consider the concurrent north-to-south polar-axis contraction (accomplished as the axis remained motionless with respect to the equatorial motions) to have caused the two original vertex-to-vertex regular polar tetrahedra to penetrate one another vertexially as their original two congruent center-of-VE-volume vertices each slid in opposite directions along their common polar-axis line, with those vertices moving toward the centers of area, respectively, of the other polar tetrahedron's polar triangle, traveling thus until those two penetrating vertices came to rest at the center of area of the opposite tetrahedron's polar triangle—the planar altitude of the octahedron being the same as the altitude of the regular tetrahedron. (See Figs. *1033.43* and *1033.47*.)

1033.44　　In this condition they represent the opposite pair of polar triangles of the regular octahedron around whose equator are arrayed the six other equiangular triangles of the regular octahedron's eight equiangular triangles. (See Fig. *1033.43*.) In this state the polarly combined and—mutually and equally—interpenetrated pair of tetrahedra occupy exactly one-half of the volume of the regular octahedron of tetravolume-4. Therefore the remaining space, with the octahedron equatorially surrounding their axial core, is also of

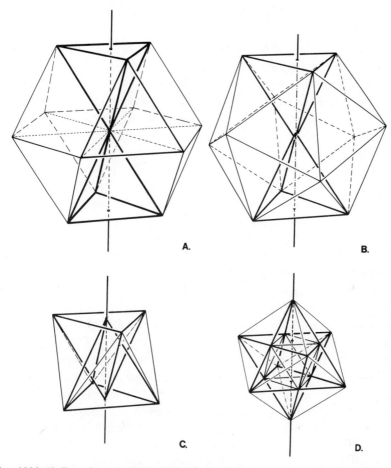

A.   B.

C.   D.

Fig. *1033.43 Two Opposite-Paired Tetrahedra Interpenetrate in Jitterbug Contraction:* As one axis remains motionless, two polar-paired, vertex-joined tetrahedra progressively interpenetrate one another to describe in mid-passage an octahedron, at *C*,
and a cube-defining star polyhedron of symmetrical congruence at *D*. (Compare Fig.
987.242A.)

tetravolume-2—i.e., one-half inside-out (space) and one-half inside-in (tet-
racore).

   1033.45   At this octahedron-forming state two of the eight vertices of the
two polar-axis tetrahedra are situated inside one another, leaving only six of
their vertices outside, and these six—always being symmetrically equidistant
from one another as well as equidistant from the system center—are now the
six vertices of the regular octahedron.

   1033.46   In the octahedron-forming state the three polar-base, corner-to-
apex-connecting-edges of each of the contracting polar-axis tetrahedra now

penetrate the other tetrahedron's three nonpolar triangle faces at their exact centers of area.

1033.47   With this same omnisymmetrical contraction continuing—with all the external vertices remaining at equal radius from the system's volumetric center—and the external vertices also equidistant chordally from one another, they find their two polar tetrahedra's mutually interpenetrating apex points breaking through the other polar triangle (at their octahedral-forming positions) at the respective centers of area of their opposite equiangular polar triangles. Their two regular-tetrahedra-shaped apex points penetrate their former polar-opposite triangles until the six mid-edges of both tetrahedra become congruent, at which symmetrical state all eight vertices of the two tetrahedra are equidistant from one another as well as from their common system center. (See Fig. *987.242A.*)

1033.48   The 12 geodesic chords omniinterconnecting these eight symmetrically omniarrayed vertices now define the regular cube, one-half of whose total volume of exactly 3-tetravolumes is symmetrically cored by the eight-pointed star core form produced by the two mutually interpenetrated tetrahedra. This symmetrical core star constitutes an inside-in tetravolume of $1\frac{1}{2}$, with the surrounding equatorial remainder of the cube-defined, insideout space being also exactly tetravolume $1\frac{1}{2}$. (See Fig. *987.242A.*)

1033.490   In this state each of the symmetrically interpenetrated tetrahedra's eight external vertices begins to approach one another as each opposite pair of each of the tetrahedra's six edges—which in the cube stage had been arrayed at their mutual mid-edges at 90 degrees to one another—now rotates in respect to those mid-edges—which six mutual tetrahedra's mid-edge points all occur at the six centers of the six square faces of the cube.

1033.491   The rotation around these six points continues until the six edge-lines of each of the two tetrahedra become congruent and the two tetrahedra's four vertices each become congruent—and the VE's original tetravolume 20 has been contracted to exactly tetravolume 1.

1033.492   Only during the symmetrical contraction of the tetravolume-3 cube to the tetravolume-1 tetrahedron did the original axial contraction cease, as the two opposing axis tetrahedra (one inside-out and one outside-out) rotate simultaneously and symmetrically on three axes (as permitted only by four-dimensionality freedoms) to become unitarily congruent as tetravolume-1—altogether constituting a cosmic allspace-filling contraction from 24 to 1, which is three octave quanta sets and 6×4 quanta leaps; i.e., six leaps of the six degrees of freedom (six inside-out and six outside-out), while providing the prime numbers 1,2,3,5 and multiples thereof, to become available for the entropic-syntropic, export-import transactions of seemingly annihilated—yet elsewhere reappearing—energy quanta conservation of the eternally regenerative Universe, whose comprehensively closed circuitry of gravitational embracement was never violated throughout the $24 \rightarrow 1$ compaction.

1033.50   Quanta Loss by Congruence

1033.51   Euler's Uncored Polyhedral Formula:

$$V + F = E + 2$$

Vector Equilibrium	$12 + 14 = 24 + 2$	
Octahedron	$6 + 8 = 12 + 2$	
Tetrahedron	$4 + 4 = 6 + 2$	

1033.52   Although superficially the tetrahedron seems to have only six vector edges, it has in fact 24. The sizeless, primitive tetrahedron—conceptual independent of size—is quadrivalent, inherently having eight potential alternate ways of turning itself inside out—four passive and four active—meaning that four positive and four negative tetrahedra are congruent. (See Secs. 460 and 461.)

1033.53   The vector equilibrium jitterbug provides the articulative model for demonstrating the always omnisymmetrical, divergently expanding or convergently contracting intertransformability of the entire primitive polyhedral hierarchy, structuring as you go in an omnitriangularly oriented evolution.

1033.54   As we explore the interbonding (valencing) of the evolving structural components, we soon discover that the universal interjointing of systems—and their foldability—permit their angularly hinged convergence into congruence of vertexes (single bonding), vectors (double bonding), faces (triple bonding), and volumetric congruence (quadri-bonding). Each of these multicongruences appears only as one vertex or one edge or one face aspect. The Eulerean topological accounting as presently practiced—innocent of the inherent synergetical hierarchy of intertransformability—accounts each of these multicongruent topological aspects as consisting of only one of such aspects. This misaccounting has prevented the physicists and chemists from conceptual identification of their data with synergetics' disclosure of nature's comprehensively rational, intercoordinate mathematical system.

1033.55   Only the topological analysis of synergetics can account for all the multicongruent—doubled, tripled, fourfolded—topological aspects by accounting for the initial tetravolume inventories of the comprehensive rhombic dodecahedron and vector equilibrium. The comprehensive rhombic dodecahedron has an initial tetravolume of 48; the vector equilibrium has an inherent tetravolume of 20; their respective initial or primitive inventories of vertexes, vectors, and faces are always present—though often imperceptibly so—at all stages in nature's comprehensive $48 \rightarrow 1$ convergence transformation.

1033.56 Only by recognizing the deceptiveness of Eulerean topology can synergetics account for the primitive total inventories of all aspects and thus conceptually demonstrate and prove the validity of Boltzmann's concepts as well as those of all quantum phenomena. Synergetics' mathematical accounting conceptually interlinks the operational data of physics and chemistry and their complex associabilities manifest in geology, biology, and other disciplines.

1033.60 Primitive Dimensionality

1033.601 Defining frequency in terms of interval requires a minimum of three intervals between four similar system events. (See Sec. *526.23*.) Defining frequency in terms of cycles requires a minimum of two cycles. Size requires time. Time requires cycles. An angle is a fraction of a cycle; angle is subcyclic. Angle is independent of time. But angle is conceptual; angle is angle independent of the length of its edges. You can be conceptually aware of angle independently of experiential time. Angular conceptioning is metaphysical; all physical phenomena occur only in time. Time and size and special-case physical reality begin with frequency. Pre-time-size conceptuality is *primitive* conceptuality. Unfrequenced angular topology is primitive. (See Sec. *527.70*.)

1033.61 Fifth Dimension Accommodates Physical Size

1033.611 Dimension begins at four. Four-dimensionality is primitive and exclusively within the primitive systems' relative topological abundances and relative interangular proportionment. Four-dimensionality is eternal, generalized, sizeless, unfrequenced.

1033.612 If the system is frequenced, it is at minimum linearly five-dimensional, surfacewise six-dimensional, and volumetrically seven-dimensional. Size is special case, temporal, terminal, and more than four-dimensional.

1033.613 Increase of relative size dimension is accomplished by multiplication of modular and cyclic frequencies, which is in turn accomplished only through subdividing a given system. Multiplication of size is accomplished only by agglomeration of whole systems in which the whole systems become the modules. In frequency modulation of both single systems or whole-system agglomerations asymmetries of internal subdivision or asymmetrical agglomeration are permitted by the indestructible symmetry of the four-dimensionality of the primitive system of cosmic reference: the tetrahedron—the minimum structural system of Universe.

1033.62 Zerovolume Tetrahedron

1033.621   The primitive tetrahedron is the four-dimensional, eight-in-one, quadrivalent, always-and-only-coexisting, inside-out and outside-out zerovolume whose four great-circle planes pass through the same nothingness center, the four-dimensionally articulatable inflection center of primitive conceptual reference.

1 tetrahedron = zerovolume

1 tetrahedron = 1 alternately–in–and–out 4th power

1 tetrahedron = 1 ½-and-½ 8th power

$\bowtie$ = the symbol of equivalence in the converging-diverging intertransforms

Tetrahedron = 1^4 $\bowtie$ (←This is the preferred notation for the four-dimensional, inside-out, outside-out, balanced mutuality of tetra intertransformability.)

0 Zerovolume Tetra & VE

4 great circles = Tetra & VE

3 great circles = Octa

6 great circles = Duo-tet Cube

12 great circles = Rhombic Dodecahedron

1033.622   Thus the tetrahedron—and its primitive, inside-out, outside-out intertransformability into the prime, whole, rational, tetravolume-numbered hierarchy of primitive-structural-system states—expands from zerovolume to its 24-tetravolume limit via the *maximum-nothingness* vector-equilibrium state, whose domain describes and embraces the primitive, nucleated, 12-around-one, closest-packed, unit-radius spheres. (See cosmic hierarchy at Sec. 982.62.)

1033.63 Prefrequency and Initial Frequency Vector Equilibrium

1033.631   The primitive tetrahedron has four planes of symmetry—i.e., is inherently four-dimensional. The cosmic hierarchy of relative tetravolumes (Sec. 982.62) is primitive, four-dimensional, and unfrequenced.

1033.632   The primitive micro vector equilibrium is inherently prefrequency and is a priori tetravolume 0. The primitive macro vector equilibrium is inherently prefrequency and is a priori tetravolume 20. We also have the primitive, prefrequency, nuclear vector equilibrium of $2^1/_2$ active and $2^1/_2$ passive phases, and the primitive, nucleated, closest-packed-about vector equilibrium of 20. The nucleated vector equilibrium of frequency^2 has a tetravolume of 160, arrived at as follows:

2-frequency volume inherently $8 \times$ primitive inherent $2\frac{1}{2}$-ness of nuclear VE $= 8 \times 2\frac{1}{2} = 20$

2-frequency volume inherently $8 \times$ primitive inherent 20-ness of nucleated VE

$2^3 = 8$, $8 \times 20 = 160$

$160 = 2^5 \times 5$, where the fifth dimension introduces time and size.

1033.633   Compare Section *1053.84* and Table *1053.849*.

1033.64   Eightness Dominance

1033.641   The quanta involvement sum of the polar pairings of octahedra would be dominant because it consists of 12 Quarter-Octahedra (i.e., $12 - 8 = 4$) = involvement dominance of four, whereas eight is the equilibrious totality vector of the 4 $\bowtie$ 4: since the eightness is the interbalancing of four, the $12 - 8$'s excess four is an unbalanced four, which alone must be either the outside-out or the inside-out four; ergo, one that produces the maximum primitive imbalance whose asymmetric proclivity invites a transformation to rectify its asymmetry. (Compare Sec. *1006.40*.)

1033.642   Thus the off-balance four invites the one quantum of six vectors released by the precessed octahedron's one-quantum "annihilation"—whose entropy cannot escape the Universe.

1033.643   The vector-equilibrious maximum nothingness becomes the spontaneous syntropic recipient of the energy quantum released from the annihilation phase of the transformation.

1033.65   Convergent-divergent Limits

1033.651   Vector equilibrium is never a shape. It is either a tetravolume 0 nothingness or a tetravolume 20 nothingness. The only difference between space nothingness and matter somethingness is vector equilibrium.

1033.652   Primitive, unfrequenced vector equilibrium is both the rationally interstaged, expansive-contractive, *minimum 0*, 1, 2, 3, 4, 5, 6→to 20 to *maximum 0*, as well as the cosmic-resonance occupant of the minimum and maximum event void existing between the primitive, systematic somethingnesses.

1033.653   The vector equilibrium has four inside-out and four outside-out self-intercancelation, *eight*-congruent, zerovolume tetrahedra, as well as *eight* centrally single-bonded tetrahedra of maximum zerovolume expansion: both invoke the cosmically intolerable vacuum voids of macro-micro-nothingness essential to the spontaneous capture of one quantum's six vectors, which—in the VE's maxi-state—structurally contracts the VE's 20-ness of spatial Universe nothingness into the 20-ness of icosahedral somethingness, just as the octa-annihilated quantum provides the always-eight-in-one, outside-out tetrahedron to fill the inside-out "black hole" tetravoid.

1033.654

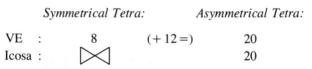

	Symmetrical Tetra:		Asymmetrical Tetra:
VE :	8	(+ 12 =)	20
Icosa :			20

1033.655   In the octahedron as the maximum conservation and quantum-annihilability model of substance (Sec. 935) the precessing vector edge of the entropic octahedron drops out 1 tetra; 1 tetra = 6 vectors = 1 quantum of energy which—as the entropically random element of radiation's nonformedness—may be effortlessly reformed by reentering the vector equilibrium to produce the icosahedron and thus to form new substance or matter.

1033.656   The vector equilibrium has 24 external vector edges: inserting the quantum set of six more makes 30 external edges whose omniintertriangulation resolves as the 30-edged icosahedron. The six added edges are inserted as contractive diagonals of the six square faces of the vector equilibrium. The contracted 30 edges = 5 energy quanta. Icosahedron = tetravolume-5. Icosahedron is the least dense of all matter.

1033.657   As we approach absolute zero, taking all the energy out of the system,* the chemical elements of which the apparatus parts consist each have unique atomic-frequency temperatures that are inherently different. This is evident to anyone who, within the same room temperature, has in swift succession touched glass, plastic, leather, or whatever it might be. Therefore, as in cryogenics we approach absolute zero (for the whole system's average temperature), the temperature of some of the elemental components of the experiment go through to the other side of zero, while others stay on this side—with the whole aggregate averaging just short of right on absolute zero. As a consequence of some components going through to the other side of zero, some of the most extraordinary things happen, such as liquids flowing in antigravity directions. This is the inside-out Universe.

1033.658   When the "black hole" phenomenon is coupled with the absolute-zero phenomenon, they represent the special-case manifests of synergetics' macro-micro-generalization extremes—i.e., both mini-maxi, zero-nothingness phases, respectively.

1033.659   Here are both the macro- and micro-divergence-convergence-limits in which the four-dimensional transformative and conversion behaviors

---

* See Secs. 205.02, 251.02, 427.01, and 443.02.

are quite different from the non-scientifically-demonstrable concept of arbitrary cutoffs of exclusively one-dimensional infinity unlimits of linear phenomena. The speed of four-dimensional light in vacuo terminates at the divergent limit. The gravitational integrity of inside-out Reverse Universe becomes convergently operative at the macrodivergence limits.

1033.66 Terminal Reversings of Evolution and Involution

1033.661　In selecting synergetics' communication tools we avoid such an unresolvable parallel-linear word as *equals*. Because there are neither positive nor negative values that add or detract from Universe, synergetics' communication also avoids the words *plus* and *minus*. We refer to *active and passive* phases. Parallel equivalence has no role in an alternatively convergent-divergent Universe. *Inflection* is also a meaningless two-dimensional linear word representing only a shadow profile of a tetrahelical wave.

1033.662　In four-dimensional conversion from convergence to divergence—and vice versa—the terminal changing reverses evolution into involution—and vice versa. Involution occurs at the system limits of expansive intertransformability. Evolution occurs at the convergent limits of system contraction.

1033.663　The macro-micro-nothingness conversion phases embrace both the maximum-system-complexity arrangements and the minimum-system-simplicity arrangements of the constant set of primitive characteristics of any and all primitive systems. A single special case system embraces both the internal and external affairs of the single atom. A plurality of special case systems and a plurality of special case atoms may associate or disassociate following the generalized interrelationship laws of chemical bonding as well as of both electromagnetics and mass-interattractiveness.

1033.664　Primitive is what you conceptualize sizelessly without words. Primitive has nothing to do with Russian or English or any special case language. My original 4-D convergent-divergent vector equilibrium conceptualizing of 1927–28 * was primitive $\bowtie$ Bow Tie: the symbol of intertransformative equivalence as well as of complementarity:

convergence $\bowtie$ divergence
$\bowtie$ Also the symbol of syntropy-entropy,
　　　and of wave and octave,
　　　$-4, -3, -2, -1,$
　　　$+1, +2, +3, +4$

---

* Also used in ''Nine Chains to the Moon,'' 1938.

1033.665   Minimum frequency = two cycles = $2 \times 360°$.

> Two cycles = $720° = 1$ tetra = 1 quantum of energy.
> Tetrahedron is the minimum unity-two experience.

1033.666   The center or nuclear sphere always has two polar axes of spin independent of surface forming or intertransforming. This is the "plus two" of the spheric shell growth around the nucleus. $NF^2 + 2$, wherefore in four primitive cosmic structural systems:

$$
\left. \begin{array}{rl}
\text{Tetra} = & 2F^2 + 2 \\
\text{Octa} = & 4F^2 + 2 \\
\text{Duo-tet Cube} = & 6F^2 + 2 \\
\text{Icosa} = & 10F^2 + 2
\end{array} \right\} 2 + 2 \left\{ \begin{array}{c} 1 \\ 2 \\ 3 \\ 5 \end{array} \right\} F^2
$$

1033.70   Geometrical 20-ness and 24-ness of Vector Equilibrium

1033.701   The maximum somethingness of the VE's 20-ness does not fill allspace, but the 24-tetravolume Duo-tet Cube (short name for the double-tetrahedron cube) does fill allspace; while the tetravolume-4-ness of the exterior octahedron (with its always-potential one-quantum annihilability) accommodates and completes the finite energy-packing inventory of discontinuous episodic Physical Scenario Universe.

1033.702   The three interior octahedra are also annihilable, since they vanish as the VE's 20-ness contracts symmetrically to the quadrivalent octahedron jitterbug stage of tetravolume 4: an additive 4-tetravolume octahedron has vanished as four of the VE's eight tetrahedra (four inside-out, four outside-out) also vanish, thereby demonstrating a 16-quanta-annihilation accomplished without impairment of either the independent motion of the system's axial twoness or its convergent-divergent, omniconcentric symmetry.

1033.703   The four of the 24-ness of the Duo-tet Cube (which is an f^2 cube: the double tetrahedron) accounts for the systemic four-dimensional planes of four-dimensional symmetry as well as for the ever-regenerative particle fourness of the quark phenomena characterizing all high-energy-system-bombardment fractionability.

1033.704 $24 \times 4 = 96$. But the number of the self-regenerative chemical elements is 92. What is missing between the VE 92 and the f^2 Duo-tet Cube's 96 is the fourness of the octahedron's function in the annihilation of energy: $92 + 4 = 24 \times 4 = 96$. The four is the disappearing octa set. The 24 is the second-power 24 unique indig turnabout increment. (See Fig. 1223.12.)

1033.71   ·We have three expendable interior octa and one expendable exterior octa. This fact accommodates and accounts both the internal and external somethingness-to-nothingness annihilations terminally occurring between the $1\rightarrow20\rightarrow1\rightarrow20$ at the macroinvolution and microevolution initiating nothingness phases, between which the total outside-out $1\rightarrow20$ quanta and the total inside-out $20\rightarrow1$ quanta intertransformabilities occur.

1033.72 The final jitterbug convergence to quadrivalent tetravolume-1 outside-out and tetravolume-1 inside-out is separated by the minimum-nothingness phases. This final conversion is accomplished only by torquing the system axis to contract it to the nothingness phase between the three-petal, triangular, inside-out and outside-out phases. (See Secs. 462.02, 464.01 and 464.02.)

1033.73 **The Quantum Leap:** Between the maximum nothingness and the minimum nothingness we witness altogether five stages of the 4-tetravolume octa vanishment in the convergent phase and five such 4-tetravolume octa growth leaps in the divergent phase. These five—together with the interior and exterior octa—constitute seven octa leaps of four quanta each. The f^2 of the inherent multiplicative two of all systems provides the *eighth fourness: the* quantum leap. (Compare Sec. 1013.60.)

1033.74 It requires 24-ness for the consideration of the total atomic behavior because the vector equilibrium is not allspace-fillingly complete in itself. It requires the exterior, inside-out, invisible-phase, eightway-fractionated, transformable octahedron superimposed on the VE's eight equiangular, triangular faces to complete the allspace-filling, two-frequency Duo-tet Cube's eight symmetrically arrayed and most-economically interconnected corners' domain involvement of 24 tetravolumes.

1033.741 The VE's involvement domain of 24 symmetrical, allspace-filling tetravolumes represents only one of the two alternate intertransformation domains of closest-packed, unit-radius spheres transforming into spaces and spaces intertransforming into spheres: ergo, it requires 48-tetravolumes to accommodate this phenomenon. To allow for each of these 48-tetravolume domains to accommodate their respective active and passive phases, it requires 96-tetravolumes. F^2 tetravoluming, which is as yet primitive, introduces an allspace-filling, symmetrical cube of 192-tetravolumes as an essential theater of omniatomic primitive interarrayings.

1033.75 The total primitively nucleated Duo-tet Cube's double-tetra unique increment of allspace filling is that which uniquely embraces the whole family of local Universe's nuclearly primitive intertransformabilities ranging through the $24\rightarrow1$ and the $1\rightarrow24$ cosmic hierarchy of rational and symmetrical "click-stop" holding patterns or minimum-effort self-stabilization states.

1033.76 The Duo-tet Cube (the maxicube) occurring between micronothingness and macronothingness shows how Universe intertransformably accommodates its entropic-syntropic energy-quanta exportings and importings within the two-frequency, allspace-filling minireality of special-case Universe. Thus the entropic-syntropic, special-case Physical Universe proves to be demonstrable within even the most allspace-crowding condition of the VE's maximum-something 20-ness and its exterior octahedron's even-more-than-maximum-something 4-tetravolume nothingness.

1033.77   This 24-ness is also a requisite of three number behavior requirements as disclosed in the min-max variabilities of octave harmonics in tetrahedral and VE cumulative closest-packing agglomerations at holistic shell levels as well as in all second-powering "surface" shell growths, as shown in three different columns in Fig. 1223.12.

1033.80   Possible Atomic Functions in Vector Equilibrium Jitterbug

1033.81   There can be nothing more primitively minivolumetric and omnisymmetrically nucleatable than 12 unit-radius spheres closest packed around one such sphere, altogether conformed as the vector equilibrium as produced in multiplication only by division. We can multiply our consideration by endlessly dividing larger into smaller and smaller, ever more highly frequenced, closest-packed spheres. Conversely, the icosahedron is the configuration of nonnucleated, omnisymmetric, unit-radius spheres closest packed circumferentially around a central space inadequate to accommodate one such unit-radius sphere. The icosahedron may be identified as the miniconfiguration of the electron function as well as the second most volumetric, initial, convergent-divergent transformation, with only the vector equilibrium being greater.

1033.82   The 20 triangular faces of the icosahedron may be considered as 10 pairs of regular tetrahedra interpenetrating as internal vertexes. The energetic functions of these 10 pairs (as described in Secs. 464 and 465) are a four-dimensional evolution like the triangles rotating in the cube, generating the double tetrahedra in the process. But according to synergetics' topological accounting it is necessary to extract one pair of double tetrahedra for the axis of spin: this leaves eight pairs of double tetra. $10 - 2 = 8$ is the same fundamental octave eightness as the eight Eighth-Octahedra that convert the eight triangular corners of the VE to the involvement domain of the nucleated cube.

1033.83   At the outset of the VE jitterbug evolution there are two polar vertical-axis triangles—if the top one points away from you, the bottom one on the table points toward you. Without itself rotating, this active-passive, triangularly poled, vertical axis permits the jitterbug evolution to rotate its equatorial components either clockwise or counterclockwise, providing for the production of two different icosahedra—an active pair and a passive pair. But since there are four VE axes that can be jitterbugged in the same manner, then there are potentially eight different icosahedra to be generated from any one vector equilibrium.

1033.84   It could be that the eight paired tetrahedra are the positrons while the eight icosahedra are the electrons. Comprehension involves all four axes available.

1033.90 Spheres and Spaces

1033.91   How can an object move through water, which is a noncompressible substance? It does so by the intertransformability of spheres becoming spaces and spaces becoming spheres. (See Sec. 1032.) This is one of the ways in which the octahedron annihilation works in allspace-filling accommodation of local transformative events. The vector equilibrium and the eight Eighth-Octahedra on the triangular facets combine to produce the primitively nucleated cube.

1033.92   The octahedron annihilation model is uniformly fractionated and redeployed eight ways to function structurally as eight asymmetric tetrahedra at the eight corners of the vector equilibrium in an intertransformable manner analogous to the one-quantum-annihilating octahedron which—in Eighth-Octahedra increments—complements the $0 \rightarrow 24$-tetravolume vector equilibrium furnished with eight corners.

1040.00 Seven Axes of Symmetry

1041.10 Seven Axes of Truncated Tetrahedron

1041.11   The prime generation of the seven axes of symmetry are the seven unique perpendiculars to the faces of the seven possible truncations of the tetrahedron:

    4 original faces

    4 triangular truncated vertexes

    <u>6</u> quadrilateral truncated edges

    14 faces of the truncated tetrahedron, which produce seven unique pairs of parallel faces whose axes, perpendicular to their respective centers of area, generate the seven axes of symmetry. (See Secs. *100.103–.05* and Fig. *1041.11.*)

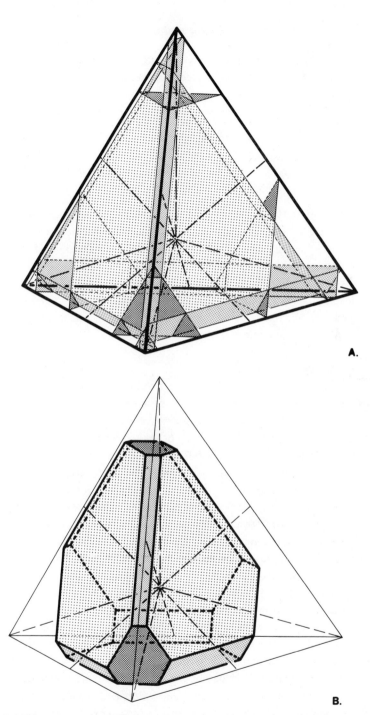

A.

B.

Fig. *1041.11 Truncated Tetrahedron Generates Seven Prime Axes of Symmetry:* Four original faces + four truncated vertexes + six truncated edges = 14 faces whose mid-points interconnect in seven axes.

1041.12   The seven unique axes of the three unique sets (4 + 4 + 6) producing the 14 planes of the truncated tetrahedron are also identifiable with:

—the 14 planes that bound and enclosingly separate all biological cells;

—the 14 facets interbonding all bubbles in the bubble complexes; and

—the 25 and 31 unique planes generated by the seven sets of foldable great circles, which are the only such foldably unbroken sets (i.e., the 3, 4, 6, and 12 sets of the vector equilibrium and the 6, 10, and 15 sets of the icosahedron).

1041.13   Various high frequencies of modular subdividings of the tetrahedron produce a variety of asymmetrical truncatabilities of the tetrahedron. The dynamics of symmetry may employ any seven sets of the 56 foldable-great-circle variations of planar orientation. Thus it follows that both the biological cell arrays and the bubble arrays display vast varieties of asymmetries in their 14 enclosing planes, so much so that this set of interidentifiability with the 14 topological characteristics of the tetrahedron, the prime structural system of Universe, has gone unnoticed until now. (See Sec. 1025.14)

1043.00   Transformative Spherical Triangle Grid System

1043.01   All the great circles of all the seven axes of symmetry together with all great-circle-trajectory interactions can be reflectively confined and trigonometrically equated with only one of the icosahedral system's 120 similar right-spherical triangles (of 90, 60, and 36 degrees, in contradistinction to the right-planar triangle of 90-, 60-, and 30-degree corners). (See Sec. 905.60.) The rational spherical excess of six degrees (of the icosahedron's 120—60 plus and 60 minus—similar tetrahedral components) is symmetrically distributed to each of the three central and three surface angles of each of the 120 tetrahedral components of the spherical icosahedron.

1043.02   This sixness phenomenon tantalizingly suggests its being the same transformative sixness as that which is manifest in the cosmically constant sixfoldedness of vectors of all the topological accountings (see Secs. 621.10 and 721); and in the sixness of equieconomical alternative degrees of freedom inherent in every event (see Sec. 537.10); as well as in the minimum of six unique interrelationships always extant between the minimum of four "star events" requisite to the definitive differentiation of a conceptual and thinkable system from out of the nonunitarily conceptual but inherently finite Universe, because of the latter's being the aggregate of locally finite, conceptually differentiable, minimum-system events (see Secs. 510 and 1051.20).

1044.00   Minimum Topological Aspects

•[*1044.00–1044.13   Minimum Topology Scenario*]

1044.01   Euler + Synergetics: The first three topological aspects of all minimum systems—vertexes, faces, and edges—were employed by Euler in his formula $V + F = E + 2$. (See Table 223.64 and Sec. 505.10.) Since synergetics' geometry embraces nuclear and angular topology, it adds four more minimum aspects to Euler's inventory of three:

$$\left.\begin{array}{l} \text{vertexes} \\ \text{faces} \\ \text{edges} \end{array}\right\} \quad \text{EULER}$$

$$\left.\begin{array}{l} \text{angles} \\ \text{insideness \& outsideness} \\ \text{convexity \& concavity} \\ \text{axis of spin} \end{array}\right\} \quad \text{SYNERGETICS}$$

1044.02   Euler discovered and developed the principle of modern engineering's structural analysis (Sec. 1007.04). He recognized that whereas all statically considered objects have a center of gravity, all dynamically considered structural components of buildings and machinery—no matter how symmetrically or asymmetrically conformed—always have a uniquely identifiable *neutral axis of gyration*. Euler did not think of his topology as either static or dynamic but as a mathematically permitted abstraction that allowed him to consider only the constant relative abundance of vertexes, faces, and edges isolated within a local area of a nonsystem. (The local consideration of the constant relative abundance of vertexes, faces, and edges applies to polyhedra as well as to cored-through polyhedra.)

1044.03   Euler's analysis failed to achieve the generalization of angles (whose convergence identified his corners), the complementary insideness and outsideness, and the convexity-concavity of all conceptual experience. Being content to play his mathematical game on an unidentified surface, he failed to conceive of systems as the initial, all-Universe separators into the tunably relevant, topologically considered set. Euler's less-than-system abstraction also occasioned his failure to identify the spin axis of any and all systems with his axis of gyration of physical objects; thus he also failed to realize that the subtraction of two vertexes from all systems for assignment as polar vertexes of the spin axis was a failure that would necessitate the "plus two" of his formula $V + F = E + 2$.

1044.04 Any and all conceptuality and any and all think-about-ability is inherently systemic (see Secs. 905.01-02). Systemic conceptuality and think-about-ability are always consequent only to consideration. Consideration means bringing stars together so that each star may be then considered integrally as unity or as an infrasystem complex of smaller systems.

1044.05 A system consists at minimum of four star events (vertexes) with four nothingness window facets and six lines of unique four-star interrelationships. As in synergetics' 14 truncation faces, Euler's three aspects result in 14 cases:

$$4 \text{ vertexes } + 4 \text{ faces } + 6 \text{ edges } = 14 \text{ cases.}$$

1044.06 Synergetics further augments Euler's inventory of three topological aspects (14 cases) with six additional and primitively constant topological aspects:

—*4th aspect* (12 cases): the 12 unique, trigonometrically integral, intercovariant vertex angles of the minimum system.

—*5th aspect* (two cases): ultravisible macrocosmic rest-of-Universe outsideness and infravisible rest-of-Universe insideness separated by the considered system; the insideness is all the integral otherness, and the outsideness is the as-yet-unconsidered irrelevance otherness.

—*6th aspect* (two cases): the multiplicative twoness of the divergent convexity and convergent concavity; there are two manifestations of *multiplicative twoness,* (a) and (b) (see Secs. 223.05–09), both of which make unity plural and at minimum two: (a) the always and only inseparable and co-occurring concavity and convexity of all systems, and (b) the always and only inseparable convergence to and divergence from system center.

—*7th aspect* (two cases): the additive twoness of the two vertexes always extracted from the system's total inventory of vertexes to serve as the poles of the system's neutral axis of spin.

—*8th aspect:* the sum of the angles externally surrounding the vertexes of any system will always equal 720 degrees less than the number of external vertexes of the system multiplied by 360 degrees.

—*9th aspect:* the sum of the angles around all the external vertexes of any system will always be evenly divided by 720 degrees, which is the angular description of one tetrahedron.

1044.07 The total of nine minimum topological aspects consists of three from Euler (14 cases) plus synergetics' inventory of six additional aspects, with 12 angular cases and six nuclear cases for a total of 18 synergetics cases. The 14 Euler cases and the 18 synergetics cases provide a total of 32 minimum topological cases.

1044.08   Topological analysis permits the generalization of all structuring in Universe as systemic.

1044.09   What we speak of as substance—a planet, water, steam, a cloud, a speck, or a pile of dust—always has both insideness and outsideness. A substance is a single system or a complex of neighboring interbonded or critical-proximity systems. Substances have inherent insideness "volumes."

1044.10   An Earthian observer can point in a describable compass direction and a describable angle of elevation toward the location in the sky where the contrails of two differently directioned jet air transports traveling at different altitudes appear to him to cross one another. Because they are flown at different altitudes, the "to-him" crossing does not mean that they touch one another; it is simply a moment when their two separate trajectories are nearest to one another. What the observer points to is a "nearest-to-one-another" moment. The observer points to an interrelationship event, which is not part of either contrail considered only by itself. This directionally identifiable interrelationship event is known as a "fix." (See Sec. 532.02.)

1044.11   The four corner fixes of an environmental tetrahedron may be pointed toward with adequate communicability to visually inform others of a specific tetrahedral presence. This is accomplished as follows: Two sky fixes must have a most economical linear interrelatedness but no insideness. Three sky fixes define a triangle between whose three edge-defining, interrelationship lines is described a plane that has no altitude—ergo, no insideness. Then the triangle described by the three sky fixes plus the position of the observer on the ground altogether describe the four corners of a tetrahedron that has six lines of observably inductable interrelatedness defining four triangular planes that observably divide all Universe into the included insideness and the excluded outsideness.

1044.12   One fix does not have insideness. Two fixes define a no-insideness linear relationship. Three fixes define a no-insideness plane. Four fixes define an insideness-including and outsideness-excluding tetrahedron, which is the minimum cosmic system and which cannot have less than 32 unique and differentially describably generalized cases of the nine irreducible-in-number unique topological aspects of the minimum system, but which in special frequenced cases may have more.

1044.13   Although not enumerated topologically (because unconsidered and because nonsimultaneously considerable) there are—in addition to the nine aspects and 32 cases—two additional ultimate conceptual aspects of the complementary macro- and microremainder of the physical Universe: all the as-yet-undiscovered—ergo, unconsidered—special cases as an epistemographic complementary to all the as-yet-undiscovered—ergo, unconsidered—generalized principles.

1050.00   Synergetic Hierarchy

1050.20   Trigonometry

1050.30   Simplest Trigonometric Solutions: *Sequence to Accompany Poster in color plate 1.*

1050.31   Stones may be broken into ever smaller stones, but they cannot be broken into no stones. They may be broken into gravel and the gravel into dust and the dust separated into crystals that are too small to be seen except through a lensed microscope; or they may be further broken apart into atoms that can be seen only through electron field microscopes. But the stones cannot be broken into nothingnesses—only into somethings. And somethings are always systems.*

1050.32   As the stones break, they have cleavage faces. They break into irregular polyhedra that are complex or simplex geometrically definable systems, each of which always has an inherent insideness and outsideness. The number of faces—hedra—of polyhedra cannot be reduced to less than four: the tetrahedron. The number of sides—gons—of a polygon cannot be reduced to less than three: the triangle. The minimum polyhedron of Universe is the tetrahedron, which requires a minimum of three triangles surrounding each of its four corners, whose four corners are omniinterconnected with a minimum of six edges that discretely outline the four triangular (minimum polygon) faces.

1050.33   Make the "V for Victory" sign with two adjacent fingers. The V is visual. The V is a specifically visible angle. The angle is an angle independent of the length of the fingers—that is, independent of the length of the sides of the angle. Angles, triangles, and tetrahedra are conceptual pattern integrities independent of size. Angles are always and only fractional parts of whole circles (of 360 degrees). Likewise, triangles are always and only components of a priori whole physical polyhedral systems (or of a plurality of whole polyhedral systems) each of 720 degrees (or whole multiples of 720 degrees) of angles surrounding all the external vertexes describing those systems. Only triangles produce structural stability. Only triangles produce pat-

---

*The energy of the blow that breaks them asunder entropically releases the energy that previously bound together the atoms of the separate somethings. Disassociative energy is radiant—entropic; associative energy is something-forming—syntropic.

tern stability. The omnitriangulated tetrahedron is the minimum structural system of Universe.

1050.34   Drawing or scribing are physical operations executed upon a physical system. Triangles can be drawn or scribed or traced or trajectoried only upon or within an a priori physical system, or defined by a constellation of three physical systems within a greater a priori system.

1050.35   There are six and only six different but always orderly intercovarying geometrical characteristics or integral parts of all triangles: three surface-angle corners *A*, *B*, and *C*, and three sides *a*, *b*, and *c*. In reality these sides are always the central angles of the scribed-upon system and they are only evidenced by their surface-arc lines.

1050.36   Individual angular values or the relative interrelationships or interratios or *functions* of these parts hold true independent of the size of the triangle. This is to say that an equiangular triangle is equiangular and humanly conceptual independent of the size of any of our special case triangular experiences. The four most useful of these functions and their symbols are:

sine = *sin*   tangent = *tan*
cosine = *cos*   cotangent = *cot*

1050.37   The science that measures the respective angle magnitudes of the six ever-orderly intercovarying angles of triangles is called *trigonometry*. All of the geometrical interrelationships of all triangles—spherical or planar—are discoveringly calculated by the same trigonometry because plane triangles are always very small spherical triangles on very large spheric systems such as high-frequency symmetric polyhedra. A circle is a spherical triangle each of whose three corner angles is 180 degrees.

1050.38   To find the value of all the central angles (sides) and surface (corner) angles of any spherical triangle, we can always start by dropping a perpendicular from any vertex of that triangle upon its opposite side—making it into two ''right'' triangles. In order to discover all six angular values of a given triangle it is necessary to know—in addition to knowing the 90-degree corner—the surface- or central-angular values *of any other two* of the to-be-solved triangle's five other parts: *A, B, a, b, c.* Many mathematicians have devised strategic formulas for coping with trigonometric solutions, most of them involving plus or minus quadrant symbols that invite errors of calculation.

1050.39   To make the trigonometry of the sea captain's celestial navigation as simple and foolproof as possible the mathematician Lord Napier (1550–1667)* evolved the following diagrams and procedures. To avoid what

---

*Napier was the first to use the decimal point; he also invented logarithms for numbers. His mathematical ingenuity contributed greatly to the attainment of world ocean supremacy by the East India Company and the Royal Navy.

is known in navigation as "the 180-degree error"—going in exactly the opposite direction from that which will get you where you want to go—Napier arranged the five non-90-degree "parts" of a triangle in a five-segment "clock."

1050.40   Napier had two equally simple ways to solve trigonometric problems without plus or minus symbols, provided that any two of the non-90-degree angles are known at the outset. His superscript ^{c} means that A^c, c^c, B^c are the 180-degree complements of A, c, B. For instance, $A^c + A = 180°$, wherefore $sin\ A^c = cos\ A;$ or $tan\ c^c = cot\ c$, etc.

1050.41   First we check-mark the two "known-in-advance" non-90-degree parts on Napier's five-segment clocklike pattern. It is clear that the two already-knowns are always either divided from one another or are side by side. In Napier's Case One the two knowns are side by side in the clock: Napier calls this the case of *Opposites*. Opposite Case see Rule 1 chosen unknown for first solution.

1050.42   In Case Two the two knowns are separated from one another in the clock: Napier calls this the case of *Adjacents*. Adjacent Case see Rule 2 first unknown to be solved.

1050.43   Napier's two easily remembered rules are:

Rule 1. The sine of any unknown part *theta* is equal to the product of the
   cosines of the two known *opposite* parts. This is written as:
   unknown's angle *theta*'s $sin = cos \cdot cos$ of its two known *opposite parts*.

Rule 2. The sine of any unknown part is equal to the product of the tangents
   of its two known *adjacent* parts. This is written as:
   unknown angle *theta's* $sin = tan \cdot tan$ of its two known *adjacent* parts.

1050.44   Next we employ the appropriate formula with the known cosine or tangent values. Next we must remove the superscript ^{c} of the complementaries, if any, by substituting cosines for sines, sines for cosines, tangents for cotangents, and cotangents for tangents.

Example: When the equation as first written is
   $$sin\ b = cos\ c^c \cdot cos\ b^c$$
the equation must be rewritten
   $$sin\ b = sin\ c \cdot sin\ b;$$
or if the equation first reads
   $$sin\ A^c = tan^c \cdot tan\ b,$$
it must be rewritten as
   $$cos\ A = cot\ c \cdot tan\ b$$
before going on to intermultiply the functions of the two knowns whose product will be the function value of the previously unknown angle *theta*. The angle values of the newly found knowns

may be located in any table of trigonometric functions or may be "remembered" by computers. When the value is found for an angle's function (*sin, cos, tan, cot*), its specific angular value may also be read out of the tables.

1052.00   Universal Integrity

1052.32   **Possibility of Rational Prime Numbers in High-energy Physics Experiments:** In recent years the experiments of the physicists, notably at the European Nuclear Research Center (CERN), seem to provide increasing confirmation of the similarities in the behaviors of electromagnetic and gravitational forces—as well as in the bonding and radioactive effects of the atomic nucleus (see Sec. 646.10). The ultimate definition of a Unified Field Theory becomes tantalizingly nearer at hand. The results and findings of the physicists' experiments should be examined in the light of synergetics' models, especially the vector equilibrium, and the comprehensive isotropicity which derives from closest-sphere-packing and provides omnirational accounting for radial and circumferential coordination. This kind of examination might account for some of the energetic behaviors of the newly described mass particles—leptons and hadrons, quarks and antiquarks—in which the second-power of their masses displays simple whole-number relationships.

1052.33   In synergetics the number of spheres on the outer surface of symmetrically complete VE aggregations is equal to two plus two times frequency to the second power times five—the prime number that is the key to the respective masses of both the VE and Icosa. The equation of prime number inherency of symmetrical structural systems ($2NF^2 + 2$; see Sec. 223.03) could be considered as describing a Unified Field Theory in which the number of vertexes (crossings or events) can be regarded as abstractions from the total field corresponding to a scenario of limited conceptuality. (Compare Secs. *419.10–20.*)

1052.350   Microsystems

1052.351   A point is always a microsystem or a plurality of microsystems—ergo, at minimum one tetrahedron.

1052.352   A line is a relationship between any two microsystems.

1052.353   A tetrahedron is defined topologically by four conceptually locatable microsystems interconnected by six interrelationship lines whose 12 ends are oriented to corner-converge in four groups of three lines each; these lines terminate in one of four infratunable microsystem corners, whose at-minimum-of-three-other corner-defining microsystems lie outside in the tune-in-able tetrahedron defined by the six lines. (See Sec. *505.83.*)

1052.354   The tetrahedron is the minimum *tunable* system. A point-to-ability is a tuned-in tetra. Each tuned-in tetra consists of four corners, each of which is an infratunable tetrasystem.

1052.355   The threeness of the quarks shows up at the three minimum convergent lines around each vertex of the minimum system consisting of only six lines.

1052.356   Topological components of systems and their infra-tune-in-able corner-vertex-locating infratunable systems ad infinitum do not and cannot exist independent of systems.

1052.357   The above describes the tunability of corners and is explanatory of the ever-reappearing quarks that disclose the primitive characteristics of all systems, which always—to any one human observer listening at any one tuning-in time—consist of infra- or ultratunable systems ad infinitum.

1052.360   Mite as Model for Quark

1052.361   Proofs must proceed from the minimum whole system to Universe and the differentiation-out of Universe of the special case conceptual system. Proofs must start from the minimum something that is the minimum structural system. All geometrical and numerical values derive from fractionation of the whole.

1052.362   At the maximum limit of the rational cosmic hierarchy of primitive structural systems we have the 120 similar and symmetrical T Quanta Module tetrahedra that agglomerate symmetrically to form the triacontahedron. (See Sec. *986.*) At the minimum limit of the hierarchy are the separate A, B, and T Quanta Modules, and at the minimum limit of allspace-filling—ergo, of all Universe structuring—we have the three-module mites consisting each of two A and one B Modules.

1052.363   The mites are the quarks. The two energy-holding A Quanta Modules and the one energy-dispersing B Quanta Module of which the mite is composited exactly correspond with the plus-two, minus-one characteristics model of the three-separate-entity functions of the quark. (See Secs. 262.04 and 262.05.)

1052.50 Syntropy and Entropy

1052.51 **Meshing and Nonmeshing:** We know from the scientifically proven knowledge derived from physical experiments that local physical systems are continually losing energy, though they may be concurrently importing or inhibiting energies. This constant energy loss is the dominant characteristic of entropy. Due to each of the local Universe system's unique complex of chemical-element periodicities the energies that are given off in an orderly manner appear to be disorderly harmonics in respect to the unique harmonic complexes released by other systems. The timings between different energies leaving different systems, like any two different-sized mechanical gears, may not necessarily mesh or synchronize with the timings of energies leaving other systems that they encounter, which encountered energy events also may be separately orderly in themselves.

1052.52 The special-case regenerative system itself may attain maximum orderliness while being acted upon by externally distributive forces. Often the reason that systems do not synchronize is that they derive from different complexes of chemical elements. Since every one of the interorbiting cosmic system's elements has its unique frequencies, the wave frequencies of the orbiting systems are like the peaks and valleys of gear teeth whose peak-and-valley perimeters have latch-key-like irregularities. We have gears that rarely interlock and must consequently remain only superficially tangent to one another. Hence they take up more room than they would if they had meshed. The centers of the two meshing gears are nearer to one another than are the centers of the same two gears when their teethed perimeters are not meshed. When meshed, they are more powerfully intermass-attracted than when nonmeshed. (See Secs. 263.02 and 522.36.)

1052.53 Gears of equal weight and of the same material might have very many little teeth or relatively few big teeth in each of their great-circle cycles. The frequencies being given off entropically do not expand in planes or lines; they expand omnidirectionally as a complex of differently timed radial spirals. As the omnispheric gears fail to mesh, they employ ever more space, and therefore we realize a physically entropic Universe that is everywhere locally broadcasting its disorderly information to our sensorial receptors. Thus it seems—to short-term, local observation—that the aggregate discards of entropically released energies of the various localities of the physical Universe are expanding and even further expending energies in an increasingly disorderly manner. The syntropic births and growths escape our attention, for they inherently withhold or withdraw information regarding their ultimately syntropic cosmic resolution of apparent disorders—a resolution withheld from Earthian observers who are preoccupied with hindsight and dismayed by the obvious only-initially-entropic disorders. But fundamental complementarity requires that there be other localities and phases of Universe wherein the Universe is reconvening, collecting, and condensively contracting in an increasingly orderly manner as complementary regenerative conservation phases of Universe thus manifesting comprehensive transitions from disorder to order, from entropy to syntropy.

1052.54   **Order and Disorder: Birth and Growth:** Entropy is locally increasing disorder; syntropy is locally increasing order. Order is obviously the complement, but not mirror-image, of disorder.* Local environments are forever complexedly altering themselves due to the myriad associative and disassociative interpatterning options of syntropy and entropy, with an overall cosmic syntropic dominance insured by an overall local entropic dominance. (See the "Principle of Universal Integrity" at Sec. 231.) Universe is a vast variety of frequency rates of eternally regenerative, explosive, entropic vs implosive, syntropic pulsation systems. Electromagnetic radiant energy is entropic; gravitational energy is syntropic.

1052.55   Both entropy and syntropy are operative in respect to planet Earth's biospheric evolution. Wherever entropy is gaining over syntropy, death prevails; wherever syntropy is gaining over entropy, life prevails.

1052.56   Entropy is decadent, putrid, repulsive, disassociative, explosive, dispersive, maximally disordering, and ultimately expansive. Syntropy is impulsive, associative, implosive, collective, maximally ordering, and ultimately compactive. Entropy and syntropy intertransform pulsively like the single rubber glove (see Sec. 507). There is an entropic, self-negating, momentary self: there is also the no-time, nondimensionable eternity of mind. Dimensioning is apprehensible only within temporal relativity. Time is experienced in our relative duration lags and gestation rates as well as in the unique frequency interrelatedness of the electromagnetic spectrum events and novents. Every time we experience the novent disconnects of momentary annihilation into eternity, naught is lost. Mind deals only with eternity—with eternal principles. What is gained to offset any loss is the residual, observational lags in accuracy inherent and operative as cognition and the relativity of awareness that we call life. (See Secs. 638.02 and 1056.20.)

* See "Principle of Irreversibility" at Sec. 229.10

1052.57 The life-propagating syntropy-entropy, birth-to-death transformations constitute the special case realizations of the complex interactive potentials of all the eternal, abstract, dimensionless, nonsubstantial, generalized principles of Universe, interplayed with the absolute "if-this-then-that" integrity of plural cosmic unity's intercomplementarity. The death and annihilation discontinuities occur as eternal generalization intervenes between the special case, "in-time," relative intersizing of the realizations.

1052.58 **Pattern Sorting and Observing:** When we are able to observe for long enough periods of time, however, we find all the gears of Universe eventually meshing, though not simultaneously. The next periodic meshing of any two of the gears might take a thousand years—or 28½ years—or 17 seconds. The important phenomenon to note is that there are great varieties of periods of nonmeshing which altogether make the physically observed totality appear to take up ever more room, and anywhere within this expansiveness the locally predominant events occurring within short spans of time appear to be omnidisorderly. When we compound that realization with the now-known millionfold greater span of electromagnetic reality and the lesser span of direct-sense ranging of the human organism, we begin to comprehend how readily humanity falls into the trap of dismay, fear, and negativism in general. Impatience engenders further myopically disorderly incrementation of information receipts. Those who are impatient for the receipt of the next *news* broadcasts are only beguiled by negative information. That is what myopia looks for. Chronic shortsightedness spontaneously seeks and tunes in only the broadcast entropy. Syntropy incasts, in contradistinction to entropic broadcast. Syntropy can be apprehended only through *overall* or comprehensive review of the totally recalled information of long-term experience.

1052.59 Man has no experimental data to suggest that energy is ever created or destroyed. Though our own overall experience leads us to the discovery of cyclic events that return upon themselves, the local, momentary, physical events seem to be giving off energy and taking up more room despite our own syntropic attempts to reestablish local order. Entropy is defined as the law of increase of the random element. But our experience in physical exploration also reveals to us that every pattern phenomenon has its complementary which is rarely a mirror-image and is most frequently invisible. As the complementary has the effect of cosmic integrity balancing, we realize there must be unseen syntropic events of Universe that are always reordering the environment. Syntropy is the law of elsewhere-importing and always-orderly regrouping of the entropic exportings of all dying systems. Aging and death here engender birth and growth elsewhere. (See Sec. *1005.611*.)

1052.60 Physical Limit and Metaphysical Absolute

1052.61   This leads us to comprehension of the significance of life on Earth. On this cosmic-energies-importing planet we find life impounding those energies, taking random receipts of cosmic radiation from the stars—more importantly the Sun—and through photosynthesis converting it into organized molecular structures. We find the biologicals making ever more intricately orderly patterns: the little seed becoming a big, superbly organized structural process, a tree, rearranging all its energy receipts from Universe in a beautiful and orderly way. And among the living we find humans and humans' minds reviewing the many brain-recorded, special case experiences and from time to time discovering generalized relationships interexisting between and coordinating the separate special-case phenomena. In pure principle these generalized principles—such as gravity—are operative and hold true throughout all experiences. The history of humanity revolves around humans' discovering these principles. Humans also in due course discover principles that encompass a plurality of principles. Humanity trends toward ever greater understanding of the significance of principles, each of which, in order to be principles, must be inherently eternal. The discovery of principles occurs only with patience. Patience is long-wave tuning and is the antithesis of impatience, which is exclusively short-wave tuning. The discovery of great principles inherently requires a periodicity of adequate increments of time. Only through the thought stimulation of discovered and periodically repeated patterns of interrelatedness can mind's discovery of generalized principles occur.

1052.62   Physical Universe expands, and as its observed components and aggregates of components are found to be larger and larger, their relative operating velocities increase to cope with their greater and greater orbital travel distances. But there seems to be a constant limit velocity of all disintegrative, entropic energy as manifest by the speed of all types of electromagnetic radiation when measured linearly in a vacuum tube. All the various types of radiation—ultraviolet, radio wave, and X-ray—reach speeds of about 186,000 miles per second, which is also 700 million miles per hour, which incidentally is a million times the speed of sound. These measurements inspired much of Einstein's exploratory thought. But we note that since light and all other radiation is entropic—ergo, concomitantly disintegrative—there is a *constant limit* of disorderliness. Here nature turns about and becomes more orderly. There is also a constant limit of orderliness; this absolute turnaround condition is that of the primitive hierarchy. We discuss this elsewhere (Sec. 440) as the limits of pattern aberration in respect to the vector equilibrium, i.e., to the absolute or zerophase of generalized nuclear systems' orderliness. Whereas the physical disintegrates entropically to a limit of velocity and disorder, the metaphysically operative mind displays a reverse pattern to that of physical entropy, wherewith to define lastingly the mind seeks the orderliness of the principles that are discovered. As the human definitions can never be perfect, the metaphysical mind of humans can only amplify and simplify the human statement of the comprehensive orderliness discovered and periodically reconfirmed by further experiences.

1052.63   From time to time humans learn a little more about a principle, but greater familiarity does not change the principles themselves. As further observation becomes more comprehensive and refined, the statement of the principle becomes ever more incisive and ever less frequently modified and improved. Since the principle itself is eternally changeless, the more accurately it is defined, the more unchangeable is the definition. The word *truth* is applicable to an earnestly attempted statement of any observed or recollected special case experience. Recollection of a plurality of truths may lead to discovery of a generalized principle intercoordinating the special case experiences. Recollection of truths leads toward discovery of generalized principles. Thus we find the metaphysical definitions of human minds tending to become ever more enduring as human mind trends toward the only absolute perfection, which is the eternal integrity of the omniinteraccommodation of all principles.

1052.64   Thus do words evolve and accumulate to fill the dictionaries as humans discover mutually shared conceptions regarding their common experiences, each of which requires unique and incisive means of identification and communicability. That all humans, always starting naked, helpless, and ignorant, have through the ages so truthfully identified over a hundred thousand experiences each of which is so unique as to deserve—indeed require—a uniquely identifying word, and that humans, despite their propensity to withhold agreement upon any mutual convention, have agreed upon some hundred thousand more or less common words and upon many more hundreds of thousands of scientific words, constitutes the greatest extant memorial in testimony of the supra-ethnic and transgeneration growth of the means of human communication, common understanding, and ultimate integration of all human concern and ever more effectively informed coordination of all human initiatives.

(*1052.641*   Vitamin D from Sunlight is essential to humans because calcium is essential to the human bone structure. Humans synthesize vitamin D through the action of the Sun's ultraviolet rays on the skin. This biochemical function is a zoological counterpart of botanical photosynthesis. But vitamin D is one of those vitamins of which humans can have an overdose. In warmer climes, where vitamin D from the Sun is adequate or excessive, humans' subconsciously functioning organisms employ their chemical-process options to develop Sunlight filters in the skin consisting of darker and darker pigments that prevent excessive absorption of radiation and avoid the overdose of vitamin D. Where there is not much Sunlight, as in the far north, human organisms had to progressively remove their pigment filters, which left only light skin that permitted maximum synthesis of vitamin D from the Sun. But dark skin was the norm. The skin pigmentation effect on human organisms is a generalized phenomenon like that of diet, wherein undernourishment alone can account for mental dullness in otherwise healthy humans. Physiognomic and physiological differentiations in humans result solely from generations of unplanned inbreeding of those types that survive most successfully under unique environmental conditions within which tribes or nations dwelt for protracted periods. Thus there is scientific evidence that there is no organic class or species differentiations of humanity. This thesis is further elaborated in my essay *No Race No Class.* Communication is ultimately independent of culture or race or class.)

1052.65   The metaphysical drive of humanity is toward total comprehension and an eternally changeless definition of all understanding. Despite the limited conditions governing our special-case human lives we can discern the syntropic cosmic trending of the metaphysical slowdown toward eternal changlessness in inverse complementation of the entropic physical trend to ever greater acceleration toward terminal velocity, frequency, and disorderliness at the speed of all radiation in vacuo. The metaphysical eternity is inherently absolute, whereas physical acceleration is terminated only by exhaustion. The physical limit is special case and suggestively alterable. The metaphysical limit is absolute and unalterable.

1052.66   The metaphysical is comprehensively generalizable. The physical is always realized only as special case experience. The metaphysical reorders the disorderly-prone physical. The metaphysical continually seeks to comprehend, master, harness, and cohere the physical. The metaphysical comprehends and reorders. Humans oscillate between the pushes of their physical incarnation and the tensing of their metaphysical propensities. This ubiquitous push-pulling propagates cosmic regenerativity.

1052.67   The regeneration may be that of a complete new baby or the local regeneration of cells in an ongoing organism. Rebirth is continual. The overall growth and refinement of information and comprehension by continuous humanity transcends the separate generations of life and steadies toward eternal unalterability; the special case physical experiences and the identification of their significance in the overall scheme of eternal cosmic regenerativity ever accelerate as the information bits multiply exponentially; wherefore the overall rate of gain of metaphysical comprehension of the physical behavior in general accelerates exponentially in respect to such arithmetical periodicities as that of the celestial cycles of the solar system.

1052.68   The physical Universe is an aggregate of frequencies. Each chemical element is uniquely identifiable in the electromagnetic spectrum by its special set of unique frequencies. These frequency sets interact to produce more complexly unique cycle frequencies, which are unheard by human ear but which resonate just as do humanly hearable musical chords or dissonances. Thus occurs a great cosmic orchestration, ranging from the microcosmic nuclear isotropicity—directly undetectable by the human senses—through the minuscule range detectable by humans, to the very complex, macrocosmic, supra-to-human-tunability symphonies of multiaggregates of isotropically interpositioned galaxies. (Compare Secs. 515.21 and *530.13*.)

1052.69   Thus develops our human awareness of the special-case physical experience events that spontaneously trigger the metaphysical faculties of humans into applying their extraordinary sorting capabilities. The more metaphysically sensitive and comprehendingly effective humans become, the more truly do they fulfill the unique cosmic function for which they were designedly included in the scheme of eternally regenerative Universe. If we seek one word that most succinctly identifies the experience we call life, it is *awareness*. Since no weight is lost as individual life terminates, and since all the chemical ingredients are as yet present and all the sense organs and their separate information-integrating brains are also intact, we have to conclude that the awareness of otherness, which we identify as the prime characteristic of human life, is indeed a weightless idea, or thought concept, of an also weightless metaphysical thinker. Life is not the corporeal chemical complex. Life is only metaphysical.

1052.70   Humans are born into their physical-sensing and information-inventorying organism not only to experience Universe but to cope with local problem-solving in support of the eternal regenerative integrity of ever complexedly intertransforming physical Universe, employing their metaphysical minds to discover the metaphysical slowdown toward the eternal generalized principles governing Universe: and thereafter to define the principles ever more adequately, incisively, and inclusively until the frequency of redefinability decreases toward zero. Thus the metaphysical processing of humanity's cognition of a generalized principle tends in time to slow toward zero. It must be noted, however, that the metaphysical mind's tools of communication with other temporal beings—including the organic self—within the temporal reality are always special case—ergo, finitely limited tools—for instance, the arbitrary symbols chosen for a Greek alphabet written with special case ink on special case paper.

1052.71   The physical accelerates to terminal and finite velocity where terminality renders the physical inherently inferior and subservient to the inherently eternal metaphysical comprehensivity's omnicoherence. Only the self-destructive, special case physical, entropic, negative evolvements accelerate to their own totally disintegrative transition into totally redistributed subfunctionings of other systems.

1052.80　Radiation-Gravitation: Electromagnetic Membrane

1052.81　**Membrane Model:** The reason why the second-power rate of interattractiveness gains in respect to the arithmetical rate of variation of the relative proximity of remote bodies is that gravity is not a linear, radial force but is a circumferentially tensional embracement force.

1052.82　We will think of two spheres inside a closed elastic membrane so smoothly intimate to each that, when the two spheres are tangent to one another, they appear as two clearly independent spheres momentarily in kissing tangency, the membrane continuity between the two being so intimately clinging as to be observationally subvisible. But as the two spheres are pulled apart, the elastic membrane is locally stretch-pulled away evenly from the surface of each sphere, and the membrane tube running between the two contracts to a progressively invisible, fine-line, spider-thread tube stretched between the two spheres. As the two spheres are pulled further apart, the tube between the two remote spheres will appear to be an invisible line-of-sight perpendicular to each of the enclosed spheres.

1052.83　Since the nuclei of the atoms are not touching one another and only the cosmic totality integrity mantle is cohering the atoms, they can be singled out in space and time array in the same manner as the much larger molecules can be thinned to a film of a single molecular thickness, cohered only by the mass interattractiveness like the vast multiplicity of atomic interattractiveness (as we have seen in Sections 644 through 646.03).

1052.84　As the spheres are next allowed to approach one another, the everywhere self-together-gathering proclivity of the elastic membrane providing the elastic tube between them will redistribute its perpendicular linear multitude of atoms back in both directions, yielding equally to the two stretched membranes around each sphere in much the same way as atoms in a thin stream of viscous maple syrup impinging vertically on a stack of pancakes will spread out in all directions to envelop the pancakes. Thus the two-way flowing stream of stretched-far-apart atoms of the omnihugging elastic membrane tightly embracing the two reapproaching-to-one-another spheres flows outwardly at 90 degrees to their perpendicular impingement to reenvelop thickly each of the two spheres. This means that the linear length of the tautly stretched tube reopens itself at the point of tangency to enclose each of the tube's separate spheres. The atoms previously invested in the remote-from-one-another, stretched-out tube of tension between the two spheres have now returned to the two spheres and have rejoined their nearest neighboring atoms around the elastic-membrane spherical sheath of the two tangent spheres.

1052.85   What had been a linear requirement becomes a surface requirement for the elastic membrane. Surfaces of omnisymmetrical geometrical objects are always second powers of the object's linear dimensions. If we were to remove one of the spheres from the omniclingingly embracing sheath, the elastic membrane would snap-contract to enclose only the remaining sphere, but the rate of atomic population gain of the spherical, surface-clinging membrane derived from the previous intersphere linear tendon is of the second power of the arithmetical rate of linear contraction of the elastic tendon. Soon the thickness of the membrane on each sphere would multiply into a plurality of closest-packed atomic layers, and the volume of the atoms will thus increase at a third-power rate in respect to an arithmetical rate of distance-halving between any two spheres. This two-sphere-embracing, few-atoms-thick, clinging elastic membrane fed into, or spread out from, an intersphere tension may be thought of as an electromagnetic membrane acting just like electric charges fed onto the convex surface of a copper Van de Graaff sphere or a copper wire (electric charges always inhabiting only the convex surfaces).

1052.86   Please now think of all the tensional forces of Universe as one single membrane containing all the radiational, explosive forces we have enumerated. Now think of the original compression sphere exploding into many parts inside the endlessly stretchable membrane, whose rate of ductility-adjustment-to-stretch equals the speed of light or radiation, c^2. Inside our tensile membrane unitary bag would be a number of individual, exploded-apart, spherical mass components, each of which is tightly embraced by the membrane—leaving only intervening perpendicular linear tubes. (See Fig. *1052.86*.)

1052.87   To understand the linear expansion rate think of making soap bubbles: Deeply layered molecules get stretched into a single layer as the single atoms guarantee the interattractiveness integrity of the area-stretching thin-out of the atoms. We now come to the balancing of the vectors of the vector equilibrium and the arrangement of the 24 external vectors—end-to-end, closing back upon themselves—in four great-circle planes, constituting an "additional" vector force magnitude of 24, embracing the outwardly and separatingly exploding 24 internal vectors, which now operate in increasing

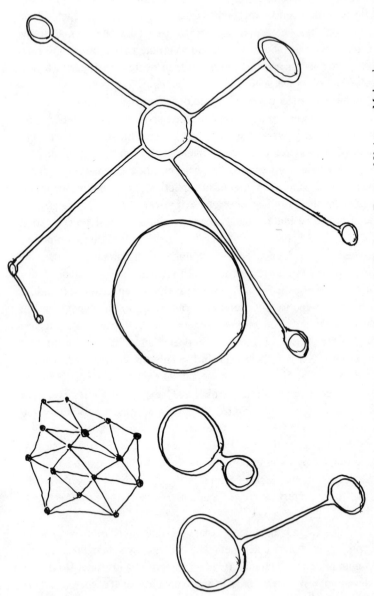

Fig. 1052.86 *Elastic Tension Membranes May Contain Explosive Forces of Universe:* Molecules can be thinned to a film of single-molecular thickness, cohered by a multiplicity of atomic interattractiveness. Such elastic membranes have a proclivity to distribute atomic attraction in a two-way flowing stream. Surfaces of geometrical objects are second powers of their linear dimensions. Thus tensional forces may contain explosive radiational forces. (From a sketch by the author.)

independence of one another—each thus producing a force of only one. We have the surface net drawing on a force resource of 24—multiplied by radius frequency to the second power—while the originally-24-force, radially explosive events separate out from one another and thus produce only separate first-power effectiveness. Hence the gravitational force's geometrical progression rate of gain—i.e., its second-power, surface-embracing finiteness closure is always at a high-energy effectiveness advantage over the disintegrative, linear, first-power, or only arithmetical progression rate of gain in force.

1052.88   The second-power rate of gain in interattractiveness occurring with each *halving* of the intervening distance of two heavenly bodies recalls Pythagoras's whole, rational-number, harmonic-octave integrity progression (or regression) occurring with each halving of the length of the tensed cord (thirding results in sharping or flatting key progressions); wherefore the gravitational-radiational, second-power, spherical surface rate of gain occurs in respect to the radial linear rate of identification of omnidirectionally propagated sound waves—at a gain of the second power of the linear. This gravitational omnisurface-embracement mathematics apprehending coincides with harmonic resonances:

Arithmetical
rate of
symmetrical
system's
radius

$$E = \text{Mass} \left(\begin{array}{l} \text{linear radial} \\ \text{shortening with} \\ \text{system contraction} \end{array} \right)^{2} \quad \leftarrow \text{Newton's gravitation}$$

$$E = \text{Mass} \left(\begin{array}{l} \text{linear radial} \\ \text{lengthening with} \\ \text{system expansion} \end{array} \right)^{2} \quad \leftarrow \text{Einstein's radiation}$$

1053.00   Superficial and Volumetric Hierarchies

1053.36   Sphere: Volume-surface Ratios: The largest number of similar triangles into which the whole surface of a sphere may be divided is 120. (See Secs. 905 and 986.) The surface triangles of each of these 120 triangles consist of one angle of 90 degrees, one of 60 degrees, and one of 36 degrees. Each of these 120 surface triangles is the fourth face of a similar tetrahedron whose three other faces are internal to the sphere. Each of these 120 tetra has the same volume as have the A or B Quanta Modules. Where the tetra is 1, the volume of the rhombic triacontahedron is approximately 5. Dividing 120 by $5 = 24 =$ quanta modules per tetra. The division of the rhombic triacontahedron of approximately tetravolume-5 by its 120 quanta modules discloses another unit system behavior of the number 24 as well as its appearance in the 24 external vector edges of the VE. (See Sec. *1224.21*.)

1053.37　　Since the surface of a sphere exactly equals the internal area of the four great circles of the sphere, and since the surface areas of each of the four triangles of the spherical tetrahedron also equal exactly one-quarter of the sphere's surface, we find that the surface area of one surface triangle of the spherical tetrahedron exactly equals the internal area of one great circle of the sphere; wherefore

1 spherical tetra's triangle　　　 $= 1$ great circle
2 spherical octa's triangles　　　 $= 1$ great circle
5 spherical icosa's triangles　　　 $= 1$ great circle
30 spherical Basic *LCD* triangles $= 1$ great circle

1053.51A　**Table:　Volumetric Hierarchy** (revised): The space quantum equals the space domain of each closest-packed nuclear sphere:

Space quantum	$= 1$
Tetrahedron	$= 1$
Nuclear vector equilibrium	$= 2^1/_2$
Nuclear icosahedron	$= 2^1/_2$
Cube	$= 3$
Octahedron	$= 4$
Rhombic triacontahedron	$= 5+$
Rhombic dodecahedron	$= 6$

1053.601　**Octahedron:** The octahedron—both numerically and geometrically—should always be considered as quadrivalent; i.e., congruent with self; i.e., doubly present.

In the volumetric hierarchy of prime-number identities we identify the octahedron's prime-number twoness and the inherent volume-fourness (in tetra terms) as volume 2^2, which produces the experiential volume 4.

1053.70　Container Structuring: Volume-surface Ratios

1053.71　When attempting to establish an international metric standard of measure for an integrated volume-weight unit to be known as "one gram" and deemed to consist of one cubic centimeter of water, the scientists overlooked the necessity for establishing a constant condition of temperature for the water. Because of expansion and contraction under changing conditions of

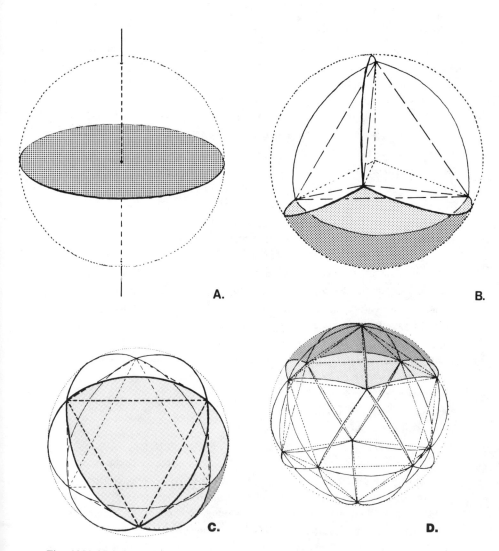

Fig. *1053.37 Spherical Great Circles Are Commensurable with Spherical Triangles of Three Prime Structural Systems: Tetra, Octa, and Icosa:*

A. Internal area of one great circle of a sphere
B. Surface triangle of spherical tetrahedron
C. Surface triangle of spherical octahedron
D. Surface triangle of spherical icosahedron
[1 great circle = 1 tetra triangle = 2 octa triangles = 5 icosa triangles = 30 basic *LCD* triangles]

temperature a constant condition of 4 degrees centigrade was later established internationally. In much the same way scientists have overlooked and as yet have made no allowance for the inherent variables in entropic and syntropic rates of energy loss or gain unique to various structurally symmetrical shapes and sizes and environmental relationships. (See Sec. *223.80,* "Energy Has Shape.") Not only do we have the hierarchy of relative volume containments respectively of equiedged tetra, cube, octa, icosa, "sphere," but we have also the relative surface-to-volume ratios of those geometries and the progressive variance in their relative structural-strength-to-surface ratios as performed by flat planes vs simple curvature; and as again augmented in strength out of the same amount of the same material when structured in compound curvature.

1053.72 In addition to all the foregoing structural-capability differentials we have the tensegrity variables (see Chap. 7), as all these relate to various structural capabilities of various energy patternings as containers to sustain their containment of the variously patterning contained energies occurring, for instance, as vacuum vs crystalline vs liquid vs gaseous vs plasmic vs electromagnetic phases; as well as the many cases of contained explosive and implosive forces. Other structural variables occur in respect to different container-contained relationships, such as those of concentrated vs distributive loadings under varying conditions of heat, vibration, or pressure; as well as in respect to the variable tensile and compressive and sheer strengths of various chemical substances used in the container structuring, and their respective heat treatments; and their sustainable strength-time limits in respect to the progressive relaxing or annealing behaviors of various alloys and their microconstituents of geometrically variant chemical, crystalline, structural, and interproximity characteristics. There are also external effects of the relative size-strength ratio variables that bring about internal interattractiveness values in the various alloys as governed by the second-power rate, i.e., frequency of recurrence and intimacy of those alloyed substances' atoms.

1053.73 As geometrical systems are symmetrically doubled in linear dimension, their surfaces increase at a rate of the second power while their volumes increase at a third-power rate. Conversely, as we symmetrically halve the linear dimensions of geometrical systems, their surfaces are reduced at a second-root rate, while their volumes decrease at a third-root rate.

1053.74 A cigar-shaped piece of steel six feet (72 inches) long, having a small hole through one end and with a midgirth diameter of six inches, has an engineering slenderness ratio (length divided by diameter) of 12 to 1: It will sink when placed on the surface of a body of water that is more than six inches deep. The same-shaped, end-pierced piece of the same steel of the same 12-to-1 slenderness ratio, when reduced symmetrically in length to three inches, becomes a sewing needle, and it will float when placed on the surface of the same body of water. Diminution of the size brought about so relatively mild a reduction in the amount of surface of the steel cigar-needle's shape in respect to the great change in volume—ergo, of weight—that its shape became so predominantly "surface" and its relative weight so negligible that only the needle's surface and the atomic-intimacy-produced surface tension of the water were importantly responsible for its interenvironmental relationship behaviors.

1053.75   For the same reasons, grasshoppers' legs in relation to a human being's legs have so favorable a volume-to-surface-tension relationship that the grasshopper can jump to a height of 100 times its own standing height (length) without hurting its delicate legs when landing, while a human can only jump and fall from a height of approximately three times his height (length) without breaking his legs.

1053.76   This same volume-to-surface differential in rate of change with size increase means that every time we double the size of a container, the contained volume increases by eight while the surface increases only fourfold. Therefore, as compared to its previous half-size state, each interior molecule of the atmosphere of the building whose size has been symmetrically doubled has only half as much building surface through which that interior molecule of atmosphere can gain or lose heat from or to the environmental conditions occurring outside the building as conductively transferable inwardly or outwardly through the building's skin. For this reason icebergs melt very slowly but accelerate progressively in the rate of melting. For the same reason a very different set of variables governs the rates of gain or loss of a system's energy as the system's size relationships are altered in respect to the environments within which they occur.

1053.77   As oil tankers are doubled in size, their payloads grow eightfold in quantity and monetary value, while their containing hulls grow only fourfold in quantity and cost. Because the surface of the tankers increases only fourfold when their lengths are doubled and their cargo volume increases eightfold, and because the power required to drive them through the sea is proportional to the ship's surface, each time the size of the tankers is doubled, the cost of delivery per cargo ton, barrel, or gallon is halved. The last decade has seen a tenfolding in the size of the transoceanic tankers in which both the cost of the ship and the transoceanic delivery costs have become so negligible that some of the first such shipowners could almost afford to give their ships away at the end of one voyage. As a consequence they have so much wealth with which to corrupt international standards of safety that they now build them approximately without safety factors—ergo, more and more oil tanker wrecks and spills.

1053.80   Growth and Decay

•[*1053.80–1053.85   Growth and Decay Scenario*]

1053.801   In chemical interbonding of atomic systems single-bonded (univalent) tetrahedra are only single-vertex-to-single-vertex congruent. This means that only one of each of any two tetrahedra's directionally differentiable four corners—which are as yet only infra- or ultratunable, only noisy subsystem, vertexial somethingnesses—are subcongruent critically intimate; that is, the magnitude of their mutual interattractiveness is greater than any other of their cosmic attracters. Singly interbonded tetrahedra are always attracted in critically intimate degree by one—and only one—of their corner-identifying infratunable systems attractively bonded with a neighboring tetrahedron's corner vertex subdifferentiable-system "points." For ages the vertexial somethingnesses only superficially apprehended by humans were experientially identified visually as "specks," audibly as noises, tactilely as prickly points, topologically as vertexes, and geometrically as sharp (corner) angles.

1053.802   Topology enumerates the critical-proximity-bonded pairs of "points" as constituting only one point and not as an almost tangent two. Topological accounting is confined to only superficially visible characteristics of systems. (See Sec. 262.02.)

1053.803   We learn experientially that lines are trajectories (Sec. 521.20), that two events and their trajectories cannot pass through the same point at the same time (Secs. 517.01–06), and that when we have such conflict or transit interference, they result in *smashes* (always separating each of the intersmashing bodies into a plurality of smaller systems, not dirt or dust), *plunge-ins* such as meteors plunging into Earth (to form more complex systems), *refractions, reflections,* or critical-proximity interrattractiveness *cotravelings* (Earth and Moon). When we do not have interference conflicts but we have two independent event trajectories converging to pass "near" ond another only at a precessionally critical-course-refracting, mass-interattractive distance, they may converge and diverge in a twist vertex exit (see Secs. 921.15 and 942.12). The term *vertex* embraces all of the foregoing system-furnished, local-focal, event cases.

1053.804   In chemical double-bonding the edge vectors of the tetrahedra—as well as the terminal vertexes—are also so critically proximate as superficially to seem to be congruent and are topologically accredited numerically only as "one" because of their superficial aspect of unity as a single hinge-pin.

1053.810 The vector equilibrium consists of eight tetrahedra each of which is edge-bonded; i.e., vertexially double-interbonded with three others, with each of their pre-time-size internal vertexes theoretically congruent as eight-in-one. Each of the pre-time-size vector equilibrium's eight tetrahedra has six vector edges ($6 \times 8 = 48$). (There are 24 internal and 24 external vector edges, 48 vector edges in all.) Each of the eight tetrahedra has four vertexes ($4 \times 8 = 32$), and in each of the tetrahedra three of these vertexes are external ($3 \times 8 = 24$): There are thus 12 externally paired sets ($24/2 = 12$) of visible vertexes. Three of each of the eight tetrahedra's vector edges ($3 \times 8 = 24$) are displayed on the outside of the vector equilibrium. (Compare Sec. *1033.020.*)

1053.811 There are 24 external vector edges of the vector equilibrium ($8 \times 3 = 24$). The other three vector edges of each of the eight tetrahedra are arrayed inwardly as 24 internal edges ($8 \times 3 = 24$), but these inwardly arrayed vector edges of the eight tetrahedra, being double-bonded or hinged together, appear as only 12 radial spokes of the vector equilibrium, which has 24 separate vectors in its four closed chordal rims of the four great-circle planes of the tetrahedra's four dimensionality; these four great circles produce the zero-volume tetrahedron. (See Sec. 441.)

1053.812 Nature never stops or even pauses at dead center. Nature contracts convergently to the center of its nuclear sphere, where each of its frequency-tuned integrities self-interfere convergently and react reflectively—ergo, omnidivergently—from their own terminally convergent self-frequency interferings. Unity is plural and at minimum two. (See Secs. 905.11 and 1070.)

1053.813 In the vector-diametered VE the convergent $2^1/_2$ phase coalesces with the divergent $2^1/_2$ phase and produces a univalent 5-ness whose consequence is also quadrivalent—producing also the vector-radiused VE's $5 \times 4 = 20$-ness of the vector equilibrium's subfrequency embracement of its eight edge-bonded, bivalent tetra and their six half-octahedra interstices.

1053.82 Life and Death

1053.821 The decaying and growing are complementary. Death is a co-function of birth: the father is dying; the child is being born. There never has been a real negative except as a positively complementary function of the oppositely directed positive.

1053.822 We do not have two Universes—"this world" and "the next world." Death is only the nonresonant, between-frequency silence of our oscillatory "no-stopover" passages through the Grand Central Station of the vector equilibrium's equilibrious center, as the lags in our cognition "realizations" time us into life's inherently aberrated imperfection aspects— somewhere off center.

1053.823 As we learn through experience to identify and comprehend ever more inclusively and precisely the generalized principles manifest in our experiences, and as we learn to communicate and share our recognitions of these manifests, we gradually reduce the lag rates in human cognition and come ever nearer to realization of the perfection.

1053.824 *Apprehension* is the physical brain's coordinate storing of all the special case, physically sensed information of otherness, integral (the child's thumb sucked by its mouth) or separate (the mother's udder sucked by the child's mouth.) *Comprehension* is the metaphysical mind's discovery of the meaningful interrelationship between the special-case information data that are neither implicit in, nor inferred by, any of the special-case information data when taken only separately—the meaning discovered by mind being the generalized principles manifest exclusively by the interrelationship variables and constants. *Awareness* means apprehending while also intuitively comprehending that the excitement over the novelty of the incoming information is significant because possibly pregnant with meaningful principles. (Compare Sec. 526.18.)

1053.825 Since "life" is experientially demonstrable to be weightless—ergo, metaphysical—its awareness and comprehension of meanings synchronize exclusively with the nonphysical intervals concentrically occurring between the only physically sensed frequencies of exclusively inanimate, radiantly propagated, electromagnetic-wave phenomena.

1053.826 Both death and life are complementary metaphysical functions interspersing and embracing our electromagnetic physical experience. Life's physical reality is constituted by the unique frequency identifications of the chemical elements and their atomic components as well as the humanly tune-in-able "color" frequencies of the electromagnetic spectrum's concentrically interpositioned occurrences (usually published by humans as a chart of positions along any one radius of the omnidirectional comprehensive concentric system). The metaphysical cognition of life-death reality is constituted exclusively by all the intervals between and beyond—inwardly and outwardly— all of the comprehensive electromagnetic phenomena sensed by human organisms.

1053.827 The music of John Cage is preoccupied with the silent intervals; his growing audience constitutes the dawning of the transition of all humanity into synchronization with the metaphysical rather than the physical. The decibel amplification of youth's "rock" music has switched its physical beat into the old silent intervals and is inducing metaphysical preoccupation in its listeners.

1053.83 Positive Visible and Integral Invisible

1053.831   To free ourselves from our preconditioned ill-chosen words of plus-minus and positive-negative, we may say operationally that there never has been a minus Universe to cofunction with Universe. There has always been cosmically integral, visible and invisible experience, which we have learned only in the past 100 years to be the consequence of whether or not we are integrally equipped organically with receiving sets having frequency tunability under the particular electromagnetic-waveband circumstances considered.

1053.832   Radiation outcasts. Radiation does not broadcast; broadcast is a planar statement; there are no planes. *Out* is inherently omnidivergent. Radiation omnicasts but does not and cannot *in*cast; it can only go-in-to-go-out. *In* is gravity.

1053.833   If radiation "goes through" a system and comes out on the other side, it does so because (1) there was no frequency interference—it just occurred between the system's occurrence frequencies—or (2) there was tangential interference and deflection thereby of the angle of travel, wherefore it did not go through; it went by.

1053.84 Cay and Decay

1053.841   In Webster's dictionary *cay* is an "emergent reef of coral or sand." We deduce that its earlier etymological meaning is a "growth," a coming together of parts (of sand or coral creatures)—ergo, we have *cay* and de-*cay*. Cay is convergently associative and syntropically cumulative. Decay is divergently disassociative and entropically dispersive.

1053.842   The nuclear vector equilibrium with a frequency of one has a double intensity (quadrivalent) tetravolume of 5 with a convergent *cay* volume of $2^1/_2$ and a divergent *decay* volume of $2^1/_2$; a congruent double $2^1/_2$ whose energy involvement potential is 5.

1053.843   In the generalized (subfrequency) case of the nuclear vector equilibrium (pulsatively impotent), *either* convergent *or* divergent (not both) quadrivalent tetravolume where frequency is half-zero, the tetravolume of the $VE^0 = 2^1/_2$.

1053.844   In the generalized (subfrequency case) of the nuclear vector equilibrium (potentially pulsative), congruently one-half-convergent and one-half-divergent quadrivalent tetravolume where frequency is zero, the half-convergent tetravolume of $2^1/_2$ compounded with the half-divergent tetravolume of $2^1/_2$ produces a double intensity two-and-a-halfness which has—an only potential—quadrivalent tetravolume of 5; ergo, $VE^0 = 5$, one-half of which is alternatively invisible; ergo, VE^0 *appears* deceptively to have a tetravolume of $2^1/_2$.

1053.845 In the generalized (subfrequency) nucleus-embracing, convergent-divergent, bivalent tetravolume vector equilibrium of frequency one, its tetravolume is 20. $VE^1 = 20$.

1053.846 In the generalized (subfrequency) nucleus-embracing, convergent-divergent vector equilibrium of frequency two, the tetravolume is 160. $VE^2 = 160$. (See Sec. 966.05 and Fig. 966.05B.)

1053.847 What must be remembered in considering all the foregoing is that unity is plural and at minimum two, as elucidated in Secs. 905.11 and 1070; wherefore the zero-frequency vector equilibrium, the VE^0 of "apparent" tetravolume $2^1/_2$, has an inherent but invisible double value that will have an operational resource effectiveness of 5, $2^1/_2$ of which is convergently effective and $2^1/_2$ divergently effective. This produces the state of equilibrium whose untenability induces cosmic resonance.

1053.848 In the symmetrical doubling of linear (radial) dimension the surface area increases four times and the volume eight times their original magnitude. In the case of the nuclear (one sphere) vector equilibrium with radius = 1 and volume = $2^1/_2$, when surrounded with 12 closest-packed, uniradius spheres and when the center of the nuclear sphere is connected to the respective centers of the 12 surrounding spheres, the distance between the center of the nuclear sphere and the center of any one of its 12 surrounding spheres is equal to 2 radii, or one *diameter* of the uniradius spheres. With radius 2, $2^1/_2 \times 8 = 20$. (Compare Sec. *1033.63*.)

Closest-packed Uniradius Spheres	Frequency	Tetravolumes
Radius 1	$VE^{0/2}$	$2^1/_2$
Radius 1	VE^0	5
Radius 2	VE^1	20
Radius 4	VE^2	160

1053.85 Inventory of Alternatives to Positive

TACTILE: —range-reachable, frequency dense, ergo interferable, ergo "solidly" or firmly touchable vs out-of-reach untunable

—cold-warm; also frequency conditions

—push-pull

AUDIBLE: —infra- or ultratunable

—sound and noise; we say "noise" when the frequencies are not differentiable but altogether overlap the frequency limit of our equipment

VISUAL: —frequency; again, electromagnetic

—infra- and ultratunable

—distance factor not a matter of resolution but of wavelength

—you can't differentiate the untunable

OLFACTORY:—sweet vs obnoxious

—*decay;* the divergent, the coming apart; decaying tends to be malodorous

—*cay* (growth); the convergent freshness tends to be olfactorily welcome

ELECTRO-
MAGNETICS:—attractions and repulsions.

What are the relative frequency ranges involved? (Compare Sec. *100.020.*)

1060.00 Omnisensorial Accommodation

1061.20 Conic Geometry of Trees

1061.21   Nature operates only convergently and divergently, never in parallel. She uses equispaced, concentric convergence and divergence. Trees grow annually by successively and concentrically producing enveloping, live, cambium-layer cones divergent from the green nuclear apex budding and of greater diameter at the tree's wide and deeply rooted base.

1061.22 Nature's approximately equispaced, concentrically conical, spherical and polyhedral convergences and divergences are all asymmetrically aberrated in respect to their symmetrical geometries of reference—in respect to which they are progressively conformed while being forever in time closely or remotely affected by the ever-changing proximities of all other systems of ever-transforming Scenario Universe.

1061.23 As with the misassumptions of "straight" lines, "flat" planes, and "absolute" solids, the misassumption of an all-embracing, rectilinearly associative and disassociative cosmic system of parallelisms has been occasioned by too-close, too-short-term, and too-limited consideration and accounting of humanity's observational experiences. Splitting a tree discloses an apparently rough parallelism of grain running vertically between the concentric cones, but it proves to be not parallel, as the concentric spacing gradually converges toward the conic apexes and diverges toward the conic tree base.

1061.24 Nature's omnidirectional growths and contractions are accomplished only convergently and divergently, even when directionally focused by combined reflective interference and refractive shunting through lenses. Even focused radiant energy does not operate in parallels but in pulsively alternating, convergent-divergent contractions and expansions of either the wirelessly beamed or wired-beam transmissions, both of which occur in concentric cones. Cones are simply rotated tetrahedra linked together first base-to-base and then apex-to-apex, repeat and repeat, with the number of concentric circles of any cross section of either the most closely or most openly spaced concentricity constituting the cyclic frequency of the special case transmitting.

1061.25 Radiation is omnidirectional entropic divergence from a nucleus; gravity is omnidirectional syntropic convergence toward all nuclei. Cross sections of gravitational convergence and radiational divergence appear as the successive concentric cambium layerings of the cross section of a tree trunk.

1070.00   Plurality of Inherent Topological Twonesses

•[*1070.00–1077.11   Geometry of Two Scenario*]

1071.00   Systematic Character of Prime Thinkability

1071.10   **Prime:** Prime means sizeless, timeless, subfrequency. Prime is prehierarchical. Prime is prefrequency. Prime is generalized, a metaphysical conceptualization experience, not a special case.

1071.20   **Systematic Realization:** The mathematician's "purely imaginative," no-thickness, no breadth—ergo, no insideness or outsideness—points, lines, and planes are nonexperienceable. All image-ing derives from experience. Conceptually imaginable point, line, and plane experiences are only systemic—i.e., they have polyhedral insideness, outsideness, and angular constancy independent of size.

1071.21   Size is always special case realizability. The mathematician's undemonstrable assumption that three points define a plane of no thickness—no radial depth—is therefore subsystemic; ergo, unthinkable, nonoperationally evidencible, and unimaginable; ergo, unemployable as constituents of proofs.

1071.22   Contrary to conventional mathematical dogma three points do not define a nonexistent—ergo, nondemonstrable—no-thickness plane; nor do they define an altitudeless triangle because there can be naught to do the defining systematically. No-thickness is neither experimentally evidencible nor conceptually feasible. System is conceptual independent of size and special case.

1071.23   Operationally omnitriangulated polyhedra may be realized only systematically—i.e., with special case dimensionality or special case radial depth of insideness. Dimensionality = special case time-size radial depth = frequency.

1071.24   Radial depth is expressed in frequency of omnidirectional wave propagations per unit of time.

1071.25   It takes a minimum of four differentially experienceable event-loci to define a system. System is primitively fourfoldedly experienceable. When humans see three stars, they see three separate special case events: there is neither special case measurability nor generalized considerability.

With inherent a priori systemic fourfoldedness there is imaginability of topological vertexes and a sixfoldedness of unique interrelatedness of the inside-from-outside differentiating thinkability. Conceptual = imaginable.

1071.26 Prime thinkability is inherently systemic. Prime epistemology is generalized thinkability. Epistemology discovers intuition.

1071.27 Intuition is the dawning awareness of the experienced, but at first unconsidered, newly occurring, unique, system-defining fourfoldedness *apprehending* and the epistemological system search for the sixfolded system interrelationships. *Comprehension,* often misidentified as "understanding," occurs when the six prehending interattractive relationships of the four-foldedness are identified.

1071.28 Structures are systems and have radial depth; wherefore "surface" triangle structures are always tetrahedra or truncated tetrahedra.

1072.00   Definability of Structural Systems

1072.10   **Proposition to Be Proven**: that structural systems are always special case operational realizations in which there is a constant relative abundance of all the topological and system characteristics, the only variable being a quantity multiplier consisting of one of the first four prime numbers—1, 2, 3, and 5—or an intermultiplied plurality of the same first four prime numbers.

1072.11

Given: definition of prime: Sec. 1071.10
Given: definition of system: Sec. 400.01
Given: definition of structure: Sec. 600.02
Given: definition of structural systems: Sec. 610.20
Given: definition of prime tetra, octa, and icosa: Sec. 1011.30
Given: definition of subfrequency: Sec. 1011.32
Given: definition of nucleus: Secs. 414 and 1012.01
Given: definition of thinkable generalization: Sec. 501
Given: definition of special case realizations: Sec. 504
Given: definition of cosmic inherency: Sec. 1073
Given: definition of two kinds of twoness: Sec. 223.05

1072.20   Generalized Topological Definability

1072.21   Generalized principles have topological system definability of angle, number, and constancy. Special cases have unique frequency dimensionability. Wherefore we propose that all recallably thinkable experiencings, physical and metaphysical, are fivefoldedly characterized:

(1) systematically,
(2) topologically
    (topo-aspectively),   generalized
                                     (metaphysical
(3) angularly,   & physical)   special
                                                     case
(4) numerically
    (topo-interabundantly);
(5) frequency definable
    (special case: physical)

1072.22   All conceptually thinkable, exclusively metaphysical experiencings are fourfoldedly characterized as above. All generalized principles are conceptually thinkable and fourfoldly definable. Generalization is conceptually (i.e., systematically) imaginable independent of (5) frequency.

1072.23   The fifth characteristic, *frequency,* is the unique *special case variable.* Physical experiencings are dependent not only on the four generalizable characteristics, but also on the fifth, frequency (i.e., size).

1072.30   Wave and Particle Definability

1072.31   Wave as a constant topological aspect is exclusively defined by angle, conceptually independent of frequency; ergo, frequency is the additional special case fifth characteristic—the generalization realized in time.

1072.32   Particle is frequency-definable special case, and wave is angularly defined generalization. The numerically unique condition of special case $5 \neq 4$ of generalizations identifies the dilemma of physics in reconciling the minimum fourfoldedness of wave definability by angles and the minimum fivefoldedness* definability of particle particularization by unique frequencies. (See Secs. 541.30, 961.46, 973.30, and *986.72*).

1073.00   Cosmic Inherency

1073.10   Four Kinds of Twoness

1073.11   Since unity is plural and, at minimum, two, the additive twoness of systemic independence of the individual system's spinnability's two axial poles, the latter's *additive* twoness must be added to something, which thinkable somethingness is the inherent systemic *multiplicative* twoness of all systems' congruent concave-convex inside-outness: this additive-two-plus-multiplicative-two *fourness* inherently produces the interrelationship $2 + 2 + 2$ *sixness* (threefold twoness) of all minimum structural-system comprehendibility.

1073.12   All systems are conceptually differentiated out of Universe.

System + environment = Universe
Universe − system = environment

1073.13   The environment is dual, consisting of the macro and micro (outsideness and insideness). Ergo, a *fourth twoness* of all prime structural systems is synergetically accountable as

$$2 + 2 + 2 + 2 = 8.$$

(See Fig. *1073.10.*)

* See Secs. *1053.12–15*.

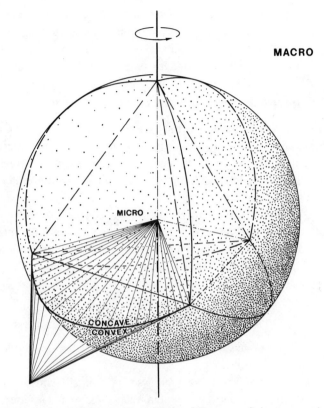

Fig. *1073.10 Cosmic Inherency: Four Kinds of Twoness:* Spin twoness is additive. Duality twoness (concave-convex) is multiplicative. The spin twoness and duality twoness together comprise a third relationship twoness. The fourth twoness is comprised of the macro-micro (insideness and outsideness) twoness.

1073.14   Integral system is threefold twoness = 6.
Integral Universe is fourfold twoness = 8.

Spin twoness 2
Duality twoness 2
Interrelationship twoness 2
Environmental twoness 2
                                                                            ─
                                                                            8

1073.15   **The Indispensable Center:** At the indispensable center of the system convergent-divergent Universe turns itself inside out. The invisible, a priori, multiplicative twoness differentially disclosed in the system's omnitopological hierarchy is manifest of the integrity of the sizeless, timeless nonconceptuality always complementing the conceptual system takeout from nonconceptual Scenario Universe's eternal regenerating. (See Sec. 1006.10.)

1073.16   Partial vacuum results as the physical atmospheric gases are re-moved; beyond those zero evacuations the electromagnetic tensing induces re-verse flows of physically demonstrable positive energy (as manifest in cryogenics, in which liquids flow antigravitationally). Vacuum = novent.

1073.20   Interrelationship Twoness: Third Kind of Twoness

1073.21   All systems have a neutral axis of spinnability, with two external polar vertexes and two interior center axis vertexes which are congruent—ergo, visible only as one vertex located at the convergence-divergence, in-tegrative-disintegrative, inbound-outbound, turnaround, neutral center of gra-vity–center of radiation of the system.

1073.22   The exterior and separate set of two polar vertexes is the additive twoness of systems, and the congruent exterior-interior set is the multiplica-tive twoness of all systems. The interior-exterior differentiating fourness has an interrelated sixness that differentiates as a unique third kind of twoness of unique interrelatedness of all systems.

1074.00   Prime Nuclear Structural Systems

1074.10   All prime nuclear structural systems have one—and only one—(unity two) interior vertex.

1074.11   Internally nuclear structural systems internally consist entirely of tetrahedra that have only one common interior vertex: omniconvertex.

1074.12   In nuclear structural systems each of the surface system's exter-nal triangles constitutes the single exterior facet of an omnisystem-occupying set of inter-triple-bonded tetrahedra, each of whose single interior-to-system vertexes are congruent with one another at the convergent nuclear center of the system.

1074.13   In all nonredundant, prime, nuclear structural systems the con-gruently interior-vertexed, omnisystem-occupying tetrahedra of all prime structural systems may all be interiorly truncated by introducing special-case frequency, which provides chordal as well as radial modular subdivisioning of the isotropic-vector-matrix intertriangulation of each radial, frequency-embracing wave layer, always accomplished while sustaining the structural ri-gidity of the system. (See Fig. *1074.13.*)

1074.20   Omnitopological Domains

1074.21   Omnitopological domains are defined in terms of the system's unique central-angle-defined insideness and its unique surface-angle-defined outsideness. (See Sec. 1006.20.)

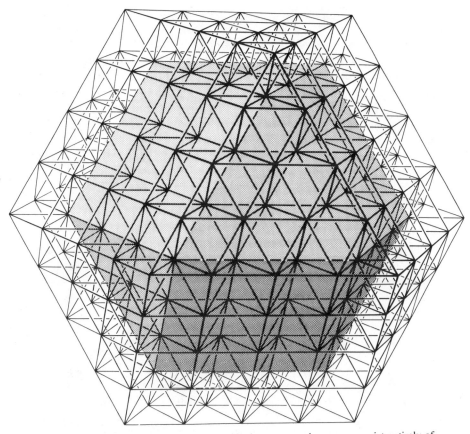

Fig. 1074.13 Nuclear Structural Systems: Nuclear structural systems consist entirely of tetrahedra having a common interior vertex. They may be interiorly truncated by introducing special case frequency, which provides chordal as well as radial modular subdivisioning of the isotropic-vector-matrix intertriangulation, while sustaining the structural rigidity of the system.

1074.30 Spin Twoness and Duality Twoness

1074.31   Having identified (a) the constant additive twoness of the vertexial poles of the axial spinnability operative in all independent systems, and (b) the multiplicative twoness characterizing the concavity and convexity congruently operative in all independent systems, we find that the first four prime numbers—1, 2, 3, and 5—are the only variables present in the Eulerean topological inventorying of all the omnitriangularly, nonredundantly stabilized, symmetrical polyhedra.

1074.32   Spin twoness is additive.

Duality twoness is multiplicative.

1075.00   Special Case: Energy and Information

1075.10   Structures are always special case. Structures are operational. Operational = physically realized. Structures always have unique size. By definition a structure is a complex of energy events interacting to produce a stable pattern.

1075.11   An energy event is always special case. Whenever we have experienced energy, we have special case. The physicist's first definition of physical is that it is an experience that is extracorporeally, remotely, instrumentally apprehensible. Metaphysical includes all the experiences that are excluded by the definition of physical. Metaphysical is always generalized principle.

1075.12   Physical is always special case. Energy is physical and always special case. Information is always special case. Energy is information: information is energy. Special case is always realized by its energetic information. Dimension is unique frequency information. Time incrementation is special case information. Concept is general: information is quantitative (special case).

1075.20   Equation of Intellect

1075.21   By thermodynamic law energy may neither be created nor lost in Universe. By synergetic postulate intellect is irrevocable and irreversibly comprehensive—both subjectively and objectively—in respect to energy.

1075.22   Intellect mensurates and modulates relative energy events and event interrelationships. The total quantity of energy operative in Universe is a constant, but a dependent, function of intellect. Universe is the integral of all metaphysical and physical phenomena.

1075.23   In respect to individual humans total energy occurs as a complex of local variables of systematically cooperative, convergent-divergent, complementary-reciprocal, intertransformation patternings of uniquely differentiable local system aspects, accountable by intellect in locally varying magnitudes of concentration. The modulations are selectable, predictable, and governable by intellect to the extent that superficial acceleration permits.

1075.24   Modulations through local transformations are arranged or valved by intellect through inherent associative-disassociative patterning of local energy-complex environments. Thus the aggregate effective energy behavior sum-totally accountable as a universal constant is engaged in its local behaviors by individual experience (and apprehended and appraised by consciously operative intellect) in widely differentiated sets of patterns in variable magnitudes of regenerative pattern concentrations.

1075.25   *Wealth* is the measurable degree of established operative advantage locally organized by generalized-principle-employing intellect over the locally occurring, differentiable behaviors of universal energy. Wealth is an irreversible advantage: it cannot be expended in a preferred reorganization of past events; it can only be expended in organizing forward events in preferential patterns.

1075.26   The *wealth* advantage increases as intellect comprehends local behaviors and acts in complementary regeneration to produce patterns advantageous to human processes. With every inventorying of local-energy behaviors by intellect, and with the informed rearrangement of them to provide wider, more frequently and precisely modulatable patterns with ever less weight of materials—ergo of energy—and fewer seconds of time per accomplished life protection, support, and accommodation function, the established wealth advantage is manifest and the documented knowledge in local Universe increases.

1076.00   Primitive Regeneration

1076.10   Prime = primitive. Primitive is generalized principle and not special case. Virgin = primitive. "Virgin soil" $\doteq$ special case. Virgin female human = special case, only because of the "human" case realization. Virginity is a generalized aspect of primitive. There can be no special-case generalized virgins. Virginity is not only prefrequency, it is pretime, pre-special-case, and pre-experienceable-dimension.

1076.11   Virgin identifies the topological insideness aspect of the coincidental insideness-outsideness of all generalized systems independently differentiated from all the macrocosmos Universe outside the virginal system, from all the microcosm Universe inside the virginal system and from the little of the cosmos Universe with which the virgin imaginably differentiates the outsideness from the insideness. And virgin is half a system because unity is plural and at minimum two, the virgin being the prime insideness of concavity to be dimensionally or experientially and operationally realized only by special-case-recognized congruence of the convex outsideness with the inside concavity.

1076.12   Male is convex; $^1/_2$ system; $^1/_2$ spin; $^1/_2$ quantum.

Female is concave; $^1/_2$ system; $^1/_2$ spin; $^1/_2$ quantum.

Engendering is a special-case phenomenon that requires fertilization. Fertilization is the systemic differentiating out of Universe that produces conceptually local Universe marrying the macrocosm to the microcosm, which realizes a new special-case system event with its own set of insideness-outsideness topological characteristics.

1076.13   Physics of the 1970s identifies:

$$^1/_2 \text{ quantum} = {}^1/_2 \text{ spin; and } 1 \text{ quantum} = 2 \left(\frac{\text{spin}}{2}\right).$$

Conception-birth comes with the realization that the aspects of the externally viewed, plus-curvature convexity that are seemingly separate from those of the internally viewed, minus-curvature concavity have no interveningly differentiating, zero-curvature sheath structurally differentiating the only timelessly (or generalized) conceptual coincidence of both the plus and minus curvature. In the alternately plus-or-minus pulsativeness frequencies of special case time the multiplicative twoness ''conception'' releases or gives birth to new, coexistent, additive twonesses as independently axially spinnable: special case spin twoness inherently coupled with the duality twoness, producing the individual unity fourness, with its primitive sixfoldedness of integral system interrelatedness and its eightfolded integral Universe environment.

1077.00   Prime Number Inherency and Constant Relative Abundance

1077.10   Since the relative interabundance of one nonspin vertex for every two faces and every three edges is a constant topological system condition, we may identify them as a constant interabundance set in terms of the number of vertexes and edges as a constant topological relationship of all symmetrical and triangularly stabilized, modularly unsubdivided, polyhedral sytems.

1077.11   We may substitute T, meaning the number of topological sytem sets, for the bracketed groups:

$$\therefore .2 + 2 = T.$$

And when the symmetrical, omninonredundantly triangulated, modularly unsubdivided systems are subjected to symmetrical modular subdivision, and the number of edge-module subdivisions is represented by F, then:

$$2 + 2NF^2 = T.$$

where the first 2 is the additive spin two; the second 2 is the multiplicative duality two; N is the prime number uniquely characterizing the system; F is the frequency of modular subdividing; and T is the number of topological sets of one vertex plus two faces equal three edges $(1 + 2 = 3)$ that exists in the symmetrical structural (because nonredundant) triangulated polyhedral system. Q.E.D.: See Sec. 223.

1100.00 Constant Zenith Projection

1100.00   CONSTANT ZENITH PROJECTION
(Formerly Triangular Geodesics Transformational Projection Model)

(1110.00   Zenith Constancy of Radial Coordination)*

(1120.00   Wrapability)

1130.00   Omnidirectional Typewriter
  1130.10   Model Studies
  1130.20   Orbital Feedback Circuitry vs Critical Path
  1131.00   Spool-wrapping of Tetrahedron
  1131.10   Omnitriangulated Strip
  1132.00   Great-circle Shunting and Switch Points
  1132.10   Great-circle Railroad Tracks of Energy
  1133.00   Information Control System of Universe

  *Titles in parentheses may be found in *Synergetics 1*

1130.00 Omnidirectional Typewriter

1130.10 Model Studies

1130.11 Hypothetical model studies are schematic probability studies. Some are planar area models, but many deal exclusively with linear probability. Comprehensive reality problems are not linear; they are omnidirectional. They deal with total system and total Universe. That is what world society is not attending to realistically and that's why we are in trouble: Synergy shows that you cannot solve comprehensive problems with exclusively local planar or local linear models.

1130.20 Orbital Feedback Circuitry vs Critical Path

1130.21 Conventional critical-path conceptioning is linear and self-under-informative. Only orbital system feedbacks are both comprehensively and incisively informative. Orbital critical feedback circuits are pulsative, tidal, importing and exporting. Critical-path elements are not overlapping linear modules in a plane: they are interspiralling complexes of regenerative feedbacks or circuits.

1130.22 When we go out to the Earth-orbiting Moon and plan to get back into the biospheric-enshrouded Earth again, we are dealing in 60,000-miles-per-hour solar system spiraling as the solar system while part of our galaxy rotates around the galaxy center at 700,000 miles per hour. This, altogether with the intergalactic motion, means we can never come back to where we were even though we safely reach Earth.

1130.23 People may think they are being realistically linear, but they are actually just increasing the radius of larger and larger spiral orbits. Each year is a Sun-spiraling circuit. Years are not linear. As humans complete their daily local circuits, the Earth spins about its axis and orbits the Sun; wherefore the critical path of progressive accomplishment that led to humans reaching the Moon and returning safely to Earth involves not a linear months-and-years progression but a complex of millions of spirals within spirals. With each year the multimillion-stranded rope of omniinterrelated local circuitry feedback closures integrates synergetically to produce a spirally orbiting, complex, system-defining set of Sun-Earth-Moon orbiting events, and this system finally reaches out to embrace the Moon as well as the Earth, all of which ever expands humanity's local Universe involvement. (See Sec. *535.20.*)

1130.24   A structural system (even such a structural system as a building) can be thought of as a multi-great-circle-faced clock, a complex of feedback circuitry where the sum-total of interferences of the pushes and pulls are everywhere synergetically and · locally regenerative. As the humans complete their daily local circuits, the Earth spins about its axis and concurrently orbits the Sun; wherefore the critical spiral path of progressive accomplishment that led to humans reaching the Moon and returning safely to Earth involves not a linear months-and-years progression but a complex of millions of spirals within spirals of an around-the-Sun-by-Earth orbiting and an around-the-Earth-by-Moon orbiting progression, wherein we progressively establish one feedback circuitry system overlapping another, and another, and so on as the year goes around.

1130.25   The reality is always systematically spiro-orbital. Orbit = circuit. For instance, all terrestrial critical-path developments inherently orbit the Sun. No path can develop as curvature-free linearity. All paths are precessionally modulated by remotely operative forces that produce curvi-wavi-spiralinear

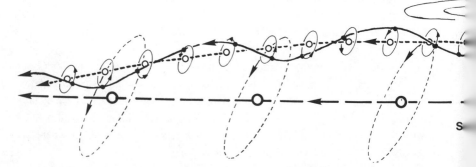

Fig. *1130.24 Reality is Spiro-orbital:* All terrestrial critical path developments inherently orbit the Sun. No path can be linear. All paths are precessionally modulated by remotely operative forces producing spiralinear paths.

paths. Increasingly complex curvi-wavi-spiralinear, system-embracing circuits are diffusive—ergo, spinoff prone; ergo, system-mass reducing; ergo, ultimately bit-by-bit self-annihilative. Spun-off simplexes may come into critical interattractiveness with other diffusely detached simplexes to form other young complex systems, to syntropically initiate new, mass-increasing, cosmically-local-traveler, complex system-defining, new intercelestial orbiting circuits.

1131.00   Spool-wrapping of Tetrahedron

1131.10   Omnitriangulated Strip

1131.11   Another model is the omnitriangulated strip tape whose width exactly equals the altitude of the regular tetrahedron's triangular face. This strip's surface has been entirely divided into a series of equilateral triangles, each of whose edges are of the same length as any edge of the regular tetrahedron. Employing this wavilinear-faced tape, we can completely and successively spool-wrap the entire surfaces of all four faces of the tetrahedron while also wrapping four of the tetrahedron's six edges and exactly paralleling the wrapping tape along the other two edges of the tetrahedron. None of the four vertexes are embracingly wrapped, but all of them are tangentially wrapped.

1131.12   The tetrahedron so wrapped has a wrapping axis running through, and perpendicular to, the midpoints of the two unwrapped edges of the tetrahedron spool. Being a regular tetrahedron, this spool may be used as a roller printing device, when its fixes are inked, to make a continuously

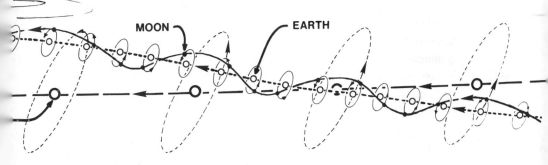

CENTER OF GALAXY

MOON   EARTH

printed strip of edge-to-edge equilateral triangles. Ergo, we have a device for projecting all of the omnidirectionally occurring and tetrahedrally observed data onto a minimum-surface system that is unwrappable onto a flat ribbon printout with four-dimensional coordination. In this method of projection the observer's viewpoint always remains perpendicular to the outside surface of the system, as in the Dymaxion map projection, where any star remains in exact perpendicular zenith to the corresponding point on the map of the world, whether the map is stretched in one flat plane or whether it is the surface of complete unitary sphericity. The same triangles are going to come out flat and the same stars are in exact zenith over their respective points, as the radii remain perpendicular to the system independent of whether the triangular area edges are arcs or chords.

1131.13   The omnitriangulated strip is an extraordinary mathematical transformation in which you can graphically accommodate the omnidirectionality of all systems in an exactly coordinated mathematical accounting. It can project and print out on a strip all gravitational and radiational data, be they in the form of stars, fishes, or anything. They are all coordinatably print-outable onto one continuous flat ribbon map. What we have is a true prototype of an *omnidirectional typewriter*. It can print out each omniembracing layer of each frequency layer of each convergent-divergent system. When you print out the omnidata on such a strip, it identifies specifically where and when each event in the transformation occurs.

1132.00 Great-circle Shunting and Switch Points

1132.01   This omnidirectional, convergent-divergent, systems-reporting device can print out the most-economical-interrelationships trackings and in-formation-coordinating routings of all systems, because it embraces the pattern of all 87 of the most economical and only available great-circle railroad tracks and no-loss-holding stations of energetic Universe; i.e., through all the closest-sphere-packed systems; i.e., through all the isotropic vector matrixes. In other words, if you want to go from here to there in Universe in the quickest and most economical way, while stopping over here and there for indefinite periods at no-extra-cost hotels, you have got to go through the 12 points of intertangency of the 25 great circles of fundamental symmetry that apply to all the atoms and their association in all seven of the fundamental symmetry subsets.

1132.02   The 31 great circles of the icosahedron always shunt the energies into local-holding great-circle orbits, while the vector equilibrium opens the switching to omniuniverse energy travel. The icosahedron is red light, holding, no-go; whereas vector equilibrium is green light, go. The six great circles of the icosahedron act as holding patterns for energies. The 25 great circles of the vector equilibrium all go through the 12 tangential contact points bridging between the 12 atomic spheres always closest packed around any one spherical atom domain.

1132.10   Great-circle Railroad Tracks of Energy

1132.11   Each of the 25 great circles of any one closest-packed sphere can be used by that special local sphere as an "until-ready," local shunt-off, holding circuit track for any traveling energy entity. This is permitted by the fact that each and all of the 25 great circles are foldable into local, bow-tie, clover-leaf, figure-eight, "chain-of-sausages," three-or-four-bladed-propeller-type patterns which, when totally interassembled, also provide full, uninterrupted, 360-degree, around-the-sphere circuitry. The energy entities can travel around locally on any one sphere's holding tracks in these local 360-degree total shuntings for as long as is "convenient" to the system.

1132.12   The 25 great circles of the vector equilibrium are the only omni-intersystem-connecting "railroad tracks" of energy in the Universe. When an energy entity holding locally on a local sphere gets a green light to get back on the grand-omni-interspheres' system tracks, it can do so by crossing over one of the 12 inter-atomic-sphere bridges. As we have seen in Sec. 450, three of the vector equilibrium's four unique sets of great circles, whose respective numbers total 25, disclose different rates of encounter with the 12 tangential "Grand Central Stations" through which the energy-entity travelers can transfer to other spheres of the omni-equiradiused, closest-packed-spherical-dynamics domains of any one elemental atomic class. Arranged in order of the number of encounters with (and entries into) the sphere-to-sphere, tangential grand-central transfer points per each great-circle cycle, they may be accounted as follows:

6 great circles go through 2 points per 360° cycle							
3 "	"	"	"	4 "	"	"	"
12 "	"	"	"	4 "	"	"	"
4 "	"	"	"	6 "	"	"	"

25 shunt holding   16 transfer opportunities
   circuits   per each spheric moment,
              of which only 12 can
              be accommodated

1132.13   Because only 12 of 16 station transfers can be accommodated, each sphere has inherently eternal retention of four energy entities. Four energy entities comprise the minimum system-defining constellation—i.e. the

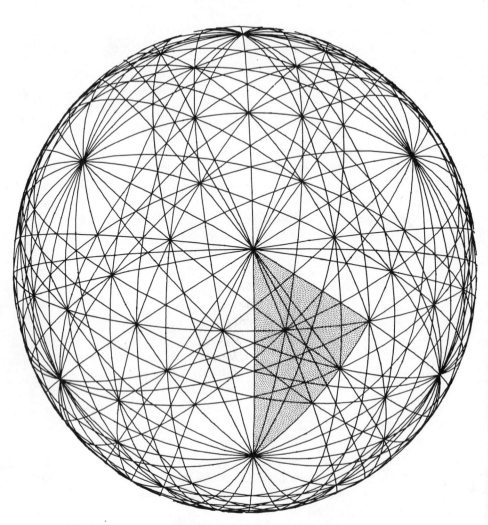

Fig. *1132.01B Composite of Vector Equilibrium and Icosahedron Great Circle Sets:*
This is a black-and-white version of color plate 32. The Basic Equilibrium 48 LCD triangle appears here shaded in the spherical grid. In this composite spherical matrix we
see all the 25 primary vector equilibrium great circles and two sets skewed-positive and
negative of the icosahedron 31 great circle sets. ($31 \times 2 = 62$. $62 + 25 = 87$. But 14 of
the 87 are redundant.) Four of the VE great circles are congruent with four of the
icosa's 10-great circle set. Three of the VE great circles are congruent with three of the
icosa's 15-great-circle set. Thus seven positive are redundant and seven negative are
redundant. ($87 - 14 = 73$.) There are 73 great circles in the composite set. (See color
plate 32.)

This composite shows the vector equilibrium great circles and the icosahedron great
circles in the two alternate ways of pumping the VE jitterbug pattern.

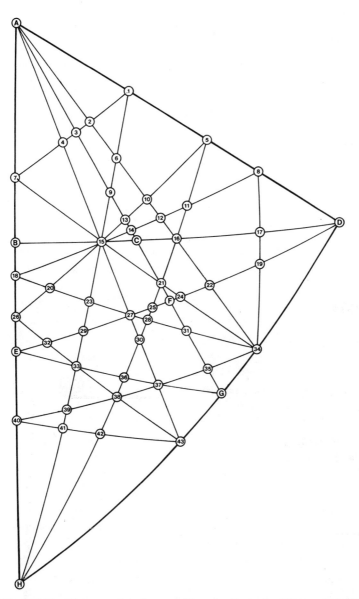

Fig. *1132.01C Net Diagram of Angles and Edges for Basic Equilibrium 48 LCD Triangle in VE-Icosa Grcd:* This is a coded detail of the basic spherical triangle shown shaded in Fig. *1132.01B* and at Fig. 453.01. It is the key to the trigonometry tables for the spherical central angles, the spherical face angles, the planar edge lengths, and the planar face angles presented at Table *1132.01D*. (The drawing shows the spherical phase: angle and edge ratios are given for both spherical and planar VE.)

tetrahedron—which is exactly one energy quantum. Thus we see that the 16 potential encounters of the 25 great-circle sphere may be identified as $^{16}/_4 = 4$ energy quanta, of which only three may be accommodated at the exits: wherefore a fourth quantum is always retained. No sphere or atom can be exhausted.

1133.00 Information Control System of Universe

1133.01 In the vector equilibrium's total of 25 great-circle circuitings, we find at any one moment four different sets of great-circle holding patterns and four energy quanta per sphere, but with exit accommodation for only three quanta. With all these beautiful local holding-circuit switches and stop-and-go controls we begin to comprehend conceptually the method by which nature can shunt, valve, hold, and transmit all information in Universe. This is the information-control system of the Universe. This is the way spheres transmit through closest-packing patterns.

1133.02 This is why transistors work; it explains why somebody was suddenly able to discover that a tiny piece of metal embraced an energy-quanta valving system having reliable regularities. Science unthinkingly spoke of this phenomenon as "solid state physics," partially because individual humans could not see those beautiful little atoms and electrons doing their acts on their railroad tracks and their respective local great-circle energy holding patterns, and partially because science has been flying blind on instruments. For over a century science has been maintaining stubbornly that there was nothing to see by looking out of the windows. They said nature does not use models in the invisible microcosm; she uses only abstract equations. This "nonconceptuality viewpoint" was fortified to the public by use of the term "solid state physics."

1133.03 In the behaviors of the vector equilibrium's 25 great circles we have the basis for the design of a nuclear omnidirectional typewriter, a programmable computer smaller than a pinhead, which is capable of storing, retrieving, and printing out all humanly acquirable information. Synergetics mathematics has the ability to convert the spherically arranged information and project it onto flat conceptual-information-printout arrays of negligible distortion. The least-possible-distorted transformational projection is icosahedral treatment employed in the Dymaxion airocean world map system. The simplest frame of reference, however, is that of the spherical tetrahedron, which transforms into the flat, omnitriangulated-grid, strip-wrapped, four-dimensionally-symmetrical tetrahedron. The tetrahedron produces a conveniently linear, four-dimensional roller printout.

1133.04 These transformational projections afford the most economical, least distorted means of translating the symmetrically omnidirectional into a flat symmetrical projection. The prime structural system of Universe, the tetrahedron, unwraps linearly to print out all possible variations of angle and frequency modulation. Here we have a conceptualizing model that can be reliably programmed to conceptualize atomic structurings at humanly discernible magnitudes. This kind of atomic-level behavior is exactly what all the computer model specialists have been missing—ergo, the magnitude of the chasm between their projective equation strategies and synergetics' four-dimensional conceptual integrity independent of size and its inherent ability to deal discretely with closest-packed atomic system proclivities and behaviors.

1238.52 **Addendum** Inspired by inferences of Secs. 1223.12, *1224.30–34* inclusive and *1238.51,* just before going to press with *Synergetics 2,* we obtained the following 71 integer, multi-intermirrored, computer-calculated and proven, volumetric (third power) Scheherazade number which we have arranged in ten, "sublimely rememberable," unique characteristic rows.

$2^{12} \cdot 3^8 \cdot 5^6 \cdot 7^6 \cdot 11^6 \cdot 13^6 \cdot 17^4 \cdot 19^3 \cdot 23^3 \cdot 29^3 \cdot 31^3 \cdot 37^3 \cdot 41^3 \cdot 43^3 \cdot 47^3$ the product of which is

616,494,535,0,868
49,2,48,0
51,88
27,49,49
00,6996,185
494,27,898
13,35,17,0
25,22,
73,66,0
864,000,000.

If all the trigonometric functions are reworked using this 71 integer number, embracing all prime numbers to 50, to the third power, employed as volumetric, cyclic unity, all functions will prove to be whole rational numbers as with the whole atomic populations.

1200.00 Numerology

1200.00   NUMEROLOGY

(1210.00   Numerology)*

1220.00   Indigs
  (1221.00   Integration of Digits)
  (1222.00   Absolute Four and Octave Wave)
  (1223.00   Wave Pulsation of Indigs)
  1224.00   Wave Pulsation of Number 24
    1224.10   Vector Equilibrium and Octave Wave
    1224.20   Recapitulation
    1224.30   Turnaround Terminals

1230.00   Scheherazade Numbers
  (1231.00   Cosmic Illions)
  1238.00   Fourteen-illion Scheherazade Number
    1238.22   Tetrahedral Complementations
    1238.28   Spherical Quadrant Phase
    1238.41   Declining Powers of Factorial Primes
    1238.51   Scheherazade Numbers

*Titles in parentheses may be found in *Synergetics 1*

1220.00 Indigs

1224.00 Wave Pulsation of Number 24

1224.10 Vector Equilibrium and Octave Wave

1224.11 The second powering of numbers apparently involves a 24-positive and 24-negative resonance phasing. The potential variables of the indigs of the second-powering of the 24 successive integers running between 0 and 25, and indigs of the 24 integers descending successively between 25 and 50, and repeating the 24 integers between 50 and 75, and the 24 integers between 75 and 100 ad infinitum, apparently account for all the equilibrious-disequilibrious, radiational-gravitational, convergent-divergent, curvi-wavilinear behaviors in respect to the vector equilibrium as well as for the unique rates of growth or contraction of closest-packed-spherical agglomerating.

1224.12 In respect to the progressive series of n^2 product numbers as expressed in congruence-in-modulo-10, a unique 24-integer series of terminal, submodulus-10, excess integers completes its series direction with 24 and makes its verse-and-reverse series at the common hinges of 25^2, 75^2, 100^2 in increments of $+24$, -24, $+24$, -24, or in a positively occurring, three-octave-wave increment sequence followed each time by a reversely occurring, three-octave-wave, unique harmonic theme.

1224.13 The three-octave, 24-integer series is manifest in the convergent-divergent, tetrahedral wave propagations of the vector equilibrium wherein the eight tetrahedra share their nuclear sphere and then share their common apex spheres as they embrace that nuclear sphere by expanding in successive triangular closest-packed sphere layers. (Compare Secs. 1012.11 and *1033.030.*)

1224.14 The lines omniinterconnecting the sphere centers of those successively embracing layers produce equiangular triangles, or electromagnetic fields, the sum of whose areas in each successive layer is always n^2 of the number in each series in that layer. In contradistinction to the triangular field, in the series of triangularly closest-packed sphere layers, every two adjacent layers' series produces the next greater n^2 number of spheres, with the number of closest-packed sphere triangles in the waxing and waning phases of the series being governed by the frequency of the wave propagation elected for consideration in each instant.

1224.20 Recapitulation

1224.21   The interwave and intervolumetric behavior of the number 24 may be considered variously as follows:

—24 A Quanta Modules per regular tetrahedron: (Tables 223.64 and 943.00; Secs. 910.11 and 942.10)

—24 modules of regular tetrahedron as cosmic bridge between equilibrious prime number one of metaphysics and disequilibrious prime number one of physical reality (Sec. 954.51)

—24 A and B Quanta Modules per Coupler (asymmetric octahedron): (Table 223.64; Secs. 954.10, 954.21, and 954.46)

—24 subparticle differentiabilities of the Coupler to provide for the 2, 3, 4, 6 combinations of proton-neutron intertransformabilities and isotopic variations: (Sec. 954.22)

—24 positive and negative basic triangles (basic equilibrium 48 *LCD* triangles) defined by the 25 great circles of the vector equilibrium: (Secs. 453.01 and 1052.30)

—24 total exterior vertexes of the vector equilibrium paired to produce 12 congruent, univalent external vertexes and to describe the eight tetrahedra, all of which share a common nuclear point to function in octavalent congruence as nuclear circuitry: (Secs. 1012.11 and *1033.030*)

—24 positively integrated vectors as the implosive, external, circumferentially embracing set of the four great circles of the vector equilibrium and the 24 negatively disintegrative, internal, radially explosive set, with both sets paired at the 12 vertexes: Secs. 450.11, *537.131*, 615.06, 905.55, 955.02, 1011.40, and 1052.30)

—24 interior and exterior A Quanta Modules of the isosceles dodecahedron: (Table 943.00)

—24 A-and-B-Quanta-Module-volume of the nucleus-embracing cube formed by applying the eight Eighth-Octahedra to the eight triangular facets of the vector equilibrium: Secs. 905.44 and 982.62)

—24 spherical right triangles of the spherical tetrahedron's three-way great-circle grid: (Sec. 905.51)

—24 highest common multiple of regular-tetrahedral-volume values of all congruently symmetric polyhedra of the hierarchy of concentric, symmetrical, rationally volumed geometries occurring within the isotropic vector matrix: (Sec. 982.70)

—24 integer series of alternately convergent-divergent sequences with 24 unique terminal suffix excesses—in respect to the series of n^2 numbers as expressed by congruence in modulo-10—which series peaks at 24 and commonly hinges at 25 to reverse descendingly again to hinge at 50 and then ascends to peak again to hinge at 75 and repeats, in this unique, three-octave, convergent-divergent, wave pulsating-propagating of harmonic themes mutingly inflected at the 25th hinge: (Sec. 1223.16)

—The 24 A or B Quanta Modules per 120 basic disequilibrium *LCD* triangles: (sec. *1053.36*)

—The inherent subdivision of any tetrahedron, regular or irregular, into 24 equal modules: Sec. 961.44)

—The cosmic hierarchy limit of 24 active tetravolumes per each sphere-into-space and each space-into-sphere intertransforming of the complex of jitterbugs: (Sec. *1033.20*)

—The 24 S Quanta Modules of the icosa-octa interrelationship within the four-frequency tetrahedron: (Sec. *988*)

—The five sets of 24 each of the T or E Quanta Modules of the rhombic triacontahedron.

1224.30 Turnaround Terminals

1224.31   The powerful 24-ness number behavior with its great-circle congruences and three-octave harmonics may have significant ramifications embracing the unique frequencies of the chemical compoundings as well as the nuclear geometry elucidated elsewhere in this work. (Sec. *1033 passim.*) The terminal-suffix excess integers of the series of second powers of numbers as expressed in congruence in modulo-10 displays the sequence of uniquely aberrating eccentricities in respect to the whole 24-integer phrases.

1224.32   The large figure "2" in the last column of the Indig Table (Fig. 1223.12B) shows that the terminal digits of the second powers of numbers turn around at the middling number 25.

1224.33   There are 24 positive and 24 negative unique numbers that reverse themselves between 0 and 50. This reflects three positive and three negative octaves with turnaround terminal zero accommodation.

1224.34   The "square" identifies that number of energy units occurring in the outer shell of all nuclear phenomena with the second-powering characteristic being that of both the gravitation and the radiational constant's surface growth.

1230.00   Scheherazade Numbers

1238.00   Fourteen-illion Scheherazade Number

1238.22   **Tetrahedral Complementations** The sphere-to-space, space-to-sphere intertransformability is a conceptual generalization holding true independent of size, which therefore permits us to consider the generalized allspace-filling complementarity of the convex (sphere) and concave (space) octahedra with the convex (sphere) and concave (space) vector equilibria; this also permits us to indulge our concentrated attention upon local special-case events without fear of missing further opportunities of enjoying total synergetically conceptual advantage regarding nonsimultaneously considerable Scenario Universe. (See Secs. 970.20 and 1032.)

1238.23   We know the fundamental intercomplementations of the external convex macrotetra and the internal concave microtetra with all conceptual systems. Looking at the four successive plus, minus, plus, minus, *XYZ* coordination quadrants, we find that a single 90-degree quadrant of one hemisphere of the spherical octahedron contains all the trigonometric functioning covariations of the whole system. When the central angle is 90 degrees, then the two small corner angles of the isosceles triangle are each 45 degrees. After 45 degrees the sines become cosines, and vice versa. At 45 degrees they balance. Thereafter all the prime numbers that can ever enter into prime trigonometric computation (in contradistinction to *complementary* function computation) occur below the number 45. What occasions irrationality is the inability of dividends to be omni-equi-divisible, due to the presence of a prime number of which the dividend is not a whole product.

1238.24   This is why we factor completely or intermultiply all of the first 14 prime numbers existing between 1 and 45 degrees. Inclusive of these 14 numbers we multiply the first eight primes to many repowerings, which produces this Scheherazade Number, which, when used as the number of units in a circle, becomes a dividend permitting omnirational computation accommodation of all the variations of all the trigonometries of Universe.

1238.25   The four vertexial stars *A, B, C, D* defining the minimum structural—ergo, triangulated—system of Universe have only four possible triangular arrangements. There are only four possible different topological vertex combinations of a minimum structural system: *ABC, ABD, ACD, BCD*. In multifrequenced, modular subdivisioning of the minimum structural system, the subdividing grid may develop eight positive and negative aspects:

ABC obverse (convex)	*ABC* reverse (concave)
ABD obverse (convex)	*ABD* reverse (concave)
ACD obverse (convex)	*ACD* reverse (concave)
BCD obverse (convex)	*BCD* reverse (concave)

1238.26

Three unopened edges *AB, AD*, BC. (Fig. *1238.26A.*)

Four edge-bonded triangles of the tetrahedron. (Fig. *1238.26B.*)

Three pairs of opened edges; three pairs of unopened edges. Each triangle has also both obverse and reverse surfaces; ergo, minimum closed system of Universe has four positive and four negative triangles—which equals eight cases of the same.

The same four triangles vertex-bond to produce the octahedron. (Fig. *1238.26C.*)

1238.27   In a spherically referenced symmetrical structural system one quadrant of one hemisphere contains all the trigonometric variables of the whole system. This is because each hemisphere constitutes a 360-degree encirclement of its pole and because a 90-degree quadrant is represented by three equi-right-angle surface-angle corners and three equi-90-degree central-angle-arc edges, half of which 90-degree surface and central angles is 45 degrees, which is the point where the sine of one angle becomes the cosine of the other and knowledge of the smallest is adequate—ergo, 45°–45° is the limit case of the smallest.

1238.28   Spherical Quadrant Phase: There is always a total of eight (four positive, four negative) unique

> interpermutative,
> intertransformative,
> interequatable,
> omniembracing

phases of all cyclically described symmetrical systems (see Sec. 610.20), within any one octave of which all the intercovariable ranging complementations of number occur. For instance, in a system such as spherical trigonometry, consisting of 360 degrees per circle or cycle, all the numerical

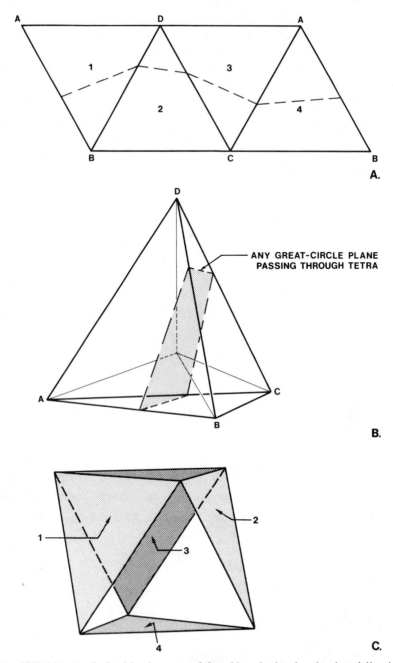

Figs. *1238.26A, B, C:* In this plane net of four hinged triangles the dotted line indicates the intersection of a great-circle plane passing through the assembled tetra.

Four edge-bonded triangles of the tetra with great-circle plane passing through.

The same four triangles may be vertex-bonded to describe an octahedron with alternate open and closed faces.

intervariabilities occur within the first 45 degrees, . ·. $45 \times 8 = 360$. Since the unit cyclic totality of the Fourteen-illion Scheherazade Number is the product of the first 15 primes, it contains all the prime numbers occurring within the 45-degree-limit numerical integer permutations of all cyclic systems together with an abundance of powers of the first eight primes, thus accommodating omnirational integrational expressibility to a 1×10^{-42} fraction of cyclic unity, a dividend so comprehensive as to permit the rational description of a 22-billion-light-year-diameter Universe in whole increments of $^1/_{10,000}$ths of one atomic nucleus diameter.

1238.29

$$\left.\begin{array}{l} (+) \cdot (+) = (+) \\ (+) \cdot (-) = (-) \\ (-) \cdot (+) = (-) \\ (-) \cdot (-) = (+) \end{array}\right\} \quad \text{Multiply}$$

$$\left.\begin{array}{l} (+)/(+) = (+) \\ (+)/(-) = (-) \\ (-)/(+) = (-) \\ (-)/(-) = (+) \end{array}\right\} \quad \text{Divide}$$

1238.41   **Declining Powers of Factorial Primes:** The recurrence of the prime number 2 is very frequent. The number of operational occasions in which we need the prime number 43 is very less frequent than the occasions in which the prime numbers 2, 3, 5, 7, and 11 occur. This Scheherazade Number provides an abundance of repowerings of the lesser prime numbers characterizing the topological and vectorial aspects of synergetics' hierarchy of prime systems and their seven prime unique symmetrical aspects (see Sec. 1040) adequate to take care of all the topological and trigonometric computations and permutations governing all the associations and disassociations of the atoms.

1238.42   We find that we can get along without multirepowerings after the second repowering of the prime number 17. The prime number 17 is all that is needed to accommodate both the positive and negative octave systems and their additional zero-nineness. You have to have the zero-nine to accommodate the noninterfered passage between octave waves by waves of the same frequency. (See Secs. 1012 and 1223.)

1238.43   The prime number 17 accommodates all the positive-negative, quanta-wave primes up to and including the number 18, which in turn accommodates the two nines of the invisible twoness of all systems. It is to be noted that the harmonics of the periodic table of the elements add up to 92:

$$
\left.\begin{array}{c} 2 \\ 8 \\ 8 \end{array}\right\} \quad 18
$$

18

18

$$
\left.\begin{array}{c} 18 \\ 18 \end{array}\right\} \quad 36
$$

$$
\underline{2}
$$

92

There are five sets of 18, though the 36 is not always so recognized. Conventional analysis of the periodic table omits from its quanta accounting the always occurring invisible additive twoness of the poles of axial rotation of all systems. (See Sec. 223.11 and Table 223.64, Col. 7.)

1238.51 Scheherazade Numbers: 47: The first prime number beyond the trigonometric limit is 47. The number 47 may be a flying increment to fill allspace, to fill out the eight triangular facets of the non-allspace-filling vector equilibrium to form the allspace-filling first nuclear cube. If 47 as a factor produces a Scheherazade Number with mirrors, it may account not only for all the specks of dust in the Universe but for all the changes of cosmic restlessness, accounting the convergent-divergent *next event,* which unbalances the even and rational whole numbers. If 47 as a factor does not produce a Scheherazade Number with mirrors, it may explain that there can be no recurring limit symmetries. It may be that 47 is the cosmic random element, the agent of infinite change.

ADDENDUM TO

Contribution to *Synergetics*

Arthur L. Loeb

Department of Visual and Environmental Studies
Carpenter Center

HARVARD UNIVERSITY

G. The Icosahedron, the Golden Section, and Fibonacci Numbers

In the following material Arthur L. Loeb augments his contribution at pages 829–32 of Synergetics 1.

The ratio $e \div d$ is denoted by τ, from the Greek $\tau o\mu\eta$, section. It satisfies the equation:

$$\frac{1}{\tau} - 1 = \tau, \text{ or } \tau = \frac{1}{1+\tau} \qquad (1)$$

Although this equation could be solved as a quadratic, the answer would be an irrational number. Because Fuller is so concerned with rational approximations, we shall here use a method of successive approximations, called "relaxation method," to approximate τ as closely as desired. To this purpose let us take a reasonable approximation, say $\tau = 1/2$. When this value is substituted in $\tau = \frac{1}{1+\tau}$, we obtain for the right-hand side $2/3$, which is not consistent with $\tau = 1/2$. However, it hints that perhaps $\tau = 2/3$ might be a better approximation. It would, in turn, make the right-hand side equal to $3/5$. This discrepancy between $2/3$ and $3/5$ is only $1/15$, whereas that between $1/2$ and $2/3$ was $1/6$. Therefore we have succeeded in decreasing the gap between the two sides of the equation, and by continuing the procedure long enough we might close the gap as nearly as desired.

The following table lists the successive approximations to τ:

τ	$1+\tau$	$1/(1+\tau)$			
$1/2$	$3/2$	$2/3 = 0.666$ . . . use as next approximation to τ			
$2/3$	$5/3$	$3/5 = 0.6$	"	"	"
$3/5$	$8/5$	$5/8 = 0.625$	"	"	"
$5/8$	$13/8$	$8/13 = 0.615$	"	"	"
$8/13$	$21/13$	$13/21 = 0.619$	"	"	"
$13/21$	$34/21$	$21/34 = 0.618$	"	"	"
$21/34$	$55/34$	$34/55 = 0.618$	"	"	"

If we want to find τ to three decimal places, the approximation $\tau = 34/55$ will do. If greater precision is desired, the procedure can be continued until successive approximations agree sufficiently. The numerators and denominators of successive approximations to τ are successive numbers in the sequence

$$1 \quad 1 \quad 2 \quad 3 \quad 5 \quad 8 \quad 13 \quad 21 \quad 34 \quad 55 \quad . . .$$

This series is called the Fibonacci series; it is commonly encountered in natural structures (pine cones, phyllotactic growth patterns of leaves and trees). Each number in this sequence equals the sum of the two preceding ones:

$a_{n+1} = a_n + a_{n-1}$, where a_{n-1}, a_n and a_{n+1} are three successive Fibonacci numbers

$$\frac{a_{n+1}}{a_n} = 1 + \frac{a_{n-1}}{a_n}$$

If we call $a_n/a_{n+1} \equiv R_n$ and $a_{n-1}/a_n \equiv R_{n-1}$

$$R_n = \frac{1}{1+R_{n-1}}$$

As the number n increases, successive values R_{n-1} and R_n approach each other more and more closely: Inspection of our table shows that the successive approximations of τ are, in fact, the ratios R_n as n increases indefinitely. When R_n and R_{n-1} are so nearly equal in magnitude that to any preset standard of precision they are indistinguishable from a common value R (this will happen at a sufficiently large value for n) then,

$$R = \frac{1}{1+R}, \text{ synonymous with } \tau = \frac{1}{1+\tau}.$$

Thus it is demonstrated that, in the limit of very large values of n, the ratio of successive Fibonacci numbers approaches the golden section!

The recursion formula $a_{n+1} = a_n + a_{n-1}$ also shows us that we can start with *any* two positive integers a_1 and a_o to generate a Fibonacci series whose limiting ratio is the golden section. For instance, if $a_o = 1$ and $a_1 = 99$:

n	a_{n-1}	a_n	a_{n-1}/a_n
1	1	99	0.0101
2	99	100	0.990
3	100	199	0.505
4	199	299	0.670
5	299	498	0.600
6	498	797	0.625
7	797	1295	0.615

By this time we have practically reached the ratio $^8/_{13}$, and it is obvious that we are approaching the same ratio as for the Fibonacci series having $a_1 = a_o = 1$

Another example:

n	a_{n-1}	a_1	a_{n-1}/a_n
1	3	2	1.50
2	2	5	0.400
3	5	7	0.714
4	7	12	0.583
5	12	19	0.632
6	19	31	0.613
7	31	50	0.620
8	50	81	0.617
9	81	131	0.618

Again, we have approached the ratio very closely, and it is apparent that the golden section ratio will be reached arbitrarily closely if one continues sufficiently long.

From Eq. (1) it follows that:

$$\tau^2 = 1 - \tau$$

Multiplying both sides of this equation by τ, and substituting for τ^2:

$$\tau^3 = \tau - \tau^2 = 2\tau - 1$$
$$\tau^4 = 2\tau^2 - \tau = 2 - 3\tau$$
$$\tau^5 = 2\tau - 3\tau^2 = 5\tau - 3$$
$$\tau^6 = 5\tau^2 - 3\tau = 5 - 8\tau$$

etc.

Since $\tau > 0$, every power of τ must be positive.

$$..2\tau - 1 > 0, \therefore \tau > {}^1/_2$$
$$2 - 3\tau > 0, \therefore \tau < {}^2/_3$$
$$5\tau - 3 > 0, \therefore \tau > {}^3/_5$$
$$5 - 8\tau > 0, \therefore \tau < {}^5/_8$$

etc.

Thus we see that τ is indeed bounded above and below by successive Fibonacci ratios, so that we have once more demonstrated that the golden section is approached in the limit by successive ratios of Fibonacci numbers.

Appendix of Tables

Table *987.132G Angles and Edges of Basic Icosahedron Triangle:* The plane projection of this spherical triangle accords with that shown at Fig. 457.30B. Planar edge lengths are ratioed to the icosa edge = 1.

In the left-hand column the complete list of spherical central angles is followed by the sequence of spherical face angles. In the right-hand column the planar edge lengths are followed by the sequence of planar face angles.

Detail key to the tables is at Fig. *987 132F*.

Icosa Table 987.132G

	SPHERICAL CENTRAL ANGLES	PLANAR EDGE LENGTHS
A.1	7. 434 809 92	0. 098 623 200 0
A.2	7. 473 084 04	0. 099 136 697 6
A.3	7. 761 243 91	0. 103 005 664 8
A.5	8. 227 129 66	0. 109 272 179 5
A.13	11. 211 433 55	0. 149 801 503 5
B.E	13. 282 525 59	0. 239 363 534 6
B.F	10. 812 316 96	0. 190 983 005 6
B.34	11. 354 628 09	0. 206 011 329 6
C.13	9. 693 723 89	0. 138 873 631 1
C.20	7. 201 242 12	0. 103 850 861 7
C.25	6. 645 371 91	0. 095 491 502 8
C.30	6. 349 948 93	0. 090 535 082 3
C.35	6. 405 037 16	0. 090 588 747 8
C.39	6. 716 268 28	0. 094 632 483 3
C.40	8. 300 774 80	0. 118 033 988 7
D.1	3. 377 507 04	0. 045 714 367 3
D.6	4. 172 280 25	0. 057 950 324 3
D.8	4. 386 177 56	0. 059 016 994 4
E.11	4. 499 294 98	0. 068 938 410 7
E.22	4. 675 036 79	0. 068 476 708 2
E.31	4. 269 282 63	0. 061 803 398 9
E.34	4. 273 238 79	0. 065 146 502 5
F.34	3. 488 005 13	0. 055 641 755 9
F.42	5. 454 720 36	0. 085 410 196 6
1.2	2. 867 486 67	0. 038 142 083 6
1.4	3. 321 598 91	0. 044 306 525 3
2.3	1. 067 453 37	0. 014 214 715 4
2.4	1. 190 705 31	0. 016 022 260 1
3.5	1. 174 468 35	0. 015 667 991 3
3.7	1. 801 498 23	0. 024 316 339 0
4.7	1. 520 969 54	0. 020 410 037 3
4.8	2. 994 501 55	0. 040 778 013 4
5.10	2. 658 120 79	0. 036 062 751 4
5.13	4. 743 940 90	0. 063 858 197 2
6.8	6. 050 821 84	0. 103 181 533 1
6.11	4. 610 950 35	0. 066 760 432 3
6.14	5. 684 213 11	0. 077 554 332 2
6.16	4. 476 071 06	0. 063 186 210 5
6.21	6. 777 786 99	0. 093 794 673 8
7.9	1. 595 408 73	0. 021 749 194 7
7.10	1. 906 868 79	0. 025 758 233 9
8.9	1. 613 156 73	0. 021 749 194 8
8.12	1. 795 236 70	0. 024 316 339 0

Appendix of Tables

Icosa Table 987.132G (*Continued*)

	SPHERICAL CENTRAL ANGLES	PLANAR EDGE LENGTHS
8.14	3. 137 695 86	0. 043 687 150 2
9.10	1. 507 502 63	0. 020 270 483 0
9.12	1. 278 129 83	0. 017 595 468 2
10.13	4. 248 120 11	0. 057 086 680 8
10.15	2. 162 899 83	0. 029 516 309 5
10.17	2. 695 860 47	0. 037 239 254 9
11.16	3. 586 955 39	0. 050 383 224 9
11.19	4. 367 084 04	0. 061 128 073 5
11.22	4. 216 785 52	0. 060 497 446 4
11.26	5. 513 331 18	0. 077 788 070 6
12.17	2. 086 284 29	0. 028 470 065 3
12.18	2. 811 400 89	0. 039 344 662 9
13.15	3. 459 802 56	0. 046 791 675 2
13.20	3. 916 638 16	0. 053 891 081 5
14.18	2. 060 087 06	0. 028 182 467 3
14.21	2. 920 002 31	0. 041 802 486 3
15.17	1. 825 294 08	0. 024 922 359 5
15.20	2. 190 236 86	0. 030 303 273 1
16.19	1. 511 494 71	0. 021 896 357 4
16.21	3. 723 797 24	0. 051 726 542 0
17.18	2. 548 068 55	0. 035 190 936 3
17.23	2. 433 978 94	0. 034 352 309 1
17.25	3. 086 929 54	0. 042 705 098 3
18.21	3. 302 711 90	0. 046 534 663 9
18.23	2. 225 637 55	0. 030 625 176 0
18.27	2. 452 873 25	0. 035 190 936 3
19.24	1. 535 510 72	0. 021 538 744 2
19.26	1. 575 434 83	0. 023 188 614 5
20.25	1. 414 201 62	0. 019 833 749 7
21.24	2. 566 599 78	0. 037 089 934 4
21.27	2. 359 154 60	0. 032 664 055 9
21.29	2. 433 978 94	0. 035 890 367 9
21.33	3. 137 695 86	0. 044 616 593 8
22.26	2. 041 231 49	0. 029 243 045 6
22.28	1. 250 993 91	0. 018 310 047 8
23.30	2. 141 728 18	0. 029 731 545 5
23.32	1. 978 721 52	0. 028 544 995 7
24.26	1. 314 921 21	0. 019 381 066 5
24.29	1. 634 821 35	0. 023 013 734 8
25.30	1. 528 205 55	0. 021 706 595 0
26.28	1. 795 236 70	0. 026 936 308 6
26.29	2. 471 740 55	0. 035 039 389 1
26.36	2. 688 270 08	0. 038 584 393 8
26.42	5. 553 615 68	0. 085 410 196 6
27.32	2. 394 957 11	0. 033 211 312 4
27.33	1. 936 967 98	0. 028 470 065 6
28.31	2. 264 732 86	0. 034 867 090 3
28.42	5. 013 976 14	0. 075 629 564 3
29.33	2. 688 270 08	0. 037 796 614 9
29.36	1. 851 745 66	0. 028 056 710 4
29.38	2. 873 538 56	0. 040 770 805 2
30.35	1. 473 159 29	0. 021 228 061 7
31.34	2. 585 402 34	0. 041 202 265 9
31.42	5. 207 455 27	0. 076 393 202 2

Icosa Table 987.132G (*Continued*)

	SPHERICAL CENTRAL ANGLES	PLANAR EDGE LENGTHS
32.35	1. 494 727 24	0. 020 805 380 4
32.37	1. 477 409 25	0. 021 730 484 4
33.37	2. 601 233 28	0. 036 418 002 1
33.38	1. 414 201 62	0. 021 220 334 0
33.40	3. 934 435 56	0. 057 635 540 4
35.39	1. 271 873 94	0. 018 594 344 1
36.41	3. 511 547 32	0. 051 445 858 4
36.42	3. 785 938 11	0. 059 774 685 9
37.39	1. 044 975 63	0. 014 621 522 8
37.40	2. 952 856 45	0. 044 671 967 1
38.40	3. 182 319 53	0. 045 851 328 4
38.41	2. 748 458 17	0. 042 440 667 9
39.40	3. 132 150 74	0. 047 003 974 1
40.41	3. 339 948 34	0. 048 632 677 9
41.42	3. 809 713 95	0. 056 940 131 1

	SPHERICAL FACE ANGLES	PLANAR FACE ANGLES
*		
1.A.2	22. 238 756 09	22. 238 756 09
2.A.3	7. 761 243 91	7. 761 243 91
3.A.5	7. 761 243 91	7. 761 243 91
5.A.13	22. 238 756 09	22. 238 756 09
E.B.34	18.	14. 477 512 19
F.B.34	18.	15. 522 487 81
13.C.20	20. 905 157 45	19. 637 522 82
20.C.25	10. 812 316 96	10. 362 477 19
25.C.30	13. 282 525 59	13. 050 747 26
30.C.35	13. 282 525 59	13. 461 247 61
35.C.39	10. 812 316 96	11. 249 247 04
39.C.40	20. 905 157 45	22. 238 756 09
1.D.8	90.	90.
6.D.8	90.	90.
B.E.34	54. 735 610 32	52. 238 756 09
11.E.22	54. 735 610 32	52. 238 756 09
22.E.31	35. 264 389 68	37. 761 243 91
31.E.34	35. 264 389 68	37. 761 243 91
B.F.34	90.	97. 761 243 91
34.F.42	90.	82. 238 756 09
A.1.2	79. 722 778 67	79. 637 522 82
D.1.4	79. 722 778 67	79. 637 522 82
2.1.4	20. 554 442 66	20. 724 954 37
A.2.1	78. 221 767 85	78. 123 721 09
A.2.3	101. 778 232 15	101. 876 278 81
A.3.2	70. 528 779 37	70. 362 477 18
A.3.5	109. 471 220 63	109. 637 522 82
2.4.1	57. 696 502 19	57. 398 766 73
2.4.7	122. 303 497 81	122. 601 233 27
A.5.3	62. 842 667 36	62. 601 233 27
A.5.13	117. 157 332 64	117. 398 766 73
D.6.8	46. 512 922 25	45. 522 487 82
8.6.14	30. 865 661 27	31. 426 764 93

Appendix of Tables

Icosa Table 987.132G (*Continued*)

	SPHERICAL FACE ANGLES	PLANAR FACE ANGLES
11.6.16	46. 512 922 25	45. 522 487 82
14.6.21	25. 242 832 96	26. 101 494 52
16.6.21	30. 865 661 27	31. 426 764 93
3.7.4	50. 032 698 38	49. 637 522 82
3.7.10	129. 967 301 62	130. 362 477 18
D.8.4	68. 176 536 45	67. 761 243 91
D.8.6	43. 646 927 11	44. 477 512 18
4.8.9	68. 176 536 45	67. 761 243 91
7.9.8	104. 215 033 04	104. 477 512 19
7.9.10	75. 784 966 96	75. 522 487 81
5.10.7	42. 393 817 63	41. 876 278 91
5.10.13	83. 403 500 48	83. 283 731 72
7.10.9	54. 202 681 89	54. 839 989 37
E.11.22	64. 828 737 83	63. 488 005 13
6.11.16	64. 828 737 83	63. 488 005 13
16.11.19	18. 840 722 77	19. 795 726 59
19.11.26	12. 661 078 80	13. 432 536 56
22.11.26	18. 840 722 77	19. 795 726 59
8.12.9	60. 585 549 01	60.
9.12.17	119. 414 450 99	120.
A.13.5	40. 908 063 75	40. 362 477 18
C.13.20	40. 908 063 75	40. 362 477 18
5.13.10	33. 851 773 96	34. 115 035 01
10.13.15	30. 480 324 57	31. 044 975 63
15.13.20	33. 851 773 96	34. 115 035 01
6.14.8	81. 111 708 18	80. 811 911 17
6.14.21	98. 888 291 82	99. 188 008 83
10.15.13	95. 382 039 90	94. 115 035 01
10.15.17	84. 617 960 10	85. 884 964 99
6.16.11	68. 789 009 70	70. 989 507 06
6.16.21	111. 210 990 30	109. 010 492 84
10.17.12	53. 022 528 57	52. 238 756 09
10.17.15	53. 022 528 57	52. 238 756 09
12.17.18	73. 954 942 86	75. 522 487 81
12.18.14	73. 614 860 76	73. 050 747 26
12.18.17	45. 504 099 05	44. 477 512 19
14.18.21	60. 881 040 19	62. 471 740 55
11.19.16	49. 992 418 20	51. 193 780 47
16.19.24	130. 007 581 80	128. 806 219 53
C.20.13	118. 403 872 47	120.
13.20.15	61. 596 127 53	60.
6.21.14	56. 012 156 42	54. 710 496 65
6.21.16	38. 059 129 17	39. 562 742 13
14.21.18	38. 059 129 17	36. 716 268 28
16.21.24	47. 869 585 24	49. 010 492 94
E.22.11	60. 585 549 01	64. 273 238 78
E.22.28	119. 414 450 99	115. 726 761 22
17.23.18	66. 139 669 29	65. 289 503 35
17.23.30	113. 860 330 71	114. 710 496 65
19.24.21	113. 411 197 08	111. 193 780 47
19.24.26	66. 588 802 92	68. 806 219 53
C.25.20	107. 669 807 11	109. 637 522 81
C.25.30	72. 330 192 89	70. 362 477 19

Icosa Table 987.132G (*Continued*)

	SPHERICAL FACE ANGLES	PLANAR FACE ANGLES
11.26.19	37. 377 368 14	37. 761 243 92
11.26.22	41. 810 314 90	44. 477 512 18
19.26.24	63. 434 948 82	60.
22.26.28	37. 377 368 14	37. 761 243 90
18.27.21	86. 676 742 88	86. 511 994 87
18.27.32	93. 323 257 12	93. 488 005 13
22.28.26	82. 056 495 26	77. 965 517 32
22.28.31	97. 943 504 74	102. 034 482 68
21.29.24	75. 385 673 59	74. 477 512 19
21.29.33	75. 385 673 59	74. 477 512 19
24.29.26	29. 228 652 83	31. 044 975 62
C.30.25	94. 471 803 73	96. 586 775 55
C.30.35	85. 528 196 27	83. 413 224 45
E.31.28	107. 502 684 11	104. 477 512 19
E.31.34	72. 497 315 89	75. 522 487 81
23.32.27	79. 287 906 24	78. 750 750 96
23.32.35	100. 712 093 76	101. 249 249 04
21.33.27	48. 657 434 21	46. 949 252 74
21.33.29	48. 657 434 21	50. 811 991 17
27.33.37	82. 685 131 58	82. 238 756 09
B.34.E	107. 669 807 11	113. 283 731 72
B.34.F	72. 330 192 89	66. 716 268 28
C.35.30	81. 270 746 28	83. 125 527 94
C.35.39	98. 729 253 72	96. 874 472 06
26.36.29	62. 842 667 36	61. 044 975 64
26.36.42	117. 157 332 64	118. 955 024 36
32.37.33	90.	90.
32.37.39	90.	90.
29.38.33	68. 119 128 65	66. 716 268 28
29.38.41	111. 880 871 35	113. 283 731 72
C.39.35	70. 528 779 37	71. 876 278 90
C.39.40	109. 471 220 63	108. 123 721 10
C.40.39	49. 797 034 11	49. 637 522 81
33.40.37	41. 409 622 11	39. 188 008 83
33.40.38	19. 498 154 83	19. 767 015 54
37.40.39	19. 498 154 83	18. 123 721 10
38.40.41	49. 797 034 11	53. 283 731 72
36.41.38	55. 690 639 53	53. 283 731 72
36.41.42	62. 154 680 23	66. 716 268 27
38.41.40	62. 154 680 23	60.
F.42.31	55. 105 900 90	60.
26.42.28	18. 699 407 09	17. 965 517 32
26.42.36	25. 544 395 55	23. 283 731 72
28.42.31	25. 544 395 55	26. 511 944 87
36.42.41	55. 105 900 90	52. 238 756 09

Table *987.137D   Angles and Edges of Basic Triangle in Vector Equilibrium Grid:*
The plane projection of this spherical triangle accords with that shown at Fig. *987.412.*
Planar edge lengths are ratioed to the vector equilibrium edge (or radius or prime
vector) = unity (as shown at line DD' at Fig. *987.412.*)

In the left-hand column the complete list of spherical central angles is followed by
the sequence of spherical face angles. In the right-hand column the planar edge lengths
are followed by the sequence of planar face angles.

Detail key to the tables is at Fig. *987.137C.*

VE Table 987.137D

	SPHERICAL CENTRAL ANGLES	PLANAR EDGE LENGTHS
A.1	5. 768 181 19	0. 082 478 61
A.2	5. 623 482 89	0. 080 396 06
A.3	5. 827 547 37	0. 083 333 33
A.6	6. 280 058 06	0. 089 854 43
A.8	8. 049 466 98	0. 042 418 25
B.E	10. 024 987 86	0. 166 666 67
B.8	11. 421 753 66	0. 173 205 08
B.14	9. 084 357 76	0. 138 675 05
B.17	8. 205 549 88	0. 125
B.25	6. 712 138 56	0. 101 759 67
B.28	6. 369 226 42	0. 096 225 05
B.30	6. 280 058 06	0. 094 758 67
B.31.	6. 586 775 55	0. 1
B.34	8. 189 205 76	0. 124 226 00
B.37	9. 084 357 76	0. 138 675 05
B.44	11. 490 459 90	0. 176 776 70
B.47	9. 901 738 15	0. 159 719 14
B.49	9. 594 068 23	0. 158 580 99
C.F	6. 353 170 92	0. 105 409 26
C.23	5. 111 089 70	0. 080 174 28
C.27	4. 120 687 22	0. 066 666 67
C.29	4. 393 529 37	0. 070 697 08
C.31	4. 306 619 10	0. 066 666 67
C.32	5. 208 719 10	0. 083 333 33
C.35	4. 125 669 50	0. 075 292 33
C.39	6. 884 359 05	0. 109 259 13
D.16	13. 262 676 01	0. 247 435 83
D.33	10. 893 394 65	0. 2
D.36	11. 536 959 03	0. 225 876 98
D.40	11. 039 484 40	0. 223 606 80
D.52	11. 309 932 47	0. 235 702 26
E.49	2. 921 328 89	0. 040 542 02
E.54	3. 504 259 65	0. 047 913 30
E.62	5. 768 181 19	0. 083 333 33
F.35	4. 366 652 03	0. 063 887 66
F.39	1. 798 709 17	0. 028 747 98
F.41	2. 262 459 23	0. 020 823 77
F.42	1. 700 938 05	0. 024 845 20
F.48	2. 921 328 89	0. 032 723 06
G.48	7. 749 366 38	0. 112 938 49
G.53	4. 860 605 64	0. 074 985 58
G.57	5. 111 089 70	0. 070 710 68

VE Table 987.137D (*Continued*)

	SPHERICAL CENTRAL ANGLES	PLANAR EDGE LENGTHS
G.58	4. 398 705 35	0. 070 710 68
G.61	4. 377 258 49	0. 060 813 03
G.63	4. 650 222 70	0. 067 092 36
G.70	8. 130 102 35	0. 117 851 13
H.73	10. 024 987 86	0. 125
H.74	9. 759 672 26	0. 121 626 06
H.75	11. 309 932 47	0. 141 421 36
1.2	1. 892 977 99	0. 027 109 41
1.4	2. 243 663 06	0. 032 192 42
1.5	4. 256 806 68	0. 061 858 96
2.3	1. 103 988 45	0. 015 813 82
2.4	1. 045 645 73	0. 015 074 26
3.6	1. 232 415 00	0. 017 674 27
3.7	1. 921 819 01	0. 027 777 77
4.7	1. 737 756 21	0. 025 038 55
4.9	3. 927 436 77	0. 057 282 20
5.9	3. 450 886 66	0. 05
5.10	5. 768 181 19	0. 086 602 54
6.8	2. 944 937 84	0. 042 418 25
6.11	3. 372 182 38	0. 049 011 50
7.11	2. 509 256 77	0. 036 419 71
7.12	3. 787 592 65	0. 055 555 56
8.14	3. 803 016 47	0. 055 470 02
9.12	2. 288 283 82	0. 033 333 33
9.15	4. 366 652 03	0. 065 465 37
10.13	3. 678 051 59	0. 057 735 03
10.15	5. 111 089 70	0. 075 592 89
10.18	4. 409 112 45	0. 066 143 78
11.14	1. 720 124 66	0. 025 213 65
11.17	3. 510 047 82	0. 052 074 72
12.17	2. 833 934 52	0. 041 666 67
12.20	3. 688 197 98	0. 055 555 56
13.16	2. 530 493 04	0. 041 239 30
13.18	4. 763 171 35	0. 072 168 78
13.19	2. 336 403 45	0. 036 084 39
14.17	2. 336 403 45	0. 034 668 76
15.20	2. 844 710 39	0. 041 996 05
15.21	2. 354 510 84	0. 036 369 65
16.19	2. 491 233 28	0. 038 918 74
16.33	7. 611 378 52	0. 124 539 97
17.22	2. 709 709 18	0. 040 972 17
17.25	2. 894 577 84	0. 044 063 23
18.21	1. 606 055 07	0. 024 056 26
18.23	1. 970 257 76	0. 030 065 36
19.23	4. 860 605 64	0. 074 299 41
19.32	6. 747 954 31	0. 108 253 18
20.22	1. 803 872 18	0. 026 724 76
20.24	1. 798 709 17	0. 027 777 78
21.23	1. 468 042 88	0. 023 144 32
21.24	3. 224 841 81	0. 048 112 52
22.25	1. 243 661 52	0. 018 501 76
22.26	1. 519 672 26	0. 023 412 67
23.27	3. 510 047 82	0. 052 835 14
23.32	6. 280 058 06	0. 104 149 45

Appendix of Tables

VE Table 987.137D (*Continued*)

SPHERICAL CENTRAL ANGLES		PLANAR EDGE LENGTHS
24.26	1. 383 267 52	0. 020 619 65
24.27	1. 063 100 90	0. 016 666 67
25.28	1. 260 862 17	0. 019 583 66
26.28	1. 841 574 29	0. 027 492 87
26.29	0. 971 157 42	0. 015 149 38
27.29	1. 140 174 88	0. 017 093 72
28.30	0. 705 165 63	0. 011 069 02
29.30	2. 232 007 50	0. 033 444 24
30.31	2. 491 233 27	0. 039 848 48
31.34	3. 244 726 48	0. 056 655 77
32.33	3. 004 491 60	0. 05
32.36	4. 860 605 64	0. 079 859 57
32.39	5. 046 112 63	0. 093 706 95
33.36	3. 822 553 73	0. 072 843 14
34.35	2. 407 359 63	0. 035 493 14
34.37	1. 306 975 56	0. 021 790 68
35.38	1. 197 183 29	0. 020 534 27
36.39	3. 688 197 98	0. 061 602 81
36.40	2. 021 624 56	0. 031 943 83
36.43	2. 279 447 45	0. 040 468 41
37.38	1. 720 124 66	0. 025 213 65
37.44	4. 551 702 04	0. 049 029 03
38.41	2. 509 256 77	0. 036 419 71
38.44	2. 170 440 16	0. 035 934 97
39.42	1. 206 107 95	0. 020 823 77
39.45	2. 709 709 18	0. 040 972 17
40.43	1. 428 490 43	0. 024 845 20
40.52	4. 860 605 64	0. 074 535 60
41.44	2. 921 328 89	0. 043 920 52
41.48	3. 981 419 27	0. 057 230 97
42.45	2. 121 615 68	0. 031 056 50
42.48	1. 958 580 13	0. 032 723 06
43.45	1. 844 300 64	0. 031 056 50
43.46	1. 509 377 34	0. 025 752 62
44.47	3. 892 484 48	0. 056 469 24
44.51	4. 125 669 50	0. 058 925 57
44.55	3. 822 553 73	0. 057 943 40
44.56	5. 111 089 70	0. 079 056 94
45.46	1. 728 356 02	0. 025 409 86
45.48	2. 466 379 40	0. 039 929 79
45.50	2. 336 403 45	0. 034 668 76
46.50	1. 071 780 85	0. 017 828 74
46.52	4. 551 702 04	0. 067 759 64
47.49	2. 460 686 44	0. 034 750 30
47.56	4. 410 537 33	0. 063 887 66
48.51	3. 450 886 66	0. 053 239 71
48.53	1. 419 452 42	0. 060 597 50
48.57	3. 719 670 97	0. 058 901 51
49.54	1. 936 213 49	0. 028 832 91
50.53	1. 419 452 42	0. 023 072 49
50.58	3. 803 016 47	0. 055 470 02
51.55	2. 288 283 82	0. 033 879 82
51.57	3. 367 623 45	0. 047 140 45
52.58	2. 726 310 99	0. 047 140 45

VE Table 987.137D (*Continued*)

	SPHERICAL CENTRAL ANGLES	PLANAR EDGE LENGTHS
53.58	2. 944 937 84	0. 042 418 25
54.56	4. 245 106 73	0. 057 495 96
54.60	2. 894 683 38	0. 041 647 53
55.56	2. 833 934 52	0. 040 655 78
55.59	2. 279 447 45	0. 033 105 16
56.59	3. 337 776 82	0. 045 175 40
56.60	3. 580 776 12	0. 049 690 40
56.65	5. 917 266 06	0. 081 311 56
56.66	6. 379 370 21	0. 090 350 79
57.61	2. 104 434 55	0. 031 716 20
59.61	3. 821 923 73	0. 052 125 46
59.64	4. 000 610 61	0. 056 033 18
60.62	4. 624 773 76	0. 062 113 00
60.66	4. 763 171 35	0. 065 446 12
61.63	2. 289 094 82	0. 033 385 47
62.66	6. 106 725 59	0. 079 859 57
62.67	3. 678 051 59	0. 05
63.64	2. 232 007 50	0. 030 965 71
63.70	5. 200 538 86	0. 072 335 19
64.65	1. 306 975 56	0. 017 828 74
64.70	4. 860 605 64	0. 065 372 05
65.66	4. 973 082 50	0. 066 221 03
65.70	5. 122 218 34	0. 067 759 64
66.67	5. 623 482 89	0. 072 843 14
66.68	2. 099 342 94	0. 028 234 62
66.69	2. 336 403 44	0. 031 000 79
66.70	8. 205 549 88	0. 106 479 43
67.68	4. 973 082 50	0. 063 737 74
67.73	5. 768 181 19	0. 075
68.69	1. 306 975 56	0. 016 773 09
68.72	4. 125 669 50	0. 053 902 46
69.70	6. 882 230 21	0. 089 456 48
69.71	2. 944 937 84	0. 038 295 10
70.71	6. 139 419 92	0. 080 845 21
70.75	7. 125 016 35	0. 094 280 90
71.72	3. 454 648 31	0. 044 097 39
71.75	3. 803 016 47	0. 048 507 13
72.73	3. 719 670 97	0. 046 853 47
72.74	1. 730 787 64	0. 022 113 83
73.74	3. 164 688 08	0. 039 645 25
74.75	5. 046 112 63	0. 063 432 39

	SPHERICAL FACE ANGLES	PLANAR FACE ANGLES
1.A.2	19. 106 605 35	19. 106 605 35
2.A.3	10. 893 394 65	10. 893 394 65
3.A.6	10. 893 394 65	10. 893 394 65
6.A.8	19. 106 605 35	19. 106 605 35
E.B.49	17. 023 866 19	14. 036 243 47
8.B.14	17. 023 866 19	16. 102 113 75
14.B.17	14. 458 287 92	13. 897 886 25
17.B.25	19. 286 325 41	19. 106 605 35

VE Table 987.137D *(Continued)*

	SPHERICAL FACE ANGLES	PLANAR FACE ANGLES
25.B.28	10. 670 695 26	10. 893 394 65
28.B.30	6. 353 170 92	6. 586 775 55
30.B.31	22. 207 654 30	23. 413 224 45
31.B.34	22. 207 654 30	26. 565 051 18
34.B.37	6. 353 170 92	7. 125 016 35
37.B.44	10. 670 695 26	11. 309 932 47
44.B.47	19. 286 325 41	18. 434 948 82
47.B.49	14. 458 287 92	12. 528 807 71
F.C.35	43. 088 723 14	36. 869 897 65
F.C.39	14. 963 217 43	15. 255 118 70
23.C.27	43. 088 723 14	40. 893 394 65
23.C.32	75. 036 782 56	79. 106 605 35
27.C.29	14. 963 217 43	13. 897 886 25
29.C.31	46. 911 276 86	46. 102 113 75
31.C.35	75. 036 782 56	71. 565 051 18
32.C.39	46. 911 276 86	56. 309 932 47
16.D.33	35. 264 389 68	30.
33.D.36	19. 471 220 63	18. 434 948 82
36.D.40	10. 024 987 86	8. 130 102 354
40.D.52	25. 239 401 82	18. 434 948 82
B.E.49	73. 221 345 12	71. 565 051 18
49.E.54	33. 557 309 76	36. 869 897 65
54.E.62	73. 221 345 12	71. 565 051 18
C.F.35	40. 202 965 89	45.
C.F.39	99. 594 068 22	90.
35.F.41	40. 202 965 89	45.
48.G.53	29. 205 932 24	29. 744 881 30
48.G.57	24. 094 842 55	26. 565 051 18
53.G.58	36. 699 225 20	33. 690 067 53
57.G.61	24. 094 842 55	26. 565 051 18
61.G.63	29. 205 932 24	29. 744 881 30
63.G.70	36. 699 225 20	33. 690 067 53
73.H.74	18. 434 948 82	18. 434 948 82
74.H.75	26. 565 051 18	26. 565 051 18
A.1.2	76. 169 775 05	76. 102 113 75
2.1.4	27. 660 449 90	27. 795 772 50
4.1.5	76. 169 775 05	76. 102 113 75
A.2.1	84. 816 211 89	84. 791 280 90
A.2.3	95. 183 788 11	95. 208 719 10
A.3.2	73. 976 820 27	73. 897 886 25
A.3.6	106. 023 179 73	106. 102 113 75
1.4.2	57. 172 967 00	56. 995 508 40
2.4.7	122. 827 033 00	123. 004 491 60
1.5.9	90.	90.
9.5.10	90.	90.
A.6.3	63. 143 728 54	63. 004 491 60
A.6.8	116. 856 271 46	116. 995 508 40
3.7.4	46. 364 701 32	46. 102 113 75
3.7.11	133. 635 298 68	133. 897 886 25
A.8.6	44. 181 377 46	43. 897 886 25
B.8.14	44. 181 377 46	43. 897 886 25
6.8.14	91. 637 245 08	92. 204 227 50
4.9.5	71. 196 157 21	70. 893 394 65
4.9.12	108. 803 842 79	109. 106 605 45

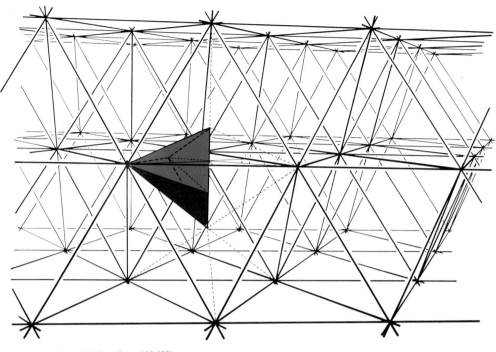

Plate 17 (See Sec. 986.422)

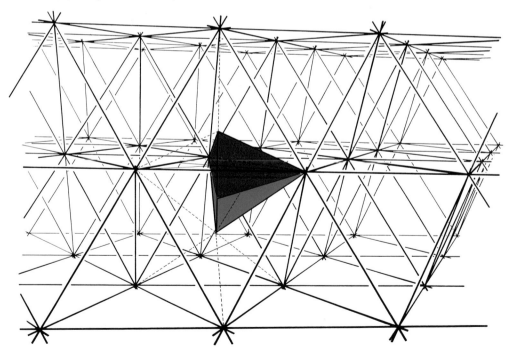

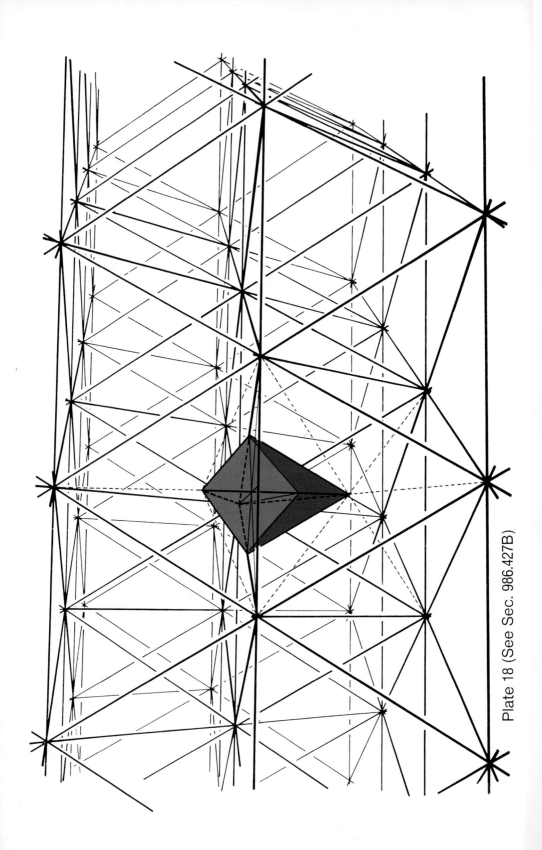

Plate 18 (See Sec. 986.427B)

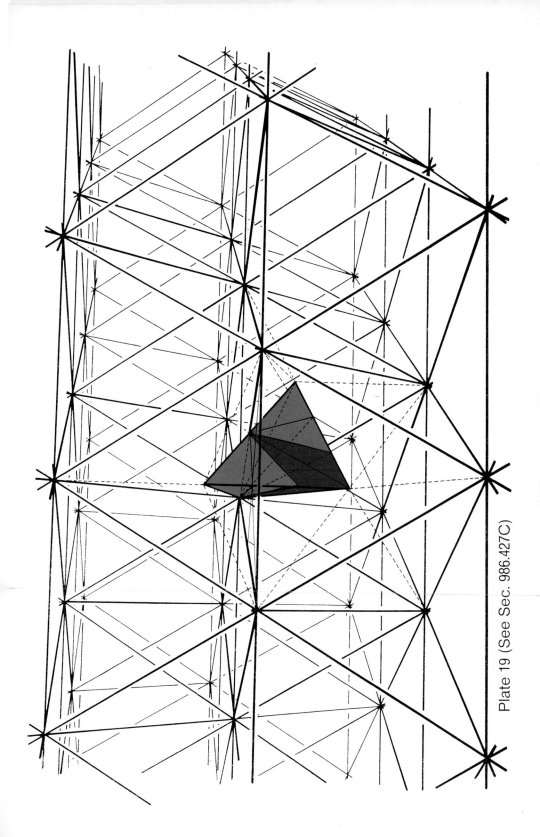

Plate 19 (See Sec. 986.427C)

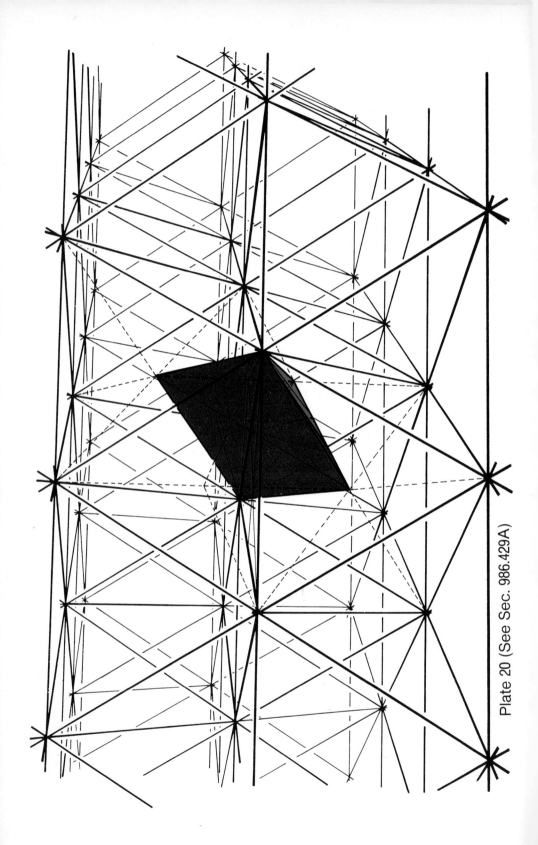

Plate 20 (See Sec. 986.429A)

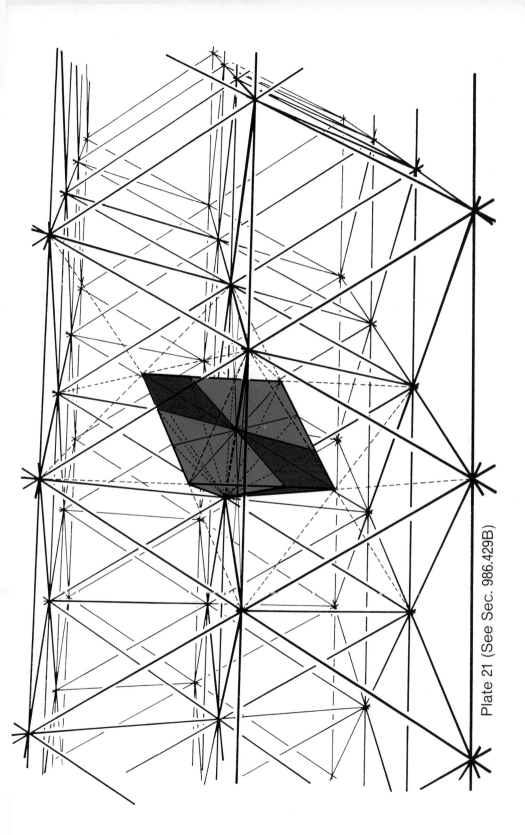

Plate 21 (See Sec. 986.429B)

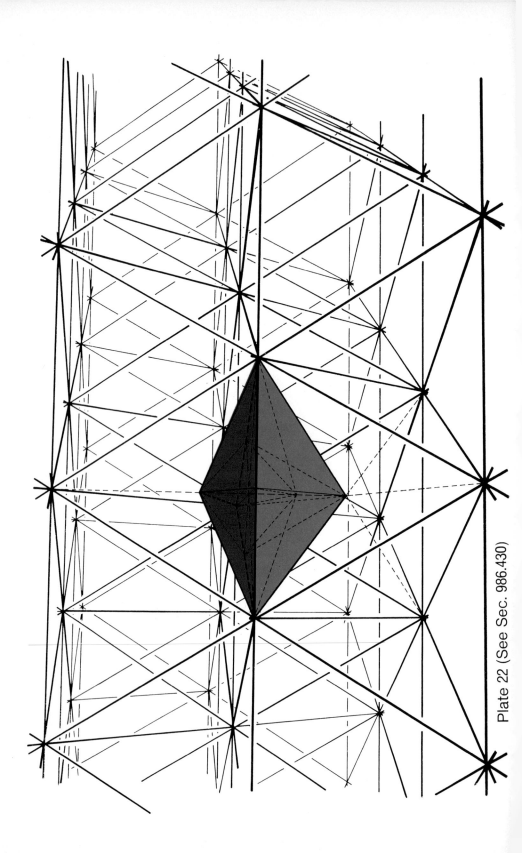

Plate 22 (See Sec. 986.430)

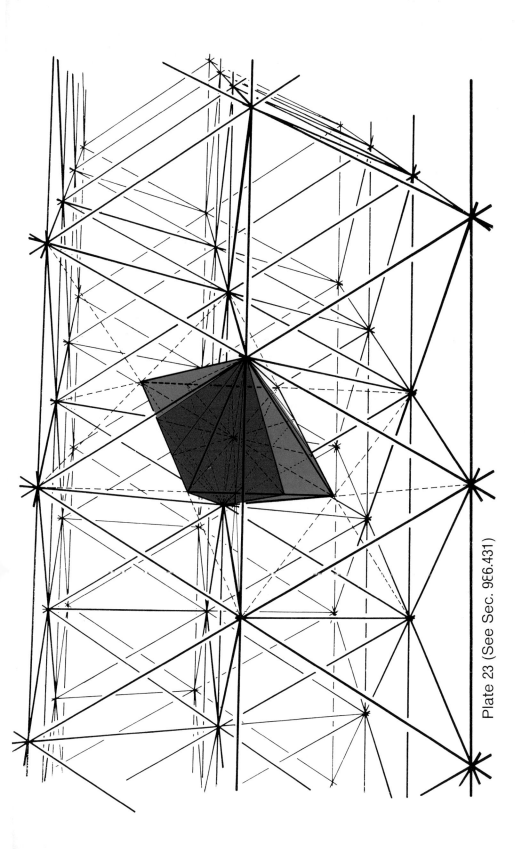

Plate 23 (See Sec. 986.431)

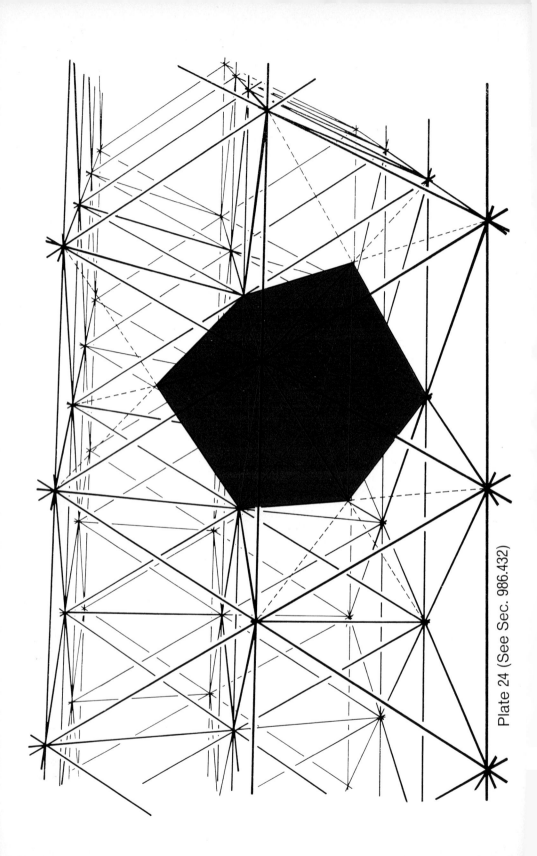

Plate 24 (See Sec. 986.432)

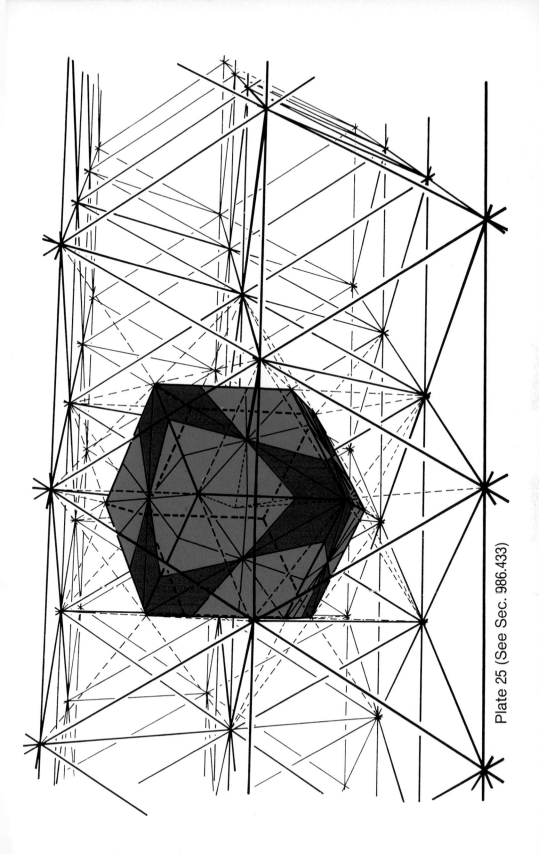

Plate 25 (See Sec. 986.433)

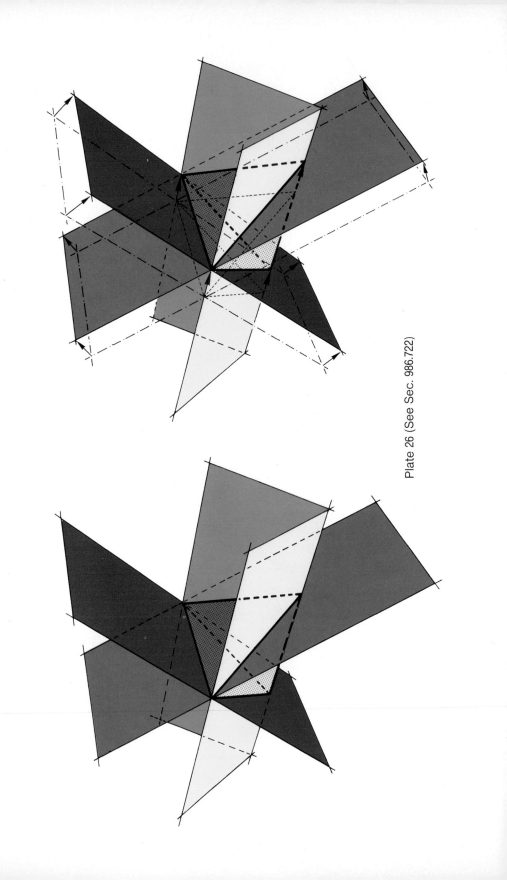

Plate 26 (See Sec. 986.722)

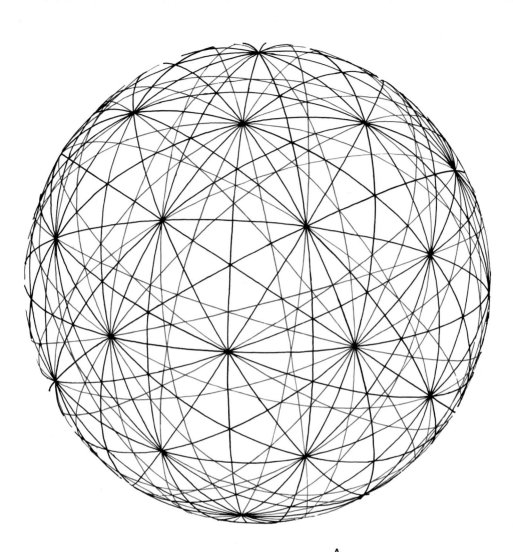

Plate 27 (See Sec. 987.132A)

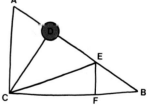

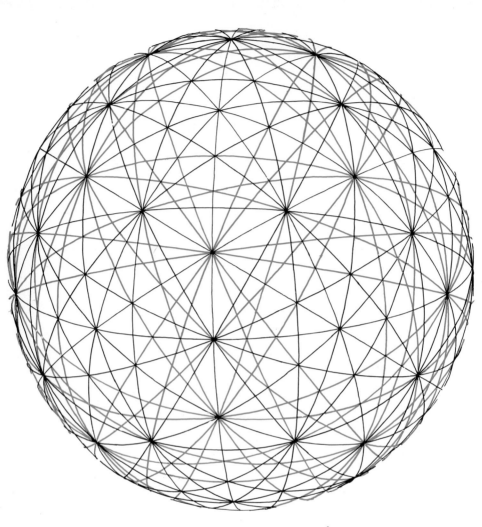

Plate 28 (See Sec. 987.132B)

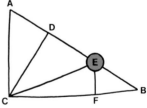

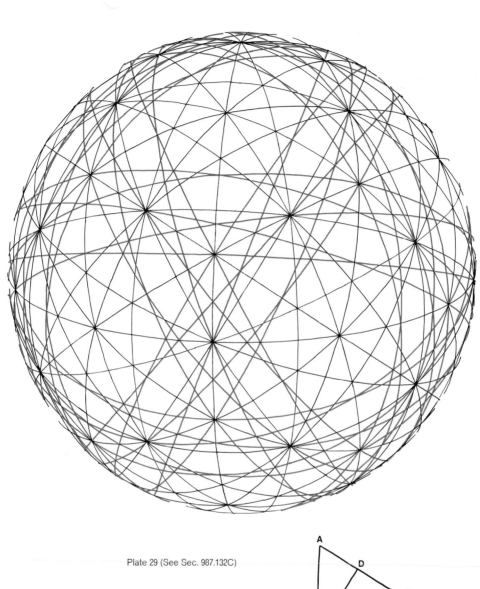

Plate 29 (See Sec. 987.132C)

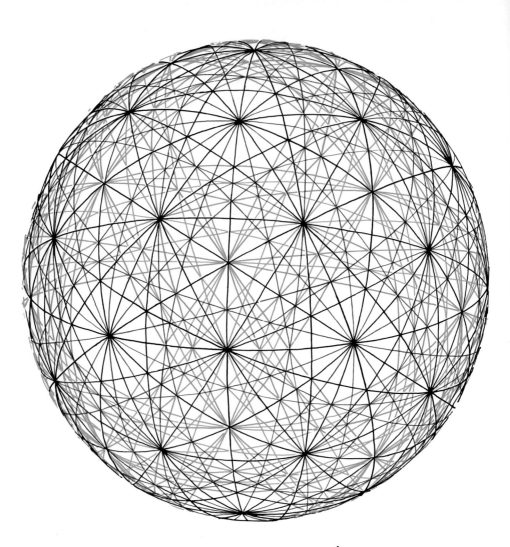

Plate 30 (See Sec. 987.132D)

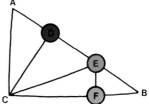

Plate 31 (See Sec. 1013.42)

A.

B.

C.

D.

E.

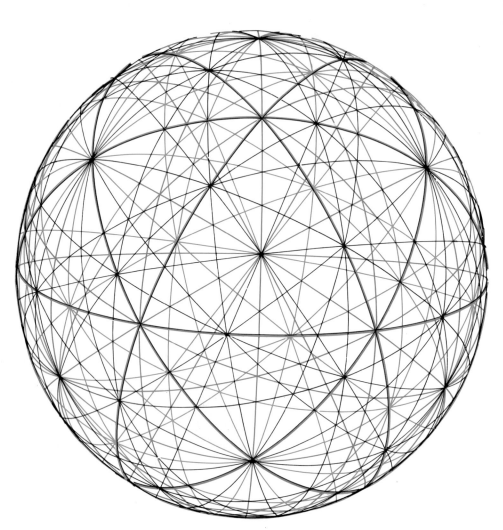

Plate 32 (See Sec. 1132.01A)

VE Table 987.137D (*Continued*)

	SPHERICAL FACE ANGLES	PLANAR FACE ANGLES
5.10.15	71. 565 051 18	70. 893 394 65
13.10.18	71. 565 051 18	70. 893 394 65
15.10.18	36. 869 897 64	38. 213 210 70
6.11.7	35. 594 453 19	35. 208 719 10
6.11.14	144. 405 546 81	144. 791 280 90
7.12.9	60. 503 791 50	60.
7.12.17	119. 496 208 50	120.
10.13.18	61. 439 174 78	60.
16.13.19	61. 439 174 78	60.
18.13.19	57. 121 650 44	60.
B.14.8	119. 059 281 07	120.
B.14.17	60. 940 718 93	60.
9.15.10	90.	90.
10.15.21	90.	90.
D.16.33	55. 462 416 21	53. 413 224 45
13.16.19	55. 462 416 21	53. 413 224 45
19.16.33	69. 075 167 57	73. 173 551 11
B.17.14	104. 763 132 62	106. 102 113 75
B.17.25	49. 859 933 85	49. 106 605 35
11.17.14	25. 376 933 52	24. 791 280 90
10.18.13	47. 130 091 12	49. 106 605 35
10.18.21	132. 869 908 88	130. 893 394 65
13.19.16	63. 143 728 55	66. 586 775 55
13.19.23	116. 856 271 45	113. 413 224 45
12.20.15	79. 480 265 11	79. 106 605 35
12.20.22	100. 519 734 89	100. 893 394 65
15.21.18	100. 410 627 55	100. 893 394 65
15.21.24	79. 589 372 45	79. 106 605 35
17.22.20	94. 335 289 37	93. 004 491 60
17.22.25	85. 664 710 63	86. 995 508 40
C.23.27	53. 300 774 80	55. 693 380 90
C.23.32	53. 300 774 80	51. 786 789 30
19.23.32	73. 398 450 40	72. 519 829 80
20.24.21	90.	90.
20.24.26	90.	90.
B.25.17	111. 012 313 79	111. 786 789 30
B.25.28	68. 987 686 21	68. 213 210 70
22.26.24	104. 900 596 69	103. 897 886 20
22.26.28	75. 099 403 31	76. 102 113 75
C.27.23	83. 736 047 28	83. 413 224 45
C.27.29	96. 263 952 72	96. 586 775 55
B.28.25	100. 410 627 55	100. 893 394 65
B.28.30	79. 589 372 45	79. 106 605 35
C.29.27	68. 813 606 02	69. 515 338 20
C.29.30	111. 186 393 99	110. 484 661 80
B.30.28	94. 096 043 76	94. 306 619 10
B.30.31	85. 903 956 24	85. 693 380 90
B.31.30	72. 024 716 19	70. 893 394 65
B.31.34	107. 975 283 81	101. 309 932 47
C.31.30	107. 975 283 81	109. 106 605 35
C.31.34	72. 024 716 19	78. 690 067 53
C.32.23	51. 887 073 50	49. 106 605 35
C.32.39	84. 399 590 82	75. 963 756 53
19.32.23	43. 713 335 68	40. 893 394 65

VE Table 987.137D (*Continued*)

	SPHERICAL FACE ANGLES	PLANAR FACE ANGLES
19.32.33	84. 399 590 82	90.
33.32.36	51. 887 073 50	63. 434 948 82
36.32.39	43. 713 335 68	40. 601 294 64
D.33.16	90.	96. 586 775 55
D.33.36	90.	101. 309 932 47
16.33.32	90.	83. 413 224 45
32.33.36	90.	78. 690 067 53
B.34.31	49. 994 799 12	52. 125 016 35
B.34.37	130. 005 200 88	127. 874 983 65
C.35.F	96. 864 566 33	98. 130 102 35
C.35.34	83. 135 433 67	81. 869 897 65
D.36.33	70. 893 394 65	60. 255 118 70
D.36.40	70. 893 394 65	81. 869 897 65
32.36.33	38. 213 210 70	37. 874 983 65
B.37.34	43. 713 335 68	45.
B.37.44	136. 286 664 32	135.
35.38.37	76. 892 506 76	74. 744 881 30
37.38.44	103. 107 493 24	105. 255 118 70
C.39.F	65. 541 166 57	74. 744 881 30
C.39.32	48. 917 666 86	47. 726 310 99
32.39.36	65. 541 166 57	57. 528 807 71
D.40.36	99. 274 499 81	90.
D.40.52	80. 725 500 19	90.
F.41.38	133. 635 298 68	127. 874 983 65
F.41.48	46. 364 701 32	52. 125 016 35
F.42.39	74. 273 101 35	77. 471 192 29
F.42.48	105. 726 898 65	102. 528 807 71
36.43.40	61. 086 164 08	52. 125 016 35
36.43.45	118. 913 835 92	127. 874 983 65
B.44.37	33. 210 910 76	33. 690 067 53
B.44.47	56. 789 089 24	63. 434 948 82
37.44.38	33. 210 910 76	29. 744 881 30
38.44.41	56. 789 089 24	53. 130 102 35
39.45.42	25. 376 933 52	29. 744 881 30
39.45.43	104. 763 132 63	97. 125 016 35
42.45.48	49. 859 933 85	53. 130 102 35
43.46.45	69. 075 167 57	74. 744 881 30
43.46.52	110. 924 832 43	105. 255 118 70
B.47.44	104. 251 755 06	98. 130 102 35
B.47.49	75. 748 244 94	81. 869 897 65
F.48.41	34. 098 126 00	37. 874 983 65
F.48.42	34. 098 126 00	32. 471 192 29
41.48.51	55. 901 874 00	60. 255 118 70
42.48.45	55. 901 874 00	49. 398 705 36
B.49.E	90.	94. 398 705 36
B.49.47	90.	85. 601 294 64
45.50.46	43. 713 335 69	45.
45.50.53	136. 286 664 31	135.
44.51.48	113. 861 046 20	108. 434 948 82
44.51.55	66. 138 953 80	71. 565 051 18
D.52.40	74. 498 640 43	71. 565 051 18
40.52.46	31. 002 719 13	36. 869 897 65
46.52.58	74. 498 640 43	71. 565 051 18
G.53.48	116. 856 271 46	112. 380 135 05

VE Table 987.137D (*Continued*)

	SPHERICAL FACE ANGLES	PLANAR FACE ANGLES
G.53.58	63. 143 728 54	67. 619 864 95
E.54.49	56. 492 066 30	57. 528 807 71
E.54.60	123. 507 933 70	122. 471 192 29
44.55.51	80. 725 500 19	74. 744 881 30
44.55.56	99. 274 499 81	105. 255 118 70
44.56.47	47. 607 954 29	45.
44.56.55	47. 607 954 29	45.
47.56.54	42. 392 045 71	45.
54.56.60	42. 392 045 71	45.
G.57.48	121. 948 059 43	120. 963 756 53
G.57.61	58. 051 940 57	59. 036 243 47
G.58.53	80. 268 524 53	78. 690 067 53
50.58.52	80. 268 524 53	78. 690 067 53
50.58.53	19. 462 950 94	22. 619 864 95
55.59.56	56. 938 103 87	60. 255 118 70
55.59.61	123. 061 896 13	119. 744 881 30
54.60.56	81. 205 315 34	77. 471 192 29
54.60.62	98. 794 684 66	102. 528 807 71
G.61.57	97. 932 889 86	94. 398 705 36
G.61.63	82. 067 110 14	85. 601 294 64
E.62.60	64. 760 598 18	63. 434 948 82
60.62.66	50. 478 803 64	51. 130 102 35
66.62.67	64. 760 598 18	63. 434 948 82
G.63.61	68. 813 606 02	64. 653 824 06
G.63.70	111. 186 393 98	115. 346 175 94
59.64.63	94. 096 043 76	90.
59.64.65	85. 903 956 24	90.
56.65.64	108. 803 842 79	105. 255 118 70
56.65.66	71. 196 157 21	74. 744 881 30
56.66.60	33. 744 613 33	32. 471 192 29
56.66.65	61. 439 174 78	60. 255 118 71
60.66.62	48. 506 020 29	49. 398 705 35
62.66.67	36. 310 191 60	37. 874 983 65
62.67.66	79. 106 605 35	78. 690 067 53
66.67.68	21. 786 789 30	22. 619 864 95
68.67.73	79. 106 605 35	78. 690 067 53
66.68.67	96. 864 566 34	97. 125 016 35
66.68.69	83. 135 433 66	82. 874 983 65
66.69.68	63. 143 728 54	64. 653 824 06
66.69.70	116. 856 271 46	115. 346 175 94
G.70.63	32. 311 533 24	30. 963 756 53
63.70.64	25. 376 933 52	25. 346 175 94
64.70.65	14. 763 132 63	15. 255 118 70
65.70.66	35. 096 801 23	36. 869 897 65
66.70.69	14. 763 132 63	15. 255 118 70
69.70.71	25. 376 933 52	25. 346 175 94
71.70.75	32. 311 533 24	30. 963 756 53
69.71.70	91. 637 245 08	90.
69.71.72	88. 362 754 92	90.
68.72.71	58. 051 940 57	57. 528 807 71
68.72.73	121. 948 059 43	122. 471 192 29
H.73.74	76. 169 775 05	75. 963 756 53
67.73.72	76. 169 775 05	75. 963 756 53
72.73.74	27. 660 449 90	28. 072 486 94

VE Table 987.137D (*Continued*)

	SPHERICAL FACE ANGLES	PLANAR FACE ANGLES
72.74.73	94. 335 289 37	94. 398 705 36
72.74.75	85. 664 710 63	85. 601 294 64
H.75.74	59. 529 640 53	59. 036 243 47
70.75.71	59. 529 640 53	59. 036 243 47
71.75.74	60. 940 718 93	61. 927 513 06

Table *1132.01D   Angles and Edges of Basic Triangle in VE-Icosa Grid:* The plane projection of this spherical triangle accords with that shown at Fig. *987.412*. Planar edge lengths are ratioed to the vector equilibrium edge (or radius or prime vector) = unity (as shown at line DD′ at Fig. *987.412*).

In the left-hand column the complete list of spherical central angles is followed by the sequence of spherical face angles. In the right-hand column the planar edge lengths are followed by the sequence of planar face angles.

Detail key to the tables is at Fig. *1132.01C*.

Combo Table 1132.01D

	SPHERICAL CENTRAL ANGLES	PLANAR EDGE LENGTHS
A.1	11. 658 290 90	0. 168 468 54
A.2	10. 812 316 96	0. 155 936 97
A.3	10. 909 891 61	0. 157 378 65
A.4	11. 211 433 55	0. 161 840 01
A.7	13. 581 110 92	0. 197 246 40
B.7	5. 890 109 71	0. 091 428 73
B.15	7. 761 243 91	0. 118 033 99
B.18	2. 952 856 44	0. 052 786 40
C.14	1. 126 133 22	0. 018 576 03
C.15	3. 132 150 74	0. 048 632 68
C.16	3. 584 117 54	0. 056 940 13
C.21	4. 568 891 00	0. 076 895 02
D.8	9. 476 737 90	0. 182 857 47
D.17	7. 761 243 91	0. 145 898 03
D.19	8. 225 780 11	0. 166 925 27
D.34	13. 282 525 59	0. 270 090 76
E.26	3. 137 695 86	0. 048 632 68
E.32	2. 771 639 30	0. 038 447 51
E.33	5. 641 161 81	0. 076 895 02
E.40	6. 777 786 99	0. 097 265 36
F.21	1. 784 279 92	0. 028 514 24
F.24	0. 898 066 00	0. 014 257 12
F.25	1. 677 667 31	0. 019 274 87
F.31	3. 686 633 84	0. 052 311 55
G.34	5. 152 423 23	0. 083 462 63
G.35	3. 090 986 42	0. 044 056 92
G.37	6. 032 116 64	0. 083 462 63
G.43	5. 659 893 73	0. 083 462 63
H.40	18. 461 614 83	0. 236 067 98
H.41	18.	0. 229 752 92
H.42	18. 303 816 06	0. 233 905 46
1.2	4. 386 177 56	0. 063 759 78
1.5	8. 491 677 11	0. 131 134 47
2.3	1. 464 602 90	0. 021 253 26
2.6	4. 172 280 25	0. 062 607 39
3.4	1. 517 999 01	0. 022 057 81
3.9	6. 411 448 06	0. 097 265 36
4.7	5. 285 096 65	0. 077 477 19
4.15	9. 693 723 90	0. 150 033 94
5.8	5. 637 683 77	0. 094 889 79
5.10	7. 537 416 10	0. 114 173 36
5.11	6. 055 858 09	0. 093 583 35
6.9	3. 176 823 04	0. 048 195 19

493

Combo Table 1132.01D (*Continued*)

	SPHERICAL CENTRAL ANGLES	PLANAR EDGE LENGTHS
6.10	4. 610 950 35	0. 072 125 50
7.15	9. 732 301 45	0. 149 302 50
8.11	7. 149 662 29	0. 114 056 96
8.17	5. 454 720 36	0. 092 274 02
9.13	2. 738 243 78	0. 043 498 39
9.15	4. 386 177 56	0. 068 776 99
10.12	2. 029 086 36	0. 033 010 15
10.13	2. 671 200 74	0. 040 540 97
11.12	2. 640 881 07	0. 040 897 42
11.16	3. 132 150 74	0. 049 844 72
12.14	2. 875 640 20	0. 044 115 61
12.16	2. 470 208 63	0. 041 468 36
13.14	1. 021 937 63	0. 016 614 91
13.15	2. 842 130 41	0. 043 498 39
14.15	2. 784 253 53	0. 042 506 52
15.18	8. 300 774 80	0. 129 299 76
15.20	6. 199 817 40	0. 103 165 49
15.21	6. 645 371 91	0. 103 165 49
15.23	5. 553 615 68	0. 098 116 21
15.27	7. 255 972 93	0. 121 278 31
16.17	7. 761 243 91	0. 130 495 17
16.21	4. 273 238 78	0. 079 911 64
16.22	5. 335 169 84	0. 087 831 40
17.19	2. 733 554 12	0. 054 237 31
18.20	3. 339 948 34	0. 049 388 11
18.26	3. 934 435 56	0. 065 247 58
19.22	4. 939 325 96	0. 086 622 13
19.34	8. 078 762 84	0. 141 995 11
20.23	3. 809 713 95	0. 055 217 59
20.26	4. 162 659 79	0. 063 759 78
21.24	2. 126 983 21	0. 031 879 89
21.25	2. 235 962 52	0. 021 012 88
22.24	2. 960 694 11	0. 048 423 24
22.34	7. 947 355 75	0. 121 380 00
23.27	3. 858 641 17	0. 055 217 59
23.29	2. 714 082 87	0. 043 878 90
24.34	9. 227 644 88	0. 135 045 38
25.27	2. 028 465 93	0. 037 753 61
25.28	1. 252 042 62	0. 025 520 44
26.32	3. 535 409 06	0. 051 582 74
27.28	1. 596 079 21	0. 027 821 62
27.29	4. 340 706 64	0. 063 759 78
27.30	2. 437 750 98	0. 045 829 94
28.30	1. 842 834 65	0. 036 418 97
28.31	3. 534 561 67	0. 049 565 37
29.32	3. 639 808 76	0. 051 582 74
29.33	3. 550 887 19	0. 054 237 31
30.36	3. 957 799 77	0. 060 690 00
30.37	4. 851 712 67	0. 070 997 56
31.34	7. 277 755 30	0. 101 300 88
31.35	3. 893 075 01	0. 061 745 41
32.33	3. 665 833 06	0. 051 582 74
33.36	4. 425 128 16	0. 059 854 42
33.38	4. 675 036 79	0. 063 759 78

Combo Table 1132.01D (*Continued*)

	SPHERICAL CENTRAL ANGLES	PLANAR EDGE LENGTHS
33.39	4. 216 785 52	0. 060 639 15
34.35	4. 803 812 44	0. 074 954 12
35.37	4. 589 200 89	0. 067 041 00
36.37	3. 187 918 80	0. 043 311 07
36.38	1. 960 609 49	0. 028 653 93
37.38	3. 889 512 26	0. 054 237 31
37.43	6. 359 720 89	0. 087 757 81
38.39	4. 499 294 99	0. 060 639 15
38.42	3. 934 940 04	0. 055 217 59
38.43	7. 761 243 91	0. 103 165 49
39.40	4. 610 950 35	0. 060 639 15
39.41	1. 964 628 74	0. 027 118 65
40.41	4. 172 280 25	0. 054 237 31
41.42	3. 377 507 04	0. 043 878 90
42.43	7. 434 809 92	0. 098 116 21

	SPHERICAL FACE ANGLES	PLANAR FACE ANGLES
1.A.2	22. 238 756 09	22. 238 756 09
2.A.3	7. 761 243 91	7. 761 243 91
3.A.4	7. 761 243 91	7. 761 243 91
4.A.7	22. 238 756 09	22. 238 756 09
7.B.15	90.	90.
15.B.18	90.	90.
14.C.15	61. 874 494 30	60.
14.C.16	118. 125 505 70	120.
15.C.21	118. 125 505 70	108. 434 948 82
16.C.21	61. 874 494 30	71. 565 051 18
8.D.17	35. 264 389 68	30.
17.D.19	19. 471 220 63	18. 434 948 82
19.D.34	35. 264 389 68	26. 565 051 18
26.E.32	73. 221 345 12	71. 565 051 18
32.E.33	33. 557 309 76	36. 869 897 64
33.E.40	73. 221 345 12	71. 565 051 18
21.F.24	99. 594 068 23	90.
21.F.25	80. 405 931 77	90.
34.G.35	65. 905 157 45	63. 434 948 82
35.G.37	48. 189 685 10	53. 130 102 35
37.G.43	65. 905 157 45	63. 434 948 82
40.H.41	13. 282 525 59	13. 282 525 59
41.H.42	10. 812 316 96	10. 812 316 96
42.H.43	20. 905 157 45	20. 905 157 45
A.1.2	68. 176 536 45	67. 761 243 91
2.1.6	43. 646 927 11	44. 477 512 19
5.1.6	68. 176 536 45	67. 761 243 91
A.2.1	90.	90.
A.2.3	90.	90.
A.3.2	82. 377 368 14	82. 238 756 09
A.3.4	97. 622 631 86	97. 761 243 91
A.4.3	74. 759 837 72	74. 477 512 19
A.4.7	105. 240 162 38	105. 522 487 81
1.5.10	75. 385 673 59	74. 477 512 19

Combo Table 1132.01D (*Continued*)

	SPHERICAL FACE ANGLES	PLANAR FACE ANGLES
8.5.11	75. 385 673 59	74. 477 512 19
10.5.11	29. 228 652 83	31. 044 975 63
1.6.2	46. 512 922 25	45. 522 487 81
1.6.10	133. 487 077 75	134. 477 512 19
A.7.4	53. 022 528 57	52. 238 756 09
B.7.15	53. 022 528 57	52. 238 756 09
4.7.15	73. 954 942 86	75. 522 487 81
D.8.17	55. 105 900 90	52. 238 756 09
5.8.11	55. 105 900 90	52. 238 756 09
11.8.17	69. 788 198 19	75. 522 487 81
3.9.6	39. 055 646 14	37. 761 243 91
3.9.15	140. 944 353 86	142. 238 756 09
5.10.6	83. 669 460 60	83. 283 731 73
5.10.12	96. 330 539 40	96. 716 268 27
5.11.8	49. 797 034 11	53. 283 731 73
5.11.12	130. 202 965 89	126. 716 268 27
10.12.11	104. 477 512 19	105. 522 487 81
10.12.14	75. 522 487 81	74. 477 512 19
9.13.10	76. 366 977 77	75. 522 487 81
9.13.15	103. 633 022 23	104. 477 512 19
C.14.12	82. 752 501 44	82. 238 756 09
C.14.15	97. 247 498 56	97. 761 243 91
B.15.7	37. 377 368 14	37. 761 243 91
B.15.18	20. 905 157 45	24. 094 842 55
C.15.14	20. 905 157 45	22. 238 756 09
C.15.21	37. 377 368 14	45.
4.15.7	31. 717 474 41	30.
4.15.9	31. 717 474 41	30.
9.15.13	37. 377 368 14	37. 761 243 91
13.15.14	20. 905 157 45	22. 238 756 09
18.15.20	20. 905 157 45	20. 905 157 45
20.15.23	37. 377 368 14	31. 717 474 41
21.15.27	31. 717 474 41	31. 717 474 41
23.15.27	31. 717 474 41	26. 565 051 18
C.16.12	54. 735 610 32	52. 238 756 09
C.16.21	70. 528 779 37	65. 905 157 45
11.16.12	54. 735 610 32	52. 238 756 09
11.16.17	70. 528 779 37	75. 522 487 81
17.16.22	54. 735 610 32	65. 905 157 45
21.16.22	54. 735 610 32	48. 189 685 10
D.17.8	90.	97. 761 243 91
D.17.19	90.	103. 282 525 59
B.18.15	69. 295 188 95	65. 905 157 45
15.18.20	41. 409 622 11	48. 189 685 10
20.18.26	69. 295 188 95	65. 905 157 45
D.19.17	70. 714 240 62	58. 282 525 59
D.19.34	109. 285 759 38	121. 717 474 41
15.20.18	117. 845 319 77	110. 905 157 45
15.20.23	62. 154 680 23	69. 094 842 55
C.21.15	24. 607 404 49	26. 565 051 18
C.21.16	47. 722 788 40	42. 529 791 38
15.21.25	107. 669 807 11	110. 905 157 45
16.22.19	106. 385 139 24	95. 659 893 73
16.22.24	73. 614 860 76	84. 340 106 27

Combo Table 1132.01D (*Continued*)

	SPHERICAL FACE ANGLES	PLANAR FACE ANGLES
15.23.20	80. 650 296 46	79. 187 683 04
15.23.27	99. 349 703 54	100. 812 316 96
F.24.21	55. 812 316 96	63. 434 948 82
F.24.34	124. 187 683 04	116. 565 051 18
F.25.21	51. 897 039 99	47. 470 208 63
F.25.28	128. 102 960 01	132. 529 791 27
E.26.32	48. 657 434 21	45.
18.26.20	48. 657 434 21	45.
20.26.32	82. 685 131 58	90.
15.27.23	49. 117 607 89	52. 622 631 86
15.27.25	92. 761 991 30	84. 847 576 77
23.27.29	38. 120 400 81	42. 529 791 37
25.28.27	90.	90.
25.28.31	90.	90.
23.29.27	61. 319 519 17	58. 282 525 59
23.29.32	118. 680 480 83	121. 717 474 41
27.30.28	40. 908 063 75	37. 377 368 14
27.30.36	139. 091 936 25	142. 622 631 86
F.31.28	42. 393 817 63	47. 470 208 63
F.31.34	137. 606 182 37	132. 529 791 37
E.32.26	58. 193 899 98	63. 434 948 82
E.32.33	121. 806 100 02	116. 565 051 18
E.33.32	24. 712 012 95	26. 565 051 18
E.33.39	94. 702 438 04	95. 152 423 23
29.33.32	60. 585 549 01	58. 282 525 59
D.34.19	36.	31. 717 474 41
G.34.35	36.	31. 717 474 41
19.34.22	36.	37. 377 368 14
22.34.24	18.	20. 905 157 45
24.34.31	18.	20. 905 157 45
31.34.35	36.	37. 377 368 14
G.35.34	78. 221 767 85	84. 847 576 77
G.35.37	101. 778 232 15	95. 152 423 23
30.36.33	95. 165 347 48	95. 659 893 73
30.36.37	84. 834 652 52	84. 340 106 27
G.37.35	30. 153 386 17	31. 717 474 41
G.37.43	54. 367 004 37	58. 282 525 59
30.37.35	95. 479 609 46	90.
33.38.36	70. 528 779 37	69. 094 842 55
33.38.39	54. 735 610 32	58. 282 525 59
36.38.37	54. 735 610 32	52. 622 631 86
33.39.38	64. 828 737 83	63. 434 948 82
33.39.40	115. 171 262 17	116. 565 051 18
E.40.39	77. 378 583 52	76. 717 474 41
H.40.41	77. 378 583 52	76. 717 474 41
39.40.41	25. 242 832 96	26. 565 051 18
H.41.40	90.	90.
H.41.42	90.	90.
H.42.41	79. 722 778 67	79. 187 683 04
H.42.43	100. 277 221 33	100. 812 316 96
G.43.37	60.	58. 282 525 59
H.43.42	60.	58. 282 525 59
37. 43.38	30.	31. 717 474 41
38.43.42	30.	31. 717 474 41

ACKNOWLEDGMENTS

In the production of *Synergetics 2* at Macmillan we are in great debt to its designer Maurice Schneps who has devoted time and effort to the project far in excess of reasonable expectation. The integration of text and graphics in the work could not have been so effective without his unfailing taste and philosophic grasp.

We were also particularly fortunate that Macmillan could engage a free-lance editor with the patience and competence of John Berseth of New York City. As copy editor he provided invaluable and sympathetic expertise in shepherding into print a manuscript that often verged on the intractable.

Mr. Schneps and Mr. Berseth played the same complementary roles in the production of the first volume; together they insured an essential continuity of style and execution.

R.B.F.
E.J.A.

CREDIT FOR ILLUSTRATIONS AND CALCULATIONS:

Most of the illustrations in *Synergetics 2* were executed by Robert Grip and Christopher Kitrick in the author's Philadelphia office during the period 1977–79. Many of the drawings are refinements of the author's original sketches; some, however, are original interpretations of geometry presented in the text.

Robert Grip and Christopher Kitrick executed the color drawings appearing at color plates 12–32. In addition, they were of great support to the author in the calculations of polyhedral angles and ratios, by the models they fabricated to test assertions in the text, and more importantly by their mathematical insights and suggestions.

The spherical trigonometry tables accompanying Figs. 987.132G, 987.137D, and 1132.01D were computed on two Texas Instruments TI-59 calculators by Kitrick and prepared by Grip. The two of them also computed the plane trigonometry tables.

The isometric projections appearing at 987.132E,F; 987.137B,C; and 1132.01B,C were plotted by a perspective program written by Grip and executed on a digital equipment DEC System 20 linked with a Tektronix 4662 Plotter. On the basis of these computer plots the illustrations at 987.132D, 987.137A, and 1132.01A were inked in color by Kitrick.

The posters at color plates 3 and 4 were redrawn and prepared for printing by Christopher Kitrick.

The following illustrations were constructed by Robert Grip, using a Texas Instruments TI-59 calculator and a PC-100 A/C printer, and they were inked by Christopher Kitrick:

100.416, 938.13, 938.15, 986.405, 986.419, 986.471, 986.502, 986.504, 987.210, 987.213, 987.221, 987.230, 987.312, 987.240, 988.12, 988.100, 1006.32, 1033.43, 1074.13, 1238.26.

R.B.F.
E.J.A.

Index

Index

Key:

Citations to *Synergetics 1* appear in Roman type—e.g., 123.45
Citations to *Synergetics 2* appear in italics—e.g., *123.45*
Main references are in boldface type—e.g., **123.45** or ***123.45***
All references are to Section Numbers

Abbreviations used occasionally:
IVM = isotropic vector matrix
VE = vector equilibrium
icosa = icosahedron
octa = octahedron
tetra = tetrahedron

AAB complex three-quanta module. *See* Mite
A & B quanta modules. *See* Modules: A & B
  quanta modules
Abacus, 1210 (pp. 734–36, 743), 1232.21
Aberrating: Aberratability, 205.05, 420.041,
  441.23, 445.11, 464.08, 539.08, 647.01,
  781.00–04, 782.10–50, 801.13, 905.64,
  981.20, 985.08, 1009.54, 1009.72,
  1053.15; *100.323, 223.06, 270.21,*
  310.12, 533.21, 537.43, 542.05, 543.22,
  901.19. 986.172, 986.751–58
  See also:
  Askew: Skew-aberrated
  Orbits are elliptical
  Wave-frequency aberrations
Aberration increment, 420.041
Aberration limit, 986.758
  See also:
  Asymmetric limits
  Rotational aberrating limit
Abhorrence of vacuum, *440.11, 1033.653*
Abortion, *1005.613–14*

Absolute. 251.02, 515.14, 1222. 1222.20:
  311.15, 504.12–14, 505.63–64, 532.17,
  543.11, 543.23, 1052.61–65
  See also:
  Constant: Constancy
  Cosmic absolutes
  Limit case
  Minimum limit case
  Regular: Regularity
  Zerophase
Absolute integrity, 445.11
Absolute network, *201.11*
Absolute velocity, 441.04, **647.00–30,**
  1106.23; *440.12, 986.518,*
  1052.65–71
Absolute zero, 205.02, 251.02, 427.01,
  443.02; *1033.657–58*
Abstraction, 220,11–12, 240.57–60, 307.01,
  502.31, 505.33, 508.10, 521.01, 538.13,
  801.13, 801.23, 905.42, 962.40,
  1012.33, 1023.16; *440.10–11,*
  505.51–53, 792.01, 986.030–32,

Axis of rotatability: Axis of rotation, 240.63, 400.60, 905.43; *269.07, 502.05(3), 1001.21, 1033.018*
Axis of spin, 222.23, **223.01–02,** 223.11, Table 223.66 (Col. 7), 223.74, 450.11–16, 457.01–10, 622.10, 622.20, 622.30; *223.09, 251.021, 265.04, 466.13–18, 527.25, 986.232, 1033.666, 1033.82 1044.01, 1044.03, 1076.13*
  See also:
  Additive twoness
  Neutral axis

B module: *See* Module: B quanta module
Baby, *790.11*
Babylonian coordinates, 1053.34, 1054.70, 1230.10
Background. *See* Cosmic background radiation
Background nothingness, *505.74, 505.80–83, 812.05*
Balance: Balancing of energies, 223.73, 310,03, 325, 430.02, 440.02, 441.20, 532.11, 532.22–23, 638.02, 640.21, 720.11, 905.48, 1053.31, 1239.31; *223.05–06, 270.13, 325.15, 532.17, 790.17, **792.40,** 936.22, 986.814, 1005.612, 1052.59*
  See also:
  Equilibrium
  Omnibalanced
  Unbalanced
Ball
  See:
  Center ball
  Earth & tennis ball
  Me ball
  Odd ball
  Ping-pong ball
  Spheres
  Stacking of oranges and cannon balls
  Tetherball
  Yin-yang
Ball bearings, 640.21, 645.01, 713.08; *792.50, 937.31*
Balloon, 703.06–16, 751.05–10, **760.00–761.06,** 1024.17–19, 1024.21; *986.095, 986.635*
Balls coming together, 411.01–07
Banana, Fig. 640.20, 641.02, 644.01; *790.18*
Bank. *See* Memory bank
Barrel: Barrel-hooping, 430.03, **705.00–06,** Fig. 705.01, Fig. 705.02, 1009.98; **790.15–17**
Basic event, 537.14–15, 614.01–05
  See also:
  Action-reaction-resultant
  Three-vector teams

Basic triangle, 902.00–10, Fig. 902.01, Fig. 902.10; *795.08–09, 986.473*
Basic triangle: Basic disequilibrium 120 LCD triangle, 417.02, 456.02–05, 612.11, **901.00–902.23, Fig. 901.03,** 905.46, 905.48, 905.52–55, **905.60–66,** 915.10–11, 915.20, 921.04, 982.56–58, Fig. 982.58, 985.04, 1053.10–15, 1053.20–21, 1053.30–35, 1104.04 footnote, 1210 (p. 754); *251.29, **795.08–09,** 986.311–312, 986.471, 986.473, 1043.01, 1053.36*
Basic triangle: Basic equilibrium 48 LCD triangle, **453.00–3, Fig. 453.01,** 905.51, 905.53, 905.72, 1053.10–15, 1053.20–21, 1053.30–35, 1053.40, Table 1053.41; *251.17, **795.08–09,** 901.19*
Basketry interweaving, *Figs. 1033.111A–E, 1033.112*
Battleship, 170
Beauty, *262.07, 542.00–04, Fig. 542.02, 793.01*
  See also Aesthetics
Becoming, 223.11, 502.13
Bee: Honey-seeking bee, 216.03, 1009.67; *326.12–13*
Begetted eightness, 415.30–42
Beginning, 961.45, 982.11
  See also:
  Eternal outset
  Event embryo
  Initiating
  Starting
Beginnings & endings, 302; *263.03, 530.11–12*
  See also:
  Biterminal
  Finite
  ıncrement
  Package
  Terminal
Beginningless, *987.031, 987.044*
  See also:
  Eternal
  Ideal
Being, 502.24
Beliefs, 203.06, 203.10, 502.10; *537.51*
  See also:
  Axioms
  Religion
Bendable: Bending, *986.632*
Benday screen, 427.15; *260.11, 260.22, 100.070*
  See also Resolution
Bernouilli, Daniel, 640.03
Bertalanffy, Ludwig von, 400.24
  See also General systems theory

Cipher, *000.103–04*
See also Null
Circle, 529.04, 539.03–10, 811.01,
   813.01–04, 982.83–84, 985.10;
   986.816–17, **1007.25, 1050.37**
See also:
Closest packing of circles
Great circles
Great circling
Circuit: Circuitry, 427.07–17, 501.06,
   522.05, 646.03, 647.02, 842.07,
   961.46–48, 981.12, 1011.30–31,
   1012.11; *267.03, 527.09, 535.21–22,*
   1007.23
See also:
Closed system: Closed circuit
Energy networks
Fail-safe alternate circuits
Feedback circuitry
Holding patterns
Hydraulic circuitry
Icosahedron as local shunting circuit
Invisible circuitry
Minimum cycle
Roundtrip circuit
Series vs parallel circuitry
Shunting
Turnaround limit
Circuit pattern tensegrity, *1033.019, Fig.*
   1033.019, 1033.020
Circular unity. *See* Cyclic unity
Circumference: Circumferential, 537.22,
   765.01; *986.874*
See also:
Embracing: Embracements
Gravity as circumferential force
Icosahedron: Circumferential closest pack-
   ing
Nuclear-circumferential
Radial-circumferential
Circumference & leverage, 1051.10–55
Circumferential field, 1051.30
Circumferential twoness, 1051.10
   See also:
   Inward-outward twoness
   Two kinds of twoness
Clear space polyhedra, 422.01
   See also:
   Allspace filling
   Self-packing
Cleavaging: Cleavages, *987.033,*
   987.100–416
   See also:
   Hemisystem cleavages
   Spin-halvings
Click-stop phases, *270.11, 987.062, 987.315*
Click-stop subdivisioning, *1033.120–28,*
   1033.75
Clock, 529.01, 530.05; *535.21*

See also:
Atomic clock
Invisible motion of hands of the clock
Closed system: Closed circuit, 224.03, 251.37,
   251.46, 331, 400.25, 501.06, 537.02,
   537.05, 538.02, 538.15, 602.01, 814.01,
   953.50, 1011.30, 1023.11–16, 1023.18,
   1053.30; *000.107, 527.09, 541.19,*
   986.317, 986.835, 1006.41,
   1033.492
See also:
Finite: Finity
Perpetual motion machine
Returning upon itself: Systems return upon
   themselves
Systematic enclosure
Closest packing of bubbles, 1025.10–14
Closest packing of circles, 982.80–84
Closest packing of rods, 412.01–02, Fig.
   412.01, 1012.35, 1107–10–42;
   792.32–40
Closest packing of spheres, 200.03, 205.06,
   222.00–53, 410.00–419.05, 420.05,
   421.01, 427.02–04, 515.31, 536.01,
   621.07, 782.30, 782.40, Fig. 930.11,
   931.61, 942.01–05, 981.01–24, 982.13,
   982.71, 1002.11–13, 1006.11–13,
   1008.11–15, 1011.35–62, 1012.15, 1210
   (p. 754); *260.30–52, 261.03–04, 268.07,*
   419.30, Fig. 419.30, 466.01, 466.31–35,
   936.17–18, 986.143, **986.150–51,**
   986.161, 986.223, 986.440, 986.741,
   986.760, 986.771–73, 987.061,
   1006.35–36, 1033.11, **1033.81,** *1052.32,*
   1053.848, Table 1053.849
See also:
Aston, F.W.
Balls coming together
Icosahedron: Circumferential closest pack-
   ing
Isotropic vector matrix
Nestability
Omnidirectional closest packing of
   spheres
Precession of two sets of 10 closest packed
   spheres
Precession of two sets of 60 closest packed
   spheres
Spheres & spaces
Stacking oranges and cannon balls
Clothesline. *See* Tensegrity clothesline
Clouds, *543.02, 790.11, 986.743*
Cloud chamber, 517.04, 517.13
Coaction: Cointeraction, *987.011, 987.042*
Coexisting: Always & only, 226.11, 400.04,
   507.03; *790.13, 792.40, 1033.621*
See also:
Cofunctions
Convex-concave

Critchlow, Keith, 950.12, 982.84
Critical path, 400.24, 537.31; *535.21–22, 1130.20–24*
See also:
General systems theory
Grand strategy of synergetics
Critical proximity, 121, 130.01–133, 240.35, 403.02, 517.101, Fig. 517.10, 517.12, **518.00–06,** 519.10, 536.02–03, 536.51, 538.14–15, 614.01, 640.30, 716.11, 726.03, 761.04, 942.12, 980.05, 985.20, 985.22, **1009.00–98,** 1024.11–21, 1025.11, 1032.23, 1054.61; *790.22, 986.635, 986.742–43, 986.835, 1009.57, Figs. 1009.57 A & B 1033.102, 1044.09, 1053.803*
See also:
Co-orbiting
Coherence
Fall-in: Fall-in proclivity
Hammerthrow
Interference
Orbital escape from critical proximity
Precession
Critical proximity threshold, 518.06
Crocodile, 400.31, 501.101
Cross-fertilizing, 216.03
Crossings, 224.20, 510.01, 514.03, 519.03, **523.00–03;** 501.21, 1007.23–24; *987.078*
See also:
Domains of crossing
Fix
Point
Vertex
Crossings, openings & trajectories, 251.02, **505.11,** 514.03, 524.31–32, 604.01; *1007.22*
See also:
Events, novents & event interrelatabilities
Fixes, discontinuities and continuities
Joint, windows & struts
Points, areas & lines
Vertexes, faces & edges
Cryogenics, 205.02, 427.01–12; *201.11, 1033.657, 1073.16*
Crystals: Crystalliness: Crystallography, 108.02, 171, 204.01, 440.05, 440.07, 615.01, 635.01, 931.40, 942.42, 961.45, 980.07, 981.20, 1005.30, 1009.67, 1025.14, 1041.01, 1042.05, 1056.20(1), 1060.03, 1061.11, 1238.21, 1239.31; *100.022, 201.11, 263.02, 531.04, 532.18, 936.12, 937.13, 937.31, 986.143, 987.325, 1041.11*
See also:
Iceland spar crystals
Liquid-crystal-vapor-incandescent phases

Rigids
Seven axes of symmetry
Trivalent
Cube, 201.03, 223.20 (c), 223.21 (c), 223.32, 223.62, 223.73–74, 223.81–91, 445.14, 454.01, 527.61–62, 615.01–07, **617.00–04,** 713.02, 905.44–45, **942.40–43,** Table 943, Table 955.41, **950.21,** 953.23, Table 963.10, 982.01–62, Table 982.62, 982.71, 1011.23, 1053.20–21, 1053.33, Table 1053.40, Table 1053.51, Fig. 1054.40, 1220.17 footnote; *251.16–17, Fig. 527.703, 537.131, 937.22, Table 954.10A, 986.047, 986.073, 986.215–16, Fig. 986.432, 987.325, 1001.23, 1006.32–33, 1053.78* allspace filler, *986.432, Table 986.440*
See also:
Domain of cube
Duo-tet cube
Minimum stable cube
Nucleated cube
Spherical cube
Triangle in cube energetic model
Truncated cube
Cube: Diagonal of, 452.07, *Fig. 463.01,* 615.01–07, Table 963.10 note, 982.21, **982.30–33,** 982.43–53; *540.11–14, 986.204, Fig. 986.210*
See also:
Prime vector
Tetra edge
Cube: Diagonal of cube as wave propagating model, 462.01–463.05, 615.07; *540.13*
Cube: Two tetrahedra as cube, 110, Fig. 110B, 223.62, 463.03, 464.07, 842.02, 982.42–48, 1009.32; *986.203, Fig. 986.209, Fig. 986.210, Color Plate 7*
See also:
Duo-tet cube
Tensegrity column
Cube & VE, 615.00–07
Cuboctahedron, 430.04, 1053.20
See also Vector equilibrium
Culture, *1052.641*
Curve: Curvature, 240.26, 624.05, 703.02, 1021.10–1025.14; *1053.71, 1076.13*
See also:
Barrel
Spherical cask
Curved space, 522.21–22, 541.04, 826.14, 1009.52, 1009.97; *325.14*
Curvilinear, 521.22; *1001.22*
See also Omnicurvilinear
Cybernetics
See:

Integration & differentiation, 105, 1054.20; *201.11, 310.14, 311.13, 326.40, 986.835, 1073.22*

Integrative-disintegrative, 231.01, **310.01,** 325, 400.11, 420.041, 541.05, 721.02, 780.24, 921.40, 972.02, 1009.30, 1030.10; *000.113, 527.09, Fig. 527.09, 541.16–19, 790.16, 1073.21*
See also Universal integrity

Integration of digits. *See* Indigs

Integrity, 400.08, 411.37, 421.10, 440.02, 502.25, 1009.37, 1009.41, 1024.25, 1056.11, 1056.13, 1056.20 (38), 1220.10; *311.16, 321.03, 537.43, 986.831, 986.850, 986.852*
See also:
Angular integrity
Cosmic integrity
Omnitensional integrity
Pattern integrity
Structural integrity
System integrity
Tensional integrity
Universal integrity
Vectorial integrity

Intellect: Intellection, 164, 400.06, 509.10, 529.201, 826.05, 1056.11, 1056.20 (17); *311.18, 504.16, 537.41, 543.02, 543.25, 986.814, 1075.20–24*
See also Wisdom

Intellect alters energy, *261.01, 1075.22, 1075.25*

Intellect: Equation of, *1075.20–26*

Intelligence. *See* Artificial intelligence

Intensity, 528.06

Interaccommodating: Interaccommodative, **163–64,** 168, 203.04, 220.04; *311.16, 504.15, 543.12, 543.22, 791.08, 792.01, 986.171*
See also Omniinteraccommodative

Interattraction. *See* Mass interattraction

Interawareness, *505.73*

Interbonding
See:
Bonds: Bonding: Interbonding
Chemical bonds
Multivalency
Valency

Interchangeable intertransformativeness, 1032.11

Intercommensurability: Intercommensurable, *987.033 footnote, 987.042, 987.050–58,* **987.057, 987.100–111**
See also Octaphase

Intercomplementary, 332, 615.07; *400.651, 1005.611*

Interconnecting, 224.07, 227.02–03, 400.53–54, 905.02, 921.15, 1023.16; *530.11*

Interconnection of any two lines in Universe, 923.10

Interconnection of any two points in Universe, 426.40, **960.08,** 961.30; *530.11, **923.15***

Interconnection of any four points in Universe, 961.30; *100.321, 530.11, Fig. 986.726*

Interconnection of systems, 400.53–54

Interconsiderability, *987.042*

Intercovariables, *000.1271*

Intereffects, 512.01, 533.01–05, 1005.53–54, 1009.60; *223.08, 533.07–12, 533.21–22*
See also:
No local change
Precession
Precession of side effects & primary effects

Interequatable
See:
Constants & variables
Intercommensurable

Interference, 108.01–02, 220.12, 516.03, **517.01–24, Fig. 517.10,** 529.24, 614.02, 710.03, 763.01–02, **1009.10–11,** 1056.20 (31); *501.23, 543.03, 1001.26, 1053.803, 1053.833*
See also:
Domains of interference
Knot
Lines cannot go through the same point at the same time
Self-interference
Tetrahedron of interferences

Interference & noninterference
See:
Discontinuity & continuity
Frequency & interval
Somethingness & nothingness
Tuning-in & tuning-out

Interfriction, 626.03

Interfunctioning covariables, 642.01

Intergeared mobility freedoms, 411.30–38

Internal & external limits, 205.01

Internuclear vector modulus, 240.40, 421.02–03, 537.21, 982.21; *540.14, 986.160–63, Fig. 986.161*
See also:
Axis of intertangency
Prime vector

Interprecess: Interprecessing, 400.61, **416.02,** 416.04, 417.01–04, 1005.12, 1005.32, 1005.50; *533.22*

Interproportionality
See:
Constants & variables
Intercommensurable

Interrelationships, Table 227.01, 227.03, 240.20, 240.25, 240.27, 240.41, 307.01, 400.02, 427.04, 509.30, 510.04, 606.02, 905.02, 905.47, 982.72, 1023.15; *266.02, **100.401–03,** 269.01–07, 310.11,*

Message content, 623.12, 633.02

Metabolism: Metabolic flow, 506.20, 826.03;
　　181, 533.12, 1005.611

Metals, 623.13, 750.11, 931.50, 1009.32;
　　533.12
　See also:
　Alloy
　Hammering sheet metal
　Heat treatment of metals
　Light on scratched metal
　Tensile strength of chrome-nickel-steel

Metals: Recirculation of, 117; *792.52, 795.03*

Metaphor, 1005.52

Metaphysical: Metaphysics, 153, 163, 220.05,
　　223.65, 501.14, 780.30, 801.23, 1056.20
　　(33), 1110.16; *504.11, 504.14, 543.24,
　　900.11, 1052.69, 1072.22, 1075.11*
　metaphysical improves the scenario, 217.03
　See also:
　Abstraction
　Conceptuality independent of size
　Contracting metaphysical Universe
　Know-how
　Mind
　Weightless

Metaphysical experience, 163

Metaphysical & physical, 142, 162, 163, 171,
　　203.10, 205.03–04, 209, 211, 217.02,
　　217.04, 221.01, 229.05, 229.10, 240.25,
　　251.27, 251.50, 302–03, 305.04, 306.01,
　　310,03, 323, 400.43, 424.02, 426.21–22,
　　426.46, 440.08, 443.01–04, 445.10–11,
　　501.01, 502.02, **513.07, 515.21, 517.05,**
　　521.01, 522.34, 524.03, 526.03, 529.06,
　　529.31, 532.14, 537.31, 620.12, 623.11,
　　625.04, 780.30, 782.50, 801.13, 905.42,
　　954.01, 954.51, 1005.50, 1053.16–17,
　　1054.71, afterpiece, p. 787; *200.06,
　　251.48, 261.01, 310.13–14,* ***326.01–50,***
　　*440.11, 533.11, 541.18, 543.22–25,
　　986.473, 986.840, 986.852, 986.854,
　　987.061, 1006.34, 1013.51–52,
　　1033.601,* ***1052.60–71,*** *1053.826–27,
　　1072.21, 1075.11, 1075.22*
　See also:
　Acceleration & deceleration
　Brain & mind
　Expanding physical Universe
　Generalized topological definability
　Information vs entropy
　Order & disorder
　Tetrahedron: One tetrahedron

Metaphysical wave patterns, 505.33

Meteors, *1053.803*

Mexican star, 955.10–14, 955.41 (6)

Michelson-Morley experiment, *935.11*

Microscope, 713.03, 1009.40, 1110.16

Microsystem, *505.83, 1052.350–57*

Middle: Middleness, 460.02, 1009.10–11,
　　1110.16; *504.14, 794.14, 937.11–15,
　　987.043*
　See also:
　Average
　Between
　Cosmic middle ground
　Macro-medio-micro
　Starting at the middle

Middle case, *937.13*

Milky Way: Milky-Way-like, 427.11, 505.02,
　　524.03, 525.02, 615.01, 640.41, 713.05,
　　740.31, 761.01, 780.22–23, 1009.30,
　　1024.17, 1220.21; *326.06, 790.22*

Millions, *See* Illions

Milton Academy, *986.096*

Mind, 211, 458.10, 508.01–02,
　　1009.70–73; *000.129–30, 262.06,
　　265.09, 311.14, 326.23, 504.15, 543.02,
　　543.05, 543.25*
　See also Brain & mind

Mind vs matter, 515.21

Mind vs muscle, 515.21; *186, 537.52, 541.18*

Miniature Universe, 311.01, 1056.20 (25)

Miniaturization, 740.20–31

Minima transformation, 1105

Minimod T. *See* Module: T quanta module

Minimum
　See:
　Conceptual minimum
　Least effort
　Limit case
　Thirty-two minimum aspects of systems

Minimum awareness. *See* Topology of
　　minimum awareness

Minimum awareness model, *505.83*

Minimum cycle, 1011.30
　See also Fourness & threeness define a cycle

Minimum effort. *See* Least effort

Minimum frequency, *1033.665*

Minimum knot, 506.13, 517.12, Fig. 517.10F;
　　1007.24

Minimum limit case, 982.84, 1011.31;
　　505.60–65

Minimum model, 503.03

Minimum nothingness, *1033.73, 1033.76*

Minimum perpetual motion machine, 116,
　　309, **330–34,** 1106.22

Minimum set, 227.02, 228.01, 309, 333,
　　510.03, 510.07, 620.01, 966.11,
　　1011.10; *505.74, 537.06, 537.131*

Minimum sphere, 223.14, 1005.50,
　　1022.10–15
　See also Tetrahedron

Minimum stable cube, 415.16, 415.21–22,
　　416.03, 615.02

Minimum system: Minimum structural system,
　　400.41–42, 401.01–07, 402.02, 608.08,

Primitive hierarchy, *000.127, 202.03, 270.24,*
  986.730, 986.840, 986.854–57, 987.033,
  987.062, 987.327, 1033.122–28
See also:
Cosmic hierarchy
Geometric hierarchy
Time-size vs primitive
Primitive & potential ***100.403,*** *1033.104,*
  1033.180–83, Table 1033.192, Table
  1033.20
Primitive regeneration, 1076.00–13
Primitive simplex module, *986.204*
See also Tetra edge
Primitive system, *270.17, 270.23*
Primitive tetrahedron, *986.854, 986.863*
Primitive unity, *987.041*
Principles
See:
Discovery of principles
Generalized principles: Family of
Pure principle
Synergetics principles
Printing. *See* Benday screen
Probability: Probability statistics, 400.24,
  503.01–02 **538.01–15,** 961.45; *505.63,*
  935.22, 986.069, 1130.11
See also:
Happening
Randomness
Probability model: Three cars, 538.10–15
Problem: Problem solving, 165, 169, 213,
  305.01, 529.07, 537.31, **537.33;** *182,*
  260.42, 311.14, 311.18, 326.24, 326.31,
  646.22, 1052.70, 1130.11
See also:
General systems theory
Mistakes
Question asking
Starting with Universe
Synergetic advantage: Principle of
Process. *See* Awareness processing
Proclivities, 905.16, 1007.15; *201.10–11*
See also:
Differentiated proclivities
Integrated synergetic proclivities
Profile
See:
No half profile
Polyhedral profiles
Profit motive, *326.08*
Program: Programming, 503.01, **509.30,**
  522.31, 1005.53, **1005.61,** 1009.66–67,
  1009.70–73, 1110.16; *181*
Progressions. *See* Volume & area progressions
Projective transformation. *See* Constant zenith
  projection
Pronouns
See:
Complex it
Ego

I
Me
Self
They
You & I
Proofs, 250.61, 306.01, 487–88, 825.26–29;
  100.102, 270.17, 986.820, 1052.361,
  1071.21
See also:
Eddington's proof of irreversibility
Experimental reverification
Propagation: Propagative, 220.11, 310.02,
  426.01–03, 445.07, 505.301, 615.07,
  639.00–02, 1032.20; *543.13, 986.571,*
  986.711, ***987.061,*** *1062.66*
See also:
Electromagnetic wave propagation
Starting at the middle
Wave propagating model
Propeller blade, 117, 516.03, 517.201,
  532.21–23
Property: Private property, 250.401–41
Proportion: Proportionality, *986.721,*
  987.033, 987.033 footnote
See also Constant proportionality
Protein shells, *986.474*
Proton & electron, 433.02, 1052.41–44,
  1055.06; *310.11, 419.30, 935.23,*
  986.121, 986.519, 986.582,
  987.321–22
Proton & neutron, 240.65, 415.11, 418.06,
  511.04, 620.06, 639.02, 921.03, 954.22,
  954.32, 954.53, 982.70, 995.03,
  1012.15; *262.04, 321.03, 419.22, Table*
  419.23, 935.22–23, Fig. 935.23,
  986.711, 986.760, 986.770–73, Table
  986.773, 987.321–22
See also:
Quantum
Three vector teams
Prototype, 464.08; *795.11*
See also Reproducibility
Proximity: Proximities, 240.36–37; *543.22*
See also Critical proximity
Proximity & remoteness, 240.37, 425.01,
  980.02; *Figs. 1009.57A & B, Fig.*
  1130.24. 1130.24
See also:
Convergence & divergence
Cosmic & local
Psychology: Psychological geometry
See:
Awareness
Conceptuality is polyhedral
Conditioned reflex
Ego
Geometry of thinking
Human tolerance limits
I
Icosahedron permits individuality

Index

Four rocket bursts
Tracer bullet sequence
Trajectory
Rods. *See* Closest packing of rods
Roemer, Ole, *935.11*
Rollability of polyhedra, 942.70
Roots: Tree root, 216.03; *793.04*
Rope: Rope-making, 505.21, **Fig. 505.41,
 506.01–15,** 522.04–09, **640.60,** Fig.
 641.01, 644.01, 711.01–04, 1005.30,
 1054.61; *325.10–16, 326.22, 535.22,
 790.21, 792.31, 936.11*
 rope of meaning, *270.14*
 See also:
 Knot
 Pattern integrity
Rotate: Rotatability, Table 223.66 col. 7,
 401.05, 905.43, **905.50–55,** 982.61;
 *201.11, 502.05, 986.726, 986.857,
 1033.017*
 See also:
 Axis of rotatability
 Centrifugal force
 Orbiting
 Precessional rotation
 Triangular-cammed model
Rotational aberrating limit, 1053.15
Rotational symmetry, *Fig. 527.08*
Roundness, 502.41(b)
 See also Sphericity
Roundtrip circuit, 522.09
 See also Turnaround limit
Rubber doughnut, 411.07, Fig. 505.41
 See also:
 Involution & evolution
 Torus
Rubber glove, 232.02, 419.02, 507.01,
 507.05, 625.05; *419.10, 526.31,
 1052.56*
 See also Annihilation
Rubber sheet topology, *270.18*
Rubber tires, 465.10, Fig. 465.10
Ruddering.
 See:
 Feedback
 Steering effect
Russell, Bertrand, *987.075*

S Module. *See* Module: S Quanta Module
Safety. *See* Failsafe advantage
Safety factors, 703.08, 723.05–06; *794.05,
 1053.77*
Sailboat: Sailing vessel, *000.104,
 000.115–16*
Sand, *100.201*
Santa Sophia dome, 764.01
Satellite sensing, 1110.02–16
 See also Telescopes mounted on satellites

Scan transmission of man by radio, 427.15,
 515.13 footnote
Scarcity: *See* Life support inadequacy
Scarcity model, 1005.61
Scenario: Scenario Universe, 217.03, 251.27,
 306.03, **320–25, Fig. 321.01,** 531.01,
 625.03–05, 780.12, 780.28, 985.07;
 *262.07–09, 265.09, 311.18, 321.04–05,
 325.10–16, 326.11, 326.31, 400.73,
 526.13, 526.32–34, 530.10–13,
 541.16–17, 543.01, 543.12, 792.04,
 792.20, 936.23, 986.048, 986.171–72,
 986.819, 987.044, 1033.103, 1073.15*
 See also:
 Finite episoding
 Finite event scenario
 Metaphysical improves the scenario
Scenario of the child, *100.010–18, 100.20*
Scenario principle, 228.00–01; *228.12,
 265.02, 1052.33*
 See also:
 Nonunitarily conceptual
 System vs scenario
Scheherazade numbers, 955.30, 1230.00–80
Science, 161, 306.01, 502.01, 532.02,
 826.04–06, 1009.80, 1056.14, 1056.20
 (14–11), 1210 p. 739; *201.11, 266.07,
 326.01, 326.03, 326.40, 440.09,
 505.51–53, 505.62, 531.06, 986.021,
 986.027, 987.075*
 See also Design science
Science & humanities: Gap between, 203.08,
 250.10–12, 826.05, 990.05; *000.124–
 31, 935.23–25*
Science opened the wrong door, 502.31,
 990.05
Science as a tool, 826.05
Scientific generalizations, 161
Scientific specialization, 203.07, 204.01
Scientists, 250.52, 502.11; *531.05*
 See also Artist-scientist
Scratches. *See* Light on scratched metal
Screw, Fig. 108.01
Scribing tools: Scribing, 986.041, 986.071,
 986.820; *1050.34*
Second, 223.11, 426.44
Seeability: Seeing, 532.16, 713.06; *266.01,
 267.01–02, 268.05, 526.24, 543.04,
 986.062*
 See also:
 Visibility
 Visual
Seeds, *793.02–03*
Self, 216.03, 411.21–23, 487–88, 538.01,
 982.11; *267.03, 440.12, Fig. 542.02,
 543.15, 1052.56*
 self is not a priori, 487
 See also:

CHART C

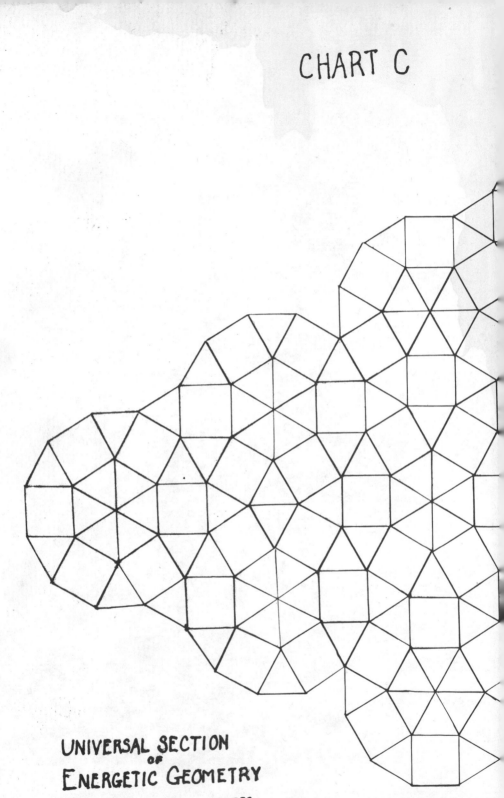

UNIVERSAL SECTION
OF
ENERGETIC GEOMETRY

VERTEXES ARE ENERGY CENTERS

X